For the following rules, x, y, and z are variables and a, b, c, . . ., w are constants.

Universal Instantiation

U.I.: $(x)\Phi x$ /∴ Φa $(x)\Phi x$ /∴ Φy

Existential Instantiation

E.I.: $(\exists x)\Phi x$ /∴ Φa
Restriction: where a is a constant that has *not* previously been introduced into the proof.

Universal Generalization

U.G.: Φy /∴ $(x)\Phi x$
Restriction: U.G. cannot be used within the scope of an assumption for C.P. or I.P. if the initial variable occurs free in the first line of the sequence for C.P. or I.P.
Restriction: U.G. must not be used if Φy contains an existential name and y is free in the line where that name is introduced.

Existential Generalization

E.G.: Φa /∴ $(\exists x)(\Phi x)$

Quantifier Negation

Q.N. $(x)\Phi x \leftrightarrow \sim(\exists x)\sim\Phi x$
      $\sim(x)\Phi x \leftrightarrow (\exists x)\sim\Phi x$
      $\sim(\exists x)\Phi x \leftrightarrow (x)\sim\Phi x$
      $(\exists x)\Phi x \leftrightarrow \sim(x)\sim\Phi x$

Identity

Id. Φx Φx
    $x = y$ $\sim\Phi y$ $x = y$ any premise
    /∴ Φy /∴ $\sim(x = y)$ /∴ $y = x$ /∴ $x = x$

Understanding Logic

Daniel E. Flage
James Madison University

PRENTICE HALL
Englewood Cliffs, New Jersey 07632

Library of Congress Cataloging-in-Publication Data

Flage, Daniel E.
   Understanding logic / Daniel E. Flage.
     p. cm.
   Includes bibliographical references and index.
   ISBN 0-02-338173-6
    1. Logic. I. Title.
  BC50.F53 1995
  160—dc20   94–35094
                         CIP

Acquisitions editor: Maggie Barbieri/Ted Bolen
Editorial Assistant: Meg McGuane
Production editor: Merrill Peterson
Interior design: Judy Allen
Cover designer: Robert Freese
Buyer: Lynn Pearlman

Acknowledgments appear on p. xii, which constitutes a continuation of the copyright page.

Published by Prentice-Hall, Inc.
A Simon & Schuster Company
Englewood Cliffs, New Jersey 07632

Printed in the United States of America

10 9 8 7 6 5 4 3 2 1

ISBN 0-02-338173-6

PRENTICE-HALL INTERNATIONAL (UK) LIMITED, *London*
PRENTICE-HALL OF AUSTRALIA PTY. LIMITED, *Sydney*
PRENTICE-HALL CANADA INC., *Toronto*
PRENTICE-HALL HISPANOAMERICANA, S.A., *Mexico*
PRENTICE-HALL OF INDIA PRIVATE LIMITED, *New Delhi*
PRENTICE-HALL OF JAPAN, INC., *Tokyo*
SIMON & SCHUSTER ASIA PTE. LTD., *Singapore*
EDITORA PRENTICE-HALL DO BRASIL, LTDA., *Rio de Janeiro*

To Dana

Contents

Preface

In our daily lives we are bombarded with requests. Advertisers ask us to buy their products. Politicians request our votes. Literature teachers ask us to accept their interpretations of Dante's *Inferno*. In many cases, these are not simple requests; they are requests based on arguments, reasons given why we should accept the truth of their claims. And in most cases, any request we receive to believe that a statement is true—and often to act on that belief—is only one of a number of competing requests. For example, each of the automakers tries to convince us that one of its cars will best fulfill our needs or desires. How do we decide among such competing claims?

One of the practical benefits derived from studying logic is that it provides us with guidelines for evaluating arguments. Studying logic will *not* help you determine whether the claims advanced for a conclusion are true, but it will give you criteria for determining whether the claims advanced, if true, provide good reasons for accepting the conclusion. Further, it will make you more sensitive to the various ways in which someone might attempt to persuade you to accept a conclusion. It will help you more critically examine the various claims advanced to accept a conclusion. Finally, by studying logic, your own argumentative abilities and problem-solving skills will be enhanced.

Using This Book

In writing this book I have attempted to cover the various topics and approaches to those topics that might be examined in an introductory logic course. In many sections I have included summaries and suggestions that my students have found helpful. I have also found that students are often more inclined to do the exercises, and thereby learn the material, if they occasionally chuckle as they go. It is my hope that some of the exercises will raise a smile on the faces of the students using the book. The solutions for all the odd-numbered exercises are included, allowing a student readily to determine whether he or she has understood the material.

Since logic instructors emphasize different topics or approaches to logic, there are various ways in which this book can be used. Here are some possible arrangements:

TRADITIONAL LOGIC COURSE

Chapter 1

Chapter 3

Chapter 4

Chapter 5

Chapter 6

Chapter 8

Chapter 9

Chapter 11

Chapter 10

INFORMAL LOGIC/CRITICAL THINKING

Chapter 1

Chapter 2

Chapter 3

Chapter 4

Chapter 8

Chapter 9

Chapter 10

Chapter 11

COURSE EMPHASIZING DEDUCTION

Chapter 1

Chapter 3, Sections 1–7

Chapter 4

Chapter 5

Chapter 6

Chapter 7, Sections 1–4

COURSE EMPHASIZING SYMBOLIC LOGIC WITH NATURAL DEDUCTION

Chapter 1

Chapter 5

Chapter 6

Chapter 7

Appendix on Truth Trees (optional)

COURSE EMPHASIZING SYMBOLIC LOGIC WITH TRUTH TREES

Chapter 1

Chapter 5

Appendix on Truth Trees, Section 1

Chapter 7, Section 1

Appendix on Truth Trees, Section 2

Chapter 7, Sections 5-6

Exercises in Chapter 7, Section 7

There are, of course, numerous variations on these sequences. At one time I taught an introductory logic course for which there was a sequel that focused on predicate logic and metatheory. While I believed students gained a great deal from working through a system of natural deduction, the sequel used the truth-tree method. So we followed approximately the outline for the Course Emphasizing Deduction, but substituted a brief examination of truth trees for the chapter on predicate logic.

Acknowledgments

This book was significantly improved by the comments from the following reviewers, to whom I give my thanks: Kit Fine, University of California, Los Angeles; James Cain, University of Rochester; Charles Kielkopf, Ohio State University; Leah Savion, Indiana University-Bloomington; Keith Burgess-Jackson, University of Texas-Arlington; Starlan Miller, Virginia Polytechnic Institute and Virginia State University; Tom Pyne, California State University, Sacramento; James Roper, Michigan State University. It has been a pleasure working with Maggie Barbieri, the philosophy and religion editor, and David Chodoff, the development editor. I also wish to thank my students, who used several versions of the manuscript in class, and my family for their love and tolerance during the writing.

Credits

Chapter One

The Language of Logic

1.1 What Is Logic?

Beginning to master any discipline without becoming hopelessly lost requires an understanding of at least the basic terms peculiar to it. Logic is no exception. Therefore, if we do not wish to be hopelessly lost as we begin to study logic, we must learn some of the basic terms peculiar to it. This is the objective of this chapter.

It is reasonable to begin by providing a preliminary definition of 'logic' and the terms found in that definition. Logic is the study of the principles or criteria used to determine whether or not an argument provides good reasons for accepting the truth of a claim. An **argument** is a set of propositions in which one or more propositions (the premises) are said to provide reasons or evidence for the truth of another proposition (the conclusion). A **proposition** is the information expressed by a declarative sentence or statement. Propositions are either **true** or **false,** that is, they either correspond to the world or they do not. **Statements** are sentences that are true or false in virtue of the propositions they express. Statements are always made in a particular language, and the truth or falsehood of a statement can depend on the context in which it is made. For example, the statement "The present president of the United States plays the saxophone" was true in mid–1993; it was false in 1990. The same proposition can be expressed by several statements in a particular language or by statements in different languages. For example, each of the following statements expresses the same proposition:

> I like ice cream.
> Ice cream is liked by me.
> Ich habe Eis gern. (German)
> Me gusto helado. (Spanish)
> J'aime la glace. (French)

Strictly speaking, truth and falsehood are only characteristics of propositions; they are *not* characteristics of arguments.[1]

Any proposition is a premise or a conclusion only in the context of a particular argument. For example, the proposition "Whenever the U.S. economy is growing, new jobs are being created" is the conclusion of the following argument, and the other two propositions are premises:

> (1) Whenever there is an increase in the Gross Domestic Product, new jobs are being created.
> (2) Whenever the U.S. economy is growing, there is an increase in the Gross Domestic Product.
> _____
> (3) Therefore, whenever the U.S. economy is growing, new jobs are being created.

But the fact that (3) was the conclusion in this argument does not prevent it from being a premise in another argument; such as:

> (4) Whenever new jobs are being created, the incumbent political party retains control of the White House.
> (3) Whenever the U.S. economy is growing, new jobs are being created.
> _____
> (5) Therefore, whenever the U.S. economy is growing, the incumbent political party retains control of the White House.

Here (3) is a premise.

To understand how arguments are evaluated, we must distinguish between two kinds of arguments, deductive and inductive. Let us begin with deductive arguments.

Deductive Arguments

A sound deductive argument provides conclusive evidence for the truth of its conclusion. An argument is **sound** if all of its premises are true and its **argument form** is **valid**. The argument form is the structural pattern of an argument. Just as many houses are *instances* of the same pattern or design—they are constructed according to a single set of blue-prints—many arguments are *instances* of the same argument form. For example, recognizing that 'whenever' means 'all times when', the two arguments above are instances of the argument form:

All *M*s are *P*s.
All *S*s are *M*s.

Therefore, all *S*s are *P*s.

'*M*', '*P*', and '*S*' are **variables** for which the terms in the arguments are substitution instances. In the first argument, "whenever there is an in-crease in the Gross Domestic Product" is the substitution instance for *M*; in the second argument, "times when new jobs are being created" is the substitution instance for *M*. In the first argument, "times when new jobs are being created" is the substitution instance for *P*; in the second argument, "the incumbent political party retains control of the White House" is the substitution instance for *P*. In both the first and second argument "whenever the U.S. economy is growing" is the substitution instance for *S*.

An argument form is **valid** if and only if the form guarantees that *if* the premises are true, the conclusion is true as well. There are instances of valid argument forms in which one or more of the premises are false. To understand this, let us again compare the form of an argument with the design of a house.

Assume you are planning to build a house that will withstand earth-quakes. In the course of your investigation, you discover that only homes of certain designs are earthquake-proof. So you choose one of those designs. But the design alone will not guarantee that your house will withstand an earthquake; if you follow the design but build a house of straw, it probably will not withstand a strong wind, let alone an earth-quake. If your house is to be earthquake-proof, you must assemble the finest building-materials according to an earthquake-proof design. A valid argument form is like the design of an earthquake-proof house: just as the design of the house guarantees that *if* you build with the finest materials your house will withstand an earthquake, so a valid argument form guarantees that *if* the premises are true, the conclusion is true as well. An argument form that does *not* guarantee the truth of the conclusion if the premises are true is an **invalid** argument form.

An unsound deductive argument fails to establish the truth of its conclusion. An argument is unsound if either (1) the argument form is valid but one or more of the premises are false, or (2) the premises are true, but the form is invalid, or (3) one or more of the premises are false and the form is invalid. The following argument illustrates the first case: the argument form is valid but one of the premises is false:

> All dogs are canines.
> All cats are dogs.
> ———————————
> Therefore, all cats are canines.

Here the conclusion is false: cats are felines, not canines. Sometimes you will draw a true conclusion on the basis of valid argument form and a false premise. For example:

> All dogs are animals.
> All cats are dogs.
> ———————————
> Therefore, all cats are animals.

This is an instance of a valid argument form, but the second premise is false. Because the second premise is false, the argument is unsound: the argument does not provide good reasons for accepting the truth of the conclusion.

Second, an argument with true premises that is an instance of an invalid argument form is unsound. Let us consider some examples. Assume someone argued as follows:

> No antelopes are dogs.
> No rabbits are antelopes.
> ———————————
> Therefore, no rabbits are dogs.

Here the premises and the conclusion are true, but the argument form is invalid. You can show that the argument form is invalid by constructing an argument of the same form with true premises and a false conclusion. This is called a **deductive counterexample.** We can represent the form of the argument as follows:

No *M* is *P*.
No *S* is *M*.
_____

Therefore, no *S* is *P*.

We replace '*M*', '*P*', and '*S*' in such a way that all the premises are true and the conclusion is false. One such instance of this argument form is:

No antelopes are dogs.
No collies are antelopes.
_____

Therefore, no collies are dogs.

Since the premises are true and the conclusion is false, we have shown that *no* argument that is an instance of the above form is valid. We have provided a refutation of the original argument by deductive counterexample.

Consider another example:

If George Bush won the presidential election in 1992, then the Republicans retained control of the White House in 1993.
George Bush did not win the presidential election in 1992.
_____

Therefore, the Republicans did not retain control of the White House in 1993.

The first premise is a conditional statement. A conditional statement is true *except* when the antecedent (the if-clause) is true and the consequent (the then-clause) is false.[2] Since George Bush did not win the election in 1992 and the Republicans did not retain control of the White House in 1993, the first premise, the second premise, and the conclusion are true. However, the argument is an instance of an invalid argument form. To represent the form of the argument, replace the statement "George Bush won the presidential election in 1992" with the statement variable *p*, and replace the statement "the Republicans retained control of the White House in 1993" with *q*. The form of the argument may be represented as follows:

If *p*, then *q*.
Not *p*.
_____

Therefore, not *q*.

As statement variables, *p* and *q* can be replaced by any statements whatsoever. So we can construct a deductive counterexample which shows that the argument form is invalid. One such instance is the following:

> If Bill Clinton won the presidential election in 1964, then the Democrats retained control of the White House in 1965.
> Bill Clinton did not win the presidential election in 1964.
>
> ———————————
>
> Therefore, the Democrats did not retain control of the White House in 1965.

The premises are true. The conclusion is false: Lyndon Johnson, a Democrat, was elected in 1964, so the Democrats retained control of the White House in 1965. This deductive counterexample shows that any argument that is an instance of the form above is invalid.

Finally, an argument that is both an instance of an invalid argument form and has one or more false premises is unsound; such an argument does not establish the truth of its conclusion. For example:

> All dogs are collies.
> No cats are dogs.
>
> ———————————
>
> Therefore, no cats are collies.

The first premise is false, so the argument does not provide good reasons for accepting the conclusion. Further, the argument is an instance of an invalid argument form. The form of the argument may be represented as follows:

> All *M* is *P*.
> No *S* is *M*.
>
> ———————————
>
> Therefore, no *S* is *P*.

It is easy to construct a deductive counterexample to show that this argument form is invalid. For example:

> All dogs are animals.
> No cats are dogs.
>
> ———————————
>
> Therefore, no cats are animals.

Logicians, as logicians, claim no special competence in determining the truth or falsehood of propositions—that is the province of the natural and social sciences. Logicians develop techniques for determining whether deductive arguments are valid or invalid. While a good deductive counterexample carries considerable rhetorical force—showing that your opponent in a debate proposed an invalid argument by means of a deductive counterexample is a good way to make points—but it is not an efficient way to demonstrate invalidity. Further, there is no comparable way to demonstrate validity. Later chapters of this book examine validity-testing techniques that are efficient and virtually mechanical.

Properly speaking, the terms 'sound', 'valid', and 'invalid' apply only to deductive arguments.

Inductive Arguments

Inductive arguments provide some, but not conclusive, evidence for the truth of their conclusions. The fact that the conclusion of an inductive argument is never certain—the fact that further evidence might call any inductive conclusion into doubt—is *not* a defect, for there are very few areas of inquiry that yield absolutely certain conclusions. Most of our beliefs about the world are based on inductive arguments. We seldom have more than inductive evidence (evidence based on inductive arguments) for the truth of the premises of a deductive argument.

There are various kinds of inductive arguments. Some inductive arguments support a general conclusion, a conclusion with respect to most or all cases; others provide evidence for a conclusion with respect to a single case or a limited number of cases. To understand this, let us consider some examples.

You are a bird-watcher. One day, you observe fifty crows and notice that each crow is black. On this basis you generalize and conclude that all crows are black. Here you are reaching a conclusion about all crows based on a small number of instances. Your argument is inductive. Each black crow you observe provides a bit more evidence that all crows are black. But given that there is a very large number of past, present, and future crows, to all of whom your conclusion applies, a conclusion based on only fifty instances is quite weak. So you attempt to strengthen the argument for your conclusion by observing more crows. You travel extensively, and wherever you go, you observe crows. For several years you observe at least fifty crows per week, crows living at many geographically diverse areas, and each crow you observe is black.

After observing several thousand crows, you have much better evidence for your conclusion that all crows are black. But your conclusion is very strong: it would take only one crow that is not black to show that your conclusion is false. You have much better evidence for the weaker conclusion that *most* crows are black.

One day you see a white bird that is the size of a crow, the shape of a crow, that caws like a crow, and engages in crowlike activities. Because this bird is similar in numerous respects to each of the thousands of crows you have observed, and differs from them only in color, you conclude that the white bird is a crow. Here you have engaged in an *argument by analogy.* You have compared one object to others on the basis of numerous properties, and since each of the birds to which you are comparing that one has the additional property of being a crow, you conclude that the white bird is also a crow. You might then develop a second argument by analogy in which you compare crows with other animals. Crows are similar to other animals insofar as their observable characteristics are causally determined by a genetic code. Since there are albino humans, dogs, cats, tigers, ravens, and so forth, it is likely that there are also albino crows. This provides a further reason to believe that the white bird is a crow. But since albinism is rare in other species, and since you have observed thousands of black crows and only one albino crow, you have very good reasons to believe that *most* crows are black.

We use inductive arguments all the time. If you diagnose a disease on the basis of a set of symptoms, you are engaging in an inductive argument: certain symptoms usually are signs of one disease, but they can also be signs of another. If you make a reasoned prediction that a certain baseball team will win the pennant, you are engaging in an inductive argument. If you predict that touching a hot stove will result in a twinge of pain because hot stoves and pain have been associated in the past, or you judge that the sun will rise tomorrow because it always has in the past, or you conclude that you would be happy with a certain model of car because several of your friends have been pleased with that model car, you are reaching a conclusion on the basis of an inductive argument. Some inductive arguments are stronger than others, that is, some provide better evidence for their conclusions than others. Chapters 8–11 examine the criteria for evaluating the strength of inductive arguments.

Given the distinction between inductive and deductive arguments, we are in a position to provide a more adequate definition of 'logic.' Logic is the study of (1) the principles used to determine whether a deductive argument is valid and (2) the principles used to evaluate the strength of an inductive argument.

EXERCISES

Using what you have just learned, indicate whether the following propositions are true or false.

1. All valid arguments have true conclusions.

2. An invalid argument can have all true premises and a false conclusion.

3. A sound argument can have a false conclusion.

4. All inductive arguments proceed from particular premises to general conclusions.

5. The premises of one argument can be conclusions of other arguments.

6. Some arguments are true.

7. The validity of an argument rests on considerations of the truth or falsehood of the premises in that argument.

8. An analogy is an example of a deductive argument.

9. A deductive counterexample will allow one to show that a deductive argument is valid.

10. No inductive arguments are valid deductive arguments.

11. A sound argument can have a false premise.

12. If the conclusion of a valid argument is false, you can infer that one of its premises is true.

13. Meteorologists and logicians mean the same thing by the word 'valid.'

14. Sometimes all the premises of an inductive argument are true and the conclusion is false.

15. The form of a deductive argument is a structural pattern found in the argument.

16. Arguments by analogy are based upon similarities among the objects mentioned in the premises.

17. If you concluded that no car runs for more than 300,000 miles because no car you have examined has run for more than 300,000 miles, you have engaged in an inductive argument.

18. You construct a deductive counterexample to a particular argument by showing that there is an argument of the same form in which all the premises are false and the conclusion is true.

19. An inductive argument can provide conclusive evidence for its conclusion.

20. Every proposition is either true or false.

1.2 *Recognizing Arguments*

Arguments are contained in essays, letters to editors, conversations, and so forth. If the techniques you learn in a logic course are to be applied in ordinary life, as they should, you must be able to identify a piece of discourse as an argument. Sometimes this is easy. Certain terms often indicate that a statement is a premise or a conclusion, giving you reason to believe you are in the presence of an argument.

The following is a partial list of **premise indicators,** words indicating that a statement is the premise of an argument:

since	because
for	as
given that	assuming that
inasmuch as	whereas (in formal motions)

The following is a partial list of **conclusion indicators,** words indicating that a statement is the conclusion of an argument:

thus	we may conclude that
therefore	it follows that
hence	it is entailed that
so	we may infer that
consequently	be it resolved that (in formal motions)

And there are certain locutions that show both:

  . . . [premise] is a reason to hold that——[conclusion]
  . . . [premise] is evidence that——[conclusion]
  . . . [premise] implies that——[conclusion]
  ——[conclusion] may be deduced from . . . [premises]
  ——[conclusion] is shown by . . . [premises]
  ——[conclusion] is entailed by . . . [premises]

——[conclusion] may be derived from . . . [premises]
it follows from . . . [premises] that——[conclusion]
we may infer from . . . [premises] that——[conclusion]

Further, if you find a conditional statement, that is, a statement of the form "if . . . then . . .", you have *probably* found a premise or conclusion of an argument. Since a conditional statement is *not* an argument, you must ask whether it functions as a premise or a conclusion.

Unfortunately, the premises and conclusion are seldom all marked by indicators. Often there is *either* a premise indicator *or* a conclusion indicator, but not both. Further, the order in which the premises and conclusion of an argument are presented has no effect on the validity of a deductive argument or the strength of an inductive argument. The premises might be presented first, or the conclusion might be presented first, or the conclusion might be nestled among the premises. For example, the same argument is presented in each of the following passages:

Since all human beings are mortals and Socrates is a human being, it follows that Socrates is a mortal.

Socrates is a mortal, for Socrates is a human being, and all human beings are mortals.

Since Socrates is a human being, we may infer that Socrates is a mortal, because all human beings are mortals.

To make matters more difficult, sometimes a premise might be considered so obvious that it is not stated, as in:

Since all human beings are mortal, Socrates is mortal.

Sometimes the conclusion is left unstated:

Socrates is a human being and we all know that all human beings are mortals.

And, of course, the premises of an argument might be scattered throughout a lengthy discourse. An essay, for example, is nothing but an extended argument for a certain conclusion (the thesis), and if you were to succinctly state the argument of an essay you would have to "disentangle" the premises for the main thesis from both the various arguments provided to support those premises and from purely descriptive and explanatory discussions. There is, however, a straightforward method for identifying the premises of an argument. If you can find the *conclusion,* you can determine which propositions are the premises by asking, *"Why should I accept this proposition as true?"* Remember, in an argument the truth of the premises provides evidence or reasons for accepting the conclusion. So by asking what reasons are given for accepting the truth of the conclusion, you should be able to discover the premises of the argument.

There are certain additional hazards of which one must be aware in searching for arguments. First, in English, words have several meanings, and what functions as a premise indicator in one context might fulfill a different function in another context. The word "since," for example, occasionally refers to a time, as in the sentence, "Since Bill Clinton became president, no Model-T Fords have been produced." Similarly, the word 'because' sometimes is used to specify the cause of something, rather than a reason that a proposition should be accepted as true. For example, you are alluding to a cause if you say, "The iron bar is hot because the molecules composing it are moving rapidly." Second, explanations might easily be mistaken for arguments, and for this reason we should look briefly at the distinction between arguments and explanations.

Assume you have a three-quart pan of boiling water on your stove, and you are asked, "Why is the water boiling?" In answering this question you give an **explanation.** You might answer, "I'm planning to make spaghetti for supper." This answers the question, "Why did you put the water on to boil?" Or you might give an explanation in terms of natural laws, that is, a **deductive nomological explanation.** Such an explanation might look like this:

(1) All water heated to 212 degrees Fahrenheit boils.
(2) The water on the stove is water heated to 212 degrees Fahrenheit.

---

(3) Therefore, the water on the stove is boiling.

This answers the question, "Why is the water boiling, rather than doing something else?" This explanation *looks* like a deductive argument, since proposition (3) is deduced from (1) and (2). How does an explanation differ from an argument?

Explanations answer the question, "Why is some *known* thing or event as it is?" You know at the outset that the water on the stove is boiling. What you are trying to discover is *why* this is so. Taken together, propositions (1) and (2) answer that question. In contrast, in an argument the premises are known or accepted first: they provide reasons why you should accept the conclusion as true. This is one reason why the conclusion of an argument is sometimes surprising. To see this, let us consider an *argument,* the conclusion of which is proposition (3).

It's the end of a long day. John is fixing a spaghetti supper and watching the national news. With the sauce completed, he places a pan of water on the stove and settles down to watch the news. Sometime later, John asks himself whether the water on stove is boiling, that is, whether it is time to add the spaghetti. Rather than wander into the kitchen to look or turn down the T.V. to determine whether he can hear the characteristic sounds of boiling water, John proposes the following argument:

(1a) Whenever you heat three quarts of water over a high flame for fifteen minutes, the water boils.
(2a) The water on the stove is three quarts of water that has been heated over a high flame for fifteen minutes.

(3) Therefore the water on the stove is boiling.

John has good grounds for believing that (1a) is true, since he's boiled water for spaghetti each of the past seventy-five evenings and has discovered that it always takes twelve to fifteen minutes for the water to boil. He has good grounds for believing (2a), since he turned the flame on high and has seen four news stories and a dozen commercials since he placed the water on the stove, and past experience provides good inductive evidence that four news stories and a dozen commercials take fifteen minutes. So, he concludes that the water on the stove is boiling on the basis of a deductive argument.

In this case, (1a) and (2a) are known or assumed to be true and entail (3). When John wanders into the kitchen and discovers that the water is *not* boiling, he is surprised. Nonetheless, the *explanation* is simple: (2a) is false. And it is easy to *explain* why (2a) is false: John forgot to pay his gas bill, and the gas company discontinued service two minutes after he went to watch the news.

In an argument, the arguer attempts to show that a certain proposition *p* is true, its truth being doubtful. In an explanation, the explainer attempts to show *why* a proposition *p* is the case, its truth being assumed.

EXERCISES

For each set of exercises below, find the premises and the conclusion of each argument. Mark the premises "P" and the conclusion "C." If a premise or conclusion is unstated, state the assumed premise or conclusion in parentheses. Restate the argument, including premise and conclusion indicators. Underline the premise indicators and circle the conclusion indicators. Indicate whether the argument is deductive or inductive. If the argument is deductive, is its form valid? If it is inductive, is it strong or weak? Are the premises true?

Example: You are given: "Since all human beings are mortals, we may conclude that Socrates is a mortal, for Socrates is a human being." Restate the argument including the premise and conclusion indicators as follows:

> P: *Since* all human beings are mortals.
> P: *For* Socrates is a human being.
> C⟨We may conclude that⟩ Socrates is a mortal.

The argument is deductive. Its form is valid. Its premises are true.

I. Each of the following passages contains one argument.

1. Since Hilda likes dark chocolate and milk chocolate, since she likes caramels and nougats, and since she likes peanut brittle, we may infer that she is fond of most kinds of candy.

2. Inasmuch as all whales feed milk to their young, it follows that no whales are fish, as no fish feed milk to their young.

3. Because all camels have humps, it follows that some cigarettes have humps, for some cigarettes are Camels.

4. That Tristan is Dan's son is shown by the facts that they have the same last name, they both have red hair, and they live in the same house.

5. Given that the Index of Leading Economic Indicators has been dropping for the last three quarters, we may infer that the economy is falling into recession.

6. The fact that every building on campus was named after a professor is evidence that most of the buildings on campus were named after Professor Hall.

7. We may infer that Lassie is a dog, since all collies are dogs.

8. Humberto attended logic class every day, studied logic for an hour every night, and did well in the course. Megan attended class occasionally, studied logic for an hour every night, and did well in the course. Gwin attended class every day, never studied at night, and failed the course. Therefore, the key to doing well in a logic course is studying nightly.

9. If I get up this morning, I'll go to work. If I go to work, I'll get caught in a traffic jam. If I get caught in a traffic jam, I'll lose my temper. If I lose my temper, I'll do something rash. If I do something rash, I'll be arrested. We may conclude that if I get up this morning, I'll be arrested. Under those circumstances, would you get up?

10. Learning logic is like learning a foreign language or learning to play the piano. You must master the vocabulary and the easier grammatical constructions before you can master the more difficult grammatical constructions. You must master the scales and finger techniques before you can play Beethoven. Similarly in logic you must master the elementary elements of the subject if you are to master the complex elements. Consequently, just as to master a language or the piano you must work with it every day, you must study logic daily to master that discipline.

II. Each of the following passages contains one argument.

1. When I was a kid, I was told that drinking coffee stunts growth. That must have been true, since Aunt Emma gave me a cup of coffee when I was three, and I only grew to be five foot ten.

2. . . . Since it is the constant and universal opinion of mankind, independent of education, custom, or law, that there are Gods; it must necessarily follow that this knowledge is implanted in our minds, or rather innate in us.

          CICERO, *Of the Nature of the Gods.*

3. Imhotep's pyramid was not much good, really, for the steps, or terraces, were not filled in, and it was less than 200 feet high.

    WILL CUPPY, *The Decline and Fall of Practically Everybody*
             (New York: Dell, 1950), p. 14.

4. It happened, then, that my father had decided to sleep in the attic one night, to be away where he could think. My mother opposed the notion strongly because, she said, the old

wooden bed up there was unsafe; it was wobbly and the heavy headboard would crash down on father's head in case the bed fell, and kill him.

JAMES THURBER, "The Night the Bed Fell," in *The Thurber Carnival* (New York: Harper Colophon Books, 1945), p. 176.

5. Editors are peculiar animals—they throw mud and bricks at you the whole year round—then they make one favorable statement which happens to agree with the facts and they think they should be hugged and kissed for it.

HARRY TRUMAN, in *The Wit and Wisdom of Harry Truman,* compiled by George S. Caldwell (New York: Stein and Day, 1966), p. 27.

6. It is likely that John Wilkes Booth first decided to dispose of Abraham Lincoln the day after the presidential election of 1864. The actor despised the President before that; in the campaign that year Booth predicted that, if Lincoln was elected, he would set up a dynasty. Lincoln had been Booth's emotional whipping boy for at least four years.

JIM BISHOP, *The Day Lincoln Was Shot* (New York: Scholastic, 1955), p. 62.

7. A great man is someone self-willed and obsessive. A self-willed and obsessive man will do everything in a self-willed and obsessive sort of way. Therefore, only self-willed and obsessive actions are to be expected from a great man.

GEORGE SZAMUELY, " 'White Hunter' Shot from the Hip," in *Insight,* vol. 6, no. 40 (October 1, 1990), p. 58.

8. Clinton's overpowering obsession was the safety of New York. His logic seems to have run in this groove: Washington would never think of taking his army south unless he had command of the sea; we know that the Royal Navy *always* retains command of the sea; therefore Washington cannot be moving his army to the South.

HAROLD A. LARRABEE, *Decision at the Chesapeake* (New York: Clarkson Potter, 1964), p. 255.

9. It seems obvious that the whole activity of the organism should conform to definite laws. If the animal were not in exact correspondence with its environment, it would cease to exist.

I. P. PAVLOV, *Conditioned Reflexes,* translated by G. V. Anrep (New York: Dover, 1960), p. 7.

10. You should pray and you should know that you are bound to pray by divine command. For the second commandment teaches that you shall not swear, curse, or conjure, but call upon the name of God in every time of need, pray, praise, and exalt him; hence that it is commanded that we pray.

MARTIN LUTHER, "On Prayer and the First
Three Petitions of the Lord's Prayer."

III. Each of the following passages contains at least one argument.

1. We are frequently asked what is the ideal number for a dinner party. . . . Seriously speaking, there is probably no ideal answer to the question. Some of the reasons will become apparent in the discussion that follows. Yet there is probably a workable minimum; and unless the guests are very close friends, that minimum much exceeds two. Back in the living room afterward, first-time acquaintances must be able to exercise options and establish small centers of mutual interest; and we suggest this can only be engineered with any degree of success among groups of at least eight. Twelve is an even happier number.

IRMA S. ROMBAUER and MARION ROMBAUER BECKER, *The Joy of Cooking* (Indianapolis: Bobbs-Merrill, 1975), p. 15.

2. Paradise is not a long sailing-journey from earth, neither is it in the moon. If it were in the moon it would sometimes bereave the light and make an eclipse.

ROBERT NYE, *Falstaff* (New York:
Random House, 1976), p. 125.

3. To the mines! tell you the duke it is not so goot to come to the mines; for, look you, the mines is not according to the disciples of the war: the concavities of it is not sufficient; for, look you, th' athversary,—you may discuss unto the duke, look you,—is digt himself four yard under the counter-mines; by Cheshu, I think 'a will plow up all, if there is not better directions.

FLUELLEN, in Shakespeare's *Henry V,* Act III, Scene 1.

4. There is no comprehensive and objective history of the telephone, telephoning as a social act, or the American Telephone and Telegraph Company, which was originally based on Bell's patents of 1876 and 1877 and has dominated American telephony ever since. Therefore, this book sets out, among other things, to fill a need.

JOHN BROOKS, *Telephone* (New York:
Harper & Row, 1976), p. xi.

5. In all Cases, whilst the Government subsists, the *Legislative is the Supream Power.* For what can give Laws to another, must needs be superiour to him: and since the Legislative is no otherwise Legislative of the Society, but by the right it has to make Laws for all the parts and for every Member of the Society, prescribing Rules to the actions, and giving power of Execution, where they are transgressed, the *Legislative* must needs be the *Supream* and all other Powers in any Members or parts of the Society, derived from and subordinate to it.

   JOHN LOCKE, *Second Treatise of Government,* Section 150.

6. The American government does not have the right, much less the obligation, to try to promote the economic and social welfare of foreign peoples. Of course, all of us are interested in combating poverty and disease wherever it exists. *But the Constitution does not empower our government to undertake that job in foreign countries,* no matter how worthwhile it might be. Therefore, except as it can be shown to promote America's national interests, the Foreign Aid program is unconstitutional.

   BARRY GOLDWATER, *The Conscience of a Conservative*
   (New York: Macfadden Books, 1960), pp.97–98.

7. More often than not, it's the child whose mother *does* belong to the PTA who gets teacher's nod [to appear on "Art Linkletter's House Party"]. One ten-year-old boy knew he just couldn't miss being selected, and he told me why: "My mother's president of the PTA, and my favorite teacher was just chosen principal."
   That's the way the world goes—it helps to have connections.

   ART LINKLETTER, *Kids Still Say the Darndest Things!*
   (New York: Bernard Geis Associates, 1961), p. 125.

8. I have said that all the reputedly powerful reactionaries are merely paper tigers. The reason is that they are divorced from the people. Look! Was not Hitler a paper tiger? Was not Hitler overthrown? I also said that the tsar of Russia, the emperor of China and Japanese imperialism were all paper tigers. As we know, they were all overthrown. U.S. imperialism has not yet been overthrown and it has the atom bomb. I believe it also will be overthrown. It, too, is a paper tiger.

   MAO TSE-TUNG, Speech at the Moscow Meeting of Communist
   and Workers' Parties (November 18, 1957).

9. I have no great faith in dreams. Athenodorus once dreamed that there was treasure in a badger's den in a wood near Rome. He found his way to the exact spot, which he had never visited before, and there in a bank was a hole leading to a den. He fetched a couple of countrymen to dig away the bank until they came to the den at the end of the hole—where they found a rotten old purse containing six mouldy coppers and a bad shilling, which was not enough to pay the countrymen for their work. And one of my tenants, a shopkeeper, dreamed once that a flight of eagles wheeled round his head and one settled on his shoulder. He took it for a sign that he would one day be Emperor, but all that happened was that a piquet of Guards visited him the next morning (they had eagles on their shields) and the corporal arrested him for some offense and brought him under military jurisdiction.

> ROBERT GRAVES, *I, Claudius* (New York: Vintage Books, 1961), p. 220.

10. Again, if the Divinity is anything, either it is a body or it is incorporeal. But neither is it incorporeal, since the incorporeal is inanimate and without senses and capable of no activity, nor is it a body, since every body is both subject to change and perishable, while the Divinity is imperishable. Therefore the Divinity does not exist.

> SEXTUS EMPIRICUS, *Selections from the Major Writings on Scepticism, Man, & God*, edited by Philip P. Hallie, translated by Sanford G. Etheridge (Indianapolis: Hackett, 1985), p. 208.

IV. Some of the following passages contain arguments; others do not. Some passages contain more than one argument. Find all the arguments in those passages that contain arguments.

1. "I was afraid of this," said Henry. "I'm not even sure there are any fish in this river."

   "There must be some fish, Henry," said Benny. "If there weren't any, this boat wouldn't have had a fishing pole on it."

   > GERTRUDE CHANDLER WARNER, *The Houseboat Mystery* (Albert Whitman & Company, 1967), p. 39.

2. It was a Cretan prophet, one of their own countrymen, who said, 'Cretans were always liars, vicious brutes, lazy gluttons'—and he told the truth!

   > Titus 1:12-13a *(New English Bible).*

3. Actions leading to heaven are in my power if I will them,
therefore I will will them.

> GEORGE BERKELEY, *Philosophical Commentaries,* entry 160.

4. When the dean was promoted to provost, the college paper
was called upon to explain to what this change in status
amounted. The paper responded:

> If geitost is goat cheese, primost is new cheese, and
> gammelost is old cheese, what is a provost?
> THE BIG CHEESE!
>
> From *Luther College Chips,* vol. 89 (April 4, 1972).

5. Consider the facts: a vampire must drink fresh human blood
at least once a week to live, and whoever suffers the bite of a
vampire turns into a vampire. Thus, the number of vampires
doubles every week, which is sufficient to show that there are
no vampires. Assume that on January 1 of last year, there
was exactly one vampire. If the number of vampires doubles
every week, then by the end of the fortieth week, there were
over a trillion vampires. But there are fewer than a trillion
people in the world. So there are no vampires.

> Adapted from "Multiplying Vampires," in *Childcraft,*
> vol. 13 (Chicago: World Book, 1987), pp. 124–127.

6. So that he that *by Conquest has a right over a Man's Person*
to destroy him if he pleases, has *not* thereby a right *over his
Estate* to possess and enjoy it. For it is the brutal force the
Aggressor has used, that gives his Adversary a right to take
away his Life, and destroy him if he pleases, as a noxious
Creature; but 'tis damage sustain'd that alone give him Title
to another Man's Goods: For though I may kill a Thief that
sets on me in the Highway, yet I may not (which seems less)
take away his Money and let him go; this would be Robbery
on my side.

> JOHN LOCKE, *Second Treatise of Government,* Section 182.

7. The Americans love a winner, and cannot tolerate a loser.
Americans despise cowards. Americans play to win; all the
time. I wouldn't give a hoot for a man who lost and laughed.
That's why Americans have never lost, and will never lose, a
war. The very thought of losing is hateful to an American.

> GENERAL GEORGE S. PATTON, JR., Address to his troops,
> July 1944, quoted in William Bancroft Mellor, *Patton:
> Fighting Man* (New York: Putnam's Sons, 1946), p. 2.

8. The doctor knows that it is the prescription slip itself, even more than what is written on it, that is often the vital ingredient for enabling a patient to get rid of whatever is ailing him. Drugs are not always necessary. Belief in recovery always is. And so the doctor may prescribe a placebo in cases where reassurance for the patient is far more useful than a famous-name pill three times a day.

    NORMAN COUSINS, *Anatomy of an Illness as Perceived by the Patient* (New York: Bantam Books, 1979) pp. 49–50.

9. For as the rain cometh down, and the snow from heaven, and returneth not thither, but watereth the earth, and maketh it bring forth and bud, that it may give seed to the sower, and bread to the eater: So shall my word be that goeth forth out of my mouth: it shall not return to me void, but it shall accomplish that which I please, and it shall prosper *in the thing* whereto I send it.

    Isaiah 55: 10-11 (King James Version).

10. The temptation to regard light and sound as nearly alike must be resisted. There are resemblances between them, and in some kinds of problems similar designs and similar equations are used. But the differences are impressive. The propagation of sound waves in air is a gross, statistical process, without scientific implications as to the nature of matter or energy. The propagation of light is an "ultimate," which reaches to the very heart of physics, cosmology, and philosophy—so much so, in fact, that we shall never have an adequate understanding of light until we understand those other giant enigmas: matter, energy, and vacuum.

    Sound cannot travel in a vacuum. Light travels best in a vacuum.

    Sound waves in air are longitudinal waves; they have no sectional pattern at all, and hence are never polarized. Light waves are transverse and may display a variety of linear, circular, or elliptical sectional patterns.

    WILLIAM A. SHURCLIFF and STANLEY S. BALLARD, *Polarized Light* (Princeton, N.J.: Van Nostrand, 1964), p. 11.

11. "Well, you're probably at Players partying and having a good time—not studying the way you should be.

    "Let's see, it's Thursday night—Ladies' Night. You're not in your room. If you were in the bathroom, you would have picked up the phone by now. I also believe after 11:00 p.m. it costs more for men to get in and you probably took Ernie, so you would have to have left by now. You may have needed to get out due to the stressful week, but going to a bar is not the way to do it, even though it is what you usually do. It's also the last Thursday before you come home, so you had to go, didn't you? Where are your priorities?

"Hope you had fun! Ha ha!"

MICHELLE BRUNECZ, "A message from Mom
on the answering machine."

12. The human body is not alone in having thousands of different enzymes—so does every other species of creature. Many of the reactions that take place in human cells also happen in the cells of other creatures. Some of the reactions, indeed, are universal, in that they take place in all cells of every type. This means that an enzyme capable of catalyzing a particular reaction may be present in the cells of wolves, octopi, moss, and bacteria, as well as in our own cells. And yet each of these enzymes, capable though it is of catalyzing one particular reaction, is characteristic of its own species. They may all be distinguished from one another.

    It follows that every species of creature has thousands of enzymes and that all those enzymes may be different. Since there are over a million different species on earth, it may be possible—judging from enzymes alone—that different proteins exist by the billions!

    ISAAC ASIMOV, *The Genetic Code* (New York:
    Signet Science Library, 1962), pp. 27–28.

13. If Englishmen had been ignorant of America and its problems until they became of service in a common struggle, the same is equally true of Americans. In 1700 the population of the American colonies was 200,000; in 1770 it had risen to over 2,000,000. Recent immigration had consisted of German and French Protestants, of Irish peasants and Scottish crofters, of whores and felons and bankrupts from London. There could be no loyalty among these immigrants, nor was it to be expected among the American born. Usually their ancestors left England in resentment and frequently their ambition had been frustrated by the economically inadequate mercantilist system. There was no comprehension of the great difficulties

facing England; Americans were concerned with immediate issues and economic advantages.

J. H. PLUMB, *England in the Eighteenth Century (1714–1815)* (Baltimore: Penguin, 1953), p. 125.

14. If you teach well, regardless of the level you teach, you will work equally as hard as any teachers, be they in a first grade or college position. Status reports have pointed out that professors are held in greater esteem than kindergarten teachers, yet one well-known authority in education wonders if it is not the kindergarten teacher who is doing the greater work for mankind.

    ROBERT L. FILBIN and STEFAN VOGEL, *So You're Going to Be a Teacher* (Woodbury, N.Y.: Barron's Educational Series, 1967), p. 18.

15. The *Dallas* phenomenon stems from something more complex than an interest in whodunit. If J. R. Ewing had not committed himself to a life of stylish wickedness—and if the part did not fit Hagman like an iron whip in a velvet glove—few viewers would care that he was near death or trouble themselves to ponder the assailant's identity. If the scheming scion of Ewing Oil were not surrounded by a nest of relatives, all pursuing their venal and venereal desires through a plot delirious in its complexity, he would be perceived as a cartoon villain among prime time's retinue of sanctified simps. If *Dallas* did not offer the rarest of series commodities—narrative surprise and character change—the attempt on J.R.'s life would be no more than a gimmick, instead of the logical climax to a season of devilish intrigue.

    "TV's *Dallas:* Whodunit?" *Time Magazine,* August 11, 1980, p. 63. Copyright 1980 Time Warner Inc. Reprinted by permisson.

16. The most wise, righteous, and gracious God doth oftentimes leave for a season his own children to manifold temptations, and the corruption of their own hearts, to chastise them for their former sins, or to discover unto them the hidden strength of corruption and deceitfulness of their hearts, that they may be humbled; and to raise them to a more close and constant dependence for their support upon himself, and to make them more watchful against all future occasions of sin, and for sundry other just and holy ends.

    Westminster Confession of Faith, ch. 5, sec. 5.

17. The first and most manifest way [to prove the existence of God] is the argument from motion. It is certain and evident to our senses that some things are in motion. Whatever is in motion is moved by another, for nothing can be in motion except it have a potentiality for that towards which it is being moved; whereas a thing moves inasmuch as it is in act. For motion is nothing else than the reduction of something from a state of potentiality into a state of actuality. Nothing, however, can be reduced from a state of potentiality into a state of actuality, unless by something already in a state of actuality. Thus that which is actually hot as fire, makes wood, which is potentially hot, to be actually hot, thereby moves and changes it. It is not possible that the same thing could be at once in a state of actuality and potentiality from the same point of view, but only from different points of view. What is actually hot cannot simultaneously be only potentially hot; still, it is simultaneously potentially cold. It is therefore impossible that from the point of view that in the same way anything should be both moved and mover, to that it should move itself. Therefore, whatever is in motion must be put in motion by another. If that by which it is put in motion be itself put in motion by another, and that by another again. This cannot go on to infinity, because then there would be no first mover, and, consequently, no other mover—seeing that subsequent mover only move inasmuch as they are put in motion by the first mover; as the staff only moves because it is put in motion by the hand. Therefore it is necessary to arrive at a First Mover, put in motion by no other; and this everyone understands to be God.

THOMAS AQUINAS, Summa Theologica, I.3,
translated by Anthony Pegis.

18. Guns don't kill people. People do.

Don't try telling that to the District of Columbia Council, though. The council is one step away from passing legislation that would hold manufacturers and dealers of handguns financially liable for shooting injuries or deaths. . . .

But their solution to these problems is as appalling as the crimes themselves. In essence, the council is saying that people who make the conscious decision to take another life aren't wholly responsible for that decision. The manufacturer, because they happen to produce the product they do, is also responsible.

That's like saying the makers of kitchen knives should be responsible for stabbing murders committed with cutlery. Or, for that matter, carmakers should be liable when people get tanked, try to drive home and plow over Aunt Fifi and Uncle Hughey as they take their nightly stroll.

Quite simply, gunmakers aren't responsible for how people choose to misuse their purchases, and to say they are is ludicrous.

KAREN ADAMS, "Off the Mark," *The Daily Texan,*
July 11, 1989, p. 4.

19. Mason said, "A lawyer isn't like a doctor. A doctor has scores of patients, some of them are young and curable, some of them old and suffering from diseases that are incurable. It's the nature of life that individuals move in a stream from birth to death. A doctor can't get so wrapped up in his patients that he suffers for them.

    "A lawyer is different. He has relatively fewer clients. Most of their troubles are curable, if a lawyer only knew exactly what to do. But whether they're curable or not, a lawyer can always better his client somewhere along the line if he can get the right combination."

ERLE STANLEY GARDNER, *The Case of the Horrified Heirs*
(William Morrow and Company, 1964), pp. 191–92.

20. I've always reckoned that looking at the new moon over your left shoulder is one of the carelessest and foolishest things a body can do. Old Hank Bunker done it once, and bragged about it; and in less than two years he got drunk and fell off the shot tower, and spread himself out so that he was just a kind of a layer, as you may say; and they slid him edgeways between two barn doors for a coffin, and buried him so, so they say, but I didn't see it. Pap told me. But anyway it all come of looking at the moon in that way, like a fool.

MARK TWAIN, *The Adventures of*
Huckleberry Finn, Chapter 10.

NOTES

1. While logicians traditionally distinguish between statements and propositions, it is by no means universally agreed that there are propositions in addition to statements. So while I write as if there are propositions in addition to statements, I leave open the question of the philosophical legitimacy of the distinction.

2. Conditional statements are discussed at greater length in Chapter 5.

Chapter Two
Meaning and Definition

2.1 Words, Information, and Emotion

We do many things with language. We tell stories, write reports, express sympathy, encourage confidence, express joy, greet people, make vows, instruct, direct, command, and so on. The words we use perform one or more of five general functions. (1) We use language to give information. For example, we might say, "Tabby is asleep." This is the **informative** function of language. (2) We use language to express or evoke emotions. Elizabeth Barrett Browning's poem "How do I love thee? Let me count the ways"[1] expresses the emotion of love. This is the **emotive** function of language. (3) We use language to request information, plead for actions, and issue orders and commands. We might ask, for example, "Did you read Dick Francis's new book?" As children we might have pled with a parent, "May my friend *please* come over to play today?" And we are all familiar with the sentences made famous by the game of *Monopoly*, "Go directly to jail. Do not pass Go. Do not collect $200." These are examples of the **directive** function of language. (4) We use language to perform various ceremonies. Marriage vows and greetings such as "Hi! How are you?" are examples of the **ceremonial** function of language. (5) Finally, we use language to make various commitments. Marriage vows, the Pledge of Allegiance, and promises, such as "I promise to meet you for lunch," are examples of the **commissive** function of language.

Of the various things we do with words, logicians are primarily concerned with the informative and emotive functions of language.[2] It is these functions of language that persuade people to accept claims as true or to act in certain ways. The following statements illustrate the differences between these two uses of language:

> Des Moines, the capital of Iowa since 1847, is one of the major centers of the insurance industry in the United States.

> The streets of Des Moines, the jewel of the Midwest, are bedecked with stately elms, fragrant flora, and lush green grass.

The first statement does little more than convey information. The second statement, using expressions such as "the jewel of the Midwest," "stately elms," "fragrant flora," and "lush green grass," tends to evoke favorable feelings toward the Iowa capital. Words that provide information have **cognitive meaning.** Words that express or evoke feelings have **emotive meaning.** This is not to say that any given word has *only* cognitive meaning or *only* emotive meaning. The second statement tells us that Des Moines's streets are lined with trees, flowers, and grass. Similarly, since Des Moines is a major insurance center, the first statement might make Des Moines emotionally appealing to insurance buffs or to people fixated on the year 1847.

Words attain emotive meanings on the basis of various associations and expectations. In the 1950s, the expression 'atomic energy' had a positive emotional appeal to many Americans. Since the United States was the first country to develop atomic energy, the words reflected a certain amount of nationalistic pride. Further, atomic energy was portrayed as safe, relatively inexpensive, and a virtually limitless source of energy. As time passed, there were several nuclear accidents and problems arose regarding the disposal of spent nuclear fuel, so for many people today the expressions 'atomic energy' and 'nuclear energy' have negative emotive meanings. Similarly, in the early 1960s the expression 'Made in Japan' had a negative emotive meaning. At that time, many products imported from Japan were not terribly reliable. Over the years, Japanese standards of engineering and manufacture improved to the extent that by the early 1990s at least one American automobile manufacturer attempted to appeal to the emotions of its potential buyers by claiming to have the same high standards of engineering as the Japanese.

It is important to distinguish between the cognitive and emotive meanings of words. *In evaluating an argument, we are concerned exclusively with the cognitive meaning of words.* We want to know whether the premises are true and how much evidence they provide for the conclusion. But we must be aware of the emotive impact of words, for in many cases the persuasive force of an argument rests upon its emotional appeal. Consider the following paragraph:

> A strong, and itself sufficient, reason for term limits is that they would restore to the legislative branch the preeminence and luster that it rightly should have. There is a kind of scorched-earth, pillage-and-burn conservatism that is always at a rolling boil, and which boils down to a brute animus against government. Those who subscribe to this vigorous but unstable faith have had jolly fun in the early 1990s as public esteem for government, and especially for Congress, has plummeted. However, that is not my kind of conservatism. I do not fathom how any American who loves the nation can relish the spectacle of the central institutions of American democracy being degraded and despised. Patriotism properly understood is not compatible with contempt for the institutions that put American democracy on display.[3]

The persuasive force of the passage rests primarily on its emotional appeal. Certainly it has more persuasive force than the following, which has approximately the same cognitive meaning:

> A good reason for term limits is that they would restore the legislative branch the status it should have. There is a kind of conservatism that is consistently opposed to government. Such conservatives have enjoyed the early 1990s as public respect for government, and especially for Congress, has decreased. However, that is not my kind of conservatism. I do not understand how any American can enjoy watching the central institutions of American democracy decreasing in esteem. Patriotism is not compatible with distaste for the institutions that put American democracy on display.

Emotional language is used by politicians, advertisers, and pundits to put a favorable "spin" on the positions they advance. For virtually any word with an unfavorable emotional meaning, there is another word with the same cognitive meaning that has a favorable emotional meaning. Here are some examples:

LESS FAVORABLE	NEUTRAL	MORE FAVORABLE
work	a job	a career
war	conflict	police action
warrior	soldier	hero
scrawny	thin	slender
bureaucrat	government employee	civil servant
crude	lacking in finesse	rustic
loud-mouthed	talkative	outspoken
indoctrination	education	edification

There is nothing wrong with emotively charged language: It is the language of poetry, the language that converts a mundane description into a glowing portrait. But in evaluating an argument, you are concerned with the cognitive meaning of words. You are concerned with the questions "Are the premises true?" and "Do the premises, if true, provide good reasons for accepting the truth of the conclusion?" Therefore it is reasonable to restate an emotionally charged argument in emotionally neutral terms: It helps you see more clearly what evidence the premises provide for the conclusion.

EXERCISES

I. For each of the following words, give another word with approximately the same cognitive meaning but with a more favorable emotive meaning.

1. 'jalopy'
2. 'shack'
3. 'boring'
4. 'stickler'
5. 'brash'
6. 'cantankerous'
7. 'lazy'
8. 'peddler'
9. 'abortion'
10. 'died'

2.2 *Words and Terms, Denotation and Connotation*

One of the topics logicians traditionally examine is the nature of definitions. This is important for several reasons. First, insofar as the evaluation of an argument often requires that we clearly understand what is claimed, definitions sometimes allow us to clarify the meaning of the statements in an argument. Second, some arguments take the definition of a term as a premise, and to evaluate such arguments we must understand the characteristics of an acceptable definition. Third, some disputes, those known as **verbal disputes,** rest on alternative meanings of terms, rather than a genuine disagreement about the facts. Once the alternative meanings are pointed out, all appearance of disagreement disappears. Consider the following examples:

1. Under–30: "Hey, man, that new red Cougar you bought is really bad!"
   Over–40: "I don't think it's such a bad car. It goes from zero to sixty in 4.3 seconds, it has nice lines, and gets over 20 miles to the gallon on the highway."

2. Two teachers are talking in the hallway:
   Ms. Hudley: "Jorge was right when he said that Mr. Boomhagen made Anastasia stand in the corner—I myself saw her standing there."
   Mr. Pate: "Jorge had no right to say that. It's the mark of disrespect when a first-grader complains to the principal about accepted classroom procedures."

Both of these are verbal disputes. The first dispute rests on alternative meanings of the word 'bad': both Under–30 and Over–40 agree the car is nice. The second dispute rests on alternative meanings of 'right'. Ms. Hudley is concerned with whether what Jorge said is true. Mr. Pate is concerned with whether it was proper for Jorge to say what he said.

While *words* are the basic elements of ordinary language, in this section we are concerned with **terms.** A term is a word or phrase that can be the subject of a sentence. Terms include common names, proper names, and descriptive phrases. Here are some examples:

Common Name	Proper Name	Descriptive phrase
author	Agatha Christie	author of *Ten Little Indians*
president	Ronald Reagan	40th President of the United States
horse	Secretariat	a winner of the Kentucky Derby
cat	Tabby	a feline animal
restaurant	Joe's Truck Stop	local greasy spoon
money	U.S. Savings Bonds	green things
students	Joan Smith, Mark Remirez	people who study
bank	Chase Manhattan Bank	New York City business
baseball team	Cincinnati Reds	heroes of summer

Words that are not terms include verbs, adverbs, nonsubstantive adjectives, conjunctions, prepositions, and nonsyntactic arrangements of words. Here are some examples of words that are not terms:

is	emotionally
green	heroically
insofar	if
write	dog redly and transcends

The last is an example of a nonsyntactic arrangement of words, that is, an arrangement of words that violates grammatical conventions.

Before we talk about words and definitions, we need to recognize the distinction between **use** and **mention**. When we make an ordinary statement, such as "Jane is crossing 1st Street," we *use* words—in this case to represent facts in the world. The statement "Jane is crossing 1st Street" is true if and only if Jane is actually crossing 1st Street. Sometimes, however, we want to talk about the words themselves. When we talk about a word, we *mention* or refer to that word. To show that we are mentioning a word, rather than using it, we place the word in single quotation marks.[4] The statement, " 'Dog' is a three-letter word" is a true statement about the word 'dog'. The statement, "Dog is a three-letter word" is false (if it is meaningful at all): here we are using the word 'dog', and a dog is an animal, not a three-letter word. Similarly, the statement " 'Car' is a noun," is true, since it mentions the word 'car', that is, it talks about the word 'car'. The statement "Some 'cars' have gasoline engines" is false, since it mentions the word 'cars' and the *word* 'cars' does not have an engine. On the other hand, the statement "Some cars have gasoline engines" is true, since we are using the word 'car' and some cars do in fact have gasoline engines.

Words are symbols. Words have meanings in certain contexts. Some words in some contexts represent things, states, or events in the world. Terms are composed of one or more words and have two kinds of meaning: denotative and connotative meaning. The **denotative meaning,** also known as the **denotation** or **extension,** of a term consists of all the things to which a term is correctly applied. For example, the word 'automobile' denotes every object that is an automobile. The **connotative meaning,** also known as the **connotation** or **intension,** of a term consists of all the characteristics or properties that are common to all the members of the class denoted by a term. For example, the word 'automobile' connotes a vehicle that carries its own power-generating and propelling mechanisms and travels on ordinary roads. These two kinds of meaning provide the basis for our discussions of definitions in subsequent sections of this chapter.

If you ask me what the connotation of the word 'gold' is, I would say gold is a metal, yellow, relatively heavy, and fairly expensive to buy. If you asked a chemist the same question, she might list some of the same characteristics, but since chemists know far more about the properties of gold than I know, she would probably list characteristics of which I know nothing. These person-to-person differences in the connotations of a term are known as **subjective connotations.** Terms also have objective connotations. The **objective connotation** of a term consists of all the characteristics common to all the things a term denotes. Since there are very few things of which anyone knows all the characteristics, the objective connotation of a term is relatively useless. Finally, there is the conventional connotation of a term. The **conventional connotation** of a term consists of the properties of a thing that the members of a certain linguistic community consider common to the things a term denotes. This is the most important of the three kinds of connotation, since it is the connotation that allows us to pick out objects and clarify the meanings of terms. Dictionary definitions purport to state conventional connotations of terms. The extent to which they do this determines the quality of the dictionary.

So far we have been concerned with descriptive connotations of terms, connotations that correspond to the cognitive meanings of terms. Many terms also have emotive connotations. Terms such as 'peace', 'love', and 'joy' have positive emotional connotations; terms such as 'war', 'hate', and 'sadness' have negative connotations. Like descriptive connotations, emotive connotations are subjective, objective, and conventional. Like conventional descriptive connotations, conventional emotive connotations can change. For example, in the eighteenth century, when a large amount of fatty tissue was a mark of prosperity, the word 'fat' had positive emotive connotations. As fashions changed, 'fat' lost its positive emotive connotations. It is important to be aware of the emotional connotations of terms because they can affect the persuasive force of an argument. In evaluating arguments and definitions, however, you should focus on the descriptive connotations of terms.

Denotations of terms do not vary from person to person. The term 'dog' denotes all dogs, past, present, and future. The term 'presently existing dogs' denotes the class of existing dogs, a class that changes from moment to moment. The term 'saber-toothed tiger' denotes all the saber-toothed tigers that existed, even though none exists now. On the other hand, since saber-toothed tigers are extinct, the term 'presently existing saber-toothed tiger' has an **empty denotation:** there is no thing that it denotes since saber-toothed tigers no longer exist. Other terms that, so far as we know, have an empty denotation include 'centaur', 'Pegasus', 'goblin', 'werewolf', 'unicorn', 'Beethoven's Eleventh Symphony', 'leprechaun', and 'Sherlock Holmes.'

While those terms have no denotation, each has a connotation. The connotation of the term acts as a standard or criterion for determining whether there is anything in the denotation of a term. For example, the term 'Beethoven's Eleventh Symphony' connotes the second symphony Ludwig van Beethoven wrote after his Ninth. Since Beethoven wrote only nine symphonies, the connotation helps us recognize that 'Beethoven's Eleventh Symphony' does not denote. The term is said to be "nondenoting" or "nonreferring." The term 'werewolf' connotes a human being who is capable of assuming the form of a wolf. The connotation of the term 'dog' is a criterion for the proper application of the term 'dog'.

Consider the terms 'rose', 'flowering plant', and 'plant'. The term 'flowering plant' is more general than the term 'rose', and the term 'plant' is more general than the term 'flowering plant'. The term 'plant' *denotes* more things than does the term 'flowering plant', which denotes more things than does the term 'rose'. On the other hand, since all flowering plants are plants, the term 'plant' *connotes* fewer properties than does the term 'flowering plant', which connotes fewer properties than does the word 'rose'. Like many words, there are relations among the denotations and connotations of the terms 'rose', 'flowering plant', and 'plant'. As related terms become more general, they usually stand in the relations of *decreasing connotation* and *increasing denotation*. When related terms become less general, they stand in relations of *increasing connotation* and *decreasing denotation*. The terms 'rose', 'flowering plant', and 'plant' stand in the following relations:

> increasing denotation: 'rose', 'flowering plant', 'plant'
> increasing connotation: 'plant', 'flowering plant', 'rose'
> decreasing denotation: 'plant', 'flowering plant', 'rose'
> decreasing connotation: 'rose', 'flowering plant', 'plant'

Here are some other examples:
increasing denotation:
  'timber wolf', 'wolf', 'canine', 'mammal', 'animal', 'thing'
  'capital murder', 'murder', 'homicide', 'crime'
increasing connotation:
  'thing', 'animal', 'mammal', 'canine', 'wolf', 'timber wolf'
  'crime', 'homicide', 'murder', 'capital murder'
decreasing denotation:
  'thing', 'animal', 'mammal', 'canine', 'wolf', 'timber wolf'
  'crime', 'homicide', 'murder', 'capital murder'
decreasing connotation:
  'timber wolf', 'wolf', 'canine', 'mammal', 'animal', 'thing'
  'capital murder', 'murder', 'homicide', 'crime'

While the orders of increasing denotation and decreasing connotation are often the same as are the orders of increasing connotation and decreasing denotation, there are cases in which they are not the same. Some terms have an empty denotation but stand in an increasing order of connotation. Here is an example:

> 'werewolf', 'green-eyed werewolf', 'green-eyed werewolf that once lived in Transylvania'

In other cases the denotation remains the same, even though the conventional connotation increases. Here is an example:

> 'dog', 'dog with a heart', 'dog with a heart and a back bone'

Since all dogs have hearts and backbones, although the properties of having a heart and having a backbone are not included in the conventional connotation of 'dog', the connotation of the terms increases. Nonetheless, the denotation of the three terms is exactly the same.

EXERCISES

I. Which of the following are terms?

1. 'bush'
2. 'either'
3. 'traveling'
4. 'Dean of the College'
5. 'mountain'
6. 'the present King of France'
7. 'Tom Sawyer'
8. 'drawing'
9. 'between'
10. 'a hare-brained idea'

II. Indicate whether the following statements are true or false. If a statement is false or meaningless, explain why it is false or meaningless.

1. Work is a four-letter word.
2. The connotation of 'schnauzer' is greater than the connotation of 'dog'.
3. 'Work' means effort directed to produce or accomplish something.
4. 'Unicorn' denotes a horse with a horn in the middle of its forehead.
5. 'Colleague' is a nine-letter word.
6. Turbo the cat is contained in the connotation of the word 'cat'.
7. The color green is connoted by the word grass.
8. Boisterous means rough and noisy.
9. The denotation of 'gnome' is the same as the denotation of 'centaur'.

10. The connotation of 'gnome' is the same as the connotation of 'centaur'.

IV. Use your knowledge of the subject in question to arrange the following sets of terms in order of increasing denotation. If you need help, consult a dictionary.

1. 'motor vehicle produced by Ford Motor Company', 'thing', 'Towncar', 'Lincoln'
2. 'mammal', 'dog', 'vertebrate', 'animal'
3. 'bacterium,' 'microorganism', 'microscopic plant,' 'organism'
4. 'political partisan', 'Democrat', 'person', 'Jimmy Carter'
5. 'bratwurst', 'food', 'sausage', 'meat'

V. Use your knowledge of the subject in question to arrange the following sets of terms in order of increasing connotation. If you need help, consult a dictionary.

1. 'animal,' 'curmudgeon', 'person', 'living thing'
2. 'bovine', 'longhorn', 'herbivore', 'animal'
3. 'rocker', 'chair', 'piece of furniture', 'home furnishing'
4. 'dictionary', 'book', 'reference book', 'printed matter'
5. 'cow with a heart', 'cow with a heart and a backbone', 'cow', 'brown cow with a heart and a backbone'

VI. Use your knowledge of the subject in question to arrange the following sets of terms in order of decreasing denotation. If you need help, consult a dictionary.

1. 'a Green Bay Packer', 'football player', 'professional football player', 'game player'
2. 'time pieces', 'Big Ben', 'clocks', 'machines'
3. 'animal', 'politician', 'thing', 'person'
4. 'major general', 'general', 'officer', 'soldier'
5. 'trees', 'evergreens', 'pines', 'Scotch pines'

VII. Use your knowledge of the subject in question to arrange the following sets of terms in order of decreasing connotation. If you need help, consult a dictionary.

1. 'fictitious entities', 'unicorns', 'mythical beasts', 'fictitious beasts'
2. 'necktie', 'bow tie', 'wearing apparel', 'things made of cloth'

3. 'book', 'textbook', 'things made of paper', 'things'
4. 'teacher', 'professor of physics', 'professor', 'person employed by an educational institution'
5. 'nose', 'part of the face', 'nostril', 'part of the body'

2.3 Why We Define

In this section we begin our discussion of definitions. There are two parts to a definition. The term that is defined is known as the **definiendum**. The word or words that define the definiendum are known as the **definiens**. For example, in the definition, " 'Ear' means the organ of hearing in humans and other vertebrates," the word 'ear' is the definiendum and the words "the organ of hearing in humans and other vertebrates" is the definiens.[5]

There are many reasons why we define words. When a new word is introduced into the language, we define it so others will know what the word means. When we confront a word with which we are unfamiliar, we look for a definition so we can know what the word means. We use definitions to remove vagueness. We introduce terms into theories by definitions. And various people might try to get us to accept their conclusions by defining a key term in a certain way. Let us consider these uses of definition in more detail.

Stipulative Definitions

There are times when we introduce new words into the language or wish to assign a new meaning to an old word. In such a case, an individual or a small part of the linguistic community *stipulates* the meaning of a word. The definition used is known as a **stipulative definition.**

We use stipulative definitions in many circumstances. Human beings are inventive, and every time something is invented, that thing is given a name. When electronic computers were invented, they needed to be given a name so that people could talk and write about them. Someone stipulated that the word 'computer' means "an electronic apparatus capable of carrying out repetitious and highly complex mathematical operations at high speeds."[6] Of course, inventions are not limited to things. We invent dances. We invent accounting procedures. And sometimes we invent words to replace other words. For example, someone once stipulated that the word 'te' could be used to replace 'he' or 'she' in gender-neutral contexts.

We also use stipulative definitions to give new meanings to old words. For example, when physicists discovered quarks, they adopted the color words 'red', 'green', and 'blue' to name those particles. This was simply a choice. When computer companies developed an instrument the movements of which allow you to point at various things on the screen, they adopted the name 'mouse'. Here there were certain analogies between the computer-mouse and a biological mouse: similar size, quick and jerky movements, a "tail," and so forth.

Finally, an author will sometimes stipulate the meaning he or she assigns to a word. This will often do away with verbal ambiguities, that is, it will specify which of a number of conventional meanings of a term is being used. For example, a biologist writing a general paper on members of the cat family might stipulate, "In this paper I use the word 'cat' to refer to any member of the genus *Felis*." Of course, anything can be stipulated. An author could go so far as to stipulate, "In this paper I use the word 'black' to refer to what we ordinarily mean by the word 'white', and I use the word 'white' to refer to what we ordinarily mean by 'black'."

A stipulative definition is an imaginative assignment of a meaning to a word, an assignment of meaning that could have been different. It is analogous to naming a newborn child. When a parent decides that his or her newborn will be called 'Amisglof', the child is henceforth called by that name. In this case, the name given to the child is analogous to the definiendum. The child is analogous to the denotation. And a description of the child—for example, "female, 21 inches long, 8 pounds 4 ounces, red hair, born August 27, 1992, the daughter of . . . , the child with a right index fingerprint of . . . ,"—is analogous to the definiens of a connotative definition, that is, it is a criterion for distinguishing the child from all others. Just as in the act of naming a child the parents cannot make a mistake—relatives' complaints about the choice of a name notwithstanding—if we stipulate that a new word has a certain meaning, we cannot make a mistake: the definition is neither true nor false. It is, however, more or less useful for our purposes and can be evaluated accordingly.

Lexical Definitions

A **lexical definition** reports a conventional meaning of a word. Dictionary definitions are prime examples of lexical definitions. Since the meaning is conventional, lexical definitions are either true or false—

depending on whether they correctly report the meaning of the word at the time and place in question. A lexical definition is true if it correctly reports one of the conventions; otherwise it is false. For example, if we define 'cat' as "a small, lithe, soft-furred animal, domesticated since ancient times and often kept as a pet or for killing mice,"[7] the definition is true: it reflects the conventional meaning of 'cat' in the contemporary United States. If we define 'dog' in the same way, the definition is false, since it does not reflect the conventional meaning of 'dog'. Of course, the conventions governing words often change over time and vary from place to place. The writers of the United States Constitution used the word 'enjoy' to mean *have* in the phrase "enjoy the right to a speedy and public trial"; this convention no longer governs the meaning of 'enjoy'. The term 'public school' in British English means a private boarding school; in American English it means a school supported by public taxes.

We use lexical definitions to learn the meanings of words, to clarify the meanings of words, and, since many words have more than one meaning, to distinguish among the meanings of a word. Since many words have more than one conventional meaning, lexical definitions help us recognize and appreciate the ambiguities in language.

Precising Definitions

Words are **ambiguous** if they have more than one meaning. For example, 'rocks' means one thing if you're planning to gravel your driveway; it means something quite different if you want your drink "on the rocks." 'Iced' has to do with frozen water when you're talking about streets, but it has to do with frosting when you're talking about cakes. 'Cat' can mean a small domestic animal, a large wild animal, a person, or a large earth-moving machine. Words are **vague** if their meanings lack clarity or precision. Examples of vague words include 'city', 'fresh', 'rich', 'poor', 'new', 'old', 'bald'. Most of the time, a bit of vagueness makes little difference. When eliminating vagueness is important, we can offer a **precising definition** to set specific limits to the definiendum.

Assume you are moving to a new community. So long as the area has all the amenities to which you have grown accustomed, it may make little difference whether you call it a town or a city or a metropolitan area. The U. S. Census Bureau finds such distinctions important, however, and offers precising definitions of terms such as 'urban area' and 'metropolitan area'. According to the Census Bureau, the term 'urban area' means an area with at least 1,000 people per square mile, and 'metropolitan area' means an area with a central city of at least 50,000 people or, if there are less than 50,000 people in the central city, at least 100,000 people in the central city and its surrounding area.[8]

Precising definitions are commonly found in specialized fields, where words from ordinary English take on technical meanings. Logicians, for example, have taken the ordinary English word 'valid' and have given it a precising definition for use within deductive logic: "An argument form is valid if and only if the truth of the premises guarantees the truth of the conclusion." Precising definitions are offered in the sciences for terms such as 'acid', 'base', 'energy', 'force', 'organic compound', 'number' and so forth. In law, 'negligence' and 'murder' have precise meanings.

A precising definition of a term assumes the conventional descriptive connotation of that term and sets limits on it. In this respect, anyone offering a precising definition lacks the freedom he or she has in offering a stipulative definition. For example, it would be unacceptable to claim that "an area of one square mile with a population of at least five people" is a precising definition of 'urban area'. However, once the definer is constrained by the conventional connotation, he or she has a significant amount of freedom regarding the points at which the limits are drawn, being constrained only by the purposes for which the precising definition is drawn. For example, it might be only for matters of convenience that the Census Bureau chose to define 'urban area' as an area of one square mile having a population of at least *1,000* people rather than 950 or 1,100 people.

Theoretical Definitions

A **theoretical definition** is used to describe an object posited by a theory. The definition shows the relationship between the definiendum and other terms in the theory. It suggests deductive consequences and further avenues of investigation (experimental and otherwise). For example, scientists define 'heat' in terms of the movement of particles. The more rapid the movement of particles, the higher the registration on the thermometer. The adequacy of this definition of 'heat' depends upon the theory of which it is a part. Insofar as the definiens of 'heat' rests on theoretical considerations, it suggests experimental procedures for determining that the definition is acceptable. If the evidence tends to confirm the theory in terms of which 'heat' is defined, scientists have reason to believe that their definition of 'heat' is correct.

Not all theoretical definitions occur within science. Philosophers also construct theoretical definitions. For example, in Plato's *Republic* the objective is to discover the nature of justice, that is, to give an adequate theoretical definition of the word 'justice'. In reading the *Republic,* we discover that there are numerous attempts at such a definition. The first attempt is roughly, " 'Justice' means doing good to your friends and evil to your enemies."[9] This is judged inadequate because inapplicable: some of those we believe to be our enemies might actually have our best interests at heart and therefore be our friends. (Consider, for example, a teacher with strict grading standards.) A second attempt at a definition is made. In each case counterexamples are considered, that is, examples which, if true, would show that the definition is inadequate. The search throughout is for a theoretical definition of 'justice' for which there are no counterexamples.

Persuasive Definitions

A **persuasive definition** is used to influence the attitudes of the hearer with respect to the thing—person, event, or state of affairs—denoted by the definiendum. The definiens contains terms that have positive or negative emotive connotations that affect the hearer's attitudes with respect to the thing denoted by the definiendum. Such definitions are often given with an eye to gaining an argumentative advantage. For example, an opponent of abortion might tell you that " 'Abortion' means the murder of innocent unborn children." A proponent of abortion rights might tell you that " 'Abortion' means giving women reproductive freedom of choice." Many terms can be alternatively defined so that they have positive or negative connotations. Here are some examples:

> 'Patriotism' means the blind commitment to the policies of a government regardless of the moral bankruptcy of those policies.
> 'Patriotism' means placing the love of your country above your personal wants.
> 'Duty' means doing what you don't want to do because someone says you should.
> 'Duty' means acting in ways that fulfill your true interests.
> 'Automation' means the wanton replacement of people with machines in the workplace solely to increase the wealth of greedy capitalists.

'Automation' means the use of machines in the workplace to increase efficiency and productivity.

'Taxation' means robbery of the people, by the government, for the government.

'Taxation' means the process by which the government acquires funds to be used for the common good.

People offer persuasive definitions to influence the attitudes of their hearers and are not primarily concerned with whether they are true or false. To determine whether the definition is true or false, it must be evaluated. For example, if someone says, " 'Abortion' means the murder of unborn children," you must ask whether abortion is the intentional taking of a human life (murder), to what extent a fetus is similar to a child that has been born, whether parental rights and responsibilities are the same for children that have been born as for those that have not been born, and so forth. In short, you must evaluate many of the arguments for one side of the abortion issue.

Persuasive definitions are commonly used to change attitudes and beliefs and can be used by people on any side of a given issue. So you should be aware of the emotional impact of the definition and ask whether the definition is plausible.

EXERCISES

I. Determine whether the following definitions are stipulative, lexical, precising, theoretical, or persuasive. Give reasons for your answers.

1. 'Gobwoff' means a golf stroke made in a creek or pond.

2. 'Energy' means mass times the speed of light squared.

3. 'Lanolin' means a fatty substance extracted from wool and used in ointments.

4. 'Cup' means a unit of liquid measure equal to .264175 liters.

5. 'Marriage' means a contractual arrangement between a woman and a man that admits them into the highest halls of human happiness.

6. 'Red mullet' means a goatfish or surmullet.

7. 'Joule' means a unit of work equal to 10^7 ergs.

8. 'Pall' means a coffin.

9. 'Politician' means a professional liar who attempts, through deception, to run a government.

10. 'Agotatae' means characters created solely to amuse logic students.

11. 'Old' means, when applied to computers, any computer that has been sold more than two days ago.

12. 'Valid' means a deductive argument in which it is impossible for all the premises to be true and the conclusion false.

13. 'Palm' means part of the inner surface of the hand which extends from the wrists to the fingers.

14. 'Id' means, in Freudian psychology, that division of the psyche from which come blind, impersonal, instinctual impulses that demand immediate gratification of primitive needs.

15. 'Impoverished' means having an annual net family income of less than $7,500.

16. 'Visitant' means a temporary resident.

17. 'Grain' means, in metallurgy, any of the individual crystalline particles forming a metal.

18. 'Money' means a person's best friend.

19. 'Middle-aged' means a man over the age of 36 or a woman over the age of 37½.

20. 'Olisthgloth' means an automobile that has passed through a car-crusher.

II. Indicate whether the following statements are true or false. Give reasons for your answers.

1. Definitions tell us the nature of things.

2. The definiens is the word defined.

3. All definitions specify the common usage of words.

4. Theoretical definitions tell us the conventional meaning of a word.

5. You can introduce a new word into a language by means of a stipulative definition.

6. It is proper to say that a lexical definition is true or false.

7. Theoretical definitions might change as new discoveries are made in the disciplines in which they are found.

8. Anyone offering a persuasive definition is primarily concerned with the truth and precision of his or her definition.

9. Precising definitions are offered to eliminate ambiguities in the definiendum.

10. Philosophical attempts to provide definitions of terms such as 'good' or 'universal' are examples of theoretical definitions.

2.4 Denotative (Extensional) Definitions

Denotative definitions and connotative definitions correspond to the denotative and connotative meanings of terms. In this section we focus on denotative definitions.

As we saw, the denotation of a term is all those things to which the term is correctly applied. In giving a denotative definition, you define a term by tying it as directly as possible to one or several objects in the term's denotation. There are three types of denotative definitions.

Ostensive Definitions

If you offer an **ostensive definition**, you literally point at a thing in a term's extension and say, "This is a. . .." For example, if I offered an ostensive definition of the term 'book', I would point at a book and say, "This is a book." While we learn some words by ostensive definition, there are obvious shortcomings. If you ask me what 'book' means and I point to a book, you might ask what I'm pointing at. I might be pointing to a packet of paper bound between pieces of heavier paper or cardboard. I might be pointing to the redness on the cover. I might be pointing to the gold letters on the cover. I might be pointing to the one-inch thickness. I might be pointing to the smooth texture. I might be pointing to something else. Some of this ambiguity can be eliminated by pointing at several examples: a thick hardbound book with a red cover, a small paperback book with a green cover, a thick paperbound book with a yellow cover, a children's book, a technical manual. In offering an ostensive definition based on numerous examples, I assume that eventually you will "see" what is common to all the examples and come to understand the meaning of the word 'book'. This is one way children learn the meanings of terms.

The ambiguity of pointing is not the only disadvantage to an ostensive definition. There are cases in which we simply cannot give an ostensive definition, since there is nothing in the denotation of a term at which we can point. If you asked me what the word 'mountain' means,

I would have no problem giving you an ostensive definition if I were in Denver, Colorado, or Charlottesville, Virginia—I'd simply take you outside and point to various large, rather pointed mounds of earth and stone to the west. If you asked me the same question when we were in Omaha, Nebraska, or Houston, Texas, I couldn't give an ostensive definition: there are no mountains near either city. The best I could do in Omaha or Houston is point at a picture of a mountain, which might raise questions regarding what I'm pointing at (the picture itself or what it represents), the size of a thing that counts as a mountain, and so forth. If you asked me to give an ostensive definition of 'atom' or 'quark', I would never be able to provide an ostensive definition: atoms and quarks are imperceptible. If you asked me to give an ostensive definition of 'bacterium', I could do so only with a pointer under a microscope. So the possibility of providing an ostensive definition sometimes depends upon geography or technology; some terms are incapable of ostensive definition.

Enumerative Definitions

A second kind of denotative definition is an **enumerative definition.** To define by enumeration, we give a (partial) list of objects in the denotation of a term. For example, if you asked me to give an enumerative definition of 'book' I might list *One Fish Two Fish Red Fish Blue Fish* (by Dr. Seuss), *The Guns of August* (by Barbara Tuchman), *Prophesy Deliverance!* (by Cornel West), *A Treatise of Human Nature* (by David Hume), *Sotah* (by Naomi Ragen), *The Doll's House* (by Evelyn Anthony), *WordPerfect for IBM Personal Computers and PC Networks* (by the WordPerfect Corporation), *The Better Homes and Gardens Cookbook,* and volume 1 of the *Encyclopedia Britannica.* While this is anything but a complete enumeration of the objects in the denotation of 'book', it is enough to allow you to know what counts as a book. On the other hand, unless you are familiar with some of the books I list in the definiendum, the enumerative definition will not be helpful.

There are very few cases in which an enumerative definition provides a complete list of the objects in the denotation of a term. We can give a complete enumeration to define the word 'ocean', namely, " 'Ocean' means the Atlantic, the Pacific, the Indian, and the Arctic." Perhaps an automobile company could give a complete enumerative definition of a discontinued model car by listing all the body identification numbers of those cars. But in most cases there are two problems: First, there is usually an indefinitely large number of objects in the denotation of a term, and, in many cases, the number of objects is constantly increasing. Second, to give a complete enumerative definition you must list the names or unique descriptions of each object in the denotation, and this can be done for very few things.

Definition by Subclass

In offering a **definition by subclass** you name the subclasses of a class denoted by a term. That is, you name various kinds of things that fall under the general term. Such definitions can be complete or incomplete. Here are some examples:

> 'Cat' means a Persian, a Siamese, an Angola, a tabby, a tiger, a gray, etc.
> 'Fish' means a trout, a blue gill, a carp, a marlin, a cod, a haddock, a sea horse, etc.
> 'Triangle' means scalene, isosceles, equilateral, right, acute, obtuse.

The first two are incomplete definitions by subclass. The third is a complete definition by subclass.

Denotative definitions are sometimes used in lexical and stipulative definitions. Since a lexical definition gives the conventional meaning of a word, it is sometimes possible to define the word by giving examples of things in the denotation. Some dictionaries do this. Even if you give a connotative lexical definition, it will often increase the reader's or hearer's understanding to mention some of the objects in the term's denotation. Since a stipulative definition is strictly arbitrary, we often give a denotative definition of the new word. For example, if I invented a machine that automatically writes logic problems, I might point to it, say "logicwrite," and so give an ostensive definition of 'logicwrite'.

EXERCISES

I. Provide a complete enumerative definition of each of the following terms.

1. 'continent'
2. 'known planets in our solar system'
3. 'New England state'
4. 'United States presidents since 1980'
5. 'Central American country'

II. Provide a partial enumerative definition of each of the following terms.

   1. 'singer'

   2. 'playwright'

   3. 'desert'

   4. 'island'

   5. 'state'

III. Provide a partial definition by subclass of each of the following terms.

   1. 'car'

   2. 'periodical'

   3. 'dog'

   4. 'time piece'

   5. 'musical instrument'

   6. 'emotion'

2.5 Connotative (Intensional) Definitions

A **connotative definition,** as we saw, states the meaning of a word by listing the properties or attributes that the word connotes. Connotative definitions are strictly verbal in the sense that you define one word in terms of other words.[10] Here we consider three kinds of connotative definitions: synonymous definitions, operational definitions, and definitions by genus and difference.

Synonymous Definitions

A common type of connotative definition is a **synonymous definition.** If we provide a synonymous definition of a term, the definiens is a single word with the same connotation as the definiendum.[11] Here are some examples:

   'Automobile' means car.
   'Bovines' means cattle.
   'Mendacious' means deceitful.
   'Odoriferous' means fragrant.

This is the kind of definition that is most commonly employed in foreign language dictionaries. For example:

> The German word *'Regen'* means rain.
> The French word *'sortie'* means exit.
> The Italian word *'andante'* means slow.
> The Spanish word *'hablar'* means speak.
> The Latin term *'rex regis'* means king.

While a synonymous definition is often an efficient way to define a word, it must be offered with great care. Many words are nearly synonymous, but have subtly different connotations. For example, 'colleagues' and 'partners' are nearly synonymous. Both words connote persons who share in an endeavor. But 'partners' connotes persons involved in a business endeavor; 'colleagues' is broader than that. Partners in a business venture are colleagues. The members of a department of English are colleagues, but they are not partners.

Operational Definitions

In an **operational definition,** the definiens specifies an experimental procedure or operation which provides a criterion for the application of a term. These definitions differ from other connotative definitions insofar as they state a procedure and claim that a certain word applies to something if and only if there is a certain result. Here are some examples:

> The word 'acid' applies to a solution if and only if a strip of blue litmus paper inserted into it turns red.
> The word 'charging' applies to a car battery if and only if the needle of a voltmeter attached to the battery points to the plus sign.
> The word 'magnet' applies to an iron bar if and only if iron filings are attracted by the ends of the bar and cling to them.
> 'Having greater mass than' applies to thing A relative to thing B if and only if when both things are placed on opposing pans of a beam balance the pan in which thing A is placed settles in a lower position than that in which thing B is placed.

In each of these examples, a certain procedure is given as a basis for the correct application of a word. For example, we are assured that a solution is an acid, and that the word 'acid' correctly applies to the solution, if and only if a piece of blue litmus paper inserted into it turns red. This is not the only test that could be run to determine whether the solution is an acid—we might have offered an operational definition in terms of the readings of less than seven on a pH-meter. What is essential to an ostensive definition is that we engage in *some* public repeatable procedure in determining whether or not a word has application.

Operational definitions are commonly used in the sciences. They provide empirical criteria for correctly applying a word to something that is not directly observable, and they do no more than that. An operational definition of 'acid', for example, provides no theoretical understanding of what it is for something to be an acid. Operational definitions provide only a *part*, often a small part, of the connotation of a term. For this reason they are sometimes judged inadequate. Nonetheless, they are often very useful for scientific purposes.

Definition by Genus and Difference

The classic form of connotative definition is a **definition by genus and difference** (definition *per genus et differentiam*). Here a word is treated as the name of a species or class of objects. We define a word by identifying a more general class in which the subclass falls (the genus) and the properties that are unique to that subclass and that *differentiate* it from other members of the genus. For example, 'girl' may be defined as "young woman." 'Girl', the definiendum, is the species name. 'Woman' is the name of the genus. 'Young' is the property that differentiates girls from other women. Here are some other examples:

SPECIES		DIFFERENCE	GENUS
'Puppy'	means	young	dog.
'Brother'	means	male	sibling.
'Tome'	means	large	book.
'Infant'	means	very young	child.
'Ice'	means	frozen	water.

Often the difference cannot be expressed in a single word. For example:

'Liver' means a large, reddish-brown organ located in the upper right side of the abdominal cavity that secretes bile and filters the blood.
'Bachelor' means unmarried male adult human.

In the first example, 'organ' is the genus, and 'large', 'reddish-brown', 'located in the upper right side of the abdominal cavity', 'secretes bile' and 'filters blood' are the difference. In the second example, 'human' is the genus, and 'unmarried', 'male', and 'adult' are the difference.

Definition by genus and difference is the most common way to define a word. Most stipulative, lexical, and persuasive definitions, and virtually all theoretical and precising definitions, are definitions by genus and difference.

EXERCISES

I. Give a synonymous definition of each of the following terms.
1. 'canine'
2. 'feline'
3. 'instructor'
4. 'booze'
5. 'circle'
6. 'magnanimous'
7. 'exacerbate'
8. 'malodorous'
9. 'melodious'
10. 'malevolent'

II. Give an operational definition of each of the following terms.
1. 'blood pressure'
2. 'radioactive'
3. 'harder than'
4. 'length of two feet'
5. 'genius'

III. Give a definition by genus and difference of each of the following terms.
1. 'professor'
2. 'buggy'
3. 'fawn'
4. 'miser'
5. 'woman'
6. 'bratwurst'
7. 'triangle'
8. 'knoll'
9. 'coronet'

8. 'husband'
9. 'kitten'
10. 'stationery'
11. 'drum'
12. 'scalpel'
13. 'bushel'

2.6 *Evaluating Connotative Definitions by Genus and Difference*

When we look up a word in a dictionary, most of the time we are seeking information: we want to know what the conventional connotation of a term is. The definition effectively provides this information to the extent that it (1) is accurate, (2) is fairly precise, and (3) succeeds in communicating the connotation of the word. But some definitions are better than others. In this section we consider five rules for evaluating connotative definitions. These rules provide guidelines for determining whether a definition could be improved *on the assumption* that the purpose for which the definition is given is to communicate the descriptive connotation of the term. Further, they apply only to definitions by genus and difference and primarily to lexical definitions. The first two rules concern accuracy and precision, guiding you in much the same way that an address guides you to a particular house: the street name allows you to find the right neighborhood and the number allows you to find the right house. The last three rules concern the communication of information. Definitions may be deemed better or worse to the extent that they follow these rules.

> Rule 1: A definition must correctly identify the genus of things denoted by the definiendum.

Consider some examples:

'Cup' (in recipes) means a unit of liquid measure.
'Sophomore' means a second-year student.
'Circle' means a closed plain curve, all points of which are equidistant from a given point called the center.

Each of these definitions identifies the correct genus; each at least gets you into the right neighborhood. When you follow the rule, there is a true universal proposition corresponding to the definition which claims that all things denoted by the definiendum are things denoted by the genus-term of the definiens. For example, the definition " 'Sophomore' means a second-year student" is acceptable on the basis of the first rule if it is true that "All sophomores are students," since 'students' is the genus-term in the definition. The other definitions are equally accept-able, since all cups in recipes are units of measure and all circles are closed plane curves. On the other hand, if a definition identifies the wrong genus, it must be rejected. For example, if I defined 'snake' as "a furry plant," the definition should be rejected because it misidenti-fies the genus in which snakes fall.

Establishing that a definition identifies the correct genus is the first step in evaluating a definition, just as finding the right street is the first step in finding your way to a particular house. But just as you'll find the right house only if you've been given the right house number, a definition successfully picks out the right class of objects only if the difference-term places the proper limits on the genus. This is the point of the second rule:

> Rule 2: A definition must correctly identify the difference that differentiates things denoted by the definiendum from other things in the same genus.

A definition can violate this rule in any of three ways. (1) A definition might completely misidentify the difference. If I said, " 'Circle' means a plain figure with four sides," the difference, 'with four sides', picks out the wrong class of plain figures. (2) If a difference-term does not suffi-ciently limit the genus, the definition is *too broad:* the definiens denotes more objects than the definiendum. (3) If a difference-term too severely limits the genus, the definition is *too narrow:* the definiens denotes fewer objects than the definiendum. Let us consider some examples to see how this is judged.

If a definition either misidentifies the difference or is too narrow, a universal proposition in which the definiendum is the subject term and the definiens is the predicate term is false. For example, if I said, " 'Book' means a written or printed work of at least 200 pages," you would in-dicate that that definition is too narrow by noting that the proposition "All books are written or printed works of at least 200 pages" is false. Many books are shorter than 200 pages. The difference-term 'of at least 200 pages' too severely limits the class of written or printed works.

If a definition is too broad, a universal proposition in which the definiens is the subject term and the definiendum is the predicate term is false. For example, if I said, " 'Human being' means featherless biped," you would indicate that the definition is too broad by noting that the proposition "All featherless bipeds are human beings" is false. The class of featherless bipeds includes plucked chickens and some dinosaurs. The difference-term 'featherless' does not place strict enough limits on the class of bipeds.

It is also possible for a definition to be *both* too broad and too narrow. Consider the definition " 'Cup' (in recipes) means a unit of liquid measure." The definition is too narrow, since cups in recipes are units of either dry or liquid measure. But the definition is also too broad, since not all units of liquid measure in recipes are cups—there are also teaspoons, tablespoons, and so forth. So you would need to narrow the definition by specifying the size of a cup. The following definition might be adequate: " 'Cup' (in recipes) means a unit of dry or liquid measure equal to a little over a quarter-liter."

Criticizing a definition on the basis of the second rule depends upon both the nature of the error and the purposes of the person who defines the word or seeks a definition. If a difference-term grossly misidentifies that which differentiates members of the species from other objects in the genus, the definition should be rejected. If the definition is too broad or too narrow, the degree to which you will fault the definition will depend upon the degree of precision you were seeking in the definition. If you are seeking a very precise definition, your tolerance will be low. If you want only "a pretty good idea" of the meaning of the term, you will probably tolerate a definition that is a bit too broad or too narrow. To return to our analogy to an address, you might be upset with an address if it takes you only to the front gate of a large estate, when you wanted to find your way to the front door of the house. The directions are not sufficiently precise to fulfill your purposes. Similarly, you might fault a set of directions that take you to the kitchen of a house, if you only wanted to find your way to the front door. Again, the directions do not comply with your purposes. Similarly, the extent to which you will fault a definition as too broad or too narrow will depend upon the purposes for which you are seeking a definition.

The final three rules concern the communication of information by a definition. A definition successfully communicates the meaning of the definiendum only if the terms in the definiens are already understood by the person hearing or seeking the definition. Obviously, many definitions that are enlightening to college students will leave a typical first grader completely in the dark. So these rules are rules of thumb, and the extent to which you are likely to fault a definition for violating one of these rules depends upon the circumstances in which the definition is offered.

Rule 3: Definitions should not be circular.

In a circular definition, some form of the definiendum is contained in the definiens. If we do not know the meaning of the definiendum, including some form of that term in the definiens usually will not clarify or explain the meaning. Here are some examples:

'Religion' means the activities of religious people.
'Football' means the game played with a football.
'Happiness' means the state of being happy.

Sometimes the circularity is not in a single definition, but in a series of definitions. Here are some examples:

'Happiness' means pleasure.
'Pleasure' means satisfaction.
'Satisfaction' means happiness.

No one of these definitions is circular, but if we want to know what 'happiness' means and successively look up 'happiness', 'pleasure', and 'satisfaction', we are as puzzled when we finish as when we started.

Nonetheless, the letter of this rule is regularly violated, and no one complains. If I look up 'sounding' in a dictionary, I am likely to find the definition, "making a sound." Since I have some idea what a sound is, the definition is informative. If I did not know what 'sound' means, I could look up that word to find out what is being made. Dictionaries would be extremely cumbersome if definitions of forms of words were not made in terms of the words of which they are forms. Further, there is a sense in which virtually any series of connotative definitions of synonymous or nearly synonymous terms will be circular, since the meanings of the terms are closely related to one another and there is only a finite number of ways in which the meaning can be expressed. The objective in giving a definition is to state the meaning of a term by means of other terms with which the person seeking a definition is likely to be familiar. The *point* of the third rule is that it is more probable that you will fulfill that objective if the definiens does not contain a form of the definiendum.

Rule 4: Generally, definitions should not be negative when they can be affirmative.

Here are some examples of affirmative and negative definitions:

'Uncouth' means crude. (affirmative)
'Uncouth' means not mannerly. (negative)
'Mammal' means any vertebrate that feeds milk from mammary glands to its young, has a body more or less covered with hair, and gives birth to its young. (affirmative)
'Mammal' means an animal that is not single-celled, that is not a reptile, that is not an amphibian, that is not a bird, and that is not a marsupial. (negative)

Often it is both more efficient and clearer to give an affirmative definition than a negative definition. For example, I could define 'oxygen' as "the known chemical element that is neither hydrogen, nor helium, nor . . ."—listing all the elements on the periodic table *except* oxygen. Such a definition would be very lengthy, and it probably would not provide the person seeking the definition the information he or she wanted. To define 'oxygen' as "a chemical element with the atomic number 8" would probably convey much of the same information and be clearer—certainly less cumbersome.

Some words are inherently negative, and these words provide exceptions to the rule. Here are some examples.

'Bald' means the absence of hair.
'Vacuum' means the absence of everything.
'Uncouth' means not mannerly.

As in the case of circular definitions, the extent, if any, to which a definition is faulted for being negative when it could be affirmative will depend upon the term and the audience. If a fairly small number of species fall under a certain genus and the person seeking the definition understands the meanings of all the species-terms except one, a negative definition might well be preferable to an affirmative definition. For example, I find it clearer to define 'uncouth' as 'not mannerly' than as 'crude', but this is in part because the word 'crude' is somewhat vague and ambiguous—a point we consider in our next rule.

Rule 5: In offering a definition we should use emotively neutral language. We should avoid obscure, figurative, vague, and ambiguous language.

Using emotive terms in a definition often obscures the conventional descriptive connotation of a word. For example, if I say " 'Abortion' means the murder of unborn children," I am making certain assumptions regarding the moral status of the fetus and the intentions of the abortionist. It seems doubtful that the objective of anyone performing or undergoing an abortion is to kill; it is clear that the objective of anyone performing or undergoing an abortion is to terminate a pregnancy. Similarly, it is a matter of considerable debate whether or at what point a fetus has the same moral status as a child who has been born—this is the primary issue in the abortion controversy. Further, my definition does not acknowledge elements contained in the conventional connotation of the term, for example, that abortion is a surgical procedure.

If we want to provide information, we should use the clearest terminology we can. Typically this means that the terminology in the definition should be as pedestrian as possible. If we use large words in the definition, there is a very good chance that the definition will be *obscure:* most people hearing the definition will not understand it. For example, if I say, " 'Path' means an itinerary occasioned by the perambulation of a populace of *homo sapiens* or nonhumanoid creatures," most hearers who did not previously know the meaning of 'path' would be no better off after hearing the definition. So keep the terminology in the definition as simple as possible.

Figurative or metaphorical language paints pictures. It is often obscure, and consequently, although figurative definitions might be extremely suggestive, they often do not convey information in the clearest way possible. For example:

> 'Dance' means poetry in motion.
> 'Bread' means the staff of life.
> 'Camel' means an animal made by a committee.

These definitions provide no clue to the conventional meanings of 'dance', 'bread', or 'camel' unless you already understand the metaphor.

A word is vague if its meaning is unclear. Using vague words in a definition does not define the limits within which a word is applied and often leaves the essential meaning of a word unclear. Here are some examples of vague definitions:

> 'Tiger' means a large striped cat.
> 'Obese' means heavy.

Since 'large' is vague, the definition of 'tiger' leaves unclear whether or not some domestic animals are tigers. The definition of 'obese' fails to tell you that you are concerned with the weight of people, that the weight must be excessive relative to some standard, and that the excessive weight is correlated with excessive amounts of fat.

A word is ambiguous if it has more than one meaning. A definition that uses ambiguous words or sentence structures will not state the essential meaning of a word. Here are some examples of ambiguous definitions:

'Clock' means a timekeeper.
'Death' means the end of life.

The definition of 'clock' leaves open the question whether the keeper of time is a device or a person. The definition of 'death' leaves open the question whether death is the cessation of life or the purpose of life.

While following the last three rules helps assure you of accurately communicating the meaning of a word, there are two other points you should keep in mind. First, definitions should always be stated in good grammatical form. Grammatical sentences are always clearer than ungrammatical sentences. Second, you should be as clear as possible about the context in which you are giving a definition. If someone asks you what 'strike' means in baseball, you must first determine whether the person is asking about the rules of the game or the newspaper headline, "Baseball Players Strike."

EXERCISES

Evaluate the following definitions on the basis of the five rules:

1. 'Dairy cow' means an animal that gives milk.
2. 'Religion' means what people practice in church.
3. 'Calendar' means a date book.
4. 'Dollar' means the primary American monetary unit.
5. 'Procrastination' means putting off until tomorrow what you should have done yesterday.
6. 'Adolescence' means a combination of vicissitudes that ensues during the second decade of the physiological maturation of a member of the species *homo sapiens*.
7. 'Regulator' means a person who regulates.

8. 'Organ' means a musical instrument consisting of sets of pipes sounded by means of compressed air, played by means of one or more keyboards, and capable of producing a wide range of musical effects.

9. 'Bill' means a statement of money owed for goods or services supplied.

10. 'Fearless' means without fear.

11. 'Zero' means the cipher representing the absence of numerocity.

12. 'Graviton' means the quantum of gravitation assumed to be an elementary particle that is its own antiparticle and that has a zero rest mass and charge and a spin of two.

13. 'Calisthenics' means movements of the arms, legs, head, and torso that are neither walking, nor running, nor sitting down.

14. 'Kindergarten' means garden of children.

15. 'Novel' means a work of fiction.

16. 'Metronome' means a mechanical or electronic toe-tapper for music.

17. 'Atom' means a small particle that is neither a molecule nor a subatomic particle.

18. 'Wine' means an alcoholic beverage made from grapes.

19. Empathy means appreciating what someone else is going through or has gone through. . . . Empathy is compassion, not agreement.
    MARIA ARAPAKIS, *Softpower* (New York: Time Warner, 1990), pp. 97–98.

20. 'Skim milk' means white water.

21. 'Index' means an alphabetical listing of names.

22. Marriage is that relation between man and woman in which the independence is equal, the dependence mutual, and the obligation reciprocal.
    LOUIS KAUFMAN ANSPACHER, Address, Boston, December 30, 1934.

23. Memory is the diary that we all carry about with us.
    OSCAR WILDE, *The Importance of Being Earnest,* Act II.

24. Art is . . . the spearhead of human development, social and individual.
    SUSANNE K. LANGER, *Philosophical Sketches* (New York: Mentor Books, 1962), p. 75.

25. A mantra . . . is a word that when repeated over and over again would transport me to a level of calmness and give me untold energy.

> ERMA BOMBECK, *Aunt Erma's Cope Book*
> (New York: Fawcett Books, 1979), p. 100.

26. Disjunctive sentences are sentences in which disjunctive joining is expressed.

> ANTOINE ARNAULD, *The Art of Thinking,* translated
> by James Dickoff and Patricia James
> (Indianapolis: Bobbs-Merrill, 1964), p. 129.

27. Faith is the substance of things hoped for, the evidence for things not seen.

> Romans 11:1 (King James Version).

28. 'Grace' means theological beneficence.

29. 'Protestant' means not Roman Catholic.

30. Life, if you're fat, is a minefield—you have to pick your way, otherwise you blow up.

> MIRIAM MARGOLYES

31. Depression is an "instead" for anger.

> DR. IRENE KASSORLA, *Putting It All Together*
> (New York: Warner Books, 1973), p. 80.

32. Politics is the science of how who gets what, when, and why.

> SIDNEY HILLMAN, *Political Primer for All Americans.*

33. 'Diet' means giving up all food that tastes good.

34. Anarchism . . . stands for the liberation of the human mind from the domination of religion; the liberation of the human body from the domination of property; liberation from the shackles and restraints of government.

> EMMA GOLDMAN, *Anarchy and Other Essays.*

35. 'Oil' means black gold.

36. Justice is a machine that, when some one has once given it the starting push, rolls on of itself.

> JOHN GALSWORTHY, *Justice,* Act II.

37. Security is when everything is settled, when nothing can happen to you; security is the denial of life.

> GERMAINE GREER, *The Female Eunuch.*

38. Mosquitoes: Flying insects with a . . . poisonous bite, which every one except hotel-managers has seen, heard, or suffered from.

EDWARD VARRALL LUCAS, *Wanderings and Diversions: The Continental Dictionary.*

39. An annibabtist is a thing I'm not a member of.

MARJORY FLEMING, *Journals, Letters, and Verses* edited by A. Esclaide (London: Sidgwick and Jackson, 1934), p. 99.

40. History is the unfolding of miscalculations.

BARBARA TUCHMAN

NOTES

1. Elizabeth Barrett Browning, *Sonnets from the Portuguese,* XLIII.

2. This is not to say that these are the *only* functions of language that are of interest to the logician. Some dicussions in more advanced courses will include examinations of the logic of imperative statements.

3. George F. Will, *Restoration: Congress, Term Limits and the Recovery of Deliberate Democracy* (New York: Free Press, 1992), pp. 8–9.

4. This is the convention I use throughout this book, although it is not the only convention used to distinguish use from mention. Some people use double quotation marks. Others italicize the word. (See, for example, *A Manual of Style,* 12th ed., rev. [Chicago: University of Chicago Press, 1969], p. 142, §6.41 and p. 143, §6.47.)

5. If you find the terms 'definiendum' and 'definiens' somewhat foreign, you might note that 'definiens' looks a bit like 'definers': the definiens are the definers of the definiendum.

6. *The Random House Dictionary of the English Language* (New York: Random House, 1966), p. 303, definition 2.

7. *Webster's New World Dictionary of the American Language,* College Edition (Cleveland: World Publishing Company, 1962), p. 229.

8. *State and Metropolitan Area Data Book 1991* (Washington, D.C.: U.S. Department of Commerce, Bureau of the Census, 1991), p. 355.

9. See Plato, *The Republic,* I, 332.

10. Think about it a bit: you cannot give an ostensive or enumerative connotative definition. You can point at properties only by pointing at things that have properties. Consider what would be involved in attempting ostensively to enumerate the properties in the connotation of the word 'dog'. A dog is an animal and it pants and it has hair and. . . . Even if you could successfully provide ostensive definitions of 'animal', 'pants', 'has hair', and so on, you would also need to point to the property of conjunctivity, that is, the property expressed by the phrase "and also having this other property," which seems impossible. Enumerative definitions list *instances* of things of a kind, while property terms are general; thus, giving a list of properties would not count as an enumerative definition.

11. As we see in discussions to follow, if the definiens consists of more than one term, it is an example of a definition by genus and difference.

Chapter Three

Informal Fallacies

Fallacies are errors in reasoning. Fallacious reasoning can be psychologically persuasive—it might convince you to accept a conclusion—but it is not logically persuasive, that is, it does not provide good reasons for accepting the conclusion. Subsequent chapters examine some *formal fallacies,* that is, deductive arguments in which the form (structure) of the argument does not guarantee that if the premises are true, so is the conclusion. In this chapter we examine *informal* or *material fallacies,* which are fallacies based on the material presented in an argument. To detect such fallacies, you must pay attention to what is being claimed in the argument. Here is an example:

All Great Danes are dogs.
Søren Kierkegaard was a great Dane.

So Søren Kierkegaard was a dog.

This might appear to be a valid deductive argument of the form:

All Xs are Ys.
S is an X.
_____

So S is a Y.

This appearance is deceptive, however. Once you recognize that 'Great Dane' in the first premise refers to a breed of dog, while 'great Dane' in the second premise refers to a Danish person who is famous or well-respected, you see that the argument does *not* show that the Danish philosopher Søren Kierkegaard was a dog.

Most informal fallacies are not this obvious. Arguments committing informal fallacies are often psychologically compelling, even though their premises do not provide good reasons for accepting their conclusions. They are common in advertising, political speeches, and letters to editors, as well as in ordinary speech. Often they are **enthymemes,** that is, arguments in which one of the premises or the conclusion is unstated. To uncover an informal fallacy, you must examine the *content* of the argument. Look for (1) ambiguous words or phrases upon which the argument turns, (2) evidence that is presumed but not stated, (3) evidence that is too weak to support the conclusion, and (4) shifts away from the issue at the heart of the argument. We examine fallacies of these several kinds in the subsequent sections.

3.1 Fallacies of Ambiguity

Language has many ambiguities. A person using the word 'cat' might be alluding to a four-legged animal that occasionally purrs, a large animal that occasionally roars, a person, or a machine that moves earth. Often you can tell precisely what a person means by a word only by examining its use in context. Similarly, statements are sometimes written or expressed in such a way that the precise referent of a term or terms is unclear. When used in the context of an argument, these ambiguities can lead to errors in reasoning. In this section we consider five fallacies of ambiguity.

Equivocation

A quick glance at a dictionary shows that many words have several meanings. If you shift from one meaning of a word to another within a piece of discourse, you **equivocate.** This is sometimes a source of humor, as in the following lines from a Marx Brothers script: " 'You act as if you had neurosis.' 'I no gotta new-rosis. My uncle he's got a flower shop—he's-a gotta new-rosis.' "[1] But when the meaning of a word shifts in the context of an argument and the persuasive force of the conclusion depends upon that shift, the argument commits the fallacy of **equivocation.** Here are some examples.

1. My boss promised me a quarterly bonus, and he was as good as his word, for my last paycheck reflected an increase in my income of twenty-five cents.

2. I've concluded that the students at the local music conservatory use CB-radios, for anyone who is interested in a person's handle is a CB user, and I heard one student say to another, "I want to get your Handel."

3. Alice sighed wearily. "I think you might do something better with time," she said, "than wasting it in asking riddles that have no answer."

   If you knew Time as well as I do," said the Hatter, "you wouldn't talk about wasting *it.* It's *him.*"

   "I don't know what you mean, said Alice.

   "Of course you don't!" the Hatter said, tossing his head contemptuously. "I dare say you never even spoke to Time."

   "Perhaps not," Alice cautiously replied, "but I know I have to beat time when I learn music."

   "Ah! That accounts for it," said the Hatter. "He won't stand beating."

   LEWIS CARROLL, Alice in Wonderland (Chapter 7)

4. All blue whales are animals. Therefore, a small blue whale is a small animal.

In the first argument there is an equivocation on 'quarterly'. Typically, a quarterly bonus is a bonus paid four times per year; here it is a bonus of twenty-five cents, that is, a quarter. In the second argument there is a confusion between a "handle," that is, what a citizen's-band radio operator calls himself or herself when on the radio, and a "Handel," that is, a piece of music by the composer George Frideric Handel. In the third argument it is the shift between the ordinary meaning of 'time' and 'Time' as a proper name that allows the Hatter to conclude, "I dare say you never even spoke to Time." In the fourth argument the ambiguity rests on the relative term 'small': even a small whale is a large animal. Relative terms such as 'large', 'small', 'good', 'bad', 'light', 'heavy', 'young', 'old', and so forth presuppose a comparison class, and you must be aware of the class. For example, while a fourteen-year-old person is young, a fourteen-year-old dog is old. Some equivocations arise when relative terms are applied across comparison classes.

Another form of equivocation occurs if you use a word in one premise and mention the word in another premise or the conclusion. You **use** a word if you make a statement with it; you **mention** a word if you talk about it. If you say, "A dog was in the yard," you *use* the word 'dog' to denote an animal that barks. If you say, "'Dog' is a three-letter word," you **mention** the word 'dog'.[2] In the following example there is an equivocation based on the confusion of use and mention:

> You should avoid four-letter words. 'Work' is a four-letter word. So you should avoid work.

The examples above are straightforward cases of equivocation. Often the equivocation is far more subtle than in the cases we have considered. For example, to notice the equivocation in the following passage, you need to notice that 'necessarily be' is assigned different meanings at different points in the passage:

> Further, all that is known by God must necessarily be; because everything known even by us must necessarily be, and God's knowledge is more certain than ours. But no contingent future event must necessarily be. Therefore no contingent future even is known by God.[3]

In the first two cases the 'necessarily be' concerns statements, that is, statements known to be true. If a statement is known to be true, it necessarily follows that the statement is true: this is what it means to *know* something. But the third instance of 'necessarily be' applies to things: a necessary thing is a thing that is not contingent, that is, *it is* a thing that must exist. It is on this equivocation that the conclusion depends.[4] Further, arguments intended to persuade are seldom as short as those we have considered, and there can be subtle shifts in the use of words from points early in the discourse to those later. For example, D. H. Fischer suggests that in Herbert Aptheker's book *American Negro Slave Revolts* the author overestimated the number of Afro-American slave revolts by shifting the meaning of 'slave revolt' in the course of his book.[5] In written form, a shift between a common noun and a proper name, between two homonyms (words that are pronounced the same), or between use and mention (if properly notated) should be easily detected. In spoken form, those hazards might be more difficult to detect, though they are no less serious.

Amphiboly

Amphibolies are arguments based on loose sentence structure. In an argument that commits the **fallacy of amphiboly,** the referent of a word or phrase is left unclear and the meaning of the phrase shifts in the course of the argument. As in the case of equivocation, imprecise sentence structure can be the source of humor, as when Captain Spaulding comments in *Animal Crackers,* "One morning I shot an elephant in my pajamas. How he got in my pajamas I don't know."[6] The logical problem arises when such imprecise phrasing occurs in the context of an argument and the persuasiveness of the conclusion rests on the loose sentence structure. Here are some examples.

1. The *Times* must be initiating divorce proceedings on behalf of Mr. and Mrs. Neumathesque, since it reported this morning, "The marriage of Ms. Merihugh Fitznagel and Mr. Ostafar Neumathesque, which we announced a few weeks ago, was a mistake, and we wish to correct it."
2. Dr. Squash gave a lecture on the causes of cancer in the biology building. So if we don't want to get cancer, we probably should avoid the biology building.
3. Over a hundred years ago when a Russian prisoner in Siberia appealed to the czar for release, the czar sent back an unpunctuated note: "Pardon Impossible To Be Executed." Upon receiving the note, the jailer released the prisoner.

In the first argument, the mistake to be corrected presumably was in the announcement, not in the marriage itself, although the wording leaves that point ambiguous. The second argument leaves unclear whether the biology building was the place where the lecture was given or the place where causes of cancer are found. In the third case, the absence of a period leaves unclear whether the czar meant "Pardon. Impossible to be executed." or "Pardon impossible. To be executed." The jailer interpreted it in the first way; the czar meant it in the second. The jailer's fate is unknown.

Notice that although both amphibolies and equivocations result from linguistic ambiguities, they are not the same. First, in an equivocation, the fallacy rests *strictly* on the ambiguous use of a *word* or words. In an amphiboly, the fallacy rests *strictly* on the defective *structure* of a sentence. Second, in an equivocation, it is typically the arguer who shifts the meaning of the word; in an amphiboly, the arguer typically interprets an ambiguous statement in a way that is different from that of the person who originally made the statement. These features should allow you to distinguish an equivocation from an amphiboly.

Accent

The meaning of a statement can shift with the emphasis you place on words in the statement. The fallacy of **accent** rests upon the ways in which you emphasize the words in a statement. Consider the statement, "We should not speak ill of our friends." Normally we take this to be a call to overlook the foibles of our friends. But if you emphasize certain words, you can draw other conclusions. Here are some examples.

1. *We* should not speak ill of our friends, but John, who is not standing in our group, can say anything he wants about them.
2. We should not *speak* ill of our friends, but we can write anything about them that we wish.
3. We should not speak ill of our *friends,* but since Hilda is not a friend, I can say anything I want about her.

A more serious form of the fallacy of accent occurs if you quote a passage out of context or only partially. In many cases, such selective quotation can shift the entire meaning of the statement. Consider the following:

1. Trying to convince John to visit the local art museum, Sally quotes a review in the *Dispatch,* "It is impossible to be too enthusiastic about the new sculpture exhibit at the Georges Museum. If you see but one exhibit this year, this is the one you will want to see."

   John replied, "Then we certainly don't want to go, since even the *Dispatch* found it 'impossible to be too enthusiastic about the exhibit,' and their critics usually look favorably on exhibitions of sculpture."

2. In a recent speech Senator Snuff said, "In my opinion, the present conditions do not warrant the use of military force in the Persian Gulf."

   Senator Bosh, who favored military intervention, said, "One can tell that the situation in the Gulf is serious, for even Senator Snuff, an avowed pacifist, said, 'In my opinion, the present conditions . . . warrant the use of military force in the Persian Gulf.' "

In each argument the conclusion reached results from incomplete quotation or quotation out of context. In the first argument, by quoting only a portion of the critics' remarks, John suggests that the critics disliked the exhibit, while looking at the statement in context indicates that they had viewed it with considerable approval. In the second argument, by deleting the 'not' from Senator Snuff's remark, Senator Bosh shifted the entire meaning of the Senator's claim.

Composition

The fallacy of **composition** occurs if either (1) you attribute characteristics true of a part to a whole or (2) you claim that something that is true of each member of a class of objects is true of the class as a whole. An object is treated as a **whole** relative to the various parts of which it is composed. My car is a whole relative to the parts of which it is composed—the engine, the fenders, the steering wheel, and so forth. A **class** is a collection of objects that have at least one characteristic in common, namely, the class-defining characteristic. The class-defining characteristic might be the only property all the objects in the class share. The fallacy of composition occurs if you shift from a **distributive** use of a word to a **collective** use of the same word. A word is used *distributively* if it applies to each and every member of a class taken individually; it is used *collectively* if it applies to a class itself—as a whole. Here are some examples.

1. Every part of my car weighs less than five hundred pounds, so my car weighs less than five hundred pounds.
2. Every player for the Washington Redskins is a better player than the corresponding player for the Green Bay Packers. So the Redskins are a better team than the Packers.
3. All the wealthiest people in Hogville attend St. Mort's Church, so St. Mort's Church is the wealthiest church in town.

The first argument ignores the fact that the weight of a car is the total of the weight of its parts. The second argument ignores the fact that the quality of a team depends on the ability of the members of a team to work together: great individual players do not guarantee a great team (although they may make it more likely). The third argument ignores the fact that the wealth of a church depends on the generosity of its members: the wealthiest people in Hogville might be the least generous people in town.

Not every inference from part to whole is illegitimate. Consider the following:

1. Every part of this engine is made of steel. Therefore, this engine is made of steel.
2. Every member of the local chapter of Phi Alpha Theta has a G.P.A. of at least 3.0. Therefore, the local chapter of Phi Alpha Theta has a G.P.A. of at least 3.0.

Since there are cases in which the characteristics of a whole depend entirely upon the characteristics of its parts, distinguishing legitimate from fallacious cases of composition requires that you know when there is and when there is not such a dependence. An engine is completely made of steel if and only if all its parts are made of steel. The G.P.A. of a group is dependent upon the G.P.A.s of its individual members. Hence, to determine whether the fallacy of composition is committed, you must know whether or not it is legitimate to transfer a characteristic from parts to a whole in a given case. An argument commits the fallacy of composition *only if* it makes a transference in an illegitimate case. That is what makes composition an *informal* fallacy.

Division

The fallacy of **division** is the mirror image of composition. The fallacy of division occurs if either (1) you attribute to a part characteristics that are true only of the corresponding whole or (2) you attribute to a member of a class a property that is true of a class of objects as a whole. It occurs if you shift from a *collective* use of a word to a *distributive* use of the same word. Here are some examples.

1. My car is red. So each part of my car is red.
2. The local chapter of the Phi Phi Phi social fraternity has a G.P.A. of 3.6. So George, a member of Phi Phi Phi, has a G.P.A. of 3.6.
3. Jean must be one of the richest women on campus since she is a member of the richest sorority on campus.

My car is red if the body of my car is red, but this does not allow me to infer anything about the color of the engine or the tires. The grade-point average of a fraternity is an average of the grade-points of its several members, but you can infer nothing about the G.P.A. of any given member. George's grade point could well be higher or lower than the average. Although the sorority to which Jean belongs is wealthy, this fact does not allow you to infer anything about Jean's financial status.

As in the case of composition, not all cases of the transference of a trait from a whole to a part are illegitimate. Consider the following:

1. This engine is made entirely of steel. Therefore, the pistons in this engine are made of steel.
2. Since I gave my wife a bouquet of roses, each flower I gave my wife is a rose.

As in the case of composition, you must consider the circumstances in which you attempt to draw an inference from the properties of a whole to the properties of its parts.

SUMMARY

To detect the five fallacies of ambiguity, look carefully at what is said in an argument. (1) Be certain that no word is used with more than one meaning: if it is, and if it affects the validity of the argument, you have found a fallacy of equivocation. (2) Be certain that there are no loosely constructed sentences: if there are, you have probably found a fallacy of amphiboly. (3) Be certain that no general statements are emphasized in an unusual way and that no statement is quoted out of context: if you find either of these, you have probably found a fallacy of accent. (4) If you find a statement that correctly attributes a property to a whole or an entire class of things and you are asked to draw a conclusion with respect to a part or a member of the class, you must ask whether you can correctly attribute the property to the part or member of the class. If you cannot, you have found a fallacy of division. (5) If you find a statement that correctly attributes a property to a part of a whole or a member of a class of things and you are asked to draw a conclusion with respect to the whole or the class, you must ask whether you can correctly attribute the property to the whole or the class. If you cannot, you have found a fallacy of division.

EXERCISES

I. Identify the fallacies of ambiguity committed in each of the following passages. Give reasons for your answers.

1. Since all plants produce chlorophyll, the General Motors plant in Detroit produces chlorophyll.

2. John: I like bratwurst better than you.
   Joan: If that's the way you feel, I never want to see you again!

3. The average American family has 2.5 children. So the Joneses, an average American family, have 2.5 children.

4. Crumbs have virtually no calories. So if you break your favorite food up into crumbs and eat the crumbs, you ingest virtually no calories.

5. The teller will give you $1,000 if and only if you go to the River Bank. But if you go to the riverbank, your feet will get muddy. Therefore, if the teller gives you $1,000, your feet will get muddy.

6. Alf: I see no good reasons to go to Chicago. I do not intend to go.
   Agnes: So you admit that there are "good reasons to go to Chicago"—those are your very words. I'm glad that you "intend to go."

7. After naming its favorite cars for the year, an automotive magazine observed that the cars on the road today are safer and more dependable than cars were ten years ago. It was comforting to know that my '76 Chevy is safer and more dependable than it was ten years ago.

8. The United States of America is the richest country in the world. So every American is wealthy.

9. A medical doctor had taken a couple years off from his practice to do graduate work. When he returned to his practice, he commented, "When I returned to my practice I felt a bit rusty. I just didn't have all those facts at my finger tips." His patient replied, "That's no problem, Doc. Just keep practicing and eventually you'll get it right."

10. Priests take a vow of poverty. The Church is a corporate body composed of priests. Therefore, the Church should not own property.

II. Identify the fallacies of ambiguity committed in each of the following passages. If no fallacy is committed, write "No Fallacy." Give reasons for your answers.

1. Caring for the basic needs of every convicted felon in this state costs the taxpayers about $25,000 per year. Since we have a multibillion-dollar budget, no one can complain about the cost of the prison system.

2. There has been a great deal of public interest in the private life of the .44-caliber killer. The press has an obligation to publish what is in the public interest. Therefore, the press has an obligation to print the details of the killer's private life.

3. A penny saved is a penny earned. So save those pennies, but feel free to spend your silver and paper money.

4. John saw a picture in Sonja's locker. Since the volume of Sonja's locker is only about three cubic feet, John must be very small.

5. My car's engine doesn't run. So my car doesn't run.

6. The master bedroom in the house I'm planning to buy is large and spacious, so the whole house is large and spacious.

7. In 1990, Arkansas was one of the poorest states in the United States. So, Sam Walton, the Arkansan who started Wal-Mart, was one of the poorest men in the United States.

8. Chris claims she interviewed for a job as an auto mechanic in the personnel office. She must not have been telling the truth, since no automobiles are repaired in the personnel office.

9. The Red King said, "Just look down the road, and tell me if you can see either of them [my messengers]."
   "I see nobody on the road," said Alice.
   "I only wish *I* had such eyes," the King remarked in a fretful tone. "To be able to see Nobody! And at that distance too! Why, it's as much as *I* can do to see real people, by this light."
   LEWIS CARROLL, *Through the Looking Glass* (Chapter 7).

10. Questioner: Would you ever hit your wife?
    Candidate: Of course not. I love my wife.
    Questioner: Suppose she attacked you with the sword you had brought back from the South Pacific as a war souvenir?
    Candidate: Well, I would push her hands aside and take the sword from her.

Questioner: But what if she were in such a frenzy, so furious and determined, that you couldn't overpower her and seize the sword?

Candidate: Gosh, I suppose that if I could keep her from lopping my head off with a sword only by hitting her with my fist to immobilize her, I would hit her.

INTERPRETATION by candidate's foe: I was saddened and alarmed to learn that my opponent believes some wives deserve to be beaten by their husbands. I can assure the people of this great land that, if they elect me, they will not be sending a wifebeater to the White House.

EDWARD GRIMSLEY, "Beware All the 'Ifs' That Might Go Boom," *Daily News-Record,* September 3, 1992. By permission of Edward Grimsley and Creators Syndicate.

3.2 *Fallacies of Relevance*

Fallacies of relevance occur if the considerations in the premises provide no reason for claiming that the conclusion is true and persuade you to accept a conclusion by shifting your considerations to something else. The persuasive force of these arguments arises from a confusion of the issues. In this section we examine eight fallacies of relevance.

Appeal to Force

The fallacy of **appeal to force** *(argumentum ad baculum)*[7] occurs if you appeal to force or the threat of force to "convince" someone to accept a conclusion. While this can be a blatant threat of the use of force, more often it is a subtle reminder that not accepting a certain conclusion will have undesirable consequences. Here are some examples.

1. Ms. Biz, head of the XYZ Computer Corporation, tells her employee, Ms. Smith, "You must always remember that we make the best computer on the market. After all, you're *currently* an employee of XYZ Computer."

2. Secretary to his boss: "I deserve a raise, for you don't want my efficiency to decrease."

3. Boss to his secretary: "You really don't want a raise. After all, you don't want me to mention your relationship with Mr. Oroschwitz to your husband."

In the first argument, Ms. Biz suggests that Ms. Smith should accept the conclusion that XYZ Computer makes the best machine on the market on pain of losing her job. In the second argument, there is a threat of decreased efficiency if the proposition "I deserve a raise" is not accepted as true. In the third argument there is a threat to expose an extramarital affair as "evidence" for the truth of the claim "You really don't want a raise."

The arguments above are *enthymematic:* A premise is assumed without being stated. The missing premise in each case is either false or questionable. Once the premise is clearly stated, you can recognize that the inference to the proposed conclusion is flawed. The arguments above rest on the following suppressed premises:

1. If Ms. Smith were not an employee of XYZ Computer Corporation, then XYZ Computer would not make the best computer on the market.
2. If you don't want decreased efficiency, then I deserve a raise.
3. If you don't want your extramarital affair exposed to your husband, then you don't want a raise.

Some further points should be noticed. In the case of an appeal to force there must be a threat made by a person who is in a position to make good on the threat. A four-year-old child who threatens not to love a parent unless she receives a new doll is not making a serious appeal to force. Further, to commit the *fallacy* of appeal to force, the threat must be given as grounds for accepting the truth of a proposition. If a robber places a gun in your ribs and says "Your money or your life," he or she is requesting that you *act* in a certain way. The robber is not committing the *fallacy* of appeal to force because you are not being asked to accept the truth of a proposition. On the other hand, if the robber said, "I deserve your money, and if you don't believe it (and act accordingly) I'll ventilate you" he or she is requesting that you accept the truth of a proposition, and therefore commits the fallacy. Finally, warnings of the natural consequences of actions are not appeals to force. If a sign on the back of your home entertainment system reads, "To prevent electrical shock, do not remove back," you might out of fear refrain from doing so; but since it is not a threat, it is not an appeal to force.

Personal Attack

An argument commits the fallacy of **personal attack** *(argumentum ad hominem)* if it attempts to *refute* the conclusion of another person's argument by attacking the person who presented the argument rather than the argument itself. *To commit this fallacy, there must be two arguers.* Instances of "mud-slinging" in political speeches are examples of personal attack. In discussing examples, however, we need to look closely at the attacks to distinguish fallacious from nonfallacious cases of personal attack.

There are three varieties of personal attack: abusive, circumstantial, and *tu quoque*. The *abusive* variety attacks the arguer's character or credibility directly in an attempt to reject the arguer's conclusions. Consider the following example:

> Senator Weak has argued that we need a national health-care program. But in the twelve years Weak has represented our state he has proven himself to be one of the biggest liars in Washington. Hence, there's no need for a national health-care program.

This argument commits the fallacy of personal attack. The critic of Senator Weak focuses exclusively on the conclusion of the argument and takes an alleged fact about the senator's character as a reason for claiming that the conclusion is false. Even if it is true that the senator occasionally lies, this does not show that the conclusion is false. If you criticize an argument, you must show one of three things. You must show either (1) that at least one of the premises is false or probably false (not supported by evidence), or (2) that the premises fail to provide evidence for the truth of the conclusion, or (3) that there is a stronger argument for the denial of the conclusion than has been advanced for the conclusion. The argument above does none of these. Nonetheless, an attack on Weak's credibility *could* show that there are reasons for *doubting* the truth of the premises of his argument, thereby showing that the evidence for the conclusion is weak. If the critic had argued as follows, it would *not* be a fallacious instance of personal attack:

> Senator Weak has argued that we need a national health-care program. The senator provides no hard evidence that the premises are true; he simply says they are. But in the dozen years Senator Weak has been in office, we've all noticed that he's a poor judge of truth—indeed, he's proven himself to be one of the biggest liars in Washington. So we have little reason to accept the truth of the premises or any conclusion that follows from them.

This argument raises questions regarding the evidence for the truth of the premises of Weak's argument, but it is *not* a direct attack on the truth of the conclusion on the basis of Weak's character. If Weak is a pathological liar, you have good reason not to take anything he says at face-value. This argument raises doubts regarding the truth of the conclusion by raising doubts regarding the truth of the premises. This is a proper form of criticism.[8]

Consider another argument:

> Smith now is arguing that abortion should be allowed, but ten years ago she was one of the foremost opponents of abortion. Can you believe anything she says?

Any position Smith might have defended at an earlier point in time is irrelevant to her present argument. Over the course of a decade, she may have come to believe that one of the premises on which her earlier arguments were based is false. The fact that at two points in time Smith defended positions that are **inconsistent** with one another, that is, two positions one of which is the denial of the other, merely distracts you from her current argument.

This argument requires further comment, since it is similar to a *legitimate* form of criticism. If in the course of an extended argument, such as an essay, you defend inconsistent claims, it follows that both claims cannot be true. Hence, there must be an error in one of the arguments in the essay. To point out such a fact might have *ad hominem* force, but it is a legitimate criticism.[9] Assume that Moore wrote an essay in which he argued (1) that the military draft should be abolished and (2) that every eighteen-year-old in the United States should be required to serve in the military for two years. Jones might legitimately attack Moore's position along the following lines:

> Moore has argued that the military draft should be abolished and that every eighteen-year-old should be compelled to engage in two years of military service. Whether you call the arrangement Moore proposes a "draft" makes little difference, for the principle is the same. If a person is drafted to serve in the military, he or she is involuntarily compelled to serve in the military. If all eighteen-year-olds are compelled to serve in the military, most of them will serve involuntarily. Hence, whether or not Moore calls it such, most of them will be drafted. Moore cannot consistently support both positions.

In pointing out a genuine inconsistency, you are basically saying, "Look! You can hold either one position or the other, but you can't hold both. Which one will it be?"

In the *circumstantial* version of personal attack, the second arguer attempts to undercut the arguments by suggesting circumstances that explain why the first arguer is defending a certain position. The second arguer tries to show that the reasons advanced by the first arguer are mere rationalizations. Here are some examples.

1. Ms. Bucks has argued that an across-the-board tax cut will stimulate the economy. What would you expect her to argue? With an annual income in six digits, Bucks would be one of the biggest gainers from such a cut.
2. Father O'Malley has argued that God exists. What would you expect from a priest?

In these arguments, appeals are made to circumstances suggesting that Ms. Bucks and Father O'Malley are personally or professionally interested in the truth of the conclusions they reached and that their arguments are mere rationalizations of positions they already accept. Such appeals ignore the arguments Bucks and O'Malley present and are, therefore, fallacious.

The third form of personal attack, called *tu quoque* (literally "you too"), rests on the appearance of inconsistency—but an inconsistency between your opponent's arguments and that person's actions. Here are some examples.

1. You have argued that I should not smoke because it's costly, harmful to my health, and once a person starts, it's very hard to quit. I can hardly accept your argument, since you smoke two packs of cigarettes every day.
2. If you think I should finish college before I get married, why did you drop out to start a family?
3. Look who's telling me to exercise and lose some weight. You're at least forty pounds overweight, and the most strenuous exercise in which you engage is twiddling your thumbs!

In each of these cases, any argument presented is ignored, and appeals are made to inconsistencies between the conclusion that has been advanced and the activities of the first arguer. The principle behind the objection is that actions speak louder than words, and if the arguer really believed what he or she was saying, he or she would be persuaded by the argument. But what persuades a person to act and what counts as good reasons for accepting the truth of a proposition are not the same thing. Many smokers will grant that they should quit for all the standard reasons: that smoking is detrimental to health, costly, frowned on in many social circles, and so forth, and the smoker might well have good evidence that all the reasons cited are true. But humans are not purely rational animals; in most cases it is the emotions that cause us to act. A smoker might quit when he or she decides that any pleasures derived from smoking are not worth the resulting shortness of breath or the complaints of his or her friends. A *tu quoque* blurs the distinction between what counts as reasons for accepting a proposition as true and the causes of actions.

Mob Appeal

An argument commits the fallacy of **mob appeal** *(argumentum ad populum)* by appealing to the emotions of the crowd—the desire to be loved, accepted, respected, and so on—rather than to the relevant facts. This appeal to emotions can be either direct or indirect.

Direct appeals to the emotions of the crowd can occur in either spoken or written form. Political speeches given before crowds of followers and written political tracts are prime occasions for mob appeal. There are appeals to patriotic sentiments. There are appeals to the great economic strides made under the guidance of the party. There are appeals to greater peace and stability at home and in the world. The candidate is described as "the defender of the middle class" or "champion of the poor" or "savior of the nation." All these rhetorical flourishes pump up the emotions of the "faithful," making them feel part of an important group, and they appeal to the emotions of the skeptical to join the group. These appeals might cause you to *act* in a certain way, but aroused emotions are not propositions, and for that reason they cannot provide evidence for the truth of another proposition. The fallacy of mob appeal occurs when you take an emotional response as a reason for the truth of a proposition.[10]

Emotional appeals are common. Speeches at sales meetings often inspire the sales force through emotional appeals. Similarly, the mission statements of companies often "sell" the company to both their potential work force and the public by emotional appeals. Often these appeals attempt to convince you that a product or a company is the best you can find by appealing to your emotions. Here is an example.

Anastasia was the top salesperson for Nogo Cosmetics this year, and this was her first year with our company. She went from a dull, low-paying job as a secretary into the exciting world of sales. Her income has soared! Her customers and close personal friends now include some of the most famous people in Hollywood, people whom she knew a year ago only as images on the screen. She has gone from being just another face in the crowd to one of the most respected persons in her community. Just think what cosmetics can do for you and your customers!

Such a sales pitch, offering prospects of wealth, prestige, excitement, and fame, might convince someone to sign on as a representative of Nogo Cosmetics. The appeal throughout is to the emotions of the listener. There is no evidence, for example, that the product is any good or that a job with that company is better than a job with some other.

Indirect mob appeals are directed at individuals and focus on their relationship to the crowd or to very special members of the crowd. A **bandwagon** argument focuses on an individual's relationship to a group. It is basically of the form, "Everyone's doing it, so you should too." Here are two examples.

1. Certainly you want to buy Lie Soap—it's America's most popular brand.
2. A recent poll shows that 68 percent of the people in this state plan to vote for Senator Smith. Shouldn't you vote for her too?

Other indirect forms of the fallacy appeal to your *vanity,* or they have *snob appeal.* Here are two examples.

1. Olisglov Vodka: For the Discriminating Drinker.
2. Toad Facial Cream: For the perfect face.

The general form of an argument committing this fallacy is: You want to be loved, esteemed, accepted, popular, and so on. Therefore you should accept such-and-such a statement (often a statement calling for some actions) as true.

Appeal to Pity

In an **appeal to pity** *(argumentum and misericordiam),* you appeal to dire circumstances in an attempt to get a conclusion accepted. Here are two examples.

1. Professor, I deserve at least a B in this course. If I don't get a B in this course, I won't be able to register for courses in my major next semester.

2. Ladies and gentlemen of the jury, the defendant is the sole support of his aged grandmother. If he is sent to jail, it will not only break her heart, she will not know where her next meal is coming from. She will be put out in the street and certainly die of exposure. The only humane thing you can do is find the defendant not guilty.

In the first argument, the arguer ignores the issue, namely, whether he or she deserves a B in the course, and appeals to the dire consequences that will follow if he or she does not receive a B. In the second argument, the lawyer attempts to evoke the pity of the jury on behalf of the defendant, but nothing the lawyer says is relevant to the question of guilt or innocence. Were such an appeal made during the sentencing phase, where it is proper procedure for the convicted to throw himself or herself on the mercy of the court and judges typically have discretion regarding the sentence, facts that might arouse the emotion of pity would be relevant. Whether the most effective way to state these facts is in emotively charged language or emotively neutral language will depend on the psychology of the judge—and is not relevant to the argument. Similarly, need is often a legitimate reason to request a raise in salary, but it is doubtful that most employers will find an emotionally charged argument more persuasive than a careful discussion of your family finances.[11]

An argument commits the fallacy of appeal to pity only if emotional appeals distract you from the facts that support or fail to support the conclusion of an argument.

Accident

An argument commits the fallacy of **accident** if it applies a general rule in a case in which that rule does not apply. Typically, the case in question falls under some other general rule. Here are two examples.

1. One should always return those things one has borrowed. So when George came to me in a drunken rage and asked for his ax back so that he could kill his neighbor, it was entirely proper for me to give it to him.

2. Members of fraternities party on Saturday nights. John is a member of Phi Beta Kappa. So John parties on Saturday nights.

The first argument appeals to a moral rule that generally holds. But there are other rules that pose greater obligations, for example, the rule that you should do what you can to preserve another person's life. Hence, the argument commits the fallacy of accident. The second argument appeals to the general rule that fraternity members party on Saturday nights. Most fraternities are social fraternities, and the rule applies, if at all, only to members of social fraternities. The argument ignores the fact that Phi Beta Kappa is an honorary fraternity.

Some students confuse the fallacy of accident with the fallacy of division. The difference between the two fallacies should be clear if you remember that in the case of accident you are applying a *general rule* to an exceptional case. In the case of division you are claiming that a *property* that is correctly applied to a whole or a class is applicable to a part or a member of a class. If you keep in mind the distinction between general statements (rules) and statements about properties, you will not confuse the fallacies.

Straw Person

Like personal attack, committing the **straw person** fallacy occurs only in the context of responding to the argument of another. There are two ways you might commit the straw person fallacy. First, you might distort the premises of the argument by claiming that the original arguer accepted a premise that he or she did not explicitly state, and then argue that your proposed premise is implausible. Second, you might distort the conclusion of the argument, argue against the conclusion as you have restated it, and hold your criticisms to apply to the original argument. If you commit the straw person fallacy, you are attacking a weak imitation of the argument rather than the flesh and blood original. Here are some examples.

1. Samantha has argued that the government should play a greater role in curtailing the skyrocketing costs of medical care. But socialized medicine is an idea whose time has gone. In all the Western countries where governments took over health care in the past four decades, the current trend is toward increasing privatization of health care. So we cannot accept Samantha's conclusion.

2. Hermione has argued in favor of national health insurance. Her argument must assume the premise that an elaborate government bureaucracy is able to provide more personalized care than is a family doctor. But such an assumption is absurd. So her conclusion must be rejected.

3. Radical feminists seek to ban pornography. But if we censored anything that offends someone, nobody would be able to say anything.

Samantha argued that the government should play a larger role in curtailing the cost of health care; there is no indication that it was an argument for socialized medicine. The conclusion attacked is the claim that the government should take over the health-care system. Even if the argument against socialized medicine is plausible, this does not affect Samantha's conclusion. In the second argument, the attack is directed against an allegedly unstated premise in the original argument, a premise that Hermione is unlikely to have accepted. The third argument ignores the premise on which the original conclusion was based. Radical feminists do not rest their case solely on offense; they are concerned about real harm to real women. These arguments illustrate the two ways in which one might commit the straw person fallacy.

Red Herring (Avoiding the Issue)

As mystery fans know, a red herring is a "false clue" that draws you away from the evidence. This meaning of the term 'red herring' derives from the practice of training hunting dogs by dragging a bag of red herrings across the trail. Red herrings have a very potent scent; only the best dogs would ignore the scent and follow the original trail. An argument commits the **red herring** fallacy if it shifts away from the issue under consideration to something different and then draws a conclusion. The basic idea is that if you can sidetrack your readers or hearers, you win the argument. Here are two examples.

1. The critics of nationalized health care contend that it would be another costly, impersonal, and inefficient bureaucracy. But there are millions of Americans for whom even basic health care is an unaffordable luxury. There are hundreds of thousands of Americans who require treatments that are beyond the meager limits provided by their insurance carriers. Only the federal government has the resources needed to fulfill these needs.

2. Proponents of a balanced-budget amendment contend that it is the only way we can assure that the government will not live beyond its means. But the proponents of the amendment ignore the fact that a balanced-budget amendment would only make deficit spending illegal. It will not deal with any of the difficult issues faced by the Con-

gress, namely, where the budget should be cut to balance taxes and spending. These decisions can be made without the amendment. So the amendment would be pointless.

In the first argument, the issue is whether nationalized health care would result in an undesirable bureaucracy. The "criticism" of that claim, however, focuses on a different issue, namely, whether nationalized health care is desirable. In the second argument, the issue is whether a constitutional amendment is the only way of assuring a balanced budget. The "criticism" of the claim, however, focuses on the fact that the members of Congress could make difficult budgetary decisions even without the amendment. Though this is true, it ignores the claim that without the amendment they are unlikely to make such decisions.

There are similarities between the red herring fallacy and the straw person fallacy. Both are concerned with replying to a claim. The straw person purports to reply to the argument for that claim. The red herring merely distracts you from the claim: it is not explicitly a reply to an argument.

Irrelevant Conclusion

An argument commits the fallacy of **irrelevant conclusion** *(ignoratio elenchi)* if its premises seem to lead you to one conclusion but an entirely different conclusion is drawn. The argument is irrelevant to the conclusion; the conclusion misses the point of the argument. Here are two examples.

1. Our elected representatives vote themselves privileges that no ordinary citizens have, and they abuse even those privileges. So we must have a constitutional convention!
2. With the demise of the Soviet Union, the major nuclear threat to the United States has been neutralized. So we can now safely disband our armed forces.

The first argument might provide reasons to vote against the incumbents. It provides little reason to believe that the only way the alleged problem can be solved is by calling a constitutional convention and changing the form of the government. The premise of the second argument might provide reasons for decreasing the number of U.S. nuclear weapons deployed, but it provides little reason to accept the more extreme conclusion that we should disband the armed forces.

SUMMARY

The premises of an argument must be relevant to the conclusion, that is, they must provide reasons for believing the conclusion is true. There are eight common ways in which an argument might be psychologically persuasive but in which the premises are irrelevant to the conclusion. (1) If the reason given for accepting a conclusion involves an implicit threat, the argument commits the fallacy of appeal to force. (2) If the reply to an argument attacks the arguer, rather than the argument, the reply commits the fallacy of personal attack. (3) If an argument appeals to the emotions of the crowd—for example, the desires to be loved, appreciated, or accepted—as reasons to accept the truth of a claim, the argument commits the fallacy of mob appeal. (4) If an argument appeals to the dire circumstances of the arguer, the argument commits the fallacy of appeal to pity. (5) If the argument applies a general rule beyond its proper domain, the argument commits the fallacy of accident. (6) If the reply to an argument distorts the premises or the conclusion, argues that the distorted premise or conclusion must be rejected, and takes this as a reply to the original argument, the reply commits the straw person fallacy. (7) If a reply to an argument is little more than a distraction from the issue at hand, the reply commits the red herring fallacy. (8) If the premises of an argument tend to support a particular conclusion, but an entirely different conclusion is drawn, the argument commits the fallacy of irrelevant conclusion.

EXERCISES

I. Identify the fallacies of relevance committed in each of the following passages. Give reasons for your answers.

1. He kept us out of war! Vote for Woodrow Wilson!

2. Showing a picture of an emaciated child living in squalid conditions, the ad reads: "Without your contributions, this child and millions like her might starve in the next year. Send all you can to SHARE."

3. You tell me that I should buy a small, fuel-efficient car. Then why do you drive that old gas-guzzling Cadillac?

4. A Lutheran College in the Midwest forbids the use of alcoholic beverages, including wine, on campus. We may conclude, therefore, that they do not use wine in their communion services.

5. And if any man shall take away from the words of the book of this prophecy, God shall take away his part out of the book of life, and out of the holy city, and *from* the things which are written in this book.

Revelation 22:19 (King James Version).

6. How do you spell 'bonds'? T-a-x-e-s! Vote NO on the bond issue!

7. All politicians are liars. No liars should be elected to public office. So an absolute monarchy is preferable to a democracy.

8. Opponents of monopolies claim that they are unfair insofar as they limit competition. But when AT&T was synonymous with the telephone company, we had the most efficient telephone system in the world. When Standard Oil dominated the petroleum industry, there was cheap gasoline for everyone. When 'Carnegie' meant steel, America dominated steel production. So, obviously, monopolies are extremely efficient.

9. General Jack D. Ripper has argued that it is absolutely essential to our future security that we immediately start mass production of the RS–100 long-range bomber. But his arguments hardly deserve serious consideration, for in a couple of weeks General Ripper will retire from the Air Force and become C.E.O. of the Hawk Corporation, which manufactures the RS–100.

10. Meg A. Bucks, president of the Noxxe Petroleum company, has argued that the government should provide petroleum companies with economic incentives for oil exploration. Her argument is reasonable only if she assumes that it is in the national interest to remain dependent on oil for the next century. But the oil reserves will be depleted within the next fifty years. So we must reject her argument.

11. Ambassador: Mr. Prime Minister, it would be fairer if your country increased its contribution to our mutual defense, for in order for us to continue paying our present contribution it will be necessary to raise the tariff on imports such as those we have been purchasing from your country.

12. The Cynics claimed that . . . if it is lawful to know one's wife, it is lawful to know one's wife in public. Now, it is lawful to know one's wife; therefore, it is lawful to know her in public.

PIERRE BAYLE, Historical and Critical Dictionary, s.v.
"Hipparchia," translated by Richard H. Popkin
(Bobbs-Merrill, 1965), p. 98.

13. The Pigeon accepts the general proposition that anything that eats eggs is a serpent, and says to Alice:

   "You're a serpent; and there's no use denying it. I suppose you'll be telling me next that you never tasted an egg!"

   "I *have* tasted eggs, certainly," said Alice, who was a very truthful child; "but little girls eat eggs quite as much as serpents do, you know."

   "I don't believe it," said the Pigeon; "but if they do, why, then they're a kind of serpent: that's all I can say."

   LEWIS CARROLL, *Alice in Wonderland* (Chapter 5).

14. The gasoline tax should not be raised. Everyone drives. Everyone needs to eat. If the gasoline tax were raised, the poor, those who generally drive the least efficient cars, would become poorer. Since the additional cost of production and transportation of food would be passed on to the consumer, the poor would be hit hardest again. Certainly many would starve. So all calls to raise the gasoline tax should be rejected.

15. Medical evidence tends to show that a diet low in cholesterol and saturated fats leads to a greater life expectancy. So if you want to live a long life, you can't eat anything tasty.

II. Identify the fallacies of relevance committed in each of the following passages. If no fallacy is committed, write "No Fallacy." Give reasons for your answers.

1. This Product Contains/Produces Chemicals Known To The State Of California To Cause Cancer, And Birth Defects Or Other Reproductive Harm.

2. Ms. Kai contends that terminally ill patients have a right to die with dignity. But murder, whether self-inflicted or other-assisted, is still murder. And murder is wrong!

3. Father to son: "Go ahead. Go to law school. Do whatever you like with your life! But if you don't come back and run the family business, I'm going to disinherit you!"

4. Senator McMurphy argued that more money should be devoted to the space program. But the space program is part of the military-industrial complex. With the end of the Cold War, it's time to decrease military spending and decrease the size of the military. So McMurphy's argument to increase funds for the space program should be rejected.

5. Glassoff Crystal—the ultimate expression of your good taste.

6. George *claims* that he was in Chicago on June 4. But George is a drug addict. He's been convicted of numerous misdemeanors. He's defaulted on numerous loans. So there's no reason to believe he was in Chicago on June 4.

7. The more formal education a person receives, the higher that person's lifetime income potential. So, since Thomas Alva Edison had little formal schooling, he must not have made much money.

8. Maggie has argued that the system of letter grades should be abolished. But such a position assumes that there are no genuine differences in the quality of work done by students, which is absurd. So the system of letter grades should not be abolished.

9. Dr. Stark has argued that the petrochemical plant in town should be closed, since it poses major health risks to the community. With over three hundred employees, that plant is the second largest employer in town. Closing the plant would throw the town into an economic recession. So we can't afford to close the plant.

10. The political polls indicate that the Democratic Presidential candidate will win the election. When economic times are tough, the incumbent usually loses. Economic times are tough and the incumbent is a Republican. So the Republican candidate will win.

11. Abortion must be retained as a legal right. Consider the teenager who finds herself pregnant. She faces rejection by her family, rejection by society, and greatly reduced educational opportunities. If the pregnancy must be brought to term, she faces a life of poverty as a social outcast.

12. Ms. Merple has argued that a civilized society cannot condone capital punishment since it is inhumane and there is always the chance of putting an innocent person to death. But consider the facts. Each convicted felon costs the taxpayer over $20,000 per year. When felons appeal their sentences, it is again the tax-payer who pays. And our prisons are overcrowded, and you know who's going to have to pay for the solution to that prob-lem! Economic viability requires that the sentences of death-row inmates be speedily carried out!

13. Try, dear friends, to make the civilized world and particularly the French people clearly hear your Fatherland's voice.

Struggle to frustrate the ignominious slanders unleashed by the French colonists.

In order to oppress our people once more, the French colonists have killed women and children. They have asked for the help of the British, Indian, and Japanese forces, using airplanes, tanks, cannons, and warships. But however modern an army is, it is powerless before the determined attitude of a whole people.

Wherever we go, they will find scorched earth and the hatred of a people who are only waiting for an opportunity to drive them out of the country.

> HO CHI MINH, "Appeal to Vietnamese Residents in France" (November 5, 1945), in *Ho Chi Minh on Revolution,* edited by Bernard B. Fall (Signet Books, 1967), p. 151.

14. The philosopher George Berkeley criticized John Locke's position on abstract ideas as follows:

> Let us see therefore how this celebrated author [John Locke] describes the general or abstract idea of a triangle. "It must be," he says, "neither oblique nor rectangular, neither equilateral, equicrural, or scalenum; but all and none of these at once. In effect it is somewhat imperfect that cannot exist; an idea, wherein some parts of several different and inconsistent ideas are put together." *(Essay on Human Understanding,* Bk. IV, chap. 7, sec. 9.) . . . That author acknowledges it does "require some pains and skill to form this general idea of a triangle." *(Ibid.)* But, had he called to mind what he says in another place, to wit, "that ideas of mixed modes wherein any inconsistent ideas are put together cannot so much as exist in the mind, i.e., be conceived" *(vide* Bk. III, chap. 10, sec. 33, *ibid.)*—I say, had this occurred to his thoughts, it is not improbable he would have owned it above all the pains and skill he was master of, to form the above-mentioned idea of a triangle, which is made up of manifest staring contradictions.
>
> GEORGE BERKELEY, *A New Theory of Vision,* Section 125.

15. In a GOP platform review (*Daily News-Record,* Aug. 13) Rep. Henry Hyde, R-Ill., expressed this vibrant thought in ten words, "George Bush has farther to climb and farther to go."

Lean-faced and Argus-eyed, President Bush is ready. Decisive challenge, bumpy mile and craggy climb, are welcome propellants. Along, of course, with the sure-grip traction of an impeccable military account. A mature, common-sense mate befitting a statesman. Incomparable foreign policy proficiency, and so on.

Why even hint at trading proven, unalloyed steel for a lead and pot-metal mixture?

VIRGIL RICHIE, "Man of Steel," *Daily News-Record,* Harrisonburg, VA, August 25, 1992, p. 6.

III. Identify the fallacies of ambiguity or fallacies of relevance in each of the following. If there is no fallacy, write "No Fallacy." Give reasons for your answers.

1. All people who favor a democratic form of government are democrats. No Republicans are Democrats. So no Republicans are people who favor a democratic form of government.

2. Water extinguishes fire. Oxygen is a part of water. So oxygen extinguishes fire.

3. German-Austria must return to the great German mother country, and not because of any economic considerations. No, and again no: even if such a union were unimportant from an economic point of view; yes, even if it were harmful, it must nevertheless take place. One blood demands one Reich.

   ADOLF HITLER, *Mein Kampf,* translated by Ralph Mannheim (New York: Houghton Mifflin, 1943), p. 3.

4. Everyone has the right to say what he or she wishes. So George has the right to make slanderous remarks about his professor.

5. Ms. DeMark has provided evidence that children who watch more than two hours of television daily do not perform as well in school as those who watch no television. But who would want to give up television? It's a source of news and weather reports. It provides large varieties of entertainment for little more than the cost of the set. Surely her conclusions are flawed.

6. Cleo read a book on zebras in the wild. So obviously Cleo has been traveling in Africa.

7. Oscar tells me that I should always drive within the speed limit. But Oscar regularly drives at speeds of well over eighty miles per hour on the interstates. So there's no reason to believe anything Oscar says.

8. Francesca claims that the government should not interfere with the personal lives of the governed. But this is just another version of the old saw that the government that

governs least governs best, which implies that the best government doesn't govern at all. But if there were no government, there would be anarchy. Anarchy is untenable. So we obviously must reject Francesca's claim.

9. The commandment says, "Thou shalt not bear false witness against thy neighbor." Since Jerusha lives two hundred miles from here, she's not my neighbor. So I can say anything about her that I wish.

10. Since buses and trains take more fuel than cars, we won't save any energy by switching from private cars to public transportation.

11. Joan contends that it is wrong to support the euthanasia movement. But people have rights everywhere. So, certainly, young people in the Far East have as many rights to their movement as anyone else.

12. Professor, you should have no trouble accepting my paper six weeks late. My parents are getting a divorce. My roommate has a drinking problem. And my dog had a very difficult pregnancy. All these things have been very trying, and I just don't know how I could survive if you didn't accept my paper late.

13. Father to son: Your grades are going to improve, or I'm going to quit paying for your college education.

14. All sorority members are women. So Josephine, a member of Sigma Alpha Psi sorority, is a woman.

15. Sheriff: We were all fond of Billy, and we want the person who killed him to be brought to justice. Jake is only being held for questioning. So far there isn't a shred of evidence that points to him.

    (The sheriff enters the jail.)

    Bad Jack: We all know how special Billy was. Pete, who took you in when your house burned down? Billy, that's who. And Mack, remember that spring when you broke your leg? Your crops would never have been planted if Bil y hadn't done it. He did something like that for each and every one of us. And what did he ask in return? Not a thing! Now we have a chance to do something for the finest man who ever lived in this town, a man who was shot in the back by that coward in jail. For Billy's sake, let's go and string him up.

16. Professor Egalf claims that a bit of skepticism with respect to one's beliefs is the mark of a rational, educated person. What would you expect from him? Egalf is a self-professed skeptic!

17. Hunting is a safe and exhilarating sport, for thousands of people go hunting every year.

18. Dr. Fernandez claims that learning a second language increases our understanding of and eases our communications with people in other cultures. But English is taught in more countries around the world than any other language. It is virtually the universal language of commerce and scholarship. So there's nothing to be gained by learning a second language.

19. "This is a pretty pass," he fumed, "when they send a businessman to a preacher. I suppose you are going to pray with me and read the Bible," he said irritably. . . .

    He proved most sullen and unco-operative until finally I was forced to say to him: "I want to tell you bluntly that you had better co-operate with us or you're going to be fired."

    "Who told you that?" he demanded.

    "Your boss," I replied. "In fact, he says that unless we can straighten you out, as much as he regrets it, you are going to be through."

    NORMAN VINCENT PEALE, *The Power of Positive Thinking* (New York: Fawcett, 1956), p. 158.

20. "Who did you pass on the road?" the King went on, holding out his hand to the Messenger for some more hay.

    "Nobody," said the Messenger.

    "Quite right," said the King: "This young lady saw him too. So of course Nobody walks much slower than you."

    "I do my best," the Messenger said in a sullen tone. "I'm sure nobody walks much faster than I do!"

    "He can't do that," said the King, "or else he'd have been here first."

    LEWIS CARROLL, *Through the Looking Glass* (Chapter 7).

3.3 Fallacies of Presumption

You commit a fallacy of presumption if you assume in the premises of your argument what you are setting out to prove, or if you assume that all the information that is relevant to accepting a conclusion is given when, in fact, it is not. In this section we examine four fallacies of presumption.

Begging the Question

The aim of an argument is to persuade someone who accepts the premises to accept the conclusion. If the conclusion is nothing more than a restatement of one of the premises, there is nothing to be persuaded of, since (by definition) the person to be persuaded already accepts the premises. An argument commits the fallacy of **begging the question** if the conclusion of the argument is nothing more than a restatement of one of the premises. The fallacy of begging the question is an informal fallacy. Since every statement entails itself, to presume the conclusion as a premise guarantees that the argument is formally valid: the problem is that statements do not provide evidence for their own truth.[12] Here are two examples.

1. Since today is Tuesday, it follows that today is Tuesday. (explicit)
2. Since Jorge is a bachelor, we may conclude that he is an unmarried man. (implicit)

In both arguments, the conclusion says nothing more than the premise. If you don't already believe that it's Tuesday, the argument provides you no reason to believe it; if you already believe on independent grounds that it's Tuesday, you discover nothing new in the conclusion. In the second argument, the conclusion does nothing more than define the word 'bachelor'. The conclusion does nothing more than restate the premise in different words.

A more sophisticated version of the fallacy of begging the question is called **arguing in a circle**. You argue in a circle if you propose a series of arguments in which the conclusion of the last argument was accepted as a premise in an earlier argument. Here are some examples.

1. I know that the Bible is the inspired word of God because I know that everything the Bible says is true. And I know that everything the Bible says is true because it is the inspired word of God.
2. "Why is giving alms to the poor the right thing to do?"
   "Because one is morally obligated to give alms to the poor."
   "But why is one morally obligated to give alms to the poor?"
   "Because it's the right thing to do!"

3. Homosexuals should be kept off the police force because they violate the antisodomy law. And we should keep the antisodomy law because it keeps homosexuals off the police force.

In each of these cases there are two arguments, and the premise of the first argument is the conclusion of the second. In each case the arguer is engaged in circular reasoning.

An **epithet** is a descriptive word or phrase used to characterize a person, thing, or idea. A third way you can commit the fallacy of begging the question is by ascribing to a person, thing, or idea an epithet that assumes what you are trying to establish. Here are two examples.

1. All the evidence shows that that criminal Smith is guilty of first-degree murder. You have no choice but to find him guilty as charged!
2. The proposed state lottery is nothing but an idiotic scheme to exploit the poor to benefit the rich. All thinking people must vote "NO" on the referendum.

In the first case, the epithet 'criminal' begs the question of Smith's guilt. In the second argument, the epithet 'idiotic scheme' begs the question whether the state lottery is a reasonable proposal.

Complex Question

You commit the fallacy of **complex question** if you implicitly ask two questions at once, one explicitly and one implicitly, and an answer to the explicit question allows you to draw a conclusion regarding the implicit question. Assume a lawyer asks you the question, "Have you stopped cheating on your taxes?" Giving any answer to this question assumes that another question has already been answered affirmatively, namely, "Did you ever cheat on your taxes?" No matter how the complex question is answered, the interrogator can respond, "Aha! So you admit that you've cheated on your taxes!" Often a complex question requires a simple "yes" or "no" answer, though it need not. Here are two examples.

1. Have you stopped cheating in this course?
2. Lefty, how did you manage to evade paying taxes for the past twenty years?

Given an answer to the first question, whether it is "yes" or "no," the interrogator can reply, "Aha! So you admit you've been cheating in this course!" If Lefty is foolish enough to answer the question—if his lawyer does not object to the form of the question—he will certainly be convicted of tax evasion.[13]

Suppressed Evidence

As a general rule, if the person presenting an argument has a vested interest in your acceptance of the conclusion—if the arguer stands to gain in some way by your accepting the conclusion—you should look very carefully at the premises to see whether they leave out any information that is relevant to judging the truth of the conclusion. An argument that commits the fallacy of **suppressed evidence** is enthymematic. It states a premise that is true but presupposes an additional premise, a false premise, the truth of which must be assumed as grounds for accepting the conclusion. It is because the argument assumes a false premise that the stated premise is sometimes described as a "half-truth": the premise is true, as far as it goes, but it does not give all the facts. Such arguments are common in advertising. Here are some examples.

1. You should use vegetable shortening in your pie crusts rather than lard, because vegetable shortening has only half the polyunsaturated fats of butter.
2. Ragic Trucks have one of the lowest sticker prices on the market. And over seventy percent of the trucks we've made in the last fifteen years are still on the road. Ragic—your best value in trucks.
3. Salesperson: This 1981 Ford is just the car for you. The odometer registers only 24,500 miles. It gets over twenty miles to the gallon on the highway. And the body is in almost mint condition.

The first argument can be fully stated as follows:

In choosing between using vegetable shortening and lard in your pie crust, you should choose that which has the lowest level of polyunsaturated fats.
Vegetable shortening has half the polyunsaturated fats of butter. (true)
Suppressed premise: Lard has more than half the polyunsaturated fats of butter. (false)

Therefore you should use vegetable shortening rather than lard in your pie crusts.

The stated premise of the first argument is true: vegetable shortening has half the polyunsaturated fats of butter. The conclusion contains a comparison between the desirability of using vegetable shortening rather than lard. For the conclusion to follow, there must be a suppressed (unstated) premise indicating that the level of polyunsaturated fats in lard is higher than that in vegetable shortening. But lard has half the polyunsaturated fats of butter—exactly the same level as vegetable shortening—so the suppressed premise is false. The argument commits the fallacy of suppressed evidence. The second argument might suppress a great deal of evidence. The fact that seventy percent of Ragic trucks made in the last fifteen years are still on the road is good evidence that Ragic Trucks are reliable only if it is *not* the case that other manufacturers can boast a better record. The fact that Ragic trucks have a relatively low initial cost is good evidence that they are a good value in trucks only if they are *not* subject to frequent, costly repairs that more than compensate for the low sticker price. The third argument assumes (1) that the mileage on the odometer is identical with the mileage on the car and (2) that the working parts of the car are in the same condition as the body. If either of these assumptions is false—for example, if the previous owner traded the car in because the engine needed a major overhaul—the salesperson's argument commits the fallacy of suppressed evidence.

Avoiding the fallacy of suppressed evidence does *not* require that we provide our argumentative opponents with evidence that tends to show our conclusion is false, but it does require that we be certain that all unstated premises are true. To detect the fallacy, you must discover suppressed premises in an argument and determine whether they are true. If a suppressed premise is false, the argument commits the fallacy of suppressed evidence.

False Dichotomy (Bifurcation)

We often argue that a certain object falls into one of two classes, note that it does not fall into the first class, and conclude that it therefore falls into the second. For example, we might argue:

> Either Helen is a male or a female.
> Helen is not a male.
> _____
> Therefore, Helen is a female.

Assuming Helen is a person, the expression "male or female" expresses a genuine dichotomy. A **dichotomy** is a division of a class into two mutually exclusive and exhaustive subclasses, that is, a division of a class such that every member of the original class is a member of one of the two subclasses and no member of the original class is a member of both subclasses. For example, the classes composed of male persons and female persons are exclusive and exhaustive: all persons fall into one class or the other and no person falls into both classes (at the same time). An argument commits the fallacy of **false dichotomy** if it presents two alternatives as the only alternatives with respect to an issue when in fact there are other options, and rejects one of the alternatives and concludes that you must accept the other: what the argument claims is a dichotomy is not. Here are two examples.

1. Given the environmental problems, either we quit using fossil fuels or we reduce the world to a cinder.
2. We can either wage an all-out war now or spend the rest of our lives living at the feet of this dictator. Obviously we don't want to spend the rest of our lives living at the feet of this dictator. So we must declare war now.

In both cases, we are invited to accept two alternatives as the only options on an issue. In both cases there seem to be additional possibilities. In the first case, we might reduce the consumption of fossil fuels through the use of more efficient engines, public transportation, and so on, and thereby check the environmental problems caused by fossil fuels. In the second case, negotiation might be an alternative to war.

Summary

Arguments committing fallacies of presumption either assume the conclusion as a premise or assume all the information is given when it is not. There are four common fallacies of presumption. (1) If an argument assumes its conclusion as a premise, it commits the fallacy of begging the question. This may also occur in a chain of arguments if a premise of one is the conclusion of another (arguing in a circle), or if a premise contains an epithet that assumes the correctness of the conclusion. (2) A complex question asks two questions at once, and answering the explicit question allows the interrogator to draw conclusions regarding the implicit question. (3) If the conclusion of an argument assumes—but does not state—a false premise, it commits the fallacy of suppressed evidence. (4) If an argument provides two alternatives as the only options when there are additional possibilities, the argument commits the fallacy of false dichotomy.

EXERCISES

I. Identify the fallacy of presumption committed in each of the following passages. Give reasons for your answers.

1. "Better dead than Red!"

2. So you think we should discuss whether to buy a new car. Very well, shall we buy a Ford or a Chevy?

3. Drug addiction is bad because it is bad to become physically or psychologically dependent upon drugs.

4. Voting for the state bond issue will not raise taxes, since all costs of administering the bonds will be drawn from the lottery fund.

5. The evidence shows that the testimony of that pathological liar Marduk is false, so he should be convicted of perjury.

6. Given the medical evidence regarding the relationship between cholesterol and heart disease, the choice is clear: give up meat or die of a heart attack!

7. Why did you steal the painting?

8. You must obey the law because it's right to do so. And we know it's right to do so because it's the law.

9. You should vote "Yes" on the referendum to legalize dog racing, for it provides a means of increasing state revenues without raising the income tax.

10. Furniture is expensive. Either you spend your money on the furniture itself, or you spend your money on the tools and wood to make it. In either case, you'll spend thousands of dollars on furniture.

11. You have a simple choice: either take our speed-reading course or fall behind on your reading assignments.

12. How did you conceal your identity for all these years?

13. Why do I know more than other people? Why, in general, am I so clever? I have never pondered over questions that are not really questions. I have never wasted my strength.

     FRIEDRICH NIETZSCHE, *Ecce Homo.*

14. "In *that* direction," the Cat said, waving its right paw round, "lives a Hatter; and in *that* direction," waving the other paw, "lives a March Hare. Visit either you like: they're both mad."

     "But I don't want to go among mad people," Alice remarked.

"Oh, you can't help that," said the cat: "we're all mad here. I'm mad. You're mad."

"How do you know I'm mad?" said Alice.

"You must be," said the Cat, "or you wouldn't have come here."

LEWIS CARROLL, *Alice in Wonderland* (Chapter 6).

15. Dr. C. Gilbert Wrenn of Tempe, Ariz., speaking in Washington recently, told about a missionary who saved his head years ago when he was captured in Africa and taken to the chief of the tribe who had every intention of "putting him in the cooking pot."

The minister tried to persuade the cannibal chief that white men were not very tasty, and that he would not make a good meal. The chief would not listen. Finally the missionary borrowed the chief's knife and cut a slab from the calf of his leg and said, "Taste and see."

The chief tasted, and spit the mouthful out in disgust. "Go," he said to the missionary as he set him free. Years later the missionary would pull up his pant leg and show where the cut was made out of his cork leg!

REV. A. PURNELL BAILEY, "Our Daily Bread," *Daily News-Record*, Harrisonburg, VA, October 6, 1992, p. 6.

II. Identify the fallacies of ambiguity, relevance, or presumption committed in each of the following passages. If no fallacy is committed, write "No Fallacy." Give reasons for your answers.

1. Anyone who cannot keep his or her personal finances in good order cannot keep public finances in good order. Alexander Hamilton, the first U.S. Secretary of the Treasury, could not keep his personal finances in good order. Therefore, Alexander Hamilton must not have been a good Secretary of the Treasury.

2. The call for a national health-care program should be rejected, for nothing the government does can assure that human life will be lengthened indefinitely.

3. All men are mortals. So all the immortals of stage, screen, and television must be women.

4. Bumper sticker: If you tease me about my age, I'll beat you with my cane.

5. Sue claims that bicycling is a good form of exercise. But bicycles are hard to see, and when a bicycle collides with a

car, the bicycle always loses. Many cyclists are injured every year because of their own negligence or unseen road hazards. Maybe Sue doesn't value her life, but bicycling's too dangerous for me.

6. Either the defendant knew what was going on in his house but did nothing about it, in which case he's lying, or he knew nothing and is a fool.

7. *Thou* shalt not steal, so I'll grab the cash and run.

8. You shouldn't take the religious arguments of John Wesley, the founder of Methodism, seriously, for Wesley was a scholastic quibbler and a critic of such modern works as John Locke's *Essay Concerning Human Understanding*.

9. When we worked through a practice examination as a group, the class completed it in less than an hour. So any student in the class should be able to complete a comparable test within an hour.

10. How do we know that "The Ride of the Valkyries" is a better piece of music than the theme from *The Sound of Music?* Because of the unanimous opinion of the experts. And how do we know who these experts are? They're the ones who hold that "The Ride of the Valkyries" is a better piece of music than the theme from *The Sound of Music.*

11. Elkie has argued that a national sales tax is a reasonable way to raise additional revenues for the federal government. Her argument is plausible only on the assumption that such a form of taxation is equitable. But a sales tax is not equitable: people are not taxed on the basis of their ability to pay. So her argument must be rejected.

12. Little girl: "My daddy says that Churchill Downs is a place where people race horses. I'm sure few people go to Churchill Downs, because it doesn't take too long to figure out that the horses always win."

13. MacMurphy's Mausoleum, the choice of the finest families in our community for over a hundred years.

14. You shouldn't take Mrs. Jones's arguments in favor of farm subsidies seriously, since she manages one of the largest agricultural enterprises in the state.

15. They're just one of a growing number of homeless families in

our community. The Smythes are a family of ten. They live in an unheated bus. Finding employment of any kind is a hit-or-miss proposition, and steady employment is little more than a dream. Winter is setting in, and the eight children have nothing warmer than T-shirts. Shouldn't you give to the Community Homeless Drive to help this family and others like it? It could be a matter of life and death.

16. I'm not backward. If I were backward, I would eat with my feet, and I don't eat with my feet.

17. At the trial of LaVale and Windshield on charges of grand larceny the District Attorney asked a prosecution witness: "What, precisely, was your job when working for those crooks LaVale and Windshield?"

18. The first musical notation was invented in about A.D. 200. We may conclude that before then everyone was a monotone.

19. Each of the atomic bombs dropped during the Second World War killed more people than were killed by any conventional bomb. So more people were killed by atomic bombs during the Second World War than by conventional bombs.

20. It's the party of the people! Vote Democratic!

21. Obviously we should support the continued construction and use of nuclear-powered electrical-generating plants, for in the past thirty years there have been fewer accidents at nuclear generating plants than at conventional power plants.

22. Dr. Swenson has provided evidence that diets high in fiber and low in polyunsaturated fats and cholesterol tend to result in fewer deaths from cancer and heart disease. But diets high in fiber have all the gustatory appeal of tree bark. Low-fat and low-cholesterol foods have no flavor at all. So unless you want to spend your life eating cardboard, you'll ignore Dr. Swenson's dietary advice.

23. Either you favor a conservative fiscal program and vote Republican, or you favor an increase in social programs and vote Democratic.

24. Lawyer to witness: "Where were you on the evening of last June 24?"

25. Help protect an endangered species! Vote Communist!

3.4 *Fallacies of Weak Induction*

The **fallacies of weak induction** occur if the premises of an argument provide *some* evidence for a conclusion, but not sufficient evidence to show that the conclusion is probably true. The evidence cited is relevant to the conclusion, but is simply not enough. In addition, in some cases various emotional ties suggest that the evidence is stronger than it is.

Appeal to Authority

Much, if not most, of our knowledge is based on the authoritative testimony of others. For example, you assume that what is taught in a class is true because your instructor is trained in the field in question. An argument commits the fallacy of **appeal to authority** if the person presenting the argument appeals to the views of someone who is *not* an expert in the field in question as if he or she were an expert, an authority. Three properties provide grounds for claiming that a person is an authority in a field. First, an expert must have education, training, and experience in the relevant field. A person with a B.S. in physics has better grounds for claiming expertise *in physics* than a person with a B.A. in English. A person with a Ph.D. in physics has better grounds for claiming expertise in physics than a person with a B.S. in physics. A person who has been a master plumber for twenty years has better grounds for claiming expertise in plumbing than a recent graduate of a vocational school. On the other hand, a recent graduate of a vocational school in auto mechanics *might* have better grounds for claiming expertise in automotive electronics than a person who has been an auto mechanic for forty years if the more experienced mechanic has not kept abreast of technological developments in automobiles, such as on-board computers.

Second, the expert should be free of bias with respect to the topic for which he or she is cited as an authority. A person's biases can affect what facts that person deems relevant to a judgment and that person's judgment of the significance of a fact or event. For example, if you are studying the American Revolution, a British historian might deem the events in the colonies of considerably less significance than would a direct descendant of Thomas Jefferson who worships his famous ancestor. Questions of bias are particularly significant when the alleged authority has a vested interest in one side of an issue. For example, when representatives of the tobacco industry testify that tobacco products are safe, many people ask whether their claims are based on unbiased research.

Finally, a person can claim expertise with respect to a certain subject matter only if there are generally recognized standards or **criteria** for justifying judgments with regard to that subject matter. In the natural and social sciences, for example, such criteria take the form of a method of inquiry. In purchasing, the best criteria for choosing a product are initial cost, reliability, ease and cost of repairs, and whether the product will fulfill the needs for which it is purchased. But there are areas in which there are no generally recognized criteria for judgment, and if there are no recognized criteria, there are no authorities in that area. Politics, religion, morality, and aesthetics are among the areas in which there are no accepted criteria. To claim that there are no recognized criteria does *not* entail that there can be no rational discussion. It merely implies that a movie critic, for example, should be willing to discuss both the criteria on the basis of which he or she judges a movie and why those criteria are preferable to other possible criteria.

If an argument appeals to an authority as the basis for accepting a conclusion, you should ask whether the alleged authority has the credentials required to be an expert in that field. If he or she does not, or if the field is one in which there are no clear criteria, the argument commits the fallacy of appeal to authority.

Appeals might be made to the authority of one person, of many people, or of a select group of people, or to tradition. Here are some examples.

1. George "the Icebox" Smith, tackle for the St. Paul Horseshoes football team, says that Bear Beer is best. So Bear Beer is the best beer.

2. Henrietta Wordfellow, chief executive officer of Noxen Petroleum Company, says that ethanol is not an efficient fuel for powering cars. So we should stick with gasoline.

3. In 1972 Richard Nixon received more popular votes than any previous presidential candidate. So Nixon must have been one of the best presidents in history.

4. The members of the First Street Baptist Ladies Aid Society agree that Aunt Sophie's double Dutch chocolate cake mix is the best cake mix on the market. Buy Aunt Sophie's!

5. In this family the parents have always arranged the marriages of their children. That's the way it ought to be done.

In the first argument we are given no reason to believe that Smith is an authority on beer. You need to inquire into Smith's credentials. If you discover that Smith is not only a football player but a master brewer as

well and that the criteria on which he bases his judgment are the criteria generally accepted in the brewing industry, you would have some
reason to believe the claim that Bear Beer is the best beer. On the other
hand, if Smith's sole credential for claiming to be an authority on beer
is that he is a famous football player, or if the sole criteria for "best
beer" is personal taste, the argument commits the fallacy of appeal to
authority. In the second argument, Wordfellow is in a position to know
the efficiency of various propellants for automobiles, but insofar as she
has a vested interest in the petroleum industry, you might question her
status as an authority on the efficiency of ethanol. To determine whether
she should be accepted as an authority on the efficiency of gasoline with
respect to ethanol, you would need to examine her arguments.[14] The
third argument appeals to the authority of the many. Electoral popular-
ity is not necessarily the mark of a great president. The fourth argument appeals to the authority of a select few. We should inquire whether
the group in question, or any group, has the best credentials necessary
for judging the quality of a cake mix. The fifth argument is an appeal
to the authority of tradition. If something has always been done in a
certain way, there is no basis for comparison; therefore, no reason is
given for claiming that that way of doing things is better than any other.
For example, if a family or society claims that the practice of arranging
marriages is the best because the practice has traditionally been followed, one might ask why it is best. Does that method provide a greater
degree of marital stability? Does it yield greater happiness for the
couple? If there is nothing with which to compare it, those questions
cannot be answered.

Who or what counts as an authority changes as the criteria for judgment in a field change. The criteria for judgment are always subject to
evaluation. If the criteria for judgment in a certain field are subject to
considerable debate, no one on either side of the debate should be
deemed an authority: if there are no accepted criteria, there are no experts.

Appeal to Ignorance

An argument commits the fallacy of **appeal to ignorance** *(argumentum
ad ignorantiam)* if it rests on the claim that since there is no evidence
that a certain claim is false, it must be true, or since there is no evidence that a claim is true, it must be false. Typically these are cases involving something that cannot be proved or, at least, has not yet been
proved. Here are two examples.

1. No one has proven that smoking marijuana leads to the use of hard drugs. So using marijuana does not lead to the use of hard drugs.

2. No one has proven that smoking marijuana does not lead to the use of hard drugs. So using marijuana does lead to the use of hard drugs.

Typically, if something is unproven—if the evidence on both sides of an issue is equal or nearly equal—you can draw no conclusions at all. As the examples indicate, if the evidence is inconclusive regarding the relationship between smoking marijuana and using harder drugs, to argue that the evidence proves one thing *just because* it does not prove the other is an instance of the fallacy of argument from ignorance.

There are cases, however, in which the lack of evidence in favor of a claim tends to show that the claim is false. For example, if a team of competent and highly respected scientists has examined the evidence for "cold fusion" and concludes that there is no evidence that it occurs, you have good grounds for claiming that cold fusion does not occur. Similarly, if no one has seen Georgette smoking a cigar, and no one has detected the telltale signs of cigar-smoking on Georgette's person (lingering odors of smoke, cigar ash, stained teeth, etc.) or in her house, there is good evidence that Georgette does not smoke cigars.

A court of law provides a case in which you can make a legitimate appeal to ignorance. In a court of law, a person is presumed innocent until proven guilty. Thus, a jury is instructed to find the defendant "not guilty" if the evidence is insufficient to show beyond a reasonable doubt that the defendant committed the crime. If the defendant is acquitted, it is presumed that the defendant did not commit the crime. Nor are courts of law the only places where presumptions prevail. If we shop in a certain store, we presume the shopkeeper is honest. We presume our neighbors are not murderers. We presume our teachers, elected officials, and financial advisors are competent unless evidence to the contrary is brought forth. All these are reasonable presumptions, and we do not commit the fallacy of appeal to ignorance by holding them.

Hasty Generalization

An argument commits the fallacy of **hasty generalization** if a general conclusion—a conclusion pertaining to all or most things of a kind—is based on an atypical case or cases. Here are some examples.

1. On Tuesday the sun was shining and it was raining. So whenever the sun shines, it rains.

2. John, a member of the Phi Beta Kappa fraternity, spends his Saturday nights studying in the library. Fred, a member of the Phi Alpha Theta fraternity, studies for twelve hours every day. So most fraternity members are studious people.

3. Joan bought a new Thunderbird, and within six months the transmission gave out. George bought a Mercury Cougar, and within three months he had problems with his carburetor. Henrietta bought a Lincoln Continental, and within two weeks she had problems with her brakes. Obviously, products of the Ford Motor Company are unreliable.

In the first argument, there is a generalization from an unusual case: the sun seldom shines when it rains. In examining the second argument your should remember that most fraternity members are members of social fraternities, while Phi Beta Kappa and Phi Alpha Theta are honorary fraternities. In the third argument, nothing has been done to show that the cases mentioned are typical—and the large number of satisfied customers of Ford suggests the cases are atypical.

The fallacy of hasty generalization occurs if you generalize from an atypical case. As such, it has nothing to do with the number of cases from which you generalize. If you conclude that Sony makes quality tape recorders on the basis of the one you own, you are not guilty of a hasty generalization: yours is a typical example of their reliable machines. To *avoid* the fallacy, however, you should look at a significant number of cases relative to the class of objects about which you draw a conclusion. The more cases you examine, the less likely it is that they will all be atypical cases.

Some students confuse cases of hasty generalization with cases of composition. The difference should be clear if you remember that in the case of hasty generalization you conclude that a general statement is true on the basis of atypical cases, whereas in the case of composition you conclude that a *property* that is correctly applied to a part of a whole or a member of a class is correctly applicable to a whole or an entire class. If you keep in mind the distinction between general statements and statements about properties, you will not confuse the fallacies.

False Cause

An argument commits the fallacy of false cause if it misidentifies the cause of an event and draws a conclusion. There are two varieties of this fallacy. The first kind is called *post hoc ergo propter hoc* ("before that, therefore because of that"). If you assume that one event is the cause of another *simply because it occurs first,* you commit the fallacy of *post hoc ergo propter hoc.* Here are two examples.

1. On Wednesday Suzanne picked up a black cat and died of a heart attack. So, if you want to live a long life, avoid black cats.

2. In 1979 Professor Jones moved to Minnesota, and within two years the state went into a recession. In 1983 she moved to Texas, and within two years the Texas economy collapsed. In 1988 Jones moved to Virginia, and the commonwealth's economy went into recession. So, if you want to avoid economic disaster, don't let Professor Jones move to your state!

There is no reason to believe either that picking up a black cat was the cause of Suzanne's death or that Professor Jones's place of residence has any significant impact on a state's economy. Hence, the proposed conclusions are unwarranted. But don't be too hasty in dismissing causal claims. Years ago the Notre Dame football team shattered tradition for a big game by wearing jerseys not of the team's usual color. They won, to most people's surprise. Is it fallacious to assume that the changed jerseys caused the victory? No. Given the context, the changed jerseys affected the players and fans psychologically, which in turn affected the play on the field, which directly caused the victory. As always, you must use judgment: don't dismiss causal claims too hastily.

The second kind of false cause is called ***non causa pro causa*** ("not the cause for the cause"). Here you incorrectly take something to be the cause of something else without any reference or allusion to the temporal order of events. Here are two examples.

1. The standards for teacher certification are increasing, but the scores students record on standardized tests are falling. To improve our children's education we should loosen the standards for teacher certification.

2. The works of great authors are subjects of discussion in literature classes. So if Bosworth can convince some English professors to use his novels in class, he will be a great author.

If there is any connection between the standards for teacher certification and the scores of students on standardized tests, it is most probably that certification standards have been increased in an attempt to improve the quality of education and thereby increase scores on standardized tests. Having a literary work discussed in classes does not make its author great; generally the quality of the literary work explains why a professor chooses to use it in a class.

Discovering the cause of something is not always an easy task. For this reason it is not always easy to determine whether what someone claims is a cause of a phenomenon is actually a cause. Sometimes a little thought will convince you that an alleged cause is not an actual cause. Other times determining whether an alleged cause is the actual cause will require investigation.

Slippery Slope

A **slippery slope argument** has the following structure. There is a slope—a chain of causes. It is slippery. Therefore, if you take even one step on the slope, you will slide all the way to the bottom. But the bottom is a bad place to be. So, you should not take the first step. The argument derives its name from the similarity to an object—a skier, for example—at the top of a slippery hill. Once the object starts sliding down, it will go all the way to the bottom. The **slippery slope fallacy** occurs when (and only when) the slope is not slippery, that is, when at least one of the alleged causal relations along the "slope" does not hold. Insofar as it is based on false claims of causal relations, the slippery slope fallacy is closely related to false cause. Here are two arguments that commit the slippery slope fallacy.

1. You don't want to start smoking tobacco, because tobacco smokers go on to smoke marijuana, and marijuana smokers go on to smoke hashish, and hashish smokers eventually go on to try cocaine, and cocaine addicts cannot function in society.

2. To consider abortion a permissible activity is the first step toward a general disregard for human life. For it is only a short step from abortion to infanticide, and another short step from infanticide to euthanasia. But if euthanasia is permissible, then it is a small step to an utter disregard for human life.

In the first case there might be some evidence that people who turn to hard drugs start with tobacco, but there is little evidence that there is a general trend for tobacco smokers to go on to use hard drugs: certainly there are many smokers who do not use other drugs. The second argument seems to rest on similarly unsupported causal claims.

There are cases in which the slope of a slippery slope argument reflects actual causal relations. Here is an example.

> You shouldn't tailgate on the highway. If the car in front of you stops suddenly, you'll run into it. If you run into that car, your car will be damaged and you'll be charged with reckless driving. If your driving was the cause of the accident, your auto insurance premiums will go up. If your auto insurance premiums go up, you'll have less money to spend on the things you enjoy, which will surely make you upset. So you shouldn't tailgate.

Here there is a genuine chain of causes; the slope is actually slippery. This argument is *not* fallacious.

Slippery slope arguments are somewhat difficult to evaluate. You have to investigate each of the alleged causal relations to see whether it holds. If they all hold, it is *not* a fallacious argument. If any one of the alleged causal relations does not hold, the argument commits the slippery slope fallacy. You should be particularly aware of cases in which you might be psychologically or sociologically persuaded that there is a causal relation, and check to see whether the evidence supports your belief.

Weak Analogy

Arguments by analogy rest on similarities between two objects, situations, or kinds of object or situation. Typically, you argue that because two objects have certain characteristics in common, it is likely that if one of them has an additional characteristic, the other one does as well. An argument commits the fallacy of **weak analogy** if there is a telling difference between the two objects compared, a difference that does away with any reason for claiming that the conclusion is warranted. Here are two examples.

1. A fetus is like a tumor insofar as it is a growth that occurs within a body. Hence, just as it is permissible to surgically remove a tumor, it is permissible to surgically remove a fetus.
2. Taxation is illegal, for taxation is little more than extortion.

The first analogy is faulty insofar as a tumor is often life-threatening, and the surgical removal of the tumor and a biopsy are often needed to determine whether it is malignant or benign. The presence of a fetus is generally not life-threatening, and the surgical removal of the fetus is not necessary to determine whether the pregnancy threatens the mother's life. Further, when left untreated, a tumor will continue to grow, while a fetus will grow only to a certain point before being expelled from a body in birth. An argument such as this does not support the claim that abortion is morally permissible. The second analogy is faulty insofar as extortion is the illegal wringing of money from a person on the basis of threats or violence, with all monetary advantages of payment going to the extortionist. Taxation is legal on the same grounds that extortion is illegal—the laws were passed by the government—and there are often benefits to the community, including the taxpayer, that are derived from paying taxes.

SUMMARY

Fallacies of weak induction are found in arguments that provide some evidence that a conclusion is true, but not sufficient evidence to justify accepting the conclusion. (1) If the conclusion of an argument is supported by an appeal to the views of a person who is not an authority in the field, the argument commits the fallacy of appeal to authority. (2) If an argument appeals to the fact that the evidence does not show that a certain statement is false (true) and concludes that it is true (false), the argument commits the fallacy of appeal to ignorance. (3) If an argument's general conclusion is based on an atypical case or cases, the argument commits the fallacy of hasty generalization. (4) If an argument claims a cause of a phenomenon that is not in fact the cause of the phenomenon, the argument commits the fallacy of false cause. (5) If an argument claims that allowing a certain action will inevitably lead to another, which will inevitably lead to another, each of which is worse than the previous action, the argument probably commits the slippery slope fallacy. (6) If the conclusion of an argument is based on comparisons between two objects that are dissimilar in important ways, the argument commits the fallacy of weak analogy.

EXERCISES

I. Identify the fallacies of weak induction that are found in the following passages. Give reasons for your answers.

1. Great artists are seldom recognized as great before they die. So if you want to be recognized as a great artist, die.

2. There's no evidence that capital punishment is a deterrent to murder, so it's not a deterrent.

3. Chevrolets are not safe cars, for Joan drove her 1952 Chevy at a high speed on a mountainous road, the brakes gave out, and she was killed.

4. We should not worry about protecting the spotted owl and the various other so-called endangered species. To claim these species must be preserved in their pure genetic state is like arguing for racial purity. But the arguments for racial purity are morally pernicious. So, the arguments for preserving endangered species are also morally pernicious.

5. If I don't get a B in this course, I won't be able to register for courses in my major next semester, and if I can't register for courses in my major next semester, completing my degree will take an additional year. Since I can't afford to spend an extra year in college, I won't be able to finish and my fourteen children (all under the age of six) will certainly starve.

6. When I go to church, I seldom have trouble sleeping. But when I go to bed at night, I frequently suffer from insomnia. So I've decided to replace my bed with a church pew.

7. For a number of years, the Ford Escort was the best-selling car in the world. So, during those years the Ford Escort was the best-built car in the world.

8. There is no evidence that the presidential primary system yields the most qualified presidential candidates, so obviously it doesn't.

9. The Pope says that using artificial birth control devices is immoral. So, using artificial birth control devices is immoral.

10. Jocelyn put her money in Gambler's Savings and Loan. Gambler's Savings went broke, and Jocelyn lost all her money. So no savings and loan institutions are safe places to put your money.

II. Identify the fallacies of weak induction that are found in the following passages. If there is no fallacy, write "No Fallacy." Give reasons for your answers.

1. As a parent, you must be a strict disciplinarian. If you allow your child to get by without eating her Brussels sprouts, she'll expect you to allow her to ignore liver. If you allow her to ignore liver, she'll assume she can get by without cleaning her

room. If you allow her to get by without cleaning her room, she'll start staying out late with her friends. If she starts staying out late with her friends, she's certain to fall in with the wrong crowd. If she falls in with the wrong crowd, she'll eventually be picked up and sent to prison for life. So, you see how important it is to be strict and make your child eat those Brussels sprouts!

2. Since St. Paul advised Timothy, "Do not drink water only, but take a little wine to help your digestion, since you are sick so often" (I Timothy 5:23), we may conclude that no churches object to the consumption of wine.

3. Father Murphy performed last rites for Monique, and she died. Father Murphy performed last rites for Roderick, and he died. Father Murphy performed last rites for Zadrick, Caroline, Hilda, Isadora, Kelvin, Glendon, Conway, and Amber. They all died. So if you don't want to die, don't let Father Murphy perform last rites.

4. It would be no crime in me to divert the *Nile* or *Danube* from its course, were I able to effect such purposes. Where then is the crime in turning a few ounces of blood from their natural channel?

   DAVID HUME, "Of Suicide."

5. The members of this family have always voted Republican. So, obviously, the Republican candidate is the one you will want to support with your vote!

6. No one has shown that using alcoholic beverages for medicinal purposes only is dangerous. So, the purely medicinal use of alcoholic beverages is perfectly safe.

7. According to the surgeon general, women should not drink alcoholic beverages during pregnancy because of the risk of birth defects.

8. Fr. Rizzini is a Roman Catholic priest, and he's married. So, all Catholic priests can now be married.

9. The only proof capable of being given that an object is visible is that people actually see it. The only proof that a sound is audible is that people hear it; and so of the other sources of our experience. In like manner, I apprehend, the sole evidence it is possible to produce that anything is desirable is that people do actually desire it.

   JOHN STUART MILL, *Utilitarianism*, chapter 4.

10. If you develop a taste for ice cream, you'll want to try chocolate sauce as a topping. If you try chocolate sauce as a topping, you'll develop a taste for candy bars. If you develop a taste for candy bars, you're certain to eat them to excess. If you eat candy to excess, you'll grow fat. If you grow fat, you'll almost certainly die prematurely of a heart attack. So, you certainly don't want to develop a taste for ice cream.

11. The President says we're coming out of our current economic slump, so it must be true.

12. During the Second World War, the Nazis murdered over six million Jews, and much of the world stood idly by. Since the Roe *v.* Wade decision in 1973, American abortionists have murdered over 40 million innocent babies. Can we afford to stand idly by and allow such a holocaust?

13. Cigarette smokers have a life expectancy that is two years less than that of nonsmokers. Pipe smokers have a life expectancy that is two years greater than that of nonsmokers. So if you want an extra couple years, you should take up a pipe.

14. There is no evidence that washing your hair every day with a strong dandruff shampoo causes baldness, so it must be safe to do so.

15. You shouldn't date. If you date, you'll fall in love. If you fall in love, you'll get married. If you get married, you'll have a bunch of kids. If you have a bunch of kids, you'll be perpetually broke, and you'll have to turn to a life of crime to make ends meet. So you shouldn't date.

III. Identify the informal fallacies in each of the following passages. If there is no fallacy, write "No Fallacy." Give reasons for your answers.

1. It's not snowing, so it's not cold.

2. It's the party of peace and prosperity! Vote Republican!

3. The federal government has no right to control the production of wine, for wine is made by pressing grapes and the First Amendment guarantees that "Congress shall make no law . . . abridging the freedom . . . of the press."

4. Hitchhiker: "I stood on Route 150 for three hours without getting a ride. As soon as I put on my stocking cap, I got a ride all the way to Capital City. So it was the cap that got me the ride, and now I always wear it when I hitch."

5. Everyone should spend a couple of years in the Army, for it certainly helped a guy in my high-school class who used to be lazy and a drug-user.

6. Boss: Is that harebrained scheme of yours going to have detrimental effects on company profits?
    Employee: No, my study suggests it will improve profits.
    Boss: Nonetheless, since you admit it's a harebrained scheme, we're going to have to make some changes around here!

7. Ms. Margroff argues that the government's deficit spending is an economic time bomb that will ultimately destroy the country. But the American people have demanded a national health-care system. We have obligations to retired people, the unemployed, and the underemployed. Defense is still a pressing need. And the tax revenues simply will not cover everything. So deficit spending is here to stay.

8. It was a unique briefcase that Ms. Nehrer lost, for her ad in the paper reads, "Lost: American Tourister briefcase with eyeglasses."

9. We must have a free press. For we must not restrict the rights of our news media to inform us of the facts as they see them and to voice their opinions on the central issues of the day.

10. We must not allow children to play with firecrackers, for Col. Oakdale, the head of the Army Demolition Squad, says that their fuses burn erratically.

11. My new car is well-designed. Therefore, its radiator is well-designed.

12. Boss to employee: You will want to increase your giving to the United Way this year. After all, you should be thankful that you're *currently* in a position to be charitable.

13. To claim that the government should decrease the size of its welfare program is like claiming that parents ought to decrease the amount of time, energy, and money they devote to the care of their children. Since it is ridiculous to suggest that parents should reduce their support of their children, it is equally ridiculous to suggest that the government should decrease its welfare program.

14. It would be terrible if the government decreased the size of its welfare program. Think of all those children who would suffer from malnutrition and exposure to the cold.

15. It is improper to charge persons bail to get out of jail, since the Eighth Amendment to the Constitution asserts that ". . . bail shall not be required."

16. Alicia has argued that recycling paper is beneficial to the environment. But her argument is reasonable only if one assumes that there are recycling centers in every city and town across the country. But any town of less than 2,500 residents is unlikely to have its own recycling center. So, we must reject her argument.

17. We should reject arguments for tighter environmental controls on industry, since such controls are certain to reduce the numbers of people employed in existing industries.

18. Given the federal deficit, the choice is clear: either we cancel our foreign aid program or the national debt will double in the next four years.

19. Block's Granulated Sugar must be the best sugar on the market: Granny Smerad has been using it for years.

20. Senator Rockingham has argued that we should increase the minimum wage. What would you expect from a senator whose primary source of campaign funds comes from labor-union war chests?

21. Professor Sun has argued that genetic manipulation holds the key to curing numerous diseases. But genetic engineering is dangerous. The bacteria used in gene manipulation experiments are extremely hard to contain. Several scientists have died as a result of their own genetic experiments. If some of those things they're working on escaped from the labs, they could destroy human life as we know it.

22. Each and every American citizen has the right to keep and bear arms. So the United States is militaristic.

23. The First Amendment forbids the government from prohibiting the free exercise of religion. Therefore, the government cannot prohibit religions from engaging in human sacrifice.

24. You don't want to smoke. Smoking is old-fashioned, passé. It's not an activity condoned by those who are with it.

25. If God is everywhere, [as] I had concluded, then He is in food. Therefore, the more I ate the godlier I would become. Impelled by this new religious fervor, I glutted myself like a fanatic.

      WOODY ALLEN, *Getting Even*
      (New York: Random House, 1971), pp. 86–87.

26. There's no evidence that there is intelligent life outside the solar system, so there isn't any.

27. Anaytus: Socrates, I think that you are too ready to speak evil of men: and, if you will take my advice, I would recommend you to be careful. Perhaps there is no city in which it is not easier to do men harm than to do them good, and this is certainly the case at Athens, as I believe that you know.

      PLATO, *Meno,* translated by Benjamin Jowett.

28. We should always help a friend in need. So, we should help our friends who become stumped during an examination.

29. Good sense is of all things in the world the most equally distributed, for everybody thinks himself so abundantly provided with it, that even those most difficult to please in all other matters do not commonly desire more of it than they already possess.

      RENÉ DESCARTES, *Discourse on Method,* translated by Elizabeth Haldane and G. R. T. Ross.

30. The Roman Catholic Church has declared that gender discrimination is a sin. So, the Catholic Church has no objection to ordaining women as priests.

31. It makes no difference what your occupation is: either you commit yourself to it fully or you fail.

32. Never let your kids play in the snow. If they play in the snow, they'll want to go sledding. If they want to go sledding, they'll want to go skiing. If they take up skiing, they'll either crash into a tree while careening down a slippery slope, or they'll want to enter Olympic competition. If they enter Olympic competition, they'll either win the gold or they won't. If they win, it'll go to their heads and you won't be able to live with them. If they don't win, they'll be so depressed you won't be able to live with them. So, unless you don't want to live with your kids, don't let them play in the snow.

33. "Chemistry for the Consumer" was an easy course. I had always thought that chemistry courses were some of the most difficult courses in the university. I now see that they're really quite simple.

34. Caffeine is an addictive drug, and its use is not prohibited by law. Alcohol is an addictive drug, and its use is not prohibited by law. Nicotine is an addictive drug, and its use is not prohibited by law. Cocaine is an addictive drug. So its use should not be prohibited by law.

35. The Sixth Amendment to the Constitution asserts that "In all criminal prosecutions, the accused shall enjoy . . . a speedy and public trial, . . ." But I talked with George, and it was clear that he didn't enjoy his murder trial at all, and it took a full twenty weeks. So, his conviction should be overturned on constitutional grounds.

36. How'd you manage to pull off the perfect bank robbery?

37. Jessica says she hopes to be married one day. Thus, I suspect Jessica will pay her divorce lawyer a retainer even before the wedding.

38. John has argued that retaining a strong military provides the best prospect for world peace. If he is correct, we must assume that members of the military are primarily peacemakers. But the military consists of soldiers, men and women trained to fight wars. So, as professional warriors, members of the military are certainly not peacemakers, and we must reject John's argument.

39. There is no evidence that a system of letter grades improves the quality of education, so the grading system should be rejected.

40. The majority of members of the Senate and the House believe that there should be relatively few restrictions on campaign contributions, so there must be good reasons not to restrict contributions.

41. A mob is no worse than the individuals in it.

42. You can tell that Dave has a high moral character by the character of his friends, for people who hang out with Dave must be of the highest moral type, or they wouldn't associate with him.

43. You should support the referendum for a state lottery, for a lottery provides a means of generating state revenues without raising taxes.

44. First Fundamentalist Church believes in predestination—it's one of the doctrines upon which the church was founded. So Ginger, who's a member of First Fundamentalist, believes in predestination.

45. Minister: You may believe that there is no harm in an exaggerated claim of youth or cheating the scale of a few pounds. It's just a little white lie you tell yourself. But let sin in the door, and you're on your way down the road that leads to hell and damnation! The little white lie becomes comfortable. So it's easier to tell a large lie—indeed, the lies are certain to get larger, for the only way to cover one lie is with another. You will lose all sense of guilt. Cheating on your income tax, you will tell yourself, is just a little lie. Cheating the butcher, the baker, the candlestick maker are just little lies. Cheating on your spouse is just a little lie. Taking the life of another is little more than a little lie. So you see what will inevitably follow from those little white lies: hellfire and damnation!

46. Perhaps there may be some one who is offended at me, when he calls to mind how he himself on a similar, or even less serious occasion, prayed and entreated the judges with many tears, and how he produced his children in court, which was a moving spectacle, together with a host of relations and friends; whereas I, who am probably in danger of my life, will do none of these things. The contrast may occur to his mind, and he may be set against me, and vote in anger because he is displeased at me on this account. Now, if there be such a person among you,—mind, I do not say that there is,—to him I may fairly reply: My friend, I am a man, and like other men, a creature of flesh and blood, and not "of wood or stone," as Homer says; and I have a family, yes, and sons, O Athenians, three in number, one almost a man, and two others who are still young; and yet I will not bring any of them hither in order to petition for an acquittal.

> SOCRATES, in Plato's *Apology,*
> translated by Benjamin Jowett.

47. Letter to a hair-product manufacturer:

> I'm writing to tell you what a wonderful dandruff shampoo
> you produce. I know you claim that it works, but you
> should know that the longer you use it, the better it works.
> I've been using your shampoo every day for the last thirty
> years. When I was twenty, I had a serious case of dandruff,
> and it helped keep it under control. By the time I was
> thirty, and my hair was beginning to thin a bit, it was
> considerably more effective. Now that I'm fifty, I no longer
> have any problem with dandruff.
> Recently, I've also been using your new head wax. It's all I
> expected: it really keeps that old chrome dome shining.
> Thank you for these wonderful products!

48. The doctrine [of body and soul] of Christian philosophers,
which was mainly Platonic in the ancient world, became
mainly Aristotelian after the eleventh century. Thomas
Aquinas (1225–74), who is officially considered the best of
the scholastics, remains to this day the standard of
philosophical orthodoxy in the Roman Catholic Church.
Teachers in educational institutions controlled by the Vatican,
while they may expound, as matters of historical interest, the
systems of Descartes or Locke, Kant or Hegel, must make it
clear that the only *true* system is that of the "seraphic
doctor." The utmost permissible license is to suggest, as his
translator does, that he is joking when he discusses what
happens at the resurrection of the body to a cannibal whose
father and mother were cannibals. Clearly the people whom
he and his parents ate have a prior right to the flesh
composing his body, so that he will be left destitute when
each claims his own. This is a real difficulty for those who
believe in the resurrection of the body, which is affirmed in
the Apostle's Creed. It is a mark of the intellectual
enfeeblement of orthodoxy in our age that it would retain the
dogma while treating as a mere pleasantry a grave discussion
of awkward problems connected with it. How real the belief
still is may be seen in the objection to cremation derived
from it, which is held by many in Protestant countries and by
almost all in Catholic countries, even when they are as
emancipated as France. When my brother was cremated at
Marseilles, the undertaker informed me that he had had

hardly any previous cases, because of the theological prejudice. It is apparently thought more difficult for Omnipotence to reassemble the parts of a human body when they have become diffused as gases than when they remain in the churchyard in the form of worms and clay. Such a view, if I were to express it, would be a mark of heresy; it is in fact, however, the prevailing opinion among the most indubitably orthodox.

BERTRAND RUSSELL, *Religion and Science*
(London: Oxford University Press, 1935), pp. 113–114.

49. U.S. imperialism invaded China's territory of Taiwan and has occupied it for the past nine years. A short while ago it sent forces to invade and occupy Lebanon. The United States has set up hundreds of military bases in many countries all over the world. China's territory of Taiwan, Lebanon and all military bases of the United States on foreign soil are so many nooses round the neck of U.S. imperialism. The nooses have been fashioned by the Americans themselves and by nobody else, and it is they themselves who have put these nooses round their own necks, handing the ends of the ropes to the Chinese people, the peoples of the Arab countries and all the peoples of the world who love peace and oppose aggression. The longer the U.S. aggressors remain in those places, the tighter the nooses round their necks will become.

MAO TSE-TUNG, Speech at the Supreme State Conference
(September 8, 1958), in *Quotations from Chairman Mao
Tse-Tung* (New York: Bantam Books, 1967), p. 41.

50. Regarding the letter, "Lake a Victim," (Oct. 28). I commend the students for their concern regarding the Newman Lake clean-up—they are an exception rather than the rule as far as caring and showing respect is concerned, and taking an interest in beautification. Please note, however, Newman Lake is *on* campus. How wonderful it would be if this caring attitude would spill over into the city—our streets, parks and lawns would no longer be eyesores.

Students litter our streets with garbage; destroy our personal property; kill our animals, urinate and regurgitate in public; have a total disregard for residential speed limits; display deplorable, discourteous driving habits; deliberately walk in front of our automobiles; crowd us off the jogging paths; allow their animals to run free (no leash); egg our cars and commit other acts of vandalism (stealing signs, banners, mail boxes, etc.); defiantly ride their bikes and walk in the center traffic lane on S. Main Street; are the biggest offenders of alcohol abuse; contribute to visual, audio and emotional pollution—the list could go on.

In view of the foregoing, I am appalled by the audacity of students to "ask the city to do its part." The city does its part by tolerating the ill-mannered, undisciplined students. If they are really sincere about a clean-up campaign, I suggest they start with their own act. The attitude of students is that this is their city and they're letting us live in it, an attitude reinforced by the fact that when infractions do occur, heads are turned the other way and punishment, if any, does not fit the crime.

The city is the victim—not Newman Lake.

VELMA CLARK, "City a Victim," *Daily News-Record,* Harrisonburg, VA, November 7, 1992, p. 6. (Used with permission of the *Daily News-Record.*)

NOTES

1. Quoted in Joe Adamson, *Groucho, Harpo, Chico, and Sometimes Zeppo* (New York: Pocket Books, 1973), p. 225.

2. Typically, when you mention a word you either place it in single quotation marks or italics. See Chapter 2, Section 2, for a discussion.

3. St. Thomas Aquinas, *Summa Theologicæ,* Book I, Question 14, Article 13, Answer 3, vol. 4, translated by Thomas Gornall (London & New York: Eyre & Spottiswoode and McGraw-Hill Book Company, copyright 1964 by Blackfriars), p. 47. In fairness to Aquinas, this is an argument he sets forth to criticize.

4. See Aquinas, *Summa Theologicæ,* vol. 4, p. 51.

5. See David Hackett Fischer, *Historians' Fallacies* (New York: Harper Colophon Books, 1970), pp. 274–275.

6. *Animal Crackers,* Paramount Pictures, 1930; quoted in Joe Adamson, *Groucho, Harpo, Chico, and Sometimes Zeppo,* p. 105.

7. Several of the fallacies have Latin names that are in common use. In such cases I include the Latin name. An *argumentum ad baculum* is literally an argument by the stick.

8. Insofar as the senator appeals only to himself as an authority on the subject, this criticism shows that he should not be trusted as an authority. You have shown that the senator's own argument commits the fallacy of appeal to authority, a fallacy discussed below.

9. This is sometimes known as a Lockean *ad hominem,* after the seventeenth-century English philosopher John Locke. In discussing ways of criticizing arguments, Locke wrote: "A third way, is to press a Man with Consequences drawn from his own Principles, or Concessions. This is already known under the Name of *Argumentum ad Hominem.*" (*An Essay Concerning Human Understanding,* edited by P. H. Nidditch [Oxford: Clarendon Press, 1975], p. 686.)

10. It seems improper to claim that politics, art, religion, law, science, and, perhaps, any other activity is a "rational activity." Reasoning and argument are used within the practice of any of these activities in an attempt to justify claims. But it is a certain type of emotional appeal that causes the practitioner of the activity to engage in it. It is often the emotional appeal of a candidate that causes us to vote for him or her, rather than any argument he or she advances. It is the emotional appeal of the possibility of finding a cure for a disease that may cause a person to dedicate his or her life to medical research. It may be the emotional appeal of the prospect of being correct that causes someone to notice the evidence favoring his or her hypothesis while overlooking potentially conflicting evidence. But questions of motivation are outside the domain of logic—they might be proper questions for psychologists and sociologists to address. A logician, as a logician, is solely concerned with whether the premises of an argument, *if true,* provide evidence for the truth of the conclusion.

11. A word should be said about moral principles. It is a matter of debate whether the justification of a moral principle such as "You should give to those in need" ultimately rests on the emotional make-up of human beings. Even if this is so, it is not the emotional make-up of human beings that functions as a premise in the argument, but rather the principle.

12. The sole exception to this is what is known as a tautology. A tautology is a statement that is true *solely* in virtue of its form. An example of a tautology is the statement, "Either it is raining or it's not raining." The problem with tautologies is that they tell us nothing about the way the world actually is. A meteorologist who sug-

gests that it will rain tomorrow unless it doesn't is not making a forecast.

13. In a court of law, a complex question is known as a leading question. The prevailing rule is that one cannot lead one's own witnesses, but one may lead "adverse" or "hostile" witnesses, witnesses whose attitudes are not favorable to one's own case.

14. If you replied to Wordfellow's argument by claiming that she cannot be accepted because, as an oil company executive, she is biased, you would be committing the fallacy of personal attack.

Chapter Four

Categorical Syllogisms

The formal study of logic began with the Greek philosopher Aristotle. Aristotle, who lived from 384 to 322 B.C., spent much of his life in Athens. He founded a school called the Lyceum, where he taught philosophy. His lectures on logic are contained in the *Prior Analytics* and the *Posterior Analytics*. Aristotle treated logic as a preliminary study to the study of other subjects.

Traditional or Aristotelian logic is the logic of categories. A category is a comprehensive division of objects. A category represents a class, set, or collection of objects, and the objects in the class might have nothing in common other than the characteristic in virtue of which they are placed in that class. Categorical logic is the logic of class inclusion and exclusion.

In this chapter we examine the nature of categorical propositions, immediate inferences from categorical propositions, standard-form categorical syllogisms, and syllogisms in ordinary English.

4.1 *Categorical Propositions*

As we learned in Chapter 1, a proposition is the information expressed by a declarative sentence or statement. Propositions are either true or false: they either correspond to the world or they do not. Some propositions are **categorical propositions,** that is, propositions that state relationships between classes, and some are not. Examples of categorical propositions include "All professors are eccentrics," "No professors are eccentrics," "Some professors are eccentrics," and "Some professors are not eccentrics." Examples of noncategorical propositions include "Today is Tuesday" and "If Fido is a dog, then Turbo is a cat."

In this section, we begin by looking at two characteristics of categorical propositions: what are known as the quantity and quality of categorical propositions. We note the traditional names for each type of categorical proposition and discuss a set of four statement forms known as **standard-form categorical statements.** Finally, we discuss an additional characteristic of categorical propositions known as distribution.

A categorical proposition expresses one of four relations between two classes. (1) You might claim that all the members of one class are members of another, for example, "All professors are eccentrics." This is an example of a **universal affirmative proposition.** It is universal in **quantity.** The quantity of a proposition tells you how many members of the first class named are, or are not, members of the second. Here you are claiming that the entire class of professors is included in the class of eccentrics. It is universal because it makes a claim regarding the entire class of professors. It is affirmative in **quality.** The quality of a proposition is either affirmative or negative. If you claim that members of the first class named are members of the second class, it is an affirmative proposition. If you deny that members of the first class named are members of the second, it is a negative proposition. The term naming the first class is known as the **subject term,** and the term naming the second class is known as the **predicate term.** Where 'S' represents the subject term and 'P' represents the predicate term, the general form of a universal affirmative proposition is:

All S is P.

(2) You might claim that no member of one class is a member of another, for example, "No professors are eccentrics." This is a **universal negative proposition.** It is universal in quantity and negative in quality. It claims that the entire class of professors is excluded from the en-

tire class of eccentrics. The general form of a universal negative proposition is:

No *S* is *P.*

(3) You might claim that at least one member of one class is a member of another, for example, "Some professors are eccentrics." This is a **particular affirmative proposition.** It is particular in quantity and affirmative in quality. It claims that there is at least one professor who is an eccentric. As logicians use the word 'some', the quantifier for particular propositions, it means that there is or exists at least one member in the subject class. So two conditions must be met for a particular affirmative proposition to be true:

(a) the subject class must contain at least one member;
(b) at least one member of the subject class must be a member of the predicate class.

The proposition "Some professors are eccentrics" is true, since (a) there is at least one professor and (b) at least one professor is an eccentric. The proposition "Some unicorns are things having one horn" is false, since there are no unicorns. The proposition "Some crows are dogs" is false, since although there is at least one crow, no crow is included in the class of dogs. The general form of a particular affirmative proposition is:

Some *S* is *P.*

Finally, (4) you might deny that at least one member of one class is a member of another, for example, "Some professors are not eccentric persons." This is a **particular negative proposition.** It is particular in quantity and negative in quality. Two conditions must be met for a particular negative proposition to be true:

(a) the subject class must contain at least one member;
(b) at least one member of the subject class must *not* be a member of the predicate class.

The proposition "Some professors are not eccentrics" is true because (a) there is at least one professor and (b) at least one professor is not a member of the class of eccentrics. The proposition "Some unicorns are not things having two horns" is false, since there are no unicorns. The proposition "Some collies are not dogs" is false, since although there is at least one collie, no collie is excluded from the class of dogs. The general form of a particular affirmative proposition is:

Some *S* is not *P*.

By a long-standing convention, a universal affirmative proposition is called an **A** proposition, a universal negative is called an **E** proposition, a particular affirmative is called an **I** proposition, and a particular negative is called an **O** proposition. These letter-names are derived from the Latin words 'AffIrmo', meaning "I affirm," and 'nEgO', meaning "I deny." As we see in Section 4.5, these letter-names are not merely a convenient shorthand for naming the kinds of propositions; they also provide the basis for naming the various syllogistic forms.

A proposition is the information expressed by a statement, and there are many statements that can express the same proposition. For example, I express the same proposition by the statement "Every dog has its day" as by the statement "All dogs are things that have a day of their own." Because some statements express the proposition more clearly than others and because it is convenient to have a uniform way of expressing **A, E, I,** and **O** propositions, logicians have deemed one statement form for each of these categorical propositions a **standard-form categorical statement.**

There are four elements in a standard-form categorical statement. (1) The *quantifier* in a standard-form categorical statement is either 'All', 'No', or 'Some'. (2) The *subject term* is the first name or descriptive phrase that picks out a class of objects. In "All professors are eccentrics" the subject term is 'professors'. In "No people who are vegetarians are meat-eaters," the subject term is 'people who are vegetarians'. (3) The *copula* is a form of the verb 'to be' that joins the subject and predicate terms. In the examples above, the copula is 'are'. (4) The *predicate term* is the second word or descriptive phrase that picks out a class of objects. In "Some professors are eccentrics," 'eccentrics' is the predicate term. In "Some herbivores are not animals that eat meat," 'animals that eat meat' is the predicate term. In short, a statement is a standard-form categorical statement if and only if:

(a) it expresses a categorical proposition;
(b) its quantifier is either 'All', 'No', or 'Some';
(c) it has a subject and a predicate term;

(d) its subject and predicate terms are joined by a copula, a form of the verb 'to be';
(e) the order of the elements in the statement is:
   Quantifier, subject term, copula, predicate term.

If a statement fails to fulfill any of these conditions, it's not a standard-form categorical statement.

Finally, **distribution** is a characteristic of some terms in some categorical propositions. A term in a categorical proposition is distributed if and only if it refers to all the members of the class denoted by the term. In an **A** proposition, the subject term is distributed. For example, in the proposition "All aardvarks are mammals" you are referring to every aardvark: you are saying that the entire class of aardvarks is contained in the class of mammals. On the other hand, the term 'mammals' is undistributed: you are not saying anything about every mammal. In an **E** proposition, both the subject term and the predicate term are distributed. For example, in the proposition "No native Texans are native Iowans" you are referring to the entire class of native Texans and the entire class of native Iowans and asserting that they have no common members. In an **I** proposition neither the subject term nor the predicate term is distributed. For example, in the proposition "Some cows are Jerseys" you are talking about neither the whole class of cows nor the whole class of Jerseys. In an **O** proposition the predicate term is distributed. For example, in the proposition "Some cats are not Siamese" you are claiming that at least one cat is excluded from the entire class of Siamese cats. On the other hand, you are making no claims about the entire class of cats, so the subject term of an **O** proposition is undistributed. In short, the subject term is distributed in a universal categorical proposition and the predicate term is distributed in a negative categorical proposition. The following chart represents the distributions of the terms in categorical propositions:

PROPOSITION	SUBJECT	PREDICATE
A: All *S* is *P*.	distributed	undistributed
E: No *S* is *P*.	distributed	distributed
I: Some *S* is *P*.	undistributed	undistributed
O: Some *S* is not *P*.	undistributed	distributed

As we see in Section 4.7, distribution is an important characteristic because it allows us to formulate several rules for judging the validity of a categorical syllogism.

EXERCISES

For each of the following standard-form categorical statements, indicate whether it is an **A, E, I,** or **O** proposition, and identify the subject and predicate terms in each.

1. All slithy toves are things that gyre and gimble in the wabe.
2. Some borogoves were mimsy things.
3. No person with a vorpal blade is a Jabberwock.
4. Some Mad Hatters are not people who beat Time.
5. Some Mad Hatters are people who do not beat Time.
6. No caterpillar who smokes a hookah is a person who would be a suitable tour-guide.
7. Some people who stand in uffish thought are not people who wander through looking-glasses.
8. Some people who wander through looking-glasses are people who become lost on large chess boards.
9. All little girls who chase white rabbits down holes and talk with Cheshire cats are girls named 'Alice'.
10. No self-respecting Jabberwock is a beast that would consider evaluating a syllogism while taking a shower.
11. Some mushrooms that are suitable for eating are mushrooms that cause little girls named 'Alice' to grow or shrink rapidly.
12. All Cheshire cats are cats who can reduce themselves to nothing more than a very broad smile.
13. No person who would qualify as a slayer of a Jabberwock is a person who is inclined to walk into a tulgey wood with anything less than a vorpal sword.
14. Some Red King who is looking for his equestrian messenger is a chess piece who might unwittingly engage in an equivocation.
15. Some Dormouse who is wont to argue over the date with the Mad Hatter is not a beast who would be opposed to distinguishing between saying what one means and meaning what one says.

4.2 Existential Import and Immediate Inference

As we noted in the last section, one of the conditions for the truth of **I** and **O** propositions is that the class denoted by the subject term contain at least one member. **Existential import** is the property of a proposition that its truth entails the existence of at least one object. So **I** and **O** propositions have existential import.

What about **A** and **E** propositions? Aristotle and some of his followers claimed that **A** and **E** propositions have existential import. This claim is known as the **Aristotelian interpretation of categorical logic.** If this interpretation is correct, then given the truth or falsehood of a categorical proposition, you can draw various immediate inferences based on the forms of the propositions alone. An **immediate inference** is an inference you can correctly draw regarding the truth value of a proposition given nothing more than the truth value of another proposition. On the Aristotelian interpretation, there are four such inferences.

(1) If a universal proposition is true, you can infer that the corresponding particular proposition is also true. This relation is known as **subalternation,** and a particular proposition is known as the **subaltern** of the universal proposition of the same quality. If the universal proposition is false, no inference can be drawn regarding the truth or falsehood of the particular proposition of the same quality. If a particular proposition is true, you can draw no inferences regarding the truth value of the universal proposition of the same quality. But if a particular proposition is false, you can infer that the corresponding universal proposition of the same quality is false. For example, if the statement "All collies are dogs" is true, you can immediately infer that the statement "Some collies are dogs" is true. If "No dogs are collies" is false, you can draw no inferences regarding the truth value of the corresponding **O** proposition. If "Some collies are T.V. stars" is true, you can draw no inferences regarding the truth value of the corresponding **A** proposition. But if "Some unicorns are not two-horned things" is false, you can infer that the corresponding **E** proposition is false.

(2) If a universal proposition is true, you can infer that a universal proposition with the same terms but the opposite quality is false. If a universal proposition is false, you can draw *no* inferences regarding the truth or falsehood of a universal proposition with the same terms but the opposite quality. To state the same point in a different way, both an **A** proposition and its corresponding **E** proposition might be false; both cannot be true. This relation is known as **contrariety** and the statements are known as **contraries.** For example, if the proposition "All collies

are dogs" is true, you can immediately infer that the proposition "No collies are dogs" is false. On the other hand, if the proposition "All T.V. stars are collies" is false, you can draw no inference regarding the truth or falsehood of the corresponding universal negative proposition.

(3) If a particular proposition is *false,* you can infer that a particular proposition with the same terms but the opposite quality is true. If a particular proposition is true, you can draw no inferences regarding the truth value of a particular proposition with the same terms but the opposite quality. To state the same point in a different way, both an I proposition and its corresponding O proposition might be true; both cannot be false. This relation is known as **subcontrariety,** and the propositions are known as **subcontraries.** For example, if the proposition "Some collies are schnauzers" is false, you can immediately infer that the proposition "Some collies are not schnauzers" is true. On the other hand, if the proposition "Some collies are T.V. stars" is true, you can draw no inference regarding the truth or falsehood of the corresponding O proposition.

(4) Finally, if a universal proposition is true, you can infer that a particular proposition with the same terms but the opposite quality is false. For example, if it is true that "All collies are dogs," it is false that "Some collies are not dogs." If a universal proposition is false, you can infer that a particular proposition with the same terms but the opposite quality is true. For example, if the proposition "No General Motors products are Chevrolets" is false, you can infer that "Some General Motors products are Chevrolets" is true. Similarly, if a particular proposition is true, you can infer that the universal proposition with the same terms but the opposite quality is false. For example, if "Some dogs are not cats" is true, you can infer that "All dogs are cats" is false. Finally, if a particular proposition is false, then the universal proposition with the same terms but the opposite quality is true. For example, if the proposition "Some cars are horses" is false, you can infer that the proposition "No cars are horses" is true. This relation is known as **contradiction,** and the statements are known as **contradictories.** For any pair of contradictories, one of the statements is true and the other false. Saying that one of a pair of contradictories is true and the other false does *not* imply that we know which one of the pair is true or false. Since they are contradictory propositions, we know that either the proposition "All crows are black" or the proposition "Some crows are not black" is true, but we might not know which is true. And if we disagree, we might both be reasonable people, since both of us might have good reasons for believing that our preferred proposition is true. Reasonable people often disagree about factual claims.

These four types of immediate inferences among categorical propositions are known as **'oppositions'**, and they are traditionally set forth in a diagram known as a Square of Opposition. The Aristotelian Square of Opposition is as follows:

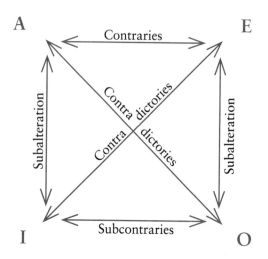

Figure 4.1 Aristotelian square of opposition

If you are given the *truth* of a universal affirmative proposition, you can follow the arrows and infer the truth value of each of the remaining propositions in the square: if an **A** proposition is true, then the corresponding **E** proposition (its contrary) is false, the corresponding **I** proposition (its subaltern) is true, and the corresponding **O** proposition (its contradictory) is false. Similarly, if you are given the *falsehood* of a particular negative proposition, you can infer that the corresponding **I** proposition (its subcontrary) is true, that the corresponding **A** proposition (its contradictory) is true, and the corresponding **E** proposition is false. Though in these two cases you can infer the truth value of each of the corresponding categorical statements in the Square, you cannot infer the truth value of each proposition in the Square if you are given that a universal proposition is false or that a particular proposition is true. For example, if "All dogs are collies" is false, you can infer that the **O** proposition "Some dogs are not collies" is true. But since both of two corresponding universal propositions can be false and both of two corresponding particular propositions can be true, you cannot infer the truth value of the corresponding **E** and **I** propositions. In this case we may refer to the truth value of the E and I propositions as undetermined: though the propositions have a truth value, you cannot know what the truth values are on the basis of inferences made by means of the Square of Opposition. The situation is parallel if you are given that a particular proposition is true.

The Aristotelian interpretation of categorical logic *assumes* that A and E propositions have existential import. It is this *assumption* that justifies several of the inferences in the Aristotelian Square of Opposition. But is that assumption true? Consider the proposition "All unicorns are horses having a single horn in the middle of their foreheads." Although there are no unicorns, the predicate term states the meaning of the subject term 'unicorn'. Doesn't this show that the proposition is true? Or we might go at it from the other side and look at I and O propositions. I and O propositions have existential import. So the propositions "Some unicorns are horses having a single horn in the middle of their foreheads" and "Some unicorns are not horses having a single horn in the middle of their foreheads" are both false, since there are no unicorns. But if a statement is false, its denial is true. The denial of "Some unicorns are not horses having a single horn in the middle of their foreheads" is its contradiction, namely, "All unicorns are horses having a single horn in the middle of their foreheads." So our earlier intuition regarding the truth of this A proposition seems correct. But "Some unicorns are horses having a single horn in the middle of their foreheads" is also false because there are no unicorns, so its denial, its contradictory "No unicorns are horses having a single horn in the middle of their foreheads," must also be true. Hence, universal propositions do not have existential import: if the subject term of a universal proposition picks out a class with no members, the proposition is trivially true.

The question of the existential import of universal propositions was a matter of some controversy in the centuries following Aristotle. But it is the nineteenth-century British logician and mathematician George Boole (1815–1864) who is credited with resolving the controversy in favor of *not* ascribing existential import to universal propositions. In his *Mathematical Analysis of Logic* (1847), Boole developed an algebraic representation of categorical logic which showed the connection between the traditional logic of terms and the logic of propositions.[1] Boole's analysis showed that particular propositions have existential import, but universal propositions do not. This interpretation of categorical logic is called the **Boolean interpretation**. In the Boolean Square of Opposition, the only relations among categorical propositions that al-

low you to make an immediate inference are the relations of contraction. The Boolean Square looks like this:

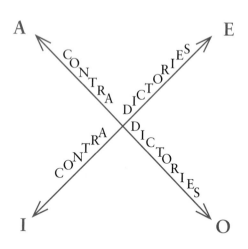

Figure 4.2 Boolean square of opposition

EXERCISES

I. Given the *Aristotelian* Square of Opposition, assume that the
statements in the first column are true. What can you
immediately infer regarding the truth value of the statements in
the second column?

1. A   E, I, O   3. I   A, E, O
2. E   A, I, O   4. O   A, E, I

II. Given the *Aristotelian* Square of Opposition, assume that the
statements in the first column are false. What can you
immediately infer regarding the truth value of the statements in
the second column?

1. A   E, I, O   3. I   A, E, O
2. E   A, I, O   4. O   A, E, I

III. Given the *Boolean* Square of Opposition, assume that the
statements in the first column are true. What can you
immediately infer regarding the truth value of the statements in
the second column?

1. A   E, I, O   3. I   A, E, O
2. E   A, I, O   4. O   A, E, I

IV. Given the *Boolean* Square of Opposition, assume that the statements in the first column are false. What can you immediately infer regarding the truth value of the statements in the second column?

1. A   E, I, O   3. I   A, E, O
2. E   A, I, O   4. O   A, E, I

4.3 *Venn Diagrams for Categorical Propositions*

Late in the nineteenth century the British logician John Venn (1834–1923) developed a pictorial means of representing categorical propositions understood according to the Boolean interpretation. These are known as Venn diagrams. Venn diagrams use circles to represent classes of objects. We see in Section 4.5 how the Venn diagram technique can be used to test the validity of syllogisms. In this section we examine how to diagram individual categorical propositions.

Consider the **A** proposition, "All collies are dogs." The *S* or subject term is 'collies' and the *P* or predicate term is 'dogs'. In a Venn diagram we represent the relationship between two terms with two intersecting circles, one for each term. This diagram has four parts:

1. The part inside the *S* circle but not inside the *P* circle (*S* and not *P*, or, for short *S*−*P*). This part represents collies that are not dogs.
2. The part inside the overlapping portion of the two circles (*S* and *P*, or, for short, *SP*). This part represents collies that are dogs.
3. The part inside the *P* circle but not inside the *S* circle (not *S* and *P*, or, for short, −*SP*). This represents dogs that are not collies.
4. The part outside of both circles (not *S* and not *P*, or, for short, −*S*−*P*). This part represents things that are neither collies nor dogs.

Now, if our **A** proposition "all collies are dogs" is true, then the entire class of collies is included in the class of dogs. This means that the class of things that are collies but not dogs *(S-P)* has no members in it; it is *empty*. We show that the class of things that are collies but not dogs is empty by shading in the part of the diagram that represents that class.

Thus a Venn diagram of any **A** proposition, including "all collies are dogs," looks like this:

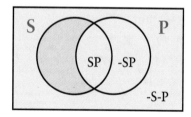

Figure 4.3

An **E** proposition—for example, "No dogs are cats"—is true if and only if the subject class has no members in common with the predicate class. In other words, an **E** proposition claims that the class of things that are both *S* and *P* is empty, so in a Venn diagram of an **E** proposition the *SP* area, the portion of the diagram representing the intersection of the two classes, is shaded:

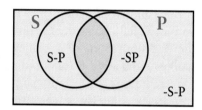

Figure 4.4

Particular propositions differ from general propositions insofar as they claim, in the case of **I** propositions, that there is at least one thing that is both *S* and *P,* or, in the case of **O** propositions, there is at least one thing that is *S* and not *P.* In a Venn diagram, an 'X' in the appropriate portion of the diagram represents the existential import of the proposition, the claim that there is at least one thing in that class. In the case of an **I** proposition—for example, "Some corn is animal fodder"—the diagram is as follows:

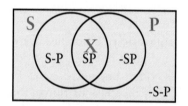

Figure 4.5

In the case of an **O** proposition, for example—"Some corn is not animal fodder"—the diagram is:

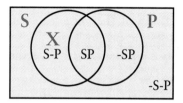

Figure 4.6

The diagrams we have considered to this point are of the forms **A** (All *S* is *P*), **E** (No *S* is *P*), **I** (Some *S* is *P*), and **O** (Some *S* is not *P*). Of course it is also possible to diagram cases in which the predicate term occurs in the subject place. Those four cases are as follows:

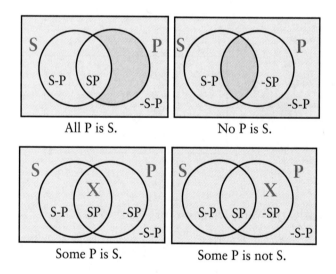

Figure 4.7

EXERCISES

Construct a Venn diagram for each of the categorical propositions in the exercise set at the end of Section 4.1.

4.4 *Conversion, Obversion, and Contraposition*

There are several statement forms that are logically equivalent to standard-form categorical statements. Two statement forms are **logically equivalent** if and only if they are true under exactly the same conditions (express the same proposition). As we will see, if two statement forms are logically equivalent, their Venn diagrams are identical. We will examine three statements forms.

Conversion

You form the **converse** of a given categorical proposition by reversing the position of the subject and the predicate terms. A categorical proposition and its converse are logically equivalent if and only if the distribution of both terms in the proposition is the same. So in the case of an E and an I proposition, you can reverse the positions of the subject and predicate terms and the resulting statement form is logically equivalent to the original. This should be obvious by a consideration of the Venn diagrams for E and I propositions, for the diagram for both "No *S* is *P*" and "No *P* is *S*" is:

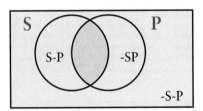

Figure 4.8

Similarly, the Venn Diagram for "Some *S* is *P*" and "Some *P* is *S*" is:

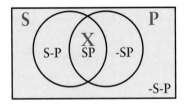

Figure 4.9

While any E or I proposition and its converse are logically equivalent, this is not the case for A and O propositions. Consider some examples.

While "All collies are dogs" is true, its converse, "All dogs are collies," is false. Similarly, while the statement "Some dogs are not collies" is true, the statement "Some collies are not dogs" is clearly false. Again, this fact can be seen by comparing the Venn diagrams for an **A** proposition and its converse and an **O** proposition and its converse.

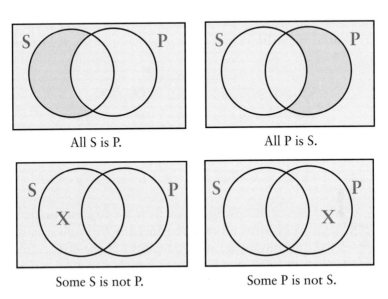

Figure 4.10

Given this, we may summarize the cases in which conversion yields logically equivalent statement forms. Where a **convertend** is a proposition to be converted, the following chart shows the cases in which conversions are logically equivalent:

CONVERSION

CONVERTEND	CONVERSE
A: All *S* is *P.*	not logically equivalent
E: No *S* is *P.*	**E:** No *P* is *S.*
I: Some *S* is *P.*	**I:** Some *P* is *S.*
O: Some *S* is not *P.*	not logically equivalent

Obversion

To understand obversion you should recognize that for every class of objects there is a **complementary class.** For any class, its complementary class contains *everything* that is not in that class. For example, the complement of the class of all dogs contains everything that is *not* a dog. The members of that class are called "non-dogs." The fact that every class has a complement provides the basis for **obversion.** You form the **obverse** of a standard-form categorical statement by changing the *quality* of the statement from affirmative to negative or from negative to affirmative, and replacing the predicate term with its complement. *For every standard-form categorical statement, there is an obverse that is logically equivalent to it.* This is summarized in the following chart:

OBVERSION

OBVERTEND	OBVERSE
A: All *S* is *P.*	**E:** No *S* is non-*P.*
E: No *S* is *P.*	**A:** All *S* is non-*P.*
I: Some *S* is *P.*	**O:** Some *S* is not non-*P.*
O: Some *S* is not *P.*	**I:** Some *S* is non-*P.*

To recognize that every standard-form categorical statement is logically equivalent to it, we may consider the Venn diagrams for each of the standard-form categorical statements. Remember, a Venn diagram for a standard-form categorical statement is divided into four areas: (1) that which is *S* and not *P (S-P),* (2) that which is both *S* and *P (SP),* (3) that which is not *S* but is *P (-SP),* and (4) the area outside the circles which is neither *S* nor *P (-S-P).* The diagram for an **A** proposition is as follows:

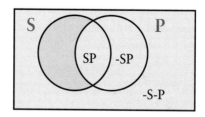

Figure 4.11

Notice that the area *S-P* is shaded, indicating that it contains no members. The obverse of an **A** proposition, namely "No *S* is non-*P*", asserts that there does not exist an *S* that is not *P,* which indicates that the section *S-P* of the diagram ought to be shaded. Hence, a consideration of the Venn diagram shows that an **A** proposition is logically equivalent to its obverse.

The Venn diagram for an E proposition also shows that the equivalence holds. The diagram for an E proposition is:

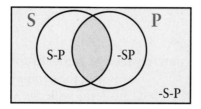

Figure 4.12

The obverse of an E proposition asserts that "All *S* is non-*P*," that is, if there is anything that is *S* then it is not *P*, which is indicated by the diagram.

The Venn diagram for an I proposition and its obverse, "Some *S* is not non-*P*," is:

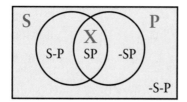

Figure 4.13

In asserting that "Some *S* is not non-*P*," one is required to place an 'X' in the portion of the diagram for *S* but not that portion that is also not *P*. *In effect,* the 'not' and the 'non-' cancel one another, although there is no rule governing such a 'not'-'non-' cancellation.

The Venn diagram for an O proposition and its obverse, "Some *S* is non-*P*," is:

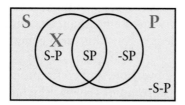

Figure 4.14

In asserting the obverse of an **O** proposition, you *in effect* force the negative quality of the **O** proposition into the predicate of the corresponding **I** proposition.

Contraposition

You form the **contrapositive** of standard-form categorical proposition by replacing the subject term with the complement of the predicate term, and replacing the predicate term with the complement of the subject term. For example, the contrapositive of an **A** proposition is the **A** proposition "All non-*P* is non-*S*." **A** and **O** propositions are logically equivalent to their contrapositives; **E** and **I** propositions are *not* logically equivalent to their contrapositives. This is summarized in the following chart:

CONTRAPOSITION

GIVEN	CONTRAPOSITIVE
A: All *S* is *P*.	**A:** All non-*S* is non-*P*.
E: No *S* is *P*.	not logically equivalent
I: Some *S* is *P*.	not logically equivalent
O: Some *S* is not *P*.	Some non-*P* is not non-*S*.

Contraposition differs from conversion and obversion insofar as in those cases in which a standard-form categorical position and its contrapositive are equivalent, you can show the equivalence by several applications of conversion and obversion. For example, you can show that an **A** proposition is equivalent to its contrapositive by means of the following steps:

"All *S* is *P*" is equivalent to "No *S* is non-*P*" by obversion, which is equivalent to "No non-*P* is *S*" by conversion, which is equivalent to "All non-*P* is non-*S*" by obversion.

In those cases in which a proposition and its contrapositive are *not* logically equivalent, you cannot attain a standard-form categorical statement: all equivalent propositions will contain either the term 'non-*S*' or 'non-*P*'.

Conversion, obversion, and contraposition can be used in conjunction with the Aristotelian or the Boolean Square of Opposition to draw immediate inferences. For example, assuming the Aristotelian Square of

Opposition, if you are given the truth of an **A** proposition of the form "All *S* is *P*," you can infer that the **I** proposition "Some *P* is *S*" is true (though not equivalent), since the truth of an **I** proposition follows from the truth of an **A** proposition by subalternation, and an **I** proposition is logically equivalent to its converse. This is called the conversion of an **A** proposition by limitation or conversion by subalternation. Similarly, given the Aristotelian Square and the truth of the **E** proposition "No *S* is *P*," you can infer the truth of the **O** proposition "Some *S* is not *P*" by subalternation, which is equivalent to its contrapositive, "Some non-*P* is not non-*S*." This is called contraposition by limitation or contraposition by subalternation.

EXERCISES

    I. State the contrapositive of each of the following, and either show that the statement is equivalent to its contrapositive by successive applications of conversion and obversion or explain why it is not equivalent.

        1. **E** No *S* is *P*.

        2. **I** Some *S* is *P*.

        3. **O** Some *S* is not *P*.

    II. By engaging in conversion and obversion, give three statements that are logically equivalent to each of the following.

        1. **A** All *S* is *P*.

        2. **E** No *S* is *P*.

        3. **I** Some *S* is *P*.

        4. **O** Some *S* is not *P*.

    III. Assuming the Aristotelian Square of Opposition, and assuming that the statement in the first column is true, what can be inferred regarding the truth or falsehood of the statement in the second column? If nothing can be inferred, write "Undetermined." (Hint: Whenever possible, eliminate 'non-' in a subject or predicate term. Whether or not it is possible to eliminate the 'non-'s, attempt to reformulate the statements so the same subject and predicate terms are in both. If it is impossible to do the latter, the truth value of the problematic statement is undeterminable.)

THE GIVEN STATEMENT	THE PROBLEMATIC STATEMENT
1. All *S* is *P*.	1. Some *S* is not *P*.
2. All *S* is *P*.	2. Some *S* is not non-*P*.
3. All *S* is *P*.	3. No *S* is non-*P*.
4. All *S* is *P*.	4. No non-*P* is *S*.
5. All *S* is *P*.	5. Some *S* is non-*P*.
6. All *S* is *P*.	6. No *P* is *S*.
7. All *S* is *P*.	7. All *P* is non-*S*.
8. All *S* is *P*.	8. All non-*P* is non-*S*.
9. All *S* is *P*.	9. Some non-*P* is non-*S*.
10. All *S* is *P*.	10. Some *P* is not non-*S*.
11. No *S* is *P*.	11. All *P* is *S*.
12. No *S* is *P*.	12. Some *S* is non-*P*.
13. No *S* is *P*.	13. Some *S* is *P*.
14. No *S* is *P*.	14. All *S* is non-*P*.
15. No *S* is *P*.	15. Some *S* is not non-*P*.
16. No *S* is *P*.	16. No *P* is non-*S*.
17. No *S* is *P*.	17. No *P* is *S*.
18. No *S* is *P*.	18. All non-*P* is non-*S*.
19. No *S* is *P*.	19. Some *P* is not non-*S*.
20. No *S* is *P*.	20. Some non-*P* is *S*.
21. Some *S* is *P*.	21. All *S* is *P*.
22. Some *S* is *P*.	22. No *P* is *S*.
23. Some *S* is *P*.	23. Some *S* is non-*P*.
24. Some *S* is *P*.	24. Some *P* is not non-*S*.
25. Some *S* is *P*.	25. No *P* is non-*S*.
26. Some *S* is *P*.	26. Some non-*P* is not non-*S*.
27. Some *S* is *P*.	27. Some non-*P* is non-*S*.
28. Some *S* is *P*.	28. Some *P* is *S*.
29. Some *S* is *P*.	29. All non-*P* is non-*S*.
30. Some *S* is *P*.	30. No non-*P* is *S*.
31. Some *S* is not *P*.	31. No *P* is *S*.
32. Some *S* is not *P*.	32. All *S* is *P*.

33. Some *S* is not *P*.
34. Some *S* is not *P*.
35. Some *S* is not *P*.
36. Some *S* is not *P*.
37. Some *S* is not *P*.
38. Some *S* is not *P*.
39. Some *S* is not *P*.
40. Some *S* is not *P*.
41. All non-*S* is *P*.
42. All non-*S* is *P*.
43. All non-*S* is *P*.
44. All non-*S* is *P*.
45. All non-*S* is *P*.
46. All non-*S* is *P*.
47. All non-*S* is *P*.
48. All non-*S* is *P*.
49. All non-*S* is *P*.
50. All non-*S* is *P*.
51. No non-*S* is *P*.
52. No non-*S* is *P*.
53. No non-*S* is *P*.
54. No non-*S* is *P*.
55. No non-*S* is *P*.
56. No non-*S* is *P*.
57. No non-*S* is *P*.
58. No non-*S* is *P*.
59. No non-*S* is *P*.
60. No non-*S* is *P*.
61. Some non-*S* is *P*.
62. Some non-*S* is *P*.
63. Some non-*S* is *P*.
64. Some non-*S* is *P*.
65. Some non-*S* is *P*.

33. No non-*P* is *S*.
34. Some *S* is non-*P*.
35. Some non-*P* is not non-*S*.
36. No *P* is non-*S*.
37. No non-*S* is *P*.
38. All non-*P* is non-*S*.
39. Some *S* is *P*.
40. All non-*P* is *S*.
41. Some *S* is not *P*.
42. Some *S* is not non-*P*.
43. No *S* is non-*P*.
44. No non-*P* is *S*.
45. Some *S* is non-*P*.
46. No *P* is *S*.
47. All *P* is non-*S*.
48. All non-*P* is non-*S*.
49. Some non-*P* is non-*S*.
50. Some *P* is not non-*S*.
51. All *P* is *S*.
52. Some *S* is non-*P*.
53. Some *S* is *P*.
54. All *S* is non-*P*.
55. Some *S* is not non-*P*.
56. No *P* is non-*S*.
57. No *P* is *S*.
58. All non-*P* is non-*S*.
59. Some *P* is not non-*S*.
60. Some non-*P* is *S*.
61. All *S* is *P*.
62. No *P* is *S*.
63. Some *S* is non-*P*.
64. Some *P* is not non-*S*.
65. No *P* is non-*S*.

66. Some non-*S* is *P.*	66. Some non-*P* is not non-*S.*
67. Some non-*S* is *P.*	67. Some non-*P* is non-*S.*
68. Some non-*S* is *P.*	68. Some *P* is *S.*
69. Some non-*S* is *P.*	69. All non-*P* is non-*S.*
70. Some non-*S* is *P.*	70. No non-*P* is *S.*
71. Some non-*S* is not *P.*	71. No *P* is *S.*
72. Some non-*S* is not *P.*	72. All *S* is *P.*
73. Some non-*S* is not *P.*	73. No non-*P* is *S.*
74. Some non-*S* is not *P.*	74. Some *S* is non-*P.*
75. Some non-*S* is not *P.*	75. Some non-*P* is not non-*S.*
76. Some non-*S* is not *P.*	76. No *P* is non-*S.*
77. Some non-*S* is not *P.*	77. No non-*S* is *P.*
78. Some non-*S* is not *P.*	78. All non-*P* is non-*S.*
79. Some non-*S* is not *P.*	79. Some *S* is *P.*
80. Some non-*S* is not *P.*	80. All non-*P* is *S.*

4.5 *Categorical Syllogisms*

A **syllogism** is a deductive argument consisting of two premises and a conclusion. A **categorical syllogism** is a special kind of syllogism, one in which both premises and the conclusion are categorical propositions and in which there are three terms, each occurring twice, and each term assigned the same meaning throughout the argument. As in the case of categorical statements, there is a standard form for categorical syllogisms. A syllogism is a **standard-form categorical syllogism** if and only if it fulfills each of the following criteria:

(a) it is a categorical syllogism;
(b) the premises and conclusion are standard-form categorical statements;
(c) the syllogism contains three different terms;
(d) each of the terms appears twice in the argument;
(e) each term is used with the same meaning throughout the argument;
(f) the predicate term of the conclusion appears in the first premise;
(g) the subject term of the conclusion appears in the second premise.

The following argument is an example of a standard form categorical syllogism:

All mortals are things that eventually die.
All human beings are mortals.

Therefore, all human beings are things that eventually die.

The argument is a categorical syllogism (a). All the propositions in the argument are standard-form categorical statements (b). There are three different terms: 'things that eventually die', 'mortals', and 'human beings' (c). Each of the terms appears twice in the argument (d). Each term is used with the same meaning throughout the argument (e). The predicate term of the conclusion appears in the first premise (f), and the subject term of the conclusion appears in the second premise (g).

Now consider the following argument:

All institutionalized persons are persons who are harmful to themselves or others.
All professors are institutionalized persons.

Therefore, all professors are persons who are harmful to themselves or others.

Though this argument *seems* to comply with criteria (a), (b), (c), (d), (f), and (g), it does not comply with criterion (e). In the first premise, 'institutionalized persons' refers to persons in psychiatric institutions. In the second premise, 'institutionalized persons' refers to persons associated with institutions of higher education. Hence, there are three terms, but one is assigned different meanings in the premises. The conclusion does not follow from the premises.

Each of the terms in a standard-form categorical syllogism has a name. The predicate term in the conclusion is known as the **major term.** The subject term in the conclusion is known as the **minor term.** The term that is in both premises but not in the conclusion—the term that "drops out" in going from the premises to the conclusion—is known as the **middle term.** Further, the premise that contains the major term is known as the **major premise,** and the premise that contains the minor term is known as the **minor premise.**

Since in a standard-form categorical syllogism you always state the major premise, then the minor premise, and finally the conclusion, you can distinguish among syllogistic forms by means of the letters used to represent each of the four kinds of the categorical statements. This is known as the **mood** of a syllogism. In stating the mood of a syllogism, you state the letter representing the major premise first, next the letter representing the minor premise, and finally the letter representing the conclusion. Thus, an argument of the mood **AAA** is composed solely of universal affirmative propositions. An argument of the mood **EIO** has a universal negative as its major premise, a particular affirmative as its minor premise, and a particular negative as its conclusion. There are sixty-four distinct moods—**AAA, AAE, AAI,** and so on.

To state only the mood of an argument is not sufficient to specify a particular form. Representing the major term of an argument as *P*, the minor term as *S*, and the middle term as *M*, we can schematically represent the form of an argument. Using this scheme, we can represent the following argument:

> Some dogs are collies.
> Some collies are rabid animals.
> _____
> Some rabid animals are dogs.

as:

> Some *P* are *M*.
> Some *M* are *S*.
> _____
> Some *S* are *P*.

This is *an* argument of the mood **III**; it consists of three **I** propositions. But it is not the *only* argument of the mood **III**. The following are also arguments of that mood:

Some *M* are *P*.	Some *P* are *M*.	Some *M* are *P*.
Some *S* are *M*.	Some *S* are *M*.	Some *M* are *S*.
_____	_____	_____
Some *S* are *P*.	Some *S* are *P*.	Some *S* are *P*.

To enumerate all possible permutations of the form of a syllogism, we must recognize that the major, minor, and middle terms in the premises can stand in any of four positions. These four positions are known as the *figures* of a syllogism. There are four figures:

FIGURE ONE	FIGURE TWO	FIGURE THREE	FIGURE FOUR
M - P	P - M	M - P	P - M
S - M	S - M	M - S	M - S
S - P	S - P	S - P	S - P

By stating both the mood and the figure, you can represent the form of any syllogistic argument. Thus, a syllogism of the mood **AAO** in the fourth figure (generally called **AAO-4**), has this form:

All *P* is *M*.
All *M* is *S*.
_____
Some *S* is not *P*.

And an **EIO-2** looks like this:

No *P* is *M*.
Some *S* is *M*.
_____
Some *S* is not *P*.

It may help you to remember the sequence of figures to notice that the position of the middle term in the figures is comparable to a shirt collar:

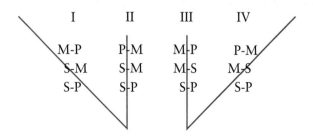

Figure 4.15

EXERCISES

I. State the mood and figure of each of the following argument forms.

1. Some *M* is *P*.
   No *S* is *M*.
   _____
   All *S* is *P*.

2. All *M* is *P*.
   All *M* is *S*.
   _____
   All *S* is *P*.

3. No *P* is *M*.
   Some *S* is not *M*.
   _____
   All *S* is *P*.

4. Some *P* is not *M*.
   Some *S* is not *M*.
   _____
   Some *S* is not *P*.

5. Some *P* is *M*.
   No *M* is *S*.
   _____
   No *S* is *P*.

6. Some *P* is *M*.
   All *M* is *S*.
   _____
   No *S* is *P*.

7. Some *M* is not *P*.
   Some *M* is not *S*.
   _____
   Some *S* is not *P*.

8. All *M* is *P*.
   All *S* is *M*.
   _____
   Some *S* is *P*.

9. No *P* is *M*.
   Some *S* is *M*.
   _____
   Some *S* is *P*.

10. No *M* is *P*.
    No *M* is *S*.
    _____
    No *S* is *P*.

11. All *P* is *M*.
    Some *S* is *M*.
    _____
    Some *S* is *P*.

12. Some *P* is not *M*.
    No *M* is *S*.
    _____
    All *S* is *P*.

13. Some *M* is *P*.
    Some *M* is not *S*.
    _____
    Some *S* is not *P*.

14. All *P* is *M*.
    All *M* is *S*.
    _____
    Some *S* is *P*.

15. Some *P* is *M*.
    Some *S* is *M*.
    _____
    No *S* is *P*.

16. No *M* is *P*.
    All *S* is *M*.
    _____
    All *S* is *P*.

17. No *P* is *M*.
    No *M* is *S*.
    _____
    No *S* is *P*.

18. Some *M* is not *P*.
    No *S* is *M*.
    _____
    Some *S* is not *P*.

19. Some *M* is *P*.
    Some *M* is *S*.
    _____
    Some *S* is *P*.

20. Some *M* is not *P*.
    All *M* is *S*.
    _____
    Some *S* is *P*.

II. State the form corresponding to each of the following moods and figures.

1. IIA-4	6. EOI-1	11. OIA-2	16. EIE-4
2. OAI-1	7. EOO-3	12. IOO-2	17. OOE-2
3. OII-4	8. AEE-2	13. EOA-1	18. AEO-4
4. IIA-2	9. EEO-1	14. OIO-2	19. EAA-3
5. IOE-3	10. AOO-1	15. AIA-3	20. IAA-3

4.6 *Venn Diagrams for Categorical Syllogisms*

Venn diagrams for categorical syllogisms have three circles, one for each term in the syllogism. The basic diagram looks like this:

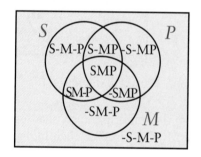

Figure 4.16

There are eight sections in the diagram representing: (1) the class of things that are S but neither M nor P (for short, S-M-P); (2) the class of things that are S and P but not M (for short, S-MP); (3) the class of things that are P but neither S nor M (for short, -S-MP); (4) the class of things that are S and M but not P (for short, SM-P). (5) the class of things that are S and M and P (for short, SPM); (6) the class of things that are M and P but not S (for short, -SMP); (7) the class of things that are M but neither S nor P (for short, -SM-P); and (8) the class of things that are neither S nor M nor P (for short, -S-M-P).

To evaluate a syllogism, you fill in the circles for each of the premises and attempt to "read off" the conclusion. To see how this works, consider a *valid* syllogism, for example, an argument of the mood and figure **AAA-1.** The schematic representation of this argument is:

All *M* is *P.*
All *S* is *M.*
———————
All *S* is *P.*

In constructing the diagram, you begin with universal premises— that is, those that involve shading empty classes. Since the major premise is an *A* proposition, we shade the portion of circle *M* that is outside circle *P.* The diagram looks like this:

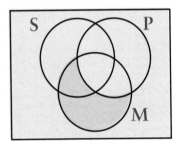

Figure 4.17

Next we diagram the minor premise, shading the portion of circle *S* that is outside circle *M.* The diagram then looks like this:

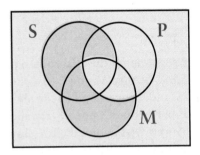

Figure 4.18

At this point the diagram is complete. Now we look at the *S* and *P* circles to see whether the conclusion is diagramed. According to the conclusion, all members of *S* are members of *P,* so the non-empty (unshaded) portion of *S* should be wholly contained in *P*. The diagram shows that this is the case. Hence, the argument is valid.

In a valid deductive argument, the conclusion is implicit in the premises. Put differently, the conclusion of a valid deductive argument gives no new information; it merely restates some of the information in the premises. So in reading the diagram to see if it includes the conclusion of the syllogism, we need only compare the two circles—those representing the *S* and *P* terms—to a diagram of the conclusion alone. The diagram for the conclusion is:

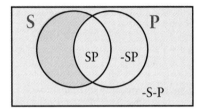

Figure 4.19

Because in both the diagram for the syllogism and the diagram for the conclusion the only unshaded portion of *S* is contained in *P*, the diagram for the syllogism shows that the argument is valid.

You might worry that there is not an *exact* match between the diagram for the conclusion and that for the syllogism. Isn't it a problem that the portion of the diagram representing things that are *S* and *P* but are not *M* is shaded? No. What is *crucial* is that the Venn diagram shows that the only non-empty portion of *S* is contained in *P*, and this is shown by the diagram. As we see below in considering arguments in which the conclusion is an **I** proposition, whenever the conclusion is affirmative, whether universal or particular, the portion of the diagram with which one is concerned is that in which all three circles overlap, the section *SMP*.

Let us look at some more cases in which both premises are universals. Consider an **EAE-2**. The schematic representation of the argument is:

No *P* is *M*.
All *S* is *M*.
──────────
No *S* is *P*.

Let us begin by diagraming the major premise:

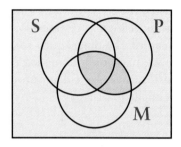

Figure 4.20

Now we diagram the minor premise:

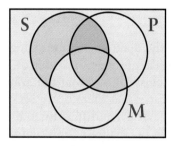

Figure 4.21

Since the conclusion is an **E** proposition, it is diagramed only if the overlapping portion of circles *S* and *P* is shaded, as it is in this case. Hence, the Venn diagram shows that an argument of the form **EAE-2** is valid.

Now consider an **AEE-3**. The schematic representation of this argument is as follows:

All *M* is *P*.
No *M* is *S*.
_____
No *S* is *P*.

Again we may diagram the major premise first:

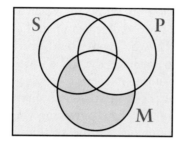

Figure 4.22

Now we diagram the minor premise:

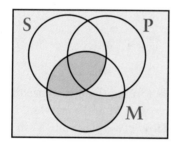

Figure 4.23

This time when we examine the result we see that the conclusion is not diagramed: the area representing the class of things that are *S* and *P* but not *M* is not shaded. In other words, the diagram shows us that the premises do not require that this class is empty: the truth of the premises does not necessitate that truth of the conclusion. The argument is invalid.

Up to this point we have considered only arguments in which both premises are universal propositions. In diagraming arguments with particular premises, we use an 'X' to denote existential import. In a valid argument the 'X' will be placed in one of the eight sections of the Venn diagram. When diagraming a syllogism with both a universal and a particular premise, there is a *prudential* rule that you should *always diagram the universal premise first.* It is wise to diagram the universal premise first because no particular premise provides you with enough information to know in which of the eight sections of the diagram to place the 'X'. For example, if you were given the particular premise "Some *M* is *S*," you would not know whether or not the *S* that is *M* is also *P*. Since the 'X' shows the existential import of a particular proposition, it *cannot* be placed (wholly or in part) in a shaded section of the diagram, since shading a section shows that the class has *no* members. By diagraming the universal premise first you sometimes eliminate one of the sections in which the 'X' could be placed.

To understand why you should diagram the universal proposition first, consider an **AII-3**, an argument whose schematic representation is as follows:

All *M* is *P*.
Some *M* is *S*.
_____

Some *S* is *P*.

Let us start by diagraming the minor premise, "Some *M* is *S*." We place an 'X' in the area where *M* and *S* overlap. But there are two such places: *SM-P* and *SMP*. Do we we place an 'X' in both? No. The premise only tells us that some *M* is *S*; it does not tell us whether or not that *M* is also *P*. So we place 'X' in the area where the circles representing *S* and *M* overlap *on* the line of the circle representing *P*. Our diagram looks like this:

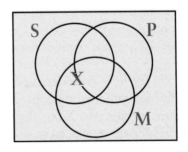

Figure 4.24

Now we diagram the major premise, "All M is P," by shading all of the M circle that is outside of P:

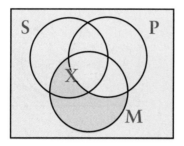

Figure 4.25

Here the 'X' is partially in a shaded area. Shading shows that the class has no members. Since nothing is in *SM-P*, we must *move* our 'X' to the area *SMP*. After the move, our diagram looks like this:

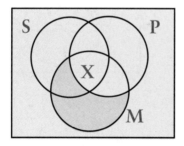

Figure 4.26

The diagram shows that the conclusion, "Some S is P," follows from the premises. The argument is valid.

Though there is nothing logically wrong with this procedure, it both is tedious and leaves open the possibility of error: we could make a mistake in moving the 'X'. The chances of error are decreased if we diagram the universal proposition first. So let us construct the diagram again, this time beginning with the universal premise, "All *M* is *P.*"

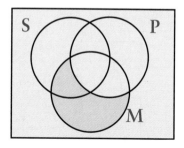

Figure 4.27

Next, we diagram the particular premise—"Some *M* is *S*"—putting an 'X' in the portion of the diagram in which the **M** circle and the **S** circle intersect. There are two such sections, but the diagramed major premise shows that *SM-P* is empty. So, the 'X' goes in the portion of the diagram in which all three circles intersect, namely *SMP.*

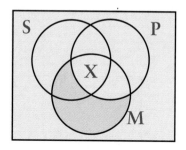

Figure 4.28

Again, the diagram shows that the syllogism is valid, but by following the prudential rule that you should diagram the universal premise before the particular, we have avoided tedium and the increased possibility of error.

Now consider an argument of the form **OAO-1**. The schematic representation of the argument is:

Some *M* is not *P.*
All *S* is *M.*
_____

Some *S* is not *P.*

In this case, the minor premise—"All *S* is *M*"—is a universal, so we begin with it:

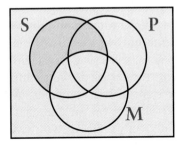

Figure 4.29

Diagraming the major premise requires that we place an 'X' in the portion of the diagram that is in the *M* circle but outside the *P* circle. Notice, however, that there are two such areas in the diagram: *SM-P* and -*SM-P*. The minor premise, which we have just diagramed, provides no grounds for claiming that the class represented by either of these two portions of the diagram is empty. The major premise specifies only that some *M* is not *P*. It says nothing about whether that "some" is or is not also *S*. Thus, to diagram the major premise we place an 'X' *in* the *M* circle and *on* the *S* circle.

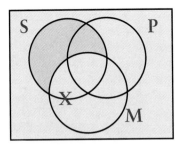

Figure 4.30

The conclusion is "Some *S* is not *P*." The diagram of the premises, however, does not allow us to know whether the thing denoted by 'X' is included in the class of things that are **S**, so the argument is invalid. If you follow the prudential rule and always diagram universal premises first, then whenever the diagraming of the premises results in an 'X' placed on a circle, the argument is invalid: the diagram shows that the premises do not entail the conclusion.

In constructing a Venn diagram, you always diagram the premises individually, looking only at the circles that represent the terms in the premise. In each case, there is a "foreign" circle cutting through the circles representing the terms in the premise, namely, the circle representing the other term in the argument. When you place an 'X' on a circle, you *always* place it on the "foreign" circle. This may easily be seen if you consider an argument with two particular premises. Consider an argument of the form **IOO-4**. The schematic representation of the argument is:

Some *P* is *M*.

Some *M* is not *S*.

Some *S* is not *P*.

Both premises are particular, so it makes no difference which premise we diagram first. Let us diagram the major premise—"Some *P* is *M*"—first, placing an 'X' in the area in which the *P*-circle and the *M*-circle intersect. Since there is no universal premise indicating that either *SMP* or -*SMP* is empty, we place the 'X' on circle-*S*:

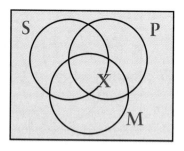

Figure 4.31

We follow the same procedure for the second premise, placing the 'X' on the **P** circle outside the **S** circle:

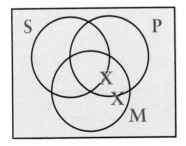

Figure 4.32

Since the conclusion—"Some *S* is not *P*"—is not diagramed, the argument is invalid.

Suggestion: Although you construct a Venn diagram *only* for the premises of an argument, many students find it *useful* to construct a *separate* diagram of the conclusion for purposes of comparison, particularly until they become comfortable with the Venn diagram technique. Thus, if you were given an argument of the mood and figure **AAE-4**,

All *P* is *M*.
All *M* is *S*.
─────────────
No *S* is *P*.

you would construct the Venn diagram for the premises as follows:

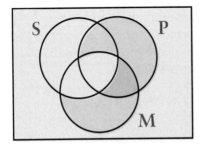

Figure 4.33

Then, off to the side, you might draw a two-circle diagram for the conclusion as follows:

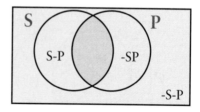

Figure 4.34

Comparing this second diagram with the diagram for the argument, you can see clearly that the conclusion is not diagramed: the argument is invalid.

EXERCISES

I. For each of the following argument forms, give the schematic representation of the argument and construct a Venn diagram to determine whether the argument is valid.

1. AAE-2	6. IIE-3	11. IOI-1	16. OEI-4
2. OEO-2	7. AOO-2	12. EEA-1	17. IAI-1
3. IEO-4	8. OOI-2	13. IOE-4	18. AII-4
4. AEO-2	9. AEE-1	14. OAO-3	19. AOE-2
5. OOA-4	10. EEO-4	15. OIO-3	20. EOO-2

II. State each of the following arguments in standard form, abbreviating terms to a single letter (either *P*, *S*, and *M* for 'major term', 'minor term', and 'middle term' or letters that will allow you to keep track of the words in the problems). State the mood and figure, and construct a Venn diagram to determine whether the argument is valid.

WELCOME TO WONDERLAND

1. All mammals are vertebrates.
   All mammals are animals.
   _____
   All animals are vertebrates.

2. No antelopes are insects.
   All fireflies are insects.

   _____

   Some fireflies are antelopes.

3. Some kangaroos are not aardvarks.
   Some kangaroos are marsupials.

   _____

   No marsupials are aardvarks.

4. Some syllogisms are exciting problems.
   Some exciting problems are sources of great frustration.

   _____

   Some sources of great frustration are syllogisms.

5. Some mad hatters are tea lovers.
   No dormice are mad hatters.

   _____

   No dormice are tea lovers.

6. All jabberwocks are things with eyes of flame.
   No jabberwocks are slithy toves.

   _____

   Some things with eyes of flame are slithy toves.

7. No lovers of the *Alice* books are Cheshire cats.
   All dormice are lovers of the *Alice* books.

   _____

   Some Cheshire cats are dormice.

8. Some tweedledums are not well-known politicians.
   No tweedledums are tweedledees.

   _____

   Some well-known politicians are tweedledees.

9. Some Cheshire cats are not aardvarks.
   No Cheshire cats are white rabbits.

   _____

   All aardvarks are white rabbits.

10. All animals that disappear except for their smiles are Cheshire cats.
    No thoughtless felines are Cheshire cats.

    _____

    All animals that disappear except for their smiles are thoughtless felines.

11. All jabberwocks are slithy toves, for some jabberwocks are not borogoves, and all borogoves are slithy toves.

12. All young women who walk through looking-glasses are women who have marvelous adventures, so some young women who walk through looking-glasses are women who

meet the red king, for some women who have marvelous adventures are not women who meet the red king.

13. Some frabjous days are not sunny days, so all frabjous days are rainy days, since some sunny days are not rainy days.

14. All mimsy borogoves are slithy toves, since no mimsy borogoves are jabberwocks, and all slithy toves are jabberwocks.

15. Since some white rabbits are animals who wear a large pocket watch, and since some animals chased by hounds are white rabbits, we may conclude that no animals chased by hounds are animals who wear a large pocket watch.

16. All readers of the *Alice* stories are persons who enjoy this set of problems, for some critical thinkers are persons who enjoy this set of problems and some critical thinkers are not readers of the *Alice* stories.

17. Since no red kings are queens of hearts, and some queens of hearts are playing cards, it follows that some playing cards are red kings.

18. Some queens of hearts are not tart-makers, so no queens of hearts are knaves of hearts, for some tart-makers are not knaves of hearts.

19. No red kings are red queens, for no red queens are knaves, and no red kings are knaves.

20. Some duchesses are rockers of pigs, for some duchesses are people who seem to rock babies, and no rockers of pigs are people who seem to rock babies.

21. Since some caterpillars are not smokers of hookahs, and all smokers of hookahs are givers of advice, we may conclude that no givers of advice are caterpillars.

22. All hatters are drinkers of tea, for some hatters are eaters of crumpets, and all eaters of crumpets are drinkers of tea.

23. No hatters are dormice, and some hatters are drinkers of tea, so no drinkers of tea are dormice.

24. No hatters are dormice, for some hatters are drinkers of tea, and all dormice are drinkers of tea.

25. No hatters are dormice, and no hatters are March hares, so some March hares are dormice.

26. Some drinkers of tea are dormice, for some hatters are not dormice, and no drinkers of tea are hatters.

27. No dormice are mad hatters, and some dormice are not March hares, so no mad hatters are March hares.

28. All mad hatters are drinkers of tea, and some mad hatters are eaters of crumpets, so some eaters of crumpets are not drinkers of tea.

29. No aardvarks are tea drinkers, for some red queens are not aardvarks and no tea drinkers are red queens.

30. Some mad hatters are tea drinkers, so no dormice are mad hatters, since all dormice are tea drinkers.

4.7 *Rules and Fallacies*

Although any categorical syllogism can be judged valid or invalid on the basis of a Venn diagram, the traditional means of judging the validity of a categorical syllogism is on the basis of six rules. These rules can be broken in seven ways, each of which is a **formal fallacy**. A formal fallacy is an error in reasoning based solely on the form of the argument, not on its content. Using the rules is faster and easier than using Venn diagrams, and, by having several alternative techniques to judge the validity of a syllogism, you can check your work to be sure you haven't erred.

The first rule is unique, for each of the other rules assumes that the first rule has *not* been broken. Rule 1: **Be certain that the syllogism is composed of exactly three terms, each of which appears twice and is assigned the same meaning throughout the syllogism.** Notice that this rule requires that you be certain that the argument you are examining is a categorical syllogism; for, by definition, a categorical syllogism must have exactly three terms, and each term must be assigned the same meaning throughout the syllogism. To break this rule is to commit the **fallacy of four terms (4T).**

There are three ways in which the fallacy of four terms can be committed. First, there might be four (or more) distinct terms in the argument. The following is an example:

All good construction companies are companies that can raise a barn in a week.
All good demolition companies are companies that can raze a barn in a week.

Therefore, all good demolition companies are good construction companies.

Second, there might be three terms, but one or more terms might be assigned different meanings at different points in the argument. For example:

> All caterpillars are animals that metamorphose into butterflies or moths.
> Some large pieces of earth-moving equipment are Caterpillars.
>
> ---
>
> Some large pieces of earth-moving equipment are animals that metamorphose into butterflies or moths.

In the major premise 'caterpillar' refers to an insect; in the minor premise 'Caterpillar' refers to a product of the Caterpillar Corporation. Since the meaning of the term 'caterpillar' shifts between the premises, the argument commits the Fallacy of Four Terms. Finally, there can be a shift in the antecedent of a pronoun. For example:

> All dogs who should eat new H*E*D (Halitosis Eradicator for Dogs) Dog Food are dogs who like it.
> All dogs with bad breath are dogs who should use new H*E*D Dog Food.
>
> ---
>
> So all dogs with bad breath are dogs who like it.

Notice that in the major premise, 'it' refers to 'H*E*D Dog Food'; in the conclusion 'it' refers to 'bad breath'. Since 'it' does not have the same meaning throughout the argument, the argument commits the fallacy of four terms.

Rule 2: **In a valid standard-form categorical syllogism, the middle term is distributed in at least one premise.** To break this rule is to commit the **fallacy of undistributed middle (UM)**. The rationale for the rule is as follows: The middle term must be distributed at least once to connect the subject and predicate terms. If the middle term is undistributed, the middle term could be referring to different subclasses of the relevant term. Consider the following instance of an **III-2:**

> Some Fords are reliable cars.
> Some Plymouths are reliable cars.
>
> ---
>
> Some Plymouths are Fords.

Reliable Fords and reliable Plymouths are entirely distinct subclasses of the class of reliable cars. Because the middle term is undistributed, the conclusion does not follow from the premises.

Rule 3: **In a valid standard form categorical syllogism, if either the major term or minor term is distributed in the conclusion, then that term must also be distributed in the corresponding premise.** If the major term is distributed in the conclusion but not in the major premise, the argument commits the **fallacy of illicit process of the major term,** or **illicit major** (IMa). If the minor term is distributed in the conclusion but not in the minor premise, the argument commits the **fallacy of illicit process of the minor term,** or **illicit minor** (IMi). The rationale for the rule is as follows: If either the major or minor term is distributed in the conclusion, the term denotes all the objects in the class. Since the conclusion of a valid deductive argument provides no new information, the sole grounds for having a term distributed in the conclusion is if it is distributed in the corresponding premise. Consider the following instance of an **OIE-4:**

Some porcupines are not marsupials.
Some marsupials are kangaroos.

No kangaroos are porcupines.

Notice that *both* the major and minor terms are distributed in the conclusion, but neither term is distributed in the premises. Hence, this argument commits *both* the fallacy of illicit major and the fallacy of illicit minor.

Rule 4: **No standard-form categorical syllogism with two negative premises is valid.** If a syllogism has two negative premises, it commits the **fallacy of exclusive premises** (EP). The rationale for the rule is that if you have two negative premises it is logically possible that you exclude too much. Consider the following instance of an **EEE-1:**

No Oldsmobile Ninety-Eights are Cadillacs.
No Sevilles are Oldsmobile Ninety-Eights.

No Sevilles are Cadillacs.

Both premises are true; the conclusion is false. The syllogism commits the fallacy of exclusive premises. Because both premises are negative propositions, they exclude too much: *no* conclusion can be drawn from the premises.

Rule 5: **If a syllogism has at least one negative premise, it must have a negative conclusion as well.** If a syllogism has a negative premise but an affirmative conclusion, it commits the fallacy of **drawing an affirmative conclusion from a negative premise** (ACNP). The rationale for the rule is as follows: If the conclusion of an argument is affirmative, it states either that "All *S* is *P*" or that "Some *S* is *P*." If one of the premises tells you that either some or all of *S* is not *M* or that some or all of *P* is not *M*, the premise does not tell you what *is* included, so you cannot draw an affirmative conclusion. Consider the following example of an **EII-3**:

> No bears are marsupials.
> Some kangaroos are marsupials.
> _____
> Some kangaroos are bears.

Both premises are true; the conclusion is false. The syllogism commits the fallacy of drawing an affirmative conclusion from a negative premise.

Rule 6: If a standard-form categorical syllogism has a particular conclusion, then it must have at least one particular premise. To break this rule is to commit the **existential fallacy (EF)**. Any syllogism with two universal premises and a particular conclusion commits the existential fallacy. Since only particular propositions have existential import, one of the premises must be particular if the conclusion is—that is, one of the premises must tell you that there actually is a thing of a certain kind if you are going to conclude that there is a thing of that kind. Consider the following instance of an **AAI-1**:

> All horned animals are dangerous animals.
> All unicorns are horned animals.
> _____
> Some unicorns are dangerous animals.

There are no unicorns, so the conclusion is false even if the premises are true. The argument commits the existential fallacy.

There are several things to remember in considering the rules. First, if an argument commits the fallacy of four terms, it is not a categorical syllogism, and consequently it cannot break any of the other rules. Also, you cannot construct a Venn diagram for an argument that commits the fallacy of four terms, since you cannot represent four classes in a three-circle diagram. Second, it is possible for an argument to commit more than one fallacy. Consider an instance of an **EEI-3**:

> No mathematicians are famous playwrights.
> No mathematicians are dramatic actors.
> _____
> Some dramatic actors are playwrights.

Both premises are negative, so the argument commits the fallacy of exclusive premises (EP; Rule 4). The premises are negative and the conclusion is affirmative, so the argument commits the fallacy of drawing an affirmative conclusion from a negative premise (ACNP; Rule 5). Both

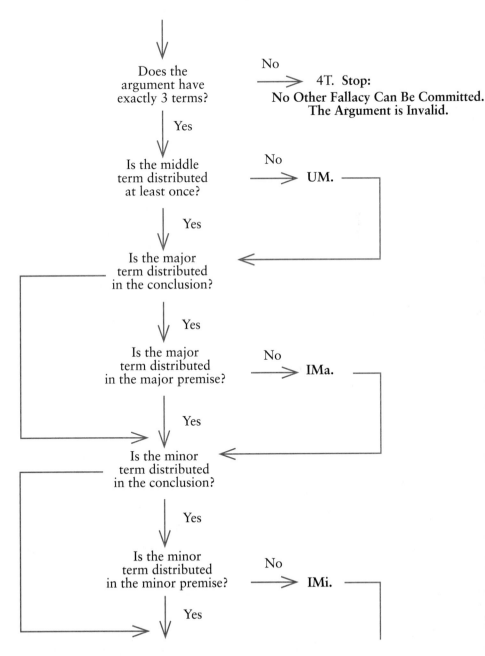

Figure 4.35 Flowchart for applying the rules

premises are universal and the conclusion is particular, so the argument commits the existential fallacy (EP; Rule 6). Finally, as long as an argument does not commit the fallacy of four terms, constructing a Venn diagram and applying the rules should lead to the same conclusion about validity.

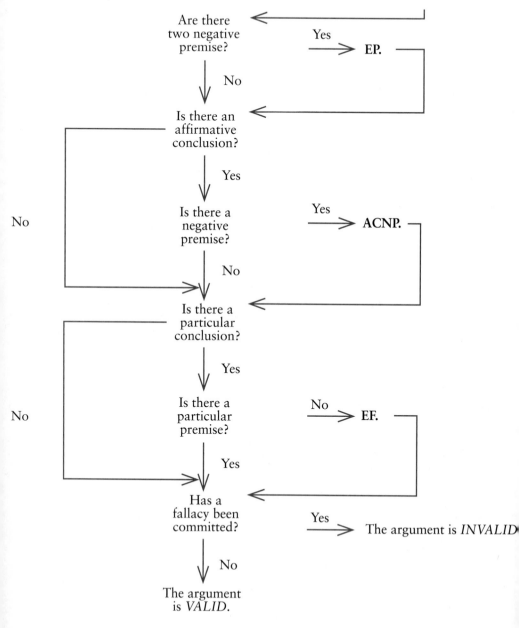

Figure 4.35 continued

Suggestion: Many students find it useful to note which terms are distributed or undistributed in an argument by making various notations in the schematic diagram for the argument. This often takes the form of a superscript. For example, if one is asked to evaluate an argument of the form **AIE-3**, one might write the schematic as follows:

All M^d is $P.^u$
Some M^u is $S.^u$
No S^d is $P.^d$

Such notations make it easy to notice that the argument commits the fallacies of illicit major (IMa) and illicit minor (IMi).

EXERCISES

I. For each of the following argument forms, give the schematic representation of the argument and use the rules to determine whether the argument is valid. If the argument is invalid, name all of the fallacies it commits. You may abbreviate fallacy names as suggested in the foregoing text.

1. AEE-1	6. AOI-1	11. OIE-1	16. EEO-2	21. EAI-2	26. IAE-1
2. OOE-4	7. EAO-4	12. EAE-3	17. IEA-3	22. AOA-3	27. IIO-1
3. EAE-3	8. IOI-2	13. IIE-4	18. EOI-4	23. OII-2	28. EOE-3
4. EEE-1	9. III-2	14. OEA-1	19. AEA-3	24. OOI-1	29. OAE-1
5. EII-3	10. IAO-3	15. AAE-4	20. AOO-4	25. EIO-4	30. AAO-4

II. If it is possible to do so, for each of the following arguments state the mood and figure, give the schematic representation of the argument, and use the rules to determine whether the argument is valid or invalid. If the argument is invalid, name all of the fallacies it commits.

HOORAY FOR HOLLYWOOD

1. Some old movies are comedies.
   No Harrison Ford films are old movies.

   Some Harrison Ford films are comedies.

2. Some old movies are not movies starring the Marx Brothers.
   All old movies are movies shown on cable T.V.
   _____

   All movies shown on cable T.V. are movies starring the Marx Brothers.

3. All Marx Brothers movies are comedies.
   No W. C. Fields movies are Marx Brothers movies.
   _____

   All comedies are W. C. Fields movies.

4. Some Marx Brothers movies are comedies.
   Some W. C. Fields movies are comedies.
   _____

   Some Marx Brothers movies are not W. C. Fields movies.

5. All David O. Selznick productions were elaborate movies.
   All David O. Selznick productions were movies completed before 1960.
   _____

   No movies completed before 1960 were elaborate movies.

6. No Marx Brothers movies are W. C. Fields movies.
   Some movies with Margaret Dumont are Marx Brothers movies.
   _____

   Some movies with Margaret Dumont are W. C. Fields movies.

7. Some old movies are movies starring the Marx Brothers.
   No serious movies are movies starring the Marx Brothers.
   _____

   No serious movies are old movies.

8. Some David O. Selznick productions are not comedies.
   Some old movies are comedies.
   _____

   Some David O. Selznick productions are old movies.

9. Some westerns are John Ford pictures.
   Some Billy Wilder pictures are not westerns.
   _____

   No John Ford pictures are Billy Wilder pictures.

10. Some westerns are not movies starring John Wayne.
    No Marx Brothers movies are movies starring John Wayne.
    _____

    All Marx Brothers movies are westerns.

11. No old movies are movies with Dolby sound, for some MGM pictures are not old movies and some MGM pictures are not movies with Dolby sound.

12. Since no MGM pictures are RKO pictures, we may conclude that some MGM pictures are not movies starring Lucille Ball, for some RKO pictures are movies starring Lucille Ball.

13. Some harpists are not persons named "Harpo," so no serious actors are harpists, for some serious actors are persons named "Harpo."

14. All westerns are action pictures, for some action pictures are not pictures featuring cowboys and horses, and all pictures featuring cowboys and horses are westerns.

15. Since all westerns are pictures featuring cowboys and horses, and some pictures featuring cowboys and horses are John Wayne movies, it follows that no John Wayne movies are westerns.

16. All Marx Brothers movies are comedies, so some comedies are not westerns, for no Marx Brothers movies are westerns.

17. Some RKO pictures are comedies, and some westerns are RKO pictures, so all westerns are comedies.

18. No night at the opera is a day at the races, for all evenings filled with duck soup are nights at the opera, and no evening filled with duck soup is a day at the races.

19. Some "Duck Soup" is not soup made by a major soup manufacturer, and some mushroom soup is soup made by a major soup manufacturer, so all mushroom soup is "Duck Soup."

20. No Marx Brothers movie is a movie starring George Burns, so no movie starring George Burns is a movie featuring Mae West, for some Marx Brothers movie is not a movie featuring Mae West.

21. Since some animal crackers are not horse feathers, and some horse feathers are things found only in old movies, we may infer that all things found only in old movies are animal crackers.

22. All events in Marx Brothers movies are instances of monkey business, so all nights in Casablanca are events in Marx Brothers movies, since some instances of monkey business are nights in Casablanca.

23. No W. C. Fields films are Marx Brothers movies, so no Mae West films are Marx Brothers movies, for some Mae West films are W. C. Fields films.

24. No person who says "Godfrey Daniels" is a person who would say "my little chickadee," so no person who drinks gin is a person who says "Godfrey Daniels," for some person who drinks gin is not a person who would say "my little chickadee."

25. Some clients of Wheeler, Dealer, and Dodge Attorneys at Law are eaters of duck soup, for no clients of Wheeler, Dealer, and Dodge Attorneys at Law are people who wear horse feathers, and all eaters of duck soup are people who wear horse feathers.

26. Since some things laced with comedy are not bowls of duck soup, and since some things laced with comedy are bundles of horse feathers, we may conclude that some bundles of horse feathers are bowls of duck soup.

27. Some movies made in the 1930s are comedies, for all Marx Brothers movies are comedies and some Marx Brothers movies are not movies made in the 1930s.

28. No Marx Brothers movies are highly dramatic movies, and no W. C. Fields movies are highly dramatic movies, so all Marx Brothers movies are W. C. Fields movies.

29. Some Marx Brothers movies are not movies starring Zeppo, for some comedies are movies starring Zeppo, and some comedies are Marx Brothers movies.

30. Since all Marx Brothers fans are "Marxists" and all Bolsheviks are Marxists, some Marx Brothers fans are Bolsheviks.

31. No movie starring Groucho is a western, and some westerns are not movies starring Zeppo, so all movies starring Zeppo are movies starring Groucho.

32. Some movies starring Harpo are movies with harp solos, so some New York Philharmonic concerts are not movies with harp solos, for some movies starring Harpo are not New York Philharmonic concerts.

33. No movie seen on late-night television is a movie in which Harpo speaks, so some movies in which Groucho asks for the secret word are not movies seen on late-night television, for all movies in which Harpo speaks are movies in which Groucho asks for the secret word.

34. All movies with a cast of thousands are movies meant to be seen on a wide screen, so no movies made for television are

movies with a cast of thousands, for some movies made for television are not movies meant to be seen on a wide screen.

35. Since all old movies are movies meant to be seen on the silver screen, and no movies meant to be seen on the silver screen are movies made for television, we may conclude that all movies made for television are old movies.

36. No W. C. Fields movies are movies in which a sucker gets an even break, but some Laurel and Hardy movies are movies in which a sucker gets an even break, so no Laurel and Hardy movies are W. C. Fields movies.

37. All fans of W. C. Fields are persons who are not all bad, so no people who hate children and dogs are persons who are not all bad, for some people who hate children and dogs are fans of W. C. Fields.

38. No W. C. Fields movie is a movie made for television, but all W. C. Fields movies are movies shot in living black and white, so all movies shot in living black and white are movies made for television.

39. No W. C. Fields movie is a movie starring Laurel and Hardy, for no W. C. Fields movie is a movie that gives a sucker an even break, and all movies starring Laurel and Hardy are movies that give a sucker an even break.

40. Some people who made it through all these exercises are not fans of old movies, and some people who should be congratulated are people who made it through all these exercises, so some people who should be congratulated are not fans of old movies.

4.8 Ordinary Language: A Translation Guide

Syllogistic arguments given in ordinary English are not always given in standard form. Sometimes they appear to have four or more terms. Sometimes the quantifier is not 'all', 'no', or 'some'. Sometimes there is no copula. **Reducing** or **translating** a nonstandard-form categorical syllogism to standard form is the first step in evaluating a syllogism. Generally this is an easy procedure, provided you keep several simple principles in mind. (1) Ask what the person presenting the argument most probably means by the several statements in the argument. Your ordinary understanding of the language is often a sufficient guide to reducing the argument to standard form. (2) *Assume* the argument is valid unless a careful examination of the possible reductions shows either that no plausible reduction will yield a valid argument or that you can obtain a valid argument in standard form only if one of the premises in the argument is clearly false. If you cannot reduce a nonstandard-form syllogism to a sound argument, assume that it is more likely that a person would make a mistake in logic than intentionally introduce a false premise.

In this section we consider some of the techniques used to reduce a nonstandard syllogisms to standard form. Some of these will be obvious; others will require a bit of thought.

1. **Synonyms,** words with the same meaning. Consider the following *valid* argument, an argument of the form **EAE-1.**

No meat-eaters are bovines.
All tigers are carnivores.
_____

No tigers are cows.

Here we have an argument in which various synonyms are used in different premises. To reduce the argument to standard form, simply replace synonyms with synonyms. The terms 'meat-eaters' and 'carnivores' are synonyms, as are the terms 'bovines' and 'cows'. So the argument can be reduced to standard form as follows:

No carnivores are cows.
All tigers are carnivores.
_____

No tigers are cows.

2. **Complementary terms.** Sometimes an argument contains two terms that pick out complementary classes, as in the following argument:

No valid argument is an argument with true premises and a false conclusion.
All invalid arguments are unsound arguments.
_____

No sound argument is an argument with true premises and a false conclusion.

Since the class of valid arguments is the complement of the class of invalid arguments, and the class of sound arguments is the complement of the class of unsound arguments, this argument can be reduced to an argument of the form **EAE-1** by replacing the minor premise with its contrapositive:

> No valid argument is an argument with true premises and a false conclusion.
> All sound arguments are valid arguments.
> _____
> No sound argument is an argument with true premises and a false conclusion.

As this case illustrates, it is common in ordinary English that a term and its complement are distinguished by prefixes such as 'in-', 'un-', and 'il-'. So 'illegal' means not legal, 'uncovered' means not covered, and 'invertebrate' means not vertebrate. You have to be a bit careful in applying this general rule, since there are exceptions. For example, 'inflammable' is synonymous with 'flammable'.

You should also notice that every argument assumes a **domain of discourse**, that is, a set of objects that are *assumed* to exist for the sake of the argument. In some cases, the limits of a domain of discourse must be recognized if you are to understand which classes are complementary. For example, members of the Senate is the complementary class to members of the House of Representatives *as long as* your domain of discourse is members of Congress. 'Barbarians' complements the term 'Greeks' *as long as* your domain of discourse is people in the ancient world (as understood from the perspective of the Greeks). If there seem to be too many terms, ask what domain of discourse is assumed in looking for complementary terms.

3. **Singular propositions.** A singular proposition is a proposition whose subject term is an individual, for example, "Socrates is a mortal" or "This book is a dull book." Singular propositions are *compound;* they make two claims. For example, "Socrates is a mortal" asserts that all the members of the class of Socrateses (there is exactly one) are mortals and that there is at least one Socrates that is a mortal. Hence, *you can treat a singular proposition as a universal proposition or as a particular proposition, and you choose how to treat it by asking what would make the syllogism valid.* Consider the following argument:

> All human beings are mortals.
> Socrates is a human being.
> _____
> Therefore, Socrates is a mortal.

The singular propositions can be treated as universal affirmatives or as particular affirmatives: both arguments of the form **AAA-1** and **AII-1** are valid. In some cases, one singular proposition in a syllogism must be treated as a universal affirmative and the other as a particular affirmative. For example:

> John is a member of Alpha Phi Omega.
> John is a member of Phi Beta Kappa.
>
> ———————————————————————————
>
> Therefore, some members of Phi Beta Kappa are members of Alpha Phi Omega.

The least bit of thought will convince you that the conclusion follows from the premises, since John is a member of both organizations. To put the argument into standard form, however, you must treat one of the premises as a universal affirmative and the other as a particular affirmative: it makes no difference which you treat as a universal and which you treat as a particular.

4. **Nonstandard quantifiers.** In ordinary English we commonly use words other than 'all', 'no', and 'some' as quantifiers. The following is a partial guide for replacing nonstandard quantifiers with standard quantifiers.

> 'Any', 'every', and 'whatever' should be replaced by 'all'.
> 'Not any' and 'none' should be replaced by 'no'.
> 'There are no' should be replaced by 'no'.
> 'There are' should be replaced by 'some'.
> 'Not all' should be replaced by "Some . . . are not . . .".

Sometimes a quantifier includes an implicit reference to the domain of discourse. If this happens, specify the domain of discourse *in both the subject and the predicate terms:*

> 'Everything' or 'anything' should be replaced by "All things that are . . . are things that are . . . ".
> 'Whenever' should be replaced by "All times that are . . . are times that are . . . ".
> 'Everyone' or 'anyone' should be replaced by "All persons who are . . . are persons who are . . . ".
> 'Nothing' should be replaced by "No things that are . . . are . . . ".

'A' and 'an' can be treated as either universal or particular quantifiers, depending *what will make the statement true.* For example, the statement "A cat is on the mat" should be replaced by "Some cat is a thing that is on the mat." "A cat is a mammal" should be replaced by "All cats are mammals."

'The' can be treated as either a universal quantifier or the mark of a singular statement. Typically one should replace "The cat is a mammal" with "All cats are mammals." On the other hand, "The present Queen of England is Elizabeth" should be treated as a singular statement, since there is exactly one present Queen of England.

If one has any question as to how to interpret a nonstandard quantifier, ask, "What interpretation of the quantifier will make the argument valid and the statement true?" This is called "the principle of charity in interpretation." If you wonder why you should be charitable in your interpretations, ask yourself, "How would you like it if someone butchered your argument?" If you apply the principle of charity in interpretation you will seldom go wrong.

5. **Predicate adjectives.** If you are given a statement that does not contain a noun in the predicate, introduce a noun. For example, if you are given, "Some cars are compact" or "No crows are red," either give the noun form of the predicate adjective, for example, "Some cars are compacts," or add a noun modified by the adjective, for example, "No crows are red birds" or "No crows are red things," depending upon what is needed to make the statement consistent with other statements in the argument.

6. **The missing copula.** Many statements in ordinary English do not contain a copula. If the copula is missing, add it and use the noun form of the given verb as the predicate. For example, if you are given, "All third graders read," restate the sentence as "All third graders are readers."

7. **It's all there, but the order's wrong.** Sometimes, all the elements of a standard-form categorical proposition are given, but the order in which they are given is not standard. In such cases, if you consider what would make the statement true, you should easily be able to reduce the statement to standard form. For example, if you are given, "Shakespeare's works are all classic works," it can be reduced to "All Shakespeare's works are classic works." (Only a real Shakespeare buff would contend it should be "All classic works are Shakespeare's works.")

8. **'Only', 'none but', 'No . . . except . . .'.** If you read a sign saying, "Only members are admitted to this club," the statement means, "You must be a member to be admitted to this club" ("Being a member is a necessary condition for admission to this club"), which reduces to the standard-form categorical proposition, "All persons who are admitted to this club are members of this club." Typically, when the quan-

tifier of a proposition is 'only', 'none but', or 'no . . . except . . .', you replace the term with 'all' and switch the positions of the subject and predicate terms given in the statement. A statement of the form "Only (none but) *S* is *P*" is reduced to "All *P* is *S*." There are some cases, however, in which the meaning of "Only *S* is *P*" is *both* "All *P* is *S*" *and* "All *S* is *P*." The procedure for deciding which is the correct reduction is this: If reducing "Only (none but) *S* is *P*" to "All *P* is *S*" will not make the argument valid, but reducing it to "All *S* is *P*" will make it valid, use the second reduction, *as long as the resulting statement is true.*

9. **'Unless'.** Sometimes you confront a proposition such as "No one reads the *Times* unless he or she is well-educated." 'Unless' requires a negation of the predicate term. Hence, the statement *could* be reduced to "No person who reads the *Times* is a non-well-educated person," which is equivalent by obversion to "All persons who read the *Times* are well-educated persons."

10. **No quantifier.** If no quantifier is given in a statement, introduce whatever quantifier seems to be intended by the person presenting the argument. Attempt to make the argument valid as long as doing so yields a true statement. For example, if you are given "Cats like milk," restate it as "All cats are likers of milk," *unless* the validity of the argument requires "Some cats are likers of milk." *In some cases it will be obvious that only a particular statement is true.* For example, if you are given "Cats are on the mat," you must restate it as, "Some cats are on the mat," for "All cats are on the mat" is obviously false.

11. **Complex quantifiers.** In addition to the cases we have considered, there are some in which the given quantifier marks a complex claim. Let us call these "complex quantifiers." An **exceptive** proposition is one beginning with 'All except' or 'All but'. Assume you are reading an advertisement for a contest and find the statement "All but employees of the XYZ Television Network are eligible." The statement asserts *both* that "All nonemployees of the XYZ Television Network are persons eligible to win the contest" and "No employees of the XYZ Television Network are persons eligible to win the contest." Other examples of quantifiers that express more than one proposition are 'Almost all', 'Not quite all', and 'Only some'. In each of these cases, the quantifier indicates that some are and some are not. Thus, if you are given the statement "Almost all cats are pets," you restate it as "Some cats are pets" and "Some cats are not pets," which admittedly does not capture its whole meaning. If a statement with such a complex quantifier is a premise of an argument, you use whichever statement will make the argument valid. If both premises of an argument include complex quantifiers, you might have to check as many as four distinct syllogisms

to determine whether the conclusion follows from any of the formulations of the premises. *But if the conclusion of a syllogism is stated with a complex quantifier, the argument will be invalid, for in such a case* ***both*** *propositions must follow from the premises.* When the conclusion has a complex quantifier, you need only show that one of the propositions will not follow.

12. **Parameters.** There are occasions in which a context or domain of discourse is assumed by a statement, although that context is not explicitly stated. If you say, for example, "Jack Nicklaus sometimes wins a golf tournament," the implicit context is "times when Jack Nicklaus plays in a golf tournament." You should reformulate the statement to make the context explicit—for example, "Some times when Jack Nicklaus plays in golf tournaments are times when Jack Nicklaus wins a golf tournament." Similarly, the statement "Flage's books are always boring" should be reduced to "All books that Flage writes are boring books." Generally, if you devote a bit of thought to a statement, you will notice whether it is necessary to specify the context of the statement by adding a word or phrase (**a parameter**) to both sides of the copula.

Finally, some practical advice, or how to keep from going crazy in ordinary English: Basically, you need do little more than ask yourself what the person presenting the argument most probably means. (1) Restate the premises and conclusion in such a way that the statements are true. (2) Ask whether there is a plausible way in which the statements can be reformulated so that the premises are true and the argument is valid. If there is no way to have a sound argument, go for true premises and a true conclusion only: assume it is more likely that errors would be made with respect to logic than with respect to truth. (3) Keep your reformulations as brief as possible. This will help keep you from being lost in the verbiage while costing nothing with respect to the analysis of the argument.

EXERCISES

I. Each of the following is a valid categorical syllogism stated in nonstandard form. Translate each syllogism into standard form. State the mood and figure of the argument, and construct a Venn diagram to show that the argument is valid.

1. Anyone who eats chocolate for breakfast has an enormous sweet tooth, so only those who support their local dentist eat

chocolate for breakfast, since whoever has a large sweet tooth supports his or her local dentist.

2. Dogs that do tricks are not kangaroos, so some zoo animals are not dogs that do tricks, for some kangaroos live in zoos.

3. Since some coins desired by coin collectors are circulating coins, and no coin coveted by a numismatist is common, we may conclude that a few rare coins are found in circulation.

4. Since no scholars are cowards and John isn't brave, it follows that John's life is not dedicated to intellectual pursuits.

5. Some people who ride cows lose the race, for none but the swift win the race, and a few cow riders are not swift persons.

6. Since racehorses are all thoroughbreds and many racehorses do not win at Belmont, it follows that some thoroughbreds are not winners at Belmont.

7. Since the cat is a carnivore, it follows that Frisky is not a feline, for Frisky is not a carnivore.

8. Ostafar doesn't hunt every duck. But since all ducks are fowl, it follows that not all fowl are hunted by Ostafar.

9. Only those who hoard money for its own sake are misers. It follows that some counting-house executives hoard money for its own sake, since some counting-house executives are real scrooges.

10. Every rabbit that Henry hunts smokes cigars. But any rabbit who smokes cigars is not a duck. So no duck is a rabbit that Henry hunts.

II. If it is possible to do so, restate the following syllogisms in standard form. State the mood and figure of the syllogism. Construct a Venn diagram to determine whether the syllogism is valid. If the syllogism is invalid, list all the rules that are broken.

1. The cat isn't a tabby, so this tabby isn't a mammal, for cats are mammals.

2. A few cats smile when they disappear, so some hedgehogs are not cats, for not everything that smiles when it disappears is a hedgehog.

3. Anyone who should be invited to a pun festival enjoys playing with language, but no one who writes logic problems should be invited to a pun festival, so no one who enjoys playing with language writes logic problems.

4. Everyone who believes that the best government is one elected by a majority of the voters is a democrat, so no Republicans believe in majority rule, since no Republicans are Democrats.

5. A few coins of the realm are not valuable to coin collectors, since every coin in circulation is a coin of the realm and only some coins in circulation are of numismatic value.

6. Dogs are not cats, for a few rats aren't cats and not any dogs are rats.

7. Not every scoundrel is a coward, but since at least one traitor is a scoundrel, it follows that some traitors are not cowards.

8. Not a single Lincoln is a compact, so some presidents weren't small, for one Lincoln was a president.

9. Some sausages are not enjoyed by fictitious German composers, for no bratwursts are enjoyed by fictitious German composers and only some sausages are bratwursts.

10. At least one cat is a Siamese, so only some dogs are Siamese, for not any canines are felines.

11. None but stone bridges are standing bridges constructed by the ancient Romans, so a bridge in Koblenz was built by the Romans, for a bridge in Koblenz is made of stone.

12. Not every dog is a hound, and not any hound is a schnauzer, so every schnauzer is a dog.

13. Any cartoon character who is flattened by a steamroller can rise to act another day, so a few people flattened by a semi don't rise to act another day, for not any person who is run over by a semi-trailer truck is a cartoon character who is flattened by a steam roller.

14. No one watches the news who is uninterested in current affairs, so every presidential candidate watches the news, given that anyone who runs for president is interested in current affairs.

15. No rabbit except Beauregard Bunny drinks corn liquor, so Beauregard Bunny is the only rabbit Amisglof hunts, for Amisglof only hunts rabbits that drink corn liquor.

16. No reader of Shakespeare reads mysteries, for not everyone who likes to solve problems reads Shakespeare, and no one reads mysteries unless he or she likes to solve problems.

17. Since every person who is a gourmet cook orders stuff from Epicure, Inc., it follows that not a single coyote who eats burgers and fries is a devotee of the Epicure Catalog, for no one who cooks fine meals eats burgers and fries.

18. Since any cat who is a gourmet cook desires a supper of mouse à la king, no desirer of a supper of mouse à la king uses the Epicure catalogue, for every cat who is a gourmet cook orders stuff from Epicure, Inc.

19. Every cat that is both well-adjusted and altruistic will not attempt to eat small elephants with large trunks, but since Seymore is not both well-adjusted and altruistic, it follows that Seymore attempts to eat small elephants with large trunks.

20. Since not quite all cats are mousers, and a few cats mistake elephants for large mice, it follows that there is a mouser now and then who mistakes elephants for mice.

4.9 Enthymemes

An **enthymeme** is an argument with an unstated premise or an unstated conclusion. Such arguments are fairly common in ordinary English, and it is usually easy to discover the missing premise or conclusion. *Assume,* until such an assumption is proven implausible, that the argument is valid. If the conclusion is missing, you appeal to the rules to determine what the conclusion must be. If a premise is missing, you appeal to the rules to determine what it must be. To make life easier, the rules may be summarized as follows:

1. Be certain there are exactly three terms.
2. Be certain the middle term is distributed exactly once.
3. Be certain no major or minor term is distributed only once.
4. Be certain the number of negative premises equals the number of negative conclusions.
5. Be certain the number of particular premises equals the number of particular conclusions.

The only additional consideration to be taken into account in evaluating an enthymematic argument is this: *If the premise or conclusion you introduce is obviously false, assume the argument is invalid.*

Now for some examples. Let's say you're given the following enthymeme:

> Given that every fictitious lawyer is a lawyer who wins every case and Marsha Perry is a fictitious lawyer, the conclusion is obvious.

Here we have the premises for a syllogism. Begin by stating the premises in standard form:

> All fictitious lawyers are lawyers who win every case.
> Marsha Perry is a fictitious lawyer.

The minor premise is a singular proposition and may be treated as a universal affirmative. Appealing to the rules, you will notice that 'Marsha Perry' must be distributed in the conclusion. So you conclude:

> Marsha Perry is a lawyer who wins every case.

The syllogism is an **AAA-1** and is clearly valid.

Now assume you are given:

> No cats are dogs, so some collies are not cats.

A premise is missing in this example. Look at the rules. The conclusion is a particular proposition, so the premise must be particular. There is one negative premise, so the missing premise must be affirmative. A particular affirmative proposition is logically equivalent to its converse, so the missing premise is *either* "Some dogs are collies" *or* "Some collies are dogs." The premise is true. Hence, the argument is *either* an **EIO-2** *or* an **EIO-4**. In either case, the argument is valid.

But now consider this enthymematic syllogism:

> All Methodists are Christians, so all Protestants are Christians.

Again you are searching for a missing premise. The conclusion is a universal affirmative, so the premise must be a universal affirmative. The minor term is distributed in the conclusion, so the minor term must be distributed in the premise. So *if the argument is valid,* it must be an **AAA-1,** and the missing premise must be:

All Protestants are Methodists.

But "All Protestants are Methodists" is certainly false: the class of Protestants includes Presbyterians, Lutherans, Baptists, and members of many other religious denominations. Since we are assuming that one is more likely to err as to validity than as to commonly known truths, we must assume that the missing premise is: "All Methodists are Protestants." This statement is true, but it means the argument is an **AAA-3,** which commits the fallacy of illicit minor. So regardless of what you do with this enthymematic argument, it is unsound. If you assume the missing premise is "All Protestants are Methodists," the syllogism is valid, but the missing premise is false. If you assume the missing premise is "All Methodists are Protestants," the premise is true but the argument is invalid.

SUMMARY

1. Ask what premises and conclusion, if any, will make the syllogism valid.

2. Ask whether those premises and conclusion are true.

3. If one of the premises or the conclusion is false, replace it with a true statement and proceed to list the fallacies.

EXERCISES

For each of the following enthymemes, find the missing premise or conclusion. Always seek a statement that will make the argument valid, and state the mood and figure of that argument. If the statement that makes the argument valid is *false,* explain why it is false and replace it with a *true* statement. If the argument is invalid, indicate which fallacies are committed. State the mood and figure for each argument. If the missing statement is logically equivalent to its converse, state all possible moods and figures of the syllogism.

  1. Since every argument of the mood and figure **AAA-1** is valid, this argument is valid.

  2. Since some millionaires are stingy and no millionaires are poor, the conclusion is obvious.

3. Since professors are intelligent and some intelligent persons are rich, I'll let you draw your own conclusions.

4. Some cats are mammals, since some cats are vertebrates.

5. Only a Dickens buff would read *A Christmas Carol* in the middle of July, so George is not a Dickens buff.

6. Some Presbyterians are not Lutherans, so some Presbyterians are not Methodists.

7. No children under three drive sports cars, so no sports-car drivers would prefer driving a Model-T Ford.

8. Anyone who masters the art of the syllogism enjoys playing logical games, so some who enjoy playing logical games are mathematicians.

9. Anyone who does not understand Plato's *Works* says, "It's all Greek to me." But since some who do not understand Plato's *Works* are fans of British philosophy, you may draw your own conclusions.

10. Not everyone who plays games with syllogisms finds syllogistic games enjoyable, for no one who finds syllogisms utterly perplexing enjoys syllogistic games.

11. No Protestants are Catholics, for no Baptists are Catholics.

12. Since no Protestants are Catholics, it follows that no Presbyterians are Catholics.

13. Since some who do these problems are not mathematically disposed, we may conclude that some who enjoy these problems are not mathematically disposed.

14. Everyone who writes for the *Times* has at least a high-school education, so no three-year-olds write for the *Times*.

15. No British solicitors are barristers, so some British lawyers are not solicitors.

4.10 Sorites

A **sorites** is a chain of enthymematic syllogisms in which the unstated conclusion of one syllogism is a premise for the next syllogism. Sometimes the conclusion of a sorites is given; sometimes it is not. If the conclusion is given, there is a four-step approach that allows you to solve the sorites. (1) Find the major term in the sorites (the predicate of the final conclusion) in one of the premises. (2) Note the other term in that premise and find the other premise with that term. (3) Restate both the premises in standard form, and draw out the conclusion. (4) Repeat steps 2 and 3 until all the premises have been used. If the conclusion is not given, pair up premises with common terms (or a term and its complement) until you find a term that does not repeat. That term will be either the major or the minor term of the sorites—you cannot tell which until you have solved the sorites. Once you find a nonrepeating term, follow steps 2, 3, and 4 above.

It is important to note that step 3 suggests that premises should be reduced to standard form as you come to them. There is a good reason for this. Typically, the reduction of one of the premises with which you begin will be clear enough. Once one premise is in standard form, the reduction of the other premise to standard form should be easy if you follow the principle that *a syllogism in ordinary English should be assumed valid until its validity is shown incompatible with an obvious truth.* If the reduction of a premise yields an obvious falsehood, even though the syllogism would be valid with that premise, ask whether there is a plausible reduction of the given premise that is true and list any fallacies committed. To see how to reduce a sorites to standard form, let us consider some examples.

You are given:

(1) Adventure films are exciting films.
(2) Documentary films are based on fact.
(3) Most documentaries aren't exciting.

Some films based on fact are not adventure films.

The major term of the sorites is 'adventure films', which is in premise (1). The other term in premise (1) is 'exciting [films]', which is also found in premise (3). So you state those two premises in standard form and use them to draw a conclusion. Stating the premises in standard form, you get this:

(1') All adventure films are exciting films.
(3') Some documentary films are not exciting films.

Given these premises you use the procedure for dealing with an enthymematic argument to draw a conclusion. There is one particular premise, so the conclusion must also be particular. There is one negative premise, so the conclusion must be negative. The term 'adventure films' is distributed in the premise, so it must be distributed in the conclusion. You conclude:

(C1) Some documentary films are not adventure films.

(C1) is the conclusion of an **AOO-2.**

Now you use (C1) with the premise (2) to draw the conclusion of the sorites. (C1) and premise (2) both contain the term 'documentary films', so to state premise (2) in standard form you use (C1) and your reformulation of (2) to reach the conclusion of the sorites:

(C1) Some documentary films are not adventure films.
(2') All documentary films are based on fact.

Some films based on fact are not adventure films.

This syllogism is an **OAO-3.**

The procedure is similar if you are *not* given the conclusion of the sorites, except that you must find a term that occurs in only one of the premises and trace that term through the sorites. You might not know until you have finished whether the term you chose is the major or minor term of the sorites. Consider the following:

(1) Some interesting activities are intellectually stimulating.
(2) No exciting activities are boring.
(3) Solving a sorites is always exciting.

Since we do not know what the conclusion is, we must look for terms that appear in only one premise. If we notice that 'boring activities' and 'interesting activities' are complementary terms, the two nonrepeating terms are 'solving a sorites' and 'intellectually stimulating activities.' Since premise (1) is in nearly standard form, let's trace 'intellectually stimulating activities' through the sorites.

We begin by stating premises (1) and (2) in standard form. Since 'boring activities' and 'interesting activities' are complementary terms, we may first reformulate (2) as (2') "No exciting activities are noninteresting activities," and then obvert to (2") "All exciting activities are interesting activities." The syllogism is:

(1') Some interesting activities are intellectually stimulating activities.
(2") All exciting activities are interesting activities.

(C1) Some exciting activities are intellectually stimulating activities.

Now using (C1) with a reformulation of (3), we can reach the conclusion of the sorites.

(C1) Some exciting activities are intellectually stimulating activities.
(3') All instances of solving a sorites are exciting activities.

(C2) Some instances of solving a sorites are intellectually stimulating activities.

As a chain of syllogisms, a sorites is like any other chain: it is only as strong as its weakest link. If one of the component syllogisms of a sorites is invalid, the whole sorites is invalid. So if you are working through a sorites and find an invalid syllogism, you can stop and declare the sorites invalid. For example, consider the following sorites:

(1) No marsupials are reptiles.
(2) No mammals are marsupials.
(3) All cats are mammals.
(4) All reptiles are animals with scales.

No animals with scales are cats.

Let's follow the major term of the sorites, 'cats', and see where it leads us. From (3) and (2) we can construct a syllogism:

(3) All cats are mammals.
(2) No mammals are marsupials.

(C1) No marsupials are cats.

The argument is an instance of an **AEE-4,** which is valid. Now you use (C1) together with premise (1) in an attempt to reach another conclusion:

(C1) No marsupials are cats.
(1) No marsupials are reptiles.

What can we conclude? Nothing! Since there are exactly three terms and both premises are negative propositions, any conclusion drawn would commit the fallacy of exclusive premises. So you explain why any conclusion drawn would yield an invalid syllogism, that is, indicate which fallacy would be committed, and declare the sorites invalid.

One last point: If you find an invalid syllogism in a sorites, you should *always* double-check your reduction of the premises to standard form before declaring the sorites invalid. Also, you should always work out as many of the valid component syllogisms in a sorites as you can, and if a conclusion is given, you should use that conclusion as the conclusion of the sorites.

EXERCISES

I. Trace the major term through each of the following sorites. State each component syllogism in standard form. State the mood and figure of each syllogism and check the rules to see if it's valid. If the sorites is invalid, explain why.[2]

1. (1) Vertebrates are all animals with backbones.
   (2) Every cat is a mammal.
   (3) No mammal is an invertebrate.

   All cats have backbones.

2. (1) Everyone who is sane can do logic.
   (2) No lunatics are fit to serve on a jury.
   (3) None of *your* sons can do logic.

   None of *your* sons is fit to serve on a jury.

3. (1) No experienced person is incompetent.
   (2) Jenkins is always blundering.
   (3) No competent person is always blundering.

   Jenkins is inexperienced.

4. (1) No deciduous trees have needles.
   (2) Every conifer has needles.
   (3) Only trees that lose their leaves are maples.
   (4) All pines are evergreens.

   Some maples aren't pines.

5. (1) All symphony orchestras play classical music.
   (2) Every Gershwin tune is a real toe-tapper.
   (3) Beethoven didn't write any Gershwin compositions.
   (4) Most groups playing classical music play Beethoven compositions.

   Some symphony orchestras play music you can tap your toes to.

6. (1) Animals that do not kick are always unexcitable.
   (2) Donkeys have no horns.
   (3) A buffalo can always toss one over a gate.
   (4) No animals that kick are easy to swallow.
   (5) No hornless animal can toss one over a gate.
   (6) All animals are excitable except buffaloes.

No animals that are easy to swallow are donkeys.

II. If it is possible to do so, solve each of the following sorites. State each component syllogism in standard form. State the mood and figure of each syllogism and check the rules to see if it is valid. If the sorites is invalid, explain why.[3]

1. (1) All puddings are nice.
   (2) This dish is a pudding.
   (3) No nice things are wholesome.

2. (1) Every politician prevaricates from time to time.
   (2) Whoever deserves to be punished should not be elected to public office.
   (3) Any liar ought to be punished.

3. (1) My gardener is well worth listening to on military subjects.
   (2) No one can remember the battle of Waterloo unless he is very old.
   (3) Nobody is really worth listening to on military subjects unless he can remember the battle of Waterloo.

4. (1) General Schwartzkopf is a West Point graduate.
   (2) Navy officers aren't army officers.
   (3) Annapolis graduates are all navy officers.
   (4) Every West Point graduate serves as an officer in the army.

5. (1) Every book that I read this year was a mystery.
   (2) Any science fiction tome is interesting.
   (3) Ostafar Neumathesque wrote at least one book I read this year.
   (4) Some technical manuals aren't science fiction books.
   (5) Ostafar Neumathesque hasn't written any interesting books.

6. (1) All the human race except my footman have a certain amount of commonsense.
   (2) No one who lives on barley-sugar can be anything but a mere baby.

(3) None but a hopscotch player knows what real happiness is.

(4) No mere baby had a grain of common sense.

(5) No engine-driver ever plays hopscotch.

(6) No footman of mine is ignorant of what real happiness is.

Notes

1. Our discussion of propositional logic begins in Chapter 5. The Boolean interpretation of an **A** proposition takes it to assert that for any object *x*, if *x* is *S*, then *x* is *P*, that is, it interprets a universal proposition as a conditional proposition. In a conditional statement, if the antecedent, the if-cause, is false, the statement is true. Hence, in cases when the antecedent claims that *x* is a nonexistent object, such as a unicorn, the universal conditional is true.

2. Exercises 2, 3, and 6 are from Lewis Carroll, *Symbolic Logic and the Game of Logic* (New York: Dover Publications, 1958), pp. 112, 113, and 121.

3. Exercises 1, 3, and 6 are from Lewis Carroll, *Symbolic Logic and the Game of Logic,* pp. 113 and 122.

Chapter Five

Propositional Logic: Truth Tables

In the twentieth century, logicians have developed a means to analyze the relationships between simple propositions. They have also developed a symbolic machinery that allows them to represent the *form* of an argument. In this chapter and the next, we develop techniques for examining arguments in which simple propositions are the fundamental elements of a logical schema. This is commonly known as **propositional logic,** or sentential logic. We examine what is known as the truth-table technique for evaluating such arguments, as well as a variation on that technique known as "reverse truth tables."

5.1 The Symbolic Language

In this section we examine compound statements whose truth value is dependent on the truth or falsehood of the statements of which they are composed. A **compound statement** contains another statement as a component. Examples of compound statements include (1) "Either today is Tuesday or today is Thursday," (2) "If tomorrow is Monday or tomorrow is Wednesday, then I have to set my alarm clock tonight," and (3) "George believes that Hildegard enjoys singing in Wagnerian operas." The first statement contains the simple statements "Today is Tuesday" and "Today is Thursday." The second statement contains the simple statements "Tomorrow is Monday," "Tomorrow is Wednesday," and "I have to set my alarm clock tonight." The third statement contains the simple statement "Hildegard enjoys singing in Wagnerian operas." The first two compound statements differ from the third in an important way: The truth of the first two compound statements depends entirely on the truth or falsehood of its simple components. Such statements—where the truth is dependent on the truth value of its simple components—are known as **truth-functionally compound statements.** The truth value of the third compound statement, however, is independent of the truth value of its simple component. George might well believe that Hildegard enjoys singing in Wagnerian operas even if Hildegard enjoys singing only rock music or if she hates singing altogether. The third statement is **non-truth-functionally compound:** The truth of the whole is independent of the truth of its component statements.

In this section we develop an artificial language that is used to represent argument forms. A natural language, such as English, allows us to communicate information, express our emotions, arouse emotions in others, and so forth, but it is an awkward language in which to evaluate arguments. Since the validity of a deductive argument is a formal characteristic of the argument, the content of an argument of a particular form makes no difference to its validity. Further, given the emotional meanings of some words, some arguments can be persuasive even if their forms are invalid. Finally, since the content of the argument is irrelevant to the argument's validity, using a natural language is cumbersome.

In our artificial language, simple statements are abbreviated to a single letter. The uppercase letters, "A, B, C, D, . . .," represent statements. For example, the statement "Humberto is a student" might be abbreviated 'H'. In addition there is a set of statement variables represented by the lowercase letters, "*p, q, r, s,* . . .". Statement variables can be replaced by *any* statement, whether simple or compound, to form an argument. Finally, there are five truth-functional connectives, '~', '&', 'v', '→', and '↔'. These connectives are defined in such a way that the truth value of the compound statements formed by using them depends entirely on the truth values of the simple statements of which they are composed. Further, as we will see, there are various English expressions which correspond to the connectives and allow us to translate English sentences into symbols.

Negation is represented by the **tilde** ('~'). Placing a tilde in front of a statement changes a true statement into a false statement and a false statement into a true statement. We may define the tilde by means of a **truth table.** A truth table represents all logically possible truth values of a statement. Since the tilde is a one-place connective, its truth table has two rows: in the first row it assumes that a statement "p" is true, while in the second row it assumes that a statement "p" is false. If "p" is true, "~p" is false; if "p" is false, "~p" is true. The truth table looks like this:

p	~p
T	F
F	T

Conjunction is represented by the **ampersand** ('&'). A statement of the form "p & q" is true if and only if both "p" and "q" are true, otherwise it is false. The truth table for conjunction is:

p	q	p & q
T	T	T
T	F	F
F	T	F
F	F	F

The two statements composing a conjunction are known as **conjuncts.** The most common English word representing conjunction is 'and', although, as shown by the translation guide to follow, it is not the only word representing conjunction.

Disjunction is represented by the **wedge** or **vee** ('v'). A statement of the form "p v q" is true except when both "p" and "q" are false. The truth table for disjunction is:

p	q	p v q
T	T	T
T	F	T
F	T	T
F	F	F

The two statements composing a disjunction are known as **disjuncts.** The most common English word denoting disjunction is 'or'. The form of disjunction defined by the truth table above is known as weak or inclusive disjunction. It does *not* apply to cases in which the meaning of 'or' is "one or the other but not both," as when a menu says "soup or salad is included with lunch." There are two reasons why we define the wedge as weak disjunction. First, the English word 'or' is ambiguous—it can have either the weak or the strong meaning. Logicians cannot tolerate ambiguity, so they stipulate the meaning of the word. Second, if it is clear that a statement expresses strong disjunction—"*p* or *q* but not both *p* and *q*"—you can construct the relevant statement:

$$(p \lor q) \ \& \ {\sim}(p \ \& \ q).$$

Notice that in this statement the tilde ranges over the entire conjunction "*p* & *q*". The tilde *always* ranges over the entire statement to its right, whether that statement is simple or complex. As we will see shortly, parentheses are used to divide compound statements into their component parts.

Material implication is represented by the **single arrow** ('$\rightarrow$'). A statement of the form "*p* $\rightarrow$ *q*" is true except when "*p*" is true and "*q*" is false. The truth table for material implication is:

p	*q*	*p* $\rightarrow$ *q*
T	T	T
T	F	F
F	T	T
F	F	T

The most common English expression for material implication is "if . . . then . . .". This is known as a **conditional statement.** The statement following the 'if' is known as the **antecedent;** the statement following the 'then' is known as the **consequent.**

Many students find it puzzling that a conditional statement is true when its antecedent is false. If we consider an example, it will become clearer why this is so. Assume the state police have set up a speed trap along a certain stretch of highway. The posted speed limit is 55 miles per hour. Under those conditions, you would grant it is true that "If I drive through the speed trap at 100 m.p.h., then I'll get a ticket." The statement is true regardless of the speed at which I drive. Whether I drive through the speed trap at 89 m.p.h. and get a ticket or drive through at 50 and do not, you would still grant that had I driven through the speed trap at 100 m.p.h., I would have gotten a ticket. The only condition in which the statement would be false is if I cruised that stretch of highway at 100 m.p.h. and did not get a ticket—and were that to happen, you would probably explain why I did not get a ticket by suggesting that the speed trap was down.

Material equivalence is represented by the **double-arrow** (↔). A statement of material equivalence is true whenever the truth values of "*p*" and "*q*" are the same, otherwise it is false. The truth table for material equivalence is:

p	*q*	*p* ↔ *q*
T	T	T
T	F	F
F	T	F
F	F	T

The most common English expression for material equivalence is "if and only if."

Notice that the tilde is a one-place connective, whereas all the other connectives are two-place connectives. Because there are two-place connectives, we introduce a set of grouping-indicators. These are parentheses, and, to make groupings more easily visible in complex statements, square brackets ([]), and braces ({}). These are the punctuation marks of our artificial language. They allow us to unambiguously indicate the truth conditions of the sentence. For example, if you are given "It is not the case that both Herman and Brunhild are bootleggers," you will notice that this is the denial of the conjunction "Herman is a bootlegger and Brunhild is a bootlegger." Since the compound statement is denied, you express it as: ~(H & B). If you were given "Herman is not a bootlegger but Brunhild is a bootlegger," the symbolic translation would be: ~H & B. In this case the tilde ranges over only "Herman is a bootlegger." If you were given "If Herman is not a bootlegger then Brunhild is a bootlegger, and if Brunhild is a bootlegger then there is moonshine in Madrid," you have a conjunction of conditional statements. It is expressed as: (~H → B) & (B → M). When using two-place connectives, it is imperative that they be grouped by means of parentheses, square brackets, and braces: only such formulae are **well-formed formulae** (WFFs).

A formula is a well-formed formula in our language under the following conditions:

1. Any simple proposition is a WFF.
2. If the proposition *p* is a WFF, then so is ~*p*.

3. If *p* and *q* are WFFs, then so are the following:
   a. (*p* & *q*)
   b. (*p* v *q*)
   c. (*p* → *q*)
   d. (*p* ↔ *q*)
4. Nothing is a WFF unless its being so follows from 1–3.

Two more points should be noticed. First, the connectives are defined in terms of statement variables, and *the variables can be replaced by a statement of any degree of complexity.* For example, the statement "If Herman is a bootlegger, then both Brunhild and Siegfried are veterinarians" would be translated into symbols as: H → (B & S). Second, the tilde ranges over the statement (of whatever degree of complexity) that is immediately to its right. For example, the statement "It is not the case that if Herman makes moonshine then if Brunhild is a bootlegger then Siegfried kills dragons" is translated: ~[H → (B → S)]; the statement "If Herman does not make moonshine, then if Brunhild is a bootlegger then Siegfried kills dragons" is translated: ~H → (B → S).

Up to this point we have noted some of the words that are translated into connectives. Since we will devote a fair amount of effort to translating English sentences into symbols, the following translation guide might be useful.

Translation Guide for Propositional Logic

The following expressions are translated ~*p*:

not *p*
it is not the case that *p*

The following expressions are translated (*p* → *q*):

If *p*, then *q*.
P only if *q*.
Q, if *p*.
Q, given that *p*.
Q, provided that *p*.
Provided that *p*, *q*.
Q, on the condition that *p*.
P implies *q*.
P entails *q*.
Q is implied by *p*.

Q is entailed by *p*.
Q is a necessary condition for *p*.
P is a sufficient condition for *q*.[1]
Q in the event that *p*.
In the event that *p*, *q*.
Q in case [that] *p*.

The following expressions are translated (*p* & *q*):

P and *q*.
P but *q*.
P yet *q*.
P however *q*.
P inasmuch as *q*.
P although *q*.
Both *p* and *q*.
P though *q*.
P even though *q*.
P nevertheless *q*.

The following expressions are translated (*P* v *Q*):

P or *q*.
Either *p* or *q*.
P unless *q*.

The following expressions are translated (*P* ↔ *Q*):

P if and only if *q*.
P just in case [that] *q*.
P is a necessary and sufficient condition for *Q*.

The following expression can be translated as *either* (~*p* & ~*q*) *or*
~(*p* v *q*):

Neither *p* nor *q*.

Finally, logicians represent conclusion indicators such as 'therefore',
'hence', 'thus', and 'so' by the symbol: '/∴'.

EXERCISES

I. Each of the following is a truth-functionally compound statement. Using your knowledge of the topics, determine which of them is true.

1. If Paris is the capital of England, then Bill Clinton is the President of Russia.

2. Either Rhode Island was settled by thirteenth-century Vikings or the White House is in Washington, D.C.

3. Rhode Island was settled by thirteenth-century Vikings just in case ancient Rome was a province of Hungary.

4. If Paris is not the capital of England, then Tipper Gore is the Queen of Hungary.

5. Either Paris is the capital of France or aquavit is popular in Norway.

6. Although Des Moines is in Iowa, neither Paris nor Berlin is in France.

7. New York City is the capital of Bulgaria only if beer is popular in Munich.

8. Beer is popular in Munich if New York City is the capital of Bulgaria.

9. Abraham Lincoln was President of the United States on the condition that either Paris is in Germany or Moscow is in Sweden.

10. If London is in England and Rome is in Italy, then neither is Moscow in Russia nor is Stockholm in Sweden.

11. The Lone Ranger rides again on the condition that if the square root of four is two then two squared is sixteen.

12. If it is neither the case that Washington is the capital of Hungary nor the case that Honolulu is the capital of Wyoming, then either the moon is made of green cheese or mice eat alligators.

13. If Roanoke is in Virginia and Raleigh is in North Carolina, then either Miami is in Florida or New York City is in Texas.

14. If Roanoke is in Virginia and either the Republicans or the Democrats control the Senate, then the moon is made of green cheese if and only if the New York Yankees play their home games in Postville, Iowa.

15. Even though Abraham Lincoln was President of the United States just in case Rhode Island is in the Arctic circle, the Lone Ranger will ride again.

16. If Beethoven wrote classical rock 'n' roll on the condition that Mozart toured with the Grateful Dead, then Amsterdam is in Holland.

17. If Beethoven wrote classical rock 'n' roll provided that Mozart toured with the Grateful Dead, then Berlin is in China.

18. If Mozart wrote classical rock 'n' roll just in case Beethoven toured with the Grateful Dead, then either the Republicans or the Democrats control the House of Commons.

19. General Patton wore army boots and Admiral Nimitz commanded a ship, in case South Dakota is in New England.

20. If South Dakota is south of North Dakota, then either both General Patton and Admiral Nimitz were graduates of West Point or West Virginia is west of Virginia.

21. If the moon is made of green cheese but the sun is made of caramel, then children commonly walk through looking glasses unless fairy tales are always true.

22. London is in England, and although Berlin is in Germany, Paris is in France; unless the fact that Edinburgh is in Scotland implies that Dublin is in Norway.

23. If the facts that London is in England and Paris is in France imply that Berlin is in Germany, then we may safely infer that the fact that Warsaw is in Poland is a sufficient condition for claiming that Moscow is in Ethiopia.

24. If it is not the case that two is less than sixty-five, then unless General Patton wrote the "Moonlight" Sonata both North Dakota and South Dakota are south of Florida.

25. The fact that General Patton wrote the "Moonlight" Sonata is a necessary condition for holding that both Beethoven and Mozart wrote music for electric guitar; just in case Shakespeare is credited for writing plays or neither Winston Churchill nor Groucho Marx smoked cigars.

II. Determine the truth value of each of the following statements. Assume that the statements A, B, and C are true, and that the statements X, Y, and Z are false.

1. A & B
2. A → X
3. X → A
4. A v B
5. X → Y
6. (A → B) v X
7. (A & X) v B
8. (A v X) & Y
9. ~(A → B) & C
10. (X → Y) v (A → B)
11. (X → Y) & (A → ~B)
12. (X → A) & (A → X)
13. [(A → B) & (X → Y)] & C
14. [(A → X) & (X → A)] v X
15. [(A → B) v (X → Y)] v C
16. [(A → X) v (X → A)] & X
17. [(A & B) & (X → A)] ↔ (X v Y)
18. [(A & B) v (X → A)] ↔ (~X & Y)
19. [(A v X) & (B ↔ C)] → [(X & B) → X]
20. [(A v X) → (B ↔ C)] → ~[(X & B) → X]
21. [(A → X) v (X → Y)] ↔ [~(A & B) → X]
22. ~{[A & (B v X)] → [(X → Y) → Z]} ↔ [(X → A) ↔ ~C]
23. ~{[~(X v (Y & A)) v Z] → [X ↔ (Y v [(A & B) → ~Z])]}
24. ~{~[(X v (~Y & A)) v Z] ↔ [~X ↔ (Y v [(A v ~B) → ~Z])]}
25. {~[~(A & Z) → (B v X)] → [((A → Y) → Z) & A]} → [A & ~B]

III. Translate the following English sentences into symbols using the statement abbreviations suggested.

ONE, TWO, THREE . . . GROAN![2]

1. If Freddy Fish studies piano, then he's working on his scales. (P, S)

2. Either Henry lost the lottery or he's deep in the heart of taxes. (L, T)

3. Ben Franklin dropped his penny in his brother's bank on the condition that he said, "A penny saved was a penny erred." (D, S)

4. George is a traveling salesman, yet he works for The Stationery Store. (G, W)

5. If Sir Galahad did not inherit Lancelot's horse Betsy, then he did not have a knight's mare. (G, K)

6. If Marie Antoinette was County Rattlesnake Queen, then either Louis paid her court or she said, "Let them eat snake!" (M, L, S)

7. The Bourbons are returning to power in France on the condition that either Mr. Daniel or his old granddad is in Paris. (B, D, G)

8. Henry Rooster will drive Ms. Maizy crazy, only if he commits a foul in the asylum's ball game or he likes to play chicken. (H, F, P)

9. George Waist will neither wed nor join the Boy Scouts provided that his motto is "Waist not want knot." (W, J, M)

10. Even though Felisha Fish is an accomplished pianist, she still works on her scales. (F, S)

11. If either George is losing weight or Brutus is a bit heavy, then Henry will say, "Diet too, Brutus?" (G, B, H)

12. St. Mort's Academy is a boy's school, just in case dissecting frogs is forbidden or the boys do not take classes with girls who wear glasses. (S, D, C)

13. It is neither the case that Henry is shopping for a new computer only if his old computer has a terminal disease, nor is it the case that Copenhagen is a small village on the condition that Hamlet is the Prince of Denmark. (N, O, C, H)

14. Patrick O'Leary has a head cold and Angus McTavish is wearing his kilt; if and only if Patrick is singing "My Wild Irish Nose" unless Angus is expecting to be drafted. (C, K, S, D)

15. If the fact that Angus McTavish is drafted entails that he is wearing his kilt, then it is not the case that he's breathing Londonderry air unless he's floating on Danny's buoy. (D, K, B, F)

16. If Freddy Fly is in the woods, then either he's not the Fly who came in from the cold, or Freddy's a nut just in case he's feeling squirrelly. (W, F, N, S)

17. Searching for a new home is a sufficient condition for taking a site-seeing bus, provided that the realtor has a van or one is looking for a house in Beverly Hills. (S, T, R, B)

18. One works for a religious organization just in case either the retirement program is out of this world or the pay is not high; but one is not an idol only if one has a business. (W, R, P, I, B)

19. Although Gustav owns a tavern and both Fred Omlisted and Henry Easinough work for Interstate Mining Company, neither Omlisted nor Easinough can purchase beer at Gustav's tavern. (G, F, H, O, E)

20. The fact that Rhonda curries favor or Alice favors curry is a necessary condition for Elise Cinnamon to propose a toast, in case thyme is not the stuff of which life is made or pepper is not the spice of life. (R, A, E, T, P)

21. If George is a buildings demolition expert, then he is an eavesdropper unless either George has the demolition contract on Autumn Leaves Apartments or it is not the case that pushing George's plunger implies that Autumn Leaves starts to fall. (D, E, C, P, A)

22. Kirk is on his guard and Ayn will have another stein of beer, given that Russ will sell his car; even though the fact that soccer is a tease can be inferred from the fact that one should seat D. Horse before D. Cart. (K, A, R, S, H)

23. It is not the case that either John French fries fish or Henry Fry fishes French out of the pond; and even though George Foot is corny, Dan Ox will not ford the stream or Phil Smith came to the bridge. (J, H, G, D, P)

24. Henry Hare will give his finacée a one-karat ring or Alice Clock will beat Gertrude Time in a game of chess, only if either a major paleontological discovery near Lake Mead implies that Francesca is working on the dino-shore or the king is a real card just in case the queen carries the day in spades. (H, A, D, F, K, Q)

25. The orchestra made a concerted effort to play Ives's Second Symphony and Frederica carried a torch for the Olympians,

in case either the fact that William shakes his spear implies that Eugene O. kneels or the queen did not serve bran flakes even though Jack was a regular fellow. (O, F, W, E, Q, J)

5.2 *Arguments and Truth Tables*

In the previous section we used truth tables to define the connectives used in propositional logic. In this section we examine the truth-table technique for determining whether an argument is valid. Recall that an argument is valid so long as it is impossible for all of its premises to be true and its conclusion false. A truth table allows us systematically to exhibit all possible combinations of truth values of the statements constituting an argument and thereby to determine whether there is any case in which all the premises are true and the conclusion false. If there is a row in which all the premises are true and the conclusion is false, the argument is invalid; otherwise the argument is valid.

Since a truth table must exhibit all possible combinations of truth values for the statements in an argument, it is imperative that we construct truth tables in a systematic way. This is easily done. For any argument, begin by noticing the number of different simple statements in the argument. If there is one simple statement, the truth table will have two rows. If there are two simple statements, the truth table will have four rows. If there are three simple statements, the truth table will have eight rows. If there are four simple statements, there will be sixteen rows, and so forth. We begin by constructing **guide columns** that specify the truth values of each of the different simple statements in the argument. In each of these columns, the simple statement will be assumed to be true half the time and false half the time. Assign truth values according to the following scheme: Starting with the first (farthest-left) column, write 'T' in each consecutive row until you have filled in half the rows in the table, then write 'F' in the remaining rows. In the second column, vary the truth value twice as often as in the first. In the third column, vary the truth value twice as often as in the second column, and so forth until you come to the last (farthest-right) guide column, in which the truth value varies every other row. For example, in a four-row truth table, the truth values vary every two rows in the first guide column, and every other row in the second guide column. In an eight-row truth table, the truth values vary every four rows in the first guide column, every two rows in the second guide column, and every other row in the third guide column. In a sixteen-row truth table, the truth value will vary every eight rows, every four rows, every two rows, and every other row, and so on for larger tables. Once the guide columns for the truth table are completed, you should have something like these:

p	q
T	T
T	F
F	T
F	F

p	q	r
T	T	T
T	T	F
T	F	T
T	F	F
F	T	T
F	T	F
F	F	T
F	F	F

p	q	r	s
T	T	T	T
T	T	T	F
T	T	F	T
T	T	F	F
T	F	T	T
T	F	T	F
T	F	F	T
T	F	F	F
F	T	T	T
F	T	T	F
F	T	F	T
F	T	F	F
F	F	T	T
F	F	T	F
F	F	F	T
F	F	F	F

Proceeding to the right, we construct a column for the premises and conclusion of our argument. If some of the premises are themselves complex statements, we must construct a column for each of the compound statements in the premises. When we have done this, if there are no rows in which all the premises are true and the conclusion false, the argument is valid; if there is at least one row in which all the premises are true and the conclusion is false, the argument is invalid. To see how this works, let us consider some examples.

Assume we are given an argument of the following form:

$$p \to q$$
$$\sim p \quad /\therefore \sim q$$

We begin by determining the number of rows in the truth table. Since there are two different simple statements, there are four rows in the truth table. We construct the guide columns for "p" and "q" by varying the truth value of "p" every two rows and varying the truth value of "*q*" every other row. The guide columns for the truth table will look like this:

p	*q*	
T	T	
T	F	
F	T	
F	F	

Next we construct a column for each of the premises and the conclusion by appealing to the definitions of the several connectives:

p	*q*	*p* → *q*	~*p*	~*q*
T	T	T	F	F
T	F	F	F	T
F	T	T	T	F
F	F	T	T	T

Finally, we look at the column for the conclusion and check every row in which the conclusion is false to determine whether there is a row in which all the premises are true. The conclusion is false in rows one and three. In row one the second premise is false, so that row will *not* show that the argument is invalid. In row three, however, both premises are true and the conclusion is false. That row shows that the argument is *invalid.* We circle the row showing that the argument is invalid and write down our judgment:

p	*q*	*p* → *q*	~*p*	~*q*	
T	T	T	F	F	
T	F	F	F	T	
F	T	T	T	F	INVALID
F	F	T	T	T	

The same procedure is followed when there are more than two simple statements in an argument, although the truth table will be more complex. Consider the following argument form:

$$p \rightarrow q$$
$$q \rightarrow r \qquad /\therefore p \rightarrow r$$

Here there are three different simple statements. So there are eight rows in the truth table, and we vary the truth value of "p" every four rows, the truth value of "q" every two rows, and the truth value of "r" in every row in our guide columns. The guide columns look like this:

p	q	r	
T	T	T	
T	T	F	
T	F	T	
T	F	F	
F	T	T	
F	T	F	
F	F	T	
F	F	F	

Next we construct a column for each of the premises and the conclusion of the argument:

p	q	r	$p \rightarrow q$	$q \rightarrow r$	$p \rightarrow r$
T	T	T	T	T	T
T	T	F	T	F	F
T	F	T	F	T	T
T	F	F	F	T	F
F	T	T	T	T	T
F	T	F	T	F	T
F	F	T	T	T	T
F	F	F	T	T	T

Now we examine each of the rows in which the conclusion is false, namely, rows two and four. In each of these rows at least one of the premises is false: in row two the second premise is false, in row four the first premise is false. Hence, there are no rows in which *both* premises are true and the conclusion is false. The argument is valid.

The procedure is the same when the premises or conclusion are more complex than in the arguments we have been considering except that we must include a column for each of the compound statements in the argument. We must take the statements apart, determine the truth values of their components, and put them back together to determine the truth values of the entire complex statement. Consider the following argument form:

$p \rightarrow (q \lor {\sim}r)$
$({\sim}r \mathbin{\&} q)$ $/\therefore$ ${\sim}q \rightarrow {\sim}p$

Since there are three different simple statements in the argument, we begin with an eight-row truth table:

p	q	r	
T	T	T	
T	T	F	
T	F	T	
T	F	F	
F	T	T	
F	T	F	
F	F	T	
F	F	F	

Since the first premise is complex, we must break it down into its simpler components to determine the truth value of the statement as a whole. To determine the truth value of "$p \rightarrow (q \lor {\sim}r)$," we must first determine the truth value of "$q \lor {\sim}r$," and to determine the truth value of "$q \lor {\sim}r$," we must first determine the truth value of "${\sim}r$." So we begin by adding a column for "${\sim}r$":

p	q	r	~r
T	T	T	F
T	T	F	T
T	F	T	F
T	F	F	T
F	T	T	F
F	T	F	T
F	F	T	F
F	F	F	T

Next, appealing to the columns for "*q*" and "*~r*," we add a column for "*q* ∨ *~r*":

p	q	r	~r	q ∨ ~r
T	T	T	F	T
T	T	F	T	T
T	F	T	F	F
T	F	F	T	T
F	T	T	F	T
F	T	F	T	T
F	F	T	F	F
F	F	F	T	T

Once this is done, we can construct a column for the entire statement "*p* → (*q* ∨ *~r*)":

p	q	r	~r	q ∨ ~r	p → (q ∨ ~r)
T	T	T	F	T	T
T	T	F	T	T	T
T	F	T	F	F	F
T	F	F	T	T	T
F	T	T	F	T	T
F	T	F	T	T	T
F	F	T	F	F	T
F	F	F	T	T	T

Next we proceed to the second premise, using the column for "~r" together with the guide column for "q":

p	q	r	~r	q ∨ ~r	p → (q ∨ ~r)	~r & q
T	T	T	F	T	T	F
T	T	F	T	T	T	T
T	F	T	F	F	F	F
T	F	F	T	T	T	F
F	T	T	F	T	T	F
F	T	F	T	T	T	T
F	F	T	F	F	T	F
F	F	F	T	T	T	F

Finally, we construct a column for the conclusion by first constructing columns for "~q" and "~p":

p	q	r	~r	q ∨ ~r	p → (q ∨ ~r)	~r & q	~q	~p	~q → ~p
T	T	T	F	T	T	F	F	F	T
T	T	F	T	T	T	T	F	F	T
T	F	T	F	F	F	F	T	F	F
T	F	F	T	T	T	F	T	F	F
F	T	T	F	T	T	F	F	T	T
F	T	F	T	T	T	T	F	T	T
F	F	T	F	F	T	F	T	T	T
F	F	F	T	T	T	F	T	T	T

In judging the validity of the argument we look *only* at the columns for the premises and the conclusion—in this case, the third, fourth, and seventh columns to the right of the guide columns. The conclusion is false only in rows three and four, and in both of those rows at least one of the premises is also false. Therefore the argument is valid.

EXERCISES

I. Construct a truth table for each of the following argument forms. Indicate whether each form is valid. If the argument is invalid, circle the row or rows that show it is invalid.

  1. *p* /∴ (*p* ∨ *q*)
  2. *p* /∴ (*p* & *q*)

3. p
   q /∴ $(p \lor q)$

4. p
   q /∴ $(p \& q)$

5. $p \rightarrow q$
   q /∴ p

6. $p \rightarrow q$
   p /∴ q

7. $p \rightarrow q$
   $\sim q$ /∴ $\sim p$

8. $p \rightarrow q$
   $\sim p \& \sim q$ /∴ $(p \lor q)$

9. $p \lor q$
   $\sim p$ /∴ $\sim q$

10. $p \& q$ /∴ p

11. $p \& q$ /∴ q

12. $p \rightarrow q$
    $q \rightarrow r$ /∴ $(\sim r \rightarrow \sim p)$

13. $p \rightarrow q$
    $p \rightarrow r$ /∴ $(q \rightarrow r)$

14. $(p \rightarrow q) \& (r \rightarrow s)$
    $p \lor r$ /∴ $q \lor s$

15. $(p \rightarrow q) \& (r \rightarrow s)$
    $p \rightarrow s$ /∴ $(\sim q \lor s)$

16. $(p \rightarrow q) \& (r \rightarrow s)$
    $\sim p \lor \sim r$ /∴ $(\sim q \lor \sim s)$

17. $(p \rightarrow q) \& (r \rightarrow s)$
    $\sim q \lor \sim s$ /∴ $(\sim p \lor \sim r)$

18. $(p \& q) \rightarrow (r \lor s)$
    $p \lor r$ /∴ $(q \lor s)$

19. $(p \rightarrow q) \rightarrow (r \rightarrow s)$
    $\sim p \lor q$ /∴ $(\sim r \lor s)$

20. $(p \& q) \leftrightarrow (r \lor s)$
    $(p \& q) \rightarrow t$
    $r \lor s$ /∴ t

II. Translate and construct a truth table for each of the following arguments using the statement abbreviations suggested for each.

Indicate whether the argument is valid. If the argument is invalid, circle the row or rows that show that it is invalid.

SOAPS!

1. If soap operas are not comedies, then the author of this book is not a soap opera addict. The author of this book is not a soap opera addict. So soap operas are not comedies. (S, A)

2. If soap operas are operas, then many bedroom scenes are sung by sopranos. Either soap operas are not operas or many bedroom scenes are not sung by sopranos. So soap operas are not operas. (S, B)

3. If a soap opera is based on Plato's *Opera,* then Socrates is up to his knees in suds. If a soap opera is based on Plato's *Opera* and Socrates is up to his knees is suds, then Socrates is up to his knees in suds. So Socrates is up to his knees in suds. (P, S)

4. Either soap operas are not based on Plato's *Opera* or the bedroom scenes are sung by a Greek chorus. The bedroom scenes are not sung by a Greek chorus. So soap operas are not based on Plato's *Opera.* (S, B)

5. If this soap opera is sponsored by a detergent company, then either Sophie's proctor spends his evenings gambling, or Sophie will leave her brother's house for a trip to the Riviera. But Sophie will not leave her brother's house for a trip to the Riviera. So Sophie's proctor spends his evenings gambling unless this soap opera is not sponsored by a detergent company. (S, P, L)

6. If Sophie makes only a cameo appearance in this soap opera, then her brother will leave her $2,000 in his will. If Sophie's brother leaves her $2,000 in his will but she does not make only a cameo appearance in this soap opera, then she will be seen in the next episode living near an Irish spring. But Sophie will not be seen in the next episode living near an Irish spring. So Sophie's brother will not leave her $2,000 in his will. (C, B, I)

7. If Sophie is guilty of robbing her butcher's freezer, then the incident will be known as the Coldgate Scandal. If Sophie is guilty of robbing her butcher's freezer, then she will be seen eating olives under a palm tree. So if Sophie will be seen

eating olives under a palm tree, then the incident will be known as the Coldgate Scandal. (S, C, P)

8. If Sophie is not involved in the Coldgate Scandal, then her brother will leave her $2,000 in his will. If Sophie is not involved in the Coldgate Scandal, her proctor will teach her how to gamble. So if Sophie is not involved in the Coldgate Scandal, then either her brother will leave her $2,000 in his will or her proctor will teacher her how to gamble. (C, B, P)

9. If Sophie is not involved in the Coldgate Scandal, then her brother will leave her $2,000 in his will. If Sophie is not involved in the Coldgate Scandal, her proctor will teach her how to gamble. So if Sophie is not involved in the Coldgate Scandal, then her brother will leave her $2,000 in his will and her proctor will teacher her how to gamble. (C, B, P)

10. Sophie vacations on the Ivory Coast and her heart is filled with joy. If Sophie's heart is filled with joy, then she will dash about the beach. If Sophie vacations on the Ivory Coast, she will dash about the beach. Therefore, Sophie will dash about the beach. (I, J, D)

11. If Sophie is a principal character in this soap opera, then she has a real zest for life. If Sophie has a real zest for life but she needs a life buoy when she goes swimming, you certainly will not want to change the dial on your television. So if you want to change the dial on your television, either Sophie is not a principal character in this soap opera or she does not need a life buoy when she goes swimming. (S, Z, L, D)

12. If Sophie's proctor does not spend his evenings gambling, Sophie will leave her brother's house for a trip to the Riviera. If Sophie leaves her brother's house for a trip to the Riviera, then she's either going to France or to her local Buick dealer. But Sophie's proctor does spend his evenings gambling and Sophie is not going to her local Buick dealer. So Sophie is going to France. (P, L, F, B)

13. Sophie will leave her brother's house and develop a real zest for life, just in case she either drives a twenty-mule team through Death Valley or makes a mad dash for the border. Sophie makes a mad dash for the border but does not develop a zest for life. So if she drives a twenty-mule team through Death Valley, she will leave her brother's house. (B, Z, T, D)

14. Sophie will leave her brother's house and develop a real zest for life, just in case she drives a twenty-mule team through Death Valley and makes a mad dash for the border. Sophie makes a mad dash for the border unless she does not develop a zest for life. So she will not drive a twenty-mule team through Death Valley unless she will leave her brother's house. (B, Z, T, D)

15. Sophie will leave her brother's house and be found splashing in the tide only if she wins the Super-Dooper Sweepstakes or sets up a tidy little house of her own. If Sophie sets up a tidy little house of her own, then she will be found splashing in the tide; and if she wins the Super-Dooper Sweepstakes, she will leave her brother's house. So Sophie will leave her brother's house and be found splashing in the tide if and only if she wins the Super-Dooper Sweepstakes or sets up a tidy little house of her own. (L, T, S, H)

16. If Sophie sets up a tidy little house of her own and her doctor lives on the shoals of Lake Walawalawap, then if Sophie is found floating facedown in the tide then her doctor will dash her to the hospital. So, if Sophie's doctor does not live on the shoals of Lake Walawalawap but he does dash her to the hospital, then either Sophie was not found floating facedown in the tide or she has not set up a tidy little house of her own. (T, L, F, D)

17. Sophie sets up a tidy little house of her own or her doctor lives on the shoals of Lake Walawalawap, only if Sophie is found floating facedown in the tide on the condition that her doctor will dash her to the hospital. So, if Sophie's doctor does not live on the shoals of Lake Walawalawap but he does dash her to the hospital, then neither was Sophie found floating facedown in the tide nor has she set up a tidy little house of her own. (T, L, F, D)

18. Sophie does not make a cameo appearance in this soap opera nor does her doctor live on the shoals of Lake Walawalawap, even though she has a zest for life only if her doctor lives on the shoals of Lake Walawalawap. If Sophie does not have a zest for life, then her body will be found floating in the tide and her part will be written out of the script. Therefore, if Sophie does not make a cameo appearance in this soap opera, her part will be written out of the script. (C, D, Z, T, P)

19. Sophie makes a cameo appearance in this soap opera but her doctor does not live on the shoals of Lake Walawalawap. So-

phie has a zest for life just in case her doctor lives on the shoals of Lake Walawalawap. If Sophie does not have a zest for life, then her body will be found floating in the tide. Therefore, if Sophie does not make a cameo appearance in this soap opera, her part will be written out of the script. (C, D, Z, T, P)

20. If Sophie's body is found floating in the tide, then either she will be written out of the script or her ghost will make an occasional appearance. If her ghost makes an occasional appearance, then the doctor will lose his mind or the soap opera will be replaced by a game show. If the soap opera will not be replaced by a game show, then Sophie will not be written out of the script. The soap opera will not be replaced by a game show. So if the doctor will not lose his mind, Sophie's body will not be found floating in the tide. (B, W, G, D, S)

5.3 *Tautology, Contradiction, Contingency, and Logical Equivalence*

The truth value of most propositions depends upon whether or not they correspond to the world. Such propositions are called **contingent propositions**. The proposition "It is raining" is contingent: it is true when it is raining, otherwise it is false. All simple propositions are contingent.

There are some compound propositions, however, that are true or false in virtue of their statement forms. A statement that is true solely in virtue of its form is known as a **tautology** or **tautological statement**. The statement "It is raining or it is not raining" is an example of a tautology. A statement that is false solely in virtue of its form is known as a **contradiction** or **self-contradictory statement**. The statement "It is raining and it is not raining" is an example of a contradiction.

You can determine whether a statement is a tautology, a contradiction, or a contingent statement on the basis of truth tables. If you construct a truth table for the form of a statement and every row in the column for that statement form contains a 'T', the proposition is a tautology. If you construct a truth table for the form of a statement and every row in the column for that propositional form contains an 'F', the proposition is a contradiction. If you construct a truth table for the form of a statement and some rows in the column for that propositional form contain a 'T' but others contain an 'F', the propositional form is contingent. Let us look at some examples.

Consider the proposition, "Either it's raining or it's not raining." The form of the statement is "*p* ∨ *-p*." So we construct a truth table for the statement form:

p	*-p*	*p* ∨ *-p*
T	F	T
F	T	T

Since the column for the form "*p* ∨ *-p*" is true in every instance, the statement form is tautologous.

Now consider the statement "It is raining but it's not raining," a statement whose form is "*p* & *-p*." We construct a truth table for the statement form:

p	*-p*	*p* & *-p*
T	F	F
F	T	F

Since the column for "*p* & *-p*" is false in every instance, the statement form is self-contradictory.

Finally, consider a statement of the form "*p* ↔ (*- q* ∨ *r*)." Again we construct a truth table:

p	*q*	*r*	*-q*	*q* ∨ *r*	*p* ↔ (*- q* ∨ *r*)
T	T	T	F	T	T
T	T	F	F	F	F
T	F	T	T	T	T
T	F	F	T	T	T
F	T	T	F	T	F
F	T	F	F	F	T
F	F	T	T	T	F
F	F	F	T	T	F

Since the column for "*p* ↔ (*- q* ∨ *r*)" is true in some rows and false in others, the statement form is contingent.

Let us try one more. Consider the statement form, "$p \to (\sim q \lor p)$."
Is it a tautology, a contingent statement, or a contradiction? Constructing a truth table will tell us.

p	q	$\sim q$	$\sim q \lor p$	$p \to (\sim q \lor p)$
T	T	F	T	T
T	F	T	T	T
F	T	F	F	T
F	F	T	T	T

Since every row in the column for "$p \to (\sim q \lor p)$" is marked 'T', the
statement form is tautologous.

There is a special case we should mention. If a statement of
material equivalence is a tautology, the two statement forms joined by
the double arrow are **logically equivalent**. Two statement forms are
logically equivalent if they express the same proposition, that is, if they
are true under exactly the same conditions. This is precisely what is
shown when we show that a statement of material equivalence is a
tautology. So to show that "$p \to q$" is logically equivalent to "$\sim p \lor q$,"
we construct a truth table for "$(p \to q) \leftrightarrow (\sim p \lor q)$":

p	q	$p \to q$	$\sim p$	$\sim p \lor q$	$(p \to q) \leftrightarrow (\sim p \lor q)$
T	T	T	F	T	T
T	F	F	F	F	T
F	T	T	T	T	T
F	F	T	F	T	T

EXERCISES

I. Use truth tables to determine whether the following statement
   forms are tautologies, contradictions, or contingent statements.

1. $p \to p$
2. $\sim p \to p$
3. $\sim(p \to p)$
4. $p \lor (\sim p \,\&\, q)$
5. $(p \,\&\, q) \lor (\sim p \,\&\, \sim q)$
6. $(p \to q) \,\&\, (q \to p)$
7. $p \leftrightarrow (q \lor r)$
8. $(p \lor \sim q) \lor (q \lor \sim r)$
9. $(p \,\&\, \sim q) \to (q \to \sim r)$
10. $(p \to q) \to [(q \to r) \to (p \to r)]$

II. Use truth tables to determine which of the following are statements of logical equivalence.

1. $(p \& q) \leftrightarrow (q \& p)$
2. $(p \rightarrow q) \leftrightarrow (q \rightarrow p)$
3. $\sim (p \lor q) \leftrightarrow (\sim p \& \sim q)$
4. $\sim (p \& q) \leftrightarrow (p \rightarrow \sim q)$
5. $(p \leftrightarrow q) \leftrightarrow [(p \& q) \lor (\sim p \& \sim q)]$
6. $(p \leftrightarrow q) \leftrightarrow [(p \rightarrow q) \lor (q \rightarrow p)]$
7. $(p \leftrightarrow q) \leftrightarrow [(p \rightarrow q) \& (\sim p \rightarrow \sim q)]$
8. $[p \& (q \lor r)] \leftrightarrow [(p \& q) \lor (p \& r)]$
9. $[p \lor (q \& r)] \leftrightarrow [(p \lor q) \& (\sim p \rightarrow r)]$
10. $[(p \& q) \lor (p \& r)] \leftrightarrow [(p \lor \sim p) \& (q \lor r)]$

5.4 Incomplete Truth Tables and Other Shortcuts

Once you have worked with truth tables for a time, you may notice that there are various shortcuts you could take and still use a truth table to determine whether an argument is valid. One of these has to do with the deconstruction of complex statements. In the previous sections, if we were given a complex statement such as "$\sim\{p \rightarrow [q \& (r \lor p)]\}$," we wrote "$r \lor p$," "$q \& (r \lor p)$," "$p \rightarrow [q \& (r \lor p)]$," and "$\sim\{p \rightarrow [q \& (r \lor p)]\}$" at the top of our truth table, and wrote a column of truth values under each. Since you have to know the truth values of each of the component propositions to determine the truth value of the proposition you are given, you cannot avoid a proliferation of columns. Nonetheless, you could write the complex proposition once and write the truth values of each component under the relevant connective. Further, since you use some of the columns *only* to determine the truth value of the complex statement, why not cross them out when you are done with them so you do not accidentally assume they must be taken into account in deciding whether or not the argument you are considering is valid? If you follow this procedure, the truth table for "$\sim\{p \rightarrow [q \& (r \lor p)]\}$" will look like this:

p	q	r	~{ p	→	[q	&	(r	v	p)]}

p	q	r	~{ p → [q & (r v p)]}
T	T	T	F T T T
T	T	F	F T T T
T	F	T	T F F T
T	F	F	T F F T
F	T	T	F T T T
F	T	F	F T F F
F	F	T	F T F T
F	F	F	F T F F

This procedure still gives you a complete truth table, but it saves paper and time and decreases the probability that you will miscopy a statement.

Even the columns-under-the-connective approach gives you more than you need. In determining the validity of an argument, not all rows are of equal importance. The only rows that make a difference are those in which the conclusion is false. What we call an **incomplete truth table** completes the column for the conclusion and only those rows in which the conclusion is false. Assume you are given the following argument form:

$p \rightarrow q$
$\sim p$ /∴ $\sim q$

Begin by constructing the guide columns for the argument form and the column for the conclusion:

p	q	$p \rightarrow q$	$\sim p$	$\sim q$
T	T			F
T	F			T
F	T			F
F	F			T

The only rows that make a difference for your judgment of validity are rows one and three. So focus on those two rows, fill in the truth values for the premises, and then judge the validity of the argument:

p	q		$p \rightarrow q$	~p	~q
T	T		T	F	F
T	F				T
F	T		T	T	F
F	F				T

Line three has two true premises and a false conclusion, so the argument is invalid.

But—as long as we make no mistakes—even this is more than we need. Let us take it as a convention when doing incomplete truth tables that you start with the conclusion and work "backward" through the premises, that is, you go from right to left as presented on the truth table and start with the top row and work down. If in any row of the truth table there is *one* false premise, that row cannot show that the argument is invalid. So, if at any point you discover that a premise in the row is false, skip the other premises in that row and go on to another row. If you find a row in which all the premises are true and the conclusion is false, you are done: that row shows that the argument is invalid. So, your incomplete truth table for the argument

$(p \ \& \ q) \rightarrow \text{~}r$
$q \leftrightarrow r \quad / \therefore \quad \text{~}(p \lor r)$

looks like this:

p	q	r		$(p \ \& \ q) \rightarrow \text{~}r$		$q \leftrightarrow r$	~$(p \lor r)$
T	T	T		T F F		T	F T
T	T	F				F	F T
T	F	T				F	F T
T	F	F		F T T		T	F T
F	T	T					F T
F	T	F					T F
F	F	T					F T
F	F	F					T F

EXERCISES

Construct an incomplete truth table for each of the following argument forms.

1. $p \rightarrow q$
   $\sim p$ /∴ $\sim q$

2. $p \rightarrow \sim q$
   q /∴ $\sim p$

3. $\sim p \leftrightarrow q$
   $\sim q$ & $(p \vee \sim p)$ /∴ q

4. $p \vee \sim p$ /∴ q & $(p$ & $q)$

5. p & $\sim p$ /∴ q

6. $p \vee q$
   $\sim q$ /∴ $\sim p$

7. p & $\sim q$
   $\sim p$ /∴ r

8. $p \rightarrow (q \vee \sim r)$
   $\sim q$ /∴ $p \rightarrow \sim r$

9. $p \leftrightarrow (q \vee \sim r)$
   $\sim q$ /∴ $p \rightarrow \sim r$

10. p & $\sim(q \vee r)$
    $r \leftrightarrow \sim p$ /∴ $\sim q$

11. p
    $p \rightarrow (q$ & $\sim r)$ /∴ r

12. $(p$ & $\sim r) \rightarrow (q \leftrightarrow r)$
    $p \vee q$ /∴ $\sim(\sim r \leftrightarrow \sim p)$

13. p & $([q \vee r] \rightarrow s)$
    $\sim s \vee \sim p$ /∴ $\sim q$ & $\sim r$

14. $(p$ & $[q \vee r]) \rightarrow s$
    $\sim s \vee \sim p$ /∴ $\sim q$ & $\sim r$

15. $(p$ & $[q \vee r]) \rightarrow s$
    $\sim s$ & $\sim p$ /∴ $\sim q \vee \sim r$

16. $(p$ & $[q \vee r]) \rightarrow (s$ & $\sim p)$
    $\sim p \leftrightarrow (\sim r \rightarrow q)$ /∴ $\sim s$

17. $(p$ & $\sim[q \vee r]) \rightarrow (s \rightarrow \sim p)$
    p & $\sim q$ /∴ $\sim s$

18. $(\sim p$ & $\sim[q \vee \sim r]) \rightarrow s$
    $\sim s$ & $\sim p$ /∴ $q \vee r$

19. $p \leftrightarrow (r \lor \sim s)$
$q \;\&\; \sim r$
$s \; / \therefore \sim q$

20. $p \rightarrow (r \lor \sim s)$
$\sim q \;\&\; r$
$s \; / \therefore \sim q \lor r$

21. $\sim p \rightarrow (r \;\&\; \sim s)$
$\sim q \leftrightarrow r$
$s \lor \sim r \; / \therefore \sim q \;\&\; p$

22. $\sim p \rightarrow (r \;\&\; \sim s)$
$\sim (q \leftrightarrow r)$
$s \;\&\; \sim r \; / \therefore \sim (q \;\&\; \sim s)$

23. $\sim p \rightarrow (r \;\&\; \sim s)$
$\sim (q \leftrightarrow r)$
$s \;\&\; r \; / \therefore \sim (q \leftrightarrow \sim q)$

24. $(p \;\&\; [q \lor r]) \leftrightarrow (s \rightarrow t)$
$\sim t \rightarrow (r \lor \sim s)$
$(p \lor \sim q) \rightarrow \sim r \; / \therefore \sim q \rightarrow s$

25. $[(p \lor q) \;\&\; (r \lor s)] \rightarrow (t \;\&\; \sim p)$
$(q \;\&\; \sim r) \rightarrow (t \;\&\; s) \; / \therefore (q \;\&\; s) \rightarrow (\sim t \lor r)$

5.5 Reverse Truth Tables

When arguments become complex, the truth-table technique for testing validity becomes tedious. If you could construct one line that shows it is possible for all the premises to be true and the conclusion false, that would be sufficient to show that the argument is invalid. This is the strategy behind the reverse truth-table technique.

Consider the argument form:

$p \rightarrow q$
$\sim p \quad / \therefore \quad \sim q$

If you constructed a complete truth table, one row would show that this argument form is invalid. In constructing a **reverse truth table,** you construct only that one row. You begin with an assumption. *Assume* that all the premises are true and the conclusion is false, then assign truth values to the components in an attempt to show that your assumption is correct. Start with the conclusion and assign truth values to its components in such a way that the conclusion is false. In this case, "q" is true, and "$\sim q$" is false:

$$p \to q \qquad \sim p \qquad / \therefore \sim q$$
$$ \text{T}$$
$$ \text{F}$$

Next, go to the premises and assign the *same* truth values to the component propositions in the premises that you have already assigned to those propositions in the conclusion. Since "q" was true in the conclusion, "q" must be true in the premises:

$$p \to q \qquad \sim p \qquad / \therefore \sim q$$
$$ \text{T} \text{T}$$
$$ \text{F}$$

Finally, you assign truth values to the remaining components of the premises in such a way that all the premises are true. Here it is easy. Since "$\sim p$" is true only if "p" is false, you assign falsehood to "p":

$$\text{T} \qquad\quad \text{T} \qquad\quad \text{F}$$
$$p \to q \qquad \sim p \qquad / \therefore \sim q$$
$$\text{F} \quad \text{T} \qquad \text{F} \qquad\quad \text{T}$$
$$\phantom{\text{F} \quad \text{T} \qquad} \text{T} \qquad\quad \text{F}$$

Given that "q" is true and "p" is false, "$p \to q$" is true:

$$p \to q \qquad \sim p \qquad / \therefore \sim q$$
$$\text{F} \quad \text{T} \qquad \text{F} \qquad\quad \text{T}$$
$$\phantom{\text{F}} \text{T} \qquad\quad \text{T} \qquad\quad \text{F}$$

The argument is invalid: you have shown that all the premises are true and the conclusion is false.

This technique also will allow you to prove that an argument form is valid; *but if more than one assignment of truth values will make the conclusion false, you will have to try each combination.* Again, *assume the argument is invalid.* Assign truth values to the conclusion so that the conclusion is false. Attempt to *consistently* assign truth values to the component statements in the premises so that the premises are all true. If the argument is *valid,* it will be impossible to consistently assign truth values in such a way that all the premises are true and the conclusion is false. As an illustration, let us consider the argument form known as *modus ponens:*

$$p \rightarrow q$$
$$p \quad /\therefore \quad q$$

Assume the conclusion is false:

$$p \rightarrow q \quad\quad p \quad\quad /\therefore q$$
$$ F$$

Now attempt to consistently assign truth values to the components of the premises so that all the premises are true. Since the second premise must be true, and since "*q*" must consistently be assigned falsehood, the assignment of truth values is as follows:

$$p \rightarrow q \quad\quad p \quad\quad /\therefore q$$
$$\text{T} \quad \text{F} \quad\quad \text{T} \quad\quad\quad \text{F}$$
$$ \text{F}$$

Notice that this makes the first premise false: it is impossible to consistently assign truth values to the simple statements in this argument form in such a way that all the premises are true and the conclusion is false. By a convention, you use the notation 'F/T' (or 'T/F') to indicate that the only way you could make all the premises true and the conclusion false is by inconsistently assigning truth values. Thus:

$$p \rightarrow q \quad\quad p \quad\quad /\therefore q$$
$$\text{T/F} \quad \text{F} \quad\quad \text{T} \quad\quad\quad \text{F}$$
$$ \text{F}$$

So far we have considered only cases in which the conclusion is a simple statement. The situation is the same in cases in which the conclusion is a compound statement with the following provision: *If there is more than one assignment of truth values to the conclusion that will make the conclusion false, and if on one assignment of truth values to the conclusion you cannot consistently assign truth values to the premises in such a way that all the premises are true and the conclusion is false, you must consider alternative assignments of truth values to the conclusion.* Consider the following argument form:

$$p \rightarrow q$$
$$q \rightarrow r \quad /\therefore \sim p \,\&\, r$$

Begin by assigning truth values to the conclusions in such a way that the conclusion is false. *One* such assignment is to assign falsehood to both "~*p*" and "*r*." But consistently assigning truth values on this basis yields the following:

$$p \rightarrow q \qquad q \rightarrow r \qquad /\therefore \sim p \;\&\; r$$

$p \rightarrow q$		$q \rightarrow r$		$/\therefore \sim p \;\&\; r$	
T/F	F	F	F	T	F
	F		T	F	
					F

Since there are three assignments of truth values to the conclusion that make the conclusion false, the fact that *one* of those assignments does *not* show that all the premises are true and the conclusion is false does not prove the argument is valid. So we must check to see whether *any* assignment of truth values will make all the premises true and the conclusion false, for example:

$p \rightarrow q$		$q \rightarrow r$		$/\therefore \sim p \;\&\; r$	
F	F	F	F	F	F
	T		T	T	
					F

This clearly shows that the argument form is invalid.

So far, so good, but there are cases in which this technique will not work. Consider the following argument form:

$$p \rightarrow q$$
$$q \rightarrow r \quad /\therefore p \lor \sim p$$

Beginning with the conclusion, try to assign truth values so that all the premises are true and the conclusion is false. Under what conditions will the conclusion—"*p* ∨ ~*p*"—be false? There are no such conditions: "*p* ∨ ~*p*" is a tautology. If you find an argument in which the conclusion is a tautology, the argument is valid. The most you would need to do is to construct a complete truth table to show that no matter what truth values are assigned to the simple components of the conclusion, the conclusion will be true.

p	$\sim p$	$(p \lor \sim p)$
T	F	T
F	F	T

   Why will this show that the argument is valid? The conditions under which an argument is valid or invalid are analogous to the conditions under which a conditional statement is true. Just as an argument is valid so long as it is impossible for all the premises to be true and the conclusion false, a conditional statement is true as long as it is not the case that the antecedent is true and the consequent false. Thus, if the conclusion of an argument is a tautology, the argument is valid: it is analogous to the case in which the consequent of a conditional statement is true.

SUMMARY

The following points spell out what is involved in the reverse truth-table technique.

1. Assign truth values to the conclusion so that the conclusion is false.

2. Attempt to *consistently* assign truth values to the premises so that all the premises are true.

3. If it is possible to consistently assign truth values to the simple propositions in the argument so that the premises are true and the conclusion is false, the argument is *invalid*.

4. If it is not possible to consistently assign truth values to the simple propositions in the argument so that the premises are true and the conclusion is false, then the argument is valid.

5. If there is more than one assignment of truth values that will make the conclusion false, that is, if the conclusion is a conjunction or a material equivalence, then if one assignment of truth values to the conclusion and the premises does *not* show that the argument is invalid, repeat the procedure until you either discover an assignment of truth values that makes the premises true and the conclusion false—in which case, the argument form is *invalid*—or until you have tested *all* assignments of truth values that make the conclusion false and has discovered that there is no consistent assignment of truth values to the premises which make them true—in which case, the argument is valid.

EXERCISES

Construct a reverse truth table to determine whether each of the following argument forms is valid or invalid.

1. p
   q /∴ p & q

2. $p \rightarrow q$
   $\sim p$ /∴ $\sim q$

3. p /∴ $p \lor q$

4. $p \lor q$
   $\sim q$ /∴ $\sim p$

5. p
   q /∴ $p \leftrightarrow q$

6. $(p$ & $q) \lor r$
   $\sim q$ /∴ $p \lor r$

7. $(p$ & $q)$ & r
   $p \lor \sim r$ /∴ q

8. $(p \lor q)$ & r
   $r \rightarrow p$ /∴ $\sim q$

9. $(p \rightarrow q) \lor r$
   $r \rightarrow \sim p$ /∴ q

10. $p \rightarrow (q \lor \sim r)$
    $\sim r \rightarrow p$ /∴ $\sim q$

11. $p \rightarrow (q$ & $\sim r)$
    $\sim r \rightarrow q$ /∴ $\sim p$

12. $p \leftrightarrow (r \rightarrow \sim q)$
    $\sim p \rightarrow r$ /∴ $\sim q$ & p

13. $p \leftrightarrow (r \rightarrow \sim q)$
    $\sim p \rightarrow r$ /∴ $\sim q \lor p$

14. $p \leftrightarrow (r \rightarrow \sim q)$
    $\sim p \rightarrow r$ /∴ $\sim q \leftrightarrow p$

15. p & $(q \leftrightarrow \sim r)$
    $r \lor (p$ & $\sim q)$ /∴ $p \lor \sim q$

16. $p \lor (q \leftrightarrow \sim r)$
    r & $(p \lor \sim q)$ /∴ $p \leftrightarrow \sim q$

17. $p \rightarrow (\sim q \lor \sim r)$
    r & $(p \lor \sim q)$ /∴ p & q

18. $p \rightarrow (\sim q \lor \sim r)$
    r & $(p \lor \sim q)$ /∴ p & $(q \lor \sim r)$

19. $p \rightarrow [q \lor (r \& s)]$
    $p \lor \sim s$
    $q \lor \sim r / \therefore \sim p \lor q$

20. $p \rightarrow [q \lor (r \& s)]$
    $p \& \sim s$
    $q \lor r / \therefore \sim p \& q$

21. $p \leftrightarrow [\sim q \& (r \leftrightarrow s)]$
    $p \lor \sim s$
    $\sim q \& r / \therefore \sim p \& q$

22. $p \& [\sim q \rightarrow (r \lor \sim s)]$
    $p \rightarrow s$
    $\sim q \rightarrow r / \therefore \sim p \rightarrow q$

23. $p \lor [q \rightarrow (\sim r \leftrightarrow s)]$
    $\sim p \rightarrow \sim s$
    $(p \& \sim s) \rightarrow r / \therefore \sim p \rightarrow q$

24. $p \lor [q \rightarrow (\sim r \leftrightarrow s)]$
    $\sim p \rightarrow \sim s$
    $(p \& \sim s) \rightarrow r / \therefore \sim p \leftrightarrow q$

25. $p \lor [q \rightarrow (\sim r \leftrightarrow s)]$
    $\sim p \leftrightarrow (\sim r \rightarrow s)$
    $(\sim p \lor s) \rightarrow \sim r / \therefore \sim s$

26. $p \lor [q \rightarrow (\sim r \leftrightarrow s)]$
    $\sim p \rightarrow t$
    $\sim p \leftrightarrow (\sim t \rightarrow s)$
    $(\sim p \lor s) \rightarrow \sim t / \therefore \sim s \lor t$

27. $p \leftrightarrow [q \rightarrow (\sim r \& s)]$
    $\sim p \rightarrow \sim t$
    $\sim p \leftrightarrow (t \rightarrow \sim s)$
    $\sim (p \lor s) \rightarrow \sim t / \therefore \sim s \& t$

28. $p \leftrightarrow [q \rightarrow (\sim r \& s)]$
    $\sim p \rightarrow \sim t$
    $\sim p \rightarrow (\sim t \& \sim s)$
    $\sim (p \lor \sim s) \rightarrow \sim t / \therefore \sim (s \& t)$

29. $p \rightarrow (\sim q \lor r)$
    $q \rightarrow (\sim r \lor s)$
    $r \rightarrow (\sim s \leftrightarrow p)$
    $\sim p \lor t / \therefore s$

30. $p \rightarrow (\sim q \vee r)$
    $q \rightarrow (\sim r \vee s)$
    $r \rightarrow (\sim s \leftrightarrow p)$
    $\sim p \ \& \ \sim t \ / \therefore \ s \ \& \ \sim t$

NOTES

1. A necessary condition is a condition in the absence of which a phenomenon will not occur. A sufficient condition is a condition that
   assures that a certain phenomenon will occur. Discussions of necessary and sufficient conditions are common when looking for causal
   conditions. See Chapter 9, Section 2.

2. This set of exercises is dedicated to the memory of those master pun-
   sters Jay Ward and Bill Scott.

Chapter Six

Propositional Logic: Natural Deduction

This chapter sets out a system of natural deduction: given a set of rules, we are going to prove that a conclusion follows from a set of premises. This method has advantages and disadvantages with respect to the truth-table technique. The major disadvantage is that it can be used *only* to show that a conclusion validly follows from a set of premises; it cannot be used to show that an argument is invalid. The advantages are that it tends to follow the ways in which we ordinarily argue and sharpen analytic or problem-solving skills: the kinds of skills you develop in working with a system of natural deduction tend to be the same kinds of skills you use in attempting to solve virtually any kind of problem in your day-to-day life.

The rules used in a system of natural deduction are introduced in three stages. First, there are nine rules of inference that allow us to construct a limited number of proofs. Second, the Rule of Replacement and five logically equivalent statement forms increase the number of proofs we can construct, although even with these rules we cannot prove the validity of all valid arguments in propositional logic. Finally, an additional five logically equivalent statement forms make it possible to prove the validity of any valid argument in propositional logic.

6.1 *The Rules of Inference*

Consider the following argument form:

$(p \ \& \ q) \rightarrow [r \lor (s \ \& \ {\sim}t)]$
$p \ \& \ q$
${\sim}r$ $/\therefore$ $s \ \& \ {\sim}t$

You could show that the argument form is valid by means of a complete truth table, but such a truth table would have thirty-two lines. Similarly, you could prove that the argument form is valid by means of a reverse truth table, but since the conclusion is a conjunction, you would have to consider each of the three cases in which the conclusion is false. On the other hand, you can do a deductive proof and show in two lines that the conclusion follows from the premises:

1. $(p \ \& \ q) \rightarrow [r \lor (s \ \& \ {\sim}t)]$
2. $p \ \& \ q$
3. ${\sim}r$ $/\therefore$ $s \ \& \ {\sim}t$
4. $r \lor (s \ \& \ {\sim}t)$ 1,2 *Modus ponens*
5. $s \ \& \ {\sim}t$ 4,3 Disjunctive syllogism

Modus ponens, sometimes known as affirming the antecedent, is an argument of the form:

$p \rightarrow q$
p $/\therefore$ q

A truth table would confirm that this argument form is valid. Since 'p' and 'q' are *statement variables,* they can be replaced by *any* statement, no matter how complex. Given both "$(p \ \& \ q) \rightarrow [r \lor (s \ \& \ {\sim}t)]$" and "$(p \ \& \ q),$" "$[r \lor (s \ \& \ {\sim}t)]$" follows as an instance of *modus ponens.* Similarly, disjunctive syllogism is an argument of the form:

$p \lor q$
${\sim}p$ $/\therefore$ q

which also can be shown to be valid by means of a truth table. Since we have already shown that "[r v (s & ~t)]" follows from the premises, and we are given "~r" as a premise, the conclusion follows from "[r v (s & ~t)]" and "~r" as an instance of disjunctive syllogism. With that we have proven that the conclusion follows from the premises, that is, we have proven that the argument is valid.

In the system of natural deduction developing here there are nine rules of inference. Each of these rules is a valid argument form and can be shown to be valid by means of truth tables. To stress that the rules can be applied with respect to a statement variable or a statement of *any* degree of complexity, we introduce four metavariables, α, β, γ, and π. The nine rules are:

Rules of Inference

1. Modus Ponens (M.P.)
   α → β
   α   /∴   β

2. Modus Tollens (M.T.)
   α → β
   ~β   /∴   ~α

3. Hypothetical Syllogism (H.S.)
   α → β
   β → γ   /∴   α → γ

4. Disjunctive Syllogism (D.S.)
   α v β
   ~α   /∴   β

5. Constructive Dilemma (C.D.)
   (α → β) & (γ → π)
   α v γ   /∴   β v π

6. Absorption (Abs.)
   α → β   /∴   α → (α & β)

7. Simplification (Simp.)
   α & β   /∴   α

8. Conjunction (Conj.)
   α
   β /∴   α & β

9. Addition (Add.)
   α   /∴   α v β

Since the metavariables in the rules can be replaced by any statement or statement variable, no matter how complex, we must be aware of what might be called the **principal connective** in a statement, the connective that holds the whole statement together. It is with respect to the principal connective that you apply the rule. If you are given the statement "p & q," the ampersand is the principal connective. If you are given the statement "(p & q) → r," the arrow is the principal connective. If you are given the statement, "{[(p v q) v r] → s}," the arrow is again the principal connective. If you are given the statement "{[(p → q) ↔ (r → s)] ↔ ~[t & (~u & ~v)]}," the second double arrow is the principal connective. Further, you must not forget that the variables might be replaced by *negative* as well as affirmative statements. So you will use *modus ponens* to conclude that "*q*," even if the premises are:

$$\sim(p \ \& \ r) \rightarrow q$$
$$\sim(p \ \& \ r) \quad /\therefore \quad q$$

Finally, in a system of natural deduction you apply the rules in a mechanical fashion: there must be a *perfect match* between the premises in an argument and the Rule of Inference to which you appeal. *None* of the following valid argument forms can be shown to be valid on the basis of *only* the nine Rules of Inference introduced up to this point:

$$p \ \& \ q \quad /\therefore \quad q$$
$$p \lor q$$
$$\sim q \quad /\therefore \quad p$$
$$p \rightarrow \sim q$$
$$q \quad /\therefore \quad \sim p$$

Each of the Rules of Inference can be used to *justify* a line of a proof. Each of these rules allows you to draw a conclusion on the basis of an *entire line or lines of the proof:* **they cannot be legitimately applied to a portion of a line of a proof.** As you might have noticed in the proof above, in doing a proof there are two columns beneath the premises. In the left-hand column, you state the conclusion you draw from one or more of the premises or previous conclusions. In the right-hand column you state the line or lines used to draw the conclusion and the name of the rule (or the abbreviation of that name) that was used to draw the conclusion. To see how this works, let us look at a few more examples.

You are given the following argument:

1. $(p \lor q) \rightarrow [r \lor (s \ \& \ t)]$
2. p
3. $\sim r \quad /\therefore \quad s$

You construct a proof by showing, in a step-by-step manner, that the conclusion follows from the premises. But how do you begin? There are several things you might do. You might stare at the rules until you see a way to apply one of them. *A better way* is to begin by noting the conclusion and asking where it is found in the argument. The conclusion, "*s*," is the first conjunct of a disjunction that is the consequent of

the first premise. What you want to do is isolate "s." The rules of in
ference apply to entire lines of a proof, so you *cannot* apply the rule of
simplification to "(s & t)" until you have isolated "(s & t)." How do
you isolate "(s & t)"? If you could isolate "[r v (s & t)]," then given
premise three, that is, "~r," you could conclude "s & t" by disjunctive
syllogism. But "[r v (s & t)]" is the consequent of a conditional statement. You can isolate the consequent of a conditional statement only
by the rule of *modus ponens,* but to apply *modus ponens* in this case
you must have "p v q." You don't have "p v q," but you do have "p."
Looking at the rules, you notice the rule of addition, which allows one
to infer "p v q" given "p" alone. At this point you have *worked backward* through the proof, and all that remains to be done is to state the
proof in a forward manner, such as the following:

1. $(p \lor q) \rightarrow [r \lor (s \ \& \ t)]$
2. p
3. ~r   /∴   s
4. $p \lor q$ 2, Add.
5. $r \lor (E \ \& \ F)$ 1,4 M.P.
6. $s \ \& \ F$ 5,3 D.S.
7. s 6 Simp.

What we should notice from thinking through the above proof is
that it is important to know where one is going. Hence, (1) you should
notice where the components of the conclusion are found in the premises. (2) It often helps to work backward from the conclusion, asking
the questions "How would I get this?" and "What do I need to get
that?" Sometimes, as in the case above, it is possible to work through
the entire proof from the end to the beginning. Other times it will at
least give you a hunch as to how to start.
   Consider another argument:

1. $(p \rightarrow q) \ \& \ (r \rightarrow t)$
2. p /∴ $q \lor t$

Now before you read on, look at the premises and conclusion, look at
the rules, and figure out how to get the conclusion. Did you get it? If
so, your reasoning *might* have gone like this: The conclusion is "q v t."
Both "q" and "t" are in the first premise, and both are consequents of
conditionals. Looking at the rules, it looks as if I could get the conclu
sion by *constructive dilemma* if I had "p v r." I do not have "p v r,"

but I do have "*p*." So by addition I can get "*p* v *r*." Your proof would look like this:

1. $(p \rightarrow q)$ & $(r \rightarrow t)$
2. *p* /∴ *q* v *t*
3. *p* v *r*   2 Add.
4. *q* v *t*   1,3 C.D.

Maybe you didn't reason in the way suggested above. Perhaps your reasoning went more like this: The conclusion is "*q* v *t*." If I could isolate "*q*," then by addition I could get "*q* v *t*." But how would I isolate "*q*"? The consequent of the conditional "*p* → *q*" is "*q*," and since I know that "*p*" by premise two, I could get "*q*" by *modus ponens* if I could isolate "*p* → *q*." But "*p* → *q*" is the first conjunct of a conjunction, so I can get "*p* → *q*" by simplification. Your proof would look like this:

1. $(p \rightarrow q)$ & $(r \rightarrow t)$
2. *p* /∴ *q* v *t*
3. *p* → *q*   1 Simp.
4. *q*   3,2 M.P.
5. *q* v *t*   4 Add.

Both of these proofs are acceptable. The first is more **elegant** than the second, that is, it is shorter, but either is acceptable. The moral of this exercise is that sometimes there are alternative ways to reach a conclusion, but your proof is acceptable as long as you apply the rules correctly.
In summary, here are five points to remember:

1. The nine rules of inference apply *only* to a complete line or two complete lines of a proof, depending upon the rule.
2. Start by looking for the components of the conclusion in the premises.
3. It is often helpful to work backward from the conclusion for at least a few steps.
4. If you don't know what to do, but you see that you could apply a rule or two that would result in simpler statements, generally it will be helpful to apply those rules.
5. The nine Rules of Inference must be applied "mechanically:" there must be an *exact match* between the premises to which you apply the rule and the form of the rule.

Advice. Learning to construct proofs is like learning a foreign language: it's a lot of fun, but if you're going to be successful, you should work on it a bit every day. The Rules of Inference are like basic elements of grammar: everything else we will do assumes you have mastered them. Students who devote at least a half hour a day, every day, to constructing proofs generally do very well.

EXERCISES

I. "Name the Rule." Each of the following is an instance of a Rule of Inference. Indicate which rule is invoked in each case.

1. A v B
   ~A   /∴   B

2. A   /∴   A v (B & ~C)

3. A → (B → C)
   A   /∴   B → C

4. A → B   /∴   A → (A & B)

5. (A → B) & (C → D)
   A v C   /∴   B v D

6. A → B
   C   /∴   (A → B) & C

7. A → (B & C)
   ~(B & C)   /∴   ~A

8. (A v C) & (D ↔ B)   /∴   A v C

9. (A & B) → C
   C → D   /∴   (A & B) → D

10. (A ↔ D) → B
    ~B   /∴   ~(A ↔ D)

11. W ↔ (X v Y)
    (Y v ~Z)   /∴   [W ↔ (X v Y)] & (Y v ~Z)

12. M   /∴   M v {[W ↔ (X v Y)] & (Y v ~Z)}

13. [A → (X & Z)] & [(B v Z) → (A & Z)]
    A v (B v Z)   /∴   (X & Z) v (A & Z)

14. [Z & (X v ~Y)] → (Z ↔ X)
    ~(Z ↔ X)   /∴   ~[Z & (X v ~Y)]

15. {~[Q v ~(Z v ~X)] v W} → (A v Q)
    (A v Q) → [A ↔ (Z & ~C)]
       /∴   {~[Q v ~(Z v ~X)] v W} → [A ↔ (Z & ~C)]

16. A → (Z v X)
    ~{B → [Q v ~(Z ↔ ~A)]}
           /∴   [A → (Z v X)] & ~{B → [Q v ~(Z ↔ ~A)]}

17. [A → (Z v X)] v ~{B → [Q v ~(Z ↔ ~A)]}
    ~[A → (Z v X)]   /∴ ~{B → [Q v ~(Z ↔ ~A)]}

18. ~{B → [Q v ~(Z ↔ ~A)]} → [A & (B → ~C)]
    ~[A & (B → ~C)]   /∴   ~~{B → [Q v ~(Z ↔ ~A)]}

19. (Q v ~B) → [X v ~(Q → ~Z)]
           /∴   (Q v ~B) → {(Q v ~B) & [X v ~(Q → ~Z)]}

20. A & ([A → (Z v X)] & ~{B → [Q v ~(Z ↔ ~A)]})
           /∴   A

II. Construct a formal proof of validity for each of the following
argument forms.

1. *p*   /∴   *p* v (*r* & *s*)

2. *p* → *q*
   q → *r*   /∴   *p* → (*q* & *r*)

3. *p*
   (*p* → *q*) & (*r* → *s*)   /∴   *q* v *s*

4. *p* v *q*
   ~*p*   /∴   *q* v *s*

5. *p*
   p → *r*   /∴   *p* & *r*

6. *p* → *q*
   q → *r*
   ~*r*   /∴   ~*p*

7. *p* → *q*
   q → *r*
   p v *q*   /∴   *q* v *r*

8. (*p* → *q*) & (*r* → *s*)
   p   /∴   *q*

9. *p* & *q*
   p → *q*   /∴   *q*

10. (*p* → *q*) & (*r* → *s*)
    p
    ~*q*   /∴   *s*

11. *p* → *q*
    (*p* & *q*) → *s*
    ~*s*   /∴   ~*p*

12. p & q
    $p \rightarrow (r \vee q)$
    ~r /∴ q

13. ~p & $(r \vee s)$
    $q \rightarrow p$ /∴   ~$q \vee (r$ & $s)$

14. $[(p \vee q) \rightarrow r]$ & $[s \rightarrow (t$ & $r)]$
    p /∴ $r \vee (t$ & $r)$

15. $(p \rightarrow q)$ & $(r \rightarrow s)$
    $r \vee p$
    ~r /∴ $q \vee s$

16. $p \rightarrow (q \vee$ ~$r)$
    $q \rightarrow ($~$r \vee s)$
    $p \vee q$
    ~$(q \vee$ ~$r)$ /∴   ~$r \vee s$

17. $p \vee (r \rightarrow s)$
    r
    ~p /∴ $s \vee$ ~s

18. $p \rightarrow q$
    $[p \rightarrow (p$ & $q)] \rightarrow r$
    ~r /∴ s

19. $p \rightarrow q$
    ~q
    $($~$p \vee s) \rightarrow (q \rightarrow s)$ /∴ $p \rightarrow s$

20. $p \rightarrow q$
    $[p \rightarrow (p$ & $q)] \rightarrow (r \rightarrow s)$
    ~$(r$ & $s)$ /∴   ~r

21. $p \rightarrow q$
    $r \vee s$
    $(q$ & $s) \rightarrow t$
    p
    ~r /∴ t

22. p
    $[p \vee (q$ & $s)] \rightarrow r$
    $r \rightarrow s$ /∴ s & $(p \vee$ ~$p)$

23. $[(p \vee q) \rightarrow r]$ & $[(s$ & $t) \rightarrow u]$
    p
    ~r /∴ u

24. $p \rightarrow q$
    $(p$ & $q) \rightarrow r$
    p /∴ $(p$ & $q)$ & r

25. $[(p \lor q) \to r]$ & $[(s \& t) \to u]$
~r
$(p \lor q) \lor (t \to s)$
~s /∴ ~$t \lor (s \leftrightarrow t)$

26. $(p \to r)$ & $(\text{~}s \to t)$
p & s
~r /∴ $(t \& p) \lor (\text{~}r \to s)$

27. $(p \lor q) \to r$
p
$r \to s$
$[(p \lor q) \& s] \to t$ /∴ $t \lor \text{~}p$

28. $p \to q$
$(p \& q) \to r$
$(p \& r) \to s$
$(p \& s) \to t$
~t /∴ ~p

29. $(p \to q)$ & $(r \to s)$
$(r \to s)$ & $(t \to u)$
p
~q /∴ s

30. $(p \to q)$ & $(r \to s)$
$(r \to s)$ & $(t \to u)$
p /∴ $(p \& q) \lor (r \& s)$

III. Translate and construct a proof of validity for each of the following arguments. Use the suggested statement letters.

HAMLET: THE PRINCE AND THE VILLAGE

1. If Hamlet is the Prince of Denmark or he is the Duke of Edinburgh, then there are ghosts about in the castle. Hamlet is the Prince of Denmark. Therefore, there are ghosts about in the castle. (H, D, G)

2. If Hamlet is a village in Wyoming, then if George runs the general store, then coffee is still available for a dime a cup. Hamlet is a village in Wyoming. If coffee is still available for a dime a cup, then Oscar will stop by the store. So, if George runs the general store, Oscar will stop by the store. (H, G, C, O)

3. If Hamlet is the Prince of Denmark or he is the Duke of Edinburgh, then his father is in a ghostly state and his

mother has remarried. Hamlet is the Prince of Denmark. Therefore, Hamlet's father is in a ghostly state. (P, D, F, M)

4. Hamlet is a village in Wyoming. If Hamlet is a village in Wyoming, then either Oscar breaks horses for a living or George runs the general store. Oscar does not break horses for a living. So, George runs the general store or Francesca runs the saloon. (H, O, G, F)

5. Either Hamlet is not fond of Ophelia or he is fond of Ophelia. If Hamlet is fond of Ophelia, then we can expect to hear a soliloquy. If Hamlet is not fond of Ophelia, then Claudius should expect a long reign. Claudius should not expect a long reign. Therefore, we can expect to hear a soliloquy. (H, S, C)

6. If Francesca runs the saloon, then either Oscar occasionally bends an elbow or he doesn't. If Oscar does not occasionally bend an elbow, then he'll be commended by Mothers Against Drunk Drovers. If Oscar occasionally bends an elbow, then he'll appear in a beer commercial. Francesca runs the saloon. So, either Oscar will appear in a beer commercial or he'll be commended by Mothers Against Drunk Drovers. (F, O, C, A)

7. If Hamlet is seeing a ghost, then either Francisco or Bernardo is seeing ghosts; and if Yorick is a jester, then there is a great deal of laughter around the castle. Hamlet is seeing a ghost. It is not the case that either Francisco or Bernardo is seeing ghosts. So Gertrude will sleep well tonight. (H, F, B, Y, L, G)

8. Oscar is a cowboy and George is a grocer. If Oscar is a cowboy or Francesca runs a saloon, then Hamilton Bromschwatz is not the mayor of Hamlet. Therefore, Hamilton Bromschwatz is not the mayor of Hamlet unless George is a grocer. (O, G, F, H)

9. If Hamlet sponsors a play, then either Rosencrantz or Guildenstern will have a job as an actor. If Hamlet sponsors a play and either Rosencrantz or Guildenstern will have a job as an actor, then either Othello will move to Denmark or the play will be the thing wherein we catch the conscience of the king. But Othello will not move to Denmark. Hamlet sponsors a play. So, the play will be the thing wherein we catch the conscience of the king. (H, R, G, O, P)

10. If Francesca allows games of poker in her saloon, then either Oscar will lose a week's pay or Sheriff Snark will raid the

joint. George runs the general store. If Oscar will lose a week's pay, then Horatio Hornswagel is an accomplished gambler; and if Sheriff Snark raids the joint, then the saloon will be closed for a week. If George runs the general store, then Francesca allows games of poker in her saloon. Horatio Hornswagel is not an accomplished gambler. So the saloon will be closed for a week unless George does not run the general store. (F, O, S, G, H, C)

11. Either Ophelia is a happy child or Polonius is an eavesdropper, and Hamlet does not cut curtains with a sword. Ophelia is not a happy child. If Polonius is an eavesdropper, then if Hamlet does not cut curtains with a sword then Claudius will die in his bed. Claudius will not die in his bed. Therefore, it is not the case that Hamlet does not cut curtains with a sword. (O, P, H, C)

12. If Francesca sells redeye, then Oscar will have a headache tomorrow morning; and if George takes bets on horse races, Sheriff Snark will raid the general store. If Horatio Hornswagel is a good gambler, then he'll win the game; and if Roosevelt Fitznagel is mayor, then the village is in good hands. Either Francesca sells redeye or Horatio Hornswagel is a good gambler. Oscar will not have a headache tomorrow morning. Therefore, Horatio will win the game. (F, O, G, S, H, W, R, V)

13. Either Polonius is killed and Claudius dies in his bed, or if Gertrude is happily married then Yorick is telling good jokes. If Polonius is killed and Claudius dies in his bed, then Marcellus is King of Denmark. If Marcellus is King of Denmark, Reynaldo is Prince of Denmark. Reynaldo is not Prince of Denmark. Yorick is not telling good jokes. If Gertrude is not happily married, then Horatio is a philosopher. So, Horatio is a philosopher. (P, C, G, Y, M, R, H)

14. If George runs the general store, then Francesca runs the saloon. If Francesca runs the saloon, then Oscar drinks redeye. If George runs the general store and Oscar drinks redeye, then Sheriff Snark takes bribes. Jezebel Bromschwatz is mayor. If Jezebel Bromschwatz is mayor, then Sheriff Snark does not take bribes. So, either George does not run the general store, or Francesca runs the saloon if and only if Oscar drinks redeye. (G, F, O, S, J)

15. Either Claudius is the rightful King of Denmark or English ambassadors are trying to take over the kingdom. If English ambassadors are trying to take over the kingdom, then Reynaldo or Yorick will have the last laugh. Reynaldo will not have the last laugh. If Yorick has the last laugh, then Bernardo and Hamlet will stand on the platform in front of the castle. If Bernardo will stand on the platform in front of the castle, then Hamlet will stand on the platform in front of the castle. Claudius is not the rightful King of Denmark. Therefore, Hamlet will stand on the platform in front of the castle. (C, E, R, Y, B, H)

16. If Francesca runs the saloon, then if George runs the general store then Jezebel Bromschwatz is mayor of Hamlet. If Sheriff Snark is not in town, then if Oscar plays a game of poker then Horatio Hornswagel loses. Francesca runs the saloon. If Francesca runs the saloon then Sheriff Snark is not in town. Oscar plays a game of poker. Therefore, either Horatio Hornswagel loses or Jezebel Bromschwatz is mayor of Hamlet. (F, G, J, S, O, H)

17. If Polonius has died, then Claudius is King of Denmark. If Polonius has died and Claudius is King of Denmark, then Reynaldo is unemployed. Either Reynaldo is unemployed or Ophelia has drowned. Hamlet is troubled. If Hamlet is troubled then Reynaldo is not unemployed. Therefore, Polonius has not died and Ophelia has drowned. (P, C, R, O, H)

18. Either Francesca moves to Denmark or George moves to Montana. If George moves to Montana, then both Jezebel Bromschwatz and Sheriff Snark will loose their source of coffee. If Francesca moves to Denmark, then Oscar will be thirsty. Oscar will not be thirsty. If Francesca does not move to Denmark, then Horatio Hornswagel will buy the saloon; and if Oscar will be thirsty then George moves to Montana. Therefore, Jezebel Bromschwatz will lose her source of coffee and Horatio Hornswagel will buy the saloon. (F, G, J, S, O, H)

19. If either Rosencrantz or Guildenstern is a good actor, then the play's the thing wherein we'll catch the conscience of the king. If either Rosencrantz or Guildenstern is a good actor, then if the play's the thing wherein we'll catch the conscience of the king then Ophelia will take a plunge into the pond. If

the play's the thing wherein we'll catch the conscience of the king, then if Ophelia will take a plunge into the pond then Claudius lives to tell the story. Rosencrantz is a good actor. Claudius does not live to tell the story. So, Hamlet dies at the end of the play. (R, G, P, O, C, H)

20. Francesca reads *Hamlet*. If Francesca reads *Hamlet,* then she moves to Denmark and Oscar develops a tremendous thirst. If Francesca reads *Hamlet* then Jezebel Bromschwatz moves to Chicago and Sheriff Snark moves to California. If Francesca moves to Denmark and Jezebel Bromschwatz moves to Chicago, then George moves to Montana. If George moves to Montana, then either Horatio Hornswagel will buy the saloon or Rustic Resorts buys the whole town. Horatio Hornswagel will not buy the saloon. If Rustic Resorts buys the whole town, then the village will die. So, the village will die. (F, M, O, J, S, G, H, R, V)

6.2 The Rule of Replacement (Part I)

Given only the rules of inference, there are obviously valid arguments that cannot be proven valid. For example, the rule of simplification allows you to infer "p" given "p & q," but it will not allow you to infer "q," even though "p & q" is true if and only if both "p" and "q" are true. Similarly, disjunctive syllogism will allow you to infer "q" given "p v q" and "$\sim p$," but it will *not* allow you to infer "p" given "p v q" and "$\sim q$." There are several ways in which this problem could be resolved. We could give alternative forms of simplification and disjunctive syllogism, but that would be merely a stop-gap measure: alternative versions of various other rules would be necessary. A second form of addition according to which given "p" you could infer "q v p" would be necessary, as would additional forms of disjunctive syllogism to deal with cases in which, given "p v (q v r)" and "$\sim r$" you could infer "p v q," or given "p v (q v r) and "$\sim q$" you could infer "p v r." An unworkably large number of rules of inference would be required, and even then not all cases would be covered.

Fortunately, the shortcomings of our current system can be overcome by adding a rule that will allow us to replace a limited number of logically equivalent, well-formed formulae *wherever they occur* in a proof. In this section we introduce the rule of replacement together with *some* of the equivalent forms that can replace each other wherever they occur within a proof, that is, whether a statement of the appropriate form constitutes an entire line of a proof or merely a part of a line. Using our metavariables, α, β, and γ, to represent statements of any degree of complexity, the Rule of Replacement and half of the equivalent forms that concern us are as follows:

RULE OF REPLACEMENT: *Any of the following logically equivalent expressions can replace each other* **wherever they occur in a proof:**

10. De Morgan's Theorems: $\sim(\alpha \,\&\, \beta) \leftrightarrow (\sim\alpha \lor \sim\beta)$
    (DeM) $\sim(\alpha \lor \beta) \leftrightarrow (\sim\alpha \,\&\, \sim\beta)$
11. Commutation (Com.): $(\alpha \lor \beta) \leftrightarrow (\beta \lor \alpha)$
                           $(\alpha \,\&\, \beta) \leftrightarrow (\beta \,\&\, \alpha)$
12. Association (Assoc.): $[\alpha \lor (\beta \lor \gamma)] \leftrightarrow [(\alpha \lor \beta) \lor \gamma]$
                           $[\alpha \,\&\, (\beta \,\&\, \gamma)] \leftrightarrow [(\alpha \,\&\, \beta) \,\&\, \gamma]$
13. Distribution (Dist.): $[\alpha \,\&\, (\beta \lor \gamma)] \leftrightarrow [(\alpha \,\&\, \beta) \lor (\alpha \,\&\, \gamma)]$
                           $[\alpha \lor (\beta \,\&\, \gamma)] \leftrightarrow [(\alpha \lor \beta) \,\&\, (\alpha \lor \gamma)]$
14. Double Negation (D.N.): $\alpha \leftrightarrow \sim\sim\alpha$

De Morgan's theorem tells you how to move the negation sign into or out of a set of parentheses when dealing with a conjunction or a disjunction. For example, if you say, "It is not the case that both Madge and Sue attend the dance," you could as well say "Either Madge doesn't attend the dance or Sue doesn't attend the dance," which leaves open the possibility that neither attends. If you say, "Mitch is not a ballplayer and Matt is not a ballplayer," you are saying "It is not the case that either Mitch or Matt is a ballplayer."

Commutation allows you to switch the positions of disjuncts or conjuncts. Obviously it does not affect the truth of the statement whether you say, "Natalie hunts tigers and Neville knits sweaters" or "Neville knits sweaters and Natalie hunts tigers." Similarly, the statements "Either Anne collects cats or Owen collects coins" and "Either Owen collects coins or Anne collects cats" are true under the same conditions.

Association allows you to move parentheses in complex disjunctions or conjunctions. The parentheses are needed to keep disjunctions and conjunctions well-formed, but their positions do not affect the truth values of the propositions. So, in terms of truth values, it makes no difference whether you say "Either Max hunts bears, or Marlene rides elephants or George does needlepoint" or "Either Max hunts bears or Marlene rides elephants, or George does needlepoint": each is true only if at least one of the disjuncts is true. Similarly, the statement "Both

Hilary and Ivy went fishing, and Ming went fishing" is logically equivalent to "Hilary went fishing, and both Ivy and Ming went fishing": each is true only if all the conjuncts are true.

Distribution deals with complex statements that include both conjunctions and disjunctions. "Bill won the election, and either George or Al lost" is true as long as Bill won and George lost, or Bill won and Al lost. "Hilary won the election or Barbara lost, and Hilary won the election or Marilyn lost" is true as long as Hilary won the election and either Barbara or Marilyn lost.

And double negation affirms what your English teachers have been telling you for years: "Dan's book isn't no good" means "Dan's book is good."

Given the rule of replacement and these equivalences, we can now construct a proof for the following argument form:

u & q
$q \rightarrow \sim(\sim s \lor r)$
$s \rightarrow [p \lor (t$ & $r)]$ /∴ $p \lor t$

The proof is as follows:

1. u & q
2. $q \rightarrow \sim(\sim s \lor r)$
3. $s \rightarrow [p \lor (t$ & $r)]$ /∴ $p \lor t$
4. q & u 1 Com.
5. q 4 Simp.
6. $\sim(\sim s \lor r)$ 2,5 M.P.
7. $\sim\sim s$ & $\sim r$ 6 DeM.
8. $\sim\sim s$ 7 Simp.
9. s 8 D.N.
10. $p \lor (t$ & $r)$ 3,9 M.P.
11. $(p \lor t)$ & $(p \lor r)$ 10 Dist.
12. $p \lor t$ 11 Simp.

The equivalences we have considered to this point do not constitute a complete list of the equivalent expressions that fall under the rule of replacement—additional equivalences are introduced in the next section. Since proofs can become more difficult as one's system of natural deduction becomes more complex, you would do well to master these equivalences before the remaining equivalences are added.

EXERCISES

I. "Name the Rule." Each of the following is justified by one of the equivalences falling under the Rule of Replacement. Indicate which equivalence is invoked in each case.

    1. ~[A v (B & C)]   /∴   ~A & ~(B & C)

    2. A & ~(C v B)   /∴   A & ~(B v C)

    3. A & (~B v C)   /∴   (A & ~B) v (A & C)

    4. (A & ~B) v (S & P)   /∴   [(A & ~B) v S] & [(A & ~B) v P]

    5. ~~(C & B)   /∴   ~(~C v ~B)

    6. C & ~~B   /∴   ~~B & C

    7. C v [B → (~B ↔ ~~G)]   /∴   C v [B → (~B ↔ G)]

    8. P & [(Q v R) & G]   /∴   [P & (Q v R)] & G

    9. P v {(Q v R) & [(Q & S) → ~(~W → ~~S)]}
       /∴   [P v (Q v R)] & {P v [(Q & S) → ~(~W → ~~S)]}

    10. [P & (Q → S)] v {Q & [(S v G) v ~S]}
        /∴   [P & (Q → S)] v {Q & [S v (G v ~S)]}

II. Construct a proof using the Rules of Inference plus De Morgan's Theorems, Commutation, Association, Distribution, and Double Negation.

    1. ~(p v q)   /∴   ~q

    2. p & (q & r)   /∴   r

    3. p
       ~(p & q)   /∴   ~q

    4. ~p → ~q
       q   /∴   p

    5. p & s   /∴   (s v q) & (s v r)

    6. p v (q v r)
       ~q   /∴   p v r

    7. p & (q & r)   /∴   p & r

    8. (p → q) & (r → s)
       p v (q & r)   /∴   q v s

    9. ~p & [q v (r & s)]   /∴   (~p & q) v (~p & s)

    10. ~[(p v q) v r]   /∴   ~q

    11. p v (q v r)
        ~p & ~q   /∴   r

12. $(p \rightarrow q) \;\&\; (q \rightarrow p)$ /∴ $(p \rightarrow p) \;\&\; (q \rightarrow q)$

13. $\sim[p \;\&\; (q \lor r)]$
    q /∴ $\sim p$

14. $\sim[p \lor (q \;\&\; r)]$
    r /∴ $\sim q$

15. $(p \;\&\; q) \lor (p \;\&\; r)$
    $\sim r$
    $q \rightarrow t$ /∴ $(t \lor s) \;\&\; (t \lor w)$

16. $p \lor \sim(q \lor r)$
    $\sim(\sim p \;\&\; q) \rightarrow s$
    $s \rightarrow w$ /∴ $(s \;\&\; w) \lor (t \;\&\; z)$

17. $(p \;\&\; q) \lor (p \;\&\; s)$
    $(s \rightarrow w) \;\&\; (q \rightarrow m)$
    $a \rightarrow \sim(m \lor w)$ /∴ $\sim a \;\&\; p$

18. $(p \;\&\; q) \lor (\sim p \;\&\; \sim q)$ /∴ $(\sim p \lor q) \;\&\; (\sim q \lor p)$

19. $(p \;\&\; q) \lor (r \;\&\; s)$
    $s \rightarrow (w \;\&\; z)$
    $\sim q$ /∴ z

20. $(p \;\&\; q) \lor (p \;\&\; r)$
    $\sim(\sim q \;\&\; \sim r) \rightarrow t$
    $\sim t \lor (x \;\&\; z)$ /∴ $(x \lor a) \;\&\; (x \lor z)$

6.3 *The Rule of Replacement (Part II)*

With the rule of replacement and the equivalent forms we have considered so far, we can construct proofs for many, but by no means all, valid arguments in propositional logic. To complete our system, we need to add several additional equivalences:

Rule of Replacement: *Any of the following logically equivalent expressions can replace each other **wherever they occur in a proof:***

15. Transposition (Trans.):	$(\alpha \rightarrow \beta) \leftrightarrow (\sim\beta \rightarrow \sim\alpha)$
	$(\sim\alpha \rightarrow \beta) \leftrightarrow (\sim\beta \rightarrow \alpha)$
16. Material Implication (Impl.):	$(\alpha \rightarrow \beta) \leftrightarrow (\sim\alpha \lor \beta)$
	$(\sim\alpha \rightarrow \beta) \leftrightarrow (\alpha \lor \beta)$

17. Material Equivalence (Equiv.): $(\alpha \leftrightarrow \beta) \leftrightarrow [(\alpha \rightarrow \beta) \,\&\, (\beta \rightarrow \alpha)]$
    $(\alpha \leftrightarrow \beta) \leftrightarrow [(\alpha \,\&\, \beta) \vee (\sim\!\alpha \,\&\, \sim\!\beta)]$

18. Exportation (Exp.): $[(\alpha \,\&\, \beta) \rightarrow \gamma] \leftrightarrow [\alpha \rightarrow (\beta \rightarrow \gamma)]$
19. Tautology (Taut.): $\alpha \leftrightarrow (\alpha \vee \alpha)$
    $\alpha \leftrightarrow (\alpha \,\&\, \alpha)$

Transposition tells you that when you switch propositions around an arrow, each must be negated to retain the same truth value. Assume it is true that "If Carmen has mumps then Steve has measles." As the truth table for the arrow shows, the statement is true as long as either the antecedent is false or the consequent is true. If the conditional is false, if Carmen has the mumps but Steve does not have the measles, its transposition is also false, that is, it is false that if Steve does not have the measles (which is true) then Carmen does not have the mumps (which is false).

Material implication is no more than a definition of the arrow. As the truth table for the arrow shows, the conditional statement "If George is President, then Dana's Vice-President" is true if either George is not President or Dana is Vice-President.

Material equivalence is no more than a definition of the double arrow. As the truth table for the double arrow shows, a biconditional is true if and only if the true values of both component propositions are the same: either they are both true or they are both false, which is precisely what the second version of material equivalence says. So the statement "Clinton is President if and only if Gore is Vice-President" is true provided that Clinton is President and Gore is Vice-President or Clinton is not President and Gore is not Vice-President. A little thought will convince you that the first version of the material equivalence is also correct, since the component conditionals are true whenever their antecedents and consequents have the same truth value.

Exportation tells you that the statement "If both Holly and Hester go to the dance, then Heloise will go to the dance" is equivalent to "If Holly goes to the dance, then if Hester goes to the dance then Heloise will go to the dance." The first statement is true except when its compound antecedent is true and the consequent is false. If you consider the second statement, you will notice that it is also true unless Heloise will *not* go to the dance even though both Holly and Hester go.

Finally, if you consider the conditions under which a conjunction or disjunction are true, it should be clear that any statement conjoined with or disjoined with itself is true under exactly the same conditions as the statement itself. So if the statement "Colin is a student" is true, then the statements "Either Colin is a student or Colin is a student" and "Colin is a student and Colin is a student" are also true.

With these equivalences our system is complete, and it is possible to prove the validity of any valid argument in propositional logic. For example, we can now construct a proof that the following argument form is valid:

p
$p \leftrightarrow q$
$\sim q \vee r$
$(r \ \& \ s) \rightarrow (t \vee t)$ $/\therefore$ $s \rightarrow t$

The proof is as follows:

1. p
2. $p \leftrightarrow q$
3. $\sim q \vee r$
4. $(r \ \& \ s) \rightarrow (t \vee t)$ $/\therefore$ $s \rightarrow t$
5. $(p \rightarrow q) \ \& \ (q \rightarrow p)$ 2 Equiv.
6. $p \rightarrow q$ 5 Simp.
7. q 1,6 M.P.
8. $q \rightarrow r$ 3 Impl.
9. r 8,7 M.P.
10. $r \rightarrow [s \rightarrow (t \vee t)]$ 4 Exp.
11. $s \rightarrow (t \vee t)$ 10,9 M.P.
12. $s \rightarrow t$ 11 Taut.

Although it is possible to prove the validity of any valid argument in propositional logic, the large number of equivalences that are available often makes it less than obvious how to begin a proof. There are, however, various rules of thumb or basic strategies that are useful to keep in mind when constructing a proof. The following is a brief list of such strategies.

RULES OF THUMB (STRATEGIES) FOR DOING
DEDUCTIVE PROOFS

1. Determine where the simple statements in the conclusion are contained in the premises.

   a. If there is a simple statement in the conclusion that is not in the premises, you will need to use addition.

b. If the conclusion is a simple statement that was not contained in the premises, you will use a combination of addition and disjunctive syllogism. For example, if the conclusion is "*r*" but "*r*" is not found in the premises, the premises will allow you to conclude both some proposition "*p*" and "*~p*," so you add "*r*" to "*p*" ("*p* ∨ *r*") and use disjunctive syllogism to conclude "*r*."

c. If the conclusion is a disjunction, it is probable that you will reach it either by addition or by constructive dilemma.

d. It is often helpful to consider equivalent forms of the conclusion.

2. Work backward from the conclusion to the premises.

a. If you can "see" what steps led to that conclusion, it will be helpful to note what those steps are. If there are alternative routes, you might also note them.

b. It is often helpful to work backward for a fair number of steps.

3. If you can use any of the Rules of Inference to break down a compound statement into its simple components, do so. (This is generally helpful, although not always necessary.) [Rules: M.P., M.T., Simp., Com., Simp.]

4. If you can use any of the Rules of Inference to eliminate a simple statement that is not in the conclusion, use it. [Rules: H.S., Simp., D.S.]

5. If there is a double arrow (↔) use the rule for material equivalence: it is usually the only way you will be able to do anything with the statement.

a. If it is the affirmation of a material equivalence, you will probably want to use the first version of the rule.

b. If it is the denial of a material equivalence, you will probably want to use the second version of the rule.

6. If there is a tilde (~) outside a set of grouping indicators, use De Morgan's to move it inside the parentheses *unless* you see how the negated compound statement can be used with M.T. or D.S. If a conditional is negated (for example, "~[A → B]"), try Impl. and then DeM.

7. If the premises contain both conditionals and disjunctions, C.D. is likely.

8. If you find a proposition of the form "*p* → (*q* → *r*)" you will probably use exportation. Exportation of a proposition of the

form "$p \rightarrow (q \rightarrow r)$" together with absorption of a proposition of
the form "$p \rightarrow q$" will allow you to conclude a proposition of
the form "$p \rightarrow r$" by hypothetical syllogism.

9. Plan ahead before using the equivalences falling under the Rule of
Replacement to *avoid* multiplying lines in the proof beyond
necessity.

10. *Most Important:* If you believe you can solve all the problems in
this book by following these rules of thumb as if they had no
exceptions, you will be disappointed.

EXERCISES

I. "Name the Rule." In each of the following, one uses either
Transposition, Material Implication, Material Equivalence,
Exportation, or Tautology to go from the premise to the
conclusion. Name the rule.

1. $p \leftrightarrow (r \vee s)$ /∴ $[p \rightarrow (r \vee s)] \ \& \ [(r \vee s) \rightarrow p]$

2. $(p \ \& \ q) \rightarrow (r \vee s)$ /∴ $p \rightarrow [q \rightarrow (r \vee s)]$

3. $p \ \& \ (q \vee q)$ /∴ $p \ \& \ q$

4. $p \vee r$ /∴ $\sim\!p \rightarrow r$

5. $[(p \ \& \sim q) \ \& \ (r \vee s)] \vee [\sim\!(p \ \& \sim q) \ \& \sim\!(r \vee s)]$
   /∴ $(p \ \& \sim q) \leftrightarrow (r \vee s)$

6. $\sim\!(p \leftrightarrow q) \vee (r \leftrightarrow \sim s)$
   /∴ $(p \leftrightarrow q) \rightarrow (r \leftrightarrow \sim s)$

7. $(p \ \& \ q) \rightarrow (r \rightarrow s)$ /∴ $[(p \ \& \ q) \ \& \ r] \rightarrow s$

8. $p \vee (q \vee r)$ /∴ $p \vee [q \vee (r \ \& \ r)]$

9. $\sim\!\{(q \ \& \ r) \vee [p \leftrightarrow (s \leftrightarrow \sim r)]\} \rightarrow (z \vee w)$
   /∴ $\{(q \ \& \ r) \vee [p \leftrightarrow (s \leftrightarrow \sim r)]\} \vee (z \vee w)$

10. $\{(q \ \& \ r) \vee [p \leftrightarrow (s \leftrightarrow \sim r)]\} \rightarrow (z \vee w)$
    /∴ $\sim\!(z \vee w) \rightarrow \sim\!\{(q \ \& \ r) \vee [p \leftrightarrow (s \leftrightarrow \sim r)]\}$

II. Construct a proof of validity for each of the following arguments
using *only* the Rules of Inference and Transposition, Material
Implication, Material Equivalence, Exportation, and Tautology.

1. p
   $\sim\!p \vee q$ /∴ q

2. $\sim\!p \vee q$
   $\sim q$ /∴ $\sim\!p$

3. $p \leftrightarrow q$
   $\sim q$ /∴ $\sim p$ & $\sim q$

4. $p \leftrightarrow q$
   $\sim(p$ & $q)$ /∴ $\sim p$ & $\sim q$

5. $(p \rightarrow q)$ & $(r \rightarrow s)$
   $\sim q$ ∨ $\sim s$ /∴ $\sim p$ ∨ $\sim r$

6. $(p \rightarrow q)$ & $(r \rightarrow q)$
   p ∨ r /∴ q

7. $p \rightarrow q$
   $p \rightarrow (q \rightarrow r)$ /∴ $p \rightarrow r$

8. $p \leftrightarrow q$
   $p \rightarrow (q \rightarrow r)$ /∴ $p \rightarrow r$

9. $p \rightarrow q$
   $\sim\sim p$ /∴ q

10. $\sim q \rightarrow p$
    $\sim p$ ∨ $\sim q$ /∴ $(p$ & $\sim q)$ ∨ $(\sim p$ & $\sim\sim q)$

11. $p \rightarrow (q$ ∨ $\sim s)$ /∴ $p \rightarrow [p \rightarrow (\sim s$ ∨ $\sim\sim q)]$

12. $p \rightarrow (\sim q \rightarrow r)$
    $\sim\sim q$ ∨ p /∴ $\sim r \rightarrow \sim\sim q$

13. $p \leftrightarrow q$
    $\sim p \rightarrow r$ /∴ $\sim q \rightarrow r$

14. $p \rightarrow q$
    $p \rightarrow [q \rightarrow (\sim r$ ∨ $s)]$ /∴ $(p$ & $r) \rightarrow s$

15. $\sim p$
    $\sim p \rightarrow s$ /∴ $\sim(\sim r \rightarrow \sim q) \rightarrow s$

16. $\sim q$
    $(\sim p$ & $q)$ ∨ $(\sim\sim p$ & $\sim q)$ /∴ $q \rightarrow q$

17. p
    $\sim p$ /∴ $(\sim\sim q \rightarrow \sim p)$ & $(\sim p \rightarrow \sim\sim q)$

18. $\sim p$
    $[\sim p$ & $(q \rightarrow r)]$ ∨ $[\sim\sim p$ & $\sim(q \rightarrow r)]$ /∴ $q \rightarrow r$

19. $p \leftrightarrow q$
    $q \rightarrow (r \rightarrow s)$
    $\sim s$ /∴ $(p$ & $r) \rightarrow t$

20. $q \rightarrow \sim p$
    $p \leftrightarrow q$
    $\sim\sim p \rightarrow (\sim q \rightarrow r)$ /∴ $\sim\sim p \rightarrow r$

III. Using the Rules of Inference and *all* the equivalences falling under
the Rule of Replacement, construct a deductive proof for each of
the following.

1. p /∴ $q \rightarrow p$

2. $p \rightarrow (q \rightarrow r)$
   $\sim r$ /∴ $\sim p \lor \sim q$

3. $p \rightarrow q$
   $q \rightarrow \sim p$ /∴ $\sim p$

4. $(p \rightarrow q)$ & $(r \rightarrow q)$
   $r \lor p$ /∴ q

5. $p \leftrightarrow q$ /∴ $\sim p \rightarrow \sim q$

6. $p \rightarrow q$
   $\sim r \rightarrow \sim q$ /∴ $p \rightarrow (p \rightarrow r)$

7. $(p \rightarrow q)$ & $(r \rightarrow s)$
   $\sim q \lor \sim s$ /∴ $p \rightarrow \sim r$

8. p & q
   $q \rightarrow (r \rightarrow s)$ /∴ $\sim r \lor s$

9. $p \rightarrow \sim q$
   q
   $\sim p \rightarrow (r \rightarrow s)$ /∴ $r \rightarrow (r$ & $s)$

10. p & q
    $(p$ & $q) \lor (\sim p$ & $\sim q)$ /∴ $q \rightarrow p$

11. $\sim p \rightarrow q$
    $\sim r \rightarrow \sim q$
    $\sim r$ /∴ p & p

12. $\sim p \lor (q$ & $r)$
    $\sim r$ /∴ $\sim p$

13. $p \lor (q$ & $r)$
    $(p \rightarrow r)$ & $(q \rightarrow s)$ /∴ $\sim s \rightarrow r$

14. $p \lor (q \lor r)$
    $\sim q$ /∴ $\sim p \rightarrow r$

15. $p \rightarrow q$
    $(q \lor p) \lor r$ /∴ $\sim q \rightarrow r$

16. $(p$ & $q)$ & r
    $q \rightarrow (r \rightarrow s)$ /∴ s

17. $\sim s \rightarrow \sim r$
    r /∴ $q \lor s$

18. $p \rightarrow q$
   $\neg p \vee \neg q$ $/\therefore$ $p \rightarrow s$

19. $p \& q$
   $q \rightarrow (r \vee s)$ $/\therefore$ $\neg s \rightarrow (\neg s \& r)$

20. $p \rightarrow (q \rightarrow r)$
   $q \& \neg r$ $/\therefore$ $\neg p$

21. $\neg(\neg p \& q)$
   $\neg(q \leftrightarrow r)$ $/\therefore$ $\neg r \rightarrow p$

22. $\neg p \rightarrow \neg q$
   $\neg(q \leftrightarrow r)$ $/\therefore$ $\neg r \rightarrow p$

23. $\neg p \leftrightarrow \neg(q \rightarrow r)$
   $\neg[(q \rightarrow r) \vee s]$ $/\therefore$ $p \leftrightarrow s$

24. $\neg[(p \& \neg q) \rightarrow (r \& s)]$
   $\neg r \rightarrow (s \vee t)$
   $\neg(t \leftrightarrow q)$ $/\therefore$ $\neg p \rightarrow t$

25. $p \leftrightarrow \neg q$
   $\neg p \rightarrow (r \& s)$
   $q \rightarrow \neg t$
   $\neg r \leftrightarrow \neg t$ $/\therefore$ $p \& \neg q$

IV. Translate and construct a deductive proof of each of the
   following. You may use the Rules of Inference together with *all*
   the equivalences falling under the Rule of Replacement. Use the
   suggested statement letters.

MURDER MOST FOUL

Cast of Characters:
   Louise Flounder, noted writer of murder mysteries
   Angela Krist, writer of murder mysteries
   Cornelius P. Hasselblatt, President of Hasselblatt Balloons, Inc.
   Jennifer Flounder, aspiring writer, niece of Louise Flounder
   Lt. Brazilton, chief homicide investigator in Swiggins Lagoon
   Sam Shovel, private investigator
   Horatio P. Hornswagel, drifter
   Larson E. Whorbunkle, heir to the Whorbunkle family fortune (of
   $2.53)
   Ima Quack, M.D., sometime medical examiner
   Rudi Ribinowitz, butler

1. Horatio P. Hornswagel was murdered and Jennifer Flounder is a prime suspect. Therefore, if Horatio P. Hornswagel was murdered, then Jennifer Flounder is a prime suspect; and if Jennifer Flounder is a prime suspect, then Horatio P. Hornswagel was murdered. (H, J)

2. Either the authors' guild of Swiggins Lagoon throws a party or Cornelius P. Hasselblatt has met with an untimely death. If the authors' guild of Swiggins Lagoon throws a party, then Angela Krist will not attend the party. If Cornelius P. Hasselblatt has met with an untimely death, then Jennifer Flounder will be the prime suspect in the murder case. Therefore, if Angela Krist attends the party, Jennifer Flounder will be the prime suspect in the murder case. (P, C, A, J)

3. A murder was committed in Swiggins Lagoon. If a murder was committed in Swiggins Lagoon and Mrs. Flounder helps investigate the case, then one of her relatives will be a prime suspect. So, if one of Mrs. Flounder's relatives is not a prime suspect, then Mrs. Flounder does not help investigate the case. (M, F, R)

4. If Lt. Brazilton smokes cigars and wears an old trench coat, then he is not taken seriously. If Lt. Brazilton is not taken seriously, then Louise Flounder will play a critical role in solving the mystery. Lt. Brazilton smokes cigars. So if Lt. Brazilton wears an old trench coat, then Louise Flounder will play a critical role in solving the mystery. (C, T, S, L)

5. A murder was committed in Swiggins Lagoon, and either Jennifer Flounder is a prime suspect or Angela Krist cracks the case wide open. If Jennifer Flounder is a prime suspect, then Louise Flounder will investigate the case; and if Angela Krist cracks the case wide open, then the Sam Shovel Detective Agency has solved another case. So if Louise Flounder does not investigate the case, then the Sam Shovel Detective Agency has solved another case. (M, J, A, L, S)

6. Either Cornelius P. Hasselblatt is dead or he isn't. If Cornelius P. Hasselblatt is dead, then Lt. Brazilton will investigate; and if Cornelius P. Hasselblat is not dead, then Angela Krist will invite Cornelius over for dinner. Lt. Brazilton will not investigate. If Angela Krist invites Cornelius over for dinner, then Horatio P. Hornswagel will settle down in Swiggins Lagoon. So either Horatio P. Hornswagel will settle down in Swiggins Lagoon or Louise Flounder will publish another mystery. (C, B, A, H, L)

7. If the Sam Shovel Detective Agency solves another case, both Louise Flounder and Angela Krist will be jailed. If Louise Floun-

der is jailed, then Jennifer Flounder will seek counsel; and if Angela Krist is jailed, then Horatio Hornswagel has been shot. But Jennifer Flounder will not seek counsel or Horatio Hornswagel has not been shot. So the Sam Shovel Detective Agency does not solve another case. (S, L, A, J, H)

8. Either Cornelius P. Hasselblatt or Horatio P. Hornswagel was murdered. Either Cornelius P. Hasselblatt or Horatio P. Hornswagel was murdered if and only if Jennifer Flounder has skipped town. But if Jennifer Flounder has skipped town, Lt. Brazilton will crack the case. So Lt. Brazilton will crack the case unless Angela Krist committed the crime. (C, H, J, B, A)

9. It is not the case that both Horatio P. Hornswagel and Cornelius P. Hasselblatt have been murdered. If Cornelius P. Hasselblatt has not been murdered, then Lt. Brazilton is out of town. Either Lt. Brazilton is not out of town or Horatio P. Hornswagel has been murdered. So Lt. Brazilton is out of town just in case Horatio P. Hornswagel has been murdered. (H, C, B)

10. Neither Cornelius P. Hasselblatt nor Horatio P. Hornswagel was murdered. If Louise Flounder is examining the case, then the fact that Cornelius P. Hasselblatt was not murdered implies that Horatio P. Hornswagel was murdered. If Jennifer Flounder is a prime suspect in the case or Angela Krist thinks something smells fishy in the affair, then Louise Flounder is examining the case. So Jennifer Flounder is not a prime suspect in the case. (C, H, L, J, A)

11. Either Lt. Brazilton is investigating or Louise Flounder has been murdered; and if the Sam Shovel Detective Agency is investigating Cornelius P. Hasselblatt, then Jennifer Flounder is in jail. The Sam Shovel Detective Agency is investigating Cornelius P. Hasselblatt. If Jennifer Flounder is in jail then Louise Flounder has not been murdered. So either Louise Flounder was murdered or she wasn't. (B, L, S, J)

12. If Angela Krist is involved in the case, then Lt. Brazilton is perplexed and Cornelius P. Hasselblatt is not dead. Either Cornelius P. Hasselblatt is dead or Mrs. Flounder is aiding in the investigation. So if Angela Krist is involved in the case, then Mrs. Flounder is aiding in the investigation. (A, B, C, F)

13. If a murder was committed in Swiggins Lagoon and Mrs. Flounder does not help investigate the case, then Lt. Brazilton is on the case. A murder was committed in Swiggins Lagoon but Lt. Brazilton is not on the case. So Mrs. Flounder helps investigate the case. (M, F, B)

14. Either Angela Krist has solved the mystery, or Louise Flounder is not in town and Lt. Brazilton is perplexed. But it is not the case that if Angela Krist has not solved the mystery then Louise Flounder is not in town and Jennifer Flounder is a prime suspect. So if Louise Flounder is in town, then Jennifer Flounder is a prime suspect or Lt. Brazilton is perplexed. (A, L, B, J)

15. If Angela Krist investigates the murder, then Louise Flounder is a suspect and Jennifer Flounder has fled the country. Either Louise Flounder is not a suspect or Lt. Brazilton is ready to make an arrest. If Louise Flounder is a suspect and Lt. Brazilton is ready to make an arrest, then if Jennifer Flounder has fled the country then Horatio P. Hornswagel is the murderer. Horatio P. Hornswagel is not the murderer. So either Angela Krist does not investigate the murder, or Horatio P. Hornswagel is the murderer just in case Jennifer Flounder has fled the country. (A, L, J, B, C, H)

16. If Horatio P. Hornswagel is dead, then a murder has been committed in Swiggins Lagoon. If Horatio P. Hornswagel is dead, then if a murder has been committed in Swiggins Lagoon, then Jennifer Flounder will be indicted for murder and Louise Flounder will join in the investigation. If Jennifer Flounder will be indicted for murder and Louise Flounder joins in the investigation, then Lt. Brazilton will crack the case. Lt. Brazilton will not crack the case. Therefore, if Horatio P. Hornswagel is dead, Louise Flounder will join in the investigation. (H, M, J, L, B)

17. If a murder was committed in Swiggins Lagoon, then Jennifer Flounder was indicted. If a murder was committed in Swiggins Lagoon and Jennifer Flounder was indicted, then Louise Flounder is not at home. Either Louise Flounder is at home, or both Angela Krist and Lt. Brazilton had a hand in the crime. So if a murder was committed in Swiggins Lagoon then Lt. Brazilton had a hand in the crime. (M, J, L, A B)

18. Mrs. Flounder is involved in the case if and only if the Sam Shovel Detective Agency is involved in the case. The indictment of Angela Krist implies that Mrs. Flounder is not involved in the case; and the indictment of Horatio P. Hornswagel implies that Mrs. Flounder is not involved in the case. Horatio P. Hornswagel has been indicted. Therefore, the Sam Shovel Detective Agency is not involved in the case. (F, S, A, H)

19. If Jennifer Flounder is the prime suspect in a murder case, then Louise Flounder will aid in the investigation. If Louise Flounder will

aid in the investigation, then Lt. Brazilton will find the killer. If Cornelius P. Hasselblatt has been murdered, then Angela Krist will have material for another book; and if Angela Krist has material for another book, then Lt. Brazilton will not find the killer. So, if Cornelius P. Hasselblatt has been murdered, then Jennifer Flounder is not the prime suspect in a murder case. (J, L, B, C, A)

20. If Lt. Brazilton and either Louise Flounder or Angela Krist are perplexed, then a red herring has entered the case. If Louise Flounder is not perplexed, then Angela Krist is perplexed. If Lt. Brazilton is not perplexed, then Angela Krist is perplexed. Therefore, if Angela Krist is not perplexed, then either Louise Flounder is perplexed or a red herring has entered the case. (B, L, A, R)

21. If both Angela Krist and Louise Flounder write murder mysteries, then the two women are rivals. Louise Flounder writes murder mysteries but the two women are not rivals. Therefore, Angela Krist does not write murder mysteries. (A, L, R)

22. Either it is not the case that either Larson E. Whorbunkle IV or Cornelius Hasselblatt has been murdered, or Angela Krist is involved in the case and if Lt. Brazilton is out of town then Jennifer Flounder is a suspect. Angela Krist is not involved in the case. Hence, Larson E. Whorbunkle IV has been murdered if and only if Cornelius P. Hasselblatt has been murdered. (L, C, A, B, J)

23. If the authors' guild of Swiggins Lagoon throws a party, then both Louise Flounder and Angela Krist will be invited. If either Angela Krist or Louise Flounder is invited, then the theme of the party will be murder. So if the authors' guild of Swiggins Lagoon throws a party, the theme of the party will be murder. (G, L, A, M)

24. Hasselblatt has been killed, and either Louise Flounder is aiding the police or Lt. Brazilton is in charge. If Lt. Brazilton is in charge, the investigation is certain to take an unusual turn. If Louise Flounder is aiding the police, then the investigation is certain to take an unusual turn. Therefore, if Hasselblatt has been killed, the investigation is certain to take an unusual turn. (H, L, B, U)

25. If Brazilton is on the case, then Dr. Quack is dead. If Brazilton is on the case, then if Dr. Quack is dead then Mrs. Flounder is meddling in the case. But Mrs. Flounder is not meddling in the case. Either Brazilton is on the case or Sam Shovel is investigating a murder. Therefore, if Sam Shovel is investigating a murder, then Sam Shovel is investigating a murder. (B, Q, F, S)

26. Jennifer Flounder is a suspect in the murder of Horatio P. Hornswagel if she had both a motive and an opportunity to kill Horatio P. Hornswagel. If Horatio was blackmailing her, then Jennifer had a motive. If Jennifer was serving wine at the party, then she had the opportunity. Horatio was blackmailing Jennifer and Jennifer was serving wine at the party. Therefore, if Jennifer is not a suspect in the murder of Horatio P. Hornswagel, then Louise Flounder is on vacation in Hawaii. (S, M, O, B, W, L)

27. If Louise Flounder is dead, then Lt. Brazilton is a suspect. If Louise Flounder is dead, then either Lt. Brazilton is not a suspect or Angela Krist is a suspect. If Dr. Quack committed the crime, then Angela Krist is not a suspect; and Dr. Quack committed the crime. So Louise Flounder is not dead. (F, B, A, Q)

28. Angela Krist was murdered just in case Lt. Brazilton is dead. Angela Krist was not murdered unless Angela Krist was not murdered. If Lt. Brazilton is not dead, then Cornelius P. Hasselblatt is not dead; and if Angela Krist was murdered, then Louise Flounder was murdered. Therefore, if Cornelius P. Hasselblatt is dead, then Louise Flounder was murdered. (A, B, C, F)

29. If Cornelius P. Hasselblatt has been murdered and Jennifer Flounder is the prime suspect, then either Lt. Brazilton will investigate the crime or Louise Flounder will have the plot for another mystery. Cornelius P. Hasselblatt has been murdered but Louise Flounder will not have a plot for another mystery. So if Jennifer Flounder is a prime suspect, then Lt. Brazilton will investigate the crime. (C, J, B, L)

30. Cornelius P. Hasselblatt is dead or Angela Krist has been stabbed, provided that a murder was committed in Swiggins Lagoon. If Cornelius P. Hasselblatt is dead, the future of Hasselblatt Balloons is up in the air. If Angela Krist has been stabbed then the final chapter of *On Whom the Bell Tolled* will not be finished. But it is neither the case that the future of Hasselblatt Balloons is up in the air nor that the last chapter of *On Whom the Bell Tolled* will not be finished. Therefore, if there was a murder in Swiggins Lagoon, then Dr. Quack is dead. (C, A, M, B, F, Q)

31. If Hasselblatt was murdered then Jennifer Flounder will be a suspect. If Jennifer Flounder is a suspect, then Louise Flounder will aid in the investigation. If Hasselblatt is murdered then Angela Krist will inherit a Porsche and Dr. Quack will perform the autopsy. But either Louise Flounder will not aid in the investigation or Dr. Quack

will not perform the autopsy, or Angela Krist will not inherit a Porsche. Therefore, Hasselblatt was not murdered. (H, J, L, A, Q)

32. Neither Cornelius P. Hasselblatt nor Horatio P. Hornswagel was murdered. Lt. Brazilton is investigating the case just in case the fact that Cornelius P. Hasselblatt was not murdered implies that Horatio P. Hornswagel was murdered. If Jennifer Flounder is a prime suspect in the case and Angela Krist thinks something smells fishy, then Lt. Brazilton is investigating the case. Therefore, if Jennifer Flounder is a prime suspect in the case, Angela Krist does not think something smells fishy. (C, H, B, J, A)

33. Either Brazilton investigates the crime, or Louise Flounder looks after the interests of her relatives or Angela Krist will write the definitive account of the case. Angela Krist does not write the definitive account of the case, but Jennifer Flounder is a prime suspect. If Jennifer Flounder is a prime suspect, then either Hasselblatt is dead or Brazilton does not investigate the crime. So if Hasselblatt is not dead then Louise Flounder looks after the interest of her relatives. (B, L, A, J, H)

34. If Dr. Quack has been murdered, then both Louise Flounder and Angela Krist will give an account of the case. Either neither Louise Flounder nor Angela Krist will give an account of the case, or Jennifer Flounder will be a suspect and Lt. Brazilton will be the chief investigator. If Jennifer Flounder will be a suspect, then Lt. Brazilton will not be the chief investigator. So, if Dr. Quack has been murdered, then Cornelius Hasselblatt is dead just in case Horatio Hornswagel has been shot. (Q, L, A, J, B, C, H)

35. If Hasselblatt is dead, then Angela Krist will be indicted for murder; if Larson E. Whorbunkle IV is dead then Mrs. Flounder will be indicted for murder. If Hasselblatt is dead and Angela Krist will be indicted for murder, then Larson E. Whorbunkle IV is dead. The fact that Ima Quack will rise to the top of the Swiggins Lagoon social register is implied by Mrs. Flounder's indictment for murder, just in case Larson E. Whorbunkle IV is dead. Mrs. Flounder will be indicted for murder. So, if Hasselblatt is dead, Ima Quack will rise to the top of the Swiggins Lagoon social register. (H, A, L, F, I)

36. If Hasselblatt has been murdered and Lt. Brazilton investigates, then cigar ash plays a significant role in the investigation. If cigar ash plays a significant role in the investigation, then either Brazilton consults Sherlock Holmes's monograph on cigar ash or he discovers that Angela Krist smokes El Ropos. If Brazilton discovers that

Angela Krist smokes El Ropos, then Angela will be indicted for murder. Although Hasselblatt has been murdered, Angela will not be indicted for murder. So if Lt. Brazilton investigates, he consults Sherlock Holmes's monograph on cigar ash. (H, B, C, S, A, I)

37. A murder was committed in Swiggins Lagoon, or Jennifer Flounder is a prime suspect and Angela Krist cracks the case wide open. If either a murder was committed in Swiggins Lagoon or Jennifer Flounder is a prime suspect, then Louise Flounder takes part in the investigation. If a murder was committed in Swiggins Lagoon or Angela Krist cracks the case wide open, then the Sam Shovel Detective Agency solves another case on the condition that Lt. Brazilton is out of town. But the Sam Shovel Detective Agency does not solve another case. So it is not the case that if Louise Flounder takes part in the investigation, then Lt. Brazilton is out of town. (M, J, A, L, B)

38. Either Jennifer Flounder is a suspect in the murder, or both Cornelius P. Hasselblatt and Horatio P. Hornswagel are dead. If Jennifer Flounder is a suspect in the murder, then Horatio P. Hornswagel is dead. If Larson E. Whorbunkle IV is the prosecuting attorney, then Cornelius P. Hasselblatt is not dead. So if Larson E. Whorbunkle IV is the prosecuting attorney, then if Horatio P. Hornswagel is not dead then the story will be made into a major motion picture. (J, C, H, L, M)

39. There was a murder in Swiggins Lagoon. So either the Sam Shovel Detective Agency will crack the case or it won't. (M, S)

40. If Lt. Brazilton is dead, then both his crumpled trench coat and his old gold Peugeot will be donated to the Smithsonian Institution. If Brazilton's old gold Peugeot will be donated to the Smithsonian Institution, then Cornelius P. Hasselblatt will get away with murder; and if Cornelius P. Hasselblatt gets away with murder then there will be a crime wave in Swiggins Lagoon. Lt. Brazilton is dead. So if Lt. Brazilton is dead and his crumpled trench coat will be donated to the Smithsonian Institution, then there will be a crime wave in Swiggins Lagoon. (B, T, P, C, S)

41. If Cornelius P. Hasselblatt will be elected mayor, then Larson E. Whorbunkle IV is running for state senate; and if Cornelius P. Hasselblatt will be elected mayor and Mrs. Flounder is not on vacation, then there will be a murder in Swiggins Lagoon. If Mrs. Flounder is on vacation then Lt. Brazilton will investigate the crime. Either Larson E. Whorbunkle IV is not running for state senate or Lt. Brazilton will not investigate the crime. If there is a murder in

Swiggins Lagoon, then Cornelius P. Hasselblatt will not be elected mayor. So Cornelius P. Hasselblatt will not be elected mayor. (C, L, F, M, B)

42. Horatio P. Hornswagel is dead. If Horatio P. Hornswagel is dead, then either he died a natural death or he was murdered. Horatio P. Hornswagel did not die a natural death, and Louise Flounder will show that her niece is innocent even though Lt. Brazilton will solve the case. If Lt. Brazilton solves the case, the citizens of Swiggins Lagoon will be shocked; and if Horatio was murdered, then Jennifer Flounder will be indicted. So Jennifer Flounder will be indicted and the citizens of Swiggins Lagoon will be shocked. (D, N, M, L, B, S, J)

43. If either there was a murder in Swiggins Lagoon or there wasn't, then Mrs. Flounder will be on the prowl. So Mrs. Flounder will be on the prowl. (M, F)

44. Both Cornelius and Horatio are dead, just in case there is a psychopathic killer in Swiggins Lagoon. That Rudi Ribinowitz is visiting Minnesota implies that there is a psychopathic killer in Swiggins Lagoon. If Cornelius is dead, then either Jennifer Flounder will be a suspect or Angela Krist committed the crime. So if Rudi Ribinowitz is visiting Minnesota and Jennifer Flounder is not a suspect, then Angela Krist committed the crime. (C, H, P, R, J, A)

45. If Horatio is dead, then Cornelius is dead. Both Horatio and Cornelius are dead, just in case Rudi Ribinowitz is a butler and Angela Krist has amorous ties to Cornelius. If Angela Krist has amorous ties to Cornelius then Cornelius is dead. If Cornelius is dead and Angela Krist has amorous ties to Cornelius, then Horatio is dead. Hence, Horatio is dead and Angela Krist has amorous ties to Cornelius, or Horatio is not dead and Angela Krist does not have amorous ties to Cornelius. (H, C, R, A)

46. If Cornelius P. Hasselblatt is murdered, then Louise Flounder will aid in the investigation; and if Horatio P. Hornswagel is murdered, then Angela Krist will aid in the investigation. So if both Cornelius P. Hasselblatt and Horatio P. Hornswagel are murdered, then both Louise Flounder and Angela Krist will aid in the investigation. (C, L, H, A)

47. If this is a classic whodunit, then the butler is guilty; and if this is a modern whodunit, then the victim's lover had a hand in the crime. So if this is either a classic or a modern whodunit, then either the butler is guilty or the victim's lover had a hand in the crime. (C, B, M, L)

48. If Jennifer Flounder murdered Hasselblatt, then Angela Krist will take over Hasselblatt Balloons and Rudi Ribinowitz retires to Argentina. Rudi Ribinowitz retires to Argentina and Jennifer Flounder murdered Hasselblatt, just in case Louise Flounder assists in the investigation. But if Angela Krist will take over Hasselblatt Balloons, then Louise Flounder does not assist in the investigation. So Jennifer Flounder did not murder Hasselblatt. (J, A, R, L)

49. Jennifer Flounder is innocent of the crime, and Angela Krist is the murderer just in case Larson E. Whorbunkle IV has fled for Argentina. If Jennifer Flounder is innocent of the crime or Rudi Ribinowitz is the butler, then Sam Shovel will crack the case wide open. If Sam Shovel cracks the case wide open, then either Larson E. Whorbunkle IV has fled for Argentina or Angela Krist is the murderer. So if Sam Shovel cracks the case wide open, then if Jennifer is innocent of the crime then Angela Krist is the murderer. (J, A, L, R, S)

50. Louise Flounder or Angela Krist will be a suspect in the case only if Horatio P. Hornswagel has stolen a murder-mystery manuscript and his body was found at the bottom of the duck pond. If Horatio P. Hornswagel's body was found at the bottom of the duck pond, then either he drowned or he was poisoned. If Horatio drowned, then he had imbibed heavily and his death will be ruled an accident. If Horatio was poisoned, then traces of poison will be found in his wine glass. Horatio P. Hornswagel's death will not be ruled an accident. Therefore, if Angela Krist will be a suspect in the case, then traces of poison will be found in Horatio's wine glass. (L, A, S, B, D, P, I, R, W)

6.4 Conditional Proof

Although we can now construct proofs for all valid arguments in propositional logic, the proofs are often long and tedious. Further, it is often unclear where we should begin and how we should proceed to show that the argument is valid. In this section and the next, we introduce two additional rules that provide us with additional strategies that can be used to construct a proof. Typically, even if using these techniques results in longer proofs, the moves we make in the proof are more obvious.

Recall that a conditional statement is true except when its antecedent is true and its consequent is false. The statement does not tell you that the antecedent is true, only that *if* it is true, the consequent is true as well. It is this fact that provides the rationale for conditional proof.

The Rule of Conditional Proof is: **Given a set of premises, you may *assume* any statement and work out the implications of that assumption with respect to the premises. You then *discharge* your assumption by forming a conditional statement in which the antecedent is the assumed statement and the consequent is the statement you have shown to follow from that assumption.**

Using the Rule of Conditional Proof is particularly useful when you have an argument with a conditional as its conclusion. Consider the argument:

$$p \rightarrow (\sim q \lor r)$$
$$q \qquad\qquad /\therefore \quad p \rightarrow r$$

You can establish that the conclusion follows from the argument by means of the following direct proof:

1. $p \rightarrow (\sim q \lor r)$
2. q $/\therefore \quad p \rightarrow r$
3. $\sim p \lor (\sim q \lor r)$ 1 Impl.
4. $(\sim p \lor \sim q) \lor r$ 3 Assoc.
5. $(\sim q \lor \sim p) \lor r$ 4 Com.
6. $\sim q \lor (\sim p \lor r)$ 5 Assoc.
7. $\sim\sim q$ 2 D.N.
8. $\sim p \lor r$ 6,7 D.S.
9. $p \rightarrow r$ 8 Impl.

On the other hand, you might *reason* as follows. The conclusion asserts that if "p" is true, then "r" is true. If I *assume* that "p" is true, then I can infer that the statement "$\sim q \lor r$" is true. If the statement "$\sim q \lor r$" is true, then the statement "$q \rightarrow r$" is true, and given "q," it follows that "r" is true. Hence, *if* (as assumed) "p" is true, then "r" is true, that is, "$p \rightarrow r$" is true. This reasoning assumes the Rule of Conditional Proof, and the proof looks like this:

1. $p \rightarrow (\sim q \lor r)$
2. q $/\therefore \quad p \rightarrow r$
    3. p ACP
    4. $\sim q \lor r$ 1,3 M.P.
    5. $q \rightarrow r$ 4 Impl.
    6. r 4,5 M.P.
7. $p \rightarrow r$ 3–6, C.P.

In line 3 you introduce your *assumption,* namely, "*p*," and justify it as an assumption for conditional proof (ACP). The lines in which the assumption is in effect are known as the **scope of the assumption,** and you indicate the scope of your assumption by indenting and drawing a vertical line to the left of the lines of the proof in which the assumption is in effect. You continue until you find the desired consequent of your conditional, in this case "*r*." You *discharge* your assumption in line 7 by stating a conditional in which the antecedent is your assumption for conditional proof and the consequent is the conclusion reached in line 6. Here you discharge your assumption with the statement "*p* → *r*," cite the lines in which the assumption was in effect and justify the conclusion by C.P. (Conditional Proof).

Two points should be noted. First, you must *always* discharge your assumptions with a conditional statement in which the antecedent is the assumption for conditional proof and the consequent is the statement in the line before you discharge the assumption. Second, although you can use a conditional proof to prove something other than the conclusion of an argument, *anything proven within the scope of the assumption for conditional proof cannot be used outside the scope of that assumption.* Consequently, if you do not want extra lines in your proof—some within the scope of your assumption and identical lines at other points in the proof—you will need to take care in deciding when to introduce an assumption.

In the example we have just considered conditional proof was used to show that the conclusion of the argument follows from the premises. In fact, the Rule of Conditional Proof can be used at *any* point in a proof. Consider the following argument form:

$\sim p \lor s$
$p \lor q$
$q \to r$
$s \to (u \,\&\, t)$ /∴ $r \lor u$

We can show that the conclusion follows by Constructive Dilemma provided that we can show that statement "$(\sim p \to r) \,\&\, (s \to u)$" follows from the premises. This can be shown by successive applications of conditional proof. The proof looks like this:

1. $\sim p \lor s$
2. $p \lor q$
3. $q \to r$

4. $s \rightarrow (u \ \& \ t)$ $/\therefore \quad r \lor u$
5. $\sim p$	ACP
7. q	2,5 D.S.
8. r	3,7 M.P.
9. $\sim p \rightarrow r$	5-8 C.P.
10. s	ACP
11. $u \ \& \ t$	4,10 M.P.
12. u	11 Simp.
13. $s \rightarrow u$ | 10-12 C.P. |
14. $(\sim p \rightarrow r) \ \& \ (s \rightarrow u)$ | 9,13 Conj. |
15. $r \lor u$ | 14,1 C.D. |

Finally, you may construct conditional proofs within the scopes of other conditional proofs. There is one restriction, however: *you must discharge your assumptions in the reverse of the order in which you make them.* Conditional proof might be said to follow last-in–first-out principles of accounting. Assume you are given:

$[(p \ \& \ q) \ \& \ r] \rightarrow s$
p $/\therefore \quad q \rightarrow (r \rightarrow s)$

You could prove the conclusion by successive instances of Exportation together with *modus ponens,* or you could construct the following conditional proof:

1. $[(p \ \& \ q) \ \& \ r] \rightarrow s$
2. p $/\therefore \quad q \rightarrow (r \rightarrow s)$
3. p	ACP
4. q	ACP
5. $p \ \& \ q$	3,4 Conj.
6. r	ACP
7. $(p \ \& \ q) \ \& \ r$	5,6 Conj.
8. s	1,7 M.P.
9. $r \rightarrow s$	6-8 C.P.
10. $q \rightarrow (r \rightarrow s)$	4-9 C.P.
11. $p \rightarrow [q \rightarrow (r \rightarrow s)]$ | 3-9 C.P. |
12. $q \rightarrow (r \rightarrow s)$ | 2,11 M.P. |

SUMMARY

1. Assume a proposition for conditional proof (ACP).
2. Beginning with the line containing the assumption, indent and draw a vertical line to the left of each line in the scope of your assumption.
3. Use the assumption with the earlier lines in the proof to draw conclusions.
4. Discharge the assumption by constructing a conditional statement of the form "$p \rightarrow q$," where "p" is the assumption for conditional proof and "q" is the conclusion reached in the previous line.
5. Assumptions for conditional proof may be made within the scope of other assumptions for conditional proof, but assumptions must be discharged in the reverse of the order in which they are made (last-in–first-out).
6. *Remember,* conclusions reached within the scope of an assumption for conditional proof *cannot* be used to justify conclusions after the assumption has been discharged.

EXERCISES

Use the rule of conditional proof to prove each of the following.

1. p /∴ $q \rightarrow p$
2. $p \& q$ /∴ $p \rightarrow q$
3. $p \lor q$
   ~p /∴ $r \rightarrow q$
4. $p \rightarrow q$
   $r \& s$ /∴ $p \rightarrow (q \& r)$
5. p
   $(p \& q) \rightarrow r$ /∴   ~$r \rightarrow$ ~q
6. $p \rightarrow (q \& $ ~$r)$
   $r \lor s$ /∴ $p \rightarrow s$
7. $(p \& q) \rightarrow r$
   $p \rightarrow q$ /∴ $(s \& p) \rightarrow r$
8. $(p \& q) \rightarrow r$
   ~$r \& p$ /∴ $s \rightarrow$ ~q
9. $p \rightarrow q$
   ~$r \rightarrow$ ~q /∴ $p \rightarrow (p \rightarrow r)$

10. $p \& q$
    $q \to (r \lor s)$ /∴ $\sim s \to (\sim s \& r)$

11. $[p \& (q \lor r)] \to s$
    $\sim q \to r$
    $\sim p \to r$ /∴ $\sim r \to (q \& s)$

12. $p \to \sim q$
    q
    $\sim p \to (r \to s)$ /∴ $r \to (r \& s)$

13. $\sim(p \& q)$
    $\sim q \to r$
    $\sim r \lor p$ /∴ $r \leftrightarrow p$

14. $p \lor (\sim q \& r)$
    $\sim[\sim p \to (\sim q \& s)]$ /∴ $q \to (\sim s \lor r)$

15. $p \to (q \& r)$
    $\sim q \lor s$
    $(q \& s) \to (r \to t)$
    $\sim t$ /∴ $\sim p \lor (t \leftrightarrow r)$

16. $(p \to q) \& r$
    $(p \& r) \to s$
    $\sim s$ /∴ $p \to (q \& \sim r)$

17. $p \to [(q \& r) \to s]$
    $\sim s$
    $p \& q$ /∴ $\sim r$

18. $q \leftrightarrow (t \lor p)$
    p
    $(q \& p) \to (r \lor s)$
    $\sim s$ /∴ r

19. $p \leftrightarrow (q \lor r)$
    r
    $(p \& r) \to (s \lor t)$
    $\sim t$ /∴ s

20. $q \to (p \& r)$
    $(\sim p \& \sim r) \lor (s \& t)$
    $s \to \sim t$ /∴ $q \to (w \leftrightarrow x)$

6.5 *Indirect Proof*

What is known alternatively as the method of **indirect proof** or proof by **reductio ad absurdum** is a variation on conditional proof. The method is straightforward. For any given "*p*" that you wish to establish, *assume* the negation of "*p*" (~*p*) as an additional premise and proceed to use the rules to construct a proof. If you can generate a self-contradictory statement, that is, a statement of the form "*p* & ~*p*," you are justified in accepting the truth of the original conclusion. The statement whose denial you assume can be the conclusion of the argument or the denial of any statement whose truth you wish to prove.

The procedure for constructing an indirect proof is basically the same as that for constructing a conditional proof. You introduce the denial of the statement you are attempting to prove as an *assumption for indirect proof* (AIP). You mark the scope of your assumption by means of a vertical line, with the lines of the proof indented. You continue until you have shown that a statement and its denial—*any* statement and its denial—follow from the premises and your assumption. Conjoin the statement and its denial and discharge your assumption by stating the denial of your assumption. As in the case of conditional proof, there can be indirect proofs within the scope of other indirect proofs, and the assumptions must be discharged in the reverse of the order in which they are introduced: last-in–first-out. Further, indirect proofs can be used in conjunction with conditional proofs, but the last-in–first-out principle continues to hold: it is permissible to construct a conditional or indirect proof within the scope of another, *but they must not overlap.*

As an example, consider the following argument:

A ∨ (B & C)
A → C   /∴   C

The conclusion of this argument can be proven to follow from the premises by either a direct proof or an indirect proof:

DIRECT PROOF		INDIRECT PROOF	
1. A v (B & C)		1. A v (B & C)	
2. A → C /∴ C		2. A → C /∴ C	
3. ~C → ~A	2 Trans.	3. ~C	AIP
4. ~~A v (B & C)	1 D.N.	4. ~A	2,3 M.T.
5. ~A → (B & C)	4 Impl.	5. B & C	1,4 D.S.
6. ~C → (B & C)	3,5 H.S.	6. C & B	5 Com.
7. ~~C v (B & C)	6 Impl.	7. C	6 Simp.
8. C v (B & C)	7 D.N.	8. C & ~C	7,3 Conj.
9. (C v B) & (C v C)	8 Dist.	9. C	3–8 I.P.
10. (C v C) & (C v B)	9 Com.		
11. C v C	10 Simp.		
12. C	11 Taut.		

Since in the indirect proof you have found that the *assumption* of the negation of the conclusion of the argument generates a contradiction, you are justified in accepting the original conclusion as true. The rationale involved is as follows: If a set of propositions entails a self-contradictory statement, at least one of those propositions is false. To prove the validity of an argument, you assume that each of its premises is true. So, if you assume the truth of an additional proposition "p" and "p" together with the premises entail a self-contradiction, "p" must be false and "~p" true. Indeed, the truth "~p" is entailed, since the truth of any proposition follows from a contradiction, as is shown by the following proof:

1. p & $\sim p$ /∴ q		
2. p	1 Simp.	
3. p v q	2 Add.	
4. $\sim p$ & p	1 Com.	
5. $\sim p$	2 Simp.	
6. q	3,5 D.S.	

As in the case of conditional proof, the method of indirect proof does not guarantee that your proofs will be shorter than direct proofs—indeed, they are often longer—but the procedure is more straightforward. Whereas it is often useful in a *direct* proof to break down complex statements into simple statements, in an indirect proof this is often a primary objective. The negation of the conclusion assumed for the indirect proof usually makes it easy to break down complex statements by means of the nine rules of inference.

SUMMARY

1. Assume the denial of the proposition you want to prove (AIP).

2. Beginning with the line containing the assumption, indent and draw a vertical line to the left of each line in the scope of your assumption.

3. Use the assumption with the earlier lines in the proof to draw conclusions.

4. When you have derived a statement "*p*" and its denial "-*p*," conjoin them and discharge your assumption by stating the proposition you want to prove.

5. Assumptions for indirect proof may be made within the scope of other assumptions for indirect or conditional proof, but assumptions must be discharged in the reverse of the order in which they are made (last-in–first-out).

6. *Remember,* conclusions reached within the scope of an assumption for indirect proof *cannot* be used to justify conclusions after the assumption has been discharged.

A FEW MORE RULES OF THUMB

1. If the conclusion is a conditional, start by assuming the antecedent (ACP) and then assume the denial of the consequent (AIP). This will allow you to establish the consequent by indirect proof and then obtain the conclusion a line later by conditional proof.

2. Use M.P., M.T., D.S., and Simp. to break down complex statements as far as possible.

3. Since it is generally helpful to break complex statements down into simpler ones, if the conclusion is a disjunction, try proceeding by indirect proof.

4. Since it is generally useful to break complex statements down into simpler statements when using either conditional or indirect proof, it is wise to break the premises down as far as possible before you make any assumptions.

EXERCISES

I. Construct an *indirect* proof for each of the following argument forms.

1. p   /∴   *q* ∨ ~*q*

2. *h*
   h → (*m* ∨ *a*)
   a → ~*p*
   p   /∴   *m*

3. *m* → *g*
   g → *a*
   a → *p*
   p → *i*
   m   /∴   *i*

4. *p* → *q*
   q ∨ *r*
   p ∨ ~*r*   /∴   *q*

5. ~*p* → (*o* & *g*)
   g ↔ *p*   /∴   *o* → *p*

6. *p* ∨ *f*
   p → (*n* ∨ *b*)
   f → *a*
   ~*a* & ~*b*   /∴   *n*

7. *p* → [~*q* ∨ (*r* & *s*)
   ~*s* & *q*   /∴   ~*p*

8. *a* → *b*
   ~(*d* & ~*c*)
   a ∨ (~*c* & *e*)   /∴   *b* ∨ ~*d*

9. *m* → *g*
   g → (*c* ∨ *h*)
   h → *d*
   ~*d*
   c → *a*   /∴   ~*m* ∨ *a*

10. *s* → *w*
    s ↔ (*b* & *y*)
    ~*w* → *b*   /∴   *w* ∨ ~*y*

II. Construct a proof of each of the following using either the rule of conditional proof, the rule of indirect proof, or a combination of the two.

1. (*m* & *f*) → (*a* ∨ ~*c*)
   g → *c*
   ~*f* → *j*
   ~*a* & *g*   /∴   ~*m* ∨ *j*

2. $\text{-}f \rightarrow (j \rightarrow p)$
   $p \rightarrow (\text{-}a \lor m)$ /∴ $(\text{-}f \& j) \rightarrow (a \rightarrow m)$

3. $p \rightarrow (\text{-} q \& r)$
   $(q \lor \text{-}r) \rightarrow s$
   $\text{-}s \lor p$ /∴ $\text{-} q$

4. $(s \& w) \lor (b \& \text{-}y)$
   $(s \rightarrow b) \& (w \rightarrow \text{-}y)$ /∴ $\text{-}y$

5. $n \leftrightarrow (h \lor s)$
   $h \rightarrow (b \& m)$
   $s \rightarrow e$
   $\text{-}e \& n$ /∴ $b \& m$

6. $p \rightarrow (q \lor r)$
   $\text{-}r \rightarrow s$
   $\text{-}s \lor p$ /∴ $q \lor r$

7. $a \lor [g \& (\text{-}d \& \text{-}e)]$
   $g \leftrightarrow e$ /∴ $\text{-}a \rightarrow \text{-}(d \& \text{-}e)$

8. $(p \& \text{-}q) \rightarrow (r \rightarrow s)$
   $p \& \text{-}s$ /∴ $\text{-} q \rightarrow \text{-}r$

9. $(h \& m) \rightarrow (k \& b)$
   $(k \lor b) \rightarrow (f \lor s)$
   $h \& \text{-}s$ /∴ $m \rightarrow f$

10. $p \& (q \lor \text{-}r)$
    $(p \& \text{-}r) \rightarrow s$
    $(\text{-}s \lor \text{-} q) \rightarrow r$ /∴ $q \lor (t \& \text{-}s)$

11. $a \rightarrow (b \& \text{-}c)$
    $\text{-}a \leftrightarrow b$ /∴ $a \rightarrow d$

12. $p \rightarrow q$
    $(p \& q) \rightarrow r$
    $(p \& r) \rightarrow s$ /∴ $p \rightarrow s$

13. $[w \& (c \lor g)] \rightarrow [g \leftrightarrow (o \rightarrow r)]$
    g
    $g \rightarrow (\text{-}r \& w)$ /∴ $\text{-}g \lor \text{-}o$

14. $p \leftrightarrow (q \lor \text{-}r)$
    $\text{-}p \& \text{-}s$ /∴ $q \leftrightarrow s$

15. $\text{-}[p \leftrightarrow (q \lor \text{-}r)]$
    $p \& \text{-}s$ /∴ $q \leftrightarrow s$

Chapter Seven
Predicate Logic: Natural Deduction

7.1 The Language of Predicate Logic

The method of propositional logic allows us to demonstrate the validity of many, but by no means all, argument forms. Consider the following two arguments:

> All dogs are mammals.
> Fido is a dog.
> _____
>
> Therefore, Fido is a mammal.

> No rats are dogs.
> Some dogs are collies.
> _____
>
> Therefore, some collies are not rats.

These arguments are valid, but to prove their validity, we must analyze the compound statements composing the arguments and modify our symbolic language. We must examine and develop symbolic representations for three kinds of statements: singular statements, particular statements, and universal statements.

"Fido is a dog" is a singular statement. A **singular statement** makes a claim about an individual, exactly one thing. There are two terms in the statement. A **term** is a word that can function as the subject or the predicate of a statement. In this premise 'Fido' is the subject term and 'dog' is the predicate term. The statement is true if and only if Fido is included in the class of dogs.

Predicates are the fundamental elements of predicate logic. We represent predicate terms by uppercase letters (A, B, C, . . . Z). The following are examples of predicate terms:

ENGLISH PREDICATE	SYMBOLIC PREDICATE
___ is a dog	D ___
___ is a building	B ___
___ is a computer	C ___
___ is rich	R ___

In each case we have only a predicate term. By adding a subject term in the blank space, we form a statement. So, "___ is a dog" becomes the statement "Fido is a dog" by placing 'Fido' in the blank.

In our symbolic language we represent subject terms by the lowercase letters from *a* to *w* (a, b, c, . . . w). These letters represent specific individuals and are called **individual constants**. So the statement "Fido is a dog" is represented by the symbol "Df" where "D ___" is the predicate "is a dog" and "f" is the constant for "Fido."

Singular statements always pertain to individuals, and they can be of any degree of complexity. Here are some examples of singular statements in English and their corresponding symbolic representations:

ENGLISH STATEMENT	SYMBOLIC TRANSLATION
Henry is poor.	Ph
Turbo is a cat.	Ct
Erin is not a student.	~Se
Josephine is not a plumber.	~Pj
If John studies, Shirley studies.	Sj → Ss
Either Bill wins the election or George wins the election.	Wb v Wg

Sally plays basketball but Dan doesn't.	Ps & ~Pd
Humberto takes the class if and only if both Gavin and Colin take the class.	Th ↔ (Tg & Tc)

The statements "Some dogs are collies" and "Some collies are not rats" are particular statements. The first is a particular affirmative statement; the second is a particular negative statement. A **particular statement** claims that there is at least one member of the class denoted by the subject term that is or is not a member of the class denoted by the predicate term. So the statement "Some collies are dogs" means "There is at least one thing that is a collie and that thing is a dog." The statement "Some collies are not rats" means "There is at least one thing that is a collie and that thing is not a cat." Since these statements are concerned with some unnamed collie or other, we introduce **individual variables** to represent whatever collie that might happen to be. We use the last three lowercase letters of the alphabet *(x, y, z)* as individual variables. Further, we introduce a **particular quantifier** to represent the English expression "there is at least one thing." The particular quantifier is formed by placing a backward *E* followed by a variable in parentheses: (∃x). Since we treat predicates in the same way for particular statements as we treated them for singular statements, our particular statements will be translated as follows:

ENGLISH STATEMENT	SYMBOLIC TRANSLATION
Some dogs are collies.	(∃x) (Dx & Cx)
Some collies are not rats.	(∃x) (Cx &~Rx)

In general, where S is the subject term and P is the predicate term, the translations and verbal meanings of the expressions are as follows:

STATEMENT FORM	SYMBOLIC REPRESENTATION	VERBAL MEANING
Some S is P.	(∃x)(Sx & Px)	There is an *x*, such that *x* is S and *x* is P.
Some S is not P.	(∃x)(Sx and ~Px)	There is an *x*, such that *x* is S and *x* is not P.

Notice that the conjunction following the quantifier is placed in parentheses. The parentheses around the statement show the **scope of the**

quantifier, that is, they show to which variables the quantifier applies. The variables within the scope of a quantifier are **bound variables.** Any variables *not* within the scope of a quantifier are **free variables.** It is only by binding the variables by a quantifier that an expression such as "Mx & Px" is converted into a proposition, a statement with a truth value. A predicate with a free variable is a **propositional function,** that is, it is a statement that will be converted into a proposition either by replacing the variable with a constant or by binding the variable by a quantifier. Propositional functions do not have a truth value. The grouping indicators (parentheses, square brackets, and braces) in propositional logic are used to convert collections of symbols into well-formed formulae; the same holds here.

The statements "All dogs are mammals" and "No rats are dogs" are universal statements. The first is a universal affirmative statement; the second is a universal negative statement. A **universal statement** makes a claim about every member of its subject class. Universal propositions are understood as conditionals. The universal affirmative proposition "All dogs are mammals" means "If anything is a dog, then it is a mammal." The universal negative statement "No rats are dogs" means "If anything is a rat then it is not a dog." The rationale for a conditional translation of a universal negative proposition is that a statement of the form "No S is P" is logically equivalent to its obverse, "All S is non-P" (see Section 4.4).[1] To translate universal statements into symbolic form we must introduce a **universal quantifier** for the English expression "for all *x*." The particular quantifier is formed by placing an *x* in parentheses: (*x*). Using the arrow ("→") to represent the material conditional, we translate universal propositions as follows:

STATEMENT FORM	SYMBOLIC REPRESENTATION	VERBAL MEANING
All S is P.	$(x)(Sx \rightarrow Px)$	For all *x*, if *x* is S then *x* is P.
No S is P.	$(x)(Sx \rightarrow -Px)$	For all *x*, if *x* is S then *x* is not P.

As in the case of particular propositions, the parentheses show the scope of the quantifier.

The language for predicate logic may be summarized as follows:

I. Atomic expressions:

   1. Individual variables: *x, y, z*

   2. Individual constants: a, b, c, . . . w

   3. Predicate letters: A, B, C, . . . Z

4. Connectives:

   a. one-place: ~

   b. two-place: &, ∨, →, ↔

5. Grouping indicators: (,), [,], {,}

6. Quantifiers: (x), (y), (z), $(\exists x)$, $(\exists y)$, $(\exists z)$

II. Well-formed formulae (WFFs):

   1. Atomic WFFs:

      a. Where Φ is a predicate letter and μ is either an individual constant or an individual variable, then Φμ is an atomic WFF.

      b. Where Φ is a predicate letter and μ and σ are either individual constants or individual variables, then Φμσ and Φσμ are atomic WFFs.

      c. Since predicates can be predicates of any degree, where Φ is a predicate letter followed by any number of individual constants or individual variables, μ, σ, τ, . . ., Φμστ . . . is an atomic WFF.

   2. Molecular WFFs: where α and β are WFFs, so are:

      a. ~α

      b. α & β

      c. α ∨ β

      e. α → β

      f. α ↔ β

   3. General WFFs: where Φ is a predicate letter and x is an individual variable, the following are WFFs:

      a. $(x)(\Phi x)$

      b. $(\exists x)(\Phi x)$

   4. Nothing is a WFF unless it can be constructed by a finite number of applications of rules 1–3.

There are various things you must take into account in translating from ordinary English into symbols. First, all of the rules for translating English words into symbols that were introduced in Chapter 5 continue to apply. Thus, "If Maggie is an aardvark then Maggie is a mammal" will be treated as a conditional statement. You introduce two predicates, "is an aardvark" and "is a mammal," and translate the statement as follows:

Am → Mm.

Similarly, if you are given the statement "If Maggie is an aardvark and all aardvarks are mammals, then Maggie is a mammal," you translate the statement as follows:

$$[Am \ \& \ (x)(Ax \rightarrow Mx)] \rightarrow Mm$$

Second, there are numerous English words that are translated into the same quantifier. For example, the following statements are translated $(x)(Sx \rightarrow Px)$:

"All S is P."
"Every S is P."
"Anything that is S is P."
"Everything that is S is P."
"Whatever is S is P."
"Whatever is S is P."
"Only P is S."
"None but P is S."[2]

(1) "Any S is P" is *usually* translated as "$(x)(Sx \rightarrow Px)$," but 'any' is ambiguous. If a statement of the form "Any S is P" is the antecedent of a conditional statement, the 'any' should be understood as particular. For example, "If any dog bites, then Rover bites" is translated: $[(\exists x)(Dx \ \& \ Bx)] \rightarrow Br$. (2) In those cases in which the statement is true and the context warrants it, that is, when the statement concerns an inclusive relationship between classes of objects, "A (An, The) S is P" is translated "$(x)(Sx \rightarrow Px)$." For example, "A (The) dog is a mammal" is translated "$(x)(Dx \rightarrow Mx)$." (3) In some cases no quantificational term is given, but the sense of the statement requires that it be understood as a universal affirmative. For example, the statement "Delicious fruits are ripe" is to be understood as "All delicious fruits are ripe pieces of fruit," that is, $(x)(Dx \rightarrow Rx)$.

The following statements are translated $(x)(Sx \rightarrow {\sim}Px)$:

"No S is P."
"Not any S is P."
"Not a single S is P."

The following statements are translated $(\exists x)(Sx \ \& \ Px)$:

"Some S is P."
"Something that is S is P."
"At least one S is P."

"There is an S that is P."
"A few S's are P's."
"Most S's are P's."[3]

In those cases in which the statement is true and the context warrants it, that is, when one is clearly concerned with at least one individual, "A (An) S is P" is translated "$(\exists x)(Sx\ \&\ Px)$." For example, "A cat is sleeping" is translated "$(\exists x)(Cx\ \&\ Sx)$."
The following statements are translated $(\exists x)(Sx\ \&\ {\sim}Px)$:

"Some S is not P."
"Something that is S is not P."
"Not every S is P."
"Not all S's are P's."[4]

In those cases in which the statement is true and the context warrants it, that is, when one is clearly concerned with at least one individual, "A (an) S is not a P" is translated "$(\exists x)(Sx\ \&\ {\sim}Px)$." For example, "A dog doesn't bark" is translated as "$(\exists x)(Dx\ \&\ {\sim}Bx)$."

Finally, there are cases in which a complex statement is embedded within a categorical statement. In such a case, you translate the complex statement at the appropriate place in the categorical statement. For example, the statement "No dog that is both well-nourished and safe at home is gassed by the animal warden" is translated:

$$(x)\{[Dx\ \&\ (Nx\ \&\ Hx)]\ \rightarrow\ {\sim}Gx\}$$

EXERCISES

Translate the following statements into symbolic form, using the abbreviations suggested.

1. All dogs are mammals. (D, M)

2. No dogs are cats. (D, C)

3. Some dogs are rabid. (D, R)

4. Some dogs are not rapid. (D, R)

5. The dog is a mammal. (D, M)

6. If a few dogs are rapid, then Fido is rabid. (D, R, f)

7. Either all dogs are rabid or some cats are rabid. (D, R, C)

8. Every dog that is rabid is a social outcast. (D, R, O)

9. If any dog is rabid, then Fido is rabid. (D, R, f)

10. If some dogs are not rabid, then some dogs are pets. (D, R, P)

11. If any dog is rabid and Fido is a dog, then Fido is rabid. (D, R, f)

12. Everything that is either an aardvark or a marsupial is a vertebrate. (A, M, V)

13. No kangaroo is a marsupial unless all kangaroos are marsupials. (K, M)

14. Every kangaroo is a marsupial on the condition that everything that is either an aardvark or a marsupial is a vertebrate. (K, M, A, V)

15. Every kangaroo that does not write is either a tea taster or a prizefighter. (K, W, T, P)

16. If any kangaroo is an author, then every kangaroo is either a tea taster or a prizefighter. (K, A, T, P)

17. If no kangaroo is an author, then some kangaroo is a prize fighter on the condition that at least one kangaroo is a marsupial. (K, A, P, M)

18. Every kangaroo who is an author is a dangerous animal, unless some kangaroo is a prizefighter on the condition that every kangaroo is a marsupial. (K, A, D, P, M)

19. If everyone who smokes is disgraceful on the condition that he is an author, then someone who smokes is not an author. (P, S, D, A)

20. It is not the case that either everyone who smokes is disgraceful on the condition that she is an author or someone who smokes is not disgraceful. (P, S, D, A)

7.2 *Quantifiers and Proofs*

Constructing proofs in predicate logic is like constructing proofs in propositional logic *except* that there are four additional rules that allow you to eliminate and introduce the quantifiers. The rules introduced in this section are rules of inference, and, like the first nine rules, they can be applied *only* to complete lines of a proof. It should be clear that the introduction of these rules is necessary for the proof, since the nineteen rules are formulated for noncategorical propositions. In this section we examine the four rules necessary to construct proofs in predicate logic.

The rules for **instantiation** allow you to take a general statement and apply it to a particular **instance,** that is, to restate it in terms of the name of a particular individual. The first rule is the rule of **universal instantiation** (U.I.). Where "Φ" represents any predicate, "x" is a variable ranging over individuals, and "a" is an arbitrarily chosen individual constant, the rule of universal instantiation asserts:

U.I.: $(x)\Phi x$ /∴ Φa

The rationale is straightforward: if Φ is true of all individuals, then Φ is true of any given individual "a." To see how this works, consider the following argument:

All humans are mortals.
Socrates is a human.

Therefore, Socrates is a mortal.

Where "Hx" is "x is a human being," "Mx" is "x is a mortal, and "s" is "Socrates," the argument is symbolized as follows:

$(x)(Hx \rightarrow Mx)$
Hs   /∴   Ms

In constructing the proof, you begin by using U.I. and proceed to apply the rules of inference. In this case, the procedure is straightforward:

1. $(x)(Hx \rightarrow Mx)$
2. Hs   /∴   Ms
3. Hs $\rightarrow$ Ms   1 U.I.
4. Ms   3,2 M.P.

While U.I. allows you to *eliminate* a universal quantifier from your proof, there are cases in which the conclusion of an argument is a universal statement, and those cases require that you *introduce* a universal quantifier into your proof. This is accomplished by the rule of **universal generalization** (U.G.). A bit of thought will convince you that you cannot legitimately move from a statement that is true of a particular individual to a corresponding universal statement. For example, even if it were true that if Amisglof gets an A in this course then she will receive a D.Phil. at Oxford, it obviously does not follow, alas, that all people who get an A in this course will receive a D.Phil. at Oxford. In fact, the *only* cases in which the conclusion of an argument can be a universal proposition are cases in which that proposition is deduced from premises all of which are universal propositions or propositions equivalent to universal propositions.[5] To account for this fact, you must, in effect, carry the generality of the premises through the argument. This is accomplished by instantiating the universal premises of an argument in which you attempt to draw a universal conclusion with a *variable*. So, there is a second version of U.I. that allows you to instantiate a universal proposition for a variable:

U.I.: $(x)\Phi x$ /∴ Φy

Notice that although the rule is stated in terms of the variables x and y, it is consistent with the rule to instantiate a statement of the form $(x)\Phi x$ as Φx. Returning to the question of universal generalization, *you can legitimately engage in universal generalization only from a statement instantiated with a variable*. So, where Φ is a predicate, and y is a variable ranging over individuals, the rule for universal generalization is as follows:

U.G.: Φy /∴ $(x)\Phi x$

To see how this works, consider the following argument:

No scientists are noted theologians.
All physicists are scientists.

_____

No physicists are noted theologians.

Where "Sx" is "x is a scientist," "Tx" is "x is a noted theologian," and "Px" is "x is a physicist," the argument is symbolized as:

$(x)(Sx \rightarrow {\sim}Tx)$
$(x)(Px \rightarrow Sx)$ /∴ $(x)(Px \rightarrow {\sim}Tx)$

We can show that the conclusion follows from the premises by hypothetical syllogism by instantiating both premises with the variable y, applying the rule of hypothetical syllogism, and applying universal generalization to the resulting conclusion. The proof is as follows:

1. $(x)(Sx \rightarrow \text{~}Tx)$
2. $(x)(Px \rightarrow Sx)$ $/\therefore$ $(x)(Px \rightarrow \text{~}Tx)$
3. $Sy \rightarrow \text{~}Ty$ 1 U.I.
4. $Py \rightarrow Sy$ 2 U.I.
5. $Py \rightarrow \text{~}Ty$ 4,3 H.S.
6. $(x)(Px \rightarrow \text{~}Tx)$ 5 U.G.

As noted above, while the rule is stated in terms of instantiating for *y*, it is fairly common practice to instantiate a statement of the form $(x)(\Phi x \rightarrow \Omega x)$ in terms of *x*. Thus, the previous proof permissibly could have been written:

1. $(x)(Sx \rightarrow \text{~}Tx)$
2. $(x)(Px \rightarrow Sx)$ $/\therefore$ $(x)(Px \rightarrow \text{~}Tx)$
3. $Sx \rightarrow \text{~}Tx$ 1 U.I.
4. $Px \rightarrow Sx$ 2 U.I.
5. $Px \rightarrow \text{~}Tx$ 4,3 H.S.
6. $(x)(Px \rightarrow \text{~}Tx)$ 5 U.G.

Existential generalization (E.G.) allows you to introduce the existential quantifier *given that a statement is true of some individual.* The rationale is clear: If it is true that George is a tuba player, for example, then it follows that something (at least one thing) is a tuba player. The general form of the rule is as follows.

E.G.: Φa $/\therefore$ $(\exists x)\Phi x$

Existential generalization is necessary to complete the proof for the following argument:

Every tove gyers in the wabe.
Ostafar is a tove.

Therefore, something gyers in the wabe.

Where "Tx" is "*x* is a tove," "Gx" is "*x* gyers in the wabe," and "*o*" is "Ostafar," the argument is translated into symbolic form as follows:

$(x)(Tx \rightarrow Gx)$

To   /∴ $(\exists x)(Gx)$

The proof is as follows:

1. $(x)(Tx \rightarrow Gx)$
2. To   /∴ $(\exists x)(Gx)$
3. To $\rightarrow$ Go   1 U.I.
4. Go   3,2 M.P.
5. $(\exists x)(Gx)$ 4 E.G.

Existential instantiation (E.I.) allows you to eliminate the existential quantifier by introducing a *hypothetical* name to represent the "at least one thing" of which the statement is true. *Notice that this is a hypothetical name*—that is, it is a name that represents someone or something, but you make no claim to know who or what that thing actually is. The reason for this should be clear. While it is true that someone is a great pianist, this will not allow you to conclude, for example, that Ostafar Neumathesque in particular is a great pianist. (Perhaps Ostafar has never sat at a piano in his life.) Because the name introduced is purely hypothetical, any proof that introduces a constant by existential instantiation must conclude by "disposing" of that hypothetical name through existential generalization. The rule of existential instantiation is stated as follows, *complete with the restriction:*

E.I.: $(\exists x)\Phi x$ /∴ Φa, where "a" is a constant that has *not* previously been introduced into the argument or in the derivation.

The implication of this restriction is that in those arguments in which you have *both* a universal statement and a particular statement, you must engage in existential instantiation *before* you engage in universal instantiation. Consider the following argument:

Some professional pianists are not tuba players.
All professional pianists are concert artists.

So some concert artists are not tuba players.

Where "Px" is "x is a professional pianist," "Tx" is "x is a tuba player," and "Cx" is "x is a concert artist," the proof is as follows:

1. $(\exists x)(Px \ \& \sim Tx)$
2. $(x)(Px \rightarrow Cx)$ $/\therefore$ $(\exists x)(Cx \ \& \sim Tx)$
3. $Pa \ \& \sim Ta$ 1 E.I.
4. $Pa \rightarrow Ca$ 2 U.I.
5. Pa 3 Simp.
6. Ca 4,5 M.P.
7. $\sim Ta \ \& \ Pa$ 3 Com.
8. $\sim Ta$ 7 Simp.
9. $Ca \ \& \sim Ta$ 6,8 Conj.
10. $(\exists x)(Cx \ \& \sim Tx)$ 9 E.G.

THINGS TO REMEMBER

1. If the premises are a combination of universal propositions and particular propositions, you should always instantiate the particular propositions first. If there is more than one particular proposition, each must be instantiated for a different constant.

2. If the conclusion is a universal proposition and all the premises are universal propositions, except for starting with U.I. for each premise and ending with U.G., the proof will be exactly like a proof in propositional logic.

3. Unless the conclusion is itself part of a complex proposition, the only way you can reach a conclusion that is a universal proposition is if all the premises are universal propositions.

4. Any quantified proposition can be instantiated more than once; *but,* if a particular (existential) proposition is instantiated more than once in a single proof, it must be instantiated by a different constant each time.

5. *The instantiation and generalization rules apply only in those cases in which a quantified statement constitutes an entire line of a proof, or a statement to be generalized constitutes an entire line of a proof.*

EXERCISES

I. Construct a proof for each of the following arguments.

1. $(x)(Px \rightarrow Qx)$
   Pa $/\therefore$ $(\exists x)Qx$

2. $(x)(Px \rightarrow Qx)$
   $(\exists x)Px$ $/\therefore$ $(\exists x)Qx$

3. $(\exists x)Px \rightarrow (x)Qx$
   Pa $/\therefore$ Qa

4. $(\exists x)Px \rightarrow (\exists x)Qx$
   $\sim(\exists x)Qx$ $/\therefore$ $\sim(\exists x)Px$

5. $(\exists x)(Px \ \& \ Qx)$ $/\therefore$ $(\exists x)Qx$

6. $(x)(Mx \rightarrow Px)$
   $(\exists x)(Mx \ \& \ Sx)$ $/\therefore$ $(\exists x)(Sx \ \& \ Px)$

7. $(x)(Mx \rightarrow \sim Px)$
   $(x)(Sx \rightarrow Mx)$ $/\therefore$ $(x)(Sx \rightarrow \sim Px)$

8. $(x)(Px \rightarrow Mx)$
   $(x)(Sx \rightarrow \sim Mx)$ $/\therefore$ $(x)(Sx \rightarrow \sim Px)$

9. $(x)(Px \rightarrow \sim Mx)$
   $(\exists x)(Mx \ \& \ \sim Sx)$ $/\therefore$ $(\exists x)(\sim Sx \ \& \ \sim Px)$

10. $(\exists x)(Mx \ \& \ \sim Px)$
    $(x)(Mx \rightarrow Sx)$ $/\therefore$ $(\exists x)(Sx \ \& \ \sim Px)$

11. $(x)(Px \rightarrow Mx)$
    $(\exists x)(Sx \ \& \ \sim Mx)$ $/\therefore$ $(\exists x)(Sx \ \& \ \sim Px)$

12. $(x)(Px \rightarrow Mx)$
    $(x)(Mx \rightarrow Sx)$
    $\sim Sa$ $/\therefore$ $\sim Pa$

13. $(x)[(Px \ \& \ Mx) \rightarrow Sx]$
    $(\exists x)(Px \ \& \ \sim Sx)$ $/\therefore$ $(\exists x)\sim Mx$

14. $(x)(Px \rightarrow Qx)$
    $(\exists x)(Px \ \& \ Sx)$
    $(\exists x)(Sx \ \& \ \sim Qx)$ $/\therefore$ $(\exists x)Qx \ \& \ (\exists y)\sim Py$

15. $(\exists x)(Px) \rightarrow (\exists x)(Qx)$
    $(x)(\sim Px \rightarrow Qx)$
    $(x)(Qx \rightarrow Px)$ $/\therefore$ $(\exists x)Qx$

16. $(x)[(Px \,\&\, Qx) \rightarrow Rx]$
    $(\exists x)(Qx \,\&\, Tx)$
    $(x)[(Tx \,\&\, Sx) \rightarrow \sim Rx]$ $/\therefore$ $(\exists x)(Px \rightarrow \sim Sx)$

17. $(x)[(Px \,\&\, Qx) \rightarrow (Rx \,\&\, Tx)]$
    $(\exists x)[(Px \,\&\, Rx) \,\&\, Qx]$ $/\therefore$ $(\exists x)(Tx \,\&\, Rx)$

18. $(x)[(Px \,\&\, Qx) \rightarrow Rx]$
    $(\exists x)(Px \,\&\, \sim Sx)$
    $(x)[(\sim Qx \,\&\, \sim Sx) \rightarrow Rx]$ $/\therefore$ $(\exists x)Rx$

19. $(x)[(Px \,\&\, Qx) \rightarrow Rx]$
    $(x)[(Rx \lor Sx) \rightarrow Tx]$
    $(\exists x)(Px \,\&\, \sim Sx)$ $/\therefore$ $(\exists x)(Qx \rightarrow Tx)$

20. $(x)[(Px \leftrightarrow Qx) \rightarrow Rx]$
    $(\exists x)[(Px \,\&\, Sx) \,\&\, Qx]$ $/\therefore$ $(\exists x)(Rx \,\&\, Sx)$

21. $(x)[(\sim Px \,\&\, \sim Qx) \rightarrow Rx]$
    $(x)[Rx \rightarrow (\sim Qx \rightarrow Sx)]$
    $(x)(Sx \rightarrow Qx)$ $/\therefore$ $(x)(\sim Qx \rightarrow Px)$

22. $(x)[\sim Px \rightarrow (Qx \,\&\, Rx)]$
    $(\exists x)(\sim Qx \,\&\, Sx)$
    $(x)[(Px \lor Qx) \rightarrow \sim Px]$ $/\therefore$ $(x)(Sx \rightarrow Rx)$

23. $(x)(Px \rightarrow Qx) \,\&\, (\exists x)[Px \,\&\, (Qx \rightarrow Rx)]$
    $(x)[Rx \rightarrow (Sx \leftrightarrow Tx)]$
    $/\therefore$ $(\exists x)[(Sx \rightarrow Tx) \,\&\, (Tx \rightarrow Sx)]$

24. $(x)[(Px \leftrightarrow Qx) \rightarrow (Rx \lor Cx)]$
    $(\exists x)[(Px \rightarrow Qx) \,\&\, \sim Rx]$
    $/\therefore$ $(\exists x)[(Cx \lor Qx) \,\&\, (Px \rightarrow Cx)]$

25. $(x)[(Px \,\&\, Qx) \rightarrow (Rx \,\&\, Sx)]$
    $(x)(Rx \rightarrow Px)$
    $(x)[(Rx \,\&\, Px) \rightarrow Qx]$ $/\therefore$ $(x)\{\sim Sx \rightarrow [Rx \leftrightarrow (Px \,\&\, Qx)]\}$

II. Translate and construct a proof for each of the following arguments. Use the suggested statement letters.

SOAPS II

1. All the young are restless. None of the old are restless. So, none of the young are old. (Y, R, O)

2. Some movers are shakers. All movers are restless. So some shakers are restless. (M, S, R)

3. Anyone who is young is bold. Someone who is wise is young. So someone who is wise is bold. (P, Y, B, W)

4. If someone is both young and restless, then everyone who is bold is attractive. Fifi is a young and restless person. So if Fifi is bold, Fifi is attractive. (P, Y, R, B, A, F)

5. Anyone who is young or attractive is either bold or restless. Fifi is a young person. Anyone who is restless is either a mover or a shaker. So, if Fifi is neither bold nor a mover, then she's a shaker. (P, Y, A, B, R, M, S, F)

6. If someone is both young and restless, then everyone who is restless is bold. Fifi is a young and restless person. So someone is both young and bold. (P, Y, R, B, F)

7. All followers of the guiding light are searchers for tomorrow. All T.V. watchers are followers of the guiding light but are not searchers for tomorrow. Therefore, all T.V. watchers are mesmerized. (F, S, W, M)

8. Anyone who is either young or restless is a searcher for tomorrow. No searchers for tomorrow are followers of the guiding light. Someone is young but not restless. So someone is not a follower of the guiding light. (P, Y, R, S, F)

9. Everyone who is young and restless is either bold or attractive. Someone is restless but not bold. So, someone is not both young and unattractive. (P, Y, R, B, A)

10. Anyone who is both young and restless is either a soap opera star or a Methodist.[6] Every soap opera star is well-known. Every Methodist is a hymn-singer. Therefore, anyone who is both young and restless is either well-known or a hymn-singer. (P, Y, R, S, M, W, H)

7.3 *Negation and Quantifier Replacement*

Just as De Morgan's Theorems indicate that changes occur when you negate a compound statement and move the negation sign inside the parentheses, so there are changes that occur when quantifiers are negated. Basically, when moving a negation sign "across" a quantifier, you replace a universal quantifier with an existential quantifier and an existential quantifier with a universal quantifier. There are four equivalences that concern quantifier negation:

Q.N. $(x)\Phi x \leftrightarrow \sim(\exists x)\sim\Phi x$
$\sim(x)\phi x \leftrightarrow (\exists x)\sim\Phi x$
$\sim(\exists x)\Phi x \leftrightarrow (x)\sim\Phi x$
$(\exists x)\Phi x \leftrightarrow \sim(x)\sim\Phi x$

Recognizing these equivalences is important for various reasons. First, the instantiation rules hold only for *unnegated* quantifiers. Second, there are cases in which one will need to apply the nine rules of inference to complex statements in which the components are quantified statements. Finally, the quantifier negation rules allow you to justify certain of your intuitions that some statements are equivalent. Let us consider an example of each of these cases.

(1) The following is a valid argument form:

$\sim(\exists x)(Px \lor \sim Qx)$ $/\therefore$ $\sim(x)Px$

To construct a proof, you proceed as follows:

1. $\sim(\exists x)(Px \lor \sim Qx)$ $/\therefore$ $\sim(x)Px$
2. $(x)\sim(Px \lor \sim Qx)$ 1 Q.N.
3. $\sim(Py \lor \sim Qy)$ 2 U.I.
4. $\sim Py \mathbin{\&} \sim\sim Qy$ 3 DeM.
5. $\sim Py$ 4 Simp.
6. $(\exists x)\sim Px$ 5 E.G.
7. $\sim(x)Px$ 6 Q.N.

(2) Since the nine rules of inference apply to *any* statements, they apply to quantified statements. Hence, given the rule of *modus tollens* together with quantifier negation, you can construct a proof of the following argument:

$(x)Px \rightarrow (\exists x)Qx$
$(x)\sim Qx$ $/\therefore$ $(\exists x)\sim Px$

The proof is as follows:

1. $(x)Px \rightarrow (\exists x)Qx$
2. $(x)\sim Qx$ $/\therefore$ $(\exists x)\sim Px$

3. ~(∃x)Qx   2 Q.N.
4. ~(x)Px   1,3 M.T.
5. (∃x)~Px   4 Q.N.

(3) Your logical intuitions suggest that the statement "No S is P" can be translated as "~(∃x)(Sx & Px)," as well as "(x)(Sx → ~Px)." Given the rules of quantifier negation, you can show that "~(∃x)(Sx & Px)" follows from "(x)(Sx → ~Px)":

1. (x)(Sx → ~Px)   /∴   ~(∃x)(Sx & Px)
2. ~(∃x)~(Sx → ~Px)   1 Q.N.
3. ~(∃x)~(~Sx v ~Px)   3 Impl.
4. ~(∃x)(~~Sx & ~~Px)   3 DeM.
5. ~(∃x)(Sx & ~~Px)   4 D.N.
6. ~(∃x)(Sx & Px)   5 D.N.

Traditionally, the relationships among universal and particular propositions have been set forth in a Square of Opposition. The Square of Opposition shows that a universal affirmative proposition and a particular negative proposition are contradictories: if one proposition is true, the other is false. It shows the same regarding a universal negative and a particular affirmative proposition. The Square of Opposition looks like this:

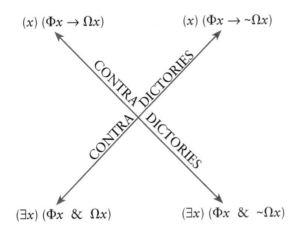

$(x) (\Phi x \to \Omega x)$ $(x) (\Phi x \to \sim\Omega x)$

CONTRADICTORIES

CONTRADICTORIES

$(\exists x) (\Phi x \ \& \ \Omega x)$ $(\exists x) (\Phi x \ \& \ \sim\Omega x)$

Given the rule of quantifier negation, it is easy to replace the universal propositions with equivalent particular propositions and see that the propositions on the corners of the square are contradictories:

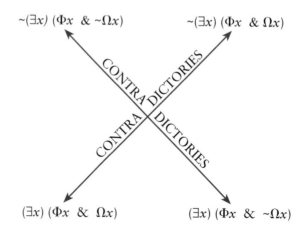

~(∃x) (Φx & ~Ωx)   ~(∃x) (Φx & Ωx)

CONTRADICTORIES

CONTRADICTORIES

(∃x) (Φx & Ωx)   (∃x) (Φx & ~Ωx)

EXERCISES

Construct a proof for each of the following arguments:

1. ~(∃x)(Px & ~Qx)
(~∃x)(Qx & ~Rx)
~Ra   /∴   ~Pa

2. ~(∃x)(Px & ~Qx)
~(x)(Qx)   /∴   ~(x)Px

3. (∃x)(Px & Qx) → (x)(Sx → Rx)
(∃x)(Sx & ~Rx)   /∴   (x)(Px → ~Qx)

4. (∃x)[Px & (Qx → Tx)] → (x)(Sx → Rx)
(∃x)(Sx & ~Rx)
(∃x)(Px & Sx)   /∴   (∃x)(Qx & Sx)

5. ~(∃x)(Px & Mx)
~(∃x)(Sx & ~Mx)   /∴   ~(∃x)(Sx & Px)

6. ~(∃x)(Px & ~Mx)
~(∃x)(Mx & Sx)   /∴   ~(∃x)(Sx & Px)

7. ~(∃x)(Mx & Px)
~(x)(Sx → ~Mx)   /∴   ~(x)(Sx → Px)

8. ~(∃x)[(Px & Qx) & ~Rx]
~(x)[Px → (Rx v ~Sx)]   /∴   ~(x)(~Qx → ~Sx)

9. ~(∃x)[Px & (~Qx & ~Rx)]
~(∃x)(Qx & ~Sx)
~(x)[Px → ~(Tx & ~Rx)]   /∴   ~(x)(Sx → ~Tx)

10. ~(∃x)[~(~Px ∨ ~Qx) & ~Rx]
    ~(∃x)[(Px & Qx) & ~Sx]
    (∃x)(Px & Qx)
    ~(∃x)[(Sx ∨ Rx) & ~Tx]   /∴   ~(x)[(Sx & Rx) → ~Tx]

7.4 *Indirect and Conditional Proof*

Indirect and conditional proof can be used in quantified proofs in basically the same way as in propositional logic, although in using both I.P. and C.P. there is a *restriction* that must be introduced with respect to *universal generalization*. The restriction is as follows:

> U.G.:   Φ*y* /∴   (*x*)Φ*x*   *but* U.G. cannot be used within the scope of an assumption for C.P. or I.P. if the initial variable occurs free in the first line of the sequence for C.P. or I.P.

The reason for the restriction is to prevent the construction of proofs for invalid arguments. The following is an invalid argument:

> (*x*)(U*x*) → (*x*)(B*x*)   /∴   (*x*)(U*x* → B*x*)

If you want to be convinced that the argument is invalid, consider the case where "U*x*" represents the propositional function "*x* is citizen of the United States" and "B*x*" represents the propositional function "*x* is a British citizen." The premise asserts that if everything in the world is a citizen of the United States, then everything in the world is a British citizen. Since the antecedent is false, the proposition is true. The conclusion, however, asserts that all citizens of the United States are British citizens, which is false. *Were it not for the restriction, one could prove that the conclusion follows from the premise as follows:*

1. (*x*)U*x* → (*x*)B*x*   /∴   (*x*)(U*x* → B*x*)
    2. U*x*   ACP
    3. (*x*)U*x*   2 U.G. *(This is illegitimate!)*
    4. (*x*)B*x*   1,3 M.P.
    5. B*x*   4 U.I.
6. U*x* → B*x*   2–5 C.P.
7. (*x*)(U*x* → B*x*)   6 U.G.

Once you take this restriction on universal generalization into account, you can use both indirect and conditional proof at any point in a proof. To see this, let us look at some examples.

Consider the argument:

$(x)(Ax \rightarrow Bx)$
$(\exists x)(Ax)$ /∴ $(\exists x)(Bx)$

Let us construct an indirect proof to show that the conclusion follows:

1. $(x)(Ax \rightarrow Bx)$
2. $(\exists x)(Ax)$ /∴ $(\exists x)(Bx)$
   3. ~$(\exists x)Bx$ AIP
   4. Ac   2 E.I.
   5. (x)~Bx   3 Q.N.
   6. ~Bc   5 U.I.
   7. Ac $\rightarrow$ Bc   1 U.I.
   8. ~Ac   7,6 M.T.
   9. Ac & ~Ac   4,8 Conj.
10. ~~$(\exists x)(Bx)$ 3–9 I.P.
11. $(\exists x)(Bx)$ 10 D.N.

Now consider this argument:

$(x)(Ax \rightarrow Bx)$ /∴ $(\exists x)(Ax) \rightarrow (\exists x)(Bx)$

Let us construct a conditional proof to show that the conclusion follows:

1. $(x)(Ax \rightarrow Bx)$ /∴ $(\exists x)(Ax) \rightarrow (\exists x)(Bx)$
   2. $(\exists x)(Ax)$ ACP
   3. Ab   2 E.I.
   4. Ab $\rightarrow$ Bb   1 U.I.
   5. Bb   4,3 M.P.
   6. $(\exists x)(Bx)$ 5 E.G.
7. $(\exists x)(Ax) \rightarrow (\exists x)(Bx)$ 2–9 C.P.

RULES OF THUMB

1. If the conclusion is a universal proposition, you will often want to assume the antecedent of the conclusion (ACP), then assume the de-

nial of the consequent (AIP). This will allow you to establish the consequent by indirect proof, establish the conditional by conditional proof, and then generalize.

2. If the conclusion is an existential (particular) proposition, you will probably want to proceed by indirect proof.

3. If the quantifier is negated in one of the premises, you will want to begin by using Q.N.

4. If you construct an indirect proof, but it becomes obvious how to construct a *direct* proof, it is always permissible to construct a direct proof and conjoin the conclusion of the direct proof with the assumption to generate the desired self-contradiction.

EXERCISES

I. Construct an indirect or conditional proof for each of the following:

1. $(x)[Px \rightarrow (Qx \ \& \ Rx)]$ /∴ $(x)(Px \rightarrow Qx)$

2. $(x)(Px \rightarrow Qx)$
   $(x)[(Qx \lor Sx) \rightarrow \sim Rx]$ /∴ $(x)(Px \rightarrow \sim Rx)$

3. $(x)[Px \rightarrow (Rx \lor \sim Sx)]$
   $(x)(Rx \rightarrow \sim Sx)$ /∴ $(x)(Px \rightarrow \sim Sx)$

4. $(x)[(Px \ \& \ Qx) \rightarrow Rx]$
   $(x)(Px \rightarrow Qx)$ /∴ $(x)[Px \rightarrow (Rx \lor Sx)]$

5. $(x)[(Px \lor Qx) \rightarrow (Rx \ \& \ Sx)]$
   $(x)[Rx \rightarrow (Qx \ \& \ \sim Sx)]$ /∴ $(x)(Qx \rightarrow \sim Sx)$

6. $(\exists x)(Px \ \& \ Qx)$
   $(x)[Px \rightarrow (Rx \rightarrow Sx)]$
   $(x)[Qx \rightarrow (\sim Rx \rightarrow \sim Sx)]$
   /∴ $(\exists x)[(Rx \ \& \ Sx) \lor (\sim Rx \ \& \ \sim Sx)]$

7. $(x)[(Px \ \& \ Qx) \rightarrow Rx]$
   $(\exists x)(Px \ \& \ \sim Rx)$ /∴ $(\exists x)\sim Qx$

8. $(x)[Px \rightarrow (Qx \leftrightarrow Rx)]$
   $(\exists x)(Qx \ \& \ \sim Rx)$ /∴ $(\exists x)\sim Px$

9. $(x)[Px \rightarrow (Rx \lor \sim Sx)]$
   $(\exists x)(Px \ \& \ \sim Rx)$ /∴ $(\exists x)(Px \ \& \ \sim Sx)$

10. $(x)(Px \rightarrow Qx)$
    $(x)(Qx \rightarrow Px)$ /∴ $(x)(Px \leftrightarrow Qx)$

11. $(x)[(Px \lor Qx) \rightarrow (Rx \,\&\, Sx)]$
    $(x)[Rx \rightarrow (Tx \lor {\sim}Px)]$ /∴ $(x)[Qx \rightarrow (Px \rightarrow Tx)]$

12. $(x)[(Px \,\&\, Qx) \rightarrow (Rx \lor Sx)]$
    $(x)[Rx \rightarrow (Tx \,\&\, {\sim}Sx)]$
    $(x)[Sx \rightarrow (Tx \,\&\, {\sim}Rx)]$ /∴ $(x)[(Px \,\&\, Qx) \rightarrow Tx]$

13. $(x)[Px \rightarrow (Qx \leftrightarrow Rx)]$
    $(\exists x)(Px \,\&\, Rx)$ /∴ $(\exists x)(Rx \,\&\, Qx)$

14. $(x)[(Qx \leftrightarrow Rx) \rightarrow Px]$
    $(\exists x)({\sim}Px \,\&\, Rx)$ /∴ $(\exists x)({\sim}Px \,\&\, {\sim}Qx)$

15. $(x)[(Qx \leftrightarrow Rx) \rightarrow {\sim}Px]$
    $(x)(Px \rightarrow Rx)$ /∴ $(x)(Px \rightarrow {\sim}Qx)$

16. $(x)[(Px \rightarrow {\sim}Qx) \rightarrow {\sim}(Px \lor Qx)]$
    $(x)(Qx \rightarrow Rx)$ /∴ $(x)(Px \rightarrow Rx)$

17. $(x)[(Px \rightarrow {\sim}Qx) \rightarrow {\sim}(Px \lor Qx)]$
    $(x)(Qx \rightarrow Rx)$
    $(x)(Rx \rightarrow Qx)$ /∴ $(\exists x)[(Px \rightarrow Rx) \,\&\, (Rx \rightarrow Px)]$

18. $(\exists x)[(Px \rightarrow {\sim}Qx) \,\&\, (Px \rightarrow {\sim}Rx)]$
    $(x)[{\sim}Px \rightarrow {\sim}({\sim}Qx \lor {\sim}Rx)]$
    /∴ $(\exists x)[(Qx \rightarrow Rx) \,\&\, (Rx \rightarrow Qx)]$

19. $(x)[Px \rightarrow {\sim}(Qx \lor Rx)]$
    $(x)[{\sim}Px \rightarrow {\sim}({\sim}Qx \lor {\sim}Rx)]$ /∴ $(x)(Qx \rightarrow Rx)$

20. $(x)[Px \leftrightarrow {\sim}(Qx \lor Rx)]$
    ${\sim}(\exists x)[{\sim}Px \,\&\, ({\sim}Qx \lor {\sim}Rx)]$ /∴ $(x)(Qx \leftrightarrow Rx)$

II. Construct a conditional or indirect proof for each of the following. Use the suggested statement letters.

YOUR MISSION, SHOULD YOU DECIDE TO ACCEPT IT . . .

1. Every spy is either knowledgeable or perplexed. Some spy is not perplexed. So, some spy is knowledgeable. (S, K, P)

2. Every hazardous mission is either fatal or salacious. So, no missions that are neither fatal nor salacious are hazardous. (M, H, F, S)

3. Every mission is either achievable or it's not. Every mission that is achievable is dangerous. Every mission that is not achievable is dangerous. Therefore, every mission is dangerous. (M, A, D)

4. No confused spy is reliable. Some spy is reliable. So some spy is not confused. (S, C, R)

5. Not every spy is resourceful. Every operative is cunning. Every cunning spy is resourceful. Hence, some spy is not an operative. (S, R, O, C)

6. All spies are cunning and resourceful persons. Some persons are not cunning. All resourceful persons are leaders. So, some people are not spies. (S, C, R, P, L)

7. All spies are cunning and resourceful persons. Some persons are not cunning. All resourceful persons are leaders. So, all spies are leaders. (S, C, R, P, L)

8. All cunning spies are resourceful. Whatever is resourceful is ingenious. Someone is cunning but not ingenious. So, someone is not a spy. (S, C, R, I, P)

9. Every hazardous mission is either fatal or salacious. Every fatal mission is disavowed. Every salacious mission is disavowed. Hence, every mission is either disavowed or not hazardous. (M, H, F, S, D)

10. Every hazardous mission is either fatal or salacious. Every fatal mission is disavowed. Every salacious mission is disavowed. Some missions are not dangerous. Therefore, some missions are not hazardous. (M, H, F, S, D)

7.5 *Proving Invalidity*

A deductive argument is valid as long as it is impossible for all of its premises to be true and its conclusion false. To show that an argument is invalid, you show that there is a case in which all the premises are true and the conclusion is false. In propositional logic this was done by means of a reverse truth table (see Chapter 5, Section 5). The technique is the same with respect to predicate logic, although you must first understand the truth conditions for universal and particular categorical propositions and then consider individual cases. So let us begin by considering the truth conditions for universal affirmative propositions.

A universal affirmative proposition of the form "All *S* is *P*" holds for all cases, that is, literally for everything in the universe. It is true just in case a massive *conjunction* of conditional statements is true. For example, the statement that "All Chevrolets are automobiles" is true just in case it is true that "if *a* is a Chevrolet, then *a* is an automobile, and if *b* is a Chevrolet then *b* is an automobile, and if *c* is a Chevrolet, then *c* is an automobile, and if . . ." In some cases, the thing named will not be a

Chevrolet—in one case, for example, it will be the rock that is currently in my shoe—and in those cases the conditional is trivially true since the antecedent is false.

The truth conditions for a universal negative statement are comparable. For example, the statement "No Fords are Chevrolets" is true just in case it is true that "If *a* is a Ford, then *a* is not a Chevrolet, and if *b* is a Ford, then *b* is not a Chevrolet, and if *c* is a Ford, then *c* is not a Chevrolet, and if . . . ."

A particular affirmative proposition of the form "Some S is P" is true as long as there is at least one thing that is both S and P. It is true just in case a massive *disjunction* of conjunctive statements is true. For example, the statement "Some automobile is a Ford" is true if it is true that "Either *a* is an automobile and *a* is a Ford, or *b* is an automobile and *b* is a Ford, or *c* is an automobile and *c* is a Ford, or . . . ." In many cases the object named will not be an automobile, so that disjunct will be false, but as long as there is one thing that is both an automobile and a Ford the disjunction will be true.

The truth conditions for a particular negative statement are comparable. For example, the statement "Some automobile is not a Chevrolet" is true just in case it is true that "either *a* is an automobile and *a* is not a Chevrolet, or *b* is an automobile and *b* is not a Chevrolet, or *c* is an automobile and *c* is not a Chevrolet, or . . . ."

It is impossible to construct the relevant conjunctions or disjunctions for the actual universe: it contains too many objects. Fortunately, to show that an argument is invalid, it is sufficient to show that in a relatively limited universe the argument form is invalid, since the objects in this limited universe will be a subset of the actual universe. So you start with a universe consisting of only one object and construct a reverse truth table to see if you can show that the argument form instantiated for that object is invalid. If the form is invalid for a universe of one object, it is invalid for any larger universe. If you cannot show the form is invalid for a universe of one object, you consider a universe consisting of two objects, or three, or four. You continue testing until you find a universe in which all the premises of the argument are true and the conclusion false. To understand how this works, let us consider some examples.

Consider the argument:

$(x)(Px \rightarrow \sim Mx)$
$(x)(Sx \rightarrow Mx)$ $/\therefore$ $(x)(Sx \rightarrow Px)$

Let us assume we have a universe consisting of exactly one object, "a." We instantiate the premises and conclusion for that object, assign truth values to the conclusion so that the conclusion is false, and attempt consistently to assign truth values to the premises so that all the premises are true. We begin as follows by assigning truth values to the conclusion:

$$Pa \rightarrow \sim Ma \qquad Sa \rightarrow Ma \qquad /\therefore \qquad Sa \rightarrow Pa$$
$$ T \quad F$$
$$ \backslash \ /$$
$$ F$$

Next we assign truth values to the premises:

$$Pa \rightarrow \sim Ma \qquad Sa \rightarrow Ma \qquad /\therefore \qquad Sa \rightarrow Pa$$
$$F \quad\ \ T \qquad\quad T \quad\ T \qquad\qquad\quad T \quad F$$
$$\backslash \ \ F \qquad\qquad\quad \backslash \ / \qquad\qquad\qquad \backslash \ /$$
$$T \qquad\qquad\qquad T \qquad\qquad\qquad\quad F$$

Here, in a universe of one object we have shown that the argument is invalid.

If you cannot show that an argument is invalid on the basis of a universe of one object, consider whether it is valid in a universe of two objects. To see how this works, consider the following argument:

$$(\exists x)(Dx \ \& \ Ex)$$
$$(\exists x)(Fx \ \& \ Ex) \qquad /\therefore \qquad (\exists x)(Dx \ \& \ Fx)$$

You begin by asking whether the argument is valid in a universe of one object, "a", by assigning truth value to the conclusion and the premises. Since the conclusion is a conjunction, we might have to consider three cases in order to show that the argument is not invalid *in a universe consisting of exactly one object:*

$$Da \ \& \ Ea \qquad Fa \ \& \ Ea \qquad /\therefore \qquad Da \ \& \ Fa$$
$$F/T \quad\ T \qquad\quad T \quad\ T \qquad\qquad\quad F \quad\ T$$
$$\backslash \ / \qquad\qquad\quad \backslash \ / \qquad\qquad\qquad\ \backslash \ /$$
$$F \qquad\qquad\qquad T \qquad\qquad\qquad\quad F$$

$$T \quad T \qquad\quad F/T \quad\ T \qquad\qquad\quad T \quad\ F$$
$$\backslash \ / \qquad\qquad\quad \backslash \ / \qquad\qquad\qquad\ \backslash \ /$$
$$T \qquad\qquad\qquad F \qquad\qquad\qquad\quad F$$

$$F/T \quad\ T \qquad\quad F/T \quad\ T \qquad\qquad\ F \quad\ F$$
$$\backslash \ / \qquad\qquad\quad \backslash \ / \qquad\qquad\qquad\ \backslash \ /$$
$$F \qquad\qquad\qquad F \qquad\qquad\qquad\quad F$$

Since it is impossible to assign values to the statements in a one-object universe in such a way that the premises are true and the conclusion is false, you ask whether the argument is valid in a two-object universe. Again you assign truth values in an attempt to find a case in which all the premises are true and the conclusion is false:

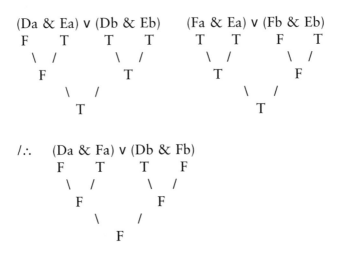

With this we have shown that for a universe of two (or more) objects, the argument form is invalid.

We can now see the pattern that is used in showing that an argument is invalid. You begin by assuming a universe composed of one object, instantiate the argument for that object, and attempt to assign truth values so that all the premises are true and the conclusion false. If it is impossible to do so, assume a universe composed of two objects, instantiate the argument for each of those two constants, treating universal propositions as *conjunctions* of singular propositions and particular propositions as *disjunctions* of singular propositions. If you are still unable to show that the argument is invalid, assume a universe of three objects and instantiate the appropriate conjunctions or disjunctions for each of the three objects. Repeat this procedure with respect to universes with increasing numbers of objects until you find a universe in which the truth-functional compound statements representing the premises are true and that representing the conclusion is false. Once you find such a universe, a universe with n objects, you have shown that the argument form is invalid for any universe with at least n objects.

EXERCISES

Show that each of the following arguments is invalid:

1. $(x)(Px \rightarrow Qx)$
   $(x)(Sx \rightarrow Qx)$ /∴ $(x)(Sx \rightarrow Px)$

2. $(x)(Px \rightarrow {\sim}Mx)$
   $(x)(Mx \rightarrow Sx)$ /∴ $(\exists x)(Sx \ \& \ Px)$

3. $(x)(Sx \rightarrow {\sim}Mx)$
   Mg /∴ Sg

4. $(x)(Mx \rightarrow {\sim}Px)$
   $(x)(Mx \rightarrow {\sim}Sx)$ /∴ $(x)(Sx \rightarrow {\sim}Px)$

5. $(x)(Px \rightarrow Qx)$
   $(\exists x)(Px \ \& \ {\sim}Sx)$ /∴ $(\exists x)(Sx \ \& \ Qx)$

6. $(x)(Px \rightarrow Qx)$
   $(\exists x)(Px \ \& \ {\sim}Sx)$ /∴ $(\exists x)Sx \ \& \ Qx$

7. $(x)(Px \rightarrow Qx)$
   $(x)(Sx \rightarrow {\sim}Qx)$ /∴ $(\exists x)(Px \ \& \ Sx)$

8. $(x)(Px \rightarrow {\sim}Qx)$
   $(\exists x)(Px \ \& \ {\sim}Sx)$ /∴ $(x)(Sx \rightarrow Px)$

9. $(\exists x)(Px \ \& \ Qx)$
   $(\exists x)(Px \ \& \ {\sim}Sx)$ /∴ $(x)(Sx \rightarrow Qx)$

10. $(\exists x)(Px \ \& \ {\sim}Qx)$
    $(\exists x)(Px \ \& \ {\sim}Sx)$ /∴ $(\exists x)(Sx \ \& \ {\sim}Qx)$

11. $(\exists x)(Px \ \& \ {\sim}Qx)$
    $(\exists x)(Px \ \& \ {\sim}Sx)$ /∴ $(\exists x)({\sim}Sx \ \& \ {\sim}Qx)$

12. $(\exists x)(Px \ \& \ {\sim}Qx)$
    $(\exists x)(Px \ \& \ {\sim}Sx)$ /∴ $(x)({\sim}Sx \rightarrow {\sim}Qx)$

13. $(\exists x)(Px \ \& \ {\sim}Qx)$
    $(\exists x)(Px \ \& \ {\sim}Sx)$ /∴ $(x)(Sx \rightarrow Qx)$

14. $(x)[(Cx \ \& \ Sx) \rightarrow {\sim}Rx]$
    $(\exists x)(Cx \ \& \ {\sim}Sx)$ /∴ $(\exists x)(Cx \ \& \ Rx)$

15. $(x)[(Mx \ \& \ Hx) \rightarrow (Fx \lor Sx)]$
    $(x)[(Mx \ \& \ Fx) \rightarrow Dx]$
    $(x)[(Mx \ \& \ Sx) \rightarrow Dx]$ /∴ $(x)(Mx \rightarrow Hx)$

7.6 *Relations and Multiple Quantification*

Up to this point we have introduced into our system only one-place (monadic) predicates such as "is a human." But there are many statements that cannot be represented in our symbolic language if it is restricted to only one-place predicates. In ordinary English you might say such things as "John is Mary's brother" or "Henry is between Sharon and Lois." To be the brother of someone or to be between two things is *to stand in a certain relation* to something else. Relations come in many forms. When two things stand in a certain relation to one another, as in the case of someone being the brother of someone else or someone being the child of someone else, two things are related; the relation is said to be *binary* or *dyadic*. When three things stand in a relation to one another, as in the case of something being between two other things, the relation is said to be *ternary* or *triadic*. If four things are related to one another, the relation is *quaternary* or *tetradic*. In general, relations can be of any degree of complexity, and if we are to represent this in our symbolic system, we must introduce multiplace predicates to represent relations of various degrees of complexity.

Multiplace or relational predicates will be represented by an uppercase letter followed by two or more lowercase letters. An expression such as "John is the brother of Mary" will be represented by "Bjm." An expression such as "Henry is between Sharon and Lois" will be represented by "Bhsl." Here are a few examples of how various relational statements are represented symbolically:

Statement	Symbolic Translation
Amisglof loves Ostafar.	Lao
Tristan is older than Angela.	Ota
George pays taxes to the Commonwealth of Virginia.	Pgtv
Dana is the mother of both Tristan and Angela.	(Mdt) & (Mda)

Notice, first, that the order in which the letters occur is significant in two respects. (a) You always read an expression "Rab" as "*a* is in relation *R* to *b*." (b) Even if it is true that *a* stands in relation *R* to *b*, this does *not* entail that *b* stands in relation *R* to *a*, that is, "Rab" does not make the same claim as "Rba." If it is true, for example, that "Tristan is older than Angela," it is certainly false that "Angela is older than Tristan." While some relations are **symmetrical**, that is, relations such that if *a* stands in relation *R* to *b,* then *b* stands in relation *R* to *a,* the overwhelming majority are not. So in translating a relational statement, you must pay attention to what stands in a particular relation to something else. Second, statements can be complex and can indicate that a single kind of relation holds between one object and two or more other objects; you must pay attention to that kind of complexity in your translations. Though it might be true that "Dana is the mother of both Tristan and Angela," there are two distinct facts asserted, namely, that "Dana is the mother of Tristan" and that "Dana is the mother of Angela."

So far we have considered only singular relational statements. To extend our quantificational system to cover relations, we must allow *multiple quantification,* that is, we must allow that there can be quantifiers within the scope of other quantifiers. In the most basic cases, that is, where there are only two quantifiers, these are understood as follows:

$(x)(y)$ For all *x* and for all *y* . . .
$(x)(\exists y)$ For all x there is a *y* such that . . .
$(\exists x)(y)$ There is an *x* such that for all *y* . . .
$(\exists x)(\exists y)$ There is an *x* such that there is a *y* such that . . .

In cases in which you make *very* general relational claims, that is, relational claims that pertain to everything in the universe, you will place the quantifiers to the left of the relational predicate. For example, if "Cxy" is the relation "*x* causes *y*" (or "*y* is caused by *x*"—this is the distinction between active and passive voice), then "$(x)(\exists y)Cxy$" would be read, "For all *x* there is a *y* such that *x* is the cause of *y,*" that is, "Everything causes something." The order of the quantifiers makes a difference, however, so if you were given "$(\exists y)(x)Cxy,$" this would be read, "There is a *y* such that for all *x, y* is caused by *x,*" that is, "Something is caused by everything." Again, "$(\exists x)(y)Cxy$" would be read, "Something causes everything," and "$(y)(\exists x)Cxy$" would be read, "Everything is caused by something."

Although there are cases in which there are no restrictions on a relation, typically relational claims are restricted to claims regarding certain kinds of things. If there are such restrictions, then, as in earlier cases, whenever you have a universal quantifier, the statement is a conditional, and whenever you have a particular (existential) quantifier, the statement is a conjunction. For example, the statement "Some dog is between George and Hildegaard" is translated

$(\exists x)(Dx \ \& \ Bxgh)$

where "Dx" is "x is a dog," "Bxyz" is "x is between y and z," "g" is "George," and "h" is "Hildegaard." The statement "Everybody loves Lucy" is translated

$$(x)(Px \to Lxl)$$

where "Px" is "x is a person," "Lxy" is "x loves y," and "l" is "Lucy." Notice that here the quantifier is 'Everybody', which means every person; it is for this reason that an accurate translation introduces "Px" to show that the domain of things is limited to persons. Similarly, although the grammatical form of "Everybody loves somebody" is similar to "Everything causes something," the 'everybody' and 'somebody' indicate that we are talking only about people. So while it is accurate to translate "Everything causes something" as "$(x)((\exists y)(Cxy)$," to translate "Everybody loves somebody" we must indicate that we are talking about people throughout. The translation is:

$$(x)(Px \to (\exists y)(Py \;\&\; Lxy))$$

Here are some more examples of translations involving multiple quantifiers:

Somebody is loved by everybody.
$(\exists x)(Px \;\&\; (y)(Py \to Lyx))$

Somebody loves everybody.
$(\exists x)(Px \;\&\; (y)(Py \to Lxy))$

Everyone competes with everyone.
$(x)(Px \to (y)(Py \to Cxy))$

No dog loves any cat.
$(x)(Dx \to (y)(Cy \to {\sim}Lxy))$
          or
$(x)(Dx \to {\sim}(\exists y)(Cy \;\&\; Lxy))$
          or
${\sim}(\exists x)(Dx \;\&\; (\exists y)(Cy \;\&\; Lxy))$

Not everyone loves himself or herself.
$(\exists x)(Px \;\&\; {\sim}Lxx)$
          or
${\sim}(x)(Px \to Lxx)$

Everybody loves somebody sometime.
$(x)(Px \rightarrow (\exists y)(Py \,\&\, (\exists z)(Tz \,\&\, Lxyz)))$

Notice that in each of these statements, every variable is bound by a quantifier. *If a variable is unbound, there is no statement.*

Though the translations above are correct, and it is intuitive to introduce the quantifiers as you come upon them, logicians always prefer uniformity in translation. Uniformity is achieved by placing the quantifiers to the left of the propositional function—or, in what is called **prenex normal form.** A statement in prenex normal form uses only affirmative quantifiers. The rule for stating propositions in prenex normal form is that a quantifier within the scope of another quantifier can be moved outside the parentheses *except* when the quantifier is in the antecedent of a conditional. If the quantifier is in the antecedent of a conditional, moving the quantifier outside the farthest-left parentheses requires changing the quantity of the quantifier: universal to particular or particular to universal. Where Φx and Ωx are one-place predicates, and θxy is a two-place predicate, the eight standard forms in prenex normal form are as follows:

All Φs stand in relation θ to all Ωs: $(x)(y)(\Phi x \rightarrow (\Omega x \rightarrow \theta xy))$
No Φs stand in relation θ to all Ωs: $(x)(y)(\Phi x \rightarrow (\Omega x \rightarrow \sim\!\theta xy))$
All Φs stand in relation θ to some Ωs: $(x)(\exists y)(\Phi x \rightarrow (\Omega x \,\&\, \theta xy))$
No Φs stand in relation θ to some Ωs: $(x)(\exists y)(\Phi x \rightarrow (\Omega x \,\&\, \sim\!\theta xy))$
Some Φs stand in relation θ to all Ωs: $(\exists x)(y)(\Phi x \,\&\, (\Omega x \rightarrow \theta xy))$
Some Φs do not stand in relation θ to all Ωs: $(\exists x)(y)(\Phi x \,\&\, (\Omega x \rightarrow \sim\!\theta xy))$
Some Φs stand in relation θ to some Ωs: $(\exists x)(\exists y)(\Phi x \,\&\, (\Omega x \,\&\, \theta xy))$
Some Φs do not stand in relation θ to some Ωs:
$(\exists x)(\exists y)(\Phi x \,\&\, (\Omega x \,\&\, \sim\!\theta xy))$

In translating, of course, you must keep the standard translation techniques in mind. For example, if you are given a statement that includes the expression "if . . ., then . . .," you *must not* assume that the objects in the consequent are the same objects in the antecedent. For example, if you are given the statement "If everybody loves somebody, then everybody is loved by somebody," you would translate it:

$\{(x)(Px \rightarrow (\exists y)(Py \,\&\, Lxy))\} \rightarrow \{(x)(Px \rightarrow (\exists y)(Py \,\&\, Lyx))\}$

The proof techniques for arguments with statements containing multiple quantifiers and relational predicates are *basically* the same as those we have considered up to this point, although we shall have to introduce an additional restriction on Universal Generalization (U.G.) and restrictions on the application of the instantiation and generalization rules.

(1) If there is a tilde (~) to the left of a quantifier, you will need to use the rule of Quantifier Negation (Q.N.) to move the tilde to the right of the quantifier. This may require several instances of Q.N. before you can instantiate. For example, if you were given "~$(x)(\exists y)Pxy$," you would first apply Q.N. to obtain "$(\exists x)$~$(\exists y)Pxy$," and then you would apply Q.N. a second time to obtain "$(\exists x)(y)($~$Pxy)$."

(2) You must instantiate quantifiers in the order in which they are presented in the proposition, beginning with the farthest-left quantifier. If you were given "$(x)(\exists y)(Px \rightarrow Qy)$," you would first instantiate for x, then for y. The first three lines of your proof might look like this:

1. $(x)(\exists y)(Px \rightarrow Qy)$
2. $(\exists y)(Pa \rightarrow Qy)$ 1 U.I.
3. $Pa \rightarrow Qb$ 2 E.I.

The restriction on existential instantiation remains, namely, that you can not instantiate for a constant that has already been introduced into the proof. It is for this reason that the existential quantifier is not instantiated for the same constant as the universal.

To understand the rationale for this restriction, consider the statement, "Everybody had a biological mother." You are concerned with two people, so the statement is symbolized as:

$(x)(\exists y)(Px \rightarrow (Px \ \& \ Myx))$

Were it not for the restrictions on the order of instantiation and existential instantiation, you could infer that someone was his or her own biological mother, which is obviously false.

(3) If you are generalizing from either statements containing only constants (existential generalization) or statements containing only free variables (universal generalization), quantifiers are added from right to left. If you had the statement in a proof, "Pa & Qb," you might engage in two instances of existential generalization as follows:

1. Pa & Qb
2. $(\exists x)(Px \ \& \ Qb)$ 1 E.G.
3. $(\exists y)(\exists x)(Px \ \& \ Qy)$ 2 E.G.

Or you might engage in two instances of existential generalization as follows:

1. Pa & Qb
2. $(\exists y)(Py \ \& \ Qb)$ 1 E.G.
3. $(\exists x)(\exists y)(Py \ \& \ Qx)$ 2 E.G.

In a quantified statement, if the quantifiers are the same, the order in which they are introduced makes no logical difference, as you can see from the following proof:

1. $(x)(y)Pxy$
2. $(y)Pxy$ 1 U.I.
3. Pxy 2 U.I.
4. $(x)Pxy$ 3 U.G.
5. $(y)(x)Pxy$ 4 U.G.

Since when the quantifiers are the same the order of generalization makes no logical difference, this is strictly a procedural rule.

(4) As we saw above, when there is a mixture of universal and existential quantifiers in a statement, the order of the quantifiers makes a difference in the meaning of the statement. For example, "$(x)(\exists y)Cxy$" might mean "Everything causes something," which means something quite different from "$(\exists x)(y)Cxy$," "Something causes everything." For this reason, there is an additional restriction that applies to Universal Generalization when dealing with multiple quantification. The restriction is as follows:

U.G. Φy $/\therefore$ $(x)\Phi x$ *but* U.G. must not be used if Φy contains a constant and y is free in the line where that name is introduced.

The restriction requires that if you have a line in your proof in which there is both a free variable and a constant, you must engage in existential generalization before you engage in universal generalization. Were it not for this restriction, you could derive the false claim that

"Something is caused by everything" from the quite possibly true claim that "Everything is the cause of something":

1. $(x)(\exists y)Cxy$
2. $(\exists y)Cxy$ 1 U.I.
3. Cxa 2 E.I.
4. $(x)Cxa$ 3 U.G. *This inference is invalid and is blocked by the restriction.*

5. $(\exists y)(x)(Cxy)$ 4 E.G.

(5) You should remember that there is a restriction on the rule of Existential Instantiation (E.I.), namely, that it requires that you introduce a *new* name into a proof. When dealing with statements involving multiple quantifiers and relations, there is also a restriction that applies to Universal Instantiation, namely, *no variable for which you instantiate by means of Universal Instantiation may be a variable that is already within the scope of an existential quantifier.* This restriction rests on considerations of what is required for most relational claims to be true: Most relations are **nonreflexive,** that is, they cannot obtain between a particular object and itself. For example, an object cannot be to the left of itself; a person cannot be the parent of himself or herself. When an object can stand in a certain relation to itself—when a relation is **reflexive**—and the validity of the argument depends on that fact, there will be a premise that tells you that the relation is reflexive. So this restriction *prevents you from inferring* that since every person has some parent, it follows that some person is its own parent, that is, the restriction blocks the following invalid inference:

1. $(x)(Px \rightarrow (\exists y)(Py \,\&\, Pyx))$
2. $Py \rightarrow (\exists y)(Py \,\&\, Pyy)$ 1 U.I. *This inference is invalid and is blocked by the restriction.*

(6) Finally, a similar restriction applies to the generalization rules: *you must not generalize in such a way that you capture variables that are already bound by other quantifiers,* that is, when generalizing you must introduce a "new" variable into the proof. The rationale here is the same as in the previous case: the restriction prevents you from incorrectly inferring that a relation is reflexive. For example, the restriction *prevents you from inferring* that since someone is the parent of *y,* everyone is the parent of himself or herself, that is, the restriction blocks the following invalid inference:

1. $(\exists x)(Px \ \& \ Pxy)$
2. $(x)(\exists x)(Px \ \& \ Pxx)$ *This inference is invalid and is blocked by the restriction.*

Given these considerations, let us consider a few examples of proofs involving multiple quantification and relations.

Suppose we were asked to translate and give a proof for the following argument: "Everyone who is related to Fran is related to George. Hazel is a person related to Fran. So Hazel is related to George." Where "Px" is "x is a person," "Rxy" is "x is related to y," "f" is "Fran," "g" is "George," and "h" is "Hazel," the translation is:

$(x)[Px \ \& \ Rxf) \to Rxg]$
Ph $\&$ Rhf   /∴   Rhg

The proof proceeds just as you would expect:

1. $(x)[(Px \ \& \ Rxf) \to Rxg]$
2. Ph $\&$ Rhf   /∴   Rhg
3. (Ph $\&$ Rhf) $\to$ Rhg   1 U.I.
4. Rhg   3,2 M.P.

In terms of proof technique, the introduction of relational predicates changes nothing.

Consider the following argument: "No six-year-old child is a grandmother. Amisglof is a six-year-old child. So Amisglof is not a grandmother." To be a grandmother is to be a grandmother of someone (or other), so where "Sx" is "x is a six-year-old," "Cx" is "x is a child," "Px" is "x is a person," "Gxy" is "x is a grandmother of y," and "a" is "Amisglof," the translation is:

$(x)[(Cx \ \& \ Sx) \to (y)(Py \to {\sim}Gxy)]$
Ca $\&$ Sa   /∴ $(y)(Py \to {\sim}Gay)$

and the proof is:

1. $(x)[(Cx \ \& \ Sx) \to (y)(Py \to {\sim}Gxy)]$
2. Ca $\&$ Sa   /∴ $(y)(Py \to {\sim}Gay)$
3. (Ca $\&$ Sa) $\to (y)(Py \to {\sim}Gay)$ 1 U.I.
4. $(y)(Py \to {\sim}Gay)$ 3,2 M.P.

Similarly, if you were given the following argument:

$(x)[Px \rightarrow (\exists y)(Qy \ \& \ Rxy)]$
$(\exists x)(Px \ \& \ Qx) \quad / \therefore \quad (\exists x)(\exists y)(Rxy)$

the proof is as follows:

1. $(x)[Px \rightarrow (\exists y)(Qy \ \& \ Rxy)]$
2. $(x)(Px \ \& \ Qx) \quad / \therefore \quad (\exists x)(\exists y)(Rxy)$
3. $Pa \ \& \ Qa$ 2 E.I.
3. $Pa \rightarrow (\exists y)(Qy \ \& \ Ray)$ 1 U.I.
4. Pa 3 Simp.
5. $(\exists y)(Qy \ \& \ Ray)$ 3,4 M.P.
6. $Qb \ \& \ Rab$ 5 E.I.
7. $Rab \ \& \ Qa$ 6 Com.
8. Rab 7 Simp.
9. $(\exists y)(Ray)$ 8 E.G.
10. $(\exists x)(\exists y)(Rxy)$ 9 E.G.

Remember that:

1. All the rules and restrictions for E.I. and U.G. continue to apply.
2. It is permissible to instantiate a particular statement more than once, *as long as it is instantiated for a different constant each time.*

EXERCISES

I. Translate each of the following into the suggested symbols:

1. Shakespeare wrote *Macbeth*. (Wxy: x wrote y; s: Shakespeare; m: *Macbeth*)

2. Shakespeare did not write *The Spy Who Came in from the Cold*. (Wxy: x wrote y; s: Shakespeare; c: *The Spy Who Came in from the Cold*)

3. If Shakespeare wrote *Hamlet* then Shakespeare wrote *Macbeth*. (Wxy: x wrote y; s: Shakespeare; h: *Hamlet*; m: Macbeth)

4. Someone is George's uncle. (Px: x is a person; Uxy: x is the uncle of y; g: George)

5. No one is George's aunt. (Px: x is a person; Axy: x is the aunt of y; g: George)

6. Some tape self-destructs. (Tx: x is a tape; Dxy: x destroys y)

7. All automobiles self-destruct. (Ax: x is an automobile; Dxy: x destroys y)

8. Anyone who is a patient of young Dr. Malone is a radio personality. (Px: x is a person; Pxy: x is a patient of y; Rx: x is a radio personality; m: young Dr. Malone)

9. All my children are residents at General Hospital. (Rx: x is a resident; Cxy: x is a child of y; Axy: x is at y; m: me; g: General Hospital)

10. Everyone has a parent. (Px: x is a person; Pxy: x is a parent of y

11. Someone is on John's left and someone is on John's right. (Px: x is a person; Rxy: x is to the right of y; Lxy: x is to the left of y; j: John)

12. Whoever is on John's right is on George's left. (Px: x is a person; Rxy: x is to the right of y; Lxy: x is to the left of y; j: John; g: George)

13. No one takes the *Times*, unless he or she is well-educated. (Px: x is a person; Txy: x takes y; W: x is well-educated; t: the *Times*)

14. No one can remember the Battle of Waterloo, unless he or she is very old. (Px: x is a person; Rxy: x can remember y; Ox: x is very old; w: the Battle of Waterloo)

15. All professional spies are better than any amateur spies. (Sx: x is a spy; Px: x is a professional; Ax: x is an amateur; Bxy: x is better than y)

16. A rolling stone gathers no moss. (Rx: x rolls; Sx: x is a stone; Mx: x is moss; Gxy: x gathers y)

17. All's fair in love and war. (Ax: x is an action (or thing); Lx: x is a state of love; Wx: x is a state of war; Ixy: x is in y; Fx: x is fair)

18. Any man who hates children and dogs cannot be all bad. (Mx: x is a man; Cx: x is a child; Dx: x is a dog; Bx: x can be all bad; Hxy: x hates y)

19. Anything that is run over by a steamroller and lives to tell about it is a cartoon character. (Tx: x is a steamroller; Rxy: x runs over y; Lxy: x lives to tell about y; Cx: x is a cartoon character)

20. Anything that is run over by a steamroller and lives to tell about it is either a toon or a friend of Wanda. (Tx: x is a

thing; S*x*: *x* is a steam roller; R*xy*: *x* runs over *y*; L*xy*: *x* lives to tell about *y*; F*xy*: *x* is a friend of *y*; C*x*: *x* is a cartoon character; w: Wanda)

II. Construct a proof for each of the following arguments. You may use direct, conditional, or indirect proof.

1. $(x)[Px \rightarrow (y)(Qy \rightarrow Rxy)]$
   $(\exists x)(Px \& Qx)$ /∴ $(\exists x)(\exists y)Rxy$

2. $(x)[Px \rightarrow (y)(Qy \rightarrow Rxy)]$
   Pa
   $(\exists x)(Px \& Qx)$ /∴ $(\exists x)Rax$

3. $(x)[Px \rightarrow (\exists x)(Qy \& Ry)]$
   $(x)(y)(\sim Rxy)$ /∴ $\sim Pa$

4. $(\exists x)[Px \& (y)(Qy \rightarrow Rxy)]$
   $(x)(Px \rightarrow Qx)$ /∴ $(\exists x)(Qx \& Rxx)$

5. $(\exists x)(\exists y)(\sim Rxy)$
   $(x)[Px \rightarrow (y)(Qy \rightarrow Rxy)]$ /∴ $(\exists x)(\exists y)(\sim Px \lor \sim Qy)$

6. $(\exists x)(y)(Qx \& \sim Rxy)$
   $(x)[Px \rightarrow (y)(Qy \rightarrow Rxy)]$ /∴ $(\exists x)(\sim Px)$

7. $(x)\{Px \rightarrow (\exists y)[Qy \& (Sy \rightarrow Rxy)]\}$
   $(\exists x)(Px \& Sx)$
   $(x)(Qx \rightarrow Sx)$ /∴ $(\exists x)(\exists y)(Rxy)$

8. $(x)\{Px \rightarrow (\exists y)[Qy \& (Sy \rightarrow Rxy)]\}$
   $(\exists x)(Px \& Sx)$
   $(x)(y)(Px \rightarrow Sy)$ /∴ $(\exists x)(Qx \& Rax)$

9. $(x)\{Px \rightarrow (\exists y)[Qy \& (Sy \rightarrow Rxy)]\}$
   $(\exists x)(Sx \& Px)$
   $(x)(y)(Rxy \rightarrow Ryx)$ /∴ $(\exists x)(\exists y)(Sy \rightarrow Ryx)$

10. $(x)\{Px \rightarrow (\exists y)[Qy \& (Sy \rightarrow Rxy)]\}$
    $(\exists x)(Px \& Sx)$
    $(x)(y)(\sim Ryx \rightarrow \sim Rxy)$ /∴ $(\exists x)(\exists y)[Px \& (Sy \rightarrow Ryx)]$

11. $(x)\{(Px \lor Qx) \rightarrow (y)[(Sy \lor Qy) \rightarrow Rxy]\}$
    $(x)(y)(Rxy \rightarrow Tyx)$ /∴ $(x)[Qx \rightarrow (y)(Qy \rightarrow Tyx)]$

12. $(x)\{(Px \lor Qx) \rightarrow (y)[(Sy \lor Qy) \rightarrow Rxy]\}$
    $(\exists x)Px \& Qx$
    $(x)(y)(Rxy \rightarrow Tyx)$ /∴ $(\exists x)[Qx \rightarrow (\exists y)(Qy \& Tyx)]$

13. $(x)\{(Px \lor Qx) \rightarrow (y)[(Sy \lor Qy) \rightarrow Rxy]\}$
    $(\exists x)(Px \& Qx)$
    $(x)(y)(Rxy \rightarrow Tyx)$ /∴ $(x)[Qx \rightarrow (\exists y)(Qy \& Tyx)]$

14. $(x)\{Px \rightarrow (\exists y)[Qy \ \& \ (Sy \rightarrow Rxy)]\}$
$(x)(Sx \rightarrow Px)$
$(x)(y)(\sim Ryx \rightarrow \sim Rxy)$
$/\therefore \quad (x)\{Sx \rightarrow (\exists y)[Qy \ \& \ (Sy \rightarrow Ryx)]\}$

15. $(x)\{Px \rightarrow (y)[(Qy \ \& \ Rxy) \rightarrow (z)(Sz \rightarrow Rxz)]\}$
$(\exists x)(y)(Px \ \& \ Rxy)$
Qb
$(x)(y)(\sim Sx \rightarrow \sim Ryx) \quad /\therefore \quad (x)(\exists y)(Sx \leftrightarrow Rxy)$

III. Translate and construct a proof for each of the following. You may use direct, conditional, or indirect proof.

POLITICS AS USUAL

1. If George is a conservative and Henry is politically to the right of George, then Henry is an ultraconservative. George is a conservative. Henry is not an ultraconservative. So Henry is not politically to the right of George. (Cx: x is a conservative; Ux: x is an ultraconservative; Rxy: x is politically to the right of y; g: George; h: Henry)

2. Anyone who is politically to the right of Henry is a conservative. George is not a conservative. So George is not politically to the right of Henry. (Cx: x is a conservative; Rxy: x is politically to the right of y; g: George; h: Henry)

3. Some politicians are liars. No liar holds truth in high regard. Therefore, some politicians do not hold truth in high regard. (Px: x is a politician; Lx: x is a liar; Hxy: x holds y in high regard; t: truth)

4. Every senator belongs to a political party. Some representatives do not belong to a political party. Therefore, some representative is not a senator. (Sx: x is a senator; Px: x is a political party; Rx: x is a representative; Rxy: x belongs to y)

5. Some politicians do not hold truth in high regard. Any politician who campaigns for a lofty cause holds truth in high regard. So, some politicians do not campaign for any lofty causes. (Px: x is a politician; Cx: x is a cause; Lx: x is lofty; Cxy: x campaigns for y; Hxy: x holds y in high regard; t: truth)

6. Some politicians are self-serving. Either George is a politician or no self-serving politician looks after George's interests. George is not a politician. So some politicians do not look after

George's interests. (P*x*: *x* is a politician; S*xy*: *x* serves *y*; I*x*: *x* is an interest; B*xy*: *x* belongs to *y*; L*xy*: *x* looks after *y*; g: George)

7. Every politician for whom I voted is honest. No honest politician was controlled by a special-interest group. No politician who was not controlled by a special-interest group was elected to an office. So, no politician for whom I voted was elected to an office. (P*x*: *x* is a politician; H*x*: *x* is honest; S*x*: *x* is a special interest group; O*x*: *x* is an office; V*xy*: *x* voted for *y*; C*xy*: *x* controlled *y*; E*xy*: *x* was elected to *y*; i: I)

8. Anyone who votes in all elections studies all the candidates. Anyone who studies all the candidates does not play chess. John is a person who votes in all elections. So John does not play chess. (P*x*: *x* is a person; E*x*: *x* is an election; V*xy*: *x* votes in *y*; C*x*: *x* is a candidate; S*xy*: *x* studies *y*; G*x*: *x* is a game of chess; P*xy*: *x* plays *y*; j: John)

9. Anyone who votes in all elections studies all the candidates. Anyone who studies all the candidates does not play chess. John is a person who plays chess. So John does not vote in all elections. (P*x*: *x* is a person; E*x*: *x* is an election; V*xy*: *x* votes in *y*; C*x*: *x* is a candidate; S*xy*: *x* studies *y*; G*x*: *x* is a game of chess; P*xy*: *x* plays *y*; j: John)

10. Anyone who votes in all elections studies all the candidates. Anyone who studies all the candidates does not play chess. Some people vote in all elections. Some people play chess. So some people study all the candidates and some people don't. (P*x*: *x* is a person; E*x*: *x* is an election; V*xy*: *x* votes in *y*; C*x*: *x* is a candidate; S*xy*: *x* studies *y*; G*x*: *x* is a game of chess; P*xy*: *x* plays *y*)

7.7 *Identity, Definite Descriptions, and Number*

Among the many relations, one is particularly useful and important. This is the relation of **identity**, or sameness. You make true identity claims in the following statements:

Lewis Carroll was Charles Lutwidge Dodgson.
George Eliot was Marian Evans Cross.
John Wilkes Booth was the murderer of Abraham Lincoln.
Ronald Reagan was the fortieth president of the United States.

Identity is to logic what equality is to mathematics, and it has many of the same properties as equality. Identity is a **transitive** relation: for any x, y, and z, if x is identical with y and y is identical with z, then x is identical with z. It is **symmetrical:** for any x and y, if x is identical with y, then y is identical with x. And it is **reflexive:** everything is identical with itself.

These facts about identity are extremely important, since they allow us, among other things, to replace names with other names in those cases in which one thing has two names. For example, if you are given the following premises:

O. Henry wrote "The Gift of the Maji."
William Sidney Porter was O. Henry.

you can infer that:

William Sidney Porter wrote "The Gift of the Maji."

To introduce identity into our logical system, we will introduce another symbol. The equality sign, '=', is the sign for identity. In addition to this, we need to introduce an additional set of rules that fall under the title of "the principle of identity" (Id.):

$$
\text{Id.} \quad
\begin{array}{l}
\Phi x \\
\underline{x = y} \\
/\therefore\ \Phi y
\end{array}
,\quad
\begin{array}{l}
\Phi x \\
\underline{\sim\!\Phi y} \\
/\therefore\ \sim\!(x = y)
\end{array}
,\quad
\begin{array}{l}
\underline{x = y} \\
/\therefore\ y = x
\end{array}
,\quad
\begin{array}{l}
\underline{\text{any premise}} \\
/\therefore\ x = x
\end{array}
$$

You should notice that since identity is a predicate, a special case falling under the first version of the rule of identity is:

$$
\begin{array}{l}
x = y \\
\underline{y = z} \\
/\therefore\quad x = z
\end{array}
$$

Given this additional rule, we can easily prove that the argument given above is valid by appealing to the principle of identity to justify the substitution of "William Sidney Porter" for "O. Henry":

1. Wog
2. p = o $/\therefore$ Wpg
3. Wpg   1,2 Id.[7]

If you look at the examples of identity statements given above, you will notice that in some cases the identity is said to hold between one person with two names. In other cases, there is an identity claimed between a person named and a person picked out on the basis of a **definite description,** that is, a phrase of the form "the so and so." Examples of definite descriptions include "the present president of the United States," "the present prime minister of the United Kingdom," and "the author of this book." Each of these complex linguistic expressions *picks out exactly one thing;* to that extent it is like a name and functions in much the same way as a name. But while a name such as "Ostafar Neumathesque" is insignificant if it names no one, or "meaningless" if you do not know the object named, a definite description can be intelligible even if it fails to pick out an object. For example, the expression "the present king of France" is intelligible, even though France has not had a monarch for over two hundred years.

Several questions arise. If you make a claim regarding the present king of France, for example, "The present king of France is bald," is that statement true or false? And how, precisely, do you provide a symbolic representation of a definite description? A definite description picks out exactly one thing—that is what makes it a *definite* description. You can represent the *uniqueness condition* of a definite description by claiming that there is at least one and at most one thing that fulfills a certain set of conditions. Where "Kx" is "x is a king of France" and "Bx" is "x is bald," you represent the statement "The present king of France is bald" as follows:

$$(\exists x)\{[Kx \ \& \ (y)(Ky \to x = y)] \ \& \ Bx\}$$

The expression, "$(\exists x)\{Kx \ \& \ (y)[(Ky \to x = y)\}$" is a **contextual definition** of the word 'the'. It specifies the meaning of the word 'the' in those and only those statements in which the sense of 'the' is "exactly one." Also, this answers the question of the truth value of the statement "The present king of France is bald": insofar as the statement claims that there is exactly one present king of France, while, as a matter of fact, there is none, the statement is false.

Considerations of this sort allow you to symbolize various numerical claims. Remember, the sense of the existential operator is "there is at least one." Hence, to claim that there is at least one x that is "P" is:

$$(\exists x)Px$$

To claim there are *no* (zero) things "x" that are "P" is:

$\sim(\exists x)Px$

To claim there is *exactly* one thing "x" that is "P" is:

$(\exists x)[Px \;\&\; (y)(Py \rightarrow x = y)]$

To claim there is *at most one* thing "x" that is "P" is:

$(x)(y)[(Px \;\&\; Py) \rightarrow x = y]$

To claim there are *at least two* things "x" that are "P" is:

$(\exists x)(\exists y)\{Px \;\&\; [Py \;\&\; \sim(x = y)]\}$

To claim there are *at most two* things that are "P" is:

$(x)(y)(z)\{[Px \;\&\; (Py \;\&\; Pz)] \rightarrow [x = y \lor (y = z \lor x = z)]\}$

To claim there are *exactly two* things that are "P" is:

$(\exists x)(\exists y)\{[Px \;\&\; (Py \;\&\; \sim(x = y))] \;\&\; (z)[Pz \rightarrow (z = x \lor z = y)]\}$

You proceed in exactly the same way to construct formulae dealing with larger numbers.

In addition to number, the relation of identity allows you to formulate the following expressions:

To claim that *only* "a" is "P" is:

$Pa \;\&\; (x)(Px \rightarrow x = a)$

To claim that *the only* "P" that is "Q" is "a" is:

$(Pa \;\&\; Qa) \;\&\; (x)[(Px \;\&\; Qx) \rightarrow x = a]$

To claim that *no* "P" *except* "a" is "Q" is:

$(Pa \;\&\; Qa) \;\&\; (x)[(Px \;\&\; Qx) \rightarrow x = a]$

To claim that *all* things that are "P" *except* "a" are "Q" is:

$(Pa \;\&\; \sim Qa) \;\&\; (x)[(Px \;\&\; \sim(x = a)) \rightarrow Qa]$

To claim that "a" is the "P" that is *most* Φ, where "M*xy*" is "*x* is more Φ than *y*," is:

Pa & (*x*){[Pa & ~(*x* = a)] → Ma*x*}

EXERCISES

I. Construct a proof for each of the following:

1. (*x*)(P*x* → Q*x*)
   Pa
   a = b   /∴   Qb

2. (*x*)(P*x* → Q*x*)
   Pa
   ~Qb   /∴   ~(a = b)

3. (*x*)(P*x* → (∃*y*)(Q*y* & R*xy*)
   Pa
   (*x*)[(*x* = a) → (*y*)(*y* = *x*)]   /∴   Qa

4. (*x*)[(∃*y*)(R*xy*) → (∃*z*)(R*zx*)]
   (*x*)(*y*)(*x* = *y*)
   (*x*)(R*xx*)   /∴   Rcb

5. (∃*x*)[P*x* & (*y*)(P*y* → R*xy*)]
   (*x*)(*y*)(R*yx* → (∃*z*)S*z*)
   (*x*)(*x* = c)   /∴   Sc

6. (∃*x*){[P*x* & (*y*)(P*y* → *x* = *y*)] & W*xt*}
   (*x*)(W*xt* → W*xe*)
   /∴   (∃*x*){[P*x* & (*y*)(P*y* → *x* = *y*)] & W*xe*}

7. Pa & ~(∃*x*)[P*x* & ~(*x* = a)]
   /∴   (∃*x*)[P*x* & (*y*)(P*y* → *x* = *y*)]

8. (∃x)(P*x* & I*x*)
   Pa & (*x*)(P*x* → *x* = a)   /∴   Ia

9. (∃*x*)(∃*y*){[(P*x* & P*y*) & ~(*x* = *y*)] & (*z*)[P*z* → (*z* = *x* v *z* = *y*)]}
   Pa
   /∴   (∃*x*)[P*x* & ~(*x* = a)]

10. (∃*x*)(∃*y*)[(F*x* & F*y*) & ~(*x* = *y*)]
    (*x*)[(F*x* v G*x*) → P*x*]
    f/∴   (∃*x*)(∃*y*)[(P*x* & P*y*) & ~(*x* = *y*)]

III. Translate each of the following statements into symbols.

1. Samuel Langhorne Clemens was Mark Twain. (c: Samuel Langhorne Clemens; t: Mark Twain)

2. The Galloping Gourmet is Graham Kerr. (Gx: x is a Galloping Gourmet; k: Graham Kerr)

3. Lynn has at least one ace. (Ax: x is an ace; Hxy: x has y; l: Lynn)

4. Pat has at most one ace. (Ax: x is an ace; Hxy: x has y; p: Pat)

5. Janette has exactly one ace. (Ax: x is an ace; Hxy: x has y; j: Janette)

6. Humberto has exactly two children. (h: Humberto; Cx: x is a child; Hxy: x and y)

7. There is no largest number. (Nx: x is a number; Lxy: x is larger than y)

8. Hornblower is the least popular reporter for the *Evening Star*. (h: Hornblower; e: the *Evening Star*; Rxy: x is a reporter for y; Lxy: x is less popular than y)

9. Dr. Muddleford is the most popular professor on campus. (m: Dr. Muddleford; c: campus; Px: x is a professor; Oxy: x is on y)

10. Any politician who kisses babies is more popular than a politician who does not kiss babies. (Px: x is a politician; Bx: x is a baby; Kxy: x kisses y; Pxy: x is more popular than y)

IV. Translate and construct a proof for each of the following.

THIS IS A STICK-UP!

1. The robber who robbed Last Transylvanian bank was Joan. So Joan robbed Last Transylvanian Bank. (Rx: x is a robber; Rxy: x robbed y; l: Last Transylvanian Bank; j: Joan)

2. Fodsworth was the only robber who got away. Herman was a robber but Herman is not Fodsworth. Therefore, Herman did not get away. (Rx: x was a robber; Gx: x got away; f: Fodsworth; h: Herman)

3. At least one bank was robbed. At most one bank was robbed. So exactly one bank was robbed. (Bx: x is a bank; Rx: x was robbed)

4. The person who robbed Last Transylvanian Bank drove a BMW. No person who drives a BMW is impoverished. So the person who robbed Last Transylvanian Bank was not impoverished. (Px: x is a man; Bx: x is a BMW; Ix: x is impoverished; Rxy: x robbed y; Dxy: x drove y; l: Last Transylvanian Bank)

5. Only Fodsworth was caught. Everyone who was caught went to jail. Everyone who went to jail was caught. So only Fodsworth went to jail. (Cx: x was caught; Wxy: x went to y; f: Fodsworth; j: jail)

6. There are at least two robbers. Gene is a robber. So, there is at least one robber who is not Gene. (Rx: x is a robber; g: Gene)

7. There are exactly two robbers. Jean is a robber. So, there is at least one robber who is not Jean. (Rx: x is a robber; j: Jean)

8. Everyone who robbed the Last Transylvanian Bank except Fodsworth was caught. Everyone who robbed the Last Transylvanian Bank was jailed if and only if he or she was caught. So, everyone who robbed the Last Transylvanian Bank except Fodsworth was jailed. (Px: x is a person; Cx: x was caught; Jx: x was jailed; Rxy: x robbed y; l: Last Transylvanian Bank; f: Fodsworth)

9. All the robbers except Fodsworth got away. Any robber who got away went to Argentina. Fodsworth went to jail. Therefore, every robber either went to Argentina or went to jail. (Rx: x is one of the robbers; Gx: x got away; Wxy: x went to y; f: Fodsworth; a: Argentina; j: jail)

10. Every robber was either a known felon or an undercover agent. Exactly one robber was an undercover agent. No undercover agent was a known felon. There were at least two robbers. So, at least one robber who was a known felon. (Rx: x was a robber; Fx: x was a known felon; Ux: x was an undercover agent)

NOTES

1. It is also equivalent to ~($\exists x$)(Sx & Px), that is, there is not an x such that x is S and x is P. Indeed, this is perhaps the more intuitive transla-

tion of "No S is P." For the time being, however, we will use the conditional translation since it provides uniformity in translation of universal statements. We introduce a rule for quantifier negation in Section 7.3, at which point we are able to prove that the two expressions are equivalent.

2. To see that this is the correct translation for statements beginning with 'Only' or 'None but', consider the statement, "None but thoroughbreds are Kentucky Derby winners." It *cannot* mean "All thoroughbreds are Kentucky Derby winners," since every horse that runs the Derby is a thoroughbred, but few win. The statement is true only if it is understood as "All Kentucky Derby winners are thoroughbreds," that is, $(x)(Kx \rightarrow Tx)$.

3. If you find it puzzling that both "A few S's are P's" and "Most S's are P's" are translated "$(\exists x)(Sx \ \& \ Px)$," consider the quantifiers. A universal quantifier claims that *every* member of the subject class is contained in the predicate class. The particular quantifier claims only that there is at least one thing in the subject class that is in the predicate class. If you claim that "*Most* S's are P's" you are not claiming that they all are, so the most the symbolism will allow you to say is that at least one is.

4. A more intuitive way to state this is $\sim(x)(Sx \rightarrow Px)$.

5. As we see in the next section, there are negations of particular propositions that are equivalent to universal propositions.

6. Should anyone question whether Methodists are both young and restless, the author attests that several years ago in a Methodist church in Texas there was a couples group that called itself "The Young and the Restless." The author also acknowledges that the name was not necessarily an accurate description of the group.

7. We should note in passing that there are contexts in which the principle of identity will *not* justify a substitution of identicals. These contexts are known as **referentially opaque.** Referentially opaque contexts include some cases of quotation as well as propositional attitudes such as believing and knowing. For example, in the statement "Joanne believes that O. Henry wrote 'The Gift of the Maji,'" 'O. Henry' is referentially opaque, that is, there is no guarantee that if you substituted "William Sidney Porter' for 'O. Henry' the resulting statement would be true. Joanne might not know that the statement "William Sidney Porter is O. Henry" is true, and if she doesn't, she would not believe that William Sidney Porter wrote "The Gift of the Maji." On referential opacity, see Willard Van Orman Quine, *Word and Object* (Cambridge: M.I.T. Press, 1960), pp. 141–56.

Chapter Eight

Analogical Arguments

The premises of an **inductive argument** provide some, but not conclusive, evidence for the truth of the conclusion. Nonetheless, many of our beliefs about the world rest on inductive arguments. They rest on the *assumption* that everything in the world operates according to certain general principles or natural laws that do not change. Although it is impossible to establish that the principles governing the operations of nature are the same at all times and in all places, the assumption that they are the same guides most of our everyday actions. You conclude that the clear liquid in a glass is water, since it looks and smells like water you have drunk in the past. You conclude that a certain glass of water will quench your thirst, because the last glass of water you drank quenched your thirst. You conclude that your friend will greet you with a smile because she has usually done so in the past. You conclude that your ten-year-old car will give you no trouble on your vacation, since you have never had a bit of trouble with it. In drawing any of these conclusions, you could be wrong.

Although no inductive argument provides conclusive evidence for its conclusion, there are various ways to evaluate the strength of the evidence for the conclusion of an inductive argument. In this chapter we examine the criteria for evaluating arguments by analogy. In the following chapters we examine criteria for evaluating other types of inductive arguments.

8.1 Analogies

Analogies are claims of similarity. If I say that the heart is analogous to a pump, I am claiming that there are at least some respects in which a heart and a pump are similar. This does not mean that analogous things are similar in all respects. A typical pump is made of metal or plastic; a heart is made of muscle. A heart and a pump are similar insofar as both move liquids.

Analogies are of different sorts and have different uses. If we already understand the similarities between two things or kinds of things, we can use analogies for purposes of illustration. Illustrative uses of analogies in literature take the form of similes and metaphors, and often convert a mundane description into a vivid verbal picture. In a **simile** a comparison between two things is made explicit by the use of words such as 'like' or 'as'. For example, rather than describing the breeze as hot, I might say that the wind struck me like molten steel from a blast furnace. Rather than saying that a man was arrogant, you might say, "he was like a cock who thought the sun had risen to hear him crow."[1] Rather than saying, "Nervously, I struggled through the State House," you might say, "Like an energetic fly in a very large cobweb, I struggled through the State House."[2] Because we already know that molten steel is very hot, that roosters are considered proud animals, and can imagine a fly energetically fighting a spider web, the similes are effective illustrations. **Metaphors** make comparisons without specifically indicating that a comparison is being made. You might metaphorically describe a particularly forceful debater by saying, "She was a tiger poised to pounce on her opponent." Rather than describing the situation in the Middle East as tumultuous, it is more striking to say, "The Middle East was a volcano, just as it is now. . . ."[3] It is because we know the characteristics of pouncing tigers and volcanos that these metaphors are striking illustrations.

Analogies are also used to explain, where something unfamiliar is made intelligible through a comparison with something familiar. For example, I might explain what a computer is by saying that a computer is like a typewriter or a calculator, but rather than writing on paper it writes on a television screen. Or I might explain what an atom is by claiming that it is like a miniature solar system. Scientific writing, especially that intended for a lay audience, is full of this type of analogy. For example, I might explain how the nineteenth-century German mathematician Georg Cantor compared the sizes of infinite sets by means of the following analogy:[4]

> If we want to talk about larger and smaller infinities, we are faced with the problem of comparing numbers that we can neither name nor write down. Our grappling with this problem is like wanting to know whether there are more beads or coins in a treasure chest but being able to count only to three. How would we find out whether the chest has more beads or coins? We might take beads and coins from the chest one by one and place them beside each other. If we run out of coins before we run out of beads, then there were more beads than coins. If we run out of beads before coins, then there were more coins than beads. If we run out of beads and coins at the same time, then there were the same number of each. It was exactly this kind of one-to-one correlation that Cantor proposed for comparing infinities.

In logic we are primarily interested in the use of analogies in arguments. In the simplest case, we construct an **argument by analogy** by comparing two things in terms of their properties and argue that since they are similar in a certain number of salient respects, the fact that one of them has another property provides reason to believe that the other one does too. In some cases, the object with an unknown property is compared to several other objects with known properties. Consider some examples.

1. Last time I had a can of Brand-X cola, it was tasty. I infer that the can of Brand-X cola I'm about to drink will be tasty.
2. I've read ten of Agatha Christie's Miss Marple mysteries. In each, Miss Marple solved the mystery. I infer that Miss Marple will solve the mystery next time I read one of Agatha Christie's Miss Marple mysteries.
3. Georgette, Henry, Bob, Monique, and Alys graduated from Area One Technical School. All five studied plumbing. All five studied with Mr. Smith, a master plumber. Georgette, Henry, Bob, and Monique are accomplished plumbers. We may infer that Alys is also an accomplished plumber.

In the first argument, there is a comparison between two cans of cola. Both are of the same brand, which implies that they are made by the same company, from the same recipe, and therefore contain the same ingredients. The first can of cola was tasty. As a result, we have good reason to believe the second can will be tasty. In the second argument, eleven books are compared. The properties of ten are known, but they are being compared only in terms of their author, their principal character, and the fact that in the ten known cases Miss Marple has solved the mystery. Still, we seem to have good reason to believe that Miss Marple will solve the next mystery I read. In the third case, five people are being compared in three respects. They all graduated from the same school and studied under the same plumbing instructor. Since four became good plumbers, we have some reason to believe that the fifth did so as well.

Though many arguments by analogy are fully stated, they are often more rhetorically effective—certainly more memorable—if they are given as a simile or a metaphor. In literature, allegories and parables are implicit analogical arguments. The difficulty with these is that the respects in which the comparisons are made and the conclusions you are asked to draw on the basis of the comparisons often are not stated. Metaphors must be *unpacked,* as it were; the implicit argument must be reconstructed. This often is tricky. If I say that books are tools, I am making a comparison between books and ordinary tools. The point of the comparison *might be* that just as tools allow you to accomplish certain physical tasks, so books allow you to accomplish certain intellectual tasks. But you would have to develop the analogical argument that is suggested by the metaphor. Since metaphors often occur within the context of a more general discussion, the clues to unpacking the metaphor usually can be drawn from the more general discussion. Typically, you will need to argue that your rendering of the analogical argument implicit in the metaphor is correct. Debate might then center on the nature of the argument.

Arguments by analogy are probably the most common arguments we use. A baker might reason that since adding a certain collection of spices to an apple pie tends to enhance its flavor, adding the same collection of spices to a peach pie would have a similar result. Since both are fruit pies, the baker might have grounds for this conclusion. Scientists argue that certain drugs will have certain effects on humans on the basis of tests on animals. The test-animals are similar in many respects to humans, so if a drug has a certain effect on the test animals, it is likely to have the same effect on humans. In common law there are arguments from precedent. These arguments are used to show that the case under consideration is similar in various respects to one on which a judicial decision has been made. And, of course, analogical arguments are used for persuasive purposes. If arguments against abortion are persuasive, it is because fetuses appear to be similar in morally relevant respects to babies and adult human beings.

EXERCISES

Some of the following passages contain analogies. Of those that do, which are arguments by analogy? If you find an analogy used nonargumentatively, what is the probable purpose of the analogy? Is it used to illustrate a point or to explain something?

1. "I mean—your eyes—your eyes, they shine like the pants of a blue serge suit."

   MR. HAMMER, in the movie *The Coconuts*
   (Paramount Famous Lasky Corporation, 1929).

2. In life, as in a game of football, the principle to follow is: hit the line hard.

   THEODORE ROOSEVELT

3. Taking an open-book test is like running the marathon. People who run the marathon on crutches seldom finish. People who use a cane seldom win. So you're best off if you don't need the book.

4. The weather was very hot. The thin, high sky was too hot to look at. Air rose up in waves from the whole prairie, as it does from a hot stove.

   LAURA INGALLS WILDER, *On the Banks of Plum Creek*
   (New York: Harper and Row, 1937), p. 192.

5. Incidentally, Della, things which seem frightfully important at the time have a habit of fading into insignificance. Events are like telephone poles, streaming back past the observation platform of a speeding train. They loom large at first, then melt into the distance, becoming so tiny they finally disappear altogether. . . . That's the way with nearly all of the things we think are so vital.

   EARLE STANLEY GRADNER, *The Case of the Perjured Parrot*
   (New York: Ballantine Books, 1939), p. 2.

6. A proposition, a picture, or a model is, in the negative sense, like a solid body that restricts the freedom of movement of others, and,

in the positive sense, like a space bounded by solid substance in which there is room for a body.

> LUDWIG WITTGENSTEIN, *Tractatus Logico-Philosophicus*,
> §4.463, translated by D. F. Pears and B. F. McGuiness
> (London: Routledge and Kegan Paul, 1961), p. 69.

7. Defining by genus and difference is like looking for a house in the city. The street is the genus, and the house number is the species.

8. The use of the right word, the exact word, is the difference between a pencil with a sharp point and a thick crayon.

> PETER MARSHALL, quoted in Catherine Marshall,
> *A Man Called Peter* (Chicago:
> People's Book Club, 1951), p. 192.

9. When a foot goes flat it's like an earthquake. First there are the tremors. Then there's the crash, when what was high is made low. Then there might be a number of aftershocks. When it's all over, life goes on pretty much as it did before. But just as you might have to do some cleaning up after an earthquake, you might need to get bigger shoes after your foot goes flat.

10. The spiritual virtue of a sacrament is like light,—although it passes among the impure, it is not polluted.

> ST. AUGUSTINE, *Tract on St. John*, Chapter 5, 15.

11. A good name is like a precious ointment; it filleth all around about, and will not easily away; for the odors of ointments are more durable than those of flowers.

> FRANCIS BACON, *Of Praise*.

12. A community is like a ship; everyone ought to be prepared to take the helm.

> HENRIK IBSEN, *An Enemy of the People*, Act I.

13. Mishaps are like knives, that either serve us or cut us, as we grasp them by the blade or the handle.

> JAMES RUSSELL LOWELL, *Cambridge Thirty Years Ago*.

14. No country on earth wastes its own heritage, its ancient treasures as we do, simply out of slothfulness. No revolution ever destroyed so much of value for the people as our Russian Revolution. Even now, when we do so much talking about our Russian traditions, it's only idle words.

> SVETLANA ALLILUYEVA, *Twenty Letters to a Friend*
> (New York: Avon Books, 1967), p. 131.

15. Our life is like some vast lake that is slowly filling with the stream of our years. As the waters creep surely upward the landmarks of the past are one by one submerged. But there shall always be memory to lift its head above the tide until the lake is overflowing.

        ALEXANDRE CHARLES AUGUSTE BISSON, *Madame X*,
        translated by J. W. McConaughy.

16. In Greek mythology the sorceress Medea, enraged at being supplanted by a rival for the affections of her husband Jason, presented the new bride with a robe possessing magic properties. The wearer of the robe immediately suffered a violent death. This death-by-indirection now finds its counterpart in what are known as "systemic insecticides." These are chemicals with extraordinary properties which are used to convert plants or animals into a sort of Medea's robe by making them actually poisonous. This is done with the purpose of killing insects that may come in contact with them, especially by sucking their juices or blood.

        RACHEL CARSON, *Silent Spring* (Boston:
        Houghton Mifflin, 1962), p. 32.

17. Time is a sort of river of passing events, and strong its current; no sooner is a thing brought to sight than it is swept by and another takes its place, and this too will be swept away.

        MARCUS AURELIUS, *Meditations,* IV, 43, translated
        by Morris Hickey Morgan.

18. A book, like a person, has its fortunes with one; is lucky or unlucky in the precise moment of its falling in our way, and often by some happy accident counts with us for something more than its independent value.

        WALTER PATER, *Marcus the Epicurean,* Chapter 6.

19. The world is a perpetual caricature of itself; at every moment it is the mockery and the contraction of what it is pretending to be.

        GEORGE SANTAYANA, *England,* "Dickens."

20. "Come, we shall have fun now!" thought Alice. "I'm glad they've begun asking riddles—I believe I can guess that," she added aloud.

    "Do you mean that you think you can find out the answer to it?" said the March Hare.

    "Exactly so," said Alice.

    "Then you should say what you mean," the March Hare went on.

    "I do," Alice hastily replied; "at least—at least I mean what I say—that's the same thing you know."

"Not the same thing a bit!" said the Hatter, "Why you might just as well say that 'I see what I eat' is the same thing as 'I eat what I see'!"

"You might just as well say," added the March Hare, "that 'I like what I get' is the same thing as 'I get what I like'!"

"You might just as well say," added the Dormouse, which seemed to be talking in its sleep, "that 'I breathe when I sleep' is the same thing as 'I sleep when I breathe'!"

LEWIS CARROLL, *Alice in Wonderland*, Chapter 7.

8.2 *Evaluating Analogical Arguments*

In this section we examine six criteria that allow us to evaluate an argument by analogy. These criteria function as guidelines for evaluating analogical arguments, although not as hard and fast rules. Generally, the more favorably you judge the argument on the basis of each of the criteria, the stronger you will judge the argument to be. In other cases, you might conclude that it is a fairly strong argument on the basis of several criteria and weak on the basis of another, and judge the argument to be weak. In such a case, you may need to develop an argument to establish that falling foul of that one criterion is sufficient to judge the entire analogical argument weak.

Let us look at each of the criteria individually, and then consider some examples.

1. The more respects in which the things being compared are similar, the stronger the argument is. In an argument by analogy, you always look at the properties the objects being compared have in common. It is on the basis of the known similarities that you infer that an unknown property in one of them is also common. The more respects in which the objects compared are similar, the more probable it is that they will be similar in yet another respect. In applying this criterion, you count the number of respects in which things are compared. But there is no magic number that distinguishes a strong analogy from a weak one: you have to judge whether the number of respects in which the objects are being compared is sufficient to warrant the conclusion. What is sufficient will vary with the complexity of the objects being compared. Consider some examples.

Assume I want to buy a new car. My current car is a 1976 Chevrolet. I am considering a new Chevrolet of approximately the same size with a comparably sized engine. My old car ran for 80,000 miles before I ran into major problems. Do I have good reason to believe that the car I am considering will serve me approximately as well? Probably not. The cars themselves are similar in only three respects: they are made by the same company, they are approximately the same size, and they have engines of approximately the same size. It would be a stronger analogy if the cars compared had the same model engine, if they were built according to the same quality-control standards, if more of the components of the cars compared were the same. In short, I would have a much stronger analogy if I compared the car I am considering with another car of the same model, since most of the parts of which they are made are similar. Let us assume my friend Fodsworth has a car of the same model I am considering, with the same model engine, and many of the same options I am considering. Assume further that Fodsworth has driven his car nearly 100,000 miles in the two years he has owned it and reports that it still "runs like a top!" Since the cars compared are similar in many respects, I would have good reason to believe that the car I am considering would serve me well for 80,000 miles on the basis of the first criterion.

2. The respects in which the things are being compared must be relevant to the conclusion. Things might be similar in many respects, but unless the respects in which the objects are similar are causally relevant to the conclusion, the similarities make no difference. In the previous example, the comparisons seem relevant, since how the cars are made is causally relevant to how long you can expect it to run. Similarly, it would have been relevant to note that Fodsworth's driving habits and the regularity with which he services his car are similar to mine, since both of those factors are causally relevant to the life-expectancy of a car. On the other hand, had I mentioned that both Fodsworth's car and the car I am considering are red, this would have been a similarity that is irrelevant to any expectations regarding the mechanical performance of the car. Irrelevant similarities do not support the conclusion. If you run into irrelevant similarities while assessing an analogy, cross them off your list of similarities and reassess the analogy on the basis of the first criterion.

3. The analogy is stronger if more things are compared. Often an analogy is based on the comparison of two things, but the argument is stronger if more objects are compared. I have some reason to believe that the car I am thinking about buying will be relatively trouble-free if Fodsworth's car is similar to it and he has had no problems in the first 100,000 miles it was driven. If there are others who own the same model car and they have had no problems with it, there is even more reason to believe that the car I am considering will serve me well. So I check with some of my other friends. Merryhugh has had a car of this model for three years and has driven it 90,000 miles with no problems. Bridget has had a car of the same model for a year and a half and has driven it 150,000 miles with no problems. Ostafar has had a car of the same model for over a year and has driven it for 60,000 miles with no problems. Since I am now considering more cars that are analogous to the one I am considering, I have better reasons to believe that the car I am considering will serve me well.

4. Relevant differences between the things compared tend to weaken the analogy. Arguments by analogy are based on similarities, but in evaluating an analogy you must ask whether there are relevant differences between the things compared. These differences are discovered by thought and investigation; they are not stated in the argument. For example, if I am wondering whether a new Chevy would serve me well, it would make little sense to compare the car I am considering with a Toyota. Chevrolets and Toyotas have many similar parts, but since they are made by different companies, they are manufactured according to different standards of engineering. Similarly, if I attempted to construct an analogy between my '76 Chevy and a new model, the argument would be weak because there are significant differences between my old car and the new one: many of the mechanical features on the old car are electronic on the new car, and it is only reasonable to assume that Chevrolet's engineering and manufacturing standards have changed somewhat over the years. You should always ask whether there are dissimilarities that weaken the analogy, and you should be particularly suspicious if there are few things compared or if they are similar in few respects.

5. When a significant number of things are similar in a significant number of respects, differences can *strengthen* the analogy. If there are a significant number of things compared and they are similar in a significant number of respects, differences can *strengthen* the analogy. For example, if I have limited the objects I am comparing to cars of the same make and model as the one I am considering, differences in the driving habits and regularity of servicing their cars might strengthen the analogy. Assume that 80 percent of Fodsworth's driving occurs at highway speeds and that he services his car every 10,000 miles. Merryhugh is a stock-car driver. Her Chevy is driven every weekend in races of 200–500 miles at speeds in excess of 100 m.p.h. and thoroughly tuned and serviced between races. Bridget services her car every 50,000 miles (whether it needs it or not, as she says). Much of her driving occurs in New York City, although twice a year she takes a three-week vacation and has toured much of the United States, Canada, and Central and

South America in her car. Ostafar religiously services his car every 2,500 miles, but all of his driving occurs in the city. These differences are important. If each car has proven reliable in spite of the differences in driving habits and care, this tends to strengthen the conclusion that the car I am considering will prove reliable.

In general, once you have shown that there is a significant number of relevant similarities between the objects providing the basis for the analogy, a certain number of dissimilarities among the objects providing the basis for the analogy tends to strengthen the argument. Generally speaking, the greater the number of similar objects providing the basis for the analogy, the greater the chances that there will be certain disanalogies among the objects that will tend to strengthen the argument.

6. The strength of the conclusion is relative to the premises. Oddly enough, the stronger the conclusion you reach, the weaker your analogy will be. Given the analogy between the car I am considering and Fodsworth's, Merryhugh's, Bridget's, and Ostafar's cars, I have some reason to believe that the car I am considering will be reliable for at least 80,000 miles. I have better reason to believe that it will be reliable for 60,000 miles, and still better reason to believe it will be reliable for 40,000 miles. If the conclusion with which I am concerned is whether I will be pleased with the car and all my friends who have comparable cars are *delighted* with theirs, I would have some evidence that I will be delighted with the car, stronger evidence that I will be pleased with the car, and still stronger evidence that I will be satisfied with the car. This shows that the reasoning becomes stronger as the conclusion becomes weaker relative to the premises.

Now that we have examined the six criteria for evaluating analogies, let us look at some examples. We start by evaluating each case on the basis of the criteria, then we note how additional considerations will tend to strengthen or weaken the argument.

Consider the following case. You are planning to buy a pair of shoes. The last five pairs you bought were made by the Pizzazz Shoe Company. Those shoes were the company's top-of-the-line shoes. You bought a black pair, a brown pair, a blue pair, a green pair, and a red pair. Each pair was extremely comfortable, kept its shine well, and lasted five to six years. As you walk into Josephine's Shoe Mart to buy a pair of orange top-of-the-line Pizzazz Shoes, you expect they will also be extremely comfortable, keep their shine, and last five to six years.

The conclusion of the argument seems well-founded. The respects in which the shoes are similar are (1) they are made by the same company and (2) they are of the same quality. The basis for your analogy contains five items, which seems like a reasonable number, although the conclusion would be stronger if there were more items in the basis. You are assuming that the manufacturing processes at Pizzazz have not changed significantly, and those processes are causally relevant to the comfort and quality of the shoes. The shoes you are planning to buy are orange, which is different from any of the Pizzazz Shoes you have bought in the past. But since you have been equally satisfied with the various colors of shoes you have bought, the color is not relevant to the comfort, shine, and life-expectancy of the shoes. The conclusion, however, is questionable: the argument would be stronger if your expectations were somewhat lower, for example, if you expected them to be relatively comfortable and expected at least three years of service from them.

If the facts were different, the strength of the analogy would change. Assume you had purchased five pairs of Pizzazz Shoes: one pair had been their top-of-the-line shoe, two pairs had been middle-quality shoes, and two pairs had been their cheap models. You had been well-satisfied with each. Since there are now more differences among the similarities, differences that suggest there is no correlation between price and the quality of the shoes, you would have better reason to believe that you would be happy with any pair of Pizzazz Shoes you bought. On the other hand, you would have less reason to have extremely high expectations regarding their top-of-the-line model, since experience shows there is no direct correlation between what you pay for the shoes and your satisfaction with them. But there might be other considerations that would weaken your conclusion. Assume that since you bought your last pair of shoes the Pizzazz Shoe Company was bought out by the Shoes-For-Less Company, a company known for its low-quality shoes. Now you would have far less reason to expect the next pair you buy under the Pizzazz label to be as satisfactory as your previous pairs.

Consider another case. The savings-and-loan company where I do business was taken over by another financial institution. The name on the sign changed from "Gambler's Savings" to "New Rotic State Bank, Oldtown Branch." Since my accounts were shifted to New Rotic State, I believe I now have my accounts at a bank, rather than at a savings and loan. My belief was based on two kinds of evidence. I compared New Rotic State to five other financial institutions I knew were genuine banks. Each was like New Rotic State Bank in the following ways: (1) each included the word 'bank' in its name, (2) deposits at each were insured by the Federal Deposit Insurance Corporation (FDIC), (3) each was open only from 9:00 a.m. until 2:00 p.m. Monday through Friday, and (4) each provided canceled checks with its checking account statements. I also compared New Rotic State to five financial institutions that I knew were savings and loans. Like New Rotic State Bank, two of those savings and loans included the word 'bank' in their names, but both described themselves as "savings banks." Deposits at none of the savings and loans were insured by the FDIC. Each of the savings and loans were open for more hours than the banks. None of the savings and loans provided canceled checks with their checking account statements.

Here there are two arguments, one based on analogies and the other based on disanalogies. New Rotic State Bank is like five other banks in four ways. The number of institutions and respects could be greater, but it provides fairly good evidence. Some respects in which the comparisons are made are more significant than others. For example, if the policies are still the same as they were three decades ago, only banks have their deposits insured by the FDIC. Hence, on the basis of the analogies to banks, I have fairly good evidence that New Rotic State Bank is a bank, rather than a savings and loan. The conclusion is strengthened by the disanalogies with savings and loans, and the argument that New Rotic State is *not* a savings and loan is approximately as strong as the argument that it is a bank. The second conclusion supports a premise for a *deductive* argument that New Rotic State is a bank, namely:

> Either New Rotic State Bank is a bank or it is a savings and loan.
> New Rotic State Bank is not a savings and loan.
> _____
> Therefore New Rotic State Bank is a bank.

Whereas in a valid deductive argument the conclusion follows with certainty, since I have only inductive evidence for the truth of the negative premise, the deductive argument does not provide conclusive evidence that New Rotic State is a bank. Nonetheless, when taken together the two inductive arguments tend to give me good reason to believe that I am now dealing with a bank. The arguments reinforce one another, and the strength of the conclusion drawn from the two arguments is greater than either alone.

Summary of the Criteria for Evaluating Analogical Arguments

In evaluating an analogical argument, ask yourself the following six questions:

1. Are the objects compared similar in a significant number of respects?

2. Are the respects in which the objects are similar causally relevant to the conclusion?

3. Is a significant number of objects being compared?

4. Are there causally relevant differences (disanalogies) between the things compared that weaken the analogy?

5. If there is a significant number of objects compared in a significant number of respects, are there differences that *strengthen* the analogy?

6. How strong is the conclusion relative to the premises?

EXERCISES

I. For each of the following analogical arguments, use the six criteria for evaluating the strength of an analogical argument to determine whether the additional considerations strengthen or weaken the argument. In each case, indicate which of the criteria will support your judgment.

1. Hormella Kies is deciding which courses to take next semester. She's considering History 492: The History of England from Earliest Times to A.D. 1000. She has liked all the history courses she has taken in the past, and as she adds this to her tentative course schedule, she fully expects to enjoy it.
a) What if Hormella has taken only History 101 and 102 in the past, and this History 492 is a senior seminar?
b) What if Hormella has taken courses in world history, oriental history, U.S. history, South American history, and European history and has enjoyed all those courses?
c) What if all the history courses she has previously taken required only a reading knowledge of modern English, but this course requires a reading knowledge of Anglo-Saxon and Old English?
d) What if Hormella has taken all the courses on English history except this one and found each at least as interesting as the one before?
e) What if Hormella was very interested in the history of the Vikings, and a good portion of the course was going to focus on the influence of Viking invasions of England in the ninth century?

f) What if Hormella thinks this is going to be the most interesting history course she has ever taken?

g) What if the courses Hormella has taken before were all courses in intellectual history, and this was a course in social and political history?

h) What if Professor Bjornsen was teaching this course, and she has enjoyed other courses she has taken with Professor Bjornsen?

i) What if this course was being offered at 8:00 a.m. and Hormella has never before taken a class in the morning?

j) What if Hormella's roommate was also going to take the course, Hormella has never been in a class with her roommate, and her roommate has no aptitude in history?

2. Ostafar Neumathesque is planning a trip on Trans-Transylvanian Airlines to Northern Slovobia. He has flown Trans-Transylvanian every year for the past six years to visit his aged mother. In each case, he found that the cabin attendants provided exceptional service, the plane arrived at its destination within an hour of the scheduled arrival time, and the pilot added to the excitement of the trip by occasionally "buzzing" flocks of sheep. Ostafar was particularly taken by the airline's policy of "serving a hogshead of wine on every flight," always consuming at least his fair share of the wine. As he packs his bags, Ostafar looks forward to an enjoyable and moderately exciting flight.

a) What if Trans-Transylvanian Airlines has recently lost a court fight with the Northern Slovobian Sheep Farmer's Association and agreed to quit "buzzing" flocks of sheep?

b) What if Ostafar booked his previous flights with Count Dracula's Travel Service, but this time he booked his flight through Frank N. Stein Travel, Inc.?

c) What if there had been a different flight crew on each of his previous trips?

d) What if Ostafar recently joined Alcoholics Anonymous?

e) What if the Amisglof-435 robotic flight attendant had been on all the previous flights and will be on this flight as well?

f) What if Ostafar has flown Trans-Transylvanian Airlines three times a year for the last ten years?

g) What if Ostafar's mother has eloped with the butcher and moved to Southern Slovobia?

h) What if Ostafar is a glutton and on previous flights the meals had consisted of sandwiches whereas on this flight the menu consists of a seven-course dinner?

i) What if all Trans-Transylvanian's cabin attendants are out on strike?

j) What if Ostafar expects this to be the most enjoyable flight he has ever taken?

3. Siegfried Hubbelschnitz is visiting the library, planning to check out a book for some light reading. Siegfried is a nuclear physicist and an avid reader of science fiction. He discovers that his favorite science-fiction author, Ostafar Neumathesque, has published a new book. Siegfried checks it out, fully expecting a moderately enjoyable evening of reading.

a) What if Siegfried has read all of Ostafar's previous books and has found each new book more enjoyable than those written earlier?

b) What if all of Ostafar's previous books were works of science fiction, but this one is an autobiography?

c) What if Siegfried finds his work extremely enjoyable and the main character in the book he checked out is an extremely competent nuclear physicist?

d) What if Siegfried has read all of Ostafar's previous books, has found each new book more enjoyable than those written earlier, and therefore expects this to be the most enjoyable book Ostafar has written?

e) What if Siegfried has read hundreds of science-fiction books, he has never read a work in science fiction he didn't like, and the book he checked out is a work in science fiction?

f) What if Siegfried has recently met Ostafar Neumathesque while on a trip to Northern Slovobia?

g) What if Siegfried has recently been married?

h) What if the books Siegfried has previously read by Ostafar Neumethesque included several works of science fiction, several biographies of famous physicists, and a history of Trans-Transylvanian Airlines?

i) What if all the books by Ostafar that Siegfried has previously read were written in Rumanian, and this one is also written in Rumanian?

j) What if Siegfried has always read in the privacy of his own home, but on his way home from the library he is kidnapped by South Slovobian terrorists?

4. Ingrid is planning her winter vacation. Since she has enjoyed skiing in the Blue Ridge Mountains, the Rockies, and the

Swiss Alps, she decides to go on a skiing vacation. Since she likes to travel and there are some similarities between the mountains in Norway and those she has previously skied, she decides to go to Norway. She expects to enjoy her trip.

a) What if Ingrid speaks fluent English, German, French, and Italian, and therefore had no trouble communicating on her previous trips, but she doesn't speak a word of Norwegian?

b) What if the best skiing is in northern Norway, where it is almost perceptually dark in winter?

c) What if Ingrid formerly went skiing with some of her closest friends, but they will not be coming along on this trip?

d) What if on other trips Ingrid has gone to a ski resort and this time she is staying in a private family home?

e) What if she expects it will be less enjoyable than her trip to Switzerland, which was her favorite trip?

f) What if she has been accompanied on previous skiing trips by a group of her closest friends, and she will be accompanied by the same group this time?

g) What if Ingrid recently broke her leg and she has never gone skiing with a broken leg?

h) What if the fjords in Norway will be frozen when she is there?

i) What if Ingrid's best friend prefers ice skating to skiing?

j) What if the Norwegian ski patrol replaces the brandy in its St. Bernards' barrels with diet cola?

5. Agatha is wondering how the university football team will do this year. Last year they had a record of 8 wins and 3 losses. Half of their starting players are returning this year. The coaching staff is the same. So she expects that they should have a winning season again this year.

a) What if one of the returning players is their All-American quarterback Hank Hunk?

b) What if one of their new recruits was the top high school fullback in the state last year?

c) What if the grass in the stadium has been replaced with astroturf?

d) What if all the roughest games on the schedule are home games?

e) What if Agatha expects their record to be at least 10 wins and 1 loss this year?

f) What if their star receiver broke his leg in practice and will be out for the season?

g) What if all the returning starters are in the offensive line, none in the defensive line?

h) What if an Associated Press pre-season poll has rated the team fourth in the country?

i) What if the coach plans to change the offense from a ground game to a passing game?

j) What if the NCAA placed the team on probation for recruiting violations?

6. On the last trading day of the year for each of the past ten years, Milan has invested in 100 shares of the XYZ Telephone Company stock. Over that time, she has observed that the stock provides dividends of approximately 6 percent on her investment and has appreciated in value at an average rate of 8 percent per year. As the last trading day of the year approaches, she plans to invest again, expecting comparable returns.

   a) What if she expects her stock to appreciate in value at the rate of 15 percent per year?

   b) What if in years past the price of the stock dropped before the last trading day of the year, and it dropped again this year?

   c) What if the phone company is planning a three-for-one split?

   d) What if the phone company is being investigated by the Federal Communications Commission for violations of several federal laws?

   e) What if the phone company has recently sold its long-distance services to another company?

   f) What if the economy has fallen into a severe recession in the last year?

   g) What if she expected only a 3 percent dividend on her investment?

   h) What if the company has a new chairman of the board?

   i) What if the value of oil company stocks are appreciating at a greater rate than phone company stocks?

   j) What if Milan decided to invest in 1,000 shares of stock, rather than 100?

7. Josiah is working on his tenth book. His previous books have sold fairly well, and each has provided him with a reasonably good livelihood for about two years. As he finishes the final chapter, he expects this book will allow him to retain his current standard of living for another year or two.

a) What if Josiah had written his previous books in Indiana, and he is writing this book in Hawaii?

b) What if his previous books were murder mysteries, and this one is also a murder mystery?

c) What if his previous books were novels, and this book is an autobiography?

d) What if the same publisher that published his previous books is going to publish this book?

e) What if each of his previous books was published by a different publisher, but this book will be published by the same company that published his last book?

f) What if each of his previous books was published under a pseudonym but this book will be published under his own name?

g) What if Josiah recently has been divorced?

h) What if Josiah's book features the same hero as that in his previous nine books?

i) What if each of Josiah's previous books was more successful than its predecessor?

j) What if each of Josiah's previous books was more successful than its predecessor and Josiah expects this to be at least as successful as his second book?

II. Evaluate each of the following analogies on the basis of the six criteria.

1. We both own a 386-25 DRAW Computer. We both bought it a year and a half ago. We both use it for about twelve hours per day. My 3½-inch drive gave out a few days ago. So you can expect that your 3½-inch drive will be giving you some trouble in the not too distant future.

2. For each of the past three years Dagmar has won a prize in the Super-Duper Sweepstakes. Each year she used a commemorative stamp on the envelope she used to submit her entry. Each year she dropped her entry into the public mailbox at the corner of Main Street and Third Avenue on a rainy day. So she reasons that if she again uses a commemorative stamp on the envelope and drops it into the mailbox on the corner of Main Street and Third Avenue on a rainy day, she'll win again.

3. Fred, Natasha, and Eudora each have a car with a 2.5-liter engine. Fred and Natasha each get 30 miles to the gallon

when driving their car. So Eudora gets 30 miles to the gallon when driving her car.

4. Every night for the past ten years, Dagwood has fixed himself a midnight snack of a large submarine sandwich. Each time he has found the sandwich tasty and satisfying. The contents of the sandwiches have varied considerably, although they've always included a variety of sandwich meats, cheeses, and lettuce. Sometimes he has included sardines and horseradish; other times he has included peanut butter and hot sauce; and still other times he has included anchovies, artichokes, and strawberry jam. As Dagwood looks into the refrigerator and takes out six kinds of sandwich meat and seven kinds of cheese, he expects to be satisfied with the resulting sandwich.

5. Being married is like owning a car. If you take good care of your car and pamper it in the appropriate ways, you'll be happy with it for many years. The same holds for a spouse. And just as trading in a car on a newer model is a very expensive proposition, you can infer that the same holds for getting a divorce.

6. Studies involving six populations of one hundred white mice show that ingesting large doses of substance X increases instances of stomach cancer. So substance X is a probable cause of stomach cancer in humans.

7. Environmental pollution is like a contagious and potentially fatal disease. If the disease is treated early and efforts are made to control the contagion, the cost of containment is fairly low and life can go on in a fairly normal way. If the disease reaches epidemic proportions, there is widespread suffering, death, and economic havoc. So efforts should be undertaken now to control pollution.

8. A flashlight is like a candle. Both provide light. Both use some fuel to produce the light. If you touch the flame that produces candlelight, you will be burned. So if you touch the bulb that produces the light in a flashlight, you will be burned.

9. Crocodiles are ancestors of dinosaurs, and crocodiles have gizzards. Birds are descendants of dinosaurs, and birds have gizzards. Therefore, dinosaurs had gizzards.

10. England nationalized health care in 1948, and by 1960 there was a two- to three-year waiting period for a child to receive

a tonsillectomy. Canada began to nationalize health care in 1965, and by 1992 there were fewer beds in children's hospitals and long waiting periods for surgical procedures. The United States is developing a national health-care program patterned after Canada's. We can expect the quality and availability of health care to decrease in the coming years.

11. The restaurant that used to advertise "Best Seafood in Town" was closed last year by the health officials after several of their customers suffered from ptomaine poisoning. The restaurant that advertises "Best Italian Food in Town" serves food that tastes of the tin cans from which it is taken. The restaurant that advertises "Best Burgers" serves only burgers that are burnt or raw—if you can ever get down through the grease to the burger itself. So if Charlie's Grill claims to serve the best food in town, you're certain to lose no matter what you order.

12. You've been in Forvel's Hardware Store some twenty times. Each time, Ms. Forvel's Rottweiler, Fido, has been wandering around the store, has come up to you, licked your hand, allowed you to pat him, and was generally friendly. Today you enter Forvel's Hardware Store and notice that Fido is chained to the gun case. You infer that if you wander over to Fido and pat him, he will be friendly.

13. After World War I the immediate demands on the U.S. military were decreased, so the United States downsized its military. When World War II began the military had to play a rapid game of catch-up. With the end of the Cold War, the immediate demands on the military are decreased, and the United States again proposes to downsize its military. But the occurrence of war is one of the few constants in history. So if the United States downsizes its military, it will eventually have to play a rapid game of catch-up.

14. In a court of law, there is a correlation between the severity of the punishment and the severity of the crime. Thus, persons convicted of petty larceny are not given sentences as severe as those convicted of murder. Similarly, there are differences in the severity of the violations of the honor code at the University. Students who sign someone else's name on an attendance sheet should not be punished as severely as those who engage in plagiarism or those who hire someone else to take an examination.

15. If the government is devoting billions of dollars annually to AIDS research, it should certainly do the same for breast-cancer research. Both are diseases, and more people die annually from breast cancer than from AIDS.

16. By eleven weeks a human fetus has all the bodily organs of an adult human being. By that age the fetus makes the various facial expressions made by children and adults alike. By that age the fetus makes fists, wakes and sleeps, and gets hiccups like adults. It is immoral to willfully deprive an adult of the means necessary for its continued existence. So it is immoral to abort a fetus.

17. If I stabbed you with a knife or shot you with a gun, I'd be charged with attempted murder. If I accidentally ran you down with a car, I'd be charged with reckless driving or, if you died, negligent homicide. Every day at work I breathe the secondhand smoke from your cigarettes. Studies show that breathing secondhand smoke causes disease and death. So you should be charged with attempted murder.

18. The federal government is like a credit-card junkie out of control. Both spend beyond their means. Both try to cover past economic excesses by seeking greater lines of credit. But since every credit-card junkie eventually comes to a day of financial reckoning, we may conclude the federal government will also come to a day of financial reckoning.

19. A mind is a bank in which ideas are deposited. Just as the more money you put into a bank the more you'll get out, the same holds for ideas placed into the mind. Just as a bank guarantees a return on your monetary investment, you are virtually guaranteed to get more ideas out of your mind than you put in. Just as the rate of return on your monetary investment is determined by when, and where, and what kind of investment you make, the same holds for your intellectual investments. Since maximizing your monetary returns requires a careful examination of your investment options, the same holds for your intellectual investments.

20. Attending a holiday party is like attending a funeral. You attend both out of a feeling of obligation. Both require putting on the appropriate face. But just as a funeral is eventually over and life can return to normal, the same holds for a holiday party.

21. In industry those in charge of large projects complete those projects in sequence: one individual is never required to complete several large projects at the same time. Businesses have only one large sales promotion at a time: though several promotions might be in various stages of planning at the same time, they never occur at the same time. Since examinations are analogous to large projects in industry or to sales promotions in business, professors should follow the lead of business and industry and schedule their final examinations at different times in the semester.

22. And they asked him, "Is it lawful to heal on the sabbath?" . . . And he said to them, "What man of you, if he has one sheep and it falls into a pit on the sabbath, will not lay hold of it and lift it out? Of how much more value is a man than a sheep! So it is lawful to do good on the sabbath."

     Matthew 12:10–12 (RSV).

23. As the [1964 Republican] convention unfolded, Rockefeller led the attacks on the so-called extremists as he dissected the party platform. . . . The governor then said, "We repudiate the efforts of irresponsible extremist groups—such as the Communists, Ku Klux Klan, the John Birch Society, and others to discredit our party by their efforts to infiltrate positions of responsibility in the party or attach themselves to its candidates."

     The attack on extremists was an attempt to include conservatives among the worst elements of American society.

     BARRY GOLDWATER with JACK CASSERLY, *Goldwater*
     (New York: St. Martin's Press, 1988), p. 232.

24. The rationale for scientizing medicine was provided by the Germ Theory of Disease. . . . Germs, as everyone knew, were invisible to ordinary people. They could be seen only by scientists skilled in microscopy, handled only by the most meticulous laboratory men. If germs caused disease, and if germs could only be ambushed by a well-stocked laboratory, then medicine without laboratories was like law without courts or theology without churches.

     BARBARA EHRENREICH and DEIRDRE ENGLISH, *For Her Own Good*
     (Garden City, NY: Doubleday Anchor Books, 1978), p. 80.

25. Not until our own time have historians been sufficiently detached from religions to understand that the [French] Revolution, in its latter stages especially, took on the character

of a religious crusade. But it is now well understood (thanks to the writings of Mathiez, Aulard, and many lesser historians), not only that the Revolution attempted to substitute the eighteenth-century religion of humanity for the traditional faiths, but also that, contrary to the belief of De Tocqueville, the new religion was *not* without God, forms of worship, and a future life. On the contrary, the new religion had its dogmas, the sacred principles of the Revolution— *Liberté et sainte égalité.* It had its form of worship, an adaptation of Catholic ceremonial, which was elaborated in connection with the civic *fêtes.* It had its saints, the heroes and martyrs of liberty. It was sustained by an emotional impulse, a mystical faith in humanity, in the ultimate regeneration of the human race.

CARL R. BECKER, *The Heavenly City of the*
Eighteenth-Century Philosophers (New Haven:
Yale University Press, 1932), p. 155.

26. Life is like a giant pinspotter in a goliath's bowling alley, with billions of humans relegated to the status of bowling pins. In the final analysis, the Pinspotter shakes us down into our proper slots and we end up exactly where we belong. If you're presently in a slot that displeases you, I suggest you begin by doing whatever is necessary to work your way into a more favorable position before the Pinspotter clamps you firmly into place.

ROBERT J. RINGER, *Looking Out for #1*
(New York: Fawcett Crest Books, 1977), p. 105.

27. "Of course, I know nothing about your course in ethics," Frazer said, "but the philosopher in search of a rational basis for deciding what's good has always reminded me of the centipede trying to decide how to walk. Simply go ahead and walk! We all know what's good, until we stop to think about it. For example, is there any doubt that health is better than sickness?"

B. F. SKINNER, *Walden Two* (New York:
Macmillan, 1948), p. 159.

28. On a shimmering summer afternoon in the third week of August [1990], the President told a large assembly of military officers from the steps of the Pentagon's river entrance that Saddam Hussein was a threat not just to the world's oil supply but to "our way of life." Comparing the Iraqi dictator

to Hitler, he said, "A half-century ago, our nation and the world paid dearly for appeasing an aggressor who should, and could, have been stopped. We are not going to make the same mistake again."

Staff of U.S. News and World Report, Triumph Without
Victory (New York: Times Books, 1992), p. 123.

29. You might ask, "If life is just a game, why play so hard to win?" To that I would answer, "Heck, if it *is* only a game, why *not* have some fun and try to win?"

     I decided I would go for all I could get, as quickly as I could get it, while I still had the opportunity to play. Recognizing that both life and business are just games made it easy for me not to take myself too seriously and, consequently, made it easier to "win." After all, if it's just a game there's no sense in viewing each move as life or death; there's no reason to be afraid to be aggressive or take chances. The reality is that there's no way you're going to get out of this thing alive, anyway, so why play a conservative game?

     ROBERT J. RINGER, Winning Through Intimidation
(New York: Fawcett Crest Books, 1974), pp. 42–43.

30. Hawking their preferred life style models, subcults clamor for our attention. In so doing, they act directly on our most vulnerable psychological property, our self-image. "Join us," they whisper, "and you become a bigger, better, more effective, more respected and less lonely person." In choosing among the fast-proliferating subcults we may only vaguely sense that our identity will be shaped by our decision, but we feel the hot urgency of their appeals and counterappeals. We are buffeted back and forth by their psychological promises.

     At the moment of choice among them, we resemble the tourist walking down Bourbon Street in New Orleans. As he strolls past the honky-tonks and clip joints, doormen grab him by the arm, spin him around, and open a door so he can catch a titillating glimpse of the naked flesh of the strippers on the platform behind the bar. Subcults reach out to capture us and appeal to our most private fantasies in ways far more powerful and subtle than any yet devised by Madison Avenue.

     ALVIN TOFFLER, Future Shock (New York:
Bantam Books, 1970), p. 311.

31. The owner of a pear orchard in California's Santa Clara Valley understands the futility of isolation.

    He treated his soil according to the best scientific research, and obtained the best trees. But he had to do more! He sprayed not only his own orchard, but also the orchards on all four sides at his own expense, to make sure that his own fruit trees would have the best possible opportunity to bring forth good fruit.

    His trees were good trees, but their fruit was dependent upon healthy neighboring trees. Isolationism doesn't work for an orchard. How true among nations. There used to be an old cry, "Let Europe stew in its own juice." Now we are so close that what stews on another continent boils over on us. A home, an orchard, or a nation cannot live unto itself!

    > REV. A. PURNELL BAILEY, "Our Daily Bread,"
    > *Daily News-Record*, Harrisonburg, VA, July 30, 1992,
    > p. 6, copyright NTM, Inc., 1992.

32. People talk about WordStar as if it were an aging American sedan, something like a '56 Mercury. It was top drawer in its day, but now it's showing its age. It doesn't have the features or the zip of the new models.

    But like an old Mercury, WordStar has another side for those who can see—it can be customized. In fact, WordStar can be patched, tweaked, and generally modified like few other programs, all in your own garage.

    > TED SILVEIRA, "WordStar Deluxe," *Profiles* 3 (1985): 32.

33. As the nineteenth century drew to a close, the town of Larkin, the seat of Larkin County, found itself embroiled in an intellectual argument which preoccupied a good many other communities: When did the new century begin?

    Tradition, accepted modes of expression and popular opinion all agreed that at midnight on 31 December 1899 an old century would die, with a new one beginning a minute later. To any practical mind, even the name of the new year, 1900, indicated that a new system of counting had begun, and to argue otherwise was ridiculous: 'Any man with horse sense can see it's a new century, elsen why would they of given it a new name?'

    Yet Earnshaw Rusk, like many thinking men and women across the state, knew that the twentieth century could not possibly begin until 31 December 1900; logic, history and mathematics all proved they were correct, but these zealots had a difficult time persuading their fellow citizens to delay celebrating until the proper date. 'Damn fools like Earnshaw cain't tell their ear from their elbow,' said one zealot. 'Any idiot knows the new century begins like we say, and I'm gonna be ringin' that church bell come New Year's Eve and Jim Bob Loomis is gonna be lightin' the fire.'

Rusk found such plans an insult to intelligence. 'Tell me,' he asked Jim Bob, 'now I want you to just tell me, how many years in a century?' . . .

'A hunnert,' Jim Bob said.

'At the time of Christ, when this all began, was there ever a year zero?'

'Not that I heerd of.'

'So the first century must have begun with the year 1.'

'I think it did.'

'So when we reached the year 99, how many years had the first century had?'

'Sound like ninety-nine.'

'It was ninety-nine, so the year 100 had nothing special about it. The second century couldn't have begun until the beginning of 101.'

JAMES MICHENER, Texas: A Novel (New York:
Random House, 1985), p. 825–26.

34. Lavoisier, the discoverer of oxygen, seems to have reasoned like this: The world is like a balance sheet—whatever is subtracted from one account must be added to another, and the bottom lines must remain in balance. According to the phlogiston theory of combustion, when sulfur or phosphorus burn, they lose phlogiston. But when sulfur and phosphorus burn, they gain weight. If losing phlogiston causes an increase in weight, then phlogiston is different from all other known substances insofar as it has negative mass. This seems unlikely. Therefore, since all other known cases of weight gain are correlated with an increase in mass, it is likely that some substance is gained in combustion, and the phlogiston theory must be rejected.

35. Pasteur argued somewhat as follows. Amyl alcohol is found as a by-product in the process of lactic acid fermentation, that is,

when sugar is changed to lactic acid. Sugar is optically active, so is lactic acid; both appear to be closely related chemically; they may contain the same unsymmetric groupings of atoms. Amyl alcohol, however, is not at all like sugar—it contains much more hydrogen, it cannot contain the same unsymmetric grouping of atoms (it is "very different"), but it rotates the plane of polarized light. How did this alcohol acquire the property of optical activity? If optical activity is found only when a compound has been produced by a life process, one may conclude that living organisms must be responsible for lactic acid fermentation. . . . Therefore, said Pasteur, let us examine the situation and see whether we can find the living organisms that bring about lactic acid fermentation.

JAMES BRYANT CONANT, *Pasteur's Study of Fermentation,* Harvard Case Histories in Experimental Science, Case 6 (Cambridge, Mass., 1952), p. 24.

36. Look round the world: Contemplate the whole and every part of it: You will find it to be nothing but one great machine, subdivided into an infinite number of lesser machines, which again admit of subdivisions, to a degree beyond what human senses and faculties can trace and explain. All these various machines, and even their most minute parts, are adjusted to each other with an accuracy, which ravishes into admiration all men, who have ever contemplated them. The curious adapting of means to ends, throughout all nature, resembles exactly, though much exceeds, the productions of human contrivance; of human design, thought, wisdom, and intelligence. Since therefore the effects resemble each other, we are led to infer, by all the rules of analogy, that the causes also resemble; and that the Author of nature is somewhat similar to the mind of man; though possessed of much larger faculties, proportioned to the grandeur of the work which he has executed. By this argument *a posteriori,* and by this argument alone, we do prove at once the existence of a Deity, and his similarity to human mind and intelligence.

DAVID HUME, *Dialogues concerning Natural Religion.*

NOTES

1. George Eliot [Marian Evans Cross], *Adam Bede* (New York: Dodd, Mead and Company, 1927), p. 331.

2. Louisa May Alcott, *Hospital Sketches* (New York: Sagamore, 1957), p. 30.

3. John Le Carré, *The Secret Pilgrim* (New York: Knopf, 1991), p. 13.

4. See George Gamow, *One Two Three . . . Infinity* (New York: Mentor Books, 1947), pp. 26–27, which provides an analogy of this kind to explain Cantor's comparison of infinities.

Chapter Nine

Mill's Methods of Experimental Inquiry

When a building burns down, a fire investigator is called in to determine the cause of the fire. When you are ill, you go to a doctor to discover the cause of your illness. If there is an accident, or a disaster, or a shortfall in company funds, someone will investigate to find out the cause of that unfortunate event. If you predict the movement of a planet in the solar system on the basis of the laws of motion and the positions of all the known planets, but, though your calculations are correct, the movement of the planet does not follow the predicted course, you might ask whether the cause of this deviation from your prediction is another planet. All these situations are complicated. In looking for "the cause" of the event, we are looking for one aspect or a small number of aspects of the event without which the event or phenomenon in question would not have occurred.

In 1843 the British philosopher John Stuart Mill published *A System of Logic*. In this book Mill developed a series of procedures for sorting through the complex elements of a situation in an attempt to discover the element or elements that produce a certain effect. These procedures have become known as Mill's Methods of Experimental Inquiry. In this chapter we examine those methods, for they are just as relevant today as they were 150 years ago.

9.1 The Methods

The Method of Agreement

When we say of two events that one is the cause and the other the effect, what do we mean? We mean, at least, that if the first event (the cause) had not occurred, then the second event (the effect) also would not have occurred. But why would anyone claim that? What kind of evidence do we take as sufficient to indicate that two events are related to one another as cause and effect? For example, why would we claim that dropping a lighted match on a bed of dry evergreen needles was the cause of the forest fire?

Two events that we claim are related to one another as cause and effect must be events of two kinds that always follow one another. If I claim that dropping a lighted match on a bed of dry evergreen needles causes the needles to burn, the only reason I have to believe that a causal relation exists between the two events is that every time anyone of whom I know has dropped a burning match on a bed of dry evergreen needles, the needles have started to burn. In addition I *assume* (this is the inductive assumption) that nature operates uniformly (that there are natural laws that hold at all times and places), and consequently that those instances of a correlation between burning matches and burning evergreen needles of which I am aware are part of a general pattern. So if I claim that dropping a burning match on a bed of dry evergreen needles *caused* the needles to burn, I am committed to the claim that at all times, if anyone drops a burning match on a bed of dry evergreen needles, the needles will burn.

To claim that an event is a cause of a phenomenon is to claim that the event is antecedent to (prior in time or simultaneous with) the phenomenon, and any event of the same kind is antecedent to a phenomenon of the same kind. The problem is that, typically, events that occur in the world are anything but simple—one complex set of conditions is followed by another complex set of conditions. The problem is sorting through the antecedent conditions to determine which of those conditions are correlated with which of the consequences. Mill's Methods provide a systematic means of eliminating circumstances in an attempt to discover the probable cause (or effect) of a phenomenon.

The Method of Agreement is straightforward: You look for cases in which one condition is consistently antecedent to another; the antecedent condition is the cause. Mill puts it this way: *"If two or more instances of the phenomenon under investigation have only one circumstance in common, the circumstance in which alone all instances agree, is the cause (or effect) of the given phenomenon."*[1] He describes the reasoning as follows:

> We shall denote antecedents by the large letters of the alphabet, and the consequences corresponding to them by the small. Let A, then, be an agent or cause, and let the object of our inquiry be to ascertain what are the effects of this cause. If we can either find, or produce, the agent A in such varieties of circumstances that the different cases have no circumstances in common except A; then whatever effect we find to be produced in all our trials, is indicated as the effect of A. Suppose, for example, that A is tried along with B and C, and that the effect is *a b c;* and suppose that A is next tried with D and E, but without B and C, and that the effect is *a d e.* Then we may reason thus: *b* and *c* are not the effects of A, for they were not produced by it in the second experiment; nor are *d* and *e,* for they were not produced in the first. Whatever is really the effect of A must have been produced in both instances; now this condition is fulfilled by no circumstance except *a.* The phenomenon *a* can not have been the effect of B or C, since it was produced where they were not; nor of D or E, since it was produced where they were not. Therefore it is the effect of A.[2]

The reasoning goes like this: You are given a complex set of conditions, which result in a complex phenomenon. If you compare several sets of antecedent conditions that are similar only with respect to one condition with the phenomena that follow and find that the phenomena are also similar only with respect to one element, you have good reason to claim that the common antecedent condition is the cause of the common element in the phenomenon.

You can use the Method of Agreement either to discover the effect of a set of conditions or to discover the cause of a phenomenon. If I wondered, for example, whether dropping a lighted match on a bed of dry evergreen needles causes the needles to burn, I could vary the experiment in each case so that the only antecedent conditions that are the same are that there is a lighted match and a bed of dry evergreen needles. I might vary the kinds of needles: pine needles, spruce needles, and fir needles. I might vary the kinds of lighted matches: book matches, kitchen matches, and so forth. If in each case I find that when a lighted match falls on a bed of dry evergreen needles the needles burn, I would have good grounds on the basis of the Method of Agreement to claim that dropping a lighted match on a bed of dry evergreen needles causes the needles to burn.

Similarly, we might know the effect and try to discover what the cause is on the basis of the Method of Agreement. Consider the following example:

> On a recent trip to the planet Zilch, there was a radiation leak. Wotan was exposed to glombitz rays, zolich rays, and ultraviolet rays. Kreimhild was exposed to glombitz rays, ultraviolet rays, and alyich rays. Brunhild was exposed to glombitz rays, blib-blib rays, and alyich rays. They all died. Upon investigating the case the Federation concluded that glombitz rays had done them in.

Why did the Federation conclude that glombitz rays had been the cause of death? Because three people died, and the only common antecedent condition was the exposure to glombitz rays. This shows that the glombitz rays are at least the probable cause of the deaths. Had more people died later and the sole common antecedent condition was the exposure to glombitz rays, there would be better evidence that those rays were the cause of death. Further, it is possible that some additional antecedent conditions were overlooked and it was either one of those conditions or some combination of conditions that was the cause of death.

The previous case contained a fairly small number of antecedent conditions. A convenient way to sort through a larger number of correlations between antecedent conditions and a phenomenon is by setting up a table that shows what conditions are present in each case. Let us let '*' represent 'present' and a blank space represent 'absent'. We have three victims: Wotan (W), Kriemhild (K), and Brunhild (B). We have five types of radiation: glombitz rays (G), zolich rays (Z), ultraviolet rays (U), alyich rays (A) and blib-blib rays (B). And we have the phenomenon, death. Our table looks like this:

Occurrence	Antecedent Conditions					Phenomenon Death
	G	Z	U	A	B	
W	*	*	*			*
K	*		*	*		*
B	*			*	*	*

Here the table shows that G is the only antecedent condition common to all instances of the phenomenon. So by the Method of Agreement, this shows that G is the probable cause of the phenomenon.

The Method of Difference

In the Method of Difference, you look for two cases whose antecedent conditions differ *only* in one respect and in which the phenomenon under investigation is present in only one case. Mill puts it this way: *"If an instance in which the phenomenon under investigation occurs, and an instance in which it does not occur, have every circumstance in common save one, that one occurring only in the former; the circumstance in which alone the two instances differ, is the effect, or the cause, or an indispensable part of the cause, of the phenomenon."*[3] He describes the reasoning as follows:

> If our object be to discover the effects of an agent A, we must procure A in some set of ascertained circumstances, as A B C, and having noted the effects produced, compare them with the effect of the remaining circumstances B C, when A is absent. If the effect of A B C is *a b c,* and the effect of B C *b c,* it is evident that the effect of A is *a.* So again, if we begin at the other end, and desire to investigate the cause of an effect *a,* we must select an instance, as *a b c,* in which the effects occurs, and in which the antecedents were A B C, and we must look for another instance in which the remaining circumstances, *b c,* occur without *a.* If the antecedents, in that instance, are B C, we know that the cause of *a* must be A: either A alone, or A in conjunction with some of the other circumstances present.[4]

The rationale is this. If there is an antecedent condition that is present when the phenomenon is present and absent when the phenomenon is absent, either that antecedent condition is the cause of the phenomenon or a partial cause of the phenomenon. In the sciences, this is the method behind the controlled experiment.

To illustrate the method, let us assume that John is shot and dies immediately. Since the only difference between John before he was shot and immediately after he died is that there was a bullet hole through his heart, the condition of being shot was the cause of death. If you want to construct a table to sort through the data, let the numerals 1–7 represent various conditions of John, 'S' represent the condition of being shot through the heart, and 'J1' and 'J2' represent John at two points in time. The table will look like this:

Occurrence	Antecedent Conditions								Phenomenon Death
	1	2	3	4	5	6	7	s	
J1	*	*	*	*	*	*	*		
J2	*	*	*	*	*	*	*	*	*

The table shows that being shot through the heart was the only condition that was present when John was dead and absent when John was alive; thus the condition of being shot through the heart was the cause of death.

Though in the previous case it is reasonable to suggest that being shot was the cause of John's death, there are other cases where the condition that differs is only a partial cause (a component of the cause) of a phenomenon. Assume you are in a chemistry lab. On the lab table there are two beakers containing a certain solution. To one beaker you add a second solution and a precipitate forms. Assume this is a carefully controlled experiment, so there are good grounds for claiming that the only difference between the solution in beaker-A and that in beaker-B is the addition of solution-X to beaker-B. For example, the temperatures of the solutions in both beakers are the same and they remain the same even after the addition of solution-X to beaker-B. If we let the numerals 1–7 represent the various chemical compounds in the original solution and 'X' represent the addition of solution-X to one of the beakers, we might construct a table that looks like this:

Occurrence	Antecedent Conditions								Phenomenon Precipitate
	1	2	3	4	5	6	7	X	
A	*	*	*	*	*	*	*		
B	*	*	*	*	*	*	*	*	*

Was the addition of solution-X *the* cause of the precipitate? This might be a bit misleading. As any chemist would say, there is something in solution-X that combined with something already in the solution in beaker-B to form the precipitate. So in this case the addition of solution-X to the beaker is a partial cause of the phenomenon.

A further word should be said about Mill's requirement that the two cases compared "have *every* circumstance in common save one." It is not clear that this condition can ever be known to be satisfied. In the chemistry example there might be a number of factors that are different with respect to the two beakers of solution: there might be minor differences in the air currents that circulate around each of the beakers, there might be slight differences in the gravitational forces acting on the solutions in the two beakers, and so forth. If there were such differences, the chemistry experiment would not properly comply with Mill's requirements for the Method of Difference. Similarly, we could tell a story about John's death that would show that a certain factor had not been—and could not be—noticed in explaining John's death. Let us assume that an instant before the bullet passed through his body John suffered a massive heart attack, but the damage to the heart caused by the bullet obliterated all evidence of the heart attack. Since we know on the basis of the *Method of Agreement* that there is a correlation between massive heart attacks and death, what would we claim as the cause of John's death? Was John "dead on his feet" when he was shot? Or would we claim that, since a heart attack is a process that takes a certain amount of time to render its lethal effect, John would have died of a heart attack if he had not been shot?

Given that we probably can never know *all* the antecedent conditions for any phenomenon, and therefore never know that two phenomenon had all antecedent conditions save one in common, does this mean that we can never use the Method of Difference? It certainly does *not* mean that we *will not* use it. For example, if civil disturbances in a part of the city followed the rendering of a certain court decision, we would claim that the court decision was a partial cause of the disturbances, since the disturbances were not present before the decision and they were present after it. The only difference we might notice in this case is the court decision. Like the Method of Agreement, the Method of Difference tends to indicate that there is a causal relation between two conditions, but it is always possible that some condition was overlooked. The problem we confront with the Method of Difference is that we are comparing only two cases, so it remains an open question whether all the antecedent conditions save one are the same in both cases. We have better reason to believe that we have isolated the *causally relevant* antecedent conditions if we have several instances in two situations that are apparently the same except for one known antecedent condition. For example, if at each of the twenty tables in the chemistry lab adding solution-X to a beaker containing some known solution is followed by observing a precipitate in the beaker, we have much better reason to believe that the addition of solution-X was a partial cause of the formation of the precipitate. But here we are not concerned solely with the Method of Difference; we are concerned both with similarities between the twenty instances of the experiment and the differences between what was observed in two beakers in each case. We are combining the first two methods. Mill's third method is such a combination of the other two.

The Joint Method of Agreement and Difference (Indirect Method of Difference)

Mill calls his third method the Indirect Method of Difference, or Joint Method of Agreement and Difference. This method combines the first two methods by looking at multiple examples of agreement and difference. Mill puts it this way: *"If two or more instances in which the phenomenon occurs have only one circumstance in common, while two or more instances in which it does not occur have nothing in common save the absence of that circumstance, the circumstance in which alone the two sets of instances differ, is the effect, or the cause, or an indispensable part of the cause, of the phenomenon."*[5] He describes the reasoning as follows:

> If we compare various instances in which *a* occurs, and find that they all have in common the circumstance A, and (as far as can be observed) no other circumstance, the Method of Agreement, so far, bears testimony to a connection between A and *a*. In order to convert this evidence of connection into proof of causation by the direct Method of Difference, we ought to be able, in some of these instances, as for example, A B C, to leave out A, and observe whether by doing so, *a* is preserved. Now supposing (what is often the case) that we are not able to try this decisive experiment; yet, provided we can by any means discover what would be its result if we could try it, the advantage will be the same. Suppose, then, that as we previously examined a variety of instances in which *a* occurred, and found them to agree in containing A, so we now observe a variety of instances in which *a* does not occur, and find them to agree in not containing A; which establishes, by the Method of Agreement, the same connection between the absence of A and the absence of *a*, which was before established between their presence. As, then, it had been shown that whenever A is present *a* is present, so, it being now shown that when A is taken away *a* is removed along with it, we have by the one proposition A B C, *a b c,* by the other B C, *b, c,* the positive and negative instances which the Method of Difference requires.[6]

The Indirect Method of Difference or Joint Method of Agreement and Difference is a combination of the previous two methods based upon multiple instances of agreement and difference. As Mill notes, however, it is very difficult to fulfill the conditions specified by the Method of Difference by finding a condition exactly like that for which you are testing except that both the antecedent condition and the phenomenon for which you are testing are absent. Nonetheless, Mill contends, the condition of difference is fulfilled by looking for cases insofar as both the antecedent condition and the phenomenon under examination are absent. So you look for both cases in which the antecedent and the phenomenon under examination are present, and cases in which both are absent. If you find both, you have stronger grounds for claiming that the antecedent condition is the cause of the phenomenon than are provided by either the Method of Agreement or the Method of Difference alone.

We have already noticed that repeated trials of a controlled experiment illustrate this method. Another example can be drawn from Walter Reed's examination of yellow fever. To prove that yellow fever was caused by the female *Culex fasciatus* mosquito that had bitten an infected yellow fever victim during the first three days of the disease, Reed's colleague Dr. Jesse Lazear first infected three people by having them bitten by such a mosquito. Each contracted the disease—Lazear, himself an experimental subject, died. Later Reed constructed a house divided into two rooms by mosquito netting. In one of these rooms, an experimental subject was exposed to repeated infected-mosquito bites. In the other room were several subjects who were not naturally immune to the disease but were protected from mosquitoes. The subject who was bitten contracted the disease; the subjects who were not bitten did not contract the disease. The two phases of the inquiry can be represented as an instance of the Indirect Method of Difference (Joint Method of Agreement and Difference): those who were bitten contracted the disease, and those who were not bitten did not contract the disease. This could be illustrated in the following table, where the numerals 1–7 represent antecedent conditions and 'B' represents being bitten by an infected mosquito:

Occurrence	Antecedent Conditions								Phenomenon Yellow Fever
	1	2	3	4	5	6	7	B	
S1	*		*				*	*	*
S2		*		*				*	*
S3					*	*		*	*
S4	*	*	*	*				*	*
S5	*	*	*	*					
S6	*	*	*	*			*		

The table shows that in each case in which yellow fever was contracted the subject was bitten by an infected mosquito, and that in those cases in which the subject was not bitten by an infected mosquito, yellow fever was not contracted.[7]

Method of Residues

Mill's fourth method is the Method of Residues. If you have a complex set of antecedent conditions and a complex phenomenon, and you can explain all but one of the elements of the phenomenon on the basis of all but one of the antecedent conditions, that is, if you have already discovered a causal correlation between some of the antecedent conditions and the elements of the phenomenon on the basis of the previous three methods, the remaining antecedent condition is causally related to the remaining element of the phenomenon. Mill puts it this way: *"Subduct from any phenomenon such part as is known by previous inductions to be the effect of certain antecedents, and the residue of the phenomenon is the effect of the remaining antecedents."*[8] He describes the reasoning as follows:

> Suppose, as before, that we have the antecedents A B C, followed by the consequent *a b c,* and that by previous inductions (founded, we will suppose, on the Method of Difference) we have ascertained the causes of some of these effects, or the effect of some of these causes; and are thence appraised that the effect of A is *a,* and the effect of B is *b.* Subtracting the sum of these effects from the total phenomenon, there remains *c,* which now, without fresh experiments, we may know to be the effect of C.[9]

Mill notes that many astronomical discoveries depend upon the Method of Residues,[10] and indeed the discovery of the planet Neptune illustrates the Method of Residues. Given the system of Newtonian mechanics, it is possible to predict the positions of each of the planets at a certain time given their positions at any previous time *on the assumption that* all the planets in the solar system are known. In 1846 the predictions did not work out: the orbit of Uranus did not comply with the predictions. Since the perturbations in the orbit of Uranus could be explained on the assumption that there was an additional planet, the French mathematician Urbain Jean Joseph Leverrier predicted the existence and location of that planet. On the basis of Leverrier's predictions, the German astronomer Johann Gottfried Galle discovered the planet Neptune. Notice the reasoning: All of the movements of the (known) planets except certain perturbations in the orbit of Uranus can be explained on the basis of the laws of Newtonian mechanics and the previous locations of the planets. So the perturbations in the orbit of Uranus can be explained by (are caused by) the gravitational attraction of an additional planet (Neptune). The same kind of reasoning led to the discovery of the planet Pluto in the early twentieth century.

The Method of Concomitant Variation

Mill's final method is the Method of Concomitant Variation. If the changes in two states of affairs vary with one another—if one increases as the other decreases or one increases (or decreases) as another does—there is reason to believe that the two states of affairs are causally related to one another. Notice, this *suggests* that there is a causal relation. It does not show *that* there is a causal relation: *that* there is a causal relation can be established only on the basis of the first three methods. Mill puts it this way: "*Whatever phenomenon varies in any manner whatever another phenomenon varies in some particular manner, is either a cause or an effect of that phenomenon, or is connected with it through some fact of causation.*"[11] He describes the reasoning as follows:

> If some modification in the antecedent A is always followed by a change in the consequent *a,* the other consequents *b* and *c* remaining the same; or *vice versa,* if every change in *a* is found to be preceded by some modification in A, none being observable in any of the other antecedents, we may safely conclude that *a* is, wholly or in part, an effect traceable to A, or at least in some way connected with it through causation.[12]

To illustrate this method, we may consider the recent finding that there is a statistical correlation between baldness and heart attacks. People who are bald have a greater tendency to suffer heart attacks than those who are not bald, and as the extent of the baldness increases, the probability of a heart attack increases proportionately. Does this show that baldness causes heart attacks? No, but it suggests either that baldness causes heart attacks or that there is some common cause of both conditions. For example, there might be a certain genetic trait that causes both baldness and a tendency to suffer heart attacks, or it might be that both those who go bald and those who tend to suffer heart attacks live a very stressful life-style, and the stress causes both. The Method of Concomitant Variation only suggests lines of further inquiry. To determine whether baldness causes heart attacks or whether they have some common cause, you would need to gather more data and see whether the Method of Agreement, the Method of Difference, or the Joint Method indicates that there is a causal connection.

As with the Method of Agreement and the Joint Method, the more data you accumulate before claiming that there is a concomitant variation, the better reason you have for claiming it is likely that there is a causal connection. If I became a fast-food junkie and discovered that my blood pressure rose proportionately with the amount of fast food I ate, there might be a causal connection. It might be that the greasy food caused an increase in blood pressure; it might be that the pressures of my job caused me both to eat out more often and caused my blood pressure to rise. It also might be purely coincidental that the increase in fast-food consumption and blood pressure happened at the same time. On the other hand, if a study were made of several thousand people and it was discovered that there was a general correlation between an increase in the amount of fast food consumed and an increase in blood pressure, there would be much better reason to believe that the concomitant variation is evidence of a causal relation. Similarly, those concomitant variations that we take to be evidence of a causal relation must fit with what we already accept as causally significant. For example, if I discovered that over a period of five years there was a concomitant variation between the use of disposable diapers in the United States and hurricane damage in Cuba—periods of higher diaper usage corresponded with periods of extensive hurricane damage in Cuba, and periods of low diaper usage corresponded with little hurricane damage—it is unlikely that anyone would claim the concomitant variation points to a causal relation. Given what we know about the conditions causing hurricanes, there is little reason to believe that the concomitant variation is anything other than coincidental. On the other hand, if I discovered there was such a concomitant variation for a period of thirty or forty years, it might suggest that further inquiry should be made into the causes of hurricanes or the causes of the use of disposable diapers.

SUMMARY

Mill's Methods of Experimental Inquiry help us search for the cause of a phenomenon. The first three methods allow us to isolate one or a small number of antecedent conditions as the cause of a phenomenon.

1. The Method of Agreement identifies the cause by showing that whenever a particular antecedent condition is present, the phenomenon is also present.

2. The Method of Difference compares two cases that differ only insofar as in one case both an antecedent condition and the phenomenon under investigation are absent.

3. The Indirect Method of Difference or Joint Method of Agreement and Difference combines the first two methods and applies both to several cases.

4. The Method of Residues allows you to determine that one of a complex set of antecedent conditions is the cause of one element of a complex phenomenon if you already know on the basis of the

other three methods that each of the remaining antecedent conditions is the cause of each of the remaining elements of the phenomenon.

5. The Method of Concomitant Variation shows it is likely that two phenomena are causally related or have a common cause if they change at the same rate. The Method of Concomitant Variation suggests that two phenomena are causally related, but determining which conditions are related as cause and effect requires the use of the first three methods.

EXERCISES

I. Use the following tables to determine the cause of the phenomenon. Is the table an example of using the Method of Agreement, the Method of Difference, or the Joint Method of Agreement and Difference?

1.

Occurrence	A	B	C	D	E	F	G	H	Phenomenon
1	*		*	*	*		*		*
2		*	*		*	*	*	*	*
3	*	*	*	*		*		*	*
4		*	*		*	*	*	*	*
5	*		*	*			*	*	*

2.

Occurrence	A	B	C	D	E	F	G	H	Phenomenon
1	*	*	*	*	*	*	*	*	*
2	*	*		*	*	*	*	*	

3.

Occurrence	A	B	C	D	E	F	G	H	Phenomenon
1		*		*		*		*	*
2	*	*	*		*		*	*	*
3		*			*	*	*		*
4	*		*		*	*	*		
5		*	*		*		*		
6	*	*			*		*	*	

4.

Occurrence	A	B	C	D	E	F	G	H	Phenomenon
1		*	*		*		*		*
2	*		*	*		*	*	*	*
3		*		*	*		*		*
4	*	*			*	*	*	*	*
5		*	*	*			*		*

5.

Occurrence	A	B	C	D	E	F	G	H	Phenomenon
1	*		*		*	*			*
2		*	*	*			*		*
3	*	*				*		*	
4				*	*		*	*	
5		*	*			*		*	*

6.

Occurrence	A	B	C	D	E	F	G	H	Phenomenon
1	*	*	*	*	*	*	*	*	*
2	*		*		*	*	*	*	

7.

Occurrence	A	B	C	D	E	F	G	H	Phenomenon
1	*	*	*		*		*	*	*
2		*		*		*		*	*
3		*		*		*	*		*
4	*		*	*		*	*		
5	*			*		*			
6			*		*		*		

8.

Occurrence	A	B	C	D	E	F	G	H	Phenomenon
1	*	*		*		*	*	*	*
2	*			*	*		*		*
3		*	*	*		*	*	*	
4	*			*	*	*		*	*
5	*	*			*		*		*
6		*	*	*		*		*	
7		*			*	*	*	*	
8	*	*	*			*	*		

9.

Occurrence	Antecedent Conditions								Phenomenon
	A	B	C	D	~A	~B	~C	~D	
1	*					*	*	*	*
2					*	*	*	*	

10.

Occurrence	Antecedent Conditions								Phenomenon
	A	B	C	D	E	F	G	H	
1	*		*		*		*		*
2		*	*	*			*		*
3	*		*	*		*	*		*
4	*	*	*	*	*		*	*	*
5		*	*				*		*
6	*	*		*	*	*			*

II. Which of Mill's Methods is illustrated in each of the following examples? Explain your choices.

1. There is a correlation between the use of disposable diapers and the shortage of space in sanitary landfills. As the number of disposable diapers increased, the shortage of space in the landfills became more acute. In periods when fewer disposable diapers were used, the shortage of space in the landfills was less acute. This suggests that the use of disposable diapers is at least a partial cause of shortage of space in landfills.

2. In the cafeteria at Yadelman Hall, there was recently a serious problem with food poisoning. Except for George and Henry, all the students who ate the turkey became dreadfully ill within twelve hours. George and Henry came down with the same malady within twenty-four hours. A careful investigation showed that they alone had spiked their coffee with an alcoholic beverage—for which they were duly expelled. The authorities concluded that the alcohol had retarded the food poisoning.

3. Bert and Nina ate Thanksgiving dinner at Joe's Truck Stop. Bert became ill afterward; Nina didn't become ill. Bert ate turkey, stuffing, cranberry sauce, pumpkin pie, and mincemeat pie. Nina ate turkey, stuffing, cranberry sauce, and mincemeat pie. So you can tell what did Bert in, can't you?

4. When Walter Reed was attempting to determine whether yellow fever was transmitted by mosquitoes, he placed three

people in a sealed room containing mosquitoes. All three caught yellow fever. One of the three died.

5. The Acme Corporation lost $500,000 last year. The accounting department suggested there could be only three causes: too many employees, increased taxes, and product loss caused by a hurricane. They estimated these costs at $150,000, $100,000, and $200,000 respectively. They suggested that the remaining $50,000 could be explained by employee theft.

6. George, Martha, and Tom ate lunch at the Red Coast Inn. George had a hamburger, fries, salad, and a diet cola. Martha had a salad, a hamburger, and a diet cola. Tom had only an order of fries. George and Tom developed an upset stomach. They concluded that the fries had caused the upset stomach.

7. During one of the smallpox epidemics in the 1790s, Edward Jenner treated many farmers and milkmaids. He observed that those who had had cowpox did not catch smallpox. He concluded that contracting cowpox causes one to be immune to smallpox.

8. Frank was not doing well in his logic class. The cause of his performance was either his study habits, the distractions of living in a dormitory, or a psychological block with respect to symbol systems. He moved into an apartment by himself, which improved his grades somewhat. He visited the academic counseling center and was coached on improving his study habits. His grades improved somewhat more. The problems that remained had to be attributed to a psychological block with respect to symbol systems.

9. Gustav, Marihugh, and Amisglof took logic. Gustav bought a new copy of the textbook, attended class every day, studied for an hour every night, and made liberal use of the professor's office hours. He passed the course. Marihugh bought a used copy of the textbook, attended class only on exam days, studied for an hour every night, and never visited the professor's office. She passed the course. Amisglof bought a new copy of the textbook, attended class every day, never studied at night, and made liberal use of the professor's office hours. She failed the course. So you can see why Gustav and Marihugh passed the course.

10. Jill and Will are siblings. They eat the same food, except Jill refuses to eat citrus fruits, tomatoes, and any other foods containing vitamin C. Jill develops scurvy. The doctor diagnoses the cause of her disease as the absence of vitamin C.

11. Two of the major causes of death in the United States are heart disease and cancer. For a number of years, the medical profession has recognized a positive correlation between cholesterol levels and heart attack. Cholesterol levels have dropped in the past ten years, but there have been no significant increases in life expectancy. People with low cholesterol levels more frequently die of cancer than do those with high cholesterol levels. This suggests that low cholesterol levels cause cancer.

12. As postal rates increase, the time it takes to have mail delivered increases. This suggests that there is a causal relationship between the rise in postal rates and the decrease in the quality of mail service.

13. Mark Twain once reported that for many years he drank two hot Scotches per day, and in all that time he'd never had a toothache. He concluded that two hot Scotches per day are a good preventative of toothache.

14. As trained physicists always do when they make a discovery, Marie Curie made measurements. With a set of instruments arranged by her and Pierre, she determined the intensity of the rays (in various elements and compounds) by measuring the conductivity of the air surrounding the radioactive elements. She then became puzzled. Pitchblende, the ore that contained the uranium and thorium, gave off rays more intense than either those of the thorium or the uranium. There must be then, she guessed, some other element or elements more intensely radioactive than either!

    ROGER BURLINGAME, *Scientists Behind the Inventors*
    (New York: Avon Books, 1960), p. 93.

15. [After his success with vaccination for chicken cholera] Pasteur was convinced now that he could also make a vaccine from a weakened strain of anthrax germs that would protect sheep and cattle from the disease. After many experiments, he found that he could weaken the anthrax germs sufficiently by heating them in a flask.

But once again he found himself involved in a bitter quarrel. The veterinarians . . . refused to believe him. They challenged him to give a public demonstration.

The test was held on a farm outside Paris. . . . Fifty sheep were used in the test. Pasteur gave his vaccine to twenty-five of them. Then two weeks later, all fifty were inoculated with a very powerful and dangerous strain of anthrax germs.

Two days later, the twenty-five that had been protected by the vaccine were alive and healthy. Eighteen of the others were dead, and the remaining seven were dying.

DAVID DIETZ, *All About Great Medical Discoveries*
(New York: Random House, 1960), p. 55.

9.2 *Necessary and Sufficient Conditions*

Although Mill constructed his Methods of Experimental Inquiry in terms of causes and effects, many of his followers divide the notion of a cause into the necessary and sufficient conditions for a phenomenon. A **necessary condition** for a phenomenon is a condition in whose absence the phenomenon in question is absent. This is expressed by a conditional statement of the form, "If the phenomenon is present, then the condition is present." A **sufficient condition** for a phenomenon is present when the phenomenon is present. This is expressed by a conditional statement of the form, "If the condition is present, then the phenomenon is present." A **necessary and sufficient** condition for a phenomenon is absent when the phenomenon is absent and present when the phenomenon is present. This is expressed by a biconditional statement of the form, "The phenomenon is present if and only if the condition is present."

The distinction between necessary and sufficient conditions is of great practical importance. For example, if you recognize that three conditions are necessary for combustion, namely, a source of heat, a combustible material, and oxygen, you are able to prevent fires by removing one of the necessary conditions. Most houses are made of combustible materials. Any house in which you would live is fairly rich in oxygen, and virtually all modern houses are wired for electricity. Electricity is a source of heat. To prevent houses from catching fire, electrical wires are insulated with a noncombustible material. Similarly, if you know that having a functioning generating system, a functioning lamp switch in the "on" position, light bulbs with filaments intact, circuit breakers in the "on" position, and so forth, are (among) the necessary and sufficient conditions for a functioning electrical lamp, and if you turn on the lamp in your apartment but the light does not come on you have a list of the possible problems: one of the necessary conditions has not been met. You might then examine the various necessary conditions to see which one has not been actualized.

How can Mill's Methods be used to determine whether a condition is necessary, sufficient, or necessary and sufficient? Since only the Method of Agreement, the Method of Difference, and the Joint Method of Agreement and Difference show *that* an antecedent condition is causally related to a phenomenon, it is only with respect to those methods that considerations of necessary and sufficient conditions arise. Given this, it should be fairly clear that the Joint Method of Agreement and Difference shows you that a certain condition is both necessary and sufficient for a phenomenon, since it shows that the antecedent condition is present when the phenomenon is present and absent when the phenomenon is absent.

What about the Method of Agreement? Whether this method is taken to show necessary or sufficient conditions depends upon whether we search for a regularly occurring phenomenon given a set of antecedent conditions, or whether we search for a set of antecedent conditions given the phenomenon. Consider the example of dropping a lighted match on a bed of dry evergreen needles. By dropping a lighted match on individual beds of dry yellow-pine needles, Scotch-pine needles, Douglas-fir needles, juniper needles, and mixed evergreen needles, and noting that in each case the needles catch fire, we have evidence that supports the conditional statement, "If a lighted match is dropped on a bed of dry evergreen needles, then the needles begin to burn." The experiment tends to show that dropping a lighted match on a bed of dry evergreen needles is a sufficient condition for the needles to burn. Does it also show that dropping a match on a bed of dry evergreen needles is a necessary condition for the burning of the needles, that is, does it show that the conditional statement "If evergreen needles burn, then a lighted match was dropped on a bed of dry evergreen needles" is true? The several cases we have considered tend to support the conditional, since in each case in which we have seen burning pine needles, a lighted match was dropped on them. But the conditional is more general than the cases we have considered, and there are cases in which evergreen needles burn when a lighted match was not dropped on them. If a burning cigarette is dropped on a bed of dry evergreen needles, the needles will burn. If lightning strikes a bed of dry evergreen needles, the needles will burn, and so forth. So if we begin with a specified set of antecedent conditions and note that a certain phenomenon is realized in each case in which the antecedent conditions are realized, the Method of Agreement tends to show that a set of antecedent conditions are sufficient for the phenomenon, but it does not show that they are necessary.

On the other hand, if we begin with the phenomenon, in this case burning evergreen needles, and look for a common antecedent condition, the Method of Agreement will tend to show that an antecedent condition is necessary for the phenomenon. For example, if the phenomenon in question is burning evergreen needles, we would look for as many cases of burning evergreen needles as we could find, and ask what antecedent condition they have in common. We might find that in some cases a burning match was dropped on the evergreen needles. In other cases a burning cigarette was dropped on them. In still other cases a bolt of lightning struck them. We then look for the characteristic or characteristics that are common to all the antecedent conditions. In this case, each of the antecedent conditions provides a significant source of heat. Hence, the investigation would tend to show that being subjected to a significant source of heat is a necessary condition for the burning of evergreen needles, that is, if evergreen needles burn, then they were subjected to a significant source of heat.

So the Method of Agreement tends to show that an antecedent condition is sufficient for a phenomenon if your investigation proceeds by asking what phenomenon occurs *given* a common set of antecedent conditions. It tends to show that an antecedent condition is necessary for a phenomenon if your investigation proceeds by asking what antecedent conditions are common to a *given* phenomenon.

Much the same can be said about the Method of Difference, although the Method of Difference tends to show that an antecedent condition is sufficient for a phenomenon if you are given the phenomenon, and that it is necessary for the phenomenon if you are given the antecedent conditions. For example, assume George came down with ptomaine poisoning, a common type of food poisoning. In your investigation, you discover that George and Samantha had dinner together and ate the same foods, except that George ate meat and Samantha did not. Under those circumstances, the Method of Difference would tend to show that eating the meat was a sufficient condition for contracting ptomaine poisoning. On the other hand, assume you knew that George and Samantha had dinner together and that they ate the same foods except that George had meat and Samantha did not. You wonder whether these differences in diet would have any effects. You later discover that George contracted ptomaine poisoning but Samantha did not. In this case, the Method of Difference tends to show that eating the meat was a necessary condition for contracting ptomaine poisoning, that is, if you contracted ptomaine poisoning, then you ate the meat.

In summary, the Joint Method of Agreement and Difference tends to show that an antecedent condition is both necessary and sufficient to a certain phenomenon. If you are investigating the phenomenon, if you are looking for the cause of a given phenomenon, the Method of Agreement tends to show that an antecedent condition is necessary for the phenomenon, and the Method of Difference tends to show that an antecedent condition is sufficient for the phenomenon. If you are investigating a set of antecedent conditions to see what effects they will have, the Method of Agreement tends to show that the antecedent conditions are sufficient for the phenomenon discovered, and the Method of Difference tends to show that the antecedent conditions are necessary for the phenomenon discovered.

EXERCISES

Look again at the second set of exercises in the previous section. Do the exercises numbered 2, 3, 4, 6, 7, 9, 10, 13, and 15 show that the antecedent conditions are necessary, sufficient, or necessary and sufficient for the phenomenon in question? Explain your answers.

NOTES

1. John Stuart Mill, *A System of Logic, Ratiocinative and Inductive: Being a Connected View of the Principles of Evidence and the Methods of Scientific Investigation*, 8th ed. (New York: Harper and Brothers, 1895), p. 280.
2. Mill, *A System of Logic*, p. 278.
3. Mill, *A System of Logic*, p. 280.
4. Mill, *A System of Logic*, p. 280.
5. Mill, *A System of Logic*, p. 284.
6. Mill, *A Method of Logic*, pp. 283–284.
7. This description of Reed's experiments was drawn from L. N.

Wood, *Walter Reed: Doctor in Uniform* (New York: Julian Messner, 1943), pp. 209–40.

8. Mill, *A System of Logic,* p. 285.

9. Mill, *A System of Logic,* p. 284.

10. Mill, *A System of Logic,* p. 306.

11. Mill, *A System of Logic,* p. 287.

12. Mill, *A System of Logic,* p. 286.

Chapter Ten

Probability and Numbers

We frequently make probability claims. We might claim:

1. The probability of a coin coming up heads in a fair toss is 1/2.
2. The probability that a 20–year-old male will live to age 85 is .27.
3. It is highly probable that George and Martha will have another child.

In each of these cases the word 'probable' has a different meaning, since a different procedure is used to determine the probability. In the first case a purely mathematical procedure is used. In the second case the probability claim is based on a large sample of men who have lived to be 85. The third is a subjective claim based on knowledge of George and Martha's attitudes toward children, their family situation, their states of health, and so forth. Corresponding to these three kinds of situations are three theories of probability: the classical theory, the relative frequency theory, and the subjective theory. These theories rest on different assumptions, although there is a common probability calculus that applies to all of them.

10.1 Probability Theories

The classical probability theory was developed in the seventeenth century by the French mathematician and philosopher Blaise Pascal (1623–1662) and the French mathematician Pierre de Fermat (1601–1655).[1] They developed the probability calculus at the request of the gambler the Chevalier de Méré, who was concerned about some practical problems at the dice tables. The theory of probability Pascal and Fermat developed is an *a priori* theory of probability, that is, it takes no account of sensory observations in computing the probability of an event. It holds that the probability of some event A is the ratio of the number of favorable outcomes (*f*) to the number of possible outcomes (*n*). The formula is:

$$P(A) = \frac{f}{n}$$

For example, the probability of drawing one of thirteen spades from a poker deck of 52 cards is $13/52$, or $1/4$. The probability of rolling an ace with one fair die is $1/6$. Similarly, the probability of tossing heads with a two-headed coin is $2/2$ or 1. The probability of tossing tails with a two-headed coin is $0/2$ or 0. An event that is certain has a probability of 1; an impossible event has a probability of 0.

The classical theory rests on two assumptions. First, it assumes that all probabilities are taken into account. Second, it assumes that all possibilities are equally probable. The second assumption is known as the **principle of indifference.** Though these assumptions are idealizations, in many circumstances they are quite reasonable. In applying the assumptions to the throw of a die, for example, the first assumption limits the possibilities to cases in which the die lands with one of its six faces up; the second assumption limits the application to a perfectly fair die. Though neither assumption holds in the real world—in some cases a die might break or land on its edge against the edge of a playing board, and no die is absolutely symmetrical—the assumptions are adequate in many cases.

Applying the classical theory of probability, you reach the following conclusions:

P(drawing a queen from a poker deck) $= 4/52 = 1/13$
P(throwing heads in a fair coin toss) $= 1/2$
P(throwing a six with a fair die) $= 1/6$
P(drawing the jack of spades from a poker deck) $= 1/52$.

The classical theory is useful for some kinds of probability calculations, namely, when there is a distinct number of possibilities; but it cannot answer all the probability questions we ask. It cannot tell you, for example, the probability that Aunt Tillie is going to live to be 70. To figure that probability, you need to know some facts about life expectancy.

In the eighteenth century, life-insurance companies began compiling mortality tables, which gave them empirical data for determining insurance rates, that is, data based on experience. Calculations are based on such empirical data, and the theory of probability is called the **relative frequency theory** of probability. The procedure for calculating the probability that Aunt Tillie will live to be 70 is the same as in the classical theory. Let us say that Aunt Tillie is 40 years old. Using data from a mortality table, you find that of an initial 10,000,000 people born, 9,241,359 are still alive at age forty. At age 70 there are 5,592,012 of the original 10,000,000 alive. Using the formula:

$$P(A) = \frac{f}{n}$$

we note that there are, at age 40, 9,241,359 possibilities, and at age 70 there are 5,592,012 favorable outcomes. So the probability that Aunt Tillie will still be alive at 70 is:

5,592,012/9,241,359 = .605[2]

The relative frequency theory of probability is commonly used in the sciences, where probabilistic predictions are based on past experience. Of course, as experience changes, the observed basis for making the predictions will also change.

Neither of these theories of probability will help calculate the probability that your favorite team will win if you are given 11-to-7 odds *in favor* of your team. Here there is a certain belief in an outcome held by individual people. The **subjective theory** of probability is based on individual beliefs. To determine the subjective probability that your favorite team will win, you need to divide the probability, namely, 11, by the total possibilities, namely, 11+7. The probability is 11/(11+7) = $^{11}/_{18}$ = .61. Since 18 represents the total number of possibilities, the subjective probability that the opponents of your team will win must be $^{7}/_{18}$ = .39; this is also the probability that your team will *not* win. On the other hand, if you were given odds of 20-to-1 *against* your team, the total number of possibilities is 21, and the probability that your team will win is $1/21$ = .05. The probability that the opposing team will win is $20/21$ = .95.

If you are given odds, they are either odds that an event *will* occur (odds for the event) or that the event will not occur (odds against the event). Further, the odds for and against an event should correspond to one another: if the odds are seven-to-three *for* an event, they should be three-to-seven *against* it. If you are given the odds *for* an event the probability with which you are concerned—that by which you will divide the total number of possibilities—is the first number given. So if the odds *in favor* of your team are seven-to-three, the probability that your team will win is $7/11$ = .64. If you are given the odds *against* an event the probability with which you are concerned—that by which you will divide the total number of possibilities—is the second number given. So if the odds *against* your team are seven-to-three, the probability that your team will win is $3/11$ = .36. There will be times, however, when you will not be explicitly told whether the odds are for or against an event. For example, if you are visiting Churchill Downs and are told that the track odds on the number seven horse are seven-to-five, this means that if you place a $5 bet and your horse wins, you will receive $7 from the cashier. The odds are against the horse. The probability that the horse will win is $5/12$ = .42.

The subjective theory of probability seems to have a difficulty that is not shared by the other theories, namely, the odds given reflect nothing more than the beliefs of the odds-makers, which change as bets are made. This is a problem only if you assume that probability is an objective property of an event. But, as we have seen, in the classical theory the number of possibilities is stipulated: actual possibilities, such as a coin landing on its edge, are ignored. Calculating according to the regularity theory rests upon estimates of favorable and possible outcomes that only approximate the facts. Calculations of the probability that a person will live to a certain age are based on mortality tables that do not reflect the most recent advances in medicine. In areas where it is assumed that actual distributions do not change, probability calculations are subject to change with improved data. Subjective probability is merely the most extreme case.

Whereas there are three theories of probability, there is a single **probability calculus.** We have already seen (1) that the formula for determining the probability of a single event is the same regardless of the theory of probability you use, namely, the ratio of favorable outcomes to possible outcomes, and (2) that all probability calculations range between a probability of zero (impossibility) and a probability of one (necessity).

But you are seldom interested in the probability of only one event. Often you want to know the probability that either or both of two or more events will occur. There are additional formulae for determining such probabilities, regardless of the theory of probability you use.

Conjunction Rules

The **restricted conjunction rule** is used to calculate the probability that two independent events will occur. Two events are **independent** of one another if and only if the occurrence of one event has no influence on the other. For example, consecutive tosses of a single coin are independent events: whatever happens on the first toss has no effect on what will happen on the second. Assume you want to know what the probability is that you will toss heads on two consecutive tosses of a fair coin. The formula for determining this is:

$$P(A \text{ and } B) = P(A) \times P(B)$$

Since the probability of tossing heads in each case in $\frac{1}{2}$, the probability of tossing heads twice is calculated as follows:

$$P(H_1 \text{ and } H_2) = \frac{1}{2} \times \frac{1}{2} = \frac{1}{4} = .25.$$

This probability can be graphically set out in a tree diagram that shows all the possibilities. Let the entries on the left represent the first toss of the coin, and those on the right represent the second:

$$
H \left\{ \begin{array}{l} H \\ T \end{array} \right.
$$
$$
T \left\{ \begin{array}{l} H \\ T \end{array} \right.
$$

Notice that there is only one case out of the four possibilities represented by the entries on the right in which only one toss of heads is correlated with a toss of heads on the first throw of the coin.

The same principle is used to calculate the probability that you will throw a one and a six while simultaneously rolling two dice. The probability of each event is $\frac{1}{6}$, so

$$P(1 \text{ and } 6) = \frac{1}{6} \times \frac{1}{6} = \frac{1}{36} = .02778.$$

Should you have any doubt of this outcome, you may construct a tree diagram to convince yourself.

Relatively few events are wholly independent. The **general conjunction rule** is used to calculate the probability of two events when the second event is dependent on the occurrence of the first. For example, let us say you wanted to calculate the probability of drawing two black aces from a poker deck. The formula for calculating this probability is:

$$P(A \text{ and } B) = P(A) \times P(B \text{ given } A)$$

Since in the second draw, the size of the deck is reduced from 52 cards to 51 cards, this fact is taken into account in the formula by the expression P(B given A). The probability of drawing a black ace on the first draw is $2/52$. Assuming that the first draw was successful, the probability of drawing the other black ace on the second draw is $1/51$. So the appropriate instance of the formula is:

$$P(D_1 \text{ and } D_2) = 2/52 \times 1/51 = 2/2652 = 1/1326 = .000754.$$

Rather than a deck of playing cards, let us say that you have an urn containing 100 balls. Of these balls 25 are red, 25 are black, and 50 are white. What is the probability of drawing a red ball on two consecutive draws, assuming that the first ball is not placed back into the urn? The probability of drawing a red ball on the first draw is $25/100$ or $1/4$. Given that one red ball is removed, the probability of drawing a red ball on the second draw is $24/99$. So the formula tells us:

$$P(R_1 \text{ and } R_2) = 1/4 \times 24/99 = 24/396 = \tfrac{2}{33} = .06061.$$

The cases we have considered with respect to both the restricted and general conjunction rules have focused on two cases; the same processes allow us to calculate the probability of three independent events. For example, the probability of throwing a one, a two, and a three on a simultaneous toss of three dice is:

$$P(1 \text{ and } 2 \text{ and } 3) = 1/6 \times 1/6 \times 1/6 = 1/216 = .00463.$$

If you have an urn containing three red balls, four blue balls, and five yellow balls, the probability of drawing a red ball on three consecutive draws (without replacement) is:

$$P(R_1 \text{ and } R_2 \text{ and } R_3) = \frac{3}{12} \times \frac{2}{11} \times \frac{1}{10} = \frac{6}{1320} = \frac{1}{220} = .00455.$$

The probability of drawing three consecutive yellow balls is:

$$P(Y_1 \text{ and } Y_2 \text{ and } Y_3) = \frac{5}{12} \times \frac{4}{11} \times \frac{3}{10} = \frac{60}{1320} = \frac{1}{22} = .0455$$

You should also notice that though we have considered two conjunction rules, the first is only a special case of the second. In cases in which two events are independent, there is no change in the probability of the second event. For example, if an urn contained four green balls and seven red balls and you were calculating the probability of drawing a green ball in each of two successive tries in which the ball drawn was *replaced* and mixed with the other balls before the second try, the probability of each event would be $\frac{4}{11}$, and the probability of the two events would be:

$$P(G_1 \text{ and } G_2) = \frac{4}{11} \times \frac{4}{11} = \frac{16}{121} = .13223.$$

Disjunction Rules

Sometimes you want to know the probability that any one of several events will occur. For example, you might want to know what the probability is that the roll of a die will yield an even number, that is, a two, a four, or a six. The disjunction rules allow us to do this. The **restricted disjunction** rule allows you to calculate the probability that one of two or more mutually exclusive events occurs. Two or more events are **mutually exclusive** if and only if they are distinct and the occurrence of one of the events precludes the occurrence of any of the others. The formula for calculating that either of two mutually exclusive events occurs is:

$$P(A \text{ or } B) = P(A) + P(B)$$

For example, the probability of rolling either a one or a three is:

$$P(1 \text{ or } 3) = \frac{1}{6} + \frac{1}{6} = \frac{2}{6} = \frac{1}{3} = .333.$$

Similarly, the probability of rolling either a one or a three or a five (that is, an odd number) is:

$$P(1 \text{ or } 3 \text{ or } 5) = \frac{1}{6} + \frac{1}{6} + \frac{1}{6} = \frac{3}{6} = \frac{1}{2} = .5.$$

And by the same means you would show that the probability of rolling one of the six sides of a die is 1:

$$P(1 \text{ or } 2 \text{ or } 3 \text{ or } 4 \text{ or } 5 \text{ or } 6) = \frac{1}{6} + \frac{1}{6} + \frac{1}{6} + \frac{1}{6} + \frac{1}{6} + \frac{1}{6}$$
$$= \frac{6}{6} = 1$$

If you have an urn containing six red balls, four blue balls, and ten yellow balls, the probability of drawing either a yellow ball or a blue ball is:

$$P(Y \text{ or } B) = \frac{10}{20} + \frac{4}{20} = \frac{14}{20} = \frac{7}{10} = .7.$$

The restricted disjunction rule can be combined with the restricted conjunction rule in computing probabilities. For example, if you wanted to calculate getting either a one or a three on two consecutive rolls of a single die, you would proceed as follows:

$$
\begin{aligned}
P(1 \text{ or } 3) \text{ and } P(1 \text{ or } 3) &= P(1 \text{ or } 3) \times P(1 \text{ or } 3) \\
&= (\tfrac{1}{6} + \tfrac{1}{6}) \times (\tfrac{1}{6} + \tfrac{1}{6}) \\
&= \tfrac{1}{3} \times \tfrac{1}{3} \\
&= \tfrac{1}{9} \\
&= .111
\end{aligned}
$$

On the other hand, if you wanted to calculate the probability of rolling one and three or two and six on a simultaneous roll of two dice, you would calculate:

$$
\begin{aligned}
P(1 \text{ and } 3) \text{ or } P(2 \text{ and } 6) &= P(1 \text{ and } 3) + P(2 \text{ and } 6) \\
&= (\tfrac{1}{6} \times \tfrac{1}{6}) + (\tfrac{1}{6} \times \tfrac{1}{6}) \\
&= \tfrac{1}{36} + \tfrac{1}{36} \\
&= \tfrac{2}{36} \\
&= \tfrac{1}{18} \\
&= .0556
\end{aligned}
$$

Since in each of the last two cases the events with which you are concerned are mutually exclusive and independent, you may use the restricted rules.

The **general disjunction rule** allows you to calculate the probability of either of two *independent* events whether or not they are mutually exclusive. As in the case of the conjunction rules, the restricted disjunction rule is a special case of the general rule. The general disjunction rule is:

$$P(A \text{ or } B) = P(A) + P(B) - P(A \text{ and } B)$$

So to calculate the probability that either of two people will live to the age of seventy, add the probabilities that each will and subtract the probability that both will. Let us say that the probability that Hortense will live to be seventy is .63 and the probability that Jorge will live to be seventy is .54. The probability that either one or the other will live to seventy is:

$$P(H \text{ or } J) = .63 + .54 - (.63 \times .54) = .83$$

If you were asked to calculate the probability that you will roll at least one four when rolling two dice, you would calculate:

$$
\begin{aligned}
P(4_1 \text{ or } 4_2) &= \tfrac{1}{6} + \tfrac{1}{6} - (\tfrac{1}{6} \times \tfrac{1}{6}) \\
&= \tfrac{2}{6} - \tfrac{1}{36} \\
&= \tfrac{11}{36} \\
&= .3056
\end{aligned}
$$

The general disjunction rule can be combined with the restricted disjunction rule to calculate the probability of a four or a six on a pair of die. On each die, the probability of rolling a four is $\tfrac{1}{6}$, and the probability of rolling a six is $\tfrac{1}{6}$. So the total probability is:

$$
\begin{aligned}
P(4 \text{ or } 6)_1 \text{ or } P(4 \text{ or } 6)_2 &= (\tfrac{1}{6} + \tfrac{1}{6}) + (\tfrac{1}{6} + \tfrac{1}{6}) \\
&\quad - [(\tfrac{1}{6} + \tfrac{1}{6}) \times (\tfrac{1}{6} + \tfrac{1}{6})] \\
&= \tfrac{2}{6} + \tfrac{2}{6} - (\tfrac{2}{6} \times \tfrac{2}{6}) \\
&= \tfrac{4}{6} - \tfrac{4}{36} \\
&= \tfrac{20}{36} \\
&= \tfrac{5}{9} \\
&= .5556
\end{aligned}
$$

Since getting a four or a six on an individual throw are exclusive events, the probability of $P(4 \text{ or } 6)_1$ is equal to the combined probabilities; the same holds for $P(4 \text{ or } 6)_2$.

The general disjunction rule can also be combined with the general conjunction rule to calculate the probability of drawing a black ball and then a white ball on pairs of draws from two urns without replacement. Let us say the first urn contains three black balls, two white balls, and one yellow ball, and the second urn contains two black balls, one white ball, and three green balls. The probability given two draws per urn is:

$$P(B \text{ and } W)_1 \text{ or } P(B \text{ and } W)_2 = [P(B) \times P(W \text{ given } B)] + [P(B) \times$$
$$P(W \text{ given } B)]$$
$$- [P(B \text{ and } W)_1 \text{ or } P(B \text{ and } W)_2]$$
$$= (\text{\%} \times \text{\%}) + (\text{\%} \times \text{\%})$$
$$- [(\text{\%} \times \text{\%}) \times (\text{\%} \times \text{\%})$$
$$= (\text{\%}_{30} + \text{\%}_{30}) - (\text{\%}_{30} \times \text{\%}_{30})$$
$$= \text{\%}_{30} - \text{\%}_{900}$$
$$= {}^{80/300}\!/ - \text{\%}_{300}$$
$$= \text{\%}_{300}$$
$$= \text{\%}_{75}$$
$$= .2533.$$

In addition to the conjunction and disjunction rules, it is useful to remember that certainty is always equal to one. Thus, if you know the probability that an event *will not* happen, you can easily calculate the probability that it *will* happen by the **negation rule:**

$$P(A) = 1 - P(\text{not-}A)$$

So, if the probability that A will not happen is .75, there is a .25 probability that A will happen.

You can also use the negation rule to calculate the probabilities of events that are *dependent*. Assume you want to calculate the probability of drawing at least one red ball in either of two successive draws (without replacement) from an urn containing three red balls and four green balls. Calculate the probability of drawing green balls on successive draws:

$$P(G_1 \text{ and } G_2) = \text{\%} \times \text{\%} = {}^{28}\!/_{42} = \text{\%} = .6667.$$

If the probability of drawing a green ball on both of two draws is ⅔, then, using the negation rule, the probability that either of the draws came out red is:

$$P(R_1 \text{ or } R_2) = 1 - \text{\%} = \text{\%} = .3333.$$

Remember, the probability calculus is the same regardless of the theory of probability you are using. Consider the following: (1) Given that the odds that Ohio State will win the Big Ten football champion-

ship are 5-to-11 and the odds that UCLA will win the Pac-10 championship are 6-to-10, there is little chance that Ohio State and UCLA will
meet in the Rose Bowl (in which the winners of these conferences play).
Assuming that the odds are correct, you do the calculations:

$$P(O \text{ and } U) = \frac{5}{16} \times \frac{6}{16} = \frac{30}{256} = .1172$$

and probably conclude it is unlikely that Ohio State and UCLA will
meet in the Rose Bowl. (2) On the other hand, assume you were given
the following argument: Given that the odds that Michigan will win
the Big Ten football championship are 11-to-4 and the odds that Washington will win the Pac-10 Championship are 8-to-3, there's a good
chance that Michigan and Washington will meet in the Rose Bowl.
Again, assuming the odds are correct, you do the calculations:

$$P(M \text{ and } W) = \frac{11}{15} \times \frac{8}{11} = \frac{88}{165} = .5333.$$

Since the probability is slightly over .5, you might not be surprised if
Michigan and Washington met in the Rose Bowl, but you probably
would not bet your house that they will.

When examining inductive arguments, remember that you must
evaluate the strength of the conclusion relative to the premises. This implies several things. First, the premises must provide good reasons for
accepting the conclusion. For example, even if there is a very high probability that the premises and the conclusion are true, the argument is
weak if the premises do not provide good reasons for accepting the conclusion. For example, you *cannot* support the claim that there is a probability of at least .9 that someone somewhere in the world will die within
the next hour on the basis of the statement that there is a probability of
.51 that at least two people in a room containing twenty-three people
have birthdays on the same day. Both the premise and the conclusion
might be true,[3] but since they are entirely unrelated to each other, the
premise provides no grounds for accepting the truth of the conclusion.

Second, if the conclusion of an argument is stated in qualitative
terms, you must have criteria that give a quantitative interpretation of
the qualitative terms. Further, your criteria might be different at different times. For example, the conclusion in the Michigan–Washington
case might be deemed quite weak if it is based on pre-season odds, since
lots of surprises arise during a typical football season; it might be considered stronger if the odds were given just before the last regular game
of the season. Even in the latter case, the claim that there is a "good
chance" the two teams will meet in the Rose Bowl, rather than a "fair

chance" or an "excellent chance" mean nothing apart from a set of criteria to interpret those qualitative claims.

EXERCISES

I. Calculate the probabilities of the following events:

1. The probability that you'll draw an ace of spades from a poker deck of 52 cards.

2. Of the 2,500 students who entered Watsamatta U. four years ago, 1,342 graduated last spring. Assuming the probability of graduating is the same for students entering this year, what is the probability that Ima Frosh, entering first-year student, will graduate in four years?

3. The odds that New Paint will win this year's derby are quoted at 7-to-13. What is the probability that New Paint will win?

4. What is the probability that you'll draw a queen from a poker deck of 52 cards?

5. From a sample of 8,472 recent college graduates, 6,841 had permanent jobs within six months of graduation. What is the probability that a particular college graduate will have a permanent job within six months?

6. Your bookie cites the odds of State winning its first football game at 5-to-3. What is the probability that State will win its first football game?

7. The odds of the Nylon Sox winning the pennant this year are cited at 47-to-62. What is the probability that the Nylon Sox will win the pennant?

8. An urn contains five red balls, six white balls, and ten green balls. What is the probability of drawing a white ball on the first draw?

9. An urn contains seventy red balls, four white balls, sixteen green balls, and twenty-five yellow balls. What is the probability of drawing a white ball on the first try?

10. A recent study shows that 3,000 Americans per year die as a result of secondhand smoke in the workplace. Assume there are 250 million people in the United States. Assume that of those, 50 million are smokers, and so cannot die of secondhand smoke. Assume further that only 100 million of

the remaining 200 million are employed. What is the probability that a person will die as the result of secondhand smoke in the workplace?

II. Calculate the probabilities of the following complex events. State the probabilities to the nearest 10,000ths place—for example, 0.0247.

1. What is the probability of tossing a six on three successive tosses of a fair die?

2. What is the probability of throwing either a four or a six on a single roll of a fair die?

3. On a simultaneous throw of three fair coins, what is the probability that the result will be:
   (a) 3 heads?
   (b) 2 heads and 1 tail?
   (c) 2 tails and 1 head?
   (d) 3 tails?

4. In a recent year, 366.9 people per 100,000 in the population died of major cardiovascular diseases, and 201.7 people per 100,000 died of cancer.[4] What is the probability that some particular individual died that year of either cardiovascular disease or cancer?

5. In 1989, 35.4 per 100,000 people between the ages of 15 and 24 died in motor vehicle accidents, and 1.7 people per 100,000 died of AIDS. What is the probability that someone between the ages of 15 and 24 died either in a motor vehicle accident or from AIDS?

6. In three draws without replacement from a standard poker deck of 52, cards, what is the probability that:
   (a) you draw a spade on each draw?
   (b) you draw an ace on the first draw, a queen on the second, and a king on the third?
   (c) you draw an ace on the first draw and queens on the next two draws?
   (d) you draw the ace of spades on the first draw, a heart on the second draw, and a king of diamonds on the third draw?
   (e) after three draws you have an ace of spades, a heart, and a king of diamonds?

7. In an urn there are six red balls, three green balls, and four yellow balls. Balls are drawn from this urn and replaced after each draw. What is the probability that:
   (a) a red ball will be drawn on each of two successive draws?

(b) a red ball will be drawn on the first draw and a green ball will be drawn on the second draw?

(c) a red ball will be drawn on the first draw and a yellow ball will be drawn on the second draw?

(d) on three successive draws, a red ball, a green ball, and a yellow ball will be drawn?

8. Assuming the situation in problem 5, what are the probabilities if the balls are drawn *without* replacement after each draw?

9. On a simultaneous throw of two fair dice, what is the probability that the total of the spots on the top faces will equal:
   (a) two?
   (b) three?
   (c) seven?
   (d) eleven?
   (e) three or six?
   (f) seven or eleven?

10. Your bookie tells you that the odds of the Green Bay Packers winning the NFC Championship are 7-to-20 and the odds of the Denver Broncos winning the AFC Championship are 10-to-18. What is the probability that the Packers will meet the Broncos in the Super Bowl (in which the respective champions play)?

11. It's late in the season, and your bookie tells you that the odds of the Washington Redskins winning the NFC Championship are 3-to-2, and the odds of the Buffalo Bills winning the AFC Championship are 4-to-3. What are the odds that the Redskins and the Bills will meet in the Super Bowl?

12. Sophie and Isabel are recent college graduates. Sophie is 22 years old. Isabel is 25 years old. The probability that Sophie will still be alive in twenty-five years is .9979, and the probability she'll be alive in fifty years is .8251. The probability that Isabel will still be alive in twenty-five years is .9571, and the probability that she'll still be alive in fifty years is .6317. What is the probability that:
   (a) either of them will be alive to attend their twenty-five-year class reunion?
   (b) both of them will be alive to attend their twenty-five-year class reunion?

(c) either of them will be alive to attend their fifty-year class reunion?

(d) both of them will be alive to attend their fifty-year class reunion?

(e) what is the probability that neither of them will be alive to attend their fifty-year class reunion?

10.2 Numbers Everywhere: What Do They Mean?

In a 1991 article the environmental activist Barry Commoner lamented the fact that in the first nineteen years that the Environmental Protection Agency operated, pollution levels dropped by only 15 to 20 percent.[5] My local newspaper informs me that the murder rate in the city last year was up 300 percent over the previous year. The price of gasoline has nearly tripled since 1972. That's the bad news.

The good news is that in the first nineteen years that the Environmental Protection Agency operated, the pollution levels dropped at least 15 percent while the population increased by 25 percent. This implies that on a per capita basis, pollution levels are between 18.75 and 25 percent better than they were in 1970. Three people were murdered in the city last year, and, while this was an increase from an all-time low of one murder the year before, the number is only half the average for the last ten years. While the price of gasoline has tripled since 1972, the value of the dollar has dropped to only a fourth of its 1972 level. So gas is cheaper than it used to be!

We are confronted with numbers all the time and asked to reach conclusions on the basis of the number we are given. But by themselves, numbers are meaningless. If you are told that there has been a statistical change, you need to ask to what the comparison is being made and whether the basis for the comparison gives you all the relevant facts. If you are told that something is "above average," you must ask which of the four meanings of 'average' is being applied: whether you are concerned with the mean, the mode, the median, or the midrange. If you are told that a poll shows that 80 percent of those surveyed favor a certain brand of soap, you should ask who was surveyed, how and when the survey was taken, and so forth.

In this section we'll look at some of the questions you should ask when confronted with numerical claims for accepting a conclusion.

Surveys

Let us say you are told that 80 percent of all Americans surveyed favor a certain brand of soap. Does that mean it is a very popular soap? Since a poll or survey is always based on a **sample,** a portion of a certain population of objects or people, the conclusion you should draw depends on who was surveyed and how the survey was conducted. The claim that 80 percent of Americans surveyed preferred a certain brand of soap *suggests* that the population on which the survey was based was a random sample of Americans. In a **random sample,** every object or person in the population in question has an equal chance of being chosen for the survey. A sample is **biased** if it does *not* give every person or object in the population in question an equal chance of being chosen for the survey. For example, if the subjects of the survey were all employees of the company making the soap or all people living in the area in which the soap is produced, there would be grounds for claiming that the sample was biased, that is, that the sample was not representative of the buying habits of the entire class of Americans.[6] So if you are asked to accept a statistical claim based on a survey, it is always proper to ask whether the sample on which the survey was based was randomly selected.

Sometimes it is easy to assure that a sample is randomly selected. Because blood circulates through the body, it makes little difference whether the nurse testing the iron content of your blood draws a sample from your left ring finger or your right leg: it is reasonable to assume that the blood is the same throughout your body. On the other hand, if you are the quality-control officer in a company making auto parts, you cannot assume that there is an equal chance that any part you take off the conveyor belt will be defective. For example, if you pull every twelfth part from the belt, it is possible that each was made by the same machines. A more random selection might be made on the basis of a throw of several dice or a stack of well-shuffled numbered cards.

When polling people, even greater care must be taken to assure that your sample is random. In 1948 it was predicted, on the basis of a telephone poll, that Harry Truman would lose the presidential election. But in 1948 virtually no telephones were found in any house in the country, and a significant number of Truman's supporters did *not* own telephones. The sample was biased: Truman won the election. So in attempting to determine whether there is a bias in the sample, there are a number of questions to ask.

First, does the method of polling itself limit the sample in a significant way? The Truman case shows that in 1948 a telephone poll was not the best method of polling, since there were proportionately more Truman supporters among those who did not own telephones than there were among those who did own phones. In the 1990s, when most people own phones but approximately a quarter of phone numbers are unlisted, choosing numbers randomly from the phone directory, rather than randomly dialing numbers, might also bias your sample. Similarly, if the demographic data show that people in certain income groups more generally return written surveys than do those in other groups, the returns on a written survey might reflect a certain bias.

Second, is the survey targeted to the right audience? If your objective is to find out whether parents of young children favor cloth or disposable diapers, you will need some device in your survey to eliminate those people who do not and have not recently had young children. You might start your survey with a question such as, "Do you have a child under the age of six?"

Third, is the timing of the survey appropriate for its objective? If your objective is to find out what the most popular shows are on television and you randomly call people between the hours of 8:00 a.m. and 5:00 p.m., asking what television program, if any, they are watching at the time, your survey is certain to show that daytime television programs are more popular than those in prime time. On the other hand, such timing would be appropriate if you are attempting to find out which daytime television programs are most popular.

Fourth, are the questions phrased in a neutral way? Most people want to give the "correct" answer to a question, so a biased question will often yield an answer that is consistent with that bias.

Fifth, are the questioners unbiased? In a personal interview, will the dress or demeanor of the questioner suggest that some of the answers are "correct"? If someone was doing a door-to-door survey to find out what soft drink was favored in a certain area, and the interviewer was wearing a T-shirt advertising a certain brand of soft drink, there would be a psychological tendency for those asked to respond in terms of the brand on the shirt. Often an interviewer's bias can be much more subtle than this. If you have a hypothesis that people prefer the taste of Brand-X Cola to any other, the intonation in your voice might be more favorable toward Brand-X than any other brand, suggesting what the "correct" answer to the question is. For this reason, the chances of an unbiased survey are increased if neither the person conducting the survey nor the person being interviewed knows what the specific objective of the survey is.

Finally, how large is the sample? If you are told that 60 percent of the participants in a nationwide taste-test preferred Brand-X Cola to any of the major brands, you should ask how many people were surveyed. Assuming the mechanics of a survey are unbiased on the basis of the criteria we have considered to this point, the greater the number of people surveyed, the greater the probability that the survey is random and the lower the probability of error. Organizations that regularly conduct surveys are able to compare the results of such things as voter-preference surveys with subsequent events, such as election results, to determine the margin of error in their surveys. The **margin of error** in a survey is the percentage by which past experience suggests actual behavior might deviate from the results of the survey within a certain "level of confidence," which is typically 95 percent. So if the results of a survey show that a certain presidential candidate can expect 48 percent of the votes and the survey has a 2 percent margin of error, this indicates that there is a 95 percent chance that the candidate will receive between 46 and 50 percent of the votes. Several years ago the Gallup organization determined that the extent to which the probability of error in its polls decreases as the size of the sample increases is as follows:

SAMPLE SIZE AND SAMPLING ERROR[7]	
NUMBER OF INTERVIEWS	MARGIN OF ERROR (IN PERCENTAGE POINTS)
4,000	±2
1,500	±3
1,000	±4
750	±4
600	±5
400	±6
200	±8
100	±11

If Gallup interviews 4,000 people and concludes that 50 percent of them will vote for a certain candidate, the margin of error shows that as many as 52 percent or as few as 48 percent might vote for the candidate. On the other hand, if Gallup reached the same conclusion from interviewing only a hundred people, as many as 69 percent or as few as 39 percent might vote for the candidate.

As the chart shows, the accuracy of a survey increases with the size of the sample, but it follows a law of diminishing returns: at a certain point the sample size must increase significantly to obtain a small increase in accuracy. If you are constructing a survey, the funds you have available might influence the degree of accuracy of your survey. If you're asked to accept a conclusion on the basis of a survey, you should ask what the margin of error is or how many people were surveyed so that you have a basis for judging the margin of error.

Average

One of the humorist Garrison Keillor's famous remarks about the fictional town of Lake Wobegon, Minnesota, is that all the children are above average. What does that mean? There are two problems with talk of averages. First, there must be a comparison class with respect to which the claim is made. If the children in Lake Wobegon are all very intelligent, they might all have I.Q.s above that of the average child in Minnesota—but, logically, they can't all have I.Q.s above that of the average child in Lake Wobegon. Second, the word 'average' has four meanings; without specifying the meaning of 'average', the statement is still ambiguous. "The average" can be the mean, the mode, the median, or the midrange. The **mean** is the arithmetic average, calculated by dividing the sum of the individual values by the total number of individuals in the reference class. For example, if our instructor tells you that the "average score" on the last test was 81.3, he or she is probably giving you the mean score. The **mode** is the number that occurs most frequently. It might be that on the last test your class took, the mode was 87, that is, of all the scores it was the one that came up most frequently. And there can be more than one mode. If on the last test ten people received an 87, ten people received a 62, and fewer than ten people received every other score, 87 and 62 would both be modes. The **median** is the number which, when the numerical data are placed in ascending order, occurs in the middle. The **midrange** is the point in the arithmetic middle of a range; it is determined by adding the highest number in the range to the lowest number and dividing by two. To understand the distinction between these four meanings of 'average' consider the following example.

Let us say I gave a test with the following results:

Jan	92
Jean	92
Leslie	80
Lou	79
Lynn	76
Pat	72
Sam	69

If I asked which student or students got the average grade on the test, you could answer that Jan, Jean, Leslie, and Lou got *an* average grade. Although Jan and Jean received the highest grades on the test, there were more students who received a 92 than any other grade, so their grade was "average": 92 is the mode. Leslie received an average score. If you add up all the scores on the test and divide by seven (the number of individuals), you get 80: 80 is the mean. Finally, Lou received an average score. Lou received a 79, and the number of students who did better than Lou is exactly equal to the number who did worse: 79 is the median. The midrange score was 80.5: no one received the midrange score.

Because the word 'average' is ambiguous, whenever you are told that something is "average," you should ask what meaning is assigned to that word.

There is a special case, however, that deserves mentioning. If you are analyzing the data from a survey and you discover that the mean, the mode, the median, and the midrange correspond quite closely to one another, you have a **normal probability distribution**. Statisticians have discovered that, in a reasonably large sample, the sampling distributions of many statistics approximate a normal probability distribution. When these statistics are plotted on a graph, the normal probability distribution will approximate a "bell curve," that is, a curve in which the highest point is at the statistical center, and there are comparable distributions in each increment on either side of the highest point. For this reason, a normal probability distribution is strong evidence that your survey was random.

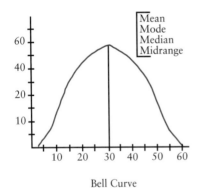

Bell Curve

Figure 10.1 Bell Curve

Summary

When you are given numbers as the basis for accepting a claim, there are various questions you as a critical reasoner should ask:

1. What is the reference class on the basis of which the comparison is being made? Is the reference class appropriate for the conclusion you are asked to draw? Is there an implicit shift in the reference class in proceeding from the premises to the conclusion? Are the numerical claims used as premises meaningful, relevant to the conclusion, and believable? These questions are of particular importance when you are asked to accept a conclusion on the basis of claims of percentages.

2. If you are given the results of a poll or survey, what reason do you have to believe that the sample used was random and the surveying techniques were unbiased?

3. If references are made to an "average" score, are these references to the mean, the mode, the median, or the midrange score?

EXERCISES

What are some of the questions you should ask when judging whether the premises in the following arguments provide good evidence for the conclusion? Explain your answers.

1. The average score on the last test was 32 percent, and my professor grades tests on a curve. Since I scored 50 percent on the test, I should have received more than a D.

2. Nine out of ten doctors surveyed smoke El Ropo Cigars. Assuming doctors do not engage in activities that are detrimental to health, smoking El Ropos must be safe.

3. When the risk of lung cancer from smoking was first announced in the mid-1960s, approximately 25 percent of Americans smoked. Since then, the number of smokers dropped to 23 percent. So the number of smokers is on the decline.

4. Between 1989 and 1991 the number of AIDS cases resulting from heterosexual intercourse increased by nearly 300 percent. So heterosexual intercourse is now the major factor in contracting AIDS.

5. A recent telephone poll shows that the socialist candidate was favored by 53 percent of those contacted. So we may conclude that the socialist candidate will win the election.

6. A recent real-estate survey shows that the average cost of a home in Yourtown is $120,000. Since the rule of thumb is that you should never spend more than three times your income on a house, we may conclude that the average annual income in Yourtown is at least $40,000.

7. The alumni office has discovered that 93 percent of last year's graduates had a job within six months of graduation. We may conclude that the college is very successful in placing its graduates in their chosen fields.

8. A certain brand of soap claims to be 99.44 percent pure.[8] So bars of that brand of soap contain little other than soap.

9. Sixty-four percent of those surveyed believe that dishonesty is a necessary condition for political leadership. Therefore, we may conclude that Americans are not committed to political honesty.

10. There's a 40 percent chance of rain today, so we may conclude that it will rain for 40 percent of the day.

11. My son is an above-average student, so fewer than 50 percent of the students in his class do better than he.

12. Four out of five people in a recent taste test preferred Grandma Sophie's chocolate cake to a leading national brand. Shouldn't you buy Aunt Sophie's?

13. The faculty at a college experienced a 2 percent pay cut in 1990 and no raise in 1991. In 1992 they were given a 2 percent pay raise. Therefore, after the raise in 1992 they received the same pay they'd received before the pay cut in 1990.

14. A survey of 7,500 Americans shows that 69 percent favor a balanced-budget amendment. So, a balanced budget amendment is favored by better than two to one.

15. Only about 40 percent of the aluminum beverage cans sold today are recycled. So, little progress has been made in aluminum recycling since the early 1970s.

NOTES

1. Fermat is also famous for Fermat's Last Theorem—that for $n > 2$, $x^n + y^n = z^n$. Fermat wrote his theorem in the margin of a mathematics books "It is impossible to divide a cube into two cubes, or a fourth power into two fourth powers, or in general any power ad infinitum into two like powers. I have found a rather marvelous proof of this, but the margin is too small to hold it." Fermat never produced the proof, and although most mathematicians believed Fermat was correct, it was not until the early 1990s that the Princeton mathematician Andrew Wiles produced what is considered a viable

proof of Fermat's Last Theorem. For a brief discussion of this see "This Equation Figures to Answer a 17th Century Puzzle," *Washington Post*, August 2, 1993, p. A3.

2. The numbers used here are from the 1958 Commissioners Standard Ordinary Mortality Table. The 1980 mortality table suggests the chances that Aunt Tillie will live to 70 are greater, approximately $753/1000 = .753$. Earlier tables would give her a lower probability of longevity. For example, the 1941 table would yield the calculation that her chances were $454548/883342 = .515$.

3. Statistics compiled by the government indicate that about two million people die annually in the United States alone. Since there are 8,760 hours in a year of 365 days, a mean-average of about 228 people die per hour. So the *odds* that someone will die in the *United States* in the next hour are 228-to-1, that is $228/229 = .9956$. The odds that someone will die in the world within the next hour are considerably higher. On the birthday problem, see Irving Adler, *Probability and Statistics for Everyman* (New York: Signet Books, 1963), pp. 52–55.

4. These statistics are drawn from *Statistical Abstract of the United States* (Washington, D.C.: U.S. Department of Commerce, 1992), p. 82. Other vital statistics mentioned in these problems are drawn from the same source.

5. Barry Commoner, "Why We Have Failed," in *Learning to Listen to the Land*, edited by Bill Willers (Covelo, CA: Island Press, 1991), p. 163.

6. If you are asked to accept a conclusion on the basis of a biased survey, the argument commits the informal fallacy of *suppressed evidence*.

7. Quoted in Charles E. Roll, Jr., and Albert H. Cantril, *Polls: Their Use and Misuse in Politics* (New York: Basic Books, 1972), p. 72.

8. If you have always wondered what this means, see David Feldman, *Why Do Clocks Run Clockwise? and Other Imponderables* (New York: Harper and Row, 1987), pp. 46–47.

Chapter Eleven
Science and Hypothetical Reasoning

In this chapter we look at the scientific method and the reasoning that method employs. We begin with a simple case that illustrates the various elements of the method, and then we look briefly at some historical examples of scientific reasoning.

One night you walk into your apartment, flip the switch on your lamp, and the light does not come on. What do you do? Perhaps you will remember the various science courses you have taken and tell yourself that the problem at hand requires an application of the scientific method. This method has several elements:

1. State the problem.
2. Collect background information.
3. Formulate a hypothesis.
4. Test the hypothesis.
5. Record your procedures and observations.
6. Draw conclusions.[1]

Let us apply these elements in the case of the nonfunctional lamp.

1. State the problem: the lamp does not work and you want to know why, with an eye to repairing the defect.

2. If you are going to figure out why the lamp does not work, you need to know a little about lamps in general and your lamp in particular. Yours is an electric lamp. Many things are necessary for an electric lamp to work. The lamp has to be connected to a source of electricity. There can be no break in the electrical circuit. If the switch is broken, or the filament in the bulb is burned out, or the bulb is not seated properly in the socket, or there is a short in one of the wires, there will be a break in the circuit, and the lamp will not work. So you gather all the information you can on lamps and electrical circuits and as much information as you can find on your particular lamp and the electrical wiring in your house.

3. Why do you gather all that information? The background information gives you necessary conditions for the proper functioning of a lamp, that is, conditions in the absence of which a lamp will not work. But none of that tells you why your lamp is not working at this time. So you formulate a **hypothesis,** that is, you make an educated guess regarding the condition that accounts for the nonfunctionality of your lamp. Hypothesis formation is a creative act; a hypothesis is not mechanically generated by engaging in the scientific method.[2] The background information you have gathered tells you some of the possible problems with the lamp. Your background investigation might even lead you to believe that some conditions more commonly account for nonfunctional lamps than do other conditions. For example, you might discover that the most common cause of dysfunctional lamps is burned-out light bulbs. So you might frame the hypothesis that the problem with your lamp is that the bulb is burned out.

4. Once you have formulated a hypothesis, you need a procedure to test the hypothesis. To do this, you formulate a conditional statement such as this: "If the bulb is burned out and I replace it with a bulb that works, then the lamp will work." The antecedent of the conditional specifies the hypothesis and the procedure in which you engage to test the hypothesis, and the consequent predicts the result of engaging in that procedure. So you test the hypothesis by changing the bulb and turning on the lamp. If the lamp lights, your experiment *tends* to **confirm** your hypothesis, that is, you have found evidence that your hypothesis is true. If the lamp fails to light, you have **refuted** the hypothesis, that is, you have shown that the hypothesis is false. The reasoning involved in this needs further comment.

Consider the case of confirming a hypothesis. Call the hypothesis and proposed procedure that form the antecedent of the conditional *H* and the prediction based upon the hypothesis *P*. What you are attempting to show is that the *H* is true. The sole basis for establishing *H* is that the prediction made is realized. So the form of the argument used is:

If *H* then *P*.
P
_____

H

This argument is an instance of affirming the consequent, which is a fallacious deductive argument (see Chapter 5, Section 2). The most we can infer is that our hypothesis is not false. If a hypothesis is rigorously and repeatedly tested without being disproved, our confidence in its truth is corroborated. In the present case, the success of the prediction provides only *some* reason to believe that by changing the bulb the lamp had been restored to a functional state, for there are numerous conditions that must hold in order for the lamp to function, and it is possible that some factor other than the changing of the bulb was responsible for returning the lamp to a functional state. For example, it might be that your superintendent had been doing some electrical work, and between the time you first tried to turn on the lamp and the time you turned on the lamp with a new bulb, she threw the switch-breaker and reactivated the circuit to the lamp.

On the other hand, if the prediction based on your hypothesis failed, you would have conclusive evidence that the antecedent of your conditional is false. The form of the argument is an instance of *modus tollens*:

If *H* then *P*.
Not-*P*.
_____

Not-*H*.

If you replace the bulb, turn on the lamp, and the lamp still does not work, it shows that the antecedent of the conditional is false: it shows *either* that the bulb is not burned out *or* that the replacement bulb does not work. You might try the new bulb in another lamp to be certain that the problem is with the hypothesis.[3] When the hypothesis fails, it is an occasion for inquiring further into necessary conditions for a functional lamp. So you change your hypothesis suggesting some other condition which, if it held, would result in a functional lamp.

5. In the present case, it is unlikely that you would record your procedures and observations. In a typical scientific experiment, on the other hand, this step is important insofar as it allows others to test the same hypothesis under similar conditions. When experiments are repeated numerous times with the same results, the evidence for the hypothesis is increased—the repetition of the experiment with the same results tends to strengthen the evidence for the truth of the hypothesis.

6. We have already noticed how the experiment helps you draw conclusions: If the predicted event occurs, there tends to be evidence for the truth of the hypothesis; if the predicted event does not occur, the hypothesis is refuted.

The case we have considered is simple and straightforward. If the lamp in your apartment does not work, you go through the various possible causes of the problem in a step-by-step manner until the lamp works again. Though it might seem so, it is not stilted to describe this as an application of the "scientific method," for we reason from hypotheses all the time. If your friend tells you how to get to his or her house, the instructions can be treated as a hypothesis to be confirmed: if you follow the instructions correctly but do not reach your destination, you have shown that the instructions were faulty. If you are a historian and want to explain why the Roman Empire fell, you might propose the hypothesis that when conditions $x, y,$ and z are realized the strength of an empire is decreased, show that these conditions were realized in the late Roman Empire and various other empires shortly before their demise, and take these conditions as probable reasons for the fall of Rome. Religious hypotheses, philosophical hypotheses, sociological hypotheses might be proposed to explain certain phenomena, and the data accepted as grounds for confirming each kind of hypothesis will differ.

In the sciences, the background information you gather before formulating a hypothesis is known as a **theory.** A scientific theory consists of a number of general, well-confirmed hypotheses that will explain why specific phenomena are as they are. The elements of a theory are often known as "natural laws." They provide very general descriptions of the world, and in a theory such statements are deductively related to one another. Returning to the lamp example, statements in the background theory might include "If there is a break in an electrical circuit, then the current will not flow through the circuit." "If the current will not flow through a circuit, then an appliance in that circuit will not function." These allow you to infer that if there is a break in an electrical circuit, then an appliance in that electrical circuit will not function. So the break in the circuit will explain why the lamp will not work, and your task is simply to discover where that break is. Your hypothesis that the problem is that the bulb is burned out might be tied into the theoretical considerations along these lines:

> If the bulb is burned out, then there is a break in the circuit.
> If there is a break in the circuit, then the appliance (lamp) will not work.
> _____
> If the bulb is burned out, then the appliance (lamp) will not work.

There is a great deal of theory that stands behind your hypothesis, and if your experimental trial *fails,* the failure might be due to the falsehood of some element in the theoretical background. Since the elements of theories are no more than well-confirmed hypotheses, they are subject to revision and modification. The history of science is filled with cases in which the failure of predictions led to modifications in the theory behind the hypothesis in question. We now look at two examples of this: Pierre and Marie Curie and the discovery of radium, and Barbara McClintock and the theory of genetic transposition.

The Curies

In the late nineteenth century, it was assumed that chemical elements were distinct and fundamentally different kinds of substances. It was assumed that carbon, for example, was fundamentally different from oxygen and could not be transformed into oxygen. The work of Pierre and Marie Curie did much to change this conception of matter.

In the early 1890s the German scientist Wilhelm von Roentgen discovered that when he sent an alternating current of electricity through a glass vacuum tube covered with black paper, some crystals on the table nearby shone. He concluded that something like light in the tube caused the crystals to shine, and he called these X-rays. In 1896 the French physicist Henri Becquerel asked whether certain substances that became radiant in sunlight also gave off these X-rays, and started working with uranium. A sample of uranium was accidentally left near some wrapped photographic plates in a dark drawer of his desk for several months, after which Becquerel discovered an image on the plates. This implied that the uranium itself was giving off these rays, that uranium did not glow because it absorbed sunlight.

Upon reading of Becquerel's discovery, Marie Curie decided she wanted to find out what made uranium give off the strange rays. First she worked solely with chemical samples containing uranium. Using an electrometer, she concluded that the more uranium there was in a sample, the more rays were given off. She eventually discovered a correlation between the readings of the electrometer and the amount of uranium in a sample. Next she wondered if such rays were given off by other metals, a question that required her to examine every known chemical element. She discovered that thorium also gave off rays like those emitted by uranium. She called the radiance of uranium and thorium "radioactivity." Finally, she decided to examine all the minerals she could obtain and see which ones were radioactive. Her investigations led to a puzzle that resulted in the discovery of radium.

Madame Curie had been examining a sample of pitchblende, a uranium ore. She knew how much uranium the ore contained and how much radioactivity that much uranium should produce. The readings on the electrometer were considerably higher than they should have been if uranium was the only radioactive substance in the pitchblende. She proposed a hypothesis: the additional amount of radiation was caused by an unknown element which she called radium.

When the hypothesis was announced in the scientific literature, the scientific community was less than impressed. "Show us some pure radium," they said. Pierre and Marie Curie devoted the next three years to extracting one decigram (1/10 gram) of pure radium from several tons of pitchblende ore. It was only at that time that the existence of radium was granted.

The discovery of radioactivity had a profound impact on the development of scientific theory. Since the demise of alchemy in the seventeenth century, chemical elements had been considered fundamental and unchangeable; radioactivity showed that this belief was false. Some elements could, through radioactive decay, be transformed into other elements. It also showed that atoms could not be solid, for the suggestion that atoms were solid would not explain either how rays could pass through apparently solid matter or how one element could be transformed into another by means of radioactive decay.

The case of the Curies illustrates several points regarding scientific inquiry. It gives an example of how a hypothesis is often formed when experimental data does not comply with the expected results, that is, the results predicted on the basis of the theories accepted and what is known on the basis of those theories at the time. Marie Curie's initial examination of pitchblende was based on the *assumption* that uranium was the only radioactive element in the ore, but when the "numbers didn't work out," when she could not account for the amount of radiation in a sample of the ore on the basis of that assumption, this suggested that there was another radioactive element or elements in the ore. But to show that the hypothesis was true required that the radium be extracted. By extracting the radium, the Curies provided **empirical evidence,** that is, evidence drawn from experience, for the existence of radium. But how could she know that she had discovered a new element once the radium had been extracted? The basis for that knowledge is the consistency between the empirical evidence and other aspects of the accepted scientific theory of the time. The results were **externally consistent** with at least some aspects of the accepted scientific theories of the time. By the time of the Curies, the Russian chemist Dmitri Ivanovich Mendeleyev had developed the periodic table of the elements, which provided a systematic understanding of the known chemical elements. But there were several gaps in the table. In 1871 Mendeleyev himself predicted the existence and chemical properties of gallium, germanium, and scandium, elements that were subsequently discovered. Because of Mendeleyev's work, there were criteria that at once allowed the Curies to identify radium as a previously unknown element and to understand its nature in a systematic way. Thus, the background theory was necessary both for the empirical confirmation of the existence of radium and the *acceptance* of its existence within the scientific community. As we see in our next example, **external consistency,** that is, the consistency between claims made by a hypothesis for which there appears to be evidence and the ongoing theoretical assumptions of a science, are crucial for the acceptance of the confirmation of a hypothesis.

Barbara McClintock

Barbara McClintock (1902–1992) was an American geneticist. She began her work in the 1920s, and throughout her career her work focused primarily on the genetics of maize *(Zea mays)*. Her early papers are listed among the classics of genetic theory. Among other accomplishments, she is credited with providing conclusive evidence for the chromosomal basis of genetics.

Dr. McClintock's research procedures illustrate the close links between hypothesis, theoretical understanding, and what you can "see" in the world. If you propose the hypothesis that a certain entity exists, your hypothesis will tell you where to look to find it, or where to look to see the consequences of the existence of such a thing. The better you understand the theory that stands behind your hypothesis, the better you understand your experimental subject and the more fully you can integrate the hypothesis into the theory. Directed by her background theory and hypotheses, McClintock had an uncanny ability to "see" the operations of the chromosomes.[4]

Maize, the central element of McClintock's research, is a complex organism. It takes several months for the plants to mature. Most geneticists preferred working with fruit flies *(Drosophilia)* or bacteria and bacteriophages (viruses that multiply in bacteria), since these organisms have a much shorter life-span than maize. So from the beginning the primary object of McClintock's research was outside the mainstream of genetic research. Furthermore, one of her most important discoveries, the discovery of the transposition of genes on a chromosome, that is, the ability to genes to change places on the chromosome and thereby affect the development of the organism, ran headlong into conflicts with accepted genetic theory.

Beginning in 1944, McClintock undertook an investigation of unstable mutations in maize. This study led to her attempt to explain how the genetic material in a single cell regulates the growth of a complex organism. She found that in a significant number of maize plants there were mutations that seemed to arise from adjacent cells. Her hypothesis was that one cell lost material that the other gained, and this resulted in a great increase in green streaks in one sector of the maize plant and greatly decreased streaks in the sector arising from the sister cell. After several years of research, she concluded that there was "a component right adjacent to a gene, and it responded [by dissociating itself] to a signal sent out from another element."[5] Such a hypothesis did not fit with accepted genetic theory in the 1940s, and McClintock developed an elaborate theoretical edifice to account for the phenomenon. She presented the theory, supported by extensive and carefully documented research, in 1951, and an expanded version in 1956. Neither presentation was enthusiastically accepted. Why? Part of the reason was that her work was outside the mainstream of genetic research at the time: her audience did not understand her work. Another reason was that there had been a shift in research emphasis to questions concerning the nature of the gene: this was the era in which research on DNA came to the forefront in genetics. McClintock's conclusions were inconsistent with the working assumption of the time that the genetic claims that were true for the bacterium *Escherichia coli* were also true for higher organisms. And her conclusions were inconsistent with what became the central dogma of genetics in the 1950s, namely, that the genetic information in DNA was not subject to modification.[6]

But McClintock's work was ultimately vindicated. In the early 1960s François Jacob and Jacques Monod argued that protein synthesis in bacteria is not regulated by the structural DNA gene itself, but by two other genes lying adjacent to the structural gene. This tied McClintock's work on maize to the mainstream of genetic research. Since that time the evidence has mounted that the genetics of protein synthesis in organisms of greatly varying degrees of complexity is consistent with the conclusions McClintock drew as early as 1951. In 1983 McClintock was awarded the Nobel Prize in physiology for her work on plant genetics.[7]

This case shows that the conclusions of science form a web. The acceptance of a theory depends, in part, upon the ways in which it can be integrated into the theoretical structures accepted at a given time. Because the discovery of radium was readily integrated into a broader theoretical framework, its existence was accepted once the element itself was extracted from pitchblende in a purified form. Because there was no theoretical framework into which McClintock's account of genetic transposition fit in the 1950s, it was ignored until it could be integrated into a modified genetic theory.

The two previous cases illustrate the importance of the integration of discoveries into the web of scientific knowledge for the acceptance of a theory. The next case allows us to consider some of the grounds for deciding among rival hypotheses.

Einstein: The General Theory of Relativity

By the late 1800s the Newtonian theory of celestial mechanics had served the scientific community for nearly 200 years, but some observations were repeatedly made that were inconsistent with predictions based on that theory. What was the reaction? Did late-nineteenth-century physicists discard Newton's laws? No. As practical people, scientists will not discard a well-confirmed hypothesis on the basis of a few problematic cases until they formulate another hypothesis that will explain both why the problematic hypothesis works where it works and why it fails where it fails. The new hypothesis would have to be more general so that it could explain the limits of the application of the old hypothesis. On the other hand, as theoretical people, scientists attempt to explain why things do not work out as the hypothesis predicts. If the hypothesis is retained, an *ad hoc* hypothesis might be proposed to explain why the earlier hypothesis did not work in a particular case. An *ad hoc* **hypothesis** is a hypothesis posed *solely* to explain why another hypothesis or theory fails in a particular case or kind of case. *Ad hoc* hypotheses can neither be tested nor explained on the basis of a more general theory. They are introduced solely to "save" some other hypothesis.

To understand the conditions under which scientists have posed *ad hoc* hypotheses, let us consider an example. When Newton formulated his laws of motion, it was assumed that there cannot be "action at a distance," that is, that if one object is to have any causal influence on another object at a distance from it, there must be an intermediate chain of objects that are affected by the first object and affect the last. To account for gravitational forces among celestial bodies, Newton posited the existence of "ether," a substance that supposedly fills the universe between such observable bodies as planets. By the late nineteenth century, physicists proposed an experiment to establish the existence of ether. Since the earth travels through space at the rate of 18 miles per second, there should be an ether wind of 18 miles per second that blows past the earth and through the spaces between its atoms. If this is so, it was hypothesized, then light should travel faster when going in the direction of the ether wind than when it travels against it. In 1881 Albert Abraham Michelson constructed an experiment to check this hypothesis. He found that the speed of light remained the same regardless of the direction in which it traveled. In 1887 Michelson and Edward Williams Morley repeated the experiment with the same result. This tended to show that there is no ether wind.

What was the reaction from the scientific community? The Irish physicist George Francis FitzGerald proposed the hypothesis, which the Dutch physicist Hendrick Antoon Lorentz put into elegant mathematical form, that the ether wind puts pressure on a moving object causing it to shrink slightly in the direction of the motion, a contraction that yields the appearance that there is no ether wind. The FitzGerald-Lorentz contraction theory, as it was called, was an *ad hoc* hypothesis to save an element of the Newtonian theory of mechanics.

As the history of science shows, Newtonian mechanics was superseded by Einstein's Theories. Einstein's Theories at once explain why Newton's Theory works very well with respect to the medium-sized objects we see every day—such things as golf balls, automobiles, and the planets of the solar system—and why its predictions fail with respect to subatomic particles and interstellar space. Einstein's Theories also assume that the speed of light is constant, disposing of the ether hypothesis. There were two crucial experiments that tended to show *both* that Einstein's General Theory of Relativity is correct and that Newton's Theory is incorrect. A **crucial experiment** is an experiment that provides strong evidence that one of two opposing hypotheses is correct by showing that the predictions of one hypothesis correspond to the observational data whereas the predictions of the other do not. The first of these crucial experiments concerned the orbit of Mercury, the plant closest to the sun. Mercury's orbit is an ellipse, and the ellipse itself rotates slowly. Newton's law of gravitation explains this on the basis of the gravitational influence of the other planets, but it predicts a slightly slower rotation than is observed. Predictions based on Einstein's General Theory were much closer to what was observed, which tended to confirm Einstein's Theory and refute Newton's. The second and more dramatic experiment occurred in 1919 during a total eclipse of the sun. Newton's physics suggested that there would be a bending of light within the gravitational field of the sun, but Einstein's theory suggested that the bending would be approximately twice as great as Newton's theory suggested. During a solar eclipse the moon blocks the sun's light, and stars very close to the sun's edge become visible. It is the light from these stars that passes through the strongest part of the sun's gravitational field. This posed three possibilities:

1. There would be no change in the apparent position of the stars, which would tend to refute both Newton's Theory and Einstein's Theory.

2. The apparent position of the stars would be close to what Newton's Theory predicted, which would tend to confirm Newton's Theory and refute Einstein's Theory.

3. The apparent position of the stars would be close to what Einstein's Theory predicted, which would tend to confirm Einstein's Theory and refute Newton's Theory.

The observed positions of the stars corresponded closely to Einstein's predictions, which at once tended to confirm his theory and refute Newton's.

Theories give an account of the world, an explanation of phenomena that integrates those phenomena into a larger picture. In the empirical sciences, the theory must be tied to what is observable, although the entities that provide the basis for the explanation are, in many cases, unobservable. If there are atoms and subatomic particles of the sorts that physicists posit, we can understand and explain many phenomena. The theory itself must be **internally consistent**, that is, it must not yield self-contradictory claims. This is the mark of rationality. Further, since the same phenomena can often be explained by more than one theory, aesthetic considerations often come into play. In the sixteenth century, movement of the planets could be predicted on the basis of the assumption that the earth is the center of the universe (the geocentric position) and the assumption that the sun is the center of the universe (the heliocentric position). A geocentric system of astronomy was developed by the second-century Greek astronomer Ptolemy. This system held that the planets revolved around the earth; but since observation showed that the planets occasionally seemed to regress in their movements, the system required that the planetary orbits contain epicycles—circular movements around a point within the orbits of the planets. On the basis of the Ptolemaic system, it was possible to calculate the positions of the planets given their positions at some other time, but the calculations were extremely complex. The Copernican system posited that the sun is the center of the universe. This assumption provided a far easier basis for calculating the movements of the planets, and it is in part because the Copernican system was simpler and more aesthetically appealing that it was accepted. In the past century, disputes in psychology raged between the Freudians, who proposed an elaborate theory of mind—including the id, the superego, and the ego, the ego being the only conscious part of the mind (that of which anyone could claim direct awareness)—and the behaviorists, who maintained that there is no mind distinct from the bodily behavior in which people engage. One of the grounds behaviorists proposed in their favor was that their theory explained everything the Freudian theory explained—but more simply: it posited fewer different kinds of things. So in choosing between two theories, both of which will explain a certain range of phenomena, considerations of simplicity often play a significant role. One theory is simpler relative to another if (1) it allows for simpler calculations, or (2) it contains fewer principles, or (3) it posits fewer different kinds of theoretical entities.

Though the examples we have considered are derived from the natural sciences, the method is the same in history and the social sciences. You cannot do controlled experiments in history, but neither can you do them in astronomy. There are certain moral constraints on experiments in sociology or psychology, but the constraints are neither more nor less severe than in medicine. Historians, for example, look for causes of events, formulate hypotheses, and test their hypotheses against the historical data. Sociologists, psychologists, and economists formulate hypotheses and test them against such things as demographic data, survey results, and census data. In concluding this chapter, we look briefly at an attempt to empirically discover the laws that govern historical development.

Arnold J. Toynbee

Is the history of the world merely a record of random and, in widely separated epochs, causally independent events, or are there discernible recurring patterns? Assuming that there are patterns of historical development, are nations the fundamental units of historical development, or does some other unit more properly constitute the unit by which historical development is to be judged? If there are patterns, what form do they take? Are the patterns linear—laws indicating that if one kind of event occurs, then another kind of event follows—or are they more complex—for example, cyclical?

Arnold J. Toynbee (1889–1975) was a British historian who proposed a theory of history based on the development of civilizations rather than nations. Toynbee's method was empirical: he attempted to discover the laws governing the growth and evolution of a civilization through a comparative study of different historical societies. His theory of history was presented in *A Study of History,* a work in twelve volumes published between 1934 and 1961.

Toynbee's hypothesis was that civilizations develop and evolve in accordance with specifiable laws. Consequently, there are recurring cycles found throughout history as one civilization forms, matures, fades away, and is replaced by another. Toynbee claimed the hypothesis came to him toward the beginning of the First World War.

> The general war of 1914 overtook me expounding Thucydides [the ancient Greek historian] to Balliol [College, Oxford] undergraduates reading for *Literae Humaniores,* and then my understanding was illuminated. The experience we were having of our world now had been experienced by Thucydides in his world already . . . . Whatever chronology might say, Thucydides' world and my world had now proved to be philosophically contemporary. And if this were the true relation between the Graeco-Roman and the Western civilizations, might not the relation between all civilizations known to us turn out to be the same?[8]

Toynbee was not the first to develop a theory of history based on the evolution of civilizations. In his *Decline of the West,* the German philosopher Oswald Spengler (1890–1936) had identified eight civilizations as the basis for his generalizations on history. Toynbee considered this too small a number for an adequate historical generalization, and Spengler had not adequately explained the conditions that account for the rise and decline of civilizations. Toynbee identified twenty-one civilizations in the history of the world, and claimed to find common patterns of growth, breakdown, decay, and dissolution in them. Civilizations are in a stage of growth when they can effectively and creatively respond to the challenges posed by their environments. They are in a stage of decline when they can no longer effectively and creatively respond to such challenges. Furthermore, civilizations are not simply subject to a period of growth followed by a period of decline and dissolution—rather, after the beginning of the decline there is a rally followed by a more rapid decline and dissolution. In the death of one civilization are the seeds from which another will inevitably develop.

Toynbee's theory of history is controversial and has been subject to criticism on a number of fronts. Perhaps the most theoretically significant criticism is that he provides no clear criteria for identifying and differentiating among civilizations. Regardless of the area in which you apply the scientific method, it is crucial that you provide clear criteria for classifying the objects with which you deal. The criteria may be developed to fulfill certain theoretical purposes—the criteria themselves are provided by means of a precising definition (see Chapter 2, Section 3)—but without such criteria the subject matter of the discipline is ambiguous. Since the primary function of a theory is to provide a framework for understanding the world, the classification of objects by means of clearly stated criteria is essential to theoretical understanding. Insofar as the notion of a civilization is central to Toynbee's theory of history, the absence of a precise set of criteria for identifying a civilization prevents us from independently testing his hypotheses against the historical data.[9]

The scientific method has allowed us to make many significant discoveries about the world around us. It provides a set of guidelines for solving problems and testing hypotheses. Historically, its application has been responsible for great advances in our understanding. Insofar as the attainment of knowledge is valuable as such, the scientific method has proven extremely valuable to humankind. Nor is this value decreased by the fact that the same method that has allowed us to discover the cures of numerous diseases also could be used to destroy life as we know it. The scientific method is a conceptual tool, and like any other tool the value resulting from its use depends on the purposes of the user. Just as a scalpel can save a life or terminate one, depending on whether it is in the hands of an accomplished surgeon or a maniac, so the scientific method can be used for good or for ill. But just as the value of the scalpel itself does not change depending on whose hands it is in, so the value of the scientific method as a tool for increasing our understanding of the world does not change with the purposes of its user.

Summary

When you use the scientific or hypothetical method to solve a problem, you state the problem, devise a hypothesis (educated guess) as to the solution to the problem, and test the hypothesis. If a prediction based on your hypothesis is realized, you have some reason to believe that your hypothesis was true. If your prediction fails, your hypothesis was false.

When used in scientific inquiry, a successful test of a hypothesis is one step toward having the truth of the hypothesis accepted. Having the truth of a hypothesis accepted, however, usually requires that it be externally consistent with an accepted theory, that is, that there be a theory which will explain the hypothesis, and, when there are several competing hypotheses, that the hypothesis in question be the simplest hypothesis available.

EXERCISES

I. Research and write a one- to two-page paper on one or more of the following. Try to show how the hypotheses posed by each scientist are consistent or inconsistent with the accepted scientific theory of the time.

1. Aristotle: the embryology of the chick.
2. William Harvey: the circulation of blood.
3. Stephen Hales: the circulation of sap in plants.
4. Louis Pasteur: the discovery of microorganisms as the basis for fermentation.
5. Sigmund Freud: the discovery of the causes of hysteria.
6. A. L. Lavoisier: the discovery of oxygen.
7. Isaac Newton: the nature of colors.
8. Galileo: the discovery of the moons of Jupiter.
9. J. C. Adams: the discovery of Neptune.
10. Wolfgang Pauli: the discovery of the neutrino.
11. J. J. Thompson: the discovery of the electron.
12. E. Tortelli: the discovery of atmospheric pressure.
13. J. Watson and F. Crick: the structure of the DNA molecule.
14. Alfred Wegener: the theory of continental drift.
15. A. A. Michelson and E. W. Morley: the impossibility of detecting the motion of the earth.

16. E. Rutherford: the artificial transmutation of the elements.

17. Konrad Lorenz: the conditions of imprinting.

18. William Beaumont: the process of digestion as chemistry.

19. F. Jacob and E. Wollman: the direct transfer of genetic material.

20. J. J. Gibson: the mechanism of perception.

21. Johannes Kepler: elliptical orbits of the planets.

22. Peter Duesberg: hypotheses on the causes of AIDS.

23. John Wesley Powell: determining the builders and age of Native American burial mounds.

24. Dorothy M. Hodgkin: determining the structure of vitamin B_{12}.

25. Rosalyn S. Yalow: developing the technique of radioimmunoassay.

26. Adam Smith: the invisible hand in economics.

27. I. P. Pavlov: conditioned response.

28. Jean Piaget: stages of cognitive development.

29. Alfred Binet: the development of the intelligent quotient (IQ).

30. John Maynard Keynes: the theory of the business cycle.

31. Margaret Mead: "feminine" and "masculine" personality traits not being linked to sex.

II. Research and write a one- to two-page paper on the causes of one or more of the following events. Clearly state your hypothesis. Indicate what evidence tends to confirm your hypothesis.

1. The First World War.

2. The Great Depression of the 1930s.

3. The rise of Japan as a military power prior to the Second World War.

4. The defeat of the United States in the Vietnam War.

5. The election of Bill Clinton as President of the United States in 1990.

NOTES

1. This list of elements of the scientific method follows that in Harvey D. Goodman, Linda E. Graham, Thomas C. Emmel, Frances M.

Slowiczek, and Yaakov Schechter, *Biology* (Orlando: Harcourt Brace Jovanovich, 1989), pp. 25–27. This is a standard list of the elements of the method, although not all the elements of the method will be used in each case. For example, in the present case it is doubtful that you will record your procedures and observations; in a scientific context you would make a careful record so someone else could repeat the same experiment.

2. Sometimes hypotheses are literally dreamed up. In the mid-nineteenth century, Frederich August Kekule discovered the ring structure of benzene. He claimed the hypothesis came to him while in a doze before the fire. "Long chains [of atoms] here and there [were] more firmly joined; all winding and turning with snake-like motion. Suddenly one of the serpents caught its own tail and the ring thus formed was exasperatingly before my eyes. I woke as if by lightning, and spent the rest of the night working out the logical consequences of the hypothesis." Quoted in Alfred B. Garrett, *The Flash of Genius* (New York: D. Van Nostrand Company, 1963), p. 86.

3. Lamp experts might correctly suggest that this is a somewhat simplified account. If the new bulb works in another lamp, but not in the problematic lamp, this does not necessarily show that the original hypothesis that the bulb was burned out was false. It is a fact that different brands of light bulbs do not seat in a socket in the same way. So, if the original bulb was Brand-X, and the bulb you use in your experimental trial is Brand-Y, it is possible that the Brand-Y bulb did not touch the electrical contact in the socket, and it did not work for that reason.

4. For some descriptions of her ability to "see" the operations of the chromosomes in cells, see Evelyn Fox Keller, *A Feeling for the Organism: The Life and Work of Barbara McClintock* (New York: W. H. Freeman and Company, 1983), pp. 117, 149, and 198.

5. Quoted in Keller, *A Feeling for the Organism*, p. 125.

6. In addition to these, some people have argued that McClintock was a victim of sexism, that her theories were ignored because she was a woman in an area dominated by men. See, for example, Evelyn Fox Keller, *Reflections on Gender and Science* (New Haven, CT: Yale University Press, 1985).

7. McClintock is certainly not unique in the history of science as a person who was correct but whose work went unnoticed for a number of years. In 1929 Alexander Fleming published a paper in which he announced the discovery of penicillin. His discovery was ignored for

a decade until, in 1939, Dr. Howard H. Florey noticed Fleming's paper and constructed his own experiments on the medicinal value of penicillin. Florey's experiments tended to confirm Fleming's conclusions, penicillin took its place in the arsenals of medicine. See Lucy Kavaler, *Mushrooms, Molds, and Miracles* (New York: Signet Books, 1965), pp. 108–110.

8. Quoted in William H. McNeill, *Arnold J. Toynbee: A Life* (New York: Oxford University Press, 1989), p. 94.

9. For a more complete account of Toynbee's theory and criticisms of it, see William H. Dray, *Philosophy of History,* Foundations of Philosophy Series (Englewood Cliffs, N.J.: Prentice-Hall, 1964), pp. 82–97.

Appendix 1
Traditional Names
for Syllogistic Forms
and Conditional Validity

In traditional (Aristotelian) logic, there are names for various argument forms. Because you might find references to these names in your readings, it is useful to become acquainted with them.

The traditional names of the syllogisms allow you to read off the mood of the syllogism on the basis of the order of the vowels in the name, the vowels denoting the kind (quantity and quality) of categorical proposition involved. *Barbara,* for example, is an argument of the form AAA-1:

> All M is P.
> All S is M.
> ———————
> All S is P.

Notice here that the vowels in the name 'Barbara' denote the kinds of categorical propositions in the argument. So, if you are given that a name represents an argument of a certain figure, it is easy to read off the mood of the argument. As an exercise, give a schematic representation of the argument forms denoted by the following names.

The arguments of the first figure are: Barbara, Celarent, Darii, and Ferio.

The arguments of the second figure are: Cesare, Camestres, Festino, and Baroco.

The arguments of the third figure are: Darapti, Felapton, Disamis, Datisi, Bocardo, and Ferason.

The arguments of the fourth figure are: Bramantip, Camenes, Dimaris, Fesapo, and Fresison.

When students have learned categorical logic by memorizing the names of the valid syllogistic forms, they have often done so by memorizing the following poem:

Barbara, Celarent, Darii, and Ferio que prioris [are first].
Cesare, Camestres, Festino, and Baroco, secundae [second].
Tertia [Third] Darapti, Felapton, Disamis, Datisi, Bocardo, and Ferason, habet: quatra insuper addit [hold: fourth are added to the above]
Bramantip, Camenes, Dimaris, Fesapo, and Fresison.

If you constructed a schematic representation of each of these argument forms, you might have noticed something surprising: on the Aristotelian interpretation there are more valid argument forms than on the Boolean interpretation of syllogistic logic. In particular, *Darapti* (AAI-3), *Ferason* (EAO-3), *Bramantip* (AAI-4), and *Fesapo* (EAO-4) are valid, whereas they are invalid on the Boolean interpretation. Why is that? On the Aristotelian interpretation universal propositions have existential import; on the Boolean interpretation they do not. To illustrate how and where this makes a difference, let us first consider *Darapti* (AAI-3), *Ferason* (EAO-3), and *Fesapo* (EAO-4). The schematic representations of these arguments are as follows:

Daraoti	*Ferason*	*Fesapo*
All M are P.	No M is P.	No P is M.
All M are S.	All M is S.	All M is S.
Some S is P.	Some S is not P.	Some S is not P.

On the Boolean interpretation, each of these commits the Existential Fallacy (EF). But if you interpret universal propositions to have existential import, then the minor premise in each case asserts that "Some M is S" as well as that "All M is S," and corresponding to each of these is a valid syllogistic form on the Boolean interpretation, namely, AII-3, EIO-3, and EIO-4. Similarly, if you interpret the major premise in the two arguments of figure three as entailing their corresponding particular affirmative or particular negatives, you will find that there is a valid form on the Boolean interpretation, namely, IAI-3 and OAO-3. On the Boolean interpretation, arguments of the mood and figure AAI-3, EAO-3, and EAO-4 are **conditionally valid**—valid *on the condition that* the middle term picks out an object that exists.

Similarly, *Bramantip* (AAI-4) is conditionally valid, although here the validity is dependent on the assumption that the major term picks out an object that exists. The schematic representation of *Bramantip* is:

All P is M.
All M is S.
_____

Some S is P.

If the major premise is interpreted as having existential import, that is, it is interpreted as asserting that "Some P is M" as well as "All P is M," the conclusion follows. On the Boolean interpretation an AAI-4 is valid *on the condition that* the major term picks out an existent object, that is, when it can be interpreted as an IAI-4.

Finally, there are five additional conditionally valid forms, namely, AAI-1, EAO-1, AAI-2, EAO-2, and AEO-4:

All M are P.	No M are P.	All P are M.
All S are M.	All S are M.	All S are M.
Some S are P.	Some S are not P.	Some S are P.

No P are M.	All P are M.
All S are M.	No M is S.
Some S are not P.	Some S is not P.

In these cases, if the minor premise is interpreted as asserting *both* a particular and a universal, the conclusion will follow on the Boolean interpretation, that is, the conclusion follows *on the condition that* the minor term picks out an existent object. Notice that in the cases of an AAI-1, EAO-1, AAI-2, EAO-2, you can substitute a particular affirmative for the minor premise to yield an argument form that is valid on the Boolean interpretation, namely, AII-1, EIO-1, AOO-2, and EIO-2. Such a simple substitution *cannot* be done in the case of an AEO-4, since an AOO-4 commits the fallacy of Undistributed Middle. Nonetheless, if the minor premise in an AEO-4 is interpreted as having existential import, that is, if it is interpreted as *both* an E proposition and an I proposition, the conclusion follows: there is not, however, a corresponding valid form in figure four. (There is, however, a corresponding valid form in figure two. Since an E proposition is logically equivalent to its converse, the minor premise of an AEO-4, "No M is S," is equivalent to "No S is M," and an AOO-2 is valid on the Boolean interpretation.)

You might ask why there are no traditional names for condition-ally valid arguments of the forms AAI-1, EAO-1, AAI-2, EAO-2, and AEO-4. The answer is that there are, but the allusion to the particular conclusion is implicit. Remember, on the Aristotelian interpretation uni-versal propositions have existential import. So if the conclusion of an argument is a universal proposition, it is taken to assert *both* a univer-sal and a particular. So the form *Barbara* represents *both* an AAA-1 *and* an AAI-1.

Cases of conditional validity are summarized in the following table:

Conditional Validity

Figure 1	Figure 2	Figure 3	Figure 4	Required Condition
AAI	AEO		AEO	S exists
EAO	EAO			
		AAI	EAO	M exists
		EAO		
			AAI	P exists

Why should we worry about conditional validity? Logicians favor the Boolean interpretation of syllogistic logic because there are univer-sal propositions having no existential import that are true (see Chapter 4, Section 2). Nonetheless, the Aristotelian assumption is quite "natu-ral," especially in cases in which most informed people would recog-nize the truth of both a universal proposition and its corresponding par-ticular. For example, if someone argued:

All musicians are people who enjoy music.
All people who practice an instrument daily are musicians.

Some people who practice an instrument daily are people who en-joy music.

most people would accept the conclusion, since most people recognize that there are people who practice an instrument daily. So if you are looking at everyday arguments, there will be cases in which an arguer will use conditionally valid forms. If the relevant assumptions of exis-tential import are true, the arguer should not be faulted.

Appendix 2
The Paradoxes of Material Implication

A conditional statement of the form "$p \to q$" is true except when the antecedent (p) is true and the consequent (q) is false. This is often seen as puzzling and paradoxical when the statement is true in virtue of a false antecedent. There is no problem with the cases in which either both the antecedent and consequent are true or in which the antecedent is true and the consequent is false, since such situations comply with our ordinary understandings of the expression "if . . . then . . ." For example, everyone will grant that the statement "If someone turns the key in your car, then the car starts" is true if you turn the key and the car starts, and that it is false if you turn the key and the car does not start. You might find it puzzling that cases in which no one turns the key and the car starts or no one turns the key and the car does not start show that the statement "If someone turns the key in your car, then the car starts" is true. Similarly, assuming that 'unicorn' is defined as a horse that has one horn in the middle of its forehead and that there are no unicorns, it might seem odd that both the statement "If Dobbin is a unicorn, then Dobbin is a horse with one horn in the middle of its forehead" and the statement "If Dobbin is a unicorn, then Dobbin is a horse with two horns in the middle of its forehead" are true. Finally, regardless of the truth value of the consequent, you might find it strange that the statement, "If the United States is in Europe, then the Dow-Jones average will drop 1,000 points next Tuesday" is true.

By definition, the material conditional is true except when the antecedent is true and the consequent is false. The truth value of a material conditional has nothing to do with the content of the statements joined by the arrow; it depends only on the truth values of its component statements. But the relation of material implication is neither the only kind of implication nor the only relationship expressed by an "If . . . then . . ." statement. In the cases that seem paradoxical, the relationship between the antecedent and the consequent is *not* the relation of material implication. In the statement "If someone turns the key in your car, then the car starts," the conditional statement expresses a *causal* relation: turning the key causes the car to start. The statement seems paradoxical if no one turns the key but the car starts because the word 'cause' is ambiguous. Causal relations are often understood as expressing both necessary and sufficient conditions for a phenomenon (see Chapter 9, Section 2), that is, as expressing the conjunction of two conditional statements: "If the key is turned, then the car starts, and if the car starts, then the key was turned," a claim of material equivalence. If the causal conditional is understood as expressing only a sufficient condition, then a false antecedent and a true consequent is less puzzling. There is more than one sufficient condition that will cause a car to start, as anyone whose car has been "hot-wired" will attest.)

In the case of the statement "If Dobbin is a unicorn, then Dobbin is a horse with two horns in the middle of its forehead," the conditional statement assumes a definitional relationship between 'unicorn' and 'a horse with two horns in the middle of its forehead'. It could be paraphrased as " 'Dobbin is a unicorn' means 'Dobbin is a horse with two horns in the middle of its forehead'," which is false. Finally, the statement "If the United States is in Europe, then the Dow-Jones average will drop 1,000 points next Tuesday" seems paradoxical only if you take the expression to express *logical* implication, for then it would show that a false statement shows that another statement is true. But this is a confusion between two meanings of 'implication'. Material implication is *only* a relation between the truth values of the antecedent and the consequent of a conditional statement. Logical implication requires more, namely, an additional premise asserting the truth of the antecedent. (*Modus ponens* expresses *logical* implication.)

So the appearance of paradox in cases in which the antecedent of a material condional is false rests upon confusions between material implication and causal claims, definitional claims, or claims of logical implication.

Appendix 3
Truth Trees

A.1 Propositional Logic

The truth-table technique allows you to determine whether any argument in propositional logic is valid, but it is not the only technique that allows you to do so. In this section we examine a technique called "truth trees." It is like the truth-table technique insofar as it is a *purely mechanical method of proof,* that is, it is a procedure which, if correctly applied, will show whether an argument is valid while requiring the user only to recognize statement forms.

The truth-tree technique proceeds by the method of *reductio ad absurdum,* that is, it assumes as an additional premise the denial of the conclusion and draws out the consequences. If the argument is valid, the additional premise will yield a contradiction, that is, for some proposition p, you will conclude both p and its denial ($\sim p$). If the argument is invalid, you will reach no contradictory conclusions. The rationale is straightforward. If the original premises *plus the denial of the conclusion* are inconsistent, then anything follows from the extended list of premises—most notably, the original conclusion. On the other hand, if the original argument is invalid, then the denial of the conclusion will yield a consistent set of premises, and no contradiction will be generated.

The truth-tree technique assumes a set of rules that are used to break complex propositions down into their simple components. Where "α" and "β" are *metavariables* that can be replaced by *any statement whatsoever, regardless of its degree of complexity and regardless of whether the statement replacing the variable is negated,* the following Rules of Inference are used to "decompose" complex statements:

Rules of Inference

Conditional	Conjunction	Disjunction	Biconditional
$\alpha \rightarrow \beta$	$\alpha \;\&\; \beta$	$\alpha \lor \beta$	$\alpha \leftrightarrow \beta$
/ \	α	/ \	/ \
~α β	β	α β	α ~α
			β ~β
Negated Conditional	Negated Conjunction	Negated Disjunction	Negated Biconditional
~$(\alpha \rightarrow \beta)$	~$(\alpha \;\&\; \beta)$	~$(\alpha \lor \beta)$	~$(\alpha \leftrightarrow \beta)$
α	/ \	~α	/ \
~β	~α ~β	~β	~α α
			β ~β

Erase or cross out all double tildes (~~).[1]

There is an important point to keep in mind when using these rules. With the exception of the rule "Erase or cross out all double tildes," *the rules pertain to an entire line of a proof.* The rules require that you look for the principal connective in an affirmative statement and the principal connective in the negated statement. Remember also that the metavariables might be replaced by *negative* as well as affirmative statements.

In constructing a truth tree, you begin by stating all the premises and the negation of the conclusion. As you apply each of the Rules of Inference, you place a check mark (✔) in front of the premise you use and construct the appropriate "branch" of the tree. If an application of a rule yields a branch containing a compound statement, that statement should be checked and the rule germane to a statement of that form should be applied. After applying a rule, read *up* the branch to see whether a statement and its negation are contained on that branch. If there is a statement and its negation, the branch is closed. You indicate that the branch is closed by placing an "X" at the end of the branch. If there is an open branch, apply a rule to another premise, appending the result to all open branches *below* it. If all the branches of the tree are closed after applying the branching rules to all the premises and any compound statements that remain after applying the rules to the premises, the argument is valid. If any branch remains open after applying the branching rules to all the premises and any compound statements that remain after applying the rules to the premises, the argument is invalid. You can see how this proof technique works by considering some examples.

Assume you are given the argument form:

$p \lor q$
$\sim q \quad /\therefore \quad p$

You begin by writing the premises followed by the denial of the conclusion in the middle of the page—you write them in the middle of the page because trees can "branch" in many directions.

$p \lor q$
$\sim q \quad /\therefore \quad p$
$\sim p$

The premises together with the denial of the conclusion are known as the "trunk" of your tree.

Next you check the first premise—the only compound premise in the argument to which a rule applies—and apply the rule by adding a "split branch" below the trunk:

$\swarrow p \lor q$
$\sim q \quad /\therefore \quad p$
$\sim p$
$/ \ \backslash$
$p \quad q$

Next, you follow each branch of the tree up through the trunk to see if you can find the denial of that statement *higher* on the tree. In this case, the branch with p at the bottom has $\sim p$ above it, and the branch with q at the bottom has $\sim q$ above it. At the bottom of each branch containing both a statement and its denial, you place an "X," indicating that the branch is "closed." Thus, as you continue, your tree looks like this:

$\swarrow p \lor q$
$\sim q \quad /\therefore \quad p$
$\sim p$
$/ \ \backslash$
$p \quad q$
$X \quad X$

If all the branches are closed, the argument is valid. We see here that all the branches are closed, so we have shown that the argument is valid.

Now assume you are given an argument of this form:

$$p \rightarrow q$$
$$\sim p \quad /\therefore \quad \sim q$$

You proceed in the same way, beginning by appending the denial of the conclusion to the trunk of the tree:

$$p \rightarrow q$$
$$\sim p \quad /\therefore \quad \sim q$$
$$q$$

Notice that the denial of the conclusion is $\sim \sim q$ and, following the last rule, we erased the double tildes. Next we check the first premise and apply the rule for the arrow, appending the result to the trunk:

$$\nu p \rightarrow q$$
$$\sim p \quad /\therefore \quad \sim q$$
$$q$$
$$/ \ \backslash$$
$$\sim p \quad q$$

Tracing the statements at the bottom of the tree up through the branches, you will notice that *neither* branch closes. Since *at least one* branch did not close, the argument is *invalid*.

The procedure is the same as the arguments become more complex, as you can see from the following argument form:

$$p \rightarrow q$$
$$q \rightarrow (r \ \& \ s)$$
$$\sim q \quad /\therefore \quad \sim p \ \& \ (r \lor s)$$

Once again, you begin by appending the denial of the conclusion to the trunk, applying all the Rules of Inference, and checking the complex statements as you go. As you append a statement at the end of each branch, you trace it back through the higher branches to determine whether that statement and its denial is found on the same branch, closing the branch if there is an inconsistent pair of statements. Following this procedure, you construct the tree for the argument:[2]

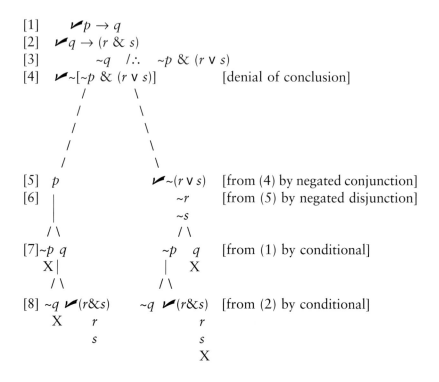

[1]   ✔$p \rightarrow q$
[2]   ✔$q \rightarrow (r \ \& \ s)$
[3]   ~q /∴   ~p & $(r \lor s)$
[4]   ✔~[~p & $(r \lor s)$]   [denial of conclusion]

[5] p ✔~$(r \lor s)$ [from (4) by negated conjunction]
[6] | ~r [from (5) by negated disjunction]
                                 ~s
     / \   / \
[7]~p q ~p q [from (1) by conditional]
   X | | X
   / \   / \
[8] ~q ✔$(r\&s)$ ~q ✔$(r\&s)$ [from (2) by conditional]
    X r r
         s s
                                  X

Notice that two branches are open. Since an argument is invalid if even one branch is open, the argument is *invalid*.

Tips for Pruning Trees

As any gardener will tell you, it is important for the health and well-being of your trees to keep them properly pruned. In the case of truth trees, it is important to keep them properly pruned for the health and well-being (sanity) of the person constructing the tree. It is important to stress, however, that *the order in which you apply the rules to the premises makes no difference with regard to determining whether the argument is valid*. These tips simply suggest ways of keeping the number of branches to a minimum.

1. Apply the rules first to statements that yield *straight* branches (that extend the trunk, but do not generate additional branches). These are the rules for the ampersand, the denial of a conditional, and the denial of a disjunction.

2. When using rules that generate split branches, apply the rules to statements in such a way that you can close one of the split branches whenever possible. (Knowing when this will work comes with practice.)

SUMMARY

1. Append the denial of the conclusion to the trunk of the truth tree.
2. Apply a rule, putting a check mark beside the compound statement to which the rule is applied.
3. Read back up each branch of the tree to see if it contains a statement and its denial.
4. If a branch contains *both* a statement and its denial, close the branch by placing an "X" at the bottom of the branch.
5. If, when all premises and the negated conclusion have been used, an "X" appears at the bottom of each branch, that is, if every branch is closed, the argument is valid. If any branch remains open, the argument is invalid.

EXERCISES

Construct a truth tree to determine whether the exercises in Chapter 5, Section 2 are valid.

A.2 Predicate Logic

The truth-tree procedure for predicate logic[3] is nothing more than an extension of the procedure for propositional logic: you construct a tree and the tree shows that the argument is valid *provided that* all the branches of the tree close. Unlike propositional logic, however, in predicate logic the truth-tree technique will *not* allow you to show that an argument is invalid.[4] To extend the truth-tree method to predicate logic, you need only notice how to eliminate quantifiers and how to deal with negative quantifiers. Beyond that, you proceed in exactly the same way in predicate logic as in propositional logic.

Rule of Quantifier Negation

If you are given a statement with a negative quantifier, check the statement, move the negation sign "across" the quantifier, and replace a universal quantifier with an existential quantifier or an existential quantifier with a universal quantifier. The resulting statements should be appended to the trunk of the tree. For example, if you are given:

$\sim(\exists x)\ (Px\ \&\ Qx)$

you write:

$$\checkmark\sim(\exists x)\ (Px\ \&\ Qx)$$
$$(x)\sim\ (Px\ \&\ Qx)$$

If you are given:

$\sim(x)\ (Px \rightarrow Qx)$

you write:

$$\checkmark\sim(x)\ (Px \rightarrow Qx)$$
$$(\exists x)\sim\ (Px \rightarrow Qx)$$

Universal Instantiation

If you are given a statement with a universal quantifier, the variables in that statement can be replaced by *any* constant whatsoever. Replacing a variable with a constant is called "instantiating" (making an instance of) a universal proposition. Further, since the variable can be replaced by any constant, you can instantiate the same statement several times. To keep track of the constants for which you have instantiated the statement, you should "check it for a constant," that is, check the statement and note the constant for which the statement has been instantiated, and add the instantiated statement to the trunk or all open branches of the tree. For example, consider the following argument:

$$(x)\ (Hx \rightarrow Mx)$$
$$Ha \quad /\therefore \quad Ma$$

Begin by appending the negation of the conclusion to the trunk:

$$(x) \ (Hx \rightarrow Mx)$$
$$Ha \qquad /\therefore \quad Ma$$
$$\sim Ma$$

Next, instantiate the universal proposition for "a" and show that you are instantiating for "a" by placing an "a" over your check mark:

$$\overset{a}{\cancel{(}}x) \ (Hx \rightarrow Mx)$$
$$Ha \qquad /\therefore \quad Ma$$
$$\sim Ma$$
$$Ha \rightarrow Ma$$

Finally, apply the rules for propositional logic to the instantiated statement:

$$\overset{a}{\cancel{\nearrow}} (x) \ (Hx \rightarrow Mx)$$
$$Ha \qquad /\therefore \quad Ma$$
$$\sim Ma$$
$$Ha \rightarrow Ma$$
$$/ \quad \backslash$$
$$\sim Ha \quad Ma$$
$$X \qquad X$$

Since both of the resulting branches close, the argument is valid.

Existential Instantiation

The procedure for existential instantiation is the same as that for universal instantiation, with this restriction: *always instantiate an existential proposition for a constant that has not previously been introduced into the tree.* The reason for the restriction should be obvious. It is true that someone is the present president of the United States. If you have already instantiated a universal proposition for Henry Kissinger *(k),* to instantiate the proposition "$(\exists x) \ (Px)$," where "Px" is "x is the present president of the United States," k would yield a false statement. Hence, although you can instantiate a particular statement any number of times for *randomly chosen constants,* you must *always* instantiate a particular statement *before* you instantiate a universal proposition for the same variable.

The procedure for instantiating a particular proposition is identical with that for instantiating a universal proposition: check the particular statement for a particular constant and append an instantiated statement to the trunk or all open branches of the tree. For example, assume you are given the following argument:

$$(\exists x)\ (Px\ \&\ {\sim}Tx)$$
$$(x)\ (Px \rightarrow Cx)\quad /\therefore\quad (\exists x)\ (Cx\ \&\ {\sim}Tx)$$

Begin by appending the denial of the conclusion to the trunk:

$$(\exists x)\ (Px\ \&\ {\sim}Tx)$$
$$(x)\ (Px \rightarrow Cx)\quad /\therefore\quad (\exists x)\ (Cx\ \&\ {\sim}Tx)$$
$${\sim}\ (\exists x)\ (Cx\ \&\ {\sim}Tx)$$

Since you have a negative quantifier, you might next use the rule for quantifier negation to change the denial of the conclusion to a universal statement:

$$(\exists x)\ (Px\ \&\ {\sim}Tx)$$
$$(x)\ (Px \rightarrow Cx)\quad /\therefore\quad (\exists x)\ (Cx\ \&\ {\sim}Tx)$$
$$\text{✔}{\sim}\ (\exists x)\ (Cx\ \&\ {\sim}Tx)$$
$$(x){\sim}\ (Cx\ \&\ {\sim}Tx)$$

Next you instantiate the first premise for "a," where "a" is a randomly chosen constant:

$$\text{✔}^{a}(\exists x)\ (Px\ \&\ {\sim}Tx)$$
$$(x)\ (Px \rightarrow Cx)\quad /\therefore\quad (\exists x)\ (Cx\ \&\ {\sim}Tx)$$
$$\text{✔}\ {\sim}\ (\exists x)\ (Cx\ \&\ {\sim}Tx)$$
$$(x)\ {\sim}\ (Cx\ \&\ {\sim}Tx)$$
$$Pa\ \&\ {\sim}Ta$$

Since you have a statement that will yield a straight branch, check the statement you have appended to the trunk and add Pa and ~Ta to the trunk:

$\cancel{(\exists x)}^a$ (Px & ~Tx)
    (x) (Px → Cx)   /∴   (∃x) (Cx & ~Tx)
$\cancel{~}$ (∃x) (Cx & ~Tx)
   (x) ~ (Cx & ~Tx)
       Pa & ~Ta
          Pa
        ~Ta

Next, instantiate the second premise for *a* and apply the appropriate rule to the resulting singular statement:

$\cancel{(\exists x)}^a$ (Px & ~Tx)
$\cancel{(x)}^a$ (Px → Cx)   /∴   (∃x) (Cx & ~Tx)
$\cancel{~}$ (∃x) (Cx & ~Tx)
   (x) ~ (Cx & ~Tx)
       Pa & ~Ta
         Pa
        ~Ta
       Pa → Ca
         / \
        / \
       /   \
    ~Pa   Ca
    X

Finally, instantiate the fourth statement in the trunk for "a," apply the appropriate rule to the resulting statement, and close the tree:

$\cancel{(\exists x)}^a$ (Px & ~Tx)
$\cancel{(x)}^a$ (Px → Cx)   /∴   (∃x) (Cx & ~Tx)
$\cancel{~}$ (∃x) (Cx & ~Tx)
$\cancel{(x)}^a$ ~ (Cx & ~Tx)
       Pa & ~Ta
         Pa
        ~Ta
       Pa → Ca
         / \
        / \
       /   \
    ~Pa   Ca
    X ~ (Ca & ~Ta)
            / \
        ~Ca Ta
         X   X

And with this, the argument is shown to be valid.

The procedure is exactly the same once you introduce relations (multiplace predicates) and more than one quantifier in a statement. For example, if you are given the following argument:

(x) $[Px \rightarrow (\exists y)$ $(Qy$ & $Rxy)]$
(x) $(Px$ & $Qx)$ $/\therefore$ $(\exists x)$ $(\exists y)$ (Rxy)

the truth tree is:

$$(x) [Px \rightarrow (\exists y) (Qy \text{ & } Rxy)]$$
$$(x) (Px \text{ & } Qx) \quad /\therefore \quad (\exists x) (\exists y) (Rxy)$$
$$\sim (\exists x) (\exists y) (Rxy)$$
$$(x) \sim (\exists y) (Rxy)$$
$$(x) (y)\sim Rxy$$
$$Pa \rightarrow (\exists y) (Qy \text{ & } Ray)$$
$$Pa \text{ & } Qa$$
$$Pa$$
$$Qa$$
$$/ \quad \backslash$$
$$\sim Pa \qquad (\exists y) (Qy \text{ & } Ray)$$
$$Qb \text{ & } Rab$$
$$Qb$$
$$Rab$$
$$(y) \sim Ray$$
$$\sim Rab$$
$$X$$

Once the system of predicate logic is expanded to include identity, two more rules are needed. The first is the **Rule for $\alpha = \beta$:**

> If any open branch contains a statement of the form "$\alpha = \beta$," where "α" and "β" represent any constant (names), you may add a statement at the bottom of the branch by replacing every instance of "α" in a statement higher in the branch with an instance of "β."

In applying the Rule for $\alpha = \beta$, you should check the statement in which you make the substitution for the constant you substitute. The rationale for this rule is as follows: A true identity claim says that there is one object that goes by two names. "George Eliot was Marian Evans Cross" and "Elizabeth II is the present queen of England" are examples of true identity statements. So the truth value of the statement "George Eliot wrote *The Mill on the Floss* " remains the same if you substitute 'Marian Evans Cross' for 'George Eliot'. Given this rule, we can easily construct a truth tree for the following argument:

> Wog
> p = o   /∴   Wpg

The truth tree is as follows:

$$\begin{array}{c}
\text{⊬Wog} \\
\text{p = o} \quad /\!\!\therefore \quad \text{Wpg} \\
\sim\text{Wpg} \\
\text{Wpg} \\
\text{X}
\end{array}$$

The second rule is the **Rule for ~($\alpha = \alpha$):**

> Close any branch that contains a sentence of the form ~($\alpha = \alpha$), where "α" represents any constant (name).

The rationale for this rule is that since every object is identical with itself, if the premises of an argument yield the negation of a claim of self-identity, the premises are inconsistent. The discovery that there is an inconsistency on the branch of a tree allows you to close the branch with an "X." So if one of the branches of your truth tree contained the following statements,

> ~ (s = b)
> a = s
> b = a

you could make replacement by the Rule of $\alpha = \beta$ and close the branch by means of the Rule for ~($\alpha = \alpha$) as follows:

$$\begin{array}{c}
\text{⊬ (s = b)} \\
\text{a = s} \\
\text{⊬b = a} \\
\text{b = s} \\
\sim \text{(s = s)} \\
\text{X}
\end{array}$$

One final point should be noted. Identity is a **symmetrical relation,** that is, for any constants or variables "α" and "β," if α is identical with β, then β is identical with α. This fact about the relation of identity may be assumed in applying the identity rules. So, if in a branch of a tree you have a statement of the form "~(α = β)" and a statement of the form "β = α," you may close the branch. So the previous example could be shortened to:

$$\sim(s = b)$$
$$a = s$$
$$\cancel{b} = a$$
$$b = s$$
$$X$$

Summary

1. Instantiate particular propositions before instantiating universal propositions.

2. Any universal or particular proposition can be instantiated for any number of constants.

3. It is permissible, and sometimes necessary, to instantiate a universal proposition for more than one constant.

EXERCISES

I. Single quantifiers and monadic predicates: construct truth trees for the exercises in Chapter 7, Section 2.

II. Multiple quantifiers and relations: construct truth trees for exercise sets II and III in Chapter 7, Section 6.

III. Identity: construct truth trees for exercise sets I and III in Chapter 7, Section 7.

Notes

1. The rules convert all compound propositions to either conjunctions or disjunctions. Straight branches are cases in which both simpler statements in the given must be true for the statement to be true.

Split branches are cases in which the simpler statements on at least one branch must be true if the statement is true.

2. The line numbers, allusions to the rules, and vertical lines are added in this tree only to make the procedures clearer; they are not proper parts of the tree.

3. This is strictly a discussion of the application of the truth-tree method to predicate logic. For a discussion of predicate logic and translation, see Chapter 7, Section 1. For a discussion of relations and multiple quantification, see Chapter 7, Section 6. For a discussion of identity, see Chapter 7, Section 7.

4. As we will see, it is possible to instantiate a quantified statement an infinite number of times. So, you can never show that the tree will remain unclosed. For the procedure to prove the invalidity of an argument in predicate logic, see Chapter 7, Section 4.

Solutions to the
Odd-Numbered Exercises

1.1

1. False
3. False
5. True
7. False
9. False
11. False
13. False
15. True
17. True
19. False

1.2.I

1. P: <u>Since</u> Hilda likes dark chocolate and milk chocolate.
   P: <u>Since</u> Hilda likes carmels and nougats.
   P: <u>Since</u> Hilda likes peanut brittle.
   C: (We may infer that) Hilda is fond of most kinds of candy.
   The argument is inductive. Assuming its premises are true, they provide good evidence for the conclusion.
3. P: <u>Because</u> all camels have humps.
   P: <u>For</u> some cigarettes are Camels.
   C: (It follows that) some cigarettes have humps.
   This is a deductive argument, but since the meaning of 'camels' and 'Camels' is not the same in the two premises, it is an invalid deductive argument.
5. P: <u>Given</u> that the Index of Leading Economic Indicators has been dropping for the last three quarters.
   C: (We may infer that) the economy is falling into recession.
   As it stands, it is an inductive argument: the premise provides some evidence for the truth of the conclusion. If you assume that there is an unstated premise, namely, "All times when the Index of Leading Economic Indicators drops for three quarters are times when the economy is falling into recession," the argument would be a valid deductive argument, and if the premises are true, a sound deductive argument.
7. P: <u>Since</u> all collies are dogs.
   (P: <u>Lassie is a collie.</u>)
   C: (We may infer that) Lassie is a dog.
   This is a deductive argument, and assuming the premises are true, it is sound.
9. P: <u>If I get up this morning, I'll go to work.</u>
   P: If I go to work, I'll get caught in a traffic jam.
   P: If I get caught in a traffic jam, I'll lose my temper.
   P: If I lose my temper, I'll do something rash.
   P: If I do something rash, I'll be arrested.
   C: (We may conclude that) if I get up this morning, I'll be arrested.
   Valid deductive argument. If the premises are true, the argument is sound.

437

1.2.II

1. P: <u>since</u> Aunt Emma gave me a cup of coffee when I was three.
   P: <u>I</u> only grew to be five foot ten.
   C: Drinking coffee stunts growth.
   Inductive. It is a poor argument, since (1) the conclusion is general and there is only one instance supporting it, and (2) the person's "shortness" might be explained in other ways, for example, genetics, lack of nutrition, etc.

3. (P: All good pyramids were more than 200 feet tall and had filled steps.)
   P: <u>for</u> the steps, or terraces, of Imhotep's pyramid were not filled in and it was less than 200 feet high.
   C: Imhotep's pyramid was not much good, really.
   This is a deductive argument, so long as you recognize the assumed premise. It is valid. It is a sound argument, if the assumed premise is true.

5. P: Editors throw mud and bricks at you the whole year round—then they make one favorable statement which happens to agree with the facts and they think they should be hugged and kissed for it.
   C: Editors are peculiar animals.
   Inductive. It's a good argument if the first premise is a good reason to claim that editors are peculiar animals.

7. P: A great man is someone self-willed and obsessive.
   P: A self-willed and obsessive man will do everything in a self-willed and obsessive sort of way.
   C: (Therefore,) only self-willed and obsessive actions are to be expected from a great man.
   Deductive. Each of the premises is a general statement; 'a' might be replaced with 'all' in each; since the conclusion is equivalent to "All great men are men who act in a self-willed and obsessive sort of way," the argument is valid. If the premises are true, the argument is sound.

9. P: If the animal were not in exact correspondence with its environment, it would cease to exist.
   C: The whole activity of the organism should conform to definite laws.
   Inductive. If the premise provides a good reason to accept the conclusion, it is a good inductive argument.

1.2.III

1. P: Back in the living room after dinner, first-time acquaintances must be able to exercise options and establish small centers of interest.
   C: The ideal number for a dinner party much exceeds two.
   Inductive. It is a good argument, since the premise provides a good reason to accept the conclusion.

3. P: <u>for,</u> the mines is not according to the disciples of the war.
   C: it is not so goot to come to the mines.
   Inductive. If the premise is true, it provides good reasons to accept the conclusion.
   P: <u>for,</u> look you, th' athversary, is digt himself four yard under the countermines.
   C: the concavities of the mine are not sufficient.
   Inductive. If the premise is true, it provides good reasons to accept the conclusion.
   There might even be a third argument:
   P: The concavities of the mine are not sufficient.
   C: The mines is not according to the disciples of the war.
   Inductive. The premise provides some evidence for the truth of the conclusion.

5. P: For what can give Laws to another, must needs be superiour to him.
   P: since the Legislative is no otherwise Legislative of the Society, but by the right it has to make Laws for all the parts and for every Member of the Society, prescribing Rules to the actions, and giving power of Execution, where they are transgressed.
   C: The *Legislative* must needs be the *Supream* power and all other Powers in any Members or parts of the Society, derived from and subordinate to it.
   Deductive. If the premises are true, the argument is sound.

7. P: More often than not, it's the child whose mother *does* belong to the PTA who gets teacher's nod [to appear on "Art Linkletter's House Party"].
   P: A ten-year-old boy's mother was the president of the PTA and his favorite teacher was just chosen principal.
   C: The boy was almost certain to be chosen to be on "Art Linkletter's House Party."
   Inductive. The premises provide good evidence for the conclusion.

9. P: Athenodorus once dreamed that there was treasure in a badger's den in a wood near Rome. He found his way to the exact spot, which he had never visited before, and there in a bank was a hole leading to a den. He fetched a couple of countrymen to dig away the bank until they came to the den at the end of the hole—where they found a rotten old purse containing six mouldy coppers and a bad shilling, which was not enough to pay the countrymen for their work.
   P: And one of my tenants, a shopkeeper, dreamed once that a flight of eagles wheeled around his head and one settled on his shoulder. He took it for a sign that he would one day be Emperor, but all that happened was that a piquet of Guards visited him the next morning (they had eagles on their shields) and the corporal arrested him for some offense and brought him under military jurisdiction.
   C: Dreams are not reliable predictors of future good fortune.
   Inductive. While the evidence is sufficient to establish that dreams cannot *always* be an indicator of future good fortune, since there are only two examples, it does not establish that they are not such indicators more often than not—the cases mentioned *might* be the odd exceptions.

1.2.IV

1. P: If there weren't any fish in the river, there wouldn't be a fishing pole on this boat.
   P: There is a fishing pole on this boat.
   C: There must be some fish in this river.
   Deductive argument. The argument is valid but the first premise is quite possibly false: as most people who have gone fishing will attest, the presence of a fishing pole on a boat does not imply there are fish in the river.

3. No argument. This is a resolution to will actions leading to heaven.

5. P: A vampire must drink fresh human blood at least once a week to live, and whoever suffers the bite of a vampire turns into a vampire.
   C: Thus, the number of vampires doubles every week.
   Deductive. Stated more explicitly, it would go like this:
   P: Every vampire bites a human (drinks fresh human blood) every week.
   P: Every person who is bitten by a vampire becomes a vampire.
   C: Every vampire causes a human to become a vampire every week.
   This is a valid deductive argument, but you might question whether the first premise is true.
   P: There was one vampire on January 1.
   P: The number of vampires doubles every week.

C: By the end of the fortieth week there will be 2^{40} (over a trillion) vampires.

P: There are not 2^{40} people in the world.

C: (So,) there was not one vampire on January 1.

This is a complex deductive argument, what is known as a *reductio ad absurdum*. It attempts to show that the first premise, which was assumed for the sake of the argument, is false. The weakest point in the argument is the second premise, since, as was noted regarding the earlier argument, it *assumes* that every vampire successfully bites a human.

7. Explanation of "why America has never lost, and will never lose a war."

9. Nonargumentative use of analogy.

11. P: It is Thursday night—Ladies's Night (at the bar).

P: You are not in your room.

P: You are not in the bathroom.

P: You probably would have left by now.

P: You usually go to the bar to relieve stress.

C: You are probably at Players (bar) partying and having a good time.

Inductive. The person who provided this (her mother's) argument granted that all the premises were true, and under ordinary circumstances the conclusion would have been true as well, but in the present case her absence was explained by a fire drill. Subordinate argument:

P: If you were in the bathroom, you would have picked up the phone by now.

(P: You have not picked up the phone by now.)

(C: You are not in the bathroom.)

Generally, a conditional statement by itself does *not* constitute an argument, but in the present case, where "Mom" continues to talk for an extended period of time, there seems to be both an implicit premise and an implicit conclusion.

     In addition to these arguments, there is a probable *explanation* of why the person to whom the call was addressed is out of the room before 11:00.

13. P: In 1700 the population of the American colonies was 200,000; in 1770 it had risen to over 2,000,000.

P: Recent immigration had consisted of German and French Protestants, of Irish peasants and Scottish crofters, of whores and felons and bankrupts from London.

(P: The primary interests of recent immigrants was with immediate issues and economic advantages.)

C: The majority of Americans were concerned with immediate issues and economic advantages.

This is a deductive argument.

     The balance is an explanation of the lack of loyalty to the British crown among the majority of American colonists.

15. Explanation of the *Dallas* phenomenon.

17. Main argument:

P: Some things in the world are in motion.

P: Whatever is moved is moved by something distinct from itself.

P: If whatever is moved is moved by something distinct from itself, then this other must be moved by yet another, which must be moved by yet another, etc.

P: There cannot be an infinite chain of movers.

C: ("Therefore) it is necessary to arrive at a First Mover, put in motion by no other; and this everyone understands to be God."

Deductive. If the premises are true, the argument is sound.

Argument for the second premise:

P: Motion is the reduction of potentiality to actuality.

P: Everything that is moved is in a state of potentiality to that toward which it is moved.

P: Nothing can be reduced from a state of potentiality to a state of actuality except by something in a state of actuality.

C: (Therefore,) whatever is in motion must be put in motion by another.

Deductive: if the premises are true, the argument is sound.

Argument for the fourth premise:

P: Assume there was an infinite chain of movers.

P: If there was an infinite chain of movers, there would be no first mover.

P: If there was no first mover, there would be no other mover.

P: There are other movers.

C: There cannot be an infinite chain of movers.

Deductive. You might suspect that there is a problem in this argument, most probably in the third premise: it assumes what the argument sets out to prove. Hence, you are not justified in accepting the conclusion of the main argument.

19. P: A doctor has scores of patients and only some of them are curable.

P: A lawyer has relatively few clients, and a lawyer can always better his client in some way if he can get the right combination.

C: A lawyer is not like a doctor.

Inductive argument (analogy). Good argument, as long as both premises are true.

2.1

1. 'car'
3. 'commonplace'
5. 'impetuous'
7. 'laid back'
9. 'miscarriage'

2.2.I

1. term
3. not a term
5. term
7. term
9. not a term

2.2.II

1. false
3. true
5. true
7. false
9. true

2.2.III

1. 'Towncar', 'Lincoln', 'Product of Ford Motor Company', 'thing'
3. 'bacterium', 'microscopic plant', 'microscopic organism', 'organism'
5. 'bratwurst', 'sausage', 'meat', 'food'

2.2.IV

1. 'living thing', 'animal', 'person', 'curmudgeon'
3. 'home furnishing', 'piece of furniture', 'chair', 'rocker'
5. 'cow', 'cow with a heart', 'cow with a heart and a backbone', 'brown cow with a heart and a backbone'

2.2.V

1. 'game player', 'football player', 'professional football player', 'a Green Bay Packer',
3. 'thing', 'animal', 'person', 'politician'
5. 'trees', 'evergreens', 'pines', 'Scotch Pines'

2.2.VI

1. 'unicorns', 'mythical beasts', 'fictitious beasts', 'fictitious entities'
3. 'textbook', 'book', 'things made of paper', 'things used in school'
5. 'nostril', 'nose', 'part of the face', 'part of the body'

2.3.I

1. stipulative
3. lexical
5. persuasive
7. theoretical
9. persuasive
11. precising
13. lexical
15. precising
17. theoretical
19. precising

2.3.II

1. false
3. false
5. true
7. true
9. true

2.4.I

1. North America, South America, Europe, Asia, Africa, Australia, Antarctica
3. Connecticut, Maine, Massachusetts, New Hampshire, Rhode Island, Vermont
5. Guatemala, British Honduras, El Salvador, Honduras, Nicaragua, Costa Rica, Panama

2.4.II

1. Frank Sinatra, Kathleen Battle, Bruce Springsteen
3. Sahara, Gobi, Mojave
5. Virginia, Iowa, California, Texas

2.4.III

1. Fords, Chevrolets, Volkswagens
3. collies, schnauzers, Irish setters
5. woodwinds, brass, strings, drums

2.5.I

1. 'dog'
3. 'teacher'
5. 'clique'
7. 'irritate'
9. 'tunelike'

2.5.II

1. A person is said to have blood pressure if and only if a number registers on the gage of the manometer attached to a person's arm.
3. Substance *A* is harder then substance *B* if and only if substance *A* can scratch substance *B*.
5. A person is said to be a genius if and only if he or she scores 140 or higher on an intelligence-quotient test.

2.5.III

1. college teacher
3. young deer
5. adult female human being
7. three-sided plane figure
9. small crown
11. young cat
13. percussion instrument
15. a dry measure

2.6.I

1. Too broad: all mammals give milk.
3. Too narrow: not all calendars take the form of a book.
5. Figurative.
7. Circular.
9. Acceptable.
11. Obscure.
13. It does not identify the genus as a type of exercise and it is negative.
15. It does not identify the genus: a novel is a book. Hence it is also too broad: it is a fictitious book.
17. Negative and circular.
19. The definition does not explicitly indicate that empathy is a psychological state. Even if this is taken for granted, the definition might be too broad: it is not clear that the definition distinguishes empathy from similar psychological states such as sympathy.
21. Too narrow: an index often includes entries that are not names. Too broad: there are listings of names that are not indexes—membership lists, for example.

23. Does not identify the genus. Figurative.
25. The definition does not acknowledge that a mantra is a word that is repeated as part of a Hindu religious practice. So the definition does not properly identify the genus.
27. Does not identify the genus. Figurative.
29. Negative. Does not give the essential meaning, namely, that it is a type of Christian religion. Too broad: does not distinguish Protestants from Orthodox Christians.
31. Does not identify the genus. Obscure.
33. Does not identify the genus. Figurative.
35. Does not identify the genus. Figurative.
37. Does not identify the genus. Negative.
39. Does not identify the genus. Negative.

3.1.I

1. Equivocation on 'plants'.
3. Division.
5. Equivocation on 'river bank'.
7. Division.
9. Equivocation on 'practice'.

3.1.II

1. Amphiboly. The wording "every convicted felon" is ambiguous, insofar as it might mean each and every felon or the totality of felons. Insofar as "every convicted felon" is understood as applying to each felon, the argument might be taken to commit the fallacy of composition.
3. Accent.
5. No fallacy. Although the engine is only a part of the car, if the engine doesn't work, the car doesn't work.
7. Division
9. No fallacy. Although there is an equivocation on 'nobody', there is no argument, so there is no fallacy.

3.2.I

1. Mob Appeal.
3. Personal Attack *(tu quoque)*.
5. Appeal to Force.
7. Irrelevant Conclusion.
9. Personal Attack.
11. Appeal to Force.
13. Accident.
15. Irrelevant Conclusion.

3.2.II

1. No fallacy: this is a warning.
3. Appeal to Force.
5. Mob Appeal: snob appeal.
7. Accident. Edison was an exception to the rule.

9. Red Herring. The "reply" to the argument does little more than distract the reader from the argument Dr. Stark provided for the closing of the petrochemical plant.
11. Appeal to Pity.
13. Mob Appeal.
15. Mob Appeal.

3.2.III

1. Equivocation on 'Democrats' ('democrats').
3. Mob Appeal.
5. Red Herring. The "reply" to the argument does little more than distract the reader from Ms. DeMark's argument.
7. Personal Attack.
9. Accent. The accent is placed on 'thou'.
11. Equivocation on 'euthanasia' ('youth in Asia').
13. Appeal to Force.
15. Mob Appeal.
17. Irrelevant Conclusion. The fact that hundreds of people go hunting every year does not show that hunting is safe.
19. Appeal to Force.

3.3.I

1. False Dichotomy.
3. Begging the Question.
5. Begging the Question: the epithet 'liar' begs the question.
7. Complex Question.
9. Suppressed Evidence.
11. False Dichotomy.
13. Complex Question.
15. Suppressed Evidence.

3.3.II

1. Accident.
3. Equivocation (on 'men' and 'mortal'/'immortal').
5. Red Herring.
7. Accent on 'thou'.
9. Division.
11. Straw person.
13. Mob Appeal (snob appeal).
15. Appeal to Pity.
17. If asked out of the blue, this would be a Complex Question, since it assumes that the witness worked for LaVale and Windshield. But since this is the prosecution's witness, it is doubtful that the District Attorney is trying to impeach him or her. So there is some doubt that, when found in context, it would be a Complex Question. Regardless of this, in calling LaVale and Windshield "crooks," it begs the question of their guilt.
19. Composition.
21. Suppressed Evidence.

23. False Dicotomy.
25. To the extent that this appeals to emotions, it might be deemed a case of Mob Appeal. But to the extent that an appeal to protect endangered species provides a reason to vote for the communist candidate, it rests on the general principle that "We should do what we can to protect endangered species." This principle applies to biological species, so in applying the general principle to a political species, it is being applied to an exceptional case, which would make it a Fallacy of Accident. Similarly, it might be claimed to a case of Equivocation: 'species' is being used to apply only to a biological species in the principle, while it is being used in a different sense to reach the conclusion.

3.4.I

1. False Cause.
3. Hasty Generalization.
5. Slippery Slope.
7. Appeal to Authority.
9. Appeal to Authority.

3.4.II

1. Slippery Slope.
3. False Cause.
5. Appeal to Authority.
7. Appeal to Authority.
9. Weak Analogy.
11. Appeal to Authority.
13. False Cause.
25. Slippery Slope.

3.4.III

1. Irrelevant Conclusion; the case might also be made for False Cause.
3. Equivocation on 'press'.
5. Hasty Generalization.
7. Red Herring.
9. Begging the Question.
11. Division.
13. Weak Analogy.
15. Accent. The quotation is incomplete. The Eighth Amendment requires that "Excessive bale shall not be required."
17. Suppressed Evidence. The case might also be made for Red Herring, since it distracts the reader from the arguments that might be made for tighter environmental controls on industry.
19. Appeal to Authority.
21. Red Herring.
23. Accident.
25. False Cause.
27. Appeal to Force.
29. Irrelevant Conclusion.
31. False Dichotomy.
33. Hasty Generalization.

35. Accent and Equivocation. The quotation is incomplete: the Amendment states: "In all criminal prosecutions, the accused shall enjoy the right to a speedy and public trial . . ." In this sentence, 'enjoy' means 'have', not 'find pleasure in'. It is the right to the trial, not the trial itself, that is "enjoyed." And the 'speedy trial' concerns the time between arrest and the trial, not the speed of the trial itself.
37. Amphiboly.
39. Appeal to Ignorance.
41. Composition.
43. Suppressed Evidence.
45. Slippery Slope and Appeal to Force: the minister claims the behavior will result in divine punishment.
47. False Cause.
49. Mob Appeal.

4.1

1. A proposition. Subject term: "slithy toves"; predicate term: "things that gyre and gimble in the wabe."
3. E proposition. Subject term: "person with a vorpal blade"; predicate term: "a Jabberwock."
5. I proposition. Subject term: "mad hatters"; predicate term: "people who do not beat Time."
7. O proposition. Subject term: "people who stand in uffish thought"; predicate term: "people who wander through looking-glasses."
9. A proposition. Subject term: "little girls who chase white rabbits down holes and talk with Cheshire cats"; predicate term: "girls named 'Alice'."
11. I proposition. Subject term: "mushrooms that are suitable for eating"; predicate term: "mushrooms that cause little girls named 'Alice' to grow or shrink rapidly."
13. E proposition. Subject term: "person who would qualify as a slayer of a Jabberwock"; predicate term: "a person who is inclined to walk into a tulgey wood with anything less than a vorpal sword."
15. O proposition. Subject term: "Dormouse who is wont to argue over the date with the Mad Hatter"; predicate term: "a beast who would be opposed to distinguishing between saying what one means and meaning what one says."

4.2.I

1. E—False
   I—True
   O—False
3. A—Undetermined
   E—False
   O—Undetermined

4.2.II

1. E—Undetermined
   I—Undetermined
   O—True
3. A—False
   E—True
   O—True

4.2.III

1. **E**—Undetermined
   I—Undetermined
   O—False
3. **A**—Undetermined
   E—False
   O—Undetermined

4.2.IV

1. **E**—Undetermined
   I—Undetermined
   O—True
3. **A**—Undetermined
   E—True
   O—Undetermined

4.3

1.

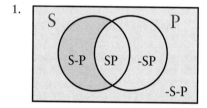

3.

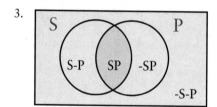

5.

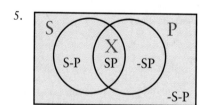

7.

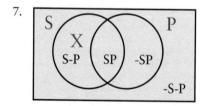

9.

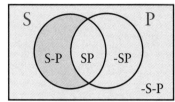

11.

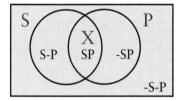

13.

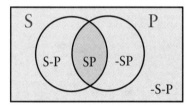

15.

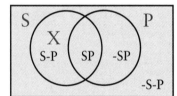

4.4.I

1. "No *S* is *P*" obverts to "All *S* is non-*P.*" But converting "All *S* is non-*P*" will not yield a logically equivalent statement. So an **E** proposition is *not* logically equivalent to its contrapositive ("No non-*P* is non-*S*").

3. "Some *S* is not *P*" obverts to "Some *S* is non-*P*", which converts to "Some non-*P* is *S*," which obverts to "Some non-*P* is not non-*S.*"

4.4.II

1. "All *S* is *P*" obverts to
   "No *S* is non-*P*," which converts to
   "No non-*P* is *S*," which obverts to
   "All non-*P* is non-*S.*"

3. "Some *S* is *P*" converts to "Some *P* is *S.*"
   "Some *S* is *P*" obverts to "Some *S* is not non-*P.*"
   "Some *P* is *S*" obverts to "Some *P* is not non-*S.*"

4.4.III

1. False
3. True
5. False
7. False
9. Undetermined
11. False
13. False
15. False
17. True
19. False
21. Undetermined
23. Undetermined
25. Undetermined
27. Undetermined
29. Undetermined
31. Undetermined
33. False
35. True
37. Undetermined
39. Undetermined
41. Undetermined
43. False (Given is equivalent to "All non-*P* is *S*.")
45. Undetermined
47. Undetermined
49. False
51. True
53. True
55. True
57. False
59. True
61. Undetermined
63. Undetermined
65. False
67. Undetermined
69. Undetermined
71. Undetermined
73. Undetermined
75. Undetermined
77. Undetermined
79. Undetermined

4.5.I

1. **IEA**-1
3. **EOA**-2
5. **IEE**-4
7. **OOO**-3
9. **EII**-2

11. **AII**-2
13. **IOO**-3
15. **IIE**-2
17. **EEE**-4
19. **III**-3

4.5.II

1. Some P is M.
   Some M is S.
   ___
   All S is P.

3. Some P is not M.
   Some M is S.
   ___
   Some S is P.

5. Some M is P.
   Some M is not S.
   ___
   No S is P.

7. No M is P.
   Some M is not S.
   ___
   Some S is not P.

9. No M is P.
   No S is M.
   ___
   Some S is not P.

11. Some P is not M.
    Some S is M.
    ___
    All S is P.

13. No M is P.
    Some S is not M.
    ___
    All S is P.

15. All M is P.
    Some M is S.
    ___
    All S is P.

17. Some P is not M.
    Some S is not M.
    ___
    No S is P.

19. No M is P.
    All M is S.
    ___
    All S is P.

4.6.I

1.   All *P* is *M*.
     All *S* is *M*.
     _____
     No *S* is *P*.

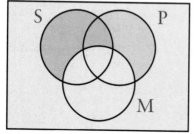

Invalid

3.   Some *P* is *M*.
     No *M* is *S*.
     _____
     Some *S* is not *P*.

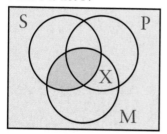

Invalid

5.   Some *P* is not *M*.
     Some *M* is not *S*.
     _____
     All *S* is *P*.

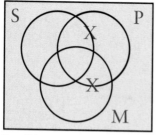

Invalid

7. All *P* is *M*.
    Some *S* is not *M*.

    Some *S* is not *P*.

    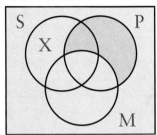

    Valid

9. All *M* is *P*.
    No *S* is *M*.

    No *S* is *P*.

    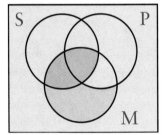

    Invalid

11. Some *M* is *P*.
    Some *S* is not *M*.

    Some *S* is *P*.

    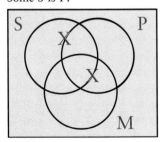

    Invalid

13. Some *P* is *M*.
    Some *M* is not *S*.

    No *S* is *P*.

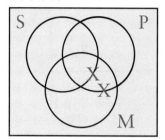

Invalid

15. Some *M* is not *P*.
    Some *M* is *S*.

    Some *S* is not *P*.

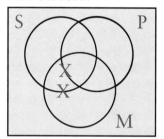

Invalid

17. Some *M* is *P*.
    All *S* is *M*.

    Some *S* is *P*.

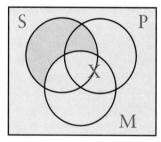

Invalid

19. All *P* is *M*.
    Some *S* is not *M*.

    No *S* is *P*.

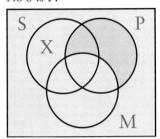

Invalid

4.6.II

1. All *M* is *V*.
   All *M* is *A*.

   All *A* is *V*.
   AAA-3

All *M* is *P*.
All *M* is *S*.

All *S* is *P*.

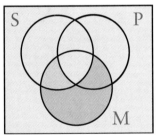

Invalid

3. Some *M* is not *L*.
   Some *M* is *P*.

   No *P* is *L*.
   OIE-3

Some *M* is not *P*.
Some *M* is *S*.

No *S* is *P*.

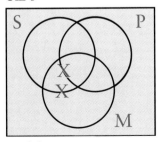

Invalid

5. Some *H* is *L*.
    No *D* is *H*.
    _____
    No *D* is *L*.
    IEE-1

Some *M* is *P*.
No *S* is *M*.
_____
No *S* is *P*.

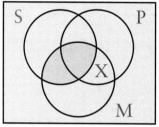

Invalid

7. All *D* are *L*.
    No *L* are *C*.
    _____
    Some *C* are *D*.
    AEI-4

All *P* are *M*.
No *M* are *S*.
_____
Some *S* are *P*.

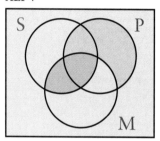

Invalid

9. No *C* are *R*.
    Some *C* are not *G*.
    _____
    All *G* are *R*.
    EOA-3

No *M* are *P*.
Some *M* are not *S*.
_____
All *S* are *P*.

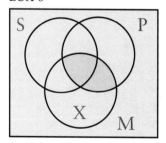

Invalid

11. All *B* are *T*.
    Some *J* are not *B*.
    _____
    All *J* are *T*.
    AOA-1

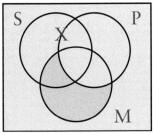

Invalid

All *M* are *P*.
Some *S* are not *M*.
_____
All *S* are *P*.

13. Some *S* are not *R*.
    Some *F* are not *S*.
    _____
    All *F* are *R*.
    OOA-1

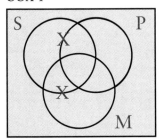

Invalid

Some *M* are not *P*.
Some *S* are not *M*.
_____
All *S* are *P*.

15. Some *R* are *W*.
    Some *C* are *R*.
    _____
    No *C* are *W*.
    IIE-1

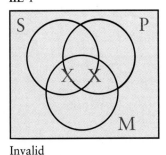

Invalid

Some *M* are *P*.
Some *S* are *M*.
_____
No *S* are *P*.

17. No *K* are *Q*.   No *P* are *M*.
     Some *Q* are *C*.   Some *M* are *S*.

     Some *C* are *K*.   Some *S* are *P*.
     EII-4

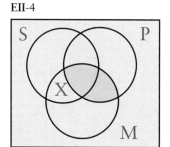

     Invalid

19. No *Q* are *K*.   No *P* are *M*.
     No *R* are *K*.   No *S* are *M*.

     No *R* are *Q*.   No *S* are *P*.
     EEE-2

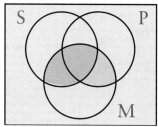

     Invalid

21. Some *C* are not *S*.   Some *P* are not *M*.
     All *S* are *G*.   All *M* are *S*.

     No *G* are *C*.   No *S* is *P*.
     OAE-4

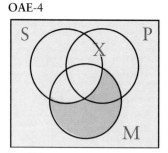

     Invalid

23. No *H* are *D*.
    Some *H* are *T*.
    ─────────────
    No *T* are *D*.
    EIE-3

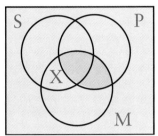

Invalid

No *M* are *P*.
Some *M* are *S*.
─────────────
No *S* is *P*.

25. No *H* are *D*.
    No *H* are *M*.
    ─────────────
    Some *M* are *D*.
    EEI-3

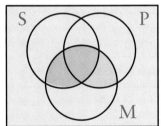

Invalid

No *M* are *P*.
No *M* are *S*.
─────────────
Some *S* are *P*.

27. Some *D* are not *M*.
    No *D* are *H*.
    ─────────────
    No *H* are *M*.
    OEE-3

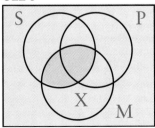

Invalid

Some *M* are not *P*.
No *M* are *S*.
─────────────
No *S* are *P*.

29. No *D* are *Q*.
    Some *Q* are not *G*.

    No *G* are *D*.
    EOE-4

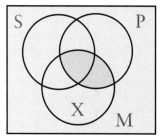

    Invalid

No *P* are *M*.
Some *M* are not *S*.

No *S* is *P*.

4.7.I

1. All *M* is *P*
   No *S* is *M*.

   No *S* is *P*.
   Invalid: IMa

3. No *M* is *P*.
   All *M* is *S*.

   No *S* is *P*.
   Invalid: IMi

5. No *M* is *P*.
   Some *M* is *S*.

   Some *S* is *P*.
   Invalid: ACNP

7. No *P* is *M*.
   All *M* is *S*.

   Some *S* is not *P*.
   Invalid: EF

9. Some *P* is *M*.
   Some *S* is *M*.

   Some *S* is *P*.
   Invalid: UM

11. Some *M* is not *P*.
    Some *S* is *M*.

    No *S* is *P*.
    Invalid: UM, IMi

13. Some *P* is *M*.
    Some *M* is *S*.

    No *S* is *P*.
    Invalid: UM, IMa, Imi

15. All *P* is *M*.
    All *M* is *S*.

    No *S* is *P*.
    Invalid: IMi

17. Some *M* is *P*.
    No *M* is *S*.

    All *S* is *P*.
    Invalid: ACNP

19. All *M* is *P*.
    No *M* is *S*.

    All *S* is *P*.
    Invalid: ACNP

21. No *P* is *M*.
    All *S* is *M*.

    Some *S* is *P*.
    Invalid: EF, ACNP

23. Some *P* is not *M*.
    Some *S* is *M*.

    Some *S* is *P*.
    Invalid: ACNP

25. No *P* is *M*.
    Some *M* is *S*.

    Some *S* is not *P*.
    Valid

27. Some *M* is *P*.
    Some *S* is *M*.

    Some *S* is not *P*.
    Invalid: UM, IMa

29. Some *M* is not *P*.
    All *S* is *M*.

    No *S* is *P*.
    Invalid: UM

4.7.II

1. **IEI-1**
   Some *M* are *C*.
   No *F* are *M*.

   Some *F* are *C*.
   Invalid: ACNP

   Some *M* are *P*.
   No *S* are *M*.

   Some *S* are *P*.

3. **EAA-4**
   No *F* are *M*.
   All *M* are *C*.

   All *C* are *F*.
   Invalid: ACNP, IMi

   No *P* are *M*.
   All *M* are *S*.

   All *S* are *P*.

5. **AAE-3**
   All *S* are *E*.
   All *S* are *C*.

   No *C* are *E*.
   Invalid: IMa, IMi

   All *M* are *P*.
   All *M* are *S*.

   No *S* are *P*.

7. **IEE-2**
   Some *O* are *M*.
   No *S* are *M*.

   No *S* are *O*.
   Invalid: IMa

   Some *P* are *M*.
   No *S* are *M*.

   No *S* are *P*.

9. **OIE-4**
   Some *B* are not *W*.
   Some *W* are *F*.

   No *F* are *B*.
   Invalid: IMa, IMi

   Some *P* are not *M*.
   Some *M* are *S*.

   No *S* are *P*.

11. **OOE-3**
    Some *M* are not *D*.
    Some *M* are not *O*.

    No *O* are *D*.
    Invalid: EP, UM

    Some *M* are not *P*.
    Some *M* are not *S*.

    No *S* is *P*.

13. **OIE-2**
    Some *H* are not *P*.   Some *P* are not *M*.
    Some *A* are *P*.   Some *S* are *M*.
    _____   _____
    No *A* are H.   No *S* are *P*.
    Invalid: IMa, IMi

15. **AIE-4**
    All *W* are *P*.   All *P* are *M*.
    Some *P* are *M*.   Some *M* are *S*.
    _____   _____
    No *M* are *W*.   No S are *P*.
    Invalid: UM, IMi

17. **IIA-1**
    Some *R* are *C*.   Some *M* are *P*.
    Some *W* are *R*.   Some *S* are *M*.
    _____   _____
    All *W* are *C*.   All *S* are *P*.
    Invalid: UM, IMi

19. **OIA-2**
    Some *D* is not *S*.   Some *P* is not *M*.
    Some *M* is *S*.   Some *S* is *M*.
    _____   _____
    All *M* is *D*.   All *S* is *P*.
    Invalid: ACNP, IMi

21. **OIA-4**
    Some *C* are not *F*.   Some *P* is not *M*.
    Some *F* are *M*.   Some *M* is *S*.
    _____   _____
    All *M* are *C*.   All *S* is *P*.
    Invalid: ACNP, IMi

23. **EIE-1**
    No *F* is *M*.   No *M* is *P*.
    Some *W* is *F*.   Some *S* is *M*.
    _____   _____
    No *W* is *M*.   No *S* is *P*.
    Invalid: IMi

25. **AEI-2**
    All *E* are *P*.   All *P* are *M*.
    No *C* are *P*.   No *S* are *M*.
    _____   _____
    Some *C* are *E*.   Some *S* are *P*.
    Invalid: ACNP

27. **AOI-3**
    All *B* are *C*.   All *M* are *P*.
    Some *B* are not *M*.   Some *M* are not *S*.
    _____   _____
    Some *M* are *C*.   Some *S* are *P*.
    Invalid: ACNP

29. **IIO-3**
    Some *C* are *Z*.   Some *M* are *P*.
    Some *C* are *M*.   Some *M* are *S*.
    _____   _____
    Some *M* are not *Z*.   Some *S* are not *P*.
    Invalid: UM, IMa

31. **EOA**-4
    No *G* is *W*.
    Some *W* is not *Z*.

    All *Z* is *G*.
    Invalid: ACNP, EP

    No *P* is *M*.
    Some *M* is not *S*.

    All *S* is *P*.

33. **EAO**-4
    No *L* is *H*.
    All *H* is *G*.

    Some *G* is not *L*.
    Invalid: EF

    No *P* is *M*.
    All *M* is *S*.

    Some *S* is not *P*.

35. **AEA**-4
    All *O* are *S*.
    No *S* are *T*.

    All *T* are *O*.
    Invalid: ACNP

    All *P* is *M*.
    No *M* is *S*.

    All *S* is *P*.

37. **AIE**-1
    All *F* are *P*.
    Some *H* are *F*.

    No *H* are *P*.
    Invalid: IMa, IMi

    All *M* are *P*.
    Some *S* are *M*.

    No *S* are *P*.

39. **AEE**-2
    All *L* are *S*.
    No *F* are *S*.

    No *F* are *L*.
    Valid

    All *P* are *M*.
    No *S* are *M*.

    No *S* are *P*.

4.8.I

1. All people with an enormous sweet-tooth are people who support their local dentist.
   All people who eat chocolate for breakfast are people with an enormous sweet-tooth.

   All people who eat chocolate for breakfast are people who support their local dentist.

   AAA-1

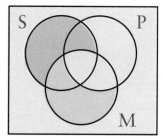

3. Some coins desired by coin collectors are coins found in circulation.
   All coins desired by coin collectors are rare coins.

   Some rare coins are coins found in circulation.
   IAI-3

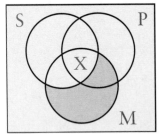

5. All winners of the race are swift-riding persons.
   Some cow-riders are not swift-riding persons.

   Some cow-riders are not winners of the race.
   AOO-2

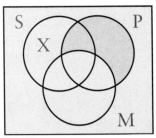

7. All cats are carnivores.
   (Some) Frisky is not a carnivore.

   (Some) Frisky is not a cat.
   AOO-2

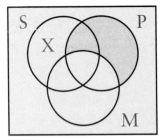

9. All misers are people who hoard money for its own sake.
    Some counting-house executives are misers.

    Some counting-house executives are people who hoard money for its own sake.
    AII-1

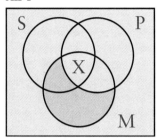

4.8.II

1. All cats are mammals.
    Some cats are not tabbies.

    Some tabbies are not mammals.
    AOO-3

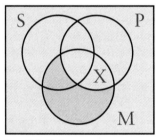

    Invalid: IMa

3. No person who writes logic problems is a person who should be invited to the pun festival.
    All persons who should be invited to the pun festival are persons who enjoy playing with language.

    No person who enjoys playing with language is a person who writes logic problems.
    EAE-4

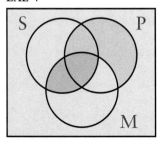

    Invalid: IMi

5. Some coins in circulation are coins of numismatic value.
    All coins in circulation are coins of the realm.

    Some coins of the realm are not coins of numismatic value.
    IAO-3

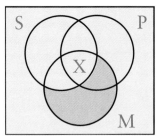

    Invalid: IMa

7. Some scoundrels are not cowards.
    Some traitors are scoundrels.

    Some traitors are not cowards.
    OIO-1

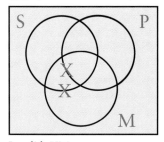

    Invalid: UM

9. No bratwursts are foods enjoyed by fictitious German composers.
    Some sausages are bratwursts.

    Some sausages are not foods enjoyed by fictitious German composers.
    EIO-1

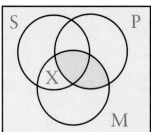

    Valid

11. All standing bridges constructed by the ancient Romans are stone bridges.
    Some bridge in Koblenz is a stone bridge.

    _____

    Some bridge in Koblenz is a standing bridge constructed by the ancient Romans.
    AII-2

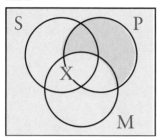

Invalid: UM
Were you to contend that the major premise should be "All stone bridges are standing bridges constructed by the ancient Romans," the argument would be of the form
AII-1, which is valid, but the major premise would clearly be false.

13. All cartoon characters who are flattened by a steamroller are cartoon characters who rise to act another day.
    No person flattened by a semi-trailer truck is a cartoon character who is flattened by a steamroller.

    _____

    Some people flattened by a semi-trailer truck are not cartoon characters who rise to act another day.
    AEO-1

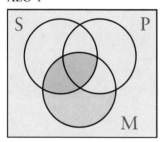

Invalid: IMa, EF

15. All rabbits that drink corn liquor are Beauregard Bunny.
    All rabbits Amisglof hunts are rabbits that drink corn liquor.

    _____

    All rabbits Amisglof hunts are Beauregard Bunny.
    AAA-1

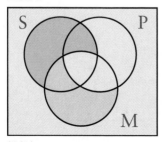

Valid

17. All persons who are gourmet cooks are devotees of the Epicure Catalog.
No person who is a gourmet cook is a person who eats burgers and fries.

No person who eats burgers and fries is a devotee of the Epicure Catalog.
AEE-3

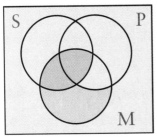

Invalid: IMa

19. No cat that is both well-adjusted and altruistic is a cat that will attempt to eat small elephants with large trunks.
(No) Seymore is a cat that is both well-adjusted and altruistic.

(All) Seymore is a cat that will attempt to eat small elephants with large trunks.
EEA-1

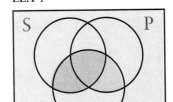

Invalid: EP, ACNP
Notice: The same fallacies are committed if one takes the singular statement to be a particular.

4.9

1. All arguments of the mood and figure AAA-1 are valid arguments.
This argument is an argument of the mood and figure AAA-1.

This argument is a valid argument.
AAA-1   Valid

3. All professors are intelligent persons.
Some intelligent persons are rich persons.

Some rich persons are professors.
AII-4   Invalid: UM
Since the conclusion is convertible, the argument might also be:
Some intelligent persons are rich persons.
All professors are intelligent persons

Some professors are rich persons.
IAI-1   Invalid: UM

5. All persons who would read *A Christmas Carol* in the middle of July are Dickens buffs.
   (No) George is a person who would read *A Christmas Carol* in the middle of July.

   (No) George is a Dickens buff.
   AEE-1   Invalid: IMa
   But you might contend that the 'only' indicates that the major premise should be understood as the converse of the premise given above:
   All Dickens buffs are persons who would read *A Christmas Carol* in the middle of July.
   (No) George is a person who would read *A Christmas Carol* in the middle of July.

   (No) George is a Dickens buff.
   AEE-2   Valid
   Note that in either formulation of the argument, the minor premise is convertible.

7. All people who would prefer driving a Model-T Ford are children under three.
   No children under three are sports-car drivers.

   No sports-car driver is a person who would prefer driving a Model-T Ford.
   AEE-4   Valid
   But the added premise is false, so the argument is more probably intended to be:
   No people who would prefer driving a Model-T Ford are children under three.
   No children under three are sports-car drivers.

   No sports-car driver is a person who would prefer driving a Model-T Ford.
   EEE-4   Invalid: EP
   But the missing premise is convertible, so the argument might also be:
   No children under three are people who would prefer driving a Model-T Ford.
   No child under three is a sports-car driver.

   No sports-car driver is a person who would prefer driving a Model-T Ford.
   EEE-3   Invalid: EP

9. All persons who do not understand Plato's *Works* are people who say, "It's all Greek to me."
   Some people who do not understand Plato's *Works* are fans of British philosophy.

   Some fans of British philosophy are people who say, "It's all Greek to me."
   If the "It's" in the expression "It's all Greek to me" does not refer to anything in particular—if it is *merely* an expression—then the argument is of the mood and figure **AII**-3, and the argument is valid. If the "It's" in the expression makes any reference, then in the major premise it refers to 'Plato's *Works*', whereas in the conclusion it refers to 'British philosophy'. In the latter case the argument commits the Fallacy of Four Terms—it is not a syllogism.

11. No Baptists are Catholics.
    All Protestants are Baptists.

    No Protestants are Catholics.
    EAE-1   Valid
    But the minor premise is false, so the argument is more probably intended to be:
    No Baptists are Catholics.
    All Baptists are Protestants.

    No Protestants are Catholics.
    EAE-3   Invalid: IMi

13. Some people who do these problems are not people who are mathematically disposed.
    All people who do these problems are people who enjoy these problems.

    ―――――――――――――――

    Some people who enjoy these problems are not people who are mathematically disposed.
    OAO-3   Valid
    Though the author of this book might like to believe that the minor premise is true, the author's belief would certainly be challenged. Hence, someone might contend that the argument should be reformulated as:
    Some people who do these problems are not people who are mathematically disposed.
    All people who enjoy these problems are people who do these problems.

    ―――――――――――――――

    Some people who enjoy these problems are not people who are mathematically disposed.
    OAO-1   Invalid: UM

15. No British solicitors are barristers.
    Some British lawyers are barristers.

    ―――――――――――――――

    Some British lawyers are not British solicitors.
    EIO-2   Valid

4.10.I

1. (1') All vertebrates are animals with backbones.
   (3') All mammals are vertebrates.

   ―――――――――――――――

   (C1) All mammals are animals with backbones.
   AAA-1   Valid
   (C1) All mammals are animals with backbones.
   (2') All cats are mammals.

   ―――――――――――――――

   All cats are animals with backbones.
   AAA-1   Valid

3. (1') All incompetent persons are inexperienced persons.
   (3') All persons who are always blundering are incompetent.

   ―――――――――――――――

   (C1) All persons who are always blundering are inexperienced persons.
   AAA-1   Valid
   (C1) All persons who are always blundering are inexperienced persons.
   (3') (All) Jenkins is a person who is always blundering.

   ―――――――――――――――

   (All) Jenkins is an inexperienced person.
   AAA-1   Valid

5. (2') All Gershwin tunes are toe-tappers.
   (3') No Beethoven compositions are Gershwin tunes.

   ―――――――――――――――

   (C1) No Beethoven compositions are toe-tappers.
   AEE-1   Valid
   (C1) No Beethoven compositions are toe-tappers.
   (4') Some groups that play classical music are groups that play Beethoven compositions.

   There are four terms, so no conclusion is entailed by the premises. The sorites is invalid.

4.10.II

1. (1') All puddings are nice things.
   (2') All dishes that are this dish are puddings.

   (C1) All dishes that are this dish are nice things.
   AAA-1   Valid
   (C1) All dishes that are this dish are nice things.
   (3') No nice things are wholesome things.

   No wholesome things are dishes that are this dish.
   AEE-4   Valid

3. (2') All people who can remember the Battle of Waterloo are very old people.
   (3') All people really worth listening to on military subjects are people who can remember the Battle of Waterloo.

   (C1) All people really worth listening to on military subjects are people who are very old.
   AAA-1   Valid
   (C1) All people really worth listening to on military subjects are people who are very old.
   (1) All gardeners of mine are really people worth listening to on military subjects.

   All gardeners of mine are very old.
   AAA-1   Valid

5. (1') All books that I read this year are mysteries.
   (3') Some book that I read this year is a book Ostafar Neumathesque wrote.

   (C1) Some book Ostafar Neumathesque wrote was a mystery.
   AII-3   Valid
   (5') No book Ostafar Neumathesque wrote is an interesting book.
   (C1) Some book Ostafar Neumathesque wrote was a mystery.

   (C2) Some mystery is not an interesting book.
   EIO-3   Valid
   (2') All science-fiction books are interesting books.
   (C2) Some mystery is not an interesting book.

   (C3) Some mysteries are not science-fiction books.
   AOO-2   Valid
   (4') Some technical manuals are not science fiction books.
   (C3) Some mysteries are not science fiction books.
   There are two negative premises, so any conclusion you would attempt to draw would at least commit the Fallacy of Exclusive Premises. The sorites is invalid.

5.1.I

1. TRUE
3. TRUE
5. TRUE
7. TRUE
9. TRUE
11. TRUE

13. TRUE
15. FALSE
17. FALSE
19. TRUE
21. TRUE
23. FALSE
25. TRUE

5.1.II

1. TRUE
3. TRUE
5. TRUE
7. TRUE
9. FALSE
11. FALSE
13. TRUE
15. TRUE
17. FALSE
19. TRUE
21. TRUE
23. TRUE
25. FALSE

5.1.III

1. P → S
3. S → D
5. ~G → ~K
7. (D v G) → B
9. M → (~W & ~J)
11. (G v B) → H
13. ~(N → O) & ~(H → C)
15. (D → K) → ~(B v F)
17. (R v B) → (S → T)
19. [G & (F & H)] & (~O & ~E)
21. D → {E v [C v ~(P → A)]}
23. ~(J v H) & [G & (~D v P)]
25. [(W → E) v (~Q & J)] → (O & F)

5.2.I.

1.

p	q	p	p v q
T	T	T	T
T	F	T	T
F	T	F	T
F	F	F	F

VALID

3.

p	q		p	q	p ∨ q
T	T		T	T	T
T	F		T	F	T
F	T		F	T	T
F	F		F	F	F

VALID

5.

p	q		p → q	q	p
T	T		T	T	T
T	F		F	F	T
F	T		T	T	F
F	F		T	F	F

INVALID

7.

p	q		p → q	~q	~p
T	T		T	F	F
T	F		F	T	F
F	T		T	F	T
F	F		T	T	T

VALID

9.

p	q		p ∨ q	~p	~q
T	T		T	F	F
T	F		T	F	T
F	T		T	T	F
F	F		F	T	T

INVALID

11.

p	q		p & q	q
T	T		T	T
T	F		F	F
F	T		F	T
F	F		F	F

VALID

13.

p	q	r		p → q	p → r	q → r
T	T	T		T	T	T
T	T	F		T	F	F
T	F	T		F	T	T
T	F	F		F	F	T
F	T	T		T	T	T
F	T	F		T	T	F
F	F	T		T	T	T
F	F	F		T	T	T

INVALID

15.

p	q	r	s	$p \rightarrow q$	$r \rightarrow s$	$[(p \rightarrow q) \,\&\, (r \rightarrow s)]$	$p \rightarrow s$	$\sim q$	$\sim q \lor s$
T	T	T	T	T	T	T	T	F	T
T	T	T	F	T	F	F	F	F	F
T	T	F	T	T	T	T	T	F	T
T	T	F	F	T	T	T	F	F	F
T	F	T	T	F	T	F	T	T	T
T	F	T	F	F	F	F	F	T	T
T	F	F	T	F	T	F	T	T	T
T	F	F	F	F	T	F	F	T	T
F	T	T	T	T	T	T	T	F	T
F	T	T	F	T	F	F	T	F	F
F	T	F	T	T	T	T	T	F	T
F	T	F	F	T	T	T	T	F	F
F	F	T	T	T	T	T	T	T	T
F	F	T	F	T	F	F	F	T	T
F	F	F	T	T	T	T	T	T	T
F	F	F	F	T	T	T	T	T	T

(The row F T F F has the values in columns "$[(p \rightarrow q) \,\&\, (r \rightarrow s)]$", "$p \rightarrow s$", "$\sim q$", and "$\sim q \lor s$" circled: T T F F)

INVALID

17.

p	q	r	s	$p \rightarrow q$	$r \rightarrow s$	$(p \rightarrow q) \,\&\, (r \rightarrow s)$	$\sim q$	$\sim s$	$\sim q \lor \sim s$	$\sim p$	$\sim r$	$\sim p \lor \sim r$
T	T	T	T	T	T	T	F	F	F	F	F	F
T	T	T	F	T	F	F	F	T	T	F	F	F
T	T	F	T	T	T	T	F	F	F	F	T	T
T	T	F	F	T	T	T	F	T	T	F	T	T
T	F	T	T	F	T	F	T	F	T	F	F	F
T	F	T	F	F	F	F	T	T	T	F	F	F
T	F	F	T	F	T	F	T	F	T	F	T	T
T	F	F	F	F	T	F	T	T	T	F	T	T
F	T	T	T	T	T	T	F	F	F	T	F	T
F	T	T	F	T	F	F	F	T	T	T	F	T
F	T	F	T	T	T	T	F	F	F	T	T	T
F	T	F	F	T	T	T	F	T	T	T	T	T
F	F	T	T	T	T	T	T	F	T	T	F	T
F	F	T	F	T	F	F	T	T	T	T	F	T
F	F	F	T	T	T	T	T	F	T	T	T	T
F	F	F	F	T	T	T	T	T	T	T	T	T

VALID

19.

p	q	r	s	$p \to q$	$r \to s$	$(p \to q) \to (r \to s)$	$\sim p$	$\sim p \lor q$	$\sim r$	$\sim r \lor s$
T	T	T	T	T	T	T	F	T	F	T
T	T	T	F	T	F	F	F	T	F	F
T	T	F	T	T	T	T	F	T	T	T
T	T	F	F	T	T	T	F	T	T	T
T	F	T	T	F	T	T	F	F	F	T
T	F	T	F	F	F	T	F	F	F	F
T	F	F	T	F	T	T	F	F	T	T
T	F	F	F	F	T	T	F	F	T	T
F	T	T	T	T	T	T	T	T	F	T
F	T	T	F	T	F	F	T	T	F	F
F	T	F	T	T	T	T	T	T	T	T
F	T	F	F	T	T	T	T	T	T	T
F	F	T	T	T	T	T	T	T	F	T
F	F	T	F	T	F	F	T	T	F	F
F	F	F	T	T	T	T	T	T	T	T
F	F	F	F	T	T	T	T	T	T	T

VALID

5.2.II

1. $\sim S \to \sim A$
   $\sim A$ $/ \therefore \sim S$

S	A	$\sim S$	$\sim A$	$\sim S \to \sim A$	$\sim S$
T	T	F	F	T	F
T	F	F	T	T	F
F	T	T	F	F	T
F	F	T	T	T	T

INVALID

3. $P \to S$
   $(P \& S) \to S$ $/ \therefore S$

P	S	$P \to S$	$P \& S$	$(P \& S) \to S$	S
T	T	T	T	T	T
T	F	F	F	T	F
F	T	T	F	T	T
F	F	T	F	T	F

INVALID

5. S → (P v L)
   ~L   /∴ P v ~S

S	P	L	P v L	S → (P v L)	~L	~S	P v ~S
T	T	T	T	T	F	F	T
T	T	F	T	T	T	F	T
T	F	T	T	T	F	F	F
T	F	F	F	F	T	F	F
F	T	T	T	T	F	T	T
F	T	F	T	T	T	T	T
F	F	T	T	T	F	T	T
F	F	F	F	T	T	T	T

VALID

7. S → C
   S → P   /∴   P → C

S	C	P	S → C	S → P	P → C
T	T	T	T	T	T
T	T	F	T	F	T
T	F	T	F	T	F
T	F	F	F	F	T
F	T	T	T	T	T
F	T	F	T	T	T
F	F	T	T	T	F
F	F	F	T	T	T

INVALID

9. ~C → B
   ~C → P   /∴   ~C → (B & P)

C	B	P	~C	~C → B	~C → P	B & P	~C → (B & P)
T	T	T	F	T	T	T	T
T	T	F	F	T	T	F	T
T	F	T	F	T	T	F	T
T	F	F	F	T	T	F	T
F	T	T	T	T	T	T	T
F	T	F	T	T	F	F	F
F	F	T	T	F	T	F	F
F	F	F	T	F	F	F	F

VALID

11. S → Z
     (Z & L) → -D   /∴   D → (-S v -L)

S	Z	L	D	S → Z	(Z & L)	-D	(Z & L) → -D	-S	-L	(-S v -L)	D → (-S v -L)
T	T	T	T	T	T	F	F	F	F	F	F
T	T	T	F	T	T	T	T	F	F	F	T
T	T	F	T	T	F	F	T	F	T	T	T
T	T	F	F	T	F	T	T	F	T	T	T
T	F	T	T	F	F	F	T	F	F	F	F
T	F	T	F	F	F	T	T	F	F	F	T
T	F	F	T	F	F	F	T	F	T	T	T
T	F	F	F	F	F	T	T	F	T	T	T
F	T	T	T	T	T	F	F	T	F	T	T
F	T	T	F	T	T	T	T	T	F	T	T
F	T	F	T	T	F	F	T	T	T	T	T
F	T	F	F	T	F	T	T	T	T	T	T
F	F	T	T	T	F	F	T	T	F	T	T
F	F	T	F	T	F	T	T	T	F	T	T
F	F	F	T	T	F	F	T	T	T	T	T
F	F	F	F	T	F	T	T	T	T	T	T

VALID

13. (B & Z) ↔ (T v D)
     D & -Z   /∴   T → B

B	Z	T	D	(B & Z)	(T v D)	(B & Z) ↔ (T v D)	-Z	D & -Z	T → B
T	T	T	T	T	T	T	F	F	T
T	T	T	F	T	T	T	F	F	T
T	T	F	T	T	T	T	F	F	T
T	T	F	F	T	F	F	F	F	T
T	F	T	T	F	T	F	T	T	T
T	F	T	F	F	T	F	T	F	T
T	F	F	T	F	T	F	T	T	T
T	F	F	F	F	F	T	T	F	T
F	T	T	T	F	T	F	F	F	F
F	T	T	F	F	T	F	F	F	F
F	T	F	T	F	T	F	F	F	T
F	T	F	F	F	F	T	F	F	T
F	F	T	T	F	T	F	T	T	F
F	F	T	F	F	T	F	T	F	F
F	F	F	T	F	T	F	T	T	T
F	F	F	F	F	F	T	T	F	T

VALID

15. (L & T) → (S ∨ H)
    (H → T) & (S → L)   /∴   (L & T) ↔ (S ∨ H)

L T S H	L & T	S ∨ H	(L & T) → (S ∨ H)	H → T	S → L	(H → T) & (S → L)	(L & T) ↔ (S ∨ H)
T T T T	T	T	T	T	T	T	T
T T T F	T	T	T	T	T	T	T
T T F T	T	T	T	T	T	T	T
T T F F	T	F	F	T	T	T	F
T F T T	F	T	T	F	T	F	F
T F T F	F	T	T	T	T	T	F
T F F T	F	T	T	F	T	F	F
T F F F	F	F	T	T	T	T	T
F T T T	F	T	T	T	F	F	F
F T T F	F	T	T	T	F	F	F
F T F T	F	T	T	T	T	T	F
F T F F	F	F	T	T	T	T	T
F F T T	F	T	T	F	F	F	F
F F T F	F	T	T	T	F	F	F
F F F T	F	T	T	F	T	F	F
F F F F	F	F	T	T	T	T	T

INVALID

17. $(T \lor L) \to (D \to F)$ $/\therefore$ $(-L \,\&\, D) \to (-F \,\&\, {\sim}T)$

T	L	D	F	$T \lor L$	$D \to F$	$(T \lor L) \to (D \to F)$	-L	-F	~T	$(-L \,\&\, D)$	$(-F \,\&\, {\sim}T)$	$(-L \,\&\, D) \to (-F \,\&\, {\sim}T)$
T	T	T	T	T	T	T	F	F	F	F	F	T
T	T	T	F	T	F	F	F	T	F	F	F	T
T	T	F	T	T	T	T	F	F	F	F	F	T
T	T	F	F	T	T	T	F	T	F	F	F	T
T	F	T	T	T	T	T	T	F	F	T	F	**F**
T	F	T	F	T	F	F	T	T	F	T	F	F
T	F	F	T	T	T	T	T	F	F	F	F	T
T	F	F	F	T	T	T	T	T	F	F	F	T
F	T	T	T	T	T	T	F	F	T	F	F	T
F	T	T	F	T	F	F	F	T	T	F	T	T
F	T	F	T	T	T	T	F	F	T	F	F	T
F	T	F	F	T	T	T	F	T	T	F	T	T
F	F	T	T	F	T	T	T	F	T	T	F	**F**
F	F	T	F	F	F	T	T	T	T	T	T	T
F	F	F	T	F	T	T	T	F	T	F	F	T
F	F	F	F	F	T	T	T	T	T	F	T	T

INVALID

19. C & -D
     Z ↔ D
     -Z → T   /∴   -C → P

C D Z T P	-D	C & -D	Z ↔ D	-Z	-Z → T	-C	-C → P
T T T T T	F	F	T	F	T	F	T
T T T T F	F	F	T	F	T	F	T
T T T F T	F	F	T	F	T	F	T
T T T F F	F	F	T	F	T	F	T
T T F T T	F	F	F	T	T	F	T
T T F T F	F	F	F	T	T	F	T
T T F F T	F	F	F	T	F	F	T
T T F F F	F	F	F	T	F	F	T
T F T T T	T	T	F	F	T	F	T
T F T T F	T	T	F	F	T	F	T
T F T F T	T	T	F	F	T	F	T
T F T F F	T	T	F	F	T	F	T
T F F T T	T	T	T	T	T	F	T
T F F T F	T	T	T	T	T	F	T
T F F F T	T	T	T	T	F	F	T
T F F F F	T	T	T	T	F	F	T
F T T T T	F	F	T	F	T	T	T
F T T T F	F	F	T	F	T	T	F
F T T F T	F	F	T	F	T	T	T
F T T F F	F	F	T	F	T	T	F
F T F T T	F	F	F	T	T	T	T
F T F T F	F	F	F	T	T	T	F
F T F F T	F	F	F	T	F	T	T
F T F F F	F	F	F	T	F	T	F
F F T T T	T	F	F	F	T	T	T
F F T T F	T	F	F	F	T	T	F
F F T F T	T	F	F	F	T	T	T
F F T F F	T	F	F	F	T	T	F
F F F T T	T	F	T	T	T	T	T
F F F T F	T	F	T	T	T	T	F
F F F F T	T	F	T	T	F	T	T
F F F F F	T	F	T	T	F	T	F

VALID

5.3.1

1.

p	p → p
T	T
F	T

Tautology

3.

p	$p \rightarrow p$	$\sim(p \rightarrow p)$
T	T	F
F	T	F

Contradiction

p	q	$p \,\&\, q$	$\sim p$	$\sim q$	$(\sim p \,\&\, \sim q)$	$(p \,\&\, q) \lor (\sim p \,\&\, \sim q)$
T	T	T	F	F	F	T
T	F	F	F	T	F	F
F	T	F	T	F	F	F
F	F	F	T	T	T	T

Contingent

7.

p	q	r	$q \lor r$	$p \leftrightarrow (q \lor r)$
T	T	T	T	T
T	T	F	T	T
T	F	T	T	T
T	F	F	F	F
F	T	T	T	F
F	T	F	T	F
F	F	T	T	F
F	F	F	F	T

Contingent

p	q	r	$\sim q$	$p \,\&\, \sim q$	$\sim r$	$q \rightarrow \sim r$	$(p \,\&\, \sim q) \rightarrow (q \rightarrow \sim r)$
T	T	T	F	F	F	F	T
T	T	F	F	F	T	T	T
T	F	T	T	T	F	T	T
T	F	F	T	T	T	T	T
F	T	T	F	F	F	F	T
F	T	F	F	F	T	T	T
F	F	T	T	F	F	T	T
F	F	F	T	F	T	T	T

Tautology

5.3.II

1.

p	q	$p \,\&\, q$	$q \,\&\, p$	$(p \,\&\, q) \leftrightarrow (q \,\&\, p)$
T	T	T	T	T
T	F	F	F	T
F	T	F	F	T
F	F	F	F	T

Logical Equivalence

3.

p	q	p ∨ q	~(p ∨ q)	~p	~q	~p & ~q	~(p ∨ q) ↔ (~p & ~q)
T	T	T	F	F	F	F	T
T	F	T	F	F	T	F	T
F	T	T	F	T	F	F	T
F	F	F	T	T	T	T	T

Logical Equivalence

5.

p	q	p ↔ q	p & q	~p	~q	~p & ~q	(p & q) ∨ (~p & ~q)	(p ↔ q) ↔ [(p & q) ∨ (~p & ~q)]
T	T	T	T	F	F	F	T	T
T	F	F	F	F	T	F	F	T
F	T	F	F	T	F	F	F	T
F	F	T	F	T	T	T	T	T

Logical Equivalence

7.

p	q	p ↔ q	p → q	~p	~q	~p → ~q	(p → q) ∨ (~p → ~q)	(p ↔ q) ↔ [(p → q) ∨ (~p → ~q)]
T	T	T	T	F	F	T	T	T
T	F	F	F	F	T	F	F	T
F	T	F	T	T	F	T	T	T
F	F	T	T	T	T	T	T	T

Logical Equivalence

9.

p	q	r	q & r	p ∨ (q & r)	p ∨ q	~p	~p → r	(p ∨ q) & (~p → r)	[p ∨ (q & r)] ↔ [(p ∨ q) & (~p → r)]
T	T	T	T	T	T	F	T	T	T
T	T	F	F	T	T	F	T	T	T
T	F	T	F	T	T	F	T	T	T
T	F	F	F	T	T	F	T	T	T
F	T	T	T	T	T	T	T	T	T
F	T	F	F	F	T	T	F	F	T
F	F	T	F	F	F	T	T	F	T
F	F	F	F	F	F	T	F	F	T

Logical Equivalence

5.4

1.

p	q		$p \to q$	$\sim p$	$\sim q$
T	T			F	F
T	F			F	T
F	T		T	T	F
F	F				T

INVALID

3.

p	q		$\sim p \leftrightarrow q$	$\sim q$ & $(p \lor \sim p)$		q
T	T					T
T	F		F T	T T	T F	F
F	T					T
F	F					F

INVALID

5.

p	q		p & $\sim p$		q
T	T				T
T	F		F F		F
F	T				T
F	F		F T		F

VALID

7.

p	q	r		p & $\sim q$		$\sim p$	r
T	T	T					T
T	T	F				F	F
T	F	T					T
T	F	F				F	F
F	T	T					T
F	T	F		F F		T	F
F	F	T					T
F	F	F		F T		T	F

VALID

9.

p	q	r		$p \leftrightarrow (q \lor \sim r)$		$\sim q$	$p \to \sim r$	
T	T	T				F	F	F
T	T	F					T	T
T	F	T		F	F F	T	F	F
T	F	F					T	T
F	T	T					T	
F	T	F					T	
F	F	T					T	
F	F	F					T	

VALID

11.

p	q	r		p	p → (q & ~r)	r
T	T	T				T
T	T	F		T	T T T	F
T	F	T				T
T	F	F				F
F	T	T				T
F	T	F				F
F	F	T				T
F	F	F				F

INVALID

13.

p	q	r	s		p & ([q ∨ r] → s)	~s ∨ ~p	~q & ~r
T	T	T	T			F F F	F F F
T	T	T	F		F T F	T T F	F F F
T	T	F	T			F F F	F F T
T	T	F	F		F T F	T T F	F F T
T	F	T	T			F F F	T F F
T	F	T	F		F T F	T T F	T F F
T	F	F	T				T T T
T	F	F	F				T T T
F	T	T	T		F T T	F T T	F F F
F	T	T	F		F T F	T T T	F F F
F	T	F	T		F T T	F T T	F F T
F	T	F	F		F T F	T T T	F F T
F	F	T	T		F T T	F T T	T F F
F	F	T	F		F T F	T T T	T F F
F	F	F	T				T T T
F	F	F	F				T T T

VALID

15.

p	q	r	s		(p & [q ∨ r]) → s	~s ∨ ~p	~q & ~r
T	T	T	T		T T T	F F F	F F F
T	T	T	F				F F F
T	T	F	T				F F T
T	T	F	F				F F T
T	F	T	T				T F F
T	F	T	F				T F F
T	F	F	T				T T T
T	F	F	F				T T T
F	T	T	T				F F F
F	T	T	F				F F F
F	T	F	T				F F T
F	T	F	F				F F T
F	F	T	T				T F F
F	F	T	F				T F F
F	F	F	T				T T T
F	F	F	F				T T T

INVALID

17.

p	q	r	s	(p & ~[q v r]) → (s → ~p)	p & ~q	~s
T	T	T	T		F F	F
T	T	T	F			T
T	T	F	T		F F	F
T	T	F	F			T
T	F	T	T	F F T T F F	T T	F
T	F	T	F			T
T	F	F	T			F
T	F	F	F			T
F	T	T	T			F
F	T	T	F			T
F	T	F	T			F
F	T	F	F			T
F	F	T	T			F
F	F	T	F			T
F	F	F	T			F
F	F	F	F			T

INVALID

19.

p	q	r	s	p ↔ (r v ~s)	q & ~r	s	~q
T	T	T	T		F F	T	F
T	T	T	F			F	F
T	T	F	T	F F F	T T	T	F
T	T	F	F			F	F
T	F	T	T		F F	T	T
T	F	T	F			T
T	F	F	T			T
T	F	F	F			T
F	T	T	T		F F	T	F
F	T	T	F			F	F
F	T	F	T	T F F	T T	T	F
F	T	F	F			F
F	F	T	T			T
F	F	T	F			T
F	F	F	T			T
F	F	F	F			T

INVALID

21.

p	q	r	s	~p → (r & ~s)	~q ↔ r	s ∨ ~r	~q & p
T	T	T	T		F F	T F	F F
T	T	T	F			F F	F F
T	T	F	T	F T F F	F T	T T	F F
T	T	F	F				F F
T	F	T	T				T T
T	F	T	F				T T
T	F	F	T				T T
T	F	F	F				T T
F	T	T	T				F
F	T	T	F				F
F	T	F	T				F
F	T	F	F				F
F	F	T	T				F
F	F	T	F				F
F	F	F	T				F
F	F	F	F				F

INVALID

23.

p	q	r	s	~p → (r & ~s)	~(q ↔ r)	s & r	~(q ↔ ~q)
T	T	T	T				T F F
T	T	T	F				T F F
T	T	F	T				T F F
T	T	F	F				T F F
T	F	T	T				T F T
T	F	T	F				T F T
T	F	F	T				T F T
T	F	F	F				T F T
F	T	T	T				T F F
F	T	T	F				T F F
F	T	F	T				T F F
F	T	F	F				T F F
F	F	T	T				T F T
F	F	T	F				T F T
F	F	F	T				T F T
F	F	F	F				T F T

VALID

25.

p	q	r	s	t	[(p ∨ q) & (r ∨ s)] → (t & -p)	(q & -r) → (t & s)	(q & s) → (-t ∨ r)
T	T	T	T	T			T T F T
T	T	T	T	F			T T T T
T	T	T	F	T			F T F T
T	T	T	F	F			F T T T
T	T	F	T	T	T T T F F F	T T	T F F F
T	T	F	T	F			T T T T
T	T	F	F	T			F T T F
T	T	F	F	F			F T T T
T	F	T	T	T			F T F T
T	F	T	T	F			F T T T
T	F	T	F	T			F T F T
T	F	T	F	F			F T T T
T	F	F	T	T			F T T F
T	F	F	T	F			F T T T
T	F	F	F	T			F T T F
T	F	F	F	F			F T T T
F	T	T	T	T			T T F T
F	T	T	T	F			T T T T
F	T	T	F	T			F T F T
F	T	T	F	F			F T T T
F	T	F	T	T	T T T T T T	T T	T F F F
F	T	F	T	F			T T T T
F	T	F	F	T			F T T F
F	T	F	F	F			F T T T
F	F	T	T	T			F T F T
F	F	T	T	F			F T T T
F	F	T	F	T			F T F T
F	F	T	F	F			F T T T
F	F	F	T	T			F T T F
F	F	F	T	F			F T T T
F	F	F	F	T			F T T F
F	F	F	F	F			F T T T

INVALID

5.5

1.   T   T   F

       p   q /∴   p & q

T/F	T	F	T	(1)
T	F/T	T	F	(2)
T/F	T/F	F	F	(3)

It is impossible to assign truth values so that all the premises are true and the conclusion is false. The argument is valid.

3.   T   F

       p   /∴   p ∨ q

     T/F   F   F

It is impossible to assign truth values so that all the premises are true and the conclusion is false. The argument is valid.

5.
```
    T   T        F
    p   q  /∴  p ↔ q
   T/F  T       F   T
    T  T/F      T   F
```
It is impossible to assign truth values so that all the premises are true and the conclusion is false. The argument is valid.

7.
```
            T        T            F
   (p & q) & r    p v -r    /∴    q
    T  T/F  T     T  T  F          F
     \ /    /      \   T
      F    /       \/
      \F /          T
```
It is impossible to assign truth values so that all the premises are true and the conclusion is false. The argument is valid.

9.
```
          T        T           F
   (p → q) v r   r → -p   /∴    q
    F  F  F  F     F              F
     \T/    /    \   T
      \ T /       \ T /
```

INVALID

11.
```
      T                T           F
   p → (q & -r)    -r → q   /∴    -p
    T   T  F  F     F   T          T
     \    \  T   T  /              F
      \    \T/    \T/
       \T/
```

INVALID

13.
```
      T                T              F
   p ↔ (r ↔ -q)    -p → r   /∴    -q v p
    F   T  T  F     F   T          T   F
     \    \  F   T  /              F\  /
      \    F/     \ T/              F
       \T/
```

INVALID

15.
```
      T                  T                F
   p & (q ↔ -r)    r v (p & -q)   /∴    p v -q
   T/F  T  F  F     F  T/F   T           F   T
     \    \  T       \   \   F            \  F
      \    \T/        \   F                F
       \F /            \F/
```
It is impossible to assign truth values so that all the premises are true and the conclusion is false. The argument is valid.

17.　　T　　　　　　　T　　　　　　　　F
$p \rightarrow (\text{-}q \lor \text{-}r)$　$r \,\&\, (p \lor \text{-}q)$　　/∴　$p \,\&\, q$
　F　　F　T　T　　F　F　　　　　　F　F
　　\　T　F　　\　　\ T　　　　　\ F /
　　　\　　\T/　　　\　　T
　　　　\T/　　　　　\T

INVALID

19.　　T　　　　　　　　T　　　T　　　　　F
$p \rightarrow [q \lor (r \,\&\, s)]$　$p \lor \text{-}s$　$q \lor \text{-}r$　/∴　$\text{-}p \lor q$
　T　　F　T　T　　T　T T/F　T　　　　T　F
　　\　　\　\T/　　\ F　　\ F　　　F　/
　　　\　　\ T/　　　T　　　F　　　　\ F
　　\ T /

It is impossible to assign truth values so that all the premises are true and the conclusion is false. The argument is valid.

21.　　T　　　　　　　　　　T　　　T　　　　　F
$p \leftrightarrow [\text{-}q \,\&\, (r \leftrightarrow s)]$　$p \lor \text{-}s$　$\text{-}q \,\&\, r$　/∴　$\text{-}p \,\&\, q$
　T　　F　　T　T　　T　T F　T　　　　T　F
　　\　T　　　\ T /　　\ F T　/　　F　/
　　　\　\ T /　　　T　　T　　　　F
　　\T/

INVALID

23.　　T　　　　　　　　　T　　　　　　T　　　　　　　F
$p \lor [q \rightarrow (\text{-}r \leftrightarrow s)]$　$\text{-}p \rightarrow \text{-}s$　$(p \,\&\, \text{-}s) \rightarrow r$　/∴　$\text{-}p \rightarrow q$
　F　F　　T　F　　F　F　F　F　T　　　　F　F
　　\　\　F　/　　T　T　\ T　/　　　T　/
　　　\　\　\T/　　\ T /　　F　/　　　\ F
　　\　T /　　　　　　　　\ T/
　　　T

INVALID

25.　　T　　　　　　　　　T　　　　　　　　T　　　　　　　F
$p \lor [q \rightarrow (\text{-}r \leftrightarrow s)]$　$\text{-}p \leftrightarrow (\text{-}r \rightarrow s)$　$(\text{-}p \lor s) \rightarrow \text{-}r$　/∴　$\text{-}s$
　F　F　　F　T　　F　　F　T　　F　T　F　　　　T
　　\　\　T　/　　T　　T　/　　T　/　T　　　　F
　　　\　\　\T/　　　\　　\T　　\T/　/
　　　\　\ T/　　　\ T /　　　\ T /
　　\ T /

INVALID

27.　　　T　　　　　　　　T　　　　　T　　　　　　　T　　　　　　　F

{p ↔ [q → (-r & s)]}　(-p → -t)　[-p ↔ (t → -s)]　[-(p ∨ s) → -t]　/∴　-s & t

　F　　T　T　F　　　F　F　　　F　F　F　　　F　F　　F　　　F　F

　　\　　\　F　/　　T　T　T　　　\　T　　　F　　T　　　T　/

　　　\　　\　　F　　\ T /　　　\　　T　　T　　　　/　　　　F

　　　　\　　F　　　　　　　　\ T /　　　　\ T

　　　　　\ T

INVALID

29.　　　T　　　　T　　　　T　　　　T　　　F

p → (-q ∨ r)　q → (-r ∨ s)　r → (-s ↔ p)　-p ∨ t　/∴　s

　F　　F　F　F　　F　F　F　　F　　F　F　　F　T　　　F

　　\　T　/　　\　T　/　　\　T　/　　T　/

　　　\　T　　　　\　T　　　　\　F　　　　T

　　　　\T　　　　　T　　　　　T

INVALID

31.　　　T　　　　　T　　　　　T　　　　　　T　　　　　　　T　　　　　　F

p → (-q ∨ r)　q → (-r ∨ s)　r → (-s & -t)　s → (r ↔ (t & -p))　-p ∨ (s & -q) /∴ s ↔ -t

　F　　F　F　F　　F　F　F　　F　F　F　　F　　F　　F　F　F　F　　F　F　　F　F

　　\　T　/　　\　T　/　　\　T　T　　\　　\　　\ T　T　　\　T　　　\　T

　　　\　T　　　　\　T　　　　\　T　　　\　　\　F　　　\　F　　　　F

　　　　T　　　　　T　　　　　T　　　　　\　T　　　　　T

　　　　　　　　　　　　　　　　　　　　　T

INVALID

33.　　　T　　T　　　　T　　　　　T　　　　　F

p ∨ q　-p ∨ (q & r)　p ∨ (-q → s)　-p ∨ -(s → t)　/∴　-p & s

　F　T　F　T　T　F　　T　F　F　　F　F　T　　　F　F

　　T　T　　　T　　　\　F　/　　T　　\ T　　　　T　/

　　　\T/　　　　　\　\T/　　　\ T /　　　　　F

　　　　　　　　　　　T

INVALID

35.　　　T　　　　　T　　　　　　T　　　　　T　　　F

p → (-q ∨ r)　-q → [r ∨ (s & -t)]　s ↔ (t → -u)　-u　/∴　s

　F　　T　T　T　　T　F　T　　F　T　F　F　　　F

　　\　F　/　F　　　\　\　F　　\　　\ T　T

　　　\　T　　\　　　\　F　　　\　F

　　　　T　　　\　　　\T　　　\ T /

　　　　　　　　　\　T　/

INVALID

37.　　T　　　　　T　　　　　　T　　　　T　　　　F
　　-p & -(-q ∨ r)　-q ∨ [r → (-s & -t)]　-s ∨ (t → u)　-u　/∴　t & -r
　　F　T　F　T　F　F　F　F　F　F　F　F　　F　F
　　T　F\　/　F　\　T　T　T　T　T　　\　T
　　\　F　\　\　T　\　T　/　　　　　F
　　\　T　/　　\　　\ T /　　　　　F
　　T/　　　　\　T　/

INVALID

39.　　T　　　　　T　　　　T　　　　T　　　　F
　　-p ∨ (q ∨ -r)　q → (r & s)　r ↔ (-s & -t)　-t ∨ (u ↔ w)　/∴　p & -w
　　F　F　F　F　F　T　F　T　F　F　F　F　　F　F
　　T\　\　T　\　F　\　F　T　T　T　　\　T
　　\　T　　　T　　\　F　\ T /　　　F
　　T　　　　　　　T

INVALID

6.1.I

1. D.S.　　11. Conj.
3. M.P.　　13. C.D.
5. C.D.　　15. H.S.
7. M.T.　　17. D.S.
9. H.S.　　19. Abs.

6.1.II

1. 1. p　/∴　p ∨ (r & s)
　 2. p ∨ (r & s)　　　　　　1 Add.

3. 1. p
　 2. (p → q) & (r → s)　/∴　q ∨ s
　 3. p ∨ r　　　　　　　　1 Add.
　 4. q ∨ s　　　　　　　　2,3 C.D.

5. 1. p
　 2. p → r　/∴　p & r
　 3. r　　　　　　　　　　1,2 M.P.
　 4. p & r　　　　　　　　1,3 Conj.

7. 1. p → q
　 2. q → r
　 3. p ∨ q　/∴　q ∨ r
　 4. (p → q) & (q → r)　　1,2 Conj.
　 5. q ∨ r　　　　　　　　4,3 C.D.

9. 1. p & q
　 2. p → q　/∴　q
　 3. p　　　　　　　　　　1 Simp.
　 4. q　　　　　　　　　　2,3 M.P.

11.   1. $p \rightarrow q$
      2. $(p \ \& \ q) \rightarrow s$
      3. $\sim s$ $/\therefore$ $\sim p$
      4. $p \rightarrow (p \ \& \ q)$ 1 Abs.
      5. $p \rightarrow s$ 4,2 H.S.
      6. $\sim p$ 5,6 M.T.

13.   1. $\sim p \ \& \ (r \lor s)$
      2. $q \rightarrow p$ $/\therefore$ $\sim q \lor (r \ \& \ s)$
      3. $\sim p$ 1 Simp.
      4. $\sim q$ 2,3 M.T.
      5. $\sim q \lor (r \ \& \ s)$ 4 Add.

15.   1. $(p \rightarrow q) \ \& \ (r \rightarrow s)$
      2. $r \lor p$
      3. $\sim r$ $/\therefore$ $q \lor s$
      4. p 2,3 D.S.
      5. $p \lor r$ 4 Add.
      6. $q \lor s$ 1 C.D.

17.   1. $p \lor (r \rightarrow s)$
      2. r
      3. $\sim p$ $/\therefore$ $s \lor \sim s$
      4. $r \rightarrow s$ 1,3 D.S.
      5. s 4,2 M.P.
      6. $s \lor \sim s$ 5 Add.

19.   1. $p \rightarrow q$
      2. $\sim q$
      3. $(\sim p \lor s) \rightarrow (q \rightarrow s)$ $/\therefore$ $p \rightarrow s$
      4. $\sim p$ 1,2 M.T.
      5. $\sim p \lor s$ 4 Add.
      6. $q \rightarrow s$ 3,5 M.P.
      7. $p \rightarrow s$ 1,6 H.S.

21.   1. $p \rightarrow q$
      2. $r \lor s$
      3. $(q \ \& \ s) \rightarrow t$
      4. p
      5. $\sim r$ $/\therefore$ t
      6. q 1,4 M.P.
      7. s 2,5 D.S.
      8. $q \ \& \ s$ 6,7 Conj.
      9. t 3,8 M.P.

23.   1. $[(p \lor q) \rightarrow r] \ \& \ [(s \ \& \ t) \rightarrow u]$
      2. p
      3. $\sim r$ $/\therefore$ u
      4. $(p \lor q) \rightarrow r$ 1 Simp
      5. $p \lor q$ 2 Add
      6. r 4,5 M.P.
      7. $r \lor u$ 6 Add
      8. u 7,3 D.S.

25.   1. $[(p \lor q) \rightarrow r]$ & $[(s$ & $t) \rightarrow u]$
    2. $\sim r$
    3. $(p \lor q) \lor (t \rightarrow s)$
    4. $\sim s$ /∴ $\sim t \lor (s \leftrightarrow t)$
    5. $(p \lor q) \rightarrow r$ 1 Simp.
    6. $\sim(p \lor q)$ 5,2 M.T.
    7. $t \rightarrow s$ 3,6 D.S.
    8. $\sim t$ 7,4 M.T.
    9. $\sim t \lor (s \leftrightarrow \sim s)$ 8 Add.

27.   1. $(p \lor q) \rightarrow r$
    2. p
    3. $r \rightarrow s$
    4. $[(p \lor q)$ & $s] \rightarrow t$ /∴ $t \lor \sim p$
    5. $(p \lor q) \rightarrow s$ 1,3 H.S.
    6. $(p \lor q) \rightarrow [(p \lor q)$ & $s]$ 5 Abs.
    7. $p \lor q$ 2 Add.
    8. $(p \lor q)$ & s 6,7 M.P.
    9. t 4,8 M.P.
    10. $t \lor \sim p$ 9 Add

29.   1. $(p \rightarrow q)$ & $(r \rightarrow s)$
    2. $(r \rightarrow s)$ & $(t \rightarrow u)$
    3. p
    4. $\sim q$ /∴ s
    5. $(p \rightarrow q)$ 1 Simp.
    6. $(r \rightarrow s)$ 2 Simp.
    7. $(p \rightarrow q)$ & $(r \rightarrow s)$ 5,6 Conj.
    8. $p \lor r$ 3 Add
    9. $q \lor s$ 7,8 C.D.
    10. s 9,4 D.S.

6.1.III

1.   1. $(H \lor D) \rightarrow G$
    2. H /∴ G
    3. $H \lor D$ 2 Add.
    4. G 1,3 M.P.

3.   1. $(P \lor D) \rightarrow (F$ & $M)$
    2. P /∴ F
    3. $P \lor D$ 2 Add.
    4. F & M 1,3 M.P.
    5. F 5 Simp.

5.   1. $\sim H \lor H$
    2. $H \rightarrow S$
    3. $\sim H \rightarrow C$
    4. $\sim C$ /∴ S
    5. $(\sim H \rightarrow C)$ & $(H \rightarrow S)$ 3,2 Conj.
    6. $C \lor S$ 5,1 C.D.
    7. S 6,4 D.S.

7. 1. [H → (F v B)] & (Y → L)
    2. H
    3. ~(F v B)   /∴   G
    4. H → (F v B)   1 Simp.
    5. ~H   4,3 M.T.
    6. H v G   2 Add.
    7. G   6,5 D.S.

9. 1. H → (R v G)
    2. [H & (R v G)] → (O v P)
    3. ~O
    4. H   /∴   P
    5. H → [H & (R v G)]   1 Abs.
    6. H → (O v P)   5,2 H.S.
    7. O v P   6,4 M.P.
    8. P   7,3 D.S.

11. 1. (O v P) & ~H
    2. ~O
    3. P → (~H → C)
    4. ~C   /∴   ~~H
    5. O v P   1 Simp.
    6. P   5,2 D.S.
    7. ~H → C   3,6 M.P.
    8. ~~H   7,4 M.T.

13. 1. (P & C) v (G → Y)
    2. (P & C) → M
    3. M → R
    4. ~R
    5. ~Y
    6. ~G → H   /∴   H
    7. ~M   3,4 M.T.
    8. ~(P & C)   2,7 M.T.
    9. G → Y   1,8 D.S.
    10. ~G   9,5 M.T.
    11. H   6,10 M.P.

15. 1. C v E
    2. E → (R v Y)
    3. ~R
    4. Y → (B & H)
    5. B → H
    6. ~C   /∴   H
    7. E   1,6 D.S.
    8. R v Y   2,7 M.P.
    9. Y   8,3 D.S.
    10. B & H   4,9 M.P.
    11. B   10 Simp.
    12. H   5,11 M.P.

17.   1. P → C
    2. (P & C) → R
    3. R v O
    4. H
    5. H → ~R   /∴   ~P & O
    6. ~R   4,5 M.P.
    7. O   3,6 D.S.
    8. P → (P & C)   1 Abs.
    9. P → R   8,2 H.S.
   10. ~P   9,6 M.T.
   11. ~P & O   10,7 Conj.

19.   1. (R v G) → P
    2. (R v G) → (P → O)
    3. P → (O → C)
    4. R
    5. ~C   /∴   H
    6. R v G   4 Add.
    7. P   1,6 M.P.
    8. P → O   2,6 M.P.
    9. O   8,7 M.P.
   10. O → C   3,7 M.P.
   11. C   10,9 M.P.
   12. C v H   11 Add.
   13. H   12,5 D.S.

6.2.I

  1.   DeM.
  3.   Dist.
  5.   DeM.
  7.   D.N.
  9.   Dist.

6.2.II

  1.   1. ~(p v q)   /∴   ~q
      2. ~p & ~q   1 DeM.
      3. ~q & ~p   2 Com.
      4. ~q   3 Simp.

  3.   1. p
      2. ~(p & q)   /∴   ~q
      3. ~p v ~q   2 DeM.
      4. ~~p   1 D.N.
      5. ~q   3,4 D.S.

  5.   1. p & s   /∴   (s v q) & (s v r)
      2. s & p   1 Com.
      3. s   2 Simp.
      4. s v (q & r)   3 Add.
      5. (s v q) & (s v r)   4 Dist.

7. 1. p & (q & r)   /∴ p & r
    2. p & (r & q)   1 Com.
    3. (p & r) & q 2 Assoc.
    4. p & r 3 Simp.

9. 1. -p & [q ∨ (r & s)]   /∴   (-p & q) ∨ (-p & s)
    2. [q ∨ (r & s)] & -p 1 Com.
    3. q ∨ (r & s)   2 Simp.
    4. (q ∨ r) & (q ∨ s)   3 Dist.
    5. (q ∨ s) & (q ∨ r)   4 Com.
    6. q ∨ s 5 Simp.
    7. -p 1 Simp.
    8. -p & (q ∨ s)   7,6 Conj.
    9. (-p & q) ∨ (-p & s)   8 Dist.

11. 1. p ∨ (q ∨ r)
    2. -p & -q /∴ r
    3. -p 2 Simp.
    4. q ∨ r 1,3 D.S.
    5. -q & -p 2 Com.
    6. -q 5 Simp.
    7. r 4,6 D.S.

13. 1. -[p & (q ∨ r)]
    2. q /∴   -p
    3. -p ∨ -(q ∨ r)   1 DeM.
    4. -(q ∨ r) ∨ -p 3 Com.
    5. q ∨ r 2 Add.
    6. --(q ∨ r)   5 D.N.
    7. -p 4,6 D.S.

15. 1. (p & q) ∨ (p & r)
     2. -r
     3. q → t   /∴   (t ∨ s) & (t ∨ w)
     4. p & (q ∨ r)   1 Dist.
     5. (q ∨ r) & p 4 Com.
     6. q ∨ r 5 Simp.
     7. r ∨ q 6 Com.
     8. q 7,2 D.S.
     9. t   3,8 M.P.
    10. t ∨ (s & w)   9 Add.
    11. (t ∨ s) & (t ∨ w)   10 Dist.

17.   1. $(p \& q) \lor (p \& s)$
      2. $(s \rightarrow w) \& (q \rightarrow m)$
      3. $a \rightarrow \lnot(m \lor w)$ $/\therefore$ $\lnot a \& p$
      4. $p \& (q \lor s)$ 1 Dist.
      5. $(q \lor s) \& p$ 4 Com.
      6. $q \lor s$ 5 Simp.
      7. $s \lor q$ 6 Com.
      8. $w \lor m$ 2,7 C.D.
      9. $m \lor w$ 8 Com.
    10. $\lnot\lnot(m \lor w)$ 9 D.N.
    11. p 4 Simp.
    12. $\lnot a$ 3,10 M.T.
    13. $\lnot a \& p$ 12,11 Conj.

19.   1. $(p \& q) \lor (r \& s)$
      2. $s \rightarrow (w \& z)$
      3. $\lnot q$ $/\therefore$ z
      4. $\lnot q \lor \lnot p$ 3 Add.
      5. $\lnot p \lor \lnot q$ 4 Com.
      6. $\lnot(p \& q)$ 5 DeM.
      7. $r \& s$ 1,6 D.S.
      8. $s \& r$ 7 Com.
      9. s 8 Simp.
    10. $w \& z$ 2,9 M.P.
    11. $z \& w$ 10 Com.
    12. z 11 Simp.

6.3.I

1. Equiv.
3. Taut.
5. Equiv.
7. Exp.
9. Impl.

6.3.II

1.   1. p
    2. $\lnot p \lor q$ $/\therefore$ q
    3. $p \rightarrow q$ 2 Impl.
    4. q 1,3 M.P.

3.   1. $p \leftrightarrow q$
    2. $\lnot q$ $/\therefore$ $\lnot p \& \lnot q$
    3. $(p \rightarrow q) \& (q \rightarrow p)$ 1 Equiv.
    4. $p \rightarrow q$ 3 Simp.
    5. $\lnot p$ 4,2 M.T.
    6. $\lnot p \& \lnot q$ 5,2 Conj.

5.   1. $(p \rightarrow q) \& (r \rightarrow s)$
    2. $\lnot q \lor \lnot s$ $/\therefore$ $\lnot p \lor \lnot r$
    3. $(\lnot q \rightarrow \lnot p) \& (r \rightarrow s)$ 1 Trans.
    5. $(\lnot q \rightarrow \lnot p) \& (\lnot s \rightarrow \lnot r)$ 3 Trans.
    6. $\lnot p \lor \lnot r$ 5,2 C.D.

7.   1. $p \rightarrow q$
     2. $p \rightarrow (q \rightarrow r)$ $/\therefore$ $p \rightarrow r$
     3. $p \rightarrow (p \& q)$ 1 Abs.
     4. $(p \& q) \rightarrow r$ 2 Exp.
     5. $p \rightarrow r$ 3,4 H.S.

9.   1. $p \rightarrow q$
     2. $\sim\sim p$ $/\therefore$ q
     3. $\sim p \vee q$ 1 Impl.
     4. q 3,2 D.S.

11. 1. $p \rightarrow (q \vee \sim s)$ $/\therefore$ $p \rightarrow [p \rightarrow (\sim s \vee \sim q)]$
     2. $(p \& p) \rightarrow (q \vee \sim s)$ 1 Taut.
     3. $p \rightarrow (p \rightarrow [q \vee \sim s])$ 2 Exp.
     4. $p \rightarrow (p \rightarrow [\sim q \rightarrow \sim s])$ 3 Impl.
     5. $p \rightarrow (p \rightarrow [\sim\sim s \rightarrow \sim q)$ 4 Trans.
     6. $p \rightarrow (p \rightarrow [\sim s \vee \sim q])$ 5 Imp.

13. 1. $p \leftrightarrow q$
     2. $\sim p \rightarrow r$ $/\therefore$ $\sim q \rightarrow r$
     3. $(p \rightarrow q) \& (q \rightarrow p)$ 1 Equiv.
     4. $p \rightarrow q$ 3 Simp.
     5. $\sim q \rightarrow \sim p$ 4 Trans.
     6. $\sim q \rightarrow \sim r$ 5,2 H.S.

15. 1. $\sim p$
     2. $\sim p \rightarrow s$ $/\therefore$ $\sim(\sim r \rightarrow \sim q) \rightarrow s$
     3. $\sim p \vee (q \rightarrow r)$ 1 Add.
     4. $p \rightarrow (q \rightarrow r)$ 3 Impl.
     5. $\sim(q \rightarrow r) \rightarrow \sim p$ 4 Trans.
     6. $\sim(q \rightarrow r) \rightarrow s$ 5,2 H.S.
     7. $\sim(\sim r \rightarrow \sim q) \rightarrow s$ 6 Trans.

17. 1. p
     2. $\sim p$ $/\therefore$ $(\sim\sim q \rightarrow \sim p) \& (\sim p \rightarrow \sim\sim q)$
     3. $p \vee [(\sim\sim q \rightarrow \sim p) \& (\sim p \rightarrow \sim\sim q)]$ 1 Add
     4. $(\sim\sim q \rightarrow \sim p) \& (\sim p \rightarrow \sim\sim q)$ 3,2 D.S.

19. 1. $p \leftrightarrow r$
     2. $q \rightarrow (r \rightarrow s)$
     3. $\sim s$ $/\therefore$ $(p \& r) \rightarrow t$
     4. $(p \rightarrow q) \& (q \rightarrow r)$ 1 Equiv.
     5. $p \rightarrow q$ 4 Simp.
     6. $p \rightarrow (r \rightarrow s)$ 5,2 H.S.
     7. $(p \& r) \rightarrow s$ 6 Exp.
     8. $\sim(p \& r)$ 7,3 M.T.
     9. $\sim(p \& r) \vee t$ 8 Add.
     10. $(p \& r) \rightarrow t$ 9 Impl.

6.3.III

1.   1. p $/\therefore$ $q \rightarrow p$
     2. $p \vee \sim q$ 1 Add.
     3. $\sim q \vee p$ 2 Com.
     4. $q \rightarrow p$ 3 Impl.

3. 1. $p \to q$
 2. $q \to -p$ $/\therefore$ $-p$
 3. $p \to -p$ 1,2 H.S.
 4. $-p \lor -p$ 3 Impl.
 5. $-p$ 4 Taut.

5. 1. $p \leftrightarrow q$ $/\therefore$ $-p \to -q$
 2. $(p \to q) \mathbin{\&} (q \to p)$ 1 Equiv.
 3. $(q \to p) \mathbin{\&} (p \to q)$ 2 Com.
 4. $q \to p$ 3 Simp.
 5. $-p \to -q$ 4 Trans.

7. 1. $(p \to q) \mathbin{\&} (r \to s)$
 2. $-q \lor -s$ $/\therefore$ $p \to -r$
 3. $(-q \to -p) \mathbin{\&} (r \to s)$ 1 Trans.
 4. $(-q \to -p) \mathbin{\&} (-s \to -r)$ 3 Trans.
 5. $-p \lor -r$ 4,2 C.D.
 6. $p \to -r$ 5 Impl.

9. 1. $p \to -q$
 2. q
 3. $-p \to (r \to s)$ $/\therefore$ $r \to (r \mathbin{\&} s)$
 4. $--q$ 2 D.N.
 5. $-p$ 1,4 M.T.
 6. $r \to s$ 3,5 M.P.
 7. $r \to (r \mathbin{\&} s)$ 6 Abs.

11. 1. $-p \to q$
 2. $-r \to -q$
 3. $-r$ $/\therefore$ $p \mathbin{\&} p$
 4. $q \to r$ 2 Trans.
 5. $-p \to r$ 1,4 H.S.
 6. $--p$ 5,3 M.T.
 7. p 6 D.N.
 8. $p \mathbin{\&} p$ 7 Taut.

13. 1. $p \lor (q \mathbin{\&} r)$
 2. $(p \to r) \mathbin{\&} (q \to s)$ $/\therefore$ $-s \to r$
 3. $(p \lor q) \mathbin{\&} (p \lor r)$ 1 Dist.
 4. $p \lor q$ 3 Simp.
 5. $r \lor s$ 2,4 C.D.
 6. $s \lor r$ 5 Com.
 7. $-s \to r$ 6 Impl.

15. 1. $p \to q$
 2. $(q \lor p) \lor r$ $/\therefore$ $-q \to r$
 3. $-q \to -p$ 1 Trans.
 4. $-q \to (-q \mathbin{\&} -p)$ 3 Abs.
 5. $-q \to -(q \lor p)$ 4 DeM.
 6. $-(q \lor p) \to r$ 2 Impl.
 7. $-q \to r$ 5,6 H.S.

17. 1. $\sim s \rightarrow \sim r$
     2. r /∴ $q \lor s$
     3. $r \rightarrow s$ 1 Trans.
     4. s 2,3 M.P.
     5. $s \lor q$ 4 Add.
     6. $q \lor s$ 5 Com.

19. 1. $p \& q$
     2. $q \rightarrow (r \lor s)$ /∴ $\sim s \rightarrow (\sim s \& r)$
     3. $q \& p$ 1 Com.
     4. q 3 Simp.
     5. $r \lor s$ 2,4 M.P.
     6. $s \lor r$ 5 Com.
     7. $\sim s \rightarrow r$ 6 Impl.
     8. $\sim s \rightarrow (\sim s \& r)$ 7 Abs.

21. 1. $\sim(\sim p \& q)$
     2. $\sim(q \leftrightarrow r)$ /∴ $\sim r \rightarrow p$
     3. $\sim[(q \& r) \lor (\sim q \& \sim r)]$ 2 Equiv.
     4. $\sim[(\sim q \& \sim r) \lor (q \& r)]$ 3 Com.
     5. $\sim(\sim q \& \sim r) \& \sim(q \& r)$ 4 DeM.
     6. $\sim(\sim q \& \sim r)$ 5 Simp.
     7. $\sim\sim q \lor \sim\sim r$ 6 DeM.
     8. $q \lor \sim\sim r$ 7 D.N.
     9. $q \lor r$ 8 D.N.
     10. $\sim q \rightarrow r$ 9 Impl.
     11. $\sim\sim p \lor \sim q$ 1 DeM.
     12. $p \lor \sim q$ 11 D.N.
     13. $\sim p \rightarrow \sim q$ 12 Impl.
     14. $\sim p \rightarrow r$ 13,10 H.S.
     15. $\sim r \rightarrow p$ 14 Trans.

23. 1. $\sim p \leftrightarrow \sim(q \rightarrow r)$
     2. $\sim[(q \rightarrow r) \lor s]$ /∴ $p \leftrightarrow s$
     3. $\sim(q \rightarrow r) \& \sim s$ 2 DeM.
     4. $[\sim p \rightarrow \sim(q \rightarrow r)] \& [\sim(q \rightarrow r) \rightarrow \sim p]$ 1 Equiv.
     5. $[\sim(q \rightarrow r) \rightarrow \sim p] \& [\sim p \rightarrow \sim(q \rightarrow r)]$ 4 Com.
     6. $\sim(q \rightarrow r) \rightarrow \sim p$ 5 Simp.
     7. $\sim(q \rightarrow r)$ 3 Simp.
     8. $\sim p$ 6,7 M.P.
     9. $\sim p \lor s$ 8 Add.
     10. $p \rightarrow s$ 9 Impl.
     11. $\sim s \& \sim(q \rightarrow r)$ 3 Com.
     12. $\sim s$ 11 Simp.
     13. $\sim s \lor p$ 12 Add.
     14. $s \rightarrow p$ 13 Impl.
     15. $(p \rightarrow s) \& (s \rightarrow p)$ 10,14 Conj.
     16. $p \leftrightarrow s$ 15 Equiv.

25. 1. $p \leftrightarrow \neg q$
     2. $\neg p \rightarrow (r \mathbin{\&} s)$
     3. $q \rightarrow \neg t$
     4. $\neg r \leftrightarrow \neg t$ /∴ $p \mathbin{\&} \neg q$
     5. $(p \rightarrow \neg q) \mathbin{\&} (\neg q \rightarrow p)$ 1 Equiv.
     6. $(\neg r \rightarrow \neg t) \mathbin{\&} (\neg t \rightarrow \neg r)$ 4 Equiv.
     7. $p \lor (r \mathbin{\&} s)$ 2 Impl.
     8. $(p \lor r) \mathbin{\&} (p \lor s)$ 7 Dist.
     9. $p \lor r$ 8 Simp.
     10. $(\neg t \rightarrow \neg r) \mathbin{\&} (\neg r \rightarrow \neg t)$ 6 Com.
     11. $\neg t \rightarrow \neg r$ 10 Simp.
     12. $q \rightarrow \neg r$ 3,11 H.S.
     13. $r \lor p$ 9 Com.
     14. $\neg r \rightarrow p$ 13 Impl.
     15. $q \rightarrow p$ 14,12 H.S.
     16. $p \rightarrow \neg q$ 5 Simp.
     17. $q \rightarrow \neg q$ 15,1 H.S.
     18. $\neg q \lor \neg q$ 17 Impl.
     19. $\neg q$ 18 Taut.
     20. $(\neg q \rightarrow p) \mathbin{\&} (p \rightarrow \neg q)$ 5 Com.
     21. $\neg q \rightarrow p$ 20 Simp.
     22. $\neg p \rightarrow \neg q$ 15 Trans.
     23. $\neg p \rightarrow p$ 22,21 H.S.
     24. $p \lor p$ 23 Impl.
     25. p 24 Taut.
     26. $p \mathbin{\&} \neg q$ 25,19 Conj.

6.3.IV

1. 1. $H \mathbin{\&} J$ /∴ $(H \rightarrow J) \mathbin{\&} (J \rightarrow H)$
    2. $(H \mathbin{\&} J) \lor (\neg H \mathbin{\&} \neg J)$ 1 Add.
    3. $H \leftrightarrow J$ 2 Equiv.
    4. $(H \rightarrow J) \mathbin{\&} (J \rightarrow H)$ 3 Equiv.

3. 1. M
    2. $(M \mathbin{\&} F) \rightarrow R$ /∴ $\neg R \rightarrow \neg F$
    3. $M \rightarrow (F \rightarrow R)$ 2 Exp.
    4. $F \rightarrow R$ 1,3 M.P.
    5. $\neg R \rightarrow \neg F$ 4 Trans.

5. 1. $M \mathbin{\&} (J \lor A)$
    2. $(J \rightarrow L) \mathbin{\&} (A \rightarrow S)$ /∴ $\neg L \rightarrow S$
    3. $(J \lor A) \mathbin{\&} M$ 1 Com.
    4. $J \lor A$ 3 Simp.
    5. $L \lor S$ 2,4 C.D.
    6. $\neg L \rightarrow S$ 5 Impl.

7.   1. S → (L & A)
     2. (L → J) & (A → H)
     3. ~J v ~H   /∴   ~S
     4. (~J → ~L) & (A → H)   2 Trans
     5. (~J → ~L) & (~H → ~A)   4 Trans.
     6. ~L v ~A   5,3 C.D.
     7. ~(L & A)   6 DeM.
     8. ~S   1,7 M.T.

9.   1. ~(H & C)
     2. ~C → B
     3. ~B v H   /∴   B ↔ H
     4. ~H v ~C   1 DeM.
     5. H → ~C   4 Impl.
     6. H → B   5,2 H.S.
     7. B → H   3 Impl.
     8. (B → H) & (H → B)   6,7 Conj.
     9. B ↔ H   8 Equiv.

11. 1. (B v L) & (S → J)
     2. S
     3. J → ~L   /∴   L v ~L
     4. (S → J) & (B v L)   1 Com
     5. S → J   4 Simp.
     6. J   5,2 M.P.
     7. ~L   3,6 M.P.
     8. ~L v L   7 Add.
     9. L v ~L   8 Com.

13. 1. (M & ~F) → B
     2. M & ~B   /∴   F
     3. M → (~F → B)   1 Exp.
     4. M   2 Simp.
     5. ~F → B   3,4 M.P.
     6. ~B & M   2 Com.
     7. ~B   6 Simp.
     8. ~~F   5,7 M.T
     9. F   8 D.N.

15. 1. A → (L & J)
     2. ~L v B
     3. (L & B) → (J → H)
     4. ~H   /∴   ~A v (H ↔ J)
     5. L → B   2 Impl.
     6. L → (L & B)   5 Abs.
     7. L → (J → H)   3,6 H.S.
     8. (L & J) → H   7 Exp.
     9. A → H   1,8 H.S.
     10. ~A   9,4 M.T.
     11. ~A v (H ↔ J)   10 Add.

17. 1. M → J
   2. (M & J) → ~L
   3. L v (A & B)   /∴   M → B
   4. M → (M & J)   1 Abs.
   5. M → ~L   4,2 H.S.
   6. (L v A) & (L v B)   3 Dist.
   7. (L v B) & (L v A)   6 Com.
   8. L v B   7 Simp.
   9. ~L → B   8 Impl.
  10. M → B   5,9 H.S.

19. 1. J → L
   2. L → B
   3. (C → A) & (A → ~B)   /∴   C → ~J
   4. J → B   1,2 H.S.
   5. C → A   3 Simp.
   6. (A → ~B) & (C → A)   3 Com.
   7. A → ~B   6 Simp.
   8. C → ~B   5,7 H.S.
   9. ~B → ~J   4 Trans.
  10. C → ~J   8,9 H.S.

21. 1. (A & L) → R
   2. L & ~R   /∴   ~A
   3. L   2 Simp.
   4. ~R & L   2 Com.
   5. ~R   4 Simp.
   6. ~(A & L)   1,5 M.T.
   7. ~A v ~L   6 DeM.
   8. ~L v ~A   7 Com.
   9. ~~L   3 D.N.
  10. ~A   8,9 D.S.

23. 1. G → (L & A)
   2. (A v L) → M   /∴   G → M
   3. ~G v (L & A)   1 Impl.
   4. (~G v L) & (~G v A)   3 Dist.
   5. ~G v L   4 Simp.
   6. (~G v L) v A   5 Add.
   7. ~G v (L v A)   6 Assoc.
   8. G → (L v A)   7 Impl.
   9. G → (A v L)   8 Com.
  10. G → M   9,2 H.S.

25. 1. B → Q
     2. B → (Q → F)
     3. -F
     4. B v S   /∴   S → S
     5. B → (B & Q)   1 Abs.
     6. (B & Q) → F   2 Exp.
     7. B → F   4,5 H.S.
     8. -B   7,3 M.T.
     9. S   4,8 D.S.
     10. S v -S   9 Add.
     11. -S v S   10 Com.
     12. S → S   11 Impl.

27. 1. F → B
     2. F → (-B v A)
     3. (Q → -A) & Q   /∴   -F
     4. F → (F & B)   1 Abs.
     5. F → (B → A)   2 Impl.
     6. (F & B) → A   5 Exp.
     7. F → A   4,6 H.S.
     8. Q → -A   3 Simp.
     9. Q & (Q → -A)   3 Com.
     10. Q   9 Simp.
     11. -A   10,8 M.P.
     12. -F   7,11 M.T.

29. 1. (C & J) → (B v L)
     2. C & -L   /∴   J → B
     3. C   2 Simp.
     4. C → [J → (B v L)]   1 Exp.
     5. J → (B v L)   4,3 M.P.
     6. -J v (B v L)   5 Impl.
     7. (-J v B) v L   6 Assoc.
     8. L v (-J v B)   7 Com.
     9. -L & C   2 Com.
     10. -L   9 Simp.
     11. -J v B   8,10 D.S.
     12. J → B   11 Impl.

31. 1. H → J
     2. J → L
     3. H → (A & Q)
     4. (-L v -Q) v -A   /∴   -H
     5. H → L   1,2 H.S.
     6. -L v (-Q v -A)   4 Assoc.
     7. L → (-Q v -A)   6 Impl.
     8. H → (-Q v -A)   5,7 H.S.
     9. H → -(Q & A)   8 DeM.
     10. H → -(A & Q)   9 Com.
     11. -(A & Q) → -H   3 Trans.
     12. H → -H   10,11 H.S.
     13. -H v -H   12 Impl.
     14. -H   13 Taut.

33.   1. B v (L v A)
     2. ~A & J
     3. J → (H v ~B)   /∴   ~H → L
     4. ~A   2 Simp.
     5. J & ~A   2 Com.
     6. J   5 Simp.
     7. H v ~B   3,6 M.P.
     8. (B v L) v A   1 Assoc.
     9. A v (B v L)   8 Com.
   10. B v L   9,4 D.S.
   11. ~B → L   10 Impl.
   12. ~H → ~B   7 Impl.
   13. ~H → L   12,11 H.S.

35.   1. (H → A) & (L → F)
     2. (H & A) → L
     3. (F → I) ↔ L
     4. F   /∴   H → I
     5. [(F → I) → L] & [L → (F → I)]   3 Equiv.
     6. H → A   1 Simp.
     7. H → (H & A)   6 Abs.
     8. H → L   7,2 H.S.
     9. [L → (F → I)] & [(F → I) → L]   5 Com.
   10. L → (F → I)   9 Simp.
   11. H → (F → I)   8,10 H.S.
   12. (H & F) → I   11 Exp.
   13. (F & H) → I   12 Com.
   14. F → (H → I)   13 Exp.
   15. H → I   14,4 M.P.

37.   1. M v (J & A)
     2. (M v J) → L
     3. (M v A) → (B → S)
     4. ~S   /∴   ~(L → B)
     5. (M v J) & (M v A)   1 Dist.
     6. M v J   5 Simp.
     7. L   2,6 M.P.
     8. (M v A) & (M v J)   5 Com.
     9. M v A   8 Simp.
   10. B → S   3,9 M.P.
   11. ~B   10,4 M.T.
   12. L & ~B   7,11 Conj.
   13. ~~L & ~B   12 D.N.
   14. ~(~L v B)   13 DeM.
   15. ~(L → B)   14 Impl.

39.
1. M /∴ $S \lor {\sim}S$
2. $M \lor {\sim}S$ 1 Add.
3. ${\sim}S \lor M$ 2 Com.
4. $S \rightarrow M$ 3 Impl.
5. $S \rightarrow (S \ \& \ M)$ 4 Abs.
6. ${\sim}S \lor (S \ \& \ M)$ 5 Impl.
7. $({\sim}S \lor S) \ \& \ ({\sim}S \lor M)$ 6 Dist.
8. ${\sim}S \lor S$ 7 Simp.
9. $S \lor {\sim}S$ 8 Com.

41.
1. $(C \rightarrow L) \ \& \ [(C \ \& \ {\sim}F) \rightarrow M]$
2. $F \rightarrow B$
3. ${\sim}L \lor {\sim}B$
4. $M \rightarrow {\sim}C$ /∴ ${\sim}C$
5. $C \rightarrow L$ 1 Simp.
6. $L \rightarrow {\sim}B$ 3 Impl.
7. $C \rightarrow {\sim}B$ 5,6 H.S.
8. ${\sim}B \rightarrow {\sim}F$ 2 Trans.
9. $C \rightarrow {\sim}F$ 7,8 H.S.
10. $[(C \ \& \ {\sim}F) \rightarrow M] \ \& \ (C \rightarrow L)$ 1 Com.
11. $[(C \ \& \ {\sim}F) \rightarrow M]$ 10 Simp.
12. $C \rightarrow (C \ \& \ {\sim}F)$ 9 Abs.
13. $C \rightarrow M$ 11,12 H.S.
14. $C \rightarrow {\sim}C$ 13,4 H.S.
15. ${\sim}C \lor {\sim}C$ 14 Impl.
16. ${\sim}C$ 15 Taut.

43.
1. $(M \lor {\sim}M) \rightarrow F$ /∴ F
2. ${\sim}(M \lor {\sim}M) \lor F$ 1 Impl.
3. $({\sim}M \ \& \ {\sim}{\sim}M) \lor F$ 2 DeM.
4. $({\sim}M \ \& \ M) \lor F$ 3 D.N.
5. $F \lor ({\sim}M \ \& \ M)$ 4 Com.
6. $(F \lor {\sim}M) \ \& \ (F \lor M)$ 5 Dist.
7. $F \lor {\sim}M$ 6 Simp.
8. ${\sim}M \lor F$ 7 Com.
9. $M \rightarrow F$ 8 Impl.
10. $(F \lor M) \ \& \ (F \lor {\sim}M)$ 6 Com.
11. $F \lor M$ 10 Simp.
12. ${\sim}F \rightarrow M$ 11 Impl.
13. ${\sim}F \rightarrow F$ 12,9 H.S.
14. $F \lor F$ 13 Impl.
15. F 14 Taut.

45. 1. H → C
     2. (H & C) ↔ (R & A)
     3. A → C
     4. (C & A) → H   /∴   (H & A) v (-H & -A)
     5. A → (A & C)   3 Abs.
     6. (A & C) → H   4 Com.
     7. A → H   5,6 H.S.
     8. [(H & C) → (R & A)] & [(R & A) → (H & C)]   2 Equiv.
     9. (H & C) → (R & A)   8 Simp.
     10. H → (H & C)   1 Abs.
     11. H → (R & A)   10,9 H.S.
     12. -H v (R & A)   11 Impl.
     13. -H v (A & R)   12 Com.
     14. (-H v A) & (-H v R)   13 Dist.
     15. -H v A   14 Simp.
     16. H → A   15 Impl.
     17. (H → A) & (A → H)   16,7 Conj.
     18. H ↔ A   17 Equiv.
     19. (H & A) v (-H & -A)   18 Equiv.

47. 1. (C → B) & (M → L)   /∴   (C v M) → (B v L)
     2. C → B   1 Simp.
     3. -C v B   2 Impl.
     4. (-C v B) v L   3 Add.
     5. -C v (B v L)   4 Assoc.
     6. (B v L) v -C   5 Com.
     7. (M → L) & (C → B)   1 Com.
     8. M → L   7 Simp.
     9. -M v L   8 Impl.
     10. (-M v L) v B   9 Add.
     11. -M v (L v B)   10 Assoc.
     12. -M v (B v L)   11 Com.
     13. (B v L) v -M   12 Com.
     14. [(B v L) v -C] & [(B v L) v -M]   6,13 Conj.
     15. (B v L) v (-C & -M)   14 Dist.
     16. (-C & -M) v (B v L)   15 Com.
     17. -(C v M) v (B v L)   16 DeM.
     18. (C v M) → (B v L)   17 Impl.

49.   1. J & (A ↔ L)
         2. (J v R) → S
         3. S → (L v A)   /∴   S → (J → A)

4. J	1 Simp.
5. J v R	4 Add.
6. S	2,5 M.P.
7. L v A	3,6 M.P.
8. (A ↔ L) & J	1 Com.
9. A ↔ L	8 Simp.
10. (A → L) & (L → A)	9 Equiv.
11. (L → A) & (A → L)	10 Com.
12. L → A	11 Simp.
13. A v L	7 Com.
14. ~A → L	13 Impl.
15. ~A → A	14,12 H.S.
16. A v A	15 Impl.
17. A	16 Taut.
18. A v (~S v ~J)	17 Add.
19. (A v ~S) v ~J	18 Assoc.
20. (~S v A) v ~J	19 Com.
21. ~S v (A v ~J)	20 Assoc.
22. S → (A v ~J)	21 Impl.
23. S → (~J v A)	22 Com.
24. S → (J → A)	23 Impl.

6.4

1.   1. p   /∴   q → p

2. q	ACP
3. p	1 Premise
4. q → p	2–3 C.P.

3.   1. p v q
         2. ~p   /∴   r → q

3. r	ACP
4. q	1,2 D.S.
5. r → q	3–4 C.P.

5.   1. p
         2. (p & q) → r   /∴   ~r → ~q

3. ~r	ACP
4. ~(p & q)	3,2 M.T.
5. ~p v ~q	4 DeM.
6. ~~p	1 D.N.
7. ~q	5,6 D.S.
8. ~r → ~q	3–7 C.P.

7. 1. $(p \ \& \ q) \rightarrow r$
    2. $p \rightarrow q$ $/\therefore$ $(s \ \& \ p) \rightarrow r$
    | 3. $s \ \& \ p$ | ACP |
    | 4. $p \ \& \ s$ | 3 Com. |
    | 5. p | 4 Simp. |
    | 6. q | 2,5 M.P. |
    | 7. $p \ \& \ q$ | 5,6 Conj. |
    | 8. r | 1,7 M.P. |
    9. $(s \ \& \ p) \rightarrow r$ 3–8 C.P.

9. 1. $p \rightarrow q$
    2. $\sim r \rightarrow \sim q$ $/\therefore$ $p \rightarrow (p \rightarrow r)$
    | 3. p | ACP |
    | 4. p | ACP |
    | 5. q | 4,1 M.P. |
    | 6. $\sim\sim q$ | 5 D.N. |
    | 7. $\sim\sim r$ | 2,6 M.T. |
    | 8. r | 7 D.N. |
    | 9. $p \rightarrow r$ | 4–8 C.P. |
    10. $p \rightarrow (p \rightarrow r)$ 3–9 C.P.

11. 1. $[p \ \& \ (q \lor r)] \rightarrow s$
    2. $\sim q \rightarrow r$
    3. $\sim p \rightarrow r$ $/\therefore$ $\sim r \rightarrow (q \ \& \ s)$
    | 4. $\sim r$ | ACP |
    | 5. $\sim\sim q$ | 2,4 M.T. |
    | 6. q | 5 D.N. |
    | 7. $\sim\sim p$ | 3,4 M.T. |
    | 8. p | 7 D.N. |
    | 9. $q \lor r$ | 6 Add. |
    | 10. $p \ \& \ (q \lor r)$ | 8,9 Conj. |
    | 11. s | 1,10 M.P. |
    | 12. $q \ \& \ s$ | 6,11 Conj. |
    13. $\sim r \rightarrow (q \ \& \ s)$ 4–12 C.P.

13. 1. $\sim(p \ \& \ q)$
    2. $\sim q \rightarrow r$
    3. $\sim r \lor p$ $/\therefore$ $r \leftrightarrow p$
    | 4. r | ACP |
    | 5. $\sim\sim r$ | 4 D.N. |
    | 6. p | 3,5 D.S. |
    | 7. $r \rightarrow p$ | 4–6 C.P. |
    | 8. p | ACP |
    | 9. $\sim p \lor \sim q$ | 1 DeM. |
    | 10. $\sim\sim p$ | 8 D.N. |
    | 11. $\sim q$ | 9,10 D.S. |
    | 12. r | 2,11 M.P |
    13. $p \rightarrow r$ 8–12 C.P.
    14. $(r \rightarrow p) \ \& \ (p \rightarrow r)$ 7,13 Conj.
    15. $r \leftrightarrow p$ 14 Equiv.

15.　　1. $p \rightarrow (q \mathbin{\&} r)$
　　　　2. $\sim q \vee s$
　　　　3. $(q \mathbin{\&} s) \rightarrow (r \rightarrow t)$
　　　　4. $\sim t$ $/\therefore$ $\sim p \vee (t \leftrightarrow r)$

5. p	ACP
6. $q \mathbin{\&} r$	5,1 M.P.
7. q	6 Simp.
8. $\sim\sim q$	7 D.N.
9. s	2,8 D.S.
10. $q \mathbin{\&} s$	7,9 Conj.
11. $r \rightarrow t$	3,10 M.P.
12. t	ACP
13. $r \mathbin{\&} q$	6 Com.
14. r	13 Simp.
15. $t \rightarrow r$	12–14 C.P.
16. $(t \rightarrow r) \mathbin{\&} (r \rightarrow t)$	15,11 Conj.
17. $t \leftrightarrow r$	16 Equiv.
18. $p \rightarrow (t \leftrightarrow r)$	5–17 C.P.
19. $\sim p \vee (t \leftrightarrow r)$	18 Impl.

17.　　1. $p \rightarrow [(q \mathbin{\&} r) \rightarrow s]$
　　　　2. $\sim s$
　　　　3. $p \mathbin{\&} q$ $/\therefore$ $\sim r$

4. p	3 Simp.
5. $q \mathbin{\&} p$	3 Com.
6. q	5 Simp.
7. $(q \mathbin{\&} r) \rightarrow s$	1,4 M.P.
8. r	ACP
9. $q \mathbin{\&} r$	6,8 Conj.
10. s	7,9 M.P.
11. $r \rightarrow s$	8–10 C.P.
12. $\sim r$	11,12 M.T.

19. 1. $p \leftrightarrow (q \vee r)$
     2. r
     3. $(p \;\&\; r) \rightarrow (s \vee t)$
     4. $\sim t$ /∴ s
	5. $\sim s$	ACP
	6. $\sim t \;\&\; \sim s$	4,5 Conj.
	7. $\sim(t \vee s)$	6 DeM.
	8. $\sim(s \vee t)$	7 Com.
	9. $\sim(p \;\&\; r)$	3,8 M.T.
	10. $\sim p \vee \sim r$	9 DeM.
	11. $p \rightarrow \sim r$	10 Impl.
	12. $\sim\sim r$	2 D.N.
	13. $\sim p$	11,12 M.T.

     14. $\sim s \rightarrow \sim p$ 5–13 C.P.
     15. $p \rightarrow s$ 15 Trans.
     16. $[p \rightarrow (q \vee r)] \;\&\; [(q \vee r) \rightarrow p)]$ 1 Equiv.
     17. $[(q \vee r) \rightarrow p\;] \;\&\; [p \rightarrow (q \vee r)]$ 16 Com.
     18. $(q \vee r) \rightarrow p$ 17 Simp.
     19. $(q \vee r) \rightarrow s$ 18,15 H.S.
     20. $r \vee q$ 2 Add.
     21. $q \vee r$ 20 Com.
     22. s 19,21 M.P.

6.5.I

1. 1. p /∴ $q \vee \sim q$
	2. $\sim(q \vee \sim q)$	AIP
	3. $\sim q \;\&\; \sim\sim q$	2 DeM.
	4. $\sim q \;\&\; q$	3 D.N.
	5. $q \;\&\; \sim q$	4 Com.

    6. $q \vee \sim q$ 2–5 I.P.

3. 1. $m \rightarrow g$
    2. $g \rightarrow a$
    3. $a \rightarrow p$
    4. $p \rightarrow i$
    5. m /∴ i
	6. $\sim i$	AIP
	7. g	1,5 M.P.
	8. a	2,7 M.P.
	9. p	3,8 M.P.
	10. i	4,9 M.P.
	11. $i \;\&\; \sim i$	10,6 Conj.

    12. i 6–11 I.P.

5. 1. $-p \rightarrow (o \,\&\, g)$
    2. $g \leftrightarrow p$ $/\therefore$ $o \rightarrow p$

3. $\sim(o \rightarrow p)$	AIP
4. $\sim(\sim o \lor p)$	3 Impl.
5. $\sim\sim o \,\&\, -p$	4 DeM.
6. $-p \,\&\, \sim\sim o$	5 Com.
7. $-p$	6 Simp.
8. $o \,\&\, g$	1,7 M.P.
9. $g \,\&\, o$	8 Com.
10. g	9 Simp.
11. $(g \rightarrow p) \,\&\, (p \rightarrow g)$	2 Equiv.
12. $g \rightarrow p$	11 Simp.
13. p	12,10 M.P.
14. $p \,\&\, -p$	13,7 Conj.
15. $o \rightarrow p$	3–14 I.P.

7. 1. $p \rightarrow [-q \lor (r \,\&\, s)]$
    2. $-s \,\&\, q$ $/\therefore$ $-p$

3. $\sim\sim p$	AIP
4. p	3 D.N.
5. $-q \lor (r \,\&\, s)$	1,4 M.P.
6. $-s$	2 Simp.
7. $q \,\&\, -s$	2 Com.
8. q	7 Simp.
9. $\sim\sim q$	9 D.N.
10. $r \,\&\, s$	5,9 D.S.
11. $s \,\&\, r$	10 Com.
12. s	11 Simp.
13. $s \,\&\, -s$	12,6 Conj.
14. $-p$	3–13 I.P.

9. 1. $m \rightarrow g$
    2. $g \rightarrow (c \lor h)$
    3. $h \rightarrow d$
    4. $-d$
    5. $c \rightarrow a$ $/\therefore$ $-m \lor a$

6. $\sim(-m \lor a)$	AIP
7. $\sim\sim m \,\&\, -a$	6 DeM.
8. $m \,\&\, -a$	7 D.N.
9. m	8 Simp.
10. $-a \,\&\, m$	8 Com.
11. $-a$	10 Simp.
12. $-c$	5,12 M.T.
13. g	1,9 M.P.
14. $c \lor h$	2,13 M.P.
15. h	14,12 D.S.
16. $-h$	3,4 M.T.
17. $h \,\&\, -h$	15,16 Conj.
18. $-m \lor a$	6–17 I.P.

6.5.II

1. 1. $(m \ \& \ f) \rightarrow (a \lor \sim c)$
    2. $g \rightarrow c$
    3. $\sim f \rightarrow j$
    4. $\sim a \ \& \ g$ $/\therefore$ $\sim m \lor j$
    > 5. m ACP
    > > 6. $\sim j$ AIP
    > > 7. $\sim\sim f$ 3,6 M.T.
    > > 8. f 7 D.N.
    > > 9. $m \ \& \ f$ 5,8 Conj.
    > > 10. $a \lor \sim c$ 1,9 M.P.
    > > 11. $\sim a$ 4 Simp.
    > > 12. $\sim c$ 9,11 D.S.
    > > 13. $g \ \& \ \sim a$ 4 Com.
    > > 14. g 13 Simp.
    > > 15. c 2,14 M.P.
    > > 16. $c \ \& \ \sim c$ 15,11 Conj.
    > 17. j 6–16 I.P.
    18. $m \rightarrow j$ 5–17 C.P.
    19. $\sim m \lor j$ 17 Impl.

3. 1. $p \rightarrow (\sim q \ \& \ r)$
    2. $(q \lor \sim r) \rightarrow s$
    3. $\sim s \lor p$ $/\therefore$ $\sim q$
    > 4. $\sim\sim q$ AIP
    > 5. q 4 D.N.
    > 6. $q \lor \sim r$ 5 Add.
    > 7. s 2,6 M.P.
    > 8. $\sim\sim s$ 7 D.N.
    > 9. p 3,8 D.S.
    > 10. $\sim q \ \& \ r$ 1,9 M.P.
    > 11. $\sim q$ 10 Simp.
    > 13. $q \ \& \ \sim q$ 5,11 Conj.
    14. $\sim q$ 4–13 I.P.

5. 1. $n \leftrightarrow (h \lor s)$
    2. $h \rightarrow (b \ \& \ m)$
    3. $s \rightarrow e$
    4. $\sim e \ \& \ n$ $/\therefore$ $b \ \& \ m$
    > 5. $\sim(b \ \& \ m)$ AIP
    > 6. $\sim h$ 5,2 M.T.
    > 7. $\sim e$ 4 Simp.
    > 8. $\sim s$ 3,7 M.T.
    > 9. $\sim h \ \& \ \sim s$ 6,8 Conj.
    > 10. $\sim(h \lor s)$ 9 DeM.
    > 11. $\sim n$ 1,11 M.T.
    > 12. $n \ \& \ \sim e$ 4 Com.
    > 13. n 12 Simp.
    > 14. $n \ \& \ \sim n$ 13,11 Conj.
    15. $b \ \& \ m$ 5–14 I.P.

7. 1. $a \lor [g \;\&\; (\text{-}d \;\&\; \text{-}e)]$
    2. $g \leftrightarrow e$ /∴ $\text{-}a \rightarrow \text{-}(d \;\&\; \text{-}e)$
       3. $\text{-}a$ ACP
       4. $g \;\&\; (\text{-}d \;\&\; \text{-}e)$ 1,3 D.S.
       5. $(\text{-}d \;\&\; \text{-}e) \;\&\; g$ 4 Com
       6. $\text{-}d \;\&\; \text{-}e$ 5 Simp.
       7. $\text{-}d$ 6 Simp.
       8. $\text{-}d \lor \text{-}\text{-}e$ 7 Add.
       9. $\text{-}(d \;\&\; \text{-}e)$ 8 DeM.
    10. $\text{-}a \rightarrow \text{-}(d \;\&\; \text{-}e)$ 3–9 C.P.

9. 1. $(h \;\&\; m) \rightarrow (k \;\&\; b)$
    2. $(k \lor b) \rightarrow (f \lor s)$
    3. $h \;\&\; \text{-}s$ /∴ $m \rightarrow f$
    4. h 3 Simp.
    5. $\text{-}s \;\&\; h$ 3 Com.
    6. $\text{-}s$ 5 Simp.
       7. m ACP
          8. $\text{-}f$ AIP
          9. $h \;\&\; m$ 4,7 Conj.
          10. $k \;\&\; b$ 1,9 M.P.
          11. k 10 Simp.
          12. $k \lor b$ 11 Add.
          13. $f \lor s$ 2,12 M.P.
          14. s 13,8 D.S.
          15. $s \;\&\; \text{-}s$ 14,6 Conj.
       16. f 8–15 I.P.
    17. $m \rightarrow f$ 7–16 C.P.

11. 1. $a \rightarrow (b \;\&\; \text{-}c)$
     2. $\text{-}a \leftrightarrow b$ /∴ $a \rightarrow d$
        3. a AIP
        4. $b \;\&\; \text{-}c$ 1,3 M.P.
        5. b 4 Simp.
        6. $(\text{-}a \rightarrow b) \;\&\; (b \rightarrow \text{-}a)$ 2 Equiv.
        7. $(b \rightarrow \text{-}a) \;\&\; (\text{-}a \rightarrow b)$ 6 Com
        8. $b \rightarrow \text{-}a$ 7 Simp.
        9. $\text{-}\text{-}a$ 3 D.N.
        10. $\text{-}b$ 8,9 M.T.
        11. $b \;\&\; \text{-}b$ 5,10 Conj.
     12. $\text{-}a$ 3–11 I.P.
     13. $\text{-}a \lor d$ 12 Add.
     14. $a \rightarrow d$ 13 Impl.

13.   1. $[w \,\&\, (c \lor g)] \to [g \leftrightarrow (o \to r)]$

      2. g

      3. $g \to (\text{-}r \,\&\, w)$ $/\therefore$ $\text{-}g \lor \text{-}o$

4. $\text{-}(\text{-}g \lor \text{-}o)$	AIP
5. $\text{-}\text{-}g \,\&\, \text{-}\text{-}o$	4 DeM.
6. $\text{-}\text{-}o \,\&\, \text{-}\text{-}g$	6 Com.
7. $\text{-}\text{-}o$	6 Simp.
8. $\text{-}r \,\&\, w$	3,2 M.P.
9. $\text{-}r$	8 Simp.
10. $\text{-}\text{-}o \,\&\, \text{-}r$	7,9 Conj.
11. $\text{-}(\text{-}o \lor r)$	10 DeM.
12. $\text{-}(o \to r)$	11 Impl.
13. $w \,\&\, \text{-}r$	8 Com.
14. w	13 Simp.
15. $w \to \{(c \lor g) \to [g \leftrightarrow (o \to r)]\}$	1 Exp.
16. $(c \lor g) \to [g \leftrightarrow (o \to r)]$	15,14 M.P.
17. $g \lor c$	2 Add.
18. $c \lor g$	17 Com.
19. $g \leftrightarrow (o \to r)$	16,18 M.P.
20. $[g \to (o \to r)] \,\&\, [(o \to r) \to g]$	19 Equiv.
21. $g \to (o \to r)$	20 Simp.
22. $o \to r$	21,2 M.P.
21. $(o \to r) \,\&\, \text{-}(o \to r)$	22,12 Conj.
22. $\text{-}g \lor \text{-}o$	4–21 I.P.

15.   1. $\text{-}[p \leftrightarrow (q \lor \text{-}r)]$

      2. $p \,\&\, \text{-}s$ $/\therefore$ $q \leftrightarrow s$

3. $\text{-}(q \leftrightarrow s)$	AIP
4. $\text{-}\{[p \,\&\, (q \lor \text{-}r)] \lor [\text{-}p \,\&\, \text{-}(q \lor \text{-}r)]\}$	1 Equiv.
5. $\text{-}[p \,\&\, (q \lor \text{-}r)] \,\&\, \text{-}[\text{-}p \,\&\, \text{-}(q \lor \text{-}r)]$	4 DeM.
6. $\text{-}[p \,\&\, (q \lor \text{-}r)]$	5 Simp.
7. $\text{-}p \lor \text{-}(q \lor \text{-}r)$	6 DeM.
8. $p \to \text{-}(q \lor \text{-}r)$	7 Impl.
9. p	2 Simp.
10. $\text{-}(q \lor \text{-}r)$	8,9 M.P.
11. $\text{-}q \,\&\, \text{-}\text{-}r$	10 DeM.
12. $\text{-}q$	11 Simp.
13. $\text{-}[(q \,\&\, s) \lor (\text{-}q \,\&\, \text{-}s)]$	3 Equiv.
14. $\text{-}(q \,\&\, s) \,\&\, \text{-}(\text{-}q \,\&\, \text{-}s)$	13 DeM.
15. $\text{-}(\text{-}q \,\&\, \text{-}s) \,\&\, \text{-}(q \,\&\, s)$	14 Com.
16. $\text{-}(\text{-}q \,\&\, \text{-}s)$	15 Simp.
17. $\text{-}\text{-}q \lor \text{-}\text{-}s$	16 DeM.
18. $q \lor \text{-}\text{-}s$	17 D.N.
19. $q \lor s$	18 D.N.
20. $\text{-}q \to s$	19 Impl.
21. $\text{-}s \,\&\, p$	2 Com.
22. $\text{-}s$	21 Simp.
23. $\text{-}\text{-}q$	20,22 M.T.
24. q	23 D.N.
25. $q \,\&\, \text{-}q$	24,12 Conj.
26. $q \leftrightarrow s$	3–25 I.P.

7.1

1. $(x)(Dx \rightarrow Mx)$
3. $(\exists x)(Dx \ \& \ Rx)$
5. $(x)(Dx \rightarrow Mx)$
7. $(x)(Dx \rightarrow Rx) \lor (\exists x)(Cx \ \& \ Rx)$
9. $(\exists x)(Dx \ \& \ Rx) \rightarrow Rf$
11. $[(\exists x)(Dx \ \& \ Rx) \ \& \ Df] \rightarrow Rf$
13. $(x)(Kx \rightarrow \sim Mx) \lor (x)(Kx \rightarrow Mx)$
15. $(x)[(Kx \ \& \ \sim Wx) \rightarrow (Tx \lor Px)]$
17. $(x)(Kx \rightarrow \sim Ax) \rightarrow [(\exists x)(Kx \ \& \ Mx) \rightarrow (\exists x)(Kx \ \& \ Px)]$
19. $(x)[(Px \ \& \ Sx) \rightarrow (Ax \rightarrow Dx)] \rightarrow (\exists x)[(Px \ \& \ Sx) \ \& \ \sim Ax]$

7.2.I

1.
   1. $(x)(Px \rightarrow Qx)$
   2. Pa $/\therefore$ $(\exists x)Qx$
   3. $Pa \rightarrow Qa$ 1 U.I.
   4. Qa 3,2 M.P.
   5. $(\exists x)Qx$ 4 E.G.

3.
   1. $(\exists x)Px \rightarrow (x)Qx$
   2. Pa $/\therefore$ Qa
   3. $(\exists x)Px$ 2 E.G.
   4. $(x)Qx$ 3,2 M.P.
   5. Qa 4 U.I.

5.
   1. $(\exists x)(Px \ \& \ Qx)$ $/\therefore$ $(\exists x)Qx$
   2. $Pa \ \& \ Qa$ 1 E.I.
   3. $Qa \ \& \ Pa$ 2 Com.
   4. Qa 3 Simp.
   5. $(\exists x)Qx$ 4 E.G.

7.
   1. $(x)(Mx \rightarrow \sim Px)$
   2. $(x)(Sx \rightarrow Mx)$ $/\therefore$ $(x)(Sx \rightarrow \sim Px)$
   3. $Mx \rightarrow \sim Px$ 1 U.I.
   4. $Sx \rightarrow Mx$ 2 U.I.
   5. $Sx \rightarrow \sim Px$ 4,3 H.S.
   6. $(x)(Sx \rightarrow \sim Px)$ 5 U.G.

9.
   1. $(x)(Px \rightarrow \sim Mx)$
   2. $(\exists x)(Mx \ \& \ \sim Sx)$ $/\therefore$ $(\exists x)(\sim Sx \ \& \ \sim Px)$
   3. $Ma \ \& \ \sim Sa$ 2 E.I.
   4. $Pa \rightarrow \sim Ma$ 1 U.I.
   5. Ma 3 Simp.
   6. $\sim Sa \ \& \ Ma$ 3 Com.
   7. $\sim Sa$ 6 Simp.
   8. $\sim\sim Ma$ 5 D.N.
   9. $\sim Pa$ 4,8 M.T.
   10. $\sim Sa \ \& \ \sim Pa$ 7,9 Conj.
   11. $(\exists x)(\sim Sx \ \& \ \sim Px)$ 10 E.G.

11. 1. $(x)(Px \rightarrow Mx)$
     2. $(\exists x)(Sx \ \& \ \sim Mx)$ /∴ $(\exists x)(Sx \ \& \ \sim Px)$
     3. $Sa \ \& \ \sim Ma$ 2 E.I.
     4. $Pa \rightarrow Ma$ 1 U.I.
     5. $\sim Ma \ \& \ Sa$ 3 Com.
     6. $\sim Ma$ 5 Simp.
     7. $\sim Pa$ 4,6 M.T.
     8. Sa 3 Simp.
     9. $Sa \ \& \ \sim Pa$ 8,7 Conj.
     10. $(\exists x)(Sx \ \& \ \sim Px)$ 9 E.G.

13. 1. $(x)[(Px \ \& \ Mx) \rightarrow Sx]$
     2. $(\exists x)(Px \ \& \ \sim Sx)$ /∴ $(\exists x)\sim Ma$
     3. $Pa \ \& \ \sim Sa$ 2 E.I.
     4. $(Pa \ \& \ Ma) \rightarrow Sa$ 1 U.I.
     5. $Pa \rightarrow (Ma \rightarrow Sa)$ 4 Exp.
     6. Pa 3 Simp.
     7. $\sim Sa \ \& \ Pa$ 3 Com.
     8. $\sim Sa$ 7 Simp.
     9. $Ma \rightarrow Sa$ 5,6 M.P.
     10. $\sim Ma$ 9,8 M.T.
     11. $(\exists x)\sim Ma$ 10 E.G.

15. 1. $(\exists x)(Px) \rightarrow (\exists x)(Qx)$
     2. $(x)(\sim Px \rightarrow Qx)$
     3. $(x)(Qx \rightarrow Px)$ /∴ $(\exists x)(Qx)$
     4. $\sim Pa \rightarrow Qa$ 2 U.I.
     5. $Qa \rightarrow Pa$ 3 U.I.
     6. $\sim Pa \rightarrow Pa$ 4,5 H.S
     7. $Pa \ v \ Pa$ 6 Impl.
     8. Pa 7 Taut.
     9. $(\exists x)(Px)$ 8 E.G.
     10. $(\exists x)(Qx)$ 1,9 M.P.

17. 1. $(x)[(Px \ \& \ Qx) \rightarrow (Rx \ \& \ Tx)]$
     2. $(\exists x)[(Px \ \& \ Rx) \ \& \ Qx]$ /∴ $(\exists x)(Tx \ \& \ Rx)$
     3. $(Pa \ \& \ Ra) \ \& \ Qa$ 2 E.I.
     4. $Qa \ \& \ (Pa \ \& \ Ra)$ 3 Com.
     5. Qa 4 Simp.
     6. $Pa \ \& \ (Ra \ \& \ Qa)$ 3 Assoc.
     7. Pa 6 Simp.
     8. $Pa \ \& \ Qa$ 7,5 Conj.
     9. $(Pa \ \& \ Qa) \rightarrow (Ra \ \& \ Ta)$ 1 U.I.
     10. $Ra \ \& \ Ta$ 9,8 M.P.
     11. $Ta \ \& \ Ra$ 10 Com.
     12. $(\exists x)(Tx \ \& \ Rx)$ 11 E.G.

19.   1. $(x)[(Px$ & $Qx) \rightarrow Rx]$
       2. $(x)[(Rx \lor Sx) \rightarrow Tx]$
       3. $(\exists x)(Px$ & $-Sx)$ $/\therefore$ $(\exists x)(Qx \rightarrow Tx)$
       4. Pa & $-Sa$ 3 E.I.
       5. Pa 4 Simp.
       6. $(Pa$ & $Qa) \rightarrow Ra$ 1 U.I.
       7. $Pa \rightarrow (Qa \rightarrow Ra)$ 6 Exp.
       8. $Qa \rightarrow Ra$ 7,5 M.P.
       9. $(Ra \lor Sa) \rightarrow Ta$ 2 U.I.
      10. $-(Ra \lor Sa) \lor Ta$ 9 Impl.
      11. $(-Ra$ & $-Sa) \lor Ta$ 10 DeM.
      12. $Ta \lor (-Ra$ & $-Sa)$ 11 Com.
      13. $(Ta \lor -Ra)$ & $(Ta \lor -Sa)$ 12 Dist.
      14. $Ta \lor -Ra$ 13 Simp.
      15. $-Ra \lor Ta$ 14 Com.
      16. $Ra \rightarrow Ta$ 15 Impl.
      17. $Qa \rightarrow Ta$ 8,16 H.S.
      18. $(\exists x)(Qx \rightarrow Tx)$ 17 E.G.

21.   1. $(x)[(-Px$ & $-Qx) \rightarrow Rx]$
       2. $(x)[Rx \rightarrow (-Qx \rightarrow Sx)]$
       3. $(x)(Sx \rightarrow Qx)$ $/\therefore$ $(x)(-Qx \rightarrow Px)$
       4. $(-Px$ & $-Qx) \rightarrow Rx$ 1 U.I.
       5. $Rx \rightarrow (-Qx \rightarrow Sx)$ 2 U.I.
       6. $Sx \rightarrow Qx$ 3 U.I.
       7. $(-Px$ & $-Qx) \rightarrow (-Qx \rightarrow Sx)$ 4,5 H.S.
       8. $[(-Px$ & $-Qx)$ & $-Qx] \rightarrow Sx$ 7 Exp.
       9. $[-Px$ & $(-Qx$ & $-Qx)] \rightarrow Sx$ 8 Assoc.
      10. $(-Px$ & $-Qx) \rightarrow Sx$ 9 Taut.
      11. $(-Px$ & $-Qx) \rightarrow Qx$ 10,6 H.S.
      12. $-Px \rightarrow (-Qx \rightarrow Qx)$ 11 Exp.
      13. $-Px \rightarrow (Qx \lor Qx)$ 12 Impl.
      14. $-Px \rightarrow Qx$ 13 Taut.
      15. $-Qx \rightarrow Px$ 14 Trans.
      16. $(x)(-Qx \rightarrow Px)$ 15 U.G.

23.   1. $(x)(Px \rightarrow Qx)$ & $(\exists x)[Px$ & $(Qx \rightarrow Rx)]$
       2. $(x)[Rx \rightarrow (Sx \leftrightarrow Tx)]$ $/\therefore$ $(\exists x)[(Sx \rightarrow Tx)$ & $(Tx \rightarrow Sx)]$
       3. $(x)(Px \rightarrow Qx)$ 1 Simp.
       4. $(\exists x)[Px$ & $(Qx \rightarrow Rx)]$ & $(x)(Px \rightarrow Qx)$ 1 Com.
       5. $(\exists x)[Px$ & $(Qx \rightarrow Rx)]$ 4 Simp.
       6. Pa & $(Qa \rightarrow Ra)$ 5 E.I.
       7. $Pa \rightarrow Qa$ 3 U.I.
       8. Pa 6 Simp.
       9. Qa 7,8 M.P.
      10. $(Qa \rightarrow Ra)$ & Pa 6 Com.
      11. $Qa \rightarrow Ra$ 10 Simp.
      12. Ra 11,9 M.P.
      13. $Ra \rightarrow (Sx \leftrightarrow Tx)$ 2 U.I.
      14. $Sx \leftrightarrow Tx$ 12,13 M.P.
      15. $(Sa \rightarrow Ta)$ & $(Ta \rightarrow Sa)$ 14 Equiv.
      16. $(\exists x)[(Sx \rightarrow Tx)$ & $(Tx \rightarrow Sx)]$ 15 E.G.

25. 1. $(x)[(Px \& Qx) \to (Rx \& Sx)]$
  2. $(x)(Rx \to Px)$
  3. $(x)[(Rx \& Px) \to Qx]$ /∴ $(x)\{-Sx \to [Rx \leftrightarrow (Px \& Qx)]\}$
  4. $(Px \& Qx) \to (Rx \& Sx)$ 1 U.I.
  5. $Rx \to Px$ 2 U.I.
  6. $(Rx \& Px) \to Qx$ 3 U.I.
  7. $-(Px \& Qx) \lor (Rx \& Sx)$ 4 Impl.
  8. $[-(Px \& Qx) \lor Rx] \& [-(Px \& Qx) \lor Sx]$ 7 Dist.
  9. $-(Px \& Qx) \lor Rx$ 8 Simp.
  10. $(Px \& Qx) \to Rx$ 9 Impl.
  11. $(Px \& Rx) \to Qx$ 6 Com.
  12. $Px \to (Rx \to Qx)$ 11 Exp.
  13. $Rx \to (Rx \to Qx)$ 5,12 H.S.
  14. $(Rx \& Rx) \to Qx$ 13 Exp.
  15. $Rx \to Qx$ 14 Taut.
  16. $-Rx \lor Qx$ 15 Impl.
  17. $-Rx \lor Px$ 5 Impl.
  18. $(-Rx \lor Px) \& (-Rx \lor Qx)$ 17,16 Conj.
  19. $-Rx \lor (Px \& Qx)$ 18 Dist.
  20. $Rx \to (Px \& Qx)$ 19 Impl.
  21. $[Rx \to (Px \& Qx)] \& [(Px \& Qx) \to Rx]$ 20,10 Conj.
  22. $Rx \leftrightarrow (Px \& Qx)$ 21 Equiv.
  23. $[Rx \leftrightarrow (Px \& Qx)] \lor Sx$ 22 Add.
  24. $Sx \lor [Rx \leftrightarrow (Px \& Qx)]$ 23 Com.
  25. $-Sx \to [Rx \leftrightarrow (Px \& Qx)]$ 24 Impl.
  26. $(x)\{-Sx \to [Rx \leftrightarrow (Px \& Qx)]\}$ 25 U.G.

7.2.II

1. 1. $(x)(Yx \to Rx)$
  2. $(x)(Ox \to -Rx)$ /∴ $(x)(Yx \to -Ox)$
  3. $Yx \to Rx$ 1 U.I.
  4. $Ox \to -Rx$ 2 U.I.
  5. $Rx \to -Ox$ 4 Trans.
  6. $Yx \to -Ox$ 3,5 H.S.
  7. $(x)(Yx \to -Ox)$ 6 U.G.

3. 1. $(x)[(Px \& Yx) \to Bx]$
  2. $(\exists x)[(Px \& Wx) \& Yx]$ /∴ $(\exists x)[(Px \& Wx) \& Bx]$
  3. $(Pa \& Wa) \& Ya$ 2 E.I.
  4. $(Pa \& Ya) \to Ba$ 1 U.I.
  5. $Pa \& (Wa \& Ya)$ 3 Assoc.
  6. Pa 4 Simp.
  7. $Ya \& (Pa \& Wa)$ 3 Com.
  8. Ya 7 Simp.
  9. $Pa \& Ya$ 6,8 Conj.
  10. Ba 4,9 M.P.
  11. $Pa \& Wa$ 3 Simp.
  12. $(Pa \& Wa) \& Ba$ 11,10 Conj.
  13. $(\exists x)[(Px \& Wx) \& Bx]$ 12 E.G.

5. 1. $(x)\{[Px \,\&\, (Yx \lor Ax)] \rightarrow (Bx \lor Rx)\}$
    2. $Pf \,\&\, Yf$
    3. $(x)[(Px \,\&\, Rx) \rightarrow (Mx \lor Sx)]$ /∴ $(\sim Bf \,\&\, \sim Mf) \rightarrow Sf$
    4. $[Pf \,\&\, (Yf \lor Af)] \rightarrow (Bf \lor Rf)$ 1 U.I.
    5. $(Pf \,\&\, Rf) \rightarrow (Mf \lor Sf)$ 3 U.I.
    6. $Pf \rightarrow [(Yf \lor Af) \rightarrow (Bf \lor Rf)]$ 4 Exp.
    7. Pf 2 Simp.
    8. $(Yf \lor Af) \rightarrow (Bf \lor Rf)$ 6,7 M.P.
    9. $Yf \,\&\, Pf$ 2 Com.
    10. Yf 9 Simp.
    11. $Yf \lor Af$ 10 Add.
    12. $Bf \lor Rf$ 8,11 M.P.
    13. $\sim Bf \rightarrow Rf$ 12 Impl.
    14. $Pf \rightarrow [Rf \rightarrow (Mf \lor Sf)]$ 5 Exp.
    15. $Rf \rightarrow (Mf \lor Sf)$ 14,7 M.P.
    16. $\sim Bf \rightarrow (Mf \lor Sf)$ 13,15 H.S.
    17. $\sim Bf \rightarrow (\sim Mf \rightarrow Sf)$ 16 Impl.
    18. $(\sim Bf \,\&\, \sim Mf) \rightarrow Sf$ 17 Exp.

7. 1. $(x)(Fx \rightarrow Sx)$
    2. $(x)[Tx \rightarrow (Fx \,\&\, \sim Sx)]$ /∴ $(x)(Tx \rightarrow Mx)$
    3. $Fx \rightarrow Sx$ 1 U.I.
    4. $Tx \rightarrow (Fx \,\&\, \sim Sx)$ 2 U.I.
    5. $\sim Fx \lor Sx$ 3 Impl.
    6. $\sim Fx \lor \sim\sim Sx$ 5 D.N.
    7. $\sim(Fx \,\&\, \sim Sx)$ 6 DeM.
    8. $\sim Tx$ 4,7 M.T.
    9. $\sim Tx \lor Mx$ 8 Add.
    10. $Tx \rightarrow Mx$ 9 Impl.
    11. $(x)(Tx \rightarrow Mx)$ 10 U.G.

9. 1. $(x)\{[Px \,\&\, (Yx \,\&\, Rx)] \rightarrow (Bx \lor Ax)\}$
    2. $(\exists x)[Px \,\&\, (Rx \,\&\, \sim Bx)]$ /∴ $(\exists x)[Px \,\&\, \sim(Yx \,\&\, \sim Ax)]$
    3. $Pa \,\&\, (Ra \,\&\, \sim Ba)$ 2 E.I.
    4. $[Pa \,\&\, (Ya \,\&\, Ra)] \rightarrow (Ba \lor Aa)$ 1 U.I.
    5. $Pa \rightarrow [(Ya \,\&\, Ra) \rightarrow (Ba \lor Aa)]$ 4 Exp.
    6. Pa 3 Simp.
    7. $(Ya \,\&\, Ra) \rightarrow (Ba \lor Aa)$ 5,6 M.P.
    8. $(Ra \,\&\, \sim Ba) \,\&\, Pa$ 3 Com.
    9. $Ra \,\&\, \sim Ba$ 8 Simp.
    10. Ra 9 Simp.
    11. $(Ra \,\&\, Ya) \rightarrow (Ba \lor Aa)$ 7 Com.
    12. $Ra \rightarrow [Ya \rightarrow (Ba \lor Aa)]$ 11 Exp.
    13. $Ya \rightarrow (Ba \lor Aa)$ 10,12 M.P.
    14. $Ya \rightarrow (Aa \lor Ba)$ 13 Com.
    15. $Ya \rightarrow (\sim Aa \rightarrow Ba)$ 14 Impl.
    16. $(Ya \,\&\, \sim Aa) \rightarrow Ba$ 15 Exp.
    17. $\sim Ba \,\&\, Ra$ 9 Com.
    18. $\sim Ba$ 17 Simp.
    19. $\sim(Ya \,\&\, \sim Aa)$ 16,18 M.T.
    20. $Pa \,\&\, \sim(Ya \,\&\, \sim Aa)$ 6,19 Conj.
    21. $(\exists x)[Px \,\&\, \sim(Yx \,\&\, \sim Ax)]$ 20 E.G.

7.3

1.   1. ~(∃x)(Px & ~Qx)
    2. ~(∃x)(Qx & ~Rx)
    3. ~Ra   /∴   ~Pa
    4. (x)~(Px & ~Qx)   1 Q.N.
    5. (x)(~Px v ~~Qx)   4 DeM.
    6. (x)(~Px v Qx)   5 D.N.
    7. (x)(Px → Qx)   6 Impl.
    8. (x)~(Qx & ~Rx)   2 Q.N.
    9. (x)(~Qx v ~~Rx)   8 DeM.
  10. (x)(~Qx v Rx)   9 D.N.
  11. (x)(Qx → Rx)   10 Impl.
  12. Pa → Qa   7 U.I.
  13. Qa → Ra   11 U.I.
  14. Pa → Ra   12,13 H.S.
  15. ~Pa   14,3 M.T.

3.   1. (∃x)(Px & Qx) → (x)(Sx → Rx)
    2. (∃x)(Sx & ~Rx)   /∴   (x)(Px → ~Qx)
    3. (∃x)(~~Sx & ~Rx)   2 D.N.
    4. (∃x)~(~Sx v Rx)   3 DeM.
    5. ~(x)(~Sx v Rx)   4 Q.N.
    6. ~(x)(Sx → Rx)   5 Impl.
    7. ~(∃x)(Px & Qx)   1,6 M.T.
    8. (x)~(Px & Qx)   7 Q.N.
    9. (x)(~Px v ~Qx)   8 DeM.
  10. (x)(Px → ~Qx)   9 Impl.

5.   1. ~(∃x)(Px & Mx)
    2. ~(∃x)(Sx & ~Mx)   /∴   ~(∃x)(Sx & Px)
    3. (x)~(Px & Mx)   1 Q.N.
    4. (x(~Px v ~Mx)   3 DeM.
    5. (x)(Px → ~Mx)   4 Impl.
    6. (x)~(Sx & ~Mx)   2 Q.N.
    7. (x)(~Sx v ~~Mx)   6 DeM.
    8. (x)(~Sx v Mx)   7 D.N.
    9. (x)(Sx → Mx)   8 Impl.
  10. Sx → Mx   9 U.I.
  11. Px → ~Mx   5 U.I.
  12. Mx → ~Px   11 Trans.
  13. Sx → ~Px   10,12 H.S.
  14. (x)(Sx → ~Px)   13 U.G.
  15. (x)(~Sx v ~Px)   14 Impl.
  16. (x)~(Sx & Px)   15 DeM.
  17. ~(∃x)(Sx & Px)   16 Q.N.

7.　　1. $-(\exists x)(Mx \ \& \ Px)$
　　　　2. $-(x)(Sx \rightarrow -Mx)$　　/∴　$-(x)(Sx \rightarrow Px)$
　　　　3. $(x)-(Mx \ \& \ Px)$　　　　　　　　　　1 Q.N.
　　　　4. $(x)(-Mx \ \lor \ -Px)$　　　　　　　　　3 DeM.
　　　　5. $(x)(Mx \rightarrow -Px)$　　　　　　　　4 Impl.
　　　　6. $(\exists x)-(Sx \rightarrow -Mx)$　　　　　　2 Q.N.
　　　　7. $(\exists x)-(-Sx \ \lor \ -Mx)$　　　　　　6 Impl.
　　　　8. $(\exists x)--(Sx \ \& \ Mx)$　　　　　　　7 DeM.
　　　　9. $(\exists x)(Sx \ \& \ Mx)$　　　　　　　　8 D.N.
　　　10. $Sa \ \& \ Ma$　　　　　　　　　　　　9 E.I.
　　　11. $Ma \rightarrow -Pa$　　　　　　　　　　5 U.I.
　　　12. $Ma \ \& \ Sa$　　　　　　　　　　　10 Com.
　　　13. Ma　　　　　　　　　　　　　　12 Simp.
　　　14. $-Pa$　　　　　　　　　　　　　11,13 M.P.
　　　15. Sa　　　　　　　　　　　　　　10 Simp.
　　　16. $Sa \ \& \ -Pa$　　　　　　　　　　　15,14 Conj.
　　　17. $(\exists x)(Sx \ \& \ -Px)$　　　　　　　16 E.G.
　　　18. $-(x)-(Sx \ \& \ -Px)$　　　　　　　17 Q.N.
　　　19. $-(x)(-Sx \ \lor \ --Px)$　　　　　　18 DeM.
　　　20. $-(x)(-Sx \ \lor \ Px)$　　　　　　　19 D.N.
　　　21. $-(x)(Sx \rightarrow Px)$　　　　　　　20 Impl.

9.　　1. $-(\exists x)[Px \ \& \ (-Qx \ \& \ -Rx)]$
　　　　2. $-(\exists x)(Qx \ \& \ -Sx)$
　　　　3. $-(x)[Px \rightarrow -(Tx \ \& \ -Rx)]$　　/∴　$-(x)(Sx \rightarrow -Tx)$
　　　　4. $(x)-[Px \ \& \ (-Qx \ \& \ -Rx)]$　　　1 Q.N.
　　　　5. $(x)[-Px \ \lor \ -(-Qx \ \& \ -Rx)]$　　4 DeM.
　　　　6. $(x)[-Px \ \lor \ --(Qx \ \lor \ Rx)]$　　5 DeM
　　　　7. $(x)[-Px \ \lor \ (Qx \ \lor \ Rx)]$　　　6 D.N.
　　　　8. $(x)[Px \rightarrow (Qx \ \lor \ Rx)]$　　　7 Impl.
　　　　9. $(x)-(Qx \ \& \ -Sx)$　　　　　　　2 Q.N.
　　　10. $(x)(-Qx \ \lor \ --Sx)$　　　　　　9 DeM.
　　　11. $(x)(-Qx \ \lor \ Sx)$　　　　　　　10 D.N.
　　　12. $(x)(Qx \rightarrow Sx)$　　　　　　　11 Impl.
　　　13. $(\exists x)-[Px \rightarrow -(Tx \ \& \ -Rx)]$　3 Q.N.
　　　14. $(\exists x)-[-Px \ \lor \ -(Tx \ \& \ -Rx)]$　13 Impl.
　　　15. $(\exists x)--[Px \ \& \ (Tx \ \& \ -Rx)]$　14 DeM.
　　　16. $(\exists x)[Px \ \& \ (Tx \ \& \ -Rx)]$　15 D.N.
　　　17. $Pa \ \& \ (Ta \ \& \ -Ra)$　　　　　　13 E.I.
　　　18. $Pa \rightarrow (Qa \ \lor \ Ra)$　　　　　8 U.I.
　　　19. Pa　　　　　　　　　　　　　17 Simp.
　　　20. $(Ta \ \& \ -Ra) \ \& \ Pa$　　　　　　17 Com.
　　　21. $Ta \ \& \ -Ra$　　　　　　　　　　20 Simp.
　　　22. $Qa \ \lor \ Ra$　　　　　　　　　　18,19 M.P.
　　　23. $Ra \ \lor \ Qa$　　　　　　　　　　22 Com.
　　　24. Ta　　　　　　　　　　　　　21 Simp.
　　　25. $-Ra \ \& \ Ta$　　　　　　　　　　21 Com.
　　　26. $-Ra$　　　　　　　　　　　　　25 Simp.
　　　27. Qa　　　　　　　　　　　　　23,26 D.S.

28. $Qa \rightarrow Sa$	11 U.I.
29. Sa	28,27 M.P.
30. Sa & Ta	29,24 Conj.
31. $\sim\sim(Sa$ & $Ta)$	30 D.N.
32. $\sim(\sim Sa \lor \sim Ta)$	31 DeM.
33. $(\exists x)\sim(\sim Sa \lor \sim Ta)$	32 E.G.
34. $\sim(x)(\sim Sa \lor \sim Ta)$	33 Q.N.
35. $\sim(x)(Sx \rightarrow \sim Tx)$	34 Impl.

7.4

1. 1. $(x)[Px \rightarrow (Qx$ & $Rx)]$ $/\therefore$ $(x)(Px \rightarrow Qx)$
      2. Px .... ACP
      3. $Px \rightarrow (Qx$ & $Rx)$ .... 1 U.I.
      4. Qx & Rx .... 2,4 M.P.
      5. Qx .... 4 Simp.
      6. $Px \rightarrow Qx$ .... 2–5 C.P.
      7. $(x)(Px \rightarrow Qx)$ .... 6 U.G.

3. 1. $(x)[Px \rightarrow (Rx \lor \sim Sx)]$
      2. $(x)(Rx \rightarrow \sim Sx)$ $/\therefore$ $(x)(Px \rightarrow \sim Sx)$
        3. Px .... ACP
        4. $\sim\sim Sx$ .... AIP
        5. $Px \rightarrow (Rx \lor \sim Sx)$ ... 1 U.I.
        6. $Rx \lor \sim Sx$ .... 3,5 M.P.
        7. $Rx \rightarrow \sim Sx$ .... 2 U.I.
        8. $\sim Rx$ .... 7,4 M.T.
        9. $\sim Sx$ .... 6,8 D.S.
        10. $\sim Sx$ & $\sim\sim Sx$ ... 4,9 Conj.
      11. $\sim Sx$ .... 4–10 I.P.
      12. $Px \rightarrow \sim Sx$ .... 3–11 C.P.
      13. $(x)(Px \rightarrow \sim Sx)$ ... 12 U.G.

5. 1. $(x)[(Px \lor Qx) \rightarrow (Rx$ & $Sx)]$
      2. $(x)[Rx \rightarrow (Qx$ & $\sim Sx)]$ $/\therefore$ $(x)(Qx \rightarrow \sim Sx)$
        3. Qx .... ACP
        4. $Qx \lor Px$ .... 3 Add.
        5. $Px \lor Qx$ .... 4 Com.
        6. $(Px \lor Qx) \rightarrow (Rx$ & $Sx)$ ... 1 U.I.
        7. Rx & Sx .... 6,5 M.P.
        8. Rx .... 7 Simp.
        9. $Rx \rightarrow (Qx$ & $\sim Sx)$ ... 2 U.I.
        10. Qx & $\sim Sx$ .... 9,8 M.P.
        11. $\sim Sx$ & Qx .... 10 Com.
        12. $\sim Sx$ .... 11 Simp.
      13. $Qx \rightarrow \sim Sx$ .... 3–12 C.P.
      14. $(x)(Qx \rightarrow \sim Sx)$ ... 13 U.I.

7. 1. $(x)[Px \& Qx) \rightarrow Rx]$
    2. $(\exists x)(Px \& \sim Rx)$ $/\therefore$ $(\exists x)\sim Qx$
    | 3. $\sim(\exists x)\sim Qx$ | AIP |
    | 4. $(x)Qx$ | 3 Q.N. |
    | 5. $Pa \& \sim Ra$ | 2 E.I. |
    | 6. $(Pa \& Qa) \rightarrow Ra$ | 1 U.I. |
    | 7. Qa | 4 U.I. |
    | 8. Pa | 5 Simp. |
    | 9. $Pa \& Qa$ | 8,7 Conj. |
    | 10. Ra | 6,9 M.P. |
    | 11. $\sim Ra \& Pa$ | 5 Com. |
    | 12. $\sim Ra$ | 11 Simp. |
    | 13. $Ra \& \sim Ra$ | 10,12 Conj. |
    14. $(\exists x)\sim Qx$ | 3–13 I.P.

9. 1. $(x)[Px \rightarrow (Rx \lor \sim Sx)]$
    2. $(\exists x)(Px \& \sim Rx)$ $/\therefore$ $(\exists x)(Px \& \sim Sx)$
    | 3. $\sim(\exists x)(Px \& \sim Sx)$ | AIP |
    | 4. $(x)\sim(Px \& \sim Sx)$ | 3 Q.N. |
    | 5. $(x)(\sim Px \lor \sim \sim Sx)$ | 4 DeM. |
    | 6. $(x)(\sim Px \lor Sx)$ | 5 D.N. |
    | 7. $(x)(Px \rightarrow Sx)$ | 6 Impl. |
    | 8. $Pa \& \sim Ra$ | 2 E.I. |
    | 9. $Pa \rightarrow Sa$ | 7 U.I. |
    | 10. Pa | 8 Simp. |
    | 11. Sa | 9,10 M.P. |
    | 12. $Pa \rightarrow (Ra \lor \sim Sa)$ | 1 U.I. |
    | 13. $Ra \lor \sim Sa$ | 12,10 M.P. |
    | 14. $\sim Ra \& Pa$ | 8 Com. |
    | 15. $\sim Ra$ | 14 Simp. |
    | 16. $\sim Sa$ | 13,15 D.S. |
    | 17. $Sa \& \sim Sa$ | 11,16 Conj. |
    18. $(\exists x)(Px \& \sim Sx)$ | 3–17 I.P.

11. 1. $(x)[(Px \lor Qx) \rightarrow (Rx \& Sx)]$
     2. $(x)[Rx \rightarrow (Tx \lor \sim Px)]$ $/\therefore$ $(x)[Qx \rightarrow (Px \rightarrow Tx)]$
     | 3. Qx | ACP |
     | 4. Px | ACP |
     | 5. $\sim Tx$ | AIP |
     | 6. $(Px \lor Qx) \rightarrow (Rx \& Sx)$ | 1 U.I. |
     | 7. $Rx \rightarrow (Tx \lor \sim Px)$ | 2 U.I. |
     | 8. $Px \lor Qx$ | 4 Add. |
     | 9. $Rx \& Sx$ | 6,8 M.P. |
     | 10. Rx | 9 Simp. |
     | 11. $Tx \lor \sim Px$ | 7,10 M.P. |
     | 12. $\sim Px$ | 11,5 D.S. |
     | 13. $Px \& \sim Px$ | 4,12 Conj. |
     | 14. Tx | 5–13 I.P. |
     | 15. $Px \rightarrow Tx$ | 4–14 C.P. |
     16. $Qx \rightarrow (Px \rightarrow Tx)$ | 3–15 C.P.
     17. $(x)[Qx \rightarrow (Px \rightarrow Tx)]$ | 16 U.G.

13. 1. $(x)[Px \rightarrow (Qx \leftrightarrow Rx)]$
     2. $(\exists x)(Px \,\&\, Rx)$ /∴ $(\exists x)(Rx \,\&\, Qx)$

3. $\sim(\exists x)(Rx \,\&\, Qx)$	AIP
4. $(x)\sim(Rx \,\&\, Qx)$	3 Q.N.
5. $Pa \,\&\, Ra$	5 E.I.
6. $Pa \rightarrow (Qa \leftrightarrow Ra)$	1 U.I.
7. Pa	5 Simp.
8. $Qa \leftrightarrow Ra$	6,7 M.P.
9. $\sim(Ra \,\&\, Qa)$	4 U.I.
10. $\sim Ra \lor \sim Qa$	9 DeM.
11. $Ra \rightarrow \sim Qa$	10 Impl.
12. $Ra \,\&\, Pa$	5 Com.
13. Ra	12 Simp.
14. $\sim Qa$	11,13 M.P.
15. $(Qx \rightarrow Ra) \,\&\, (Ra \rightarrow Qa)$	8 Equiv.
16. $(Ra \rightarrow Qa) \,\&\, (Qx \rightarrow Ra)$	15 Com.
17. $Ra \rightarrow Qa$	16 Simp.
18. Qa	17,13 M.P.
19. $Qa \,\&\, \sim Qa$	18,14 Conj.
20. $(\exists x)(Rx \,\&\, Qx)$	3–19 I.P.

15. 1. $(x)[(Qx \leftrightarrow Rx) \rightarrow \sim Px]$
     2. $(x)(Px \rightarrow Rx)$ /∴ $(x)(Px \rightarrow \sim Qx)$

3. Px	ACP
4. $\sim\sim Qx$	AIP
5. $Px \rightarrow Rx$	2 U.I.
6. Rx	5,3 M.P.
7. $(Qx \leftrightarrow Rx) \rightarrow \sim Px$	1 U.I.
8. $\sim\sim Px$	3 D.N.
9. $\sim(Qx \leftrightarrow Rx)$	7,8 M.T.
10. $\sim[(Qx \,\&\, Rx) \lor (\sim Qx \,\&\, \sim Rx)]$	10 Equiv.
11. $\sim(Qx \,\&\, Rx) \,\&\, \sim(\sim Qx \,\&\, \sim Rx)$	10 DeM.
12. $\sim(Qx \,\&\, Rx)$	11 Simp.
13. $\sim Qx \lor \sim Rx$	12 DeM.
14. $Qx \rightarrow \sim Rx$	13 Impl.
15. Qx	4 D.N.
16. $\sim Rx$	14,15 M.P.
17. $Rx \,\&\, \sim Rx$	6,16 Conj.
18. $\sim Qx$	4–17 I.P.
19. $Px \rightarrow \sim Qx$	3–18 C.P.
20. $(x)(Px \rightarrow \sim Qx)$	19 U.G.

17. 1. $(x)[(Px \rightarrow \sim Qx \rightarrow \sim(Px \lor Qx]$
     2. $(x)(Qx \rightarrow Rx)$
     3. $(x)(Rx \rightarrow Qx)$ /∴ $(\exists x)[(Px \rightarrow Rx) \& (Rx \rightarrow Px)]$

4.	$\sim(\exists x)[(Px \rightarrow Rx) \& (Rx \rightarrow Px)]$	AIP
5.	$(x)\sim[(Px \rightarrow Rx) \& (Rx \rightarrow Px)]$	4 Q.N.
6.	$\sim[(Px \rightarrow Rx) \& (Rx \rightarrow Px)]$	5 U.I.
7.	$\sim(Px \rightarrow Rx) \lor \sim(Rx \rightarrow Px)$	6 DeM.
8.	$(Px \rightarrow \sim Qx) \rightarrow \sim(Px \lor Qx)$	1 U.I.
9.	$\sim(Px \rightarrow \sim Qx) \lor \sim(Px \lor Qx)$	8 Impl.
10.	$\sim(\sim Px \lor \sim Qx) \lor \sim(Px \lor Qx)$	9 Impl.
11.	$\sim\sim(Px \& Qx) \lor \sim(Px \lor Qx)$	10 De.M.
12.	$(Px \& Qx) \lor \sim(Px \lor Qx)$	11 D.N.
13.	$(Px \& Qx) \lor (\sim Px \& \sim Qx)$	12 DeM.
14.	$(Px \leftrightarrow Qx)$	13 Equiv.
15.	$(Px \rightarrow Qx) \& (Qx \rightarrow Px)$	14 Equiv.
16.	$Qx \rightarrow Rx$	2 U.I.
17.	$Rx \rightarrow Qx$	3 U.I.
18.	$Px \rightarrow Qx$	15 Simp.
19.	$Px \rightarrow Rx$	18,16 H.S.
20.	$\sim\sim(Px \rightarrow Rx)$	19 D.N.
21.	$\sim(Rx \rightarrow Px)$	7,20 D.S.
22.	$(Qx \rightarrow Px) \& (Px \rightarrow Qx)$	15 Com.
23.	$Qx \rightarrow Px$	22 Simp.
24.	$Rx \rightarrow Px$	17,23 H.S.
25.	$(Rx \rightarrow Px) \& \sim(Rx \rightarrow Px)$	24,21 Conj.

26. $(\exists x)[(Px \rightarrow Rx) \& (Rx \rightarrow Px)]$ 4–25 I.P.

19. 1. $(x)[Px \rightarrow \sim(Qx \lor Rx)]$
     2. $(x)[\sim Px \rightarrow \sim(\sim Qx \lor \sim Rx)]$ /∴ $(x)(Qx \leftrightarrow Rx)$

3.	Qx	ACP
4.	$Px \rightarrow \sim(Qx \lor Rx)$	1 U.I.
5.	$Qx \lor Rx$	3 Add.
6.	$\sim\sim(Qx \lor Rx)$	5 D.N.
7.	$\sim Px$	4,6 M.T.
8.	$\sim Px \rightarrow \sim(\sim Qx \lor \sim Rx)$	2 U.I.
9.	$\sim(\sim Qx \lor \sim Rx)$	8,7 M.P.
10.	$\sim\sim(Qx \& Rx)$	9 DeM.
11.	$Qx \& Rx$	10 D.N.
12.	$Rx \& Qx$	11 Com.
13.	Rx	12 Simp.

14. $Qx \rightarrow Rx$ 3–13 C.P.
  15. Rx ACP
  16. $Px \rightarrow \sim(Qx \vee Rx)$ 1 U.I.
  17. $Rx \vee Qx$ 15 Add.
  18. $Qx \vee Rx$ 17 Com.
  19. $\sim\sim(Qx \vee Rx)$ 18 D.N.
  20. $\sim Px$ 16,19 M.T.
  21. $\sim Px \rightarrow \sim(\sim Qx \vee \sim Rx)$ 2 U.I.
  22. $\sim(\sim Qx \vee \sim Rx)$ 21,20 M.P.
  23. $\sim\sim(Qx \& Rx)$ 22 DeM.
  24. $Qx \& Rx$ 23 D.N.
  25. Qx 24 Simp.
26. $Rx \rightarrow Qx$ 15–25 C.P.
27. $(Qx \rightarrow Rx) \& (Rx \rightarrow Qx)$ 14,26 Conj.
28. $(Qx \leftrightarrow Rx)$ 27 Equiv.
29. $(x)(Qx \leftrightarrow Rx)$ 28 U.G.

7.5

1. $Pa \rightarrow Qa$ $Sa \rightarrow Qa$ $/\therefore$ $Sa \rightarrow Pa$
    F   T   T   T   T   F
     \   /   \   /   \   /
      T   T   F

3. $Sg \rightarrow \sim Mg$ Mg $/\therefore$ Sg
   F   T   T   F
   \   F
    T

5. $Pa \rightarrow Qa$ $Pa \& \sim Sa$ $/\therefore$ $Sa \& Qa$
   T   T   T   F   F   T
   \   /   \   T   F
    T   T

7. $Pa \rightarrow Qa$ $Sa \rightarrow \sim Qa$ $/\therefore$ $Pa \& Sa$
   F   F   F   F   F   F
   \   /   \   T   F
    T   T

9. $[(Pa \& Qa) \vee (Pb \& Qb)]$ $[(Pa \& \sim Sa) \vee (Pb \& \sim Sb)$ $/\therefore$ $[(Sa \rightarrow Qa) \& (Sb \rightarrow Qb)]$
     T   F   T   T   T   T   T   F   T   F   F   T
       F   T   \   F   \   T   F   T
        \   /   F   T   \   /
         T   T   F

11. $[(Pa \& \sim Qa) \vee (Pb \& \sim Qb)]$ $[(Pa \& \sim Sa) \vee (Pb \& \sim Sb)] /\therefore$ $[(\sim Sa \& \sim Qa) \vee (\sim Sb \& \sim Qb)]$
     T   F   T   T   T   T   T   F   T   F   F   T
      \   T   \   F   \   F   \   T   F   T   T   F
     T   F   F   T   F   F
       \   /   \   /   \   /
         T   T   F

13. (P*a* & ~Q*a*) v (P*b* & ~Q*b*)   (P*a* & ~S*a*) v (P*b* & ~S*b*)   /∴   (S*a* → Q*a*) & (S*b* → Q*b*)
       T   F   T   T   T   T   T   F   T   F   F   T
         \ T   \ F   \ F   \ T   \ /   \ /
          T   F   F   T   F   T
           \ /   \ /   \ /
            T   T   F

15. [(M*a* & H*a*) → (F*a* v S*a*)] [(M*a* & F*a*) → D*a*] [(M*a* & S*a*) → D*a*] /∴ (M*a* → H*a*)
       T   F   F T   T   F   T   T   F   T   T   T   T   T   T   T   F
           F   T   F   /   T   /   F
             \   /   \   /   \   /
              T   T   T

7.6.I

1. W*sm*
3. W*sh* → W*sm*
5. (*x*)(P*x* → ~A*xg*) or ~(∃*x*)(P*x* & A*xg*)
7. (*x*)(A*x* → D*xx*)
9. (*x*)[C*xm* → (R*x* & A*xg*)]
11. (∃*x*)(P*x* & L*xj*) & (∃*x*)(P*x* & R*xj*)
13. (*x*)[(P*x* & T*xt*) → W*x*]
15. (*x*){(S*x* & P*x*) → (*y*)[(S*y* & A*y*) → B*xy*]}
17. (*x*)[A*x* → (*y*){[(L*y* v W*y*) & I*xy*] → F*x*}]
19. (*x*){T*x* → (*y*)[[S*y* & R*yx*] & L*xy*] → C*x*]}

7.6.II

1.   1. (*x*)[P*x* → (*y*)(Q*y* → R*xy*)]
     2. (∃*x*)(P*x* & Q*x*)   /∴   (∃*x*)(∃*y*)R*xy*
     3. P*a* & Q*a*   2 E.I.
     4. P*a*   3 Simp.
     5. P*a* → (*y*)(Q*y* → R*ay*)   1 U.I.
     6. P*b* & Q*b*   2 E.I.
     7. Q*b* & P*b*   6 Com.
     8. Q*b*   7 Simp.
     9. (*y*)(Q*y* → R*ay*)   5,4 M.P.
    10. Q*b* → R*ab*   9 U.I.
    11. R*ab*   10,8 M.P.
    12. (∃*y*)R*ay*   11 E.G.
    13. (∃*x*)(∃*y*)R*xy*   12 E.G.

3. 1. $(x)[Px \rightarrow (\exists y)(Qy \& Rxy)]$
    2. $(x)(y)(\sim Rxy)$ $/\therefore$ $\sim Pa$
3. Pa	AIP
4. $Pa \rightarrow (\exists y)(Qy \& Ray)$	1 U.I.
5. $(\exists y)(Qy \& Ray)$	3,4 M.P.
6. $Qb \& Rab$	5 E.I.
7. $Rab \& Qb$	6 Com.
8. Rab	7 Simp.
9. $(y)(\sim Ray)$	2 U.I.
10. $\sim Rab$	9 U.I.
11. $Rab \& \sim Rab$	8,10 Conj.
    12. $\sim Pa$ 3–11 I.P.

5. 1. $(\exists x)(\exists y)(\sim Rxy)$
    2. $(x)[Px \rightarrow (y)(Qy \rightarrow Rxy)]$ $/\therefore$ $(\exists x)(\exists y)(\sim Px \lor \sim Qy)$
3. $\sim(\exists x)(\exists y)(\sim Px \lor \sim Qy)$	AIP
4. $(x)\sim(\exists y)(\sim Px \lor \sim Qy)$	3 Q.N.
5. $(x)(y)\sim(\sim Px \lor \sim Qy)$	4 Q.N.
6. $(\exists y)(\sim Ray)$	1 E.I.
7. $\sim Rab$	6 E.I.
8. $(x)(y)\sim\sim(Px \& Qy)$	5 DeM.
9. $(x)(y)(Px \& Qy)$	8 D.N.
10. $(y)(Pa \& Qy)$	9 U.I.
11. $Pa \& Qb$	10 U.I.
12. $Pa \rightarrow (y)(Qy \rightarrow Ray)$	2 U.I.
13. Pa	11 Simp.
14. $(y)(Qy \rightarrow Ray)$	12,13 M.P.
15. $Qb \rightarrow Rab$	14 U.I.
16. $Qb \& Pa$	11 Com.
17. Qb	16 Simp.
18. Rab	15,17 M.P.
19. $Rab \& \sim Rab$	19,7 Conj.
    20. $(\exists x)(\exists y)(\sim Px \lor \sim Qy)$ 3–19 I.P.

7. 1. $(x)\{Px \rightarrow (\exists y)[Qy \& (Sy \rightarrow Rxy)]\}$
    2. $(\exists x)(Px \& Sx)$
    3. $(x)(Qx \rightarrow Sx)$ $/\therefore$ $(\exists x)(\exists y)(Rxy)$
4. $Pa \& Sa$	2 E.I.
5. Pa	4 Simp.
6. $Pa \rightarrow (\exists y)[Qy \& (Sy \rightarrow Ray)]$	1 U.I.
7. $(\exists y)[Qy \& (Sy \rightarrow Ray)]$	6,5 M.P.
8. $Qb \& (Sb \rightarrow Rab)$	7 E.I.
9. Qb	8 Simp.
10. $Qb \rightarrow Sb$	3 U.I.
11. Sb	10,11 M.P.
12. $(Sb \rightarrow Rab) \& Qb$	8 Com.
13. $Sb \rightarrow Rab$	12 Simp.
14. Rab	13,11 M.P.
15. $(\exists y)Ray$	14 E.G.
16. $(\exists x)(\exists y)Rxy$	15 E.G.

9. 1. $(x)\{Px \to (\exists y)[Qy \ \& \ (Sy \to Rxy)]\}$
    2. $(\exists x)(Sx \ \& \ Px)$
    3. $(x)(y)(Rxy \to Ryx)$ /∴ $(\exists x)(\exists y)(Sy \to Ryyx)$
    4. $Sa \ \& \ Pa$ 2 E.I.
    5. $Pa \to (\exists y)[Qy \ \& \ (Sy \to Ray)]$ 1 U.I.
    6. $Pa \ \& \ Sa$ 4 Com.
    7. Pa 6 Simp.
    8. $(\exists y)[Qy \ \& \ (Sy \to Ray)]$ 5,7 M.P.
    9. $Qb \ \& \ (Sb \to Rab)$ 8 E.I.
    10. $(Sb \to Rab) \ \& \ Qb$ 9 Com.
    11. $Sb \to Rab$ 10 Simp.
    12. $(y)(Ray \to Rya)$ 3 U.I.
    13. $Rab \to Rba$ 12 U.I.
    14. $Sb \to Rba$ 11,13 H.S.
    15. $(\exists y)(Sy \to Rya)$ 14 E.I.
    16. $(\exists x)(\exists y)(Sy \to Rya)$ 15 E.I.

11. 1. $(x)\{(Px \lor Qx) \to (y)[(Sy \lor Qy) \to Rxy]\}$
    2. $(x)(y)(Rxy \to Tyx)$ /∴ $(x)[Qx \to (y)(Qy \to Tyx)]$
    3. Qx ACP
    4. $Qx \lor Px$ 3 Add.
    5. $Px \lor Qx$ 4 Com.
    6. $(Px \lor Qx) \to (y)[(Sy \lor Qy) \to Rxy]$ 1 U.I.
    7. $(y)[(Sy \lor Qy) \to Rxy]$ 6,5 M.P.
    8. $(Sy \lor Qy) \to Rxy$ 7 U.I.
    9. Qy ACP
    10. $Qy \lor Sy$ 9 Add.
    11. $Sy \lor Qy$ 10 Com.
    12. Rxy 8,11 M.P.
    13. $Qy \to Rxy$ 9–12 C.P.
    14. $(y)(Rxy \to Tyx)$ 2 U.I.
    15. $Rxy \to Tyx$ 14 U.I.
    16. $Qy \to Tyx$ 13,15 H.S.
    17. $(y)(Qy \to Tyx)$ 16 U.G.
    18. $Qx \to (y)(Qy \to Tyx)$ 3–17 C.P.
    19. $(x)[Qx \to (y)(Qy \to Tyx)]$ 18 U.G.

13. 1. $(x)\{(Px \lor Qx) \rightarrow (y)[(Sy \lor Qy) \rightarrow Rxy]\}$
     2. $(\exists x)(Px \,\&\, Qx)$
     3. $(x)(y)(Rxy \rightarrow Tyx)$ $/\therefore$ $(x)[Qx \rightarrow (\exists y)(Qy \,\&\, Tyx)]$

4. Qx	ACP
5. $\sim(\exists y)(Qy \,\&\, Tyx)$	AIP
6. $(y)\sim(Qy \,\&\, Tyx)$	5 Q.N.
7. $(Px \lor Qx) \rightarrow (y)[(Sy \lor Qy) \rightarrow Rxy]$	1 U.I.
8. $Qx \lor Px$	4 Add.
9. $Px \lor Qx$	8 Com.
10. $(y)[(Sy \lor Qy) \rightarrow Rxy]$	7,9 M.P.
11. $Pb \,\&\, Qb$	2 E.I.
12. $Qb \,\&\, Pb$	11 Com.
13. Qb	12 Simp.
14. $(Sb \lor Qb) \rightarrow Rxb$	10 U.I.
15. $Qb \lor Sb$	13 Add.
16. $Sb \lor Qb$	15 Com.
17. Rxb	14,16 M.P.
18. $\sim(Qb \,\&\, Tbx)$	6 U.I.
19. $\sim Qb \lor \sim Tbx$	18 DeM.
20. $Qb \rightarrow \sim Tbx$	19 Impl.
21. $\sim Tbx$	20,13 M.P.
22. $(y)(Rxy \rightarrow Tyx)$	3 U.I.
23. $Rxb \rightarrow Tbx$	22 U.I.
24. Tbx	23,17 M.P.
25. $Tbx \,\&\, \sim Tbx$	24,21 Conj.
26. $(\exists y)(Qy \,\&\, Tyx)$	5–25 I.P.
27. $Qx \rightarrow (\exists y)(Qy \,\&\, Tyx)$	4–26 C.P.
28. $(x)[Qx \rightarrow (\exists y)(Qy \,\&\, Tyx)]$	27 U.G.

15. 1. $(x)\{Px \rightarrow (y)[(Qy \,\&\, Rxy) \rightarrow (z)(Sz \rightarrow Rxz)]\}$
     2. $(\exists x)(y)(Px \,\&\, Rxy)$
     3. Qb
     4. $(x)(y)(\sim Sx \rightarrow \sim Ryx)$ $/\therefore$ $(x)(\exists y)(Sx \leftrightarrow Rxy)$

5. $(y)(Pa \,\&\, Ray)$	2 E.I.
6. $Pa \,\&\, Rab$	5 U.I.
7. $Pa \rightarrow (y)[(Qy \,\&\, Ray) \rightarrow (z)(Sz \rightarrow Raz)]$	1 U.I.
8. Pa	6 Simp.
9. $(y)[(Qy \,\&\, Ray) \rightarrow (z)(Sz \rightarrow Raz)]$	7,8 M.P.
10. $Rab \,\&\, Pa$	6 Com.
11. Rab	10 Simp.
12. $(Qb \,\&\, Rab) \rightarrow (z)(Sz \rightarrow Raz)$	9 U.I.
13. $Qb \,\&\, Rab$	3,11 Conj.
14. $(z)(Sz \rightarrow Raz)$	12,13 M.P.
15. $Sx \rightarrow Rax$	14 U.I.
16. $(y)(\sim Sx \rightarrow \sim Ryx)$	4 U.I.
17. $\sim Sx \rightarrow \sim Rax$	16 U.I.
18. $Rax \rightarrow Sx$	17 Trans.
19. $(Sx \rightarrow Rax) \,\&\, (Rax \rightarrow Sx)$	15,18 Conj.
20. $Sx \leftrightarrow Rax$	19 Equiv.
21. $(\exists y)(Sx \leftrightarrow Ryx)$	20 E.G.
22. $(x)(\exists y)(Sx \leftrightarrow Ryx)$	21 U.G.

7.6.III

1.   1. (Cg & Rhg) → Uh
   2. Cg
   3. ~Uh   /∴   ~Rhg
   4. Cg → (Rhg → Uh)   1 Exp.
   5. Rhg → Uh   2,4 M.P.
   6. ~Rhg   5,3 M.T.

3.   1. (∃x)(Px & Lx)
   2. (x)(Lx → ~Hxt)   /∴   (∃x)(Px & ~Hxt)
   3. Pa & La   1 E.I.
   4. La → ~Hat   2 U.I.
   5. Pa   3 Simp.
   6. La & Pa   3 Com.
   7. La   6 Simp.
   8. ~Hat   4,7 M.P.
   9. Pa & ~Hat   5,8 Conj.
   10. (∃x)(Px & ~Hxt)   9 E.G.

5.   1. (∃x)(Px & ~Hxt)
   2. (x){[Px & (∃y)[(Cy & Ly) & Cxy]] → Hxt}
                      /∴   (∃x){Px & ~(∃y)[(Cx & Lx) & Cxy]}
   3. Pa & ~Hat   1 E.I.
   4. [Pa & (∃y)[(Cy & Ly) & Cay]] → Hat   2 U.I.
   5. Pa   3 Simp.
   6. ~Hat & Pa   3 Com.
   7. ~Hat   6 Simp.
   8. Pa → [(∃y)[(Cy & Ly) & Cay] → Hat]   4 Exp.
   9. (∃y)[(Cy & Ly) & Cay] → Hat   8,5 M.P.
   10. ~(∃y)[(Cy & Ly) & Cay]   9,7 M.T.
   11. Pa & ~(∃y)[(Cy & Ly) & Cay]   5,10 Conj.
   12. (∃x){Px & ~(∃y)[(Cy & Ly) & Cxy]}   11 E.G.

7. 1. $(x)[(Px \& Vix) \to Hx]$
    2. $(x)[(Px \& Hx) \to \text{-}(\exists y)(Sy \& Cyx)]$
    3. $(x)\{[Px \& \text{-}(\exists y)(Sy \& Cyx)] \to \text{-}(\exists z)(Oz \& Exz)\}$
       $/\therefore\ (x)[(Px \& Vix) \to \text{-}(\exists z)(Oz \& Exz)\}$

4. $(Px \& Vix) \to Hx$	1 U.I.
5. $(Px \& Hx) \to \text{-}(\exists y)(Sy \& Cyx)$	2 U.I.
6. $[Px \& \text{-}(\exists y)(Sy \& Cyx)] \to \text{-}(\exists z)(Oz \& Exz)$	3 U.I.
7. $(Hx \& Px) \to \text{-}(\exists y)(Sy \& Cyx)$	5 Com.
8. $Hx \to [Px \to \text{-}(\exists y)(Sy \& Cyx)]$	7 Exp.
9. $(Px \& Vix \to [Px \to \text{-}(\exists y)(Sy \& Cyx)]$	4,8 H.S.
10. $[(Px \& Vix) \& Px] \to \text{-}(\exists y)(Sy \& Cyx)$	9 Exp.
11. $[Px \& (Vix \& Px)] \to \text{-}(\exists y)(Sy \& Cyx)$	10 Assoc.
12. $[Px \& (Px \& Vix)] \to \text{-}(\exists y)(Sy \& Cyx)$	11 Com.
13. $[(Px \& Px) \& Vix] \to \text{-}(\exists y)(Sy \& Cyx)$	12 Assoc.
14. $(Px \& Vix) \to \text{-}(\exists y)(Sy \& Cyx)$	13 Taut.
15. $[\text{-}(\exists y)(Sy \& Cyx) \& Px] \to \text{-}(\exists z)(Ox \& Exz)$	6 Com.
16. $\text{-}(\exists y)(Sy \& Cyx) \to [Px \to \text{-}(\exists z)(Oz \& Exz)]$	15 Exp.
17. $(Px \& Vix) \to [Px \to \text{-}(\exists z)(Oz \& Exz)]$	14,16 H.S.
18. $[(Px \& Vix) \& Px] \to \text{-}(\exists z)(Oz \& Exz)$	17 Exp.
19. $[Px \& (Vix \& Px)] \to \text{-}(\exists z)(Oz \& Exz)$	18 Assoc.
20. $[Px \& (Px \& Vix)] \to \text{-}(\exists z)(Oz \& Exz)$	19 Com.
21. $[(Px \& Px) \& Vix] \to \text{-}(\exists z)(Oz \& Exz)$	20 Assoc.
22. $(Px \& Vix) \to \text{-}(\exists z)(Oz \& Exz)$	21 Taut.
23. $(x)[(Px \& Vix) \to \text{-}(\exists z)(Oz \& Exz)]$	22 U.G.

9. 1. $(x)\{[Px \& (y)(Ey \to Vxy)] \to (z)(Cz \to Sxz)\}$
    2. $(x)\{[Px \& (z)(Cz \to Sxz)] \to (y)(Gy \to \text{-}Pxy)\}$
    3. $Pj \& (\exists y)(Gy \& Pjy)$ $/\therefore$ $(\exists y)(Ey \& \text{-}Vjy)$

4. $[Pj \& (y)(Ey \to Vjy)] \to (z)(Cz \to Sjz)$	1 U.I.
5. $Pj \to [(y)(Ey \to Vjy) \to (z)(Cz \to Sjz)]$	4 Exp.
6. Pj	3 Simp.
7. $(y)(Ey \to Vjy) \to (z)(Cz \to Sjz)$	5,6 M.P.
8. $[Pj \& (z)(Cz \to Sjz)] \to (y)(Gy \to \text{-}Pjy)$	2 U.I.
9. $Pj \to [(z)(Cz \to Sjz) \to (y)(Gy \to \text{-}Pjy)]$	8 Exp.
10. $(z)(Cz \to Sjz) \to (y)(Gy \to \text{-}Pjy)$	9,6 M.P.
11. $(y)(Ey \to Vjy) \to (y)(Gy \to \text{-}Pjy)$	7,10 H.S.
12. $(\exists y)(Gy \& Pjy) \& Pj$	3 Com.
13. $(\exists y)(Gy \& Pjy)$	12 Simp.
14. $\text{-}(y)\text{-}(Gy \& Pjy)$	13 Q.N.
15. $\text{-}(y)(\text{-}Gy \lor \text{-}Pjy)$	14 DeM.
16. $\text{-}(y)(Gy \to \text{-}Pjy)$	15 Impl.
17. $\text{-}(y)(Ey \to Vjy)$	11,16 M.T.
18. $(\exists y)\text{-}(Ey \to Vjy)$	17 Q.N.
19. $(\exists y)\text{-}(\text{-}Ey \lor Vjy)$	18 Impl.
20. $(\exists y)\text{-}\text{-}(Ey \& \text{-}Vjy)$	19 DeM.
21. $(\exists y)(Ey \& \text{-}Vjy)$	20 D.N.

7.7.I

1.   1. $(x)(Px \to Qx)$
   2. Pa
   3. $a = b$ /∴ Qb
   4. $Pb \to Qb$ 1 U.I.
   5. Pb 2,3 Id.
   6. Qb 4,5 M.P.

3.   1. $(x)(Px \to (\exists y)(Qy \ \& \ Rxy))$
   2. Pa
   3. $(x)[(x = a) \to (y)(y = x)]$ /∴ Qa
   4. $Pa \to (\exists y)(Qy \ \& \ Ray)$ 1 U.I.
   5. $(\exists y)(Qy \ \& \ Ray)$ 4,2 M.P.
   6. $Qb \ \& \ Rab$ 5 E.I.
   7. $(a = a) \to (y)(y = a)$ 3 U.I.
   8. $a = a$ pr. Id.
   9. $(y)(y = a)$ 7,8 M.P.
  10. Qb 6 Simp.
  11. $b = a$ 9 U.I.
  12. Qa 11,10 Id.

5.   1. $(\exists x)[Px \ \& \ (y)(Py \to Rxy)]$
   2. $(x)(y)(Ryx \to (\exists z)Sz)$
   3. $(x)(x = c)$ /∴ Sc
   4. $Pa \ \& \ (y)(Py \to Ray)$ 1 E.I.
   5. Pa 4 Simp.
   6. $(y)(Py \to Ray) \ \& \ Pa$ 4 Com.
   7. $(y)(Py \to Ray)$ 6 Simp.
   8. $Pa \to Raa$ 7 U.I.
   9. Raa 8,5 M.P.
  10. $(y)[Rya \to (\exists z)Sz]$ 2 U.I.
  11. $Raa \to (\exists z)Sz$ 10 U.I.
  12. $(\exists z)Sz$ 9,11 M.P.
  13. Sb 12 E.I.
  14. $b = c$ 3 U.I.
  15. Sc 13,14 Id.

7.   1. $Pa \ \& \ \text{-}(\exists x)[Px \ \& \ \text{-}(x = a)]$ /∴ $(\exists x)[Px \ \& \ (y)(Py \to x = y)]$
   2. $\text{-}(\exists x)[Px \ \& \ \text{-}(x = a)] \ \& \ Pa$ 1 Com.
   3. $\text{-}(\exists x)[Px \ \& \ \text{-}(x = a)]$ 2 Simp.
   4. $(x)\text{-}[Px \ \& \ \text{-}(x = a)]$ 3 Q.N.
   5. $\text{-}[Py \ \& \ \text{-}(y = a)]$ 4 U.I.
   6. $\text{-}Py \lor \text{-}\text{-}(y = a)$ 5 DeM.
   7. $\text{-}Py \lor (y = a)$ 6 D.N.
   8. $Py \to (y = a)$ 7 Impl.
   9. $(y)[Py \to (y = a)]$ 8 U.G.
  10. Pa 1 Simp.
  11. $Pa \ \& \ (y)[Py \to (y = a)]$ 10,9 Conj.
  12. $(\exists x)\{Px \ \& \ (y)[Py \to (y = x)]\}$ 11 E.G.

9.   1. $(\exists x)(\exists y)\{[(Px \ \& \ Py) \ \& \ \sim(x = y)] \ \& \ (z)[Pz \rightarrow (z = x \lor z = y)]\}$

      2. Pa /∴ $(\exists x)[Px \ \& \ \sim(x = a)]$

3. $\sim(\exists x)[Px \ \& \ \sim(x = a)]$	AIP
4. $(x)\sim[Px \ \& \ \sim(x = a)]$	3 Q.N.
5. $(\exists y)\{[(Pb \ \& \ Py) \ \& \ \sim(b = y)] \ \& \ (z)[(Pz \rightarrow (z = b \lor z = y)]\}$	1 E.I.
6. $[(Pb \ \& \ Pc) \ \& \ \sim(b = c)] \ \& \ (z)[(Pz \rightarrow (z = b \lor z = c)]$	5 E.I.
7. $(Pb \ \& \ Pc) \ \& \ \sim(b = c)$	6 Simp.
8. $Pb \ \& \ Pc$	7 Simp.
9. $\sim(b = c) \ \& \ (Pb \ \& \ Pc)$	7 Com.
10. $\sim(b = c)$	9 Simp.
11. $(z)(Pz \rightarrow (z = b \lor z = c)] \ \& \ [(Pb \ \& \ Pc) \ \& \ \sim(b = c)]$	6 Com.
12. $(z)[Pz \rightarrow (z = b \lor z = c)]$	11 Simp.
13. $Pa \rightarrow (a = b \lor a = c)$	12 U.I.
14. $a = b \lor a = c$	13,2 M.P.
15. $\sim[Pb \ \& \ \sim(b = a)]$	4 U.I.
16. $\sim Pb \lor \sim\sim(b = a)$	15 DeM.
17. $\sim Pb \lor b = a$	16 D.N.
18. $Pb \rightarrow b = a$	17 Impl.
19. Pb	8 Simp.
20. $b = a$	18,19 M.P.
21. $\sim[Pc \ \& \ \sim(c = a)]$	4 U.I.
22. $\sim Pc \lor \sim\sim(c = a)$	21 DeM.
23. $\sim Pc \lor c = a$	22 D.N.
24. $Pc \rightarrow c = a$	23 Impl.
25. $Pc \ \& \ Pb$	8 Com
26. Pc	25 Simp.
27. $c = a$	24,26 M.P.
28. $a = c$	27 Id.
29. $b = c$	20,28 Id.
30. $(b = c) \ \& \ \sim(b = c)$	29,10 Conj.

   31. $(\exists x)[Px \ \& \ \sim(x = a)]$ 3–30 I.P.

7.7.II

1. $c = t$
3. $(\exists x)(Ax \ \& \ Hlx)$
5. $(\exists x)\{(Ax \ \& \ Hjx) \ \& \ (y)[(Ay \ \& \ Hjy) \rightarrow x = y]\}$
7. $\sim(\exists x)[Nx \ \& \ (y)(Ny \rightarrow Lyx)]$
9. $(Pm \ \& \ Omc) \ \& \ (x)\{[(Px \ \& \ Oxc) \ \& \ \sim(x = m)] \rightarrow Pmx\}$

7.7.III

1.   1. $(\exists x)\{[(Rx \ \& \ Rxl) \ \& \ (y)[(Ry \ \& \ Ryl) \rightarrow x = y]] \ \& \ x = j\}$ /∴ Rjl

2. $[(Ra \ \& \ Ral) \ \& \ (y)[(Ry \ \& \ Ryl) \rightarrow a = y]] \ \& \ a = j$	1 E.I.
3. $a = j \ \& \ [(Ra \ \& \ Ral) \ \& \ (y)[(Ry \ \& \ Ryl) \rightarrow a = y]]$	2 Com.
4. $a = j$	3 Simp.
5. $(Ra \ \& \ Ral) \ \& \ [(y)[(Ry \ \& \ Ryl) \rightarrow a = y] \ \& \ a = j]$	2 Assoc.
6. $Ra \ \& \ Ral$	5 Simp.
7. $Ral \ \& \ Ra$	6 Com.
8. Ral	7 Simp.
9. Rjl	8,4 Id.

3. 1. $(\exists x)(Bx \ \& \ Rx)$
   2. $(x)(y)\{[(Bx \ \& \ Rx) \ \& \ (By \ \& \ Ry)] \rightarrow x = y\}$
   $\qquad /\therefore \ (\exists x)\{(Bx \ \& \ Rx) \ \& \ (y)[(By \ \& \ Ry) \rightarrow x = y]\}$
   3. $Ba \ \& \ Ra$ $\qquad\qquad\qquad\qquad\qquad\qquad$ 1 E.I.
   4. $(y)\{[(Ba \ \& \ Ra) \ \& \ (By \ \& \ Ry)] \rightarrow a = y\}$ $\qquad$ 2 U.I.
   5. $[(Ba \ \& \ Ra) \ \& \ (By \ \& \ Ry)] \rightarrow a = y$ $\qquad$ 4 U.I.
   6. $(Ba \ \& \ Ra) \rightarrow [(By \ \& \ Ry)] \rightarrow a = y]$ $\qquad$ 5 Exp.
   7. $(By \ \& \ Ry) \rightarrow a = y$ $\qquad\qquad\qquad\qquad$ 6,3 M.P.
   8. $(y)[(By \ \& \ Ry) \rightarrow a = y]$ $\qquad\qquad\qquad$ 7 U.G.
   9. $(Ba \ \& \ Ra) \ \& \ (y)[(By \ \& \ Ry) \rightarrow a = y]$ $\qquad$ 3,8 Conj.
   10. $(\exists x)\{(Bx \ \& \ Rx) \ \& \ (y)[(By \ \& \ Ry) \rightarrow x = y]\}$ $\quad$ 9 E.G.

5. 1. $Cf \ \& \ (x)(Cx \rightarrow x = f)$
   2. $(x)(Cx \rightarrow Wxj)$
   3. $(x)(Wxj \rightarrow Cx)$ $\quad /\therefore \quad Wfj \ \& \ (x)(Wxj \rightarrow x = f)$
   4. Cf $\qquad\qquad\qquad\qquad\qquad$ 1 Simp.
   5. $Cf \rightarrow Wfj$ $\qquad\qquad\qquad\quad$ 2 U.I.
   6. Wfj $\qquad\qquad\qquad\qquad\quad$ 5,4 M.P.
   7. $(x)(Cx \rightarrow x = f) \ \& \ Cf$ $\qquad$ 1 Com.
   8. $(x)(Cx \rightarrow x = f)$ $\qquad\qquad$ 7 Simp.
   9. $Cx \rightarrow x = f$ $\qquad\qquad\qquad$ 8 U.I.
   10. $Wxj \rightarrow Cx$ $\qquad\qquad\qquad$ 3 U.I.
   11. $Wxj \rightarrow x = f$ $\qquad\qquad\quad$ 10,9 H.S.
   12. $(x)(Wxj \rightarrow x = f)$ $\qquad\quad$ 11 U.G.
   13. $Wfj \ \& \ (x)(Wxj \rightarrow x = f)$ $\quad$ 6,12 Conj.

7. 1. $(\exists x)(\exists y)\{[Rx \ \& \ [Ry \ \& \ \sim(x = y)]] \ \& \ (z)[Rz \rightarrow (z = x \lor z = y)]\}$
   2. Rj $\quad /\therefore \qquad\qquad (\exists x)\{Rx \ \& \ \sim(x = j)\}$
   3. $\sim(\exists x)[Rx \ \& \ \sim(x = j)]$ $\qquad\qquad\qquad\qquad$ AIP
   4. $(x)\sim[Rx \ \& \ \sim(x = j)]$ $\qquad\qquad\qquad\qquad$ 3 Q.N.
   5. $(\exists y)\{[Ra \ \& \ [Ry \ \& \ \sim(a = y)]] \ \& \ (z)[Rz \rightarrow (z = a \lor z = y)]\}$ 1 E.I.
   6. $[Ra \ \& \ [Rb \ \& \ \sim(a = b)]] \ \& \ (z)[Rz \rightarrow (z = a \lor z = b)]$ 6 E.I.
   7. $Ra \ \& \ [Rb \ \& \ \sim(a = b)]$ $\qquad\qquad\qquad\qquad$ 6 Simp.
   8. Ra $\qquad\qquad\qquad\qquad\qquad\qquad\qquad$ 7 Simp.
   9. $[Rb \ \& \ \sim(a = b)] \ \& \ Ra$ $\qquad\qquad\qquad\quad$ 7 Com.
   10. $Rb \ \& \ \sim(a = b)$ $\qquad\qquad\qquad\qquad\quad$ 9 Simp.
   11. Rb $\qquad\qquad\qquad\qquad\qquad\qquad\quad$ 10 Simp.
   12. $\sim(a = b) \ \& \ Rb$ $\qquad\qquad\qquad\qquad\quad$ 10 Com.
   13. $\sim(a = b)$ $\qquad\qquad\qquad\qquad\qquad\quad$ 12 Simp.
   14. $\sim[Ra \ \& \ \sim(a = j)]$ $\qquad\qquad\qquad\quad$ 4 U.I.
   15. $\sim Ra \lor \sim\sim(a = j)$ $\qquad\qquad\qquad\quad$ 14 DeM.
   16. $\sim Ra \lor (a = j)$ $\qquad\qquad\qquad\qquad\quad$ 15 D.N.
   17. $Ra \rightarrow (a = j)$ $\qquad\qquad\qquad\qquad\quad$ 16 Impl.
   18. $a = j$ $\qquad\qquad\qquad\qquad\qquad\qquad$ 17,8 M.P.
   19. $\sim[Rb \ \& \ \sim(b = j)]$ $\qquad\qquad\qquad\quad$ 4 U.I.
   20. $\sim Rb \lor \sim\sim(b = j)$ $\qquad\qquad\qquad\quad$ 19 DeM.
   21. $\sim Rb \lor (b = j)$ $\qquad\qquad\qquad\qquad\quad$ 20 D.N.
   22. $Rb \rightarrow (b = j)$ $\qquad\qquad\qquad\qquad\quad$ 21 Impl.
   23. $b = j$ $\qquad\qquad\qquad\qquad\qquad\qquad$ 22,11 M.P.
   24. $j = b$ $\qquad\qquad\qquad\qquad\qquad\qquad$ 23 Id.
   25. $a = b$ $\qquad\qquad\qquad\qquad\qquad\qquad$ 18,24 Id.
   26. $(a = b) \ \& \ \sim(a = b)$ $\qquad\qquad\qquad\quad$ 25,13 Conj.
   27. $(\exists x)\{Rx \ \& \ \sim(x = j)\}$ $\qquad\qquad\qquad$ 3–26 I.P.

9. 1. $(Rf$ & $\sim Gf)$ & $(x)\{[Rx$ & $\sim(x = f)] \rightarrow Gx\}$
    2. $(x)[(Rx$ & $Gx) \rightarrow Wxa]$
    3. Wfj $/\therefore$ $(x)[Rx \rightarrow (Wxa \vee Wxj)]$

4. $\sim(x)[Rx \rightarrow (Wxa \vee Wxj)]$	AIP
5. $(\exists x)\sim[Rx \rightarrow (Wxa \vee Wxj)]$	4 Q.N.
6. $\sim[Rb \rightarrow (Wba \vee Wbj)]$	5 E.I.
7. $\sim[\sim Rb \vee (Wba \vee Wbj)]$	6 Impl.
8. $\sim\sim Rb \vee \sim(Wba \vee Wbj)$	7 DeM.
9. Rb & $\sim(Wba \vee Wbj)$	8 D.N.
10. Rb	9 Simp.
11. $\sim(Wba \vee Wbj)$ & Rb	10 Com.
12. $\sim(Wba \vee Wbj)$	11 Simp.
13. $\sim Wba$ & $\sim Wbj$	12 DeM.
14. $\sim Wba$	13 Simp.
15. $(Rb$ & $Gb) \rightarrow Wba$	2 U.I.
16. $Rb \rightarrow (Gb \rightarrow Wba)$	15 Exp.
17. $Gb \rightarrow Wba$	16,10 M.P.
18. $\sim Gb$	17,14 M.T.
19. $(x)\{[Rx$ & $\sim(x = f)] \rightarrow Gx\}$ & $(Rf$ & $\sim Gf)$	1 Com.
20. $(x)\{[Rx$ & $\sim(x = f)] \rightarrow Gx\}$	19 Simp.
21. $[Rb$ & $\sim(b = f)] \rightarrow Gb$	20 U.I.
22. $Rb \rightarrow [\sim(b = f) \rightarrow Gb]$	21 Exp.
23. $\sim(b = f) \rightarrow Gb$	22,10 M.P.
24. $\sim\sim(b = f)$	23,18 M.T.
25. $b = f$	24 D.N.
26. $f = b$	25 Id.
27. Wbj	3,26 Id.
28. $\sim Wbj$ & $\sim Wba$	13 Com.
29. $\sim Wbj$	28 Simp.
30. Wbj & $\sim Wbj$	27,29 Conj.
31. $(x)[Rx \rightarrow (Wxa \vee Wxj)]$	4–30 I.P.

8.1

1. Mere comparison.
3. Argument.
5. Argument.
7. Illustrative.
9. Illustrative.
11. Illustrative.
13. Illustrative.
15. Illustrative.
17. Illustrative.
19. Illustrative.

8.2.I

1. a) Weakens the analogy: there is a significant difference between introductory history courses and a senior seminar.
    b) Strenthens the analogy: the course is analogous to a significant number of courses Hormella took and enjoyed, and there are significant differences in the content of the courses.

c) Weakens the analogy: this is a significant difference.

d) Strengthens the analogy: the course she's planning to take is analogous in more respects to the other courses she's taken.

e) Strengthens the analogy: the course is analogous to more things in which she is interested.

f) Weakens the analogy: the conclusion is too strong.

g) Weakens the analogy: there are relatively few respects in which the course Hormella is planning to take is analogous to those she has taken in the past.

h) Strengthens the analogy: similar in more respects to other courses.

i) Weakens the analogy: this is a respect in which the course is dissimilar to other courses she's taken.

j) Weakens the analogy: this is a respect in which the course is dissimilar to other courses she's taken.

3. a) Strengthens the analogy: the conclusion of the argument was that it would be a moderately enjoyable evening of reading, which is a weak conclusion relative to this additional premise.

b) Weakens the analogy: dissimilar to previous cases.

c) Strengthens the analogy: similar in more respects to things in which Siegfried is interested.

d) Weakens the analogy: conclusion too strong.

e) Strengthens the analogy: more objects compared.

f) Neither strengthens nor weakens the analogy.

g) Neither strengthens nor weakens the analogy.

h) Strengthens the analogy: if Siegfried enjoyed them all, it tends to show that regardless of the differences in subject matter, Ostafar's books are enjoyable.

i) Strengthens the analogy: similar in more respects.

j) Weakens the analogy: dissimilarity in a respect.

5. a) Strengthens the analogy: similar in more respects.

b) Strengthens the analogy: relevant factor.

c) Weakens the analogy: dissimilarity in a respect, but it doesn't seriously weaken the analogy, since it is reasonable to believe the team has played a lot of games on astroturf.

d) Strengthens the analogy: since teams generally do better at home, this is a relevant respect.

e) Weakens the analogy: conclusion too strong relative to the premises.

f) Weakens the analogy: relevant factor.

g) Weakens the analogy: relevant factor.

h) Neither strengthens nor weakens the analogy: this is not a relevant factor.

i) Weakens the analogy: difference in a respect.

j) Neither strengthens nor weakens the analogy.

7. a) Weakens the analogy slightly, if at all. Where one writes can make a difference to an author's writing, but generally that is not a relevant consideration.

b) Strengthens the analogy: similar in more respects.

c) Weakens the analogy: dissimilar in a respect.

d) Strengthens the analogy: similar in more respects.

e) Strengthens the analogy, but slightly: differences in publisher seem to be irrelevant to Josiah's success, so the fact that he is sticking with the same publisher who brought out his previous book might slightly increase his chance of continued success.

f) Weakens the analogy: relevant difference: he would not have the advantage of name recognition.

g) Neither strengthens nor weakens the analogy.

h) Strengthens the analogy: similar in more respects.

i) Strengthens the analogy: relevant consideration.

j) Strengthens the analogy: weak conclusion relative to the premises.

8.2.II

1. Similar in many respects. Few objects compared. Factors are relevant, e.g., hours of use. The conclusion is too strong relative to the premises. Weak analogy.

3. Compared in only one respect, engine size. Only three objects compared. The conclusion is too strong. Weak analogy.

5. There are indefinitely many objects compared in an indefinitely large number of ways. "Pampering" seems to be relevant in both cases. There are very significant differences between machines and people. But the conclusion seems warranted by the premises. Fairly strong analogy.

7. There are indefinitely many objects compared in an indefinitely large number of ways. The conclusion seems reasonable. Strong analogy.

9. There are large numbers of objects that are similar in large numbers of respects. Strong analogy.

11. There are only a few objects that are compared in one respect, namely, calling themselves "The best." What they call themselves should be irrelevant to the actual quality of the food. The conclusion is strong. Weak analogy.

13. There are two cases considered. The only respect in which they are similar is the immediate decrease in the demands on the military. There are significant disanalogies between the end of the First World War and the end of the cold war in terms of the threat and nature of hostilities. The analogy is weak.

15. There are significant disanalogies here. AIDS is a contagious disease; breast cancer is not. Research on AIDS is relatively recent; cancer research has been going on for some time. There is the possibility of a vaccine for AIDS; it is doubtful that a vaccine can be developed for breast cancer. Weak analogy.

17. There is an indefinite number of individual cases compared. They are compared in only one respect, namely, they are actions that can cause death. There are several disanalogies. Stabbings and shootings are actions that are intended to cause harm; smoking is not. The analogy here is closer to the case of the car accident. But even here there are differences. A car accident causes immediate injury; secondhand smoke is injurious over an extended period of time. Whereas the accident victim cannot avoid the accident, the potential victim of secondhand smoke could look for a different job. Finally, the conclusion is far too strong: the smoker does not intend to kill anyone by his or her smoking, which is necessary for a charge of murder. Weak analogy.

19. Monetary and mental investments are compared in three ways. There is an indefinite number of objects. There are differences, but they seem not to distract from the analogy. The conclusion seems reasonable. Strong analogy.

21. Though there is a number of respects in which higher education is analogous to a business, there are far more respects in which they are dissimilar. In a typical situation, alas, the timing of final examinations is not an option. Weak analogy.

23. There are numerous dissimilarities between the Communists, the Ku Klux Klan, the John Birch Society, and the conservative elements of the Republican Party in 1964. Weak analogy.

25. There are numerous religious traditions implicitly compared with the French Revolution. They are compared in a fair number of relevant respects. These similarities stand in spite of various dissimilarities. The conclusion is not terribly strong relative to the premises. Strong analogy.
27. Weak analogy. No respects are compared directly.
29. Innumerable cases of lives and games are implicitly compared. They are compared with respect to the attitudes you might take toward a game, suggesting that the same attitude might be taken toward life. There are numerous dissimilarities. Nonetheless, it is a fairly strong analogy if you grant the initial comparison between life and a game.
31. There are numerous cases implicitly compared with respect to the question of isolationism. There are numerous respects in which they are similar. There are also numerous differences, but the differences tend to strengthen the analogy. Strong analogy.
33. There are two analogies here. The first is an analogy between two numbering systems: since the first two digits of the year change, the name of the century must change as well. This is irrelevant. The analogy is weak. The second analogy is based on a comparison of the beginning of the twentieth century to the beginning of the second century. They are compared in two respects: they must last 100 years. The comparisons are relevant. There are no relevant disanalogies. The analogy is good.
35. There is an indefinite number of objects compared. They are compared with respect to optical activity and what Pasteur knew in other cases to produce optical activity. There are few relevant differences. Strong analogy.

9.1.I

1. Method of Agreement
3. Joint Method of Agreement and Difference
5. Joint Method of Agreement and Difference
7. Joint Method of Agreement and Difference
9. Method of Difference

9.1.II

1. Method of Concomitant Variation
3. Method of Difference
5. Method of Residues
7. Method of Agreement
9. Joint Method of Agreement and Difference
11. Method of Concomitant Variation
13. Method of Agreement
15. Joint Method of Agreement and Difference

9.2

3. Method of Difference: the pumpkin pie was a sufficient condition for Bert's illness.
7. Method of Agreement: if the phenomenon in question is the immunity to smallpox, this shows that having contracted cowpox is a necessary condition for immunity to smallpox.
9. Joint Method of Agreement and Difference: necessary and sufficient condition for the phenomenon.

13. Method of Agreement: if the phenomenon under investigation is the preventative of toothache, Twain can be taken to have concluded that drinking two hot Scotches per day is a necessary condition for the phenomenon.
15. Joint Method of Agreement and Difference: both a necessary and a sufficient condition for the phenomenon.

10.1.I

1. $1/52 = .0192$
3. $7/(7+13) = 7/20 = .35$
5. $6,841/8,472 = .8075$
7. $47/(47+62) = 47/109 = .4312$
9. $4/(70+4+16) = 4/90 = .0444$

10.1.II

1. $P(6 \text{ and } 6 \text{ and } 6) = 1/6 \times 1/6 \times 1/6 = 1/216 = .0046$
3. (a) $P(H_1 \text{ and } H_2 \text{ and } H_3) = (1/2 \times 1/2 \times 1/2) = 1/8 = .1250$
   (b) $P[(H_1 \text{ and } H_2 \text{ and } T_3) \text{ or } (H_1 \text{ and } T_2 \text{ and } H_3) \text{ or } (T_1 \text{ and } H_2 \text{ and } H_3)$
   $= [(1/2 \times 1/2 \times 1/2) + (1/2 \times 1/2 \times 1/2) + (1/2 \times 1/2 \times 1/2)]$
   $= [1/8 + 1/8 + 1/8]$
   $= 3/8$
   $= .3750$
   (c) $P[(T_1 \text{ and } T_2 \text{ and } H_3) \text{ or } (T_1 \text{ and } H_2 \text{ and } T_3) \text{ or } (H_1 \text{ and } T_2 \text{ and } T_3)$
   $= [(1/2 \times 1/2 \times 1/2) + (1/2 \times 1/2 \times 1/2) + (1/2 \times 1/2 \times 1/2)]$
   $= [1/8 + 1/8 + 1/8]$
   $= 3/8$
   $= .3750$
   (d) $P(T_1 \text{ and } T_2 \text{ and } T_3) = (1/2 \times 1/2 \times 1/2) = 1/8 = .1250$
5. $P(D_1 \text{ or } D_2) = (35.4/100,000 + 1.7/100,000) = (.000354 + .000017) = .000371$
   $\approx .0004$
7. (a) $P(D_1 1 \text{ and } D_2) = 6/13 \times 6/13 = 36/169 = .2130$
   (b) $P(D_1 1 \text{ and } D_2) = 6/13 \times 3/13 = 18/169 = .1065$
   (c) $P(D_1 1 \text{ and } D_2) = 6/13 \times 4/13 = 24/169 = .1420$
   (d) $P(D_1 1 \text{ and } D_2 \text{ and } D_3) = 6/13 \times 3/13 \times 4/13 = 72/2197 = .0328$
9. To solve some of these, you need to remember that there are various combinations of numbers on the dice that can yield the total.
   (a) $P(1_1 \text{ and } 1_2 2) = 1/6 \times 1/6 = 1/36 = .0278$
   (b) $P[(1_1 \text{ and } 2_2) \text{ or } (2_1 \text{ and } 1_2)]$
   $= (1/6 \times 1/6) + (1/6 \times 1/6) = 1/36 + 1/36$
   $= 2/36 = 1/18 = .0556$
   (c) $P[(1_1 \text{ and } 6_2) \text{ or } (2_1 \text{ and } 5_2) \text{ or } (3_1 \text{ and } 4_2) \text{ or } (4_1 \text{ and } 3_2) \text{ or } (5_1 \text{ and } 2_2) \text{ or } (6_1$ and $1_2)]$
   $= (1/6 \times 1/6) + (1/6 \times 1/6) + (1/6 \times 1/6) + (1/6 \times 1/6) + (1/6 \times 1/6) + (1/6 \times 1/6)$
   $= 1/36 + 1/36 + 1/36 + 1/36 + 1/36 + 1/36$
   $= 6/36 = 1/6 = .1667$
   (d) $P[(5_1 \text{ and } 6_2) \text{ or } (6_1 \text{ and } 5_2)]$
   $= (1/6 \times 1/6) + (1/6 \times 1/6) = 1/36 + 1/36$
   $= 2/36 = 1/18 = .0556$

(e) $P\{[(1_1 \text{ and } 2_2) \text{ or } (2_1 \text{ and } 1_2)] \text{ or } [(1_1 \text{ and } 5_2) \text{ or } (2_1 \text{ and } 4_2) \text{ or } (3_1 \text{ and } 3_2) \text{ or } (4_1 \text{ and } 2_2) \text{ or } (5_1 \text{ and } 1_2)]\}$
= $[(1/6 \times 1/6) + (1/6 \times 1/6)] + [(1/6 \times 1/6) + (1/6 \times 1/6) + (1/6 \times 1/6) + (1/6 \times 1/6) + (1/6 \times 1/6)]$
= $[(1/36) + (1/36)] + [(1/36) + (1/36) + (1/36) + (1/36) + (1/36)]$
= $2/36 + 5/36 = 7/36 = .1944$

(f) $P\{[(1_1 \text{ and } 6_2) \text{ or } (2_1 \text{ and } 5_2) \text{ or } (3_1 \text{ and } 4_2) \text{ or } (4_1 \text{ and } 3_2) \text{ or } (5_1 \text{ and } 2_2) \text{ or } (6_1 \text{ and } 1_2)] \text{ or } [(5_1 \text{ and } 6_2) \text{ or } (6_1 \text{ and } 5_2)]\}$
= $[(1/6 \times 1/6) + (1/6 \times 1/6) + (1/6 \times 1/6) + (1/6 \times 1/6) + (1/6 \times 1/6)] + [(1/6 \times 1/6) + (1/6 \times 1/6)]\}$
= $6/36 + 2/36 = 8/36 = .2222$

11. Probability of the Redskins winning = $3/5 = .6000$
Probability of the Bills winning = $4/7 = .5714$
Probability of both winning = $3/5 \times 4/7 = .3429$

10.2

1. According to what meaning of 'average' was 32 percent the "average score"? If it was the mode, the most common score, it could well be that 50 percent was well below the mean, which is the basis for the professor's curve.

3. To what extent has the population increased since the mid-1960s? Is 23 percent of the current population a smaller number than 25 percent of the population in the mid-1960s?

5. Was the survey unbiased?

7. What is the proportion of the graduates that have jobs in their chosen fields?

9. Was the survey unbiased?

11. What does 'average' mean in the premise?

13. Was the 2 percent raise based on the present salary or the salary before the reduction?

15. What proportion of aluminum cans was recycled in the early 1970s? What raw number of aluminum beverage cans were produced in the early 1970s as opposed to the present?

APPENDIX 3.1 Exercises from 5.2, Set I.

1. 　　　　p /∴ $(p \lor q)$
　✔~$(p \lor q)$
　　　~p
　　　~q
　　　X　　VALID

3. 　　　　p
　　　　q /∴ $(p \lor q)$
　✔~$(p \lor q)$
　　　~p
　　　~q
　　　X　　VALID

5. $\mathrel{\rlap{\hspace{0.1em}/}{\vDash}} p \to q$
    $\quad q \quad /\therefore \quad p$
    $\quad {\sim}p$
    $\quad / \ \backslash$
    $\quad {\sim}p \quad q \quad$ INVALID

7. $\mathrel{\rlap{\hspace{0.1em}/}{\vDash}} p \to q$
    $\quad {\sim}q \quad /\therefore \quad {\sim}p$
    $\quad p$
    $\quad / \ \backslash$
    $\quad {\sim}p \quad q$
    $\quad \text{X} \quad \text{X} \quad$ VALID

9. $\mathrel{\rlap{\hspace{0.1em}/}{\vDash}} p \vee q$
    $\quad {\sim}p \quad /\therefore \quad {\sim}q$
    $\quad q$
    $\quad / \ \backslash$
    $\quad p \quad q$
    $\quad \text{X} \qquad$ INVALID

11. $\mathrel{\rlap{\hspace{0.1em}/}{\vDash}} p \mathrel{\&} q \quad /\therefore \quad q$
    $\quad {\sim}q$
    $\quad p$
    $\quad q$
    $\quad \text{X} \quad$ VALID

13. $\quad \mathrel{\rlap{\hspace{0.1em}/}{\vDash}} p \to q$
    $\quad \mathrel{\rlap{\hspace{0.1em}/}{\vDash}} p \to r \quad /\therefore \quad (q \to r)$
    $\mathrel{\rlap{\hspace{0.1em}/}{\vDash}} {\sim}(q \to r)$
    $\quad\quad q$
    $\quad\quad {\sim}r$
    $\quad\quad / \ \backslash$
    $\quad {\sim}p \quad r$
    $\quad / \ \backslash \ \text{X}$
    $\quad {\sim}p \quad q \quad$ INVALID

15. $\blacktriangleright(p \rightarrow q)\ \&\ (r \rightarrow s)$
$\quad\quad\quad \blacktriangleright p \rightarrow s\ \ /\therefore\ \ (\sim q \lor s)$
$\quad\quad \blacktriangleright \sim(\sim q \lor s)$
$\quad\quad\quad\quad q$
$\quad\quad\quad\quad \sim s$
$\quad\quad\quad \blacktriangleright p \rightarrow q$
$\quad\quad\quad \blacktriangleright r \rightarrow s$
$\quad\quad\quad\quad /\ \backslash$
$\quad\quad\quad \sim r\quad s$
$\quad\quad\quad /\ \backslash\ \ X$
$\quad\quad \sim p\quad s$
$\quad\quad /\ \backslash\ \ X$
$\quad \sim p\quad q \quad\quad$ INVALID

17. $\blacktriangleright(p \rightarrow q)\ \&\ (r \rightarrow s)$
$\quad\quad\quad \blacktriangleright \sim q \lor \sim s\ /\therefore\ \ (\sim p \lor \sim r)$
$\quad\quad \blacktriangleright \sim(\sim p \lor \sim r)$
$\quad\quad\quad\quad p$
$\quad\quad\quad\quad r$
$\quad\quad\quad \blacktriangleright p \rightarrow q$
$\quad\quad\quad \blacktriangleright r \rightarrow s$
$\quad\quad\quad\quad /\ \backslash$
$\quad\quad\quad \sim p\quad q$
$\quad\quad\quad X\ /\ \backslash$
$\quad\quad\quad\quad \sim r\quad s$
$\quad\quad\quad\quad X\ /\ \backslash$
$\quad\quad\quad\quad\quad \sim q\ \ \sim s$
$\quad\quad\quad\quad\quad X\quad X\quad$ VALID

19. $\blacktriangleright(p \rightarrow q) \rightarrow (r \rightarrow s)$
$\quad\quad\quad \blacktriangleright \sim p \lor q\ \ /\therefore\ \ (\sim r \lor s)$
$\quad\quad \blacktriangleright \sim(\sim r \lor s)$
$\quad\quad\quad\quad r$
$\quad\quad\quad\quad \sim s$
$\quad\quad\quad\quad /\ \backslash$
$\quad\quad\quad /\quad\ \backslash$
$\blacktriangleright \sim(p \rightarrow q)\quad \blacktriangleright r \rightarrow s$
$\quad\quad p \quad\quad\quad\quad /\ \backslash$
$\quad\quad \sim q \quad\quad\quad \sim r\quad s$
$\quad\quad /\ \backslash \quad\quad\quad X\quad X$
$\quad \sim p\quad q$
$\quad X\quad X \quad\quad\quad\quad$ VALID

APPENDIX 3.1 Exercises from 5.2, Set II.

1. $\blacktriangleright S \rightarrow A$
$\quad\quad \sim A\ /\therefore\ \ \sim S$
$\quad\quad\ S$
$\quad\quad /\ \backslash$
$\quad \sim S\quad A$
$\quad X\quad X\quad\quad$ VALID

3.   ✔P→ S
```
      ✔(P & S)→ S  /∴   S
                ~S
                / \
              ~P   S
              / \  X
   ✔~(P & S)   S
       / \     X
     ~P  ~S          INVALID
```

5.   ✔S → (P v L)
```
       ~L   /∴   P v ~S
   ✔~(P v ~S)
        ~P
         S
        / \
      ~S  ✔P v L
      X    / \
          P  L
          X  X   VALID
```

7.   ✔S → C
```
     ✔S → P /∴  P → C
   ✔~(P → C)
        P
       ~C
       / \
     ~S   C
     / \  X
   ~S  P     INVALID
```

9.   ✔~C → B
```
      ✔~C → P /∴  ~C → (B & P)
   ✔~[~C → (B & P)]
         ~C
      ✔~(B & P)
         / \
        C   B
        X  / \
          C   P
          X  / \
            ~B  ~P
            X   X   VALID
```

11.   ✔S → Z
    ✔(Z & L) → ~D /∴ D → (~S v ~L)
     ✔~[D → (~S v ~L)]
         D
     ✔~(~S v ~L)
        S
        L
       / \
      ~S Z
      X / \
        /   \
   ✔~(Z & L) ~D
     / \   X
   ~Z ~L
   X X   VALID

13.   (B & D) ↔ (T v D)
       ✔D & ~Z /∴ T → B
      ✔~(T → B)
        T
       ~B
       D
      ~Z
      / \
     /   \
    /   \
  ✔B & D   ~(B & D)
   T v D ✔~(T v D)
    B   ~T
    D   ~D
    X   X   VALID

15.

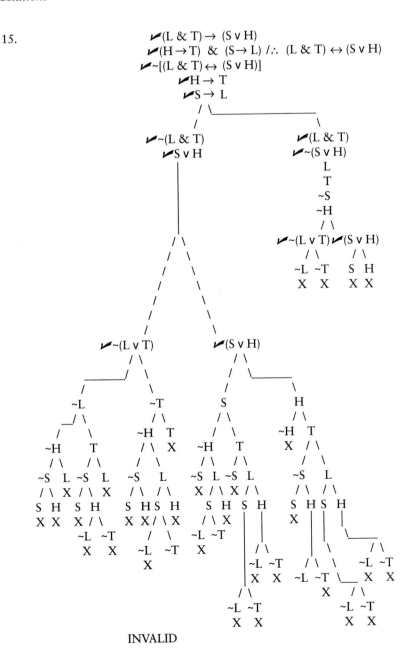

INVALID

17.   ✔(T ∨ L) → (D → F) /∴   (~L & D) → (~F & ~T)
    ✔~[(~L & D) → (~F & ~T)]
        ✔(~L & D)
        ✔~(~F & ~T)
             ~L
              D
             / \
            /   \
           /   \
          /   \
    ✔~(T ∨ L)   ✔D → F
       ~T   / \
       ~L   ~D F
       / \   X / \
      F T   F T
        X
            INVALID

19.   ✔C & ~D
       Z ↔ D
       ~Z → T   /∴ ~C → P
    ✔~(~C → P)
       ~C
       ~P
        C
       ~D
        X   VALID

APPENDIX 3.1.I Exercises from 7.2, Set I.

1. ✔(x)(Px → Qx)
           Pa /∴   (∃x)Qx
        ✔~(∃x)Qx
     ✔(x)~Qx
        ~Qa
        Pa→Qa
         / \
       ~Pa   Qa
        X   X

3. ✔(∃x) Px→(x)Qx
        Pa   /∴ Qa
        ~Qa
        / \
✔~(∃x)Px ✔(x)Qx
   ✔(x)~Px Qa
     ~Pa   X
       X

5. ✔(∃x)(Px & Qx)   /∴ (∃x) Qx
     ✔~(∃x)Qx
       ✔(x)~Qx
        ✔Pa & Qa
           Pa
           Qa
          ~Qa
           X

7.   ✔(x)(Mx → ~Px)
     ✔(x) (Sx → Mx)   /∴ (x)(Sx →~Px)
     ✔~(x)(Sx → ~Px)
     ✔(∃x)~(Sx → ~Px)
       ✔~(Sa → ~Pa)
           Sa
           Pa
     ✔Ma → ~Pa
         / \
      ~Ma ~Pa
        | X
   ✔Sa   Ma
     / \
   ~Sa Ma
    X   X

9.   ✓(x)(Px → ~Mx)
    ✓(∃x)(Mx & ~Sx) /∴   (∃x)(~Sx & ~Px)
    ✓~(∃x)(~Sx & ~Px)
    ✓(x)~(~Sx & ~Px)
       ✓Ma & ~Sa
         Ma
         ~Sa
     ✓~(~Sa & ~Pa)
        / \
       Sa Pa
       X |
      ✓Pa →~Ma
         / \
      ~Pa ~Ma
        X X

11.   ✓(x)(Px → Mx)
    ✓(∃x)(Sx & ~Mx) /∴ (∃x)(Sx & ~Px)
    ✓~(∃x)(Sx & ~Px)
    ✓(x)~(Sx & ~Px)
       ✓Sa & ~Ma
         Sa
        ~Ma
     ✓~(Sa & ~Pa)
        / \
      ~Sa Pa
      X |
      ✓Pa → Ma
         / \
      ~Pa Ma
      X   X

13.   ✓(x)[(Px & Mx) → Sx]
      ✓(∃x)(Px & ~Sx) /∴   (∃x)~Mx
      ✓~(∃x)~Mx
       ✓(x)Mx
        ✓Pa & ~Sa
          Pa
         ~Sa
         Ma
     ✓(Pa & Ma) → Sa
         / \
     ✓~(Pa & Ma) Sa
       / \   X
     ~Pa ~Ma
      X X

15.   ✔$(\exists x)(Px) \rightarrow (\exists x)(Qx)$
      ✔$(x)(\sim Px \rightarrow Qx)$
        $(x)(Qx \rightarrow Px)$ $/\therefore$ $(\exists x)Qx$
        ✔$\sim(\exists x)Qx$
         ✔$(x)\sim Qx$
          / \
         /   \
       /   \
 ✔$\sim(\exists x)(Px)$ ✔$(\exists x)(Qx)$
   ✔$(x)\sim Px$ Qa
     $\sim Qa$ $\sim Qa$
     $\sim Pa$ X
  ✔$\sim Pa \rightarrow Qa$
     / \
    Pa Qa
    X   X

17.   ✔$(x)[(Px \ \& \ Qx) \rightarrow (Rx \ \& \ Tx)]$
      ✔$(\exists x)[Px \ \& \ Rx) \ \& \ Qx]$ $/\therefore$ $(\exists x)(Tx \ \& \ Rx)$
        ✔$\sim(\exists x)(Tx \ \& \ Rx)$
         ✔$(x)\sim(Tx \ \& \ Rx)$
       ✔$(Pa \ \& \ Ra) \ \& \ (Qa)$
          ✔$Pa \ \& \ Ra$
           Qa
           Pa
           Ra
        ✔$\sim(Ta \ \& \ Ra)$
          / \
        $\sim Ta$ $\sim Ra$
         | X
    ✔$(Pa \ \& \ Qa) \rightarrow (Ra \ \& \ Ta)$
         / \
        /   \
       /   \
  ✔$\sim(Pa \ \& \ Qa)$ ✔$Ra \ \& \ Ta$
    / \ Ra
  $\sim Pa$ $\sim Qa$ Ta
   X   X   X

19. ✓(x)[(Px & Qx) → Rx]
   ✓(x)[(Rx ∨ Sx) → Tx]
     ✓(∃x)(Px & ~Sx) /∴   (∃x)(Qx → Tx)
    ✓~(∃x)(Qx → Tx)
     ✓(x)~(Qx → Tx)
       ✓Pa & ~Sa
         Pa
         ~Sa
      ✓~(Qa → Ta)
         Qa
         ~Ta
   ✓(Pa & Qa) → Ra
        / \
   ✓~(Pa & Qa) Ra
     / \
   ~Pa ~Qa
    X   X
     ✓ (Ra ∨ Sa) → Ta
        / \
    ✓~(Ra ∨ Sa) Ta
     ~Ra   X
     ~Sa
      X

21. ✓(x)[(~Px & ~Qx) → Rx]
   ✓(x)[Rx → (~Qx → Sx)]
     ✓(x)(Sx → Qx) /∴   (x)(~Qx → Px)
    ✓~(x)(~Qx → Px)
   ✓(∃x)~(~Qx → Px)
     ✓~(~Qa → Pa)
       ~Qa
       ~Pa
  ✓(~Pa & ~Qa) → Ra
        / \
      /   \
     /   \
    /   \
~(~Pa & ~Qa)   Ra
  / \
 Pa Qa
  X X
           ✓Ra → (~Qa → Sa)
             / \
          ~Ra ✓~Qa → Sa
           X   / \
               Qa Sa
               X |
                  ✓Sa → Qa
                   / \
                ~Sa Qa
                 X X

23.   ✔(x)(Px → Qx) & (∃x)[Px & (Qx → Rx)]
      ✔(x)[Rx → (Sx → Tx)]   /∴   (∃x) [(Sx → Tx) & (Tx → Sx)]
  ✔~(∃x)[(Sx → Tx) & (Tx → Sx)]
   ✔(x)~[(Sx → Tx) & (Tx → Sx)]
       ✔(x)(Px → Qx)
      ✔(∃x)[Px & (Qx → Rx)]
       ✔Pa & (Qa → Ra)
         Pa
     ✔Qa → Ra
     ✔Pa → Qa
       / \
     ~Pa   Qa
      X   / \
         ~Qa   Ra
         X |
           ✔Ra → (Sa → Ta)
             / \
         ~Ra   ✔Sa → Ta
         X   / \
                Sa   ~Sa
                Ta   ~Ta
  ✔~[(Sa → Ta) & (Ta → Sa)]   ✔~[(Sa → Ta) & (Ta → Sa)]
      / \   / \
  ~(Sa → Ta)   ✔~(Ta → Sa)   ✔~(Sa → Ta)   ✔~(Ta → Sa)
     Sa   Ta   Sa   Ta
    ~Ta   ~Sa   ~Ta   ~Sa
     X   X   X   X

25.   ☒(x)[(Px & Qx) → (Rx & Sx)]
         ☒(x) (Rx → Px)
      ☒(x)[(Rx & Px) → Qx]
                   /∴   (x){~Sx → [Rx ↔ (Px & Qx)]}
      ☑~(x){~Sx → [Rx ↔ (Px & Qx)]}
   ☒(∃x)~{~Sx → [Rx ↔ (Px & Qx)]}
      ☑~{~Sa → [Ra ↔ (Pa & Qa)]}
            ~Sa
      ☑~[Ra ↔ (Pa & Qa)]
        ☑(Pa & Qa) → (Ra & Sa)
                   / \
      ☑~(Pa & Qa)   ☑Ra & Sa
        ☑Ra → Pa   Ra
   ☑(Ra & Pa) → Qa   Sa
              / \   X
             /   \
            /   \
          ~Ra   Ra
   ☑Pa & Qa   ☑~(Pa & Qa)
        Pa   / \
        Qa   /   \
        / \   /   \
     ~Pa ~Qa ~Pa   ~Qa
      X   X   / \   / \
             ~Ra Pa   /   \
              X   X   /   \
                     /   \
                   ~Ra   Pa
                    X   / \
              ☑~(Ra & Pa)   Qa
                  / \   X
                ~Ra ~Pa
                 X   X

APPENDIX 3.1 Exercises from 7.2, Set II.

1.　✓(x)(Yx → Rx)
　　✓(x)(Ox → ~Rx)　　/∴　(x)(Yx → ~Ox)
　　✓~(x)(Yx → ~Ox)
　　✓(∃x)~(Yx → ~Ox)
　　　　✓~(Ya → ~Oa)
　　　　　　Ya
　　　　　　Oa
　　　　✓Ya → Ra
　　　　　／＼
　　　　~Ya　Ra
　　　　　X　✓Oa → ~Ra
　　　　　　　　／＼
　　　　　　　~Oa　~Ra
　　　　　　　　X　　X

3.　✓(x)[(Px & Yx) → Bx]
　　✓(∃x)[(Px & Wx) & Yx]　/∴　(∃x)[(Px & Wx) & Bx]
　　✓~(∃x)[(Px & Wx) & Bx]
　　✓(x)~[(Px & Wx) & Bx]
　　　✓(Pa & Wa) & Ya
　　　　✓Pa & Wa
　　　　　Ya
　　　　　Pa
　　　　　Wa
　　✓(Pa & Ya) → Ba
　　　　　／＼
　✓(Pa & Ya)　＼
　　／＼　　　　＼
~Pa　~Ya　　Ba
　X　　X　✓~[(Pa & Wa) & Ba]
　　　　　　　／＼
　　　✓~(Pa & Wa)　　~Ba
　　　　／＼　　　　　X
　　　~Pa　~Wa
　　　　X　　X

5. $\cancel{f}(x)\{[Px \ \& \ (Yx \ \lor \ Ax)] \to (Bx \ \lor \ Rx)\}$
        $\cancel{\hspace{2pt}}Pf \ \& \ Yf$
    $\cancel{f}(x)[(Px \ \& \ Rx) \to (Mx \ \lor \ Sx)]$
          /∴ $(\sim Bf \ \& \ \sim Mf) \to Sf$
  $\cancel{\hspace{2pt}}\sim[(\sim Bf \ \& \ \sim Mf) \to Sf]$
      $\cancel{\hspace{2pt}}(\sim Bf \ \& \ \sim Mf)$
         $\sim Sf$
         $\sim Bf$
         $\sim Mf$
          Pf
          Yf
    $\cancel{\hspace{2pt}}(Pf \ \& \ Rf) \to (Mf \ \lor \ Sf)$
           / \
  $\cancel{\hspace{2pt}}\sim(Pf \ \& \ Rf)$ $\cancel{\hspace{2pt}}Mf \ \lor \ Sf$
      / \   / \
    $\sim Pf$ \ Mf Sf
     X   \   X   X
        $\sim Rf$
      $\cancel{\hspace{2pt}}[Pf \ \& \ (Yf \ \lor \ Af)] \to (Bf \ \lor \ Rf)$
              / \
    $\cancel{\hspace{2pt}}\sim[Pf \ \& \ (Yf \ \lor \ Af)]$ $Bf \ \lor \ Rf$
       / \   / \
    $\sim Pf$ $\cancel{\hspace{2pt}}\sim(Yf \ \lor \ Af)$ Bf Rf
     X $\sim Yf$ X X
             $\sim Af$
              X

7. $\cancel{a}(x)(Fx \to Sx)$
    $\cancel{a}(x)[Tx \to (Fx \ \& \sim Sx)]$ /∴ $(x)(Tx \to Mx)$
   $\cancel{\hspace{2pt}}\sim(x)(Tx \to Mx)$
  $\cancel{a}(\exists x)\sim(Tx \to Mx)$
    $\cancel{\hspace{2pt}}\sim(Ta \to Ma)$
        Ta
       $\sim Ma$
    $\cancel{\hspace{2pt}}Ta \to (Fa \ \& \sim Sa)$
       / \
    $\sim Ta$ $\cancel{\hspace{2pt}}(Fa \ \& \sim Sa)$
     X Fa
          $\sim Sa$
        $\cancel{\hspace{2pt}}Fa \to Sa$
          / \
        $\sim Fa$ Sa
         X   X

9. $\checkmark^{a}(x)\{[Px \ \& \ (Yx \ \& \ Rx)] \to (Bx \lor Ax)\}$
     $\checkmark^{a}(\exists x)[Px \ \& \ (Rx \ \& \ {\sim}Bx)]$ /∴ $(\exists x)[Px \ \& \ {\sim}(Yx \ \& \ {\sim}Ax)]$
     $\checkmark{\sim}(\exists x)[Px \ \& \ {\sim}(Yx \ \& \ {\sim}Ax)]$
     $\checkmark^{a}(x){\sim}[Px \ \& \ {\sim}(Yx \ \& \ {\sim}Ax)]$
          $\checkmark Pa \ \& \ (Ra \ \& \ {\sim}Ba)$
                    Pa
               $\checkmark(Ra \ \& \ {\sim}Ba)$
                    Ra
                   ${\sim}Ba$
     $\checkmark[Pa \ \& \ (Ya \ \& \ Ra)] \to (Ba \lor Aa)$
                   / \
     $\checkmark{\sim}[Pa \ \& \ (Ya \ \& \ Ra)]$ $\checkmark Ba \lor Aa$
              / \   / \
        ${\sim}Pa$ $\checkmark{\sim}(Ya \ \& \ Ra)$ Ba \
          X   / \   X   \
                      /   \   \
                     /   \   \
                  ${\sim}Ya$ ${\sim}Ra$ Aa
     $\checkmark{\sim}[Pa \ \& \ {\sim}(Ya \ \& \ {\sim}Aa)]$ X $\checkmark{\sim}[Pa \ \& \ {\sim}(Ya \ \& \ {\sim}Aa)]$
          / \   / \
       ${\sim}Pa$ $\checkmark Ya \ \& \ {\sim}Aa$ ${\sim}Pa$ $\checkmark Ya \ \& \ {\sim}Aa$
        X Ya X Ya
                ${\sim}Aa$ ${\sim}Aa$
                 X   X

APPENDIX 3.II Exercises from 7.6, Set II.

1. $\checkmark^{a}(x)[Px \to (y)(Qy \to Rxy)]$
     $\checkmark^{a}(\exists x)(Px \ \& \ Qx)$ /∴ $(\exists x)(\exists y)Rxy$
          $\checkmark{\sim}(\exists x)(\exists y)Rxy$
          $\checkmark(x){\sim}(\exists y)Rxy$
          $\checkmark^{a}(x)(y){\sim}Rxy$
          $\checkmark Pa \ \& \ Qa$
               Pa
               Qa
          $\checkmark Pa \to (y)(Qy \to Ray)$
               / \
            ${\sim}Pa$ $\checkmark^{a}(y)(Qy \to Ray)$
             X $\checkmark Qa \to Raa$
                         / \
                      ${\sim}Qa$ Raa
                        X $\checkmark^{a}(y){\sim}Ray$
                            ${\sim}Raa$
                             X

3. $(x)[Px \rightarrow (\exists y)(Qy \,\&\, Rxy)]$
   $(x)(y)(\sim Rxy)$ $/\therefore$ $\sim Pa$
         Pa
       $Pa \rightarrow (\exists y)(Qy \,\&\, Ray)$
         $/\ \backslash$
       $\sim Pa$ $(\exists y)(Qy \,\&\, Ray)$
        X $Qb \,\&\, Rab$
               Qb
               Rab
               $(y)\sim Ray$
               $\sim Rab$
                X

5. $(\exists x)(\exists y)(\sim Rxy)$
        $(x)[Px \rightarrow (y)(Qy \rightarrow Rxy)]$ $/\therefore$ $(\exists x)(\exists y)(\sim Px \,\lor\, \sim Qy)$
      $\sim(\exists x)(\exists y)(\sim Px \,\lor\, \sim Qy)$
      $(x)\sim(\exists y)(\sim Px \,\lor\, \sim Qy)$
      $(x)(y)\sim(\sim Px \,\lor\, \sim Qy)$
        $(\exists y)\sim Ray$
          $\sim Rab$
      $(y)\sim(\sim Pa \,\lor\, \sim Qy)$
       $\sim(\sim Pa \,\lor\, \sim Qb)$
          Pa
          Qb
       $Pa \rightarrow (y)(Qy \rightarrow Ray)$
          $/\ \backslash$
       $\sim Pa$ $(y)(Qy \rightarrow Ray)$
        X $Qa \rightarrow Rab$
              $/\ \backslash$
           $\sim Qb$ Rab
            X   X

7.　　☑(x){Px → (∃y)[Qy & (Sy → Rxy)]}
　　　☑(∃x)(Px & Sx)
　　　☑(x)(Qx → Sx)　/∴　(∃x)(∃y)(Rxy)
　　☑~(∃x)(∃y)(Rxy)
　　☑(x)~(∃y)(Rxy)
　　　☑(x)(y)~Rxy
　　　　☑Pa & Sa
　　　　　Pa
　　　　　Sa
　　　☑Pa → (∃y)[Qy & (Sy → Ray)]
　　　　　/ \
　　　~Pa　☑(∃y)[Qy & (Sy → Ray)]
　　　　X　☑Qb & (Sb → Rab)
　　　　　　Qb
　　　　☑Sb → Rab
　　　　☑(y)~Ray
　　　　☑Qb → Sb
　　　　　~Rab
　　　　　　/ \
　　　　~Sb　　Rab
　　　　/ \　　X
　　~Qb　Sb
　　X　　X

9.　　　☑(x){Px → (∃y)[Qy & (Sy → Rxy)]}
　　　☑(∃x)(Sx & Px)
　　☑(x)(y)(Rxy → Ryx)　/∴　(∃x)(∃y)(Sx → Rxy)
　☑~(∃x)(∃y)(Sx → Rxy)
　　☑(x)~(∃y)(Sx → Rxy)
　　☑(x)(y)~(Sx → Rxy)
　　　　☑Sa & Pa
　　　　　Sa
　　　　　Pa
　　　☑Pa → (∃y)[Qy & (Sy → Ray)]
　　　　　/ \
　　　~Pa　☑(∃y)[Qy & (Sy → Ray)]
　　　X　☑Qb & (Sb → Rab)
　　　　　　Qb
　　　　☑Sb → Rab
　　　　☑(y)~(Sb → Rby)
　　　　☑~(Sb → Rba)
　　　　　Sb
　　　　~Rba
　　　　　/ \
　　　~Sb　Rab
　　　X　☑(y)(Ray → Rya)
　　　　☑(Rab → Rba)
　　　　　　/ \
　　　~Rab　Rba
　　　　X　　X

11. $(x)\{(Px \lor Qx) \to (y)[(Sy \lor Qy) \to Rxy]\}$
     $(x)(y)(Rxy \to Tyx)$ /∴ $(x)[Qx \to (y)(Qy \to Tyx)]$
     $\sim(x)[Qx \to (y)(Qy \to Tyx)]$
     $(\exists x)\sim[Qx \to (y)(Qy \to Tyx)]$
     $\sim[Qa \to (y)(Qy \to Tya)]$
          Qa
     $\sim(y)(Qy \to Tya)$
     $(\exists y)\sim(Qy \to Tya)$
     $\sim(Qb \to Tba)$
         Qb
         $\sim Tba$
    $(Pa \lor Qa) \to (y)[(Sy \lor Qy) \to Ray]$
            / \
   $\sim(Pa \lor Qa)$ $(y)[(Sy \lor Qy) \to Ray]$
      $\sim Pa$ $(Sb \lor Qb) \to Rab$
      $\sim Qa$ / \
       X $\sim(Sb \lor Qb)$ \
             $\sim Sb$ \
             $\sim Qb$ Rab
               X $(y)(Ray \to Tya)$
                  $Rab \to Tba$
                   / \
                $\sim Rab$ Tba
                 X   X

13. $(x)\{(Px \lor Qx) \to (y)[(Sy \lor Qy) \to Rxy]\}$
     $(\exists x)(Px \,\&\, Qx)$
     $(x)(y)(Rxy \to Tyx)$ /∴ $(\exists x)(y)(Qy \to Tyx)$
   $\sim(\exists x)(y)(Qy \to Tyx)$
   $(x)\sim(y)(Qy \to Tyx)$
   $(x)(\exists y)\sim(Qy \to Tyx)$
       $Pa \,\&\, Qa$
         Pa
         Qa
   $(Pa \lor Qa) \to (y)[(Sy \lor Qy) \to Ray]$
          / \
  $\sim(Pa \lor Qa)$ $(y)[(Sy \lor Qy) \to Ray]$
     $\sim Pa$ $(\exists y)\sim(Qy \to Tya)$
     $\sim Qa$ $\sim(Qb \to Tba)$
      X Qb
           $\sim Tba$
         $(y)(Ray \to Tya)$
        $Rab \to Tba$
          / \
         / Tba
        /   X
      $\sim Rab$
    $(Sb \lor Qb) \to Rab$
         / \
   $\sim(Sa \lor Qb)$ Rab
      $\sim Sb$ X
      $\sim Qb$
        X

15. ⌐(x){(Px → (y)[(Qy & Rxy) → (z)(Sz → Rxz)]}
   ⌐(∃x)(y)(Px & Rxy)
                  Qb
   ⌐(x)(y)(~Sx → ~Ryx)   /∴   (x)(∃y)(Sx ↔ Ryx)
   ⌐~(x)(∃y)(Sx ↔ Ryx)
   ⌐(∃x)~(∃y)(Sx ↔ Ryx)
   ⌐(∃x)(y)~(Sx ↔ Ryx)
        ⌐(y)(Pa & Ray)
           ⌐Pa & Rab
               Pa
              Rab
        ⌐Pa →(y)[(Qy & Ray) → (z)(Sz → Raz)]
               / \
           ~Pa   ⌐(y)[(Qy & Ray) → (z)(Sz → Raz)]
            X   ⌐(Qb & Rab) → (z)(Sz → Raz)
                        / \
              ⌐~(Qb & Rab)   ⌐(z)(Sz → Raz)
                   / \   ⌐(y)~(Sc → Ryc)
              ~Qb   ~Rab   ⌐(y)(~Sc → ~Ryc)
               X   X   ⌐~Sc → ~Rac
                             ⌐Sc → Rac
                             ⌐~(Sc ↔ Rac)
                                  / \
                                 /   \
                                /   \
                               /   \
                              /   \
                           ~Sc   Sc
                           Rac   ~Rac
                          / \   / \
                     Sc   ~Rac   /   \
                     X   X   /   \
                                Sc   ~Rac
                               / \   / \
                            ~Sc Rac   ~Sc Rac
                             X   X   X   X

APPENDIX 3.2.II Exercises from 7.6, Set III.

1. ⌐(Cg & Rhg) → Uh
                Cg
                ~Uh   /∴   ~Rhg
                Rhg
                / \
       ⌐~(Cg & Rhg)   Uh
          / \   X
       ~Cg ~Rhg
        X   X

3.   ✓(∃x)(Px & Lx)
     ✓(x)(Lx → ~Hxt)   /∴   (∃x)(Px & ~Hxt)
  ✓~(∃x)(Px & ~Hxt)
   ✓(x)~(Px & ~Hxt)
     ✓Pa & La
       Pa
       La
    ✓La → ~Hat
       / \
    ~La ~Hat
     X   ✓~(Pa & ~Hat)
         / \
       ~Pa Hat
       X   X

5.   ✓(∃x)(Px & ~Hxt)
  ✓(x){[Px & (∃y)[(Cy & Ly) & Cxy]] → Hxt}
       /∴ (∃x){Px & ~(∃y)[(Cy & Ly) & Cxy]}
  ✓~(∃x){Px & ~(∃y)[(Cy & Ly) & Cxy]}
   ✓(x)~{Px & ~(∃y)[(Cy & Ly) & Cxy]}
     ✓Pa & ~Hat
       Pa
      ~Hat
     ✓~{Pa & ~(∃y)[(Cy & Ly) & Cay]}
       / \
     ~Pa ✓(∃y)[(Cy & Ly) & Cay]
       ✓(Cb & Lb) & Cab
       ✓Cb & Lb
        Cab
        Cb
        Lb
      ✓{[Pa & (∃y)[(Cy & Ly) & Cay]] → Hat}
         / \
  ✓~[Pa & (∃y)[(Cy & Ly) & Cay]] Hat
    / \   X
  ~Pa ✓~(∃y)[(Cy & Ly) & Cay]
  X ✓(x)~[(Cy & Ly) & Cay]
    ✓~[(Cb & Lb) & Cab]
       / \
   ✓~(Cb & Lb) ~Cab
    / \   X
   ~Cb ~Lb
   X   X

7.   ✓(x)[(Px & Vix) → Hx]
    ✓(x)[(Px & Hx) → ~(∃y)(Sy & Cyx)]
  ✓(x){[Px & ~(∃y)(Sy & Cyx)] → ~(∃z)(Oz & Exz)}
        /∴   (x)[(Px & Vix) → ~(∃z)(Oz & Exz)]
    ✓~(x)[(Px & Vix) → ~(∃z)(Oz & Exz)]
     ✓(∃x)~[(Px & Vix) → ~(∃z)(Oz & Exz)]
      ✓~[(Pa & Via) → ~(∃z)(Oz & Eaz)]
         ✓ Pa & Via
        ✓(∃z)(Oz & Eaz)
            Pa
            Via
         ✓(Pa & Via) → Ha
           / \
   ✓~(Pa & Via) Ha
      / \   ✓(Pa & Ha) → ~(∃y)(Sy & Cya)
    ~Pa ~Via   / \
     X   X   ~(Pa & Ha) ✓~(∃y)(Sy & Cya)
             / \   ✓(y)~(Sy & Cya)
         ~Pa   ~Ha ✓[Pa & ~(∃y)(Sy & Cya)] → ~(∃z)(Oz & Eaz)
          X   X   ✓Oc & Eac
                     Oc
                     Eac
                   / \
                 /   \
                /   \
              /   \
            /   \
          /   \
        /   \
      /   \
     /   \
    /   \
 ✓~[Pa & ~(∃y)(Sy & Cya)]   ✓~(∃z)(Oz & Eaz)
     / \   ✓(z)~(Oz & Eaz)
   ~Pa ✓(∃y)(Sy & Cya)   ✓~(Oc & Eac)
    X   ✓Sb & Cba   / \
         Sb   ~Oc ~Eac
         Cba   X   X
       ✓~(Sb & Cba)
          / \
        ~Sb ~Cba
         X   X

9. ✓(x){[Px & (y)(Ey → Vxy)] → (z)(Cz → Sxz)}
    ✓(x){[Px & (z)(Cz → Sxz)] → (y)(Gy → ~Pxy)}
        ✓Pj & (∃y)(Gy & Pjy)   /∴   (∃y)(Ey & ~Vjy)
        ✓~(∃y)(Ey & ~Vjy)
        ✓(y) ~(Ey & ~Vjy)
                Pj
            ✓(∃y)(Gy & Pjy)
            ✓Ga & Pja
                Ga
                Pja
            ✓[Pj & (z)(Cz → Sjz)] → (y)(Gy → ~Pjy)
                        / \
    ✓~[Pj & (z)(Cz → Sjz)]   ✓(y)(Gy → ~Pjy)
            / \   ✓Ga → ~Pja
          /   \   / \
         /   \   ~Ga   ~Pja
        /   \   X   X
      ~Pj   ✓~(z)(Cz → Sjz)
       X   ✓(∃z)~(Cz → Sjz)
               ✓~(Cb → Sjb)
                   Cb
                  ~Sjb
            ✓[Pj & (y)(Ey → Vjy)] → (z)(Cz → Sjz)
                        / \
    ✓~[Pj & (y)(Ey → Vjy)]   ✓(z)(Cz → Sjz)
            / \   ✓Cb → Sjb
          ~Pj \   / \
           X   \   ~Cb   Sjb
                 \   X   X
            ✓~(y)(Ey → Vjy)
            ✓(∃y)~(Ey → Vjy)
            ✓~(Ec → Vjc)
                Ec
               ~Vjc
            ✓~(Ec & ~Vjc)
                  / \
               ~Ec   Vjc
                X   X

APPENDIX 3.2.III Exercises from 7.7, Set I.

1. $(x)(Px \to Qx)$
      Pa
      $a = b$ /∴ Qb
      $\sim Qb$
      $Pa \to Qa$
        / \
    $\sim Pa$ Qa
    X Qb
          X

3. $(x)[Px \to (\exists y)(Qy \ \& \ Rxy)]$
        Pa
  $(x)[(x = a) \to (y)(y = x)]$ /∴ Qa
        $\sim Qa$
     $Pa \to (\exists y)(Qy \ \& \ Ray)$
        / \
    $\sim Pa$ $(\exists y)(Qy \ \& \ Ray)$
    X $Qb \ \& \ Rab$
          Qb
          Rab
        $(a = a) \to (y)(y = a)$
           / \
      $\sim(a = a)$ $(y)(y = a)$
        X $b = a$
               Qa
               X

5. $(\exists x)[Px \ \& \ (y)(Py \to Rxy)]$
     $(x)(y)(Ryx \to (\exists z)Sz)$
     $(x)(x = c)$ /∴ Sc
      $\sim Sc$
   $Pa \ \& \ (y)(Py \to Ray)$
      Pa
     $(y)(Py \to Ray)$
      $Pa \to Raa$
       / \
    $\sim Pa$ Raa
    X $(y)(Rya \to (\exists z)Sz)$
       $Raa \to (\exists z)Sz$
       / \
     $\sim Raa$ $(\exists z)Sz$
     X Sb
         $b = c$
         Sc
         X

7. ✓Pa & ~(∃x)[Px & ~(x = a)]   /∴   (∃x)[Px & (y)(Py→ x = y)]
   ~(∃x)[Px & (y)(Py→ x = y)]
   ✓(x)~[Px & (y)(Py→ x = y)]
                   Pa
         ✓~(∃x)[Px & ~(x = a)]
         ✓(x)~[Px & ~(x = a)]
         ✓~[Pa & (y)(Py→ a = y)]
                   / \
         ~Pa   ✓~(y)(Py→ a = y)
          X   ✓(∃y)~(Py→ a = y)
               ✓~(Pb→ a = b)
                   Pb
                 ~(a = b)
               ✓~[Pb & ~(b = a)]
                   / \
                 ~Pb   (b = a)
                  X   X

9. ✓(∃x)(∃y){[(Px & Py) & ~(x = y)] & (z)[Pz→ (z = x ∨ z = y)]}
                Pa /∴   (∃x)[Px & ~(x = a)]
         ✓~(∃x)[Px & ~(x = a)]
         ✓✓(x)~[Px & ~(x = a)]
      ✓(∃y){[(Pb & Py) & ~(b = y)] & (z)(Pz→ (z = b ∨ z = y)]}
      ✓[(Pb & Pc) & ~(b = c)] & (z)[Pz→ (z = b ∨ z = c)]
         ✓(Pb & Pc) & ~(b = c)
         ✓(z)[Pz→ (z = b ∨ z = c)]
           ✓Pb & Pc
           ~(b = c)
              Pb
              Pc
         ✓~[Pb & ~(b = a)]
              / \
         ~Pb   ✓b = a
          X   ✓Pc→ (c = b ∨ c = c)
                   / \
              ~Pc   ✓(c = b ∨ c = c)
               X   / \
                       c = b   c = c
                        X   ✓~[Pc & ~(c = a)]
                                / \
                             ~Pc   c = a
                              X   b = c
                                     X

APPENDIX 3.2.III Exercises from 7.7, Set III.

1. $\swarrow^{a}(\exists x)\{[(Rx \ \& \ Rxl) \ \& \ (y)[(Ry \ \& \ Ryl) \rightarrow x = y]] \ \& \ x = j\}$ $/\therefore$ Rjl

               $\sim Rjl$

          $\swarrow[(Ra \ \& \ Ral) \ \& \ (y)[(Ry \ \& \ Ryl) \rightarrow a = y]] \ \& \ a = j$

          $\swarrow(Ra \ \& \ Ral) \ \& \ (y)[(Ry \ \& \ Ryl) \rightarrow a = y]$

                   $a = j$

             $\swarrow Ra \ \& \ Ral$

          $(y)[(Ry \ \& \ Ryl) \rightarrow a = y]$

                Ra

             $\swarrow^{j}Ral$

                Rjl

                X

3. $\swarrow^{a}(\exists x)(Bx \ \& \ Rx)$

        $\swarrow^{a}(x)(y)\{[(Bx \ \& \ Rx) \ \& \ (By \ \& \ Ry)] \rightarrow x = y\}$

           $/\therefore$ $(\exists x)\{(Bx \ \& \ Rx) \ \& \ (y)[(By \ \& \ Ry) \rightarrow x = y]\}$

     $\swarrow \sim(\exists x)\{(Bx \ \& \ Rx) \ \& \ (y)[(By \ \& \ Ry) \rightarrow x = y]\}$

     $\swarrow^{a}(x)\sim\{(Bx \ \& \ Rx) \ \& \ (y)[(By \ \& \ Ry) \rightarrow x = y]\}$

              $\swarrow Ba \ \& \ Ra$

                Ba

                Ra

     $\swarrow \sim\{(Ba \ \& \ Ra) \ \& \ (y)[(By \ \& \ Ry) \rightarrow a = y]\}$

                $/ \ \backslash$

   $\swarrow \sim(Ba \ \& \ Ra)$ $\swarrow^{b}\sim(y)[(By \ \& \ Ry) \rightarrow a = y]$

      $/ \ \backslash$ $\swarrow(\exists y)\sim[(By \ \& \ Ry) \rightarrow a = y]$

   $\sim Ba$ $\sim Ra$ $\swarrow \sim[(Bb \ \& \ Rb) \rightarrow a = b]$

    X   X $\swarrow Bb \ \& \ Rb$

                $\sim(a = b)$

                Bb

                Rb

          $\swarrow^{b}(y)\{[(Ba \ \& \ Ra) \ \& \ (By \ \& \ Ry)] \rightarrow a = y\}$

         $\swarrow[(Ba \ \& \ Ra) \ \& \ (Bb \ \& \ Rb)] \rightarrow a = b$

                   $/ \ \backslash$

                 $/$ $a = b$

    $\swarrow \sim[(Ba \ \& \ Ra) \ \& \ (Bb \ \& \ Rb)]$ X

           $/ \ \backslash$

   $\swarrow \sim(Ba \ \& \ Ra)$ $\swarrow \sim(Ba \ \& \ Rb)$

      $/ \ \backslash$ $/ \ \backslash$

   $\sim Ba$ $\sim Ra$ $\sim Bb$ $\sim Rb$

     X   X   X   X

5. ✓ Cf & (x)(Cx →x = f)
    ✓ (x)(Cx →Wxj)
    ✓ (x)(Wxj →Cx)   /∴   Wfj & (x)(Wxj →x = f)
    ✓ ~[Wfj & (x)(Wxj →x = f)]
              Cf
    ✓ (x)(Cx →x = f)
      ✓ Cf →Wfj
         / \
      ~Cf   Wfj
       X   / \
        ~Wfj ✓ ~(x)(Wxj →x = f)
          X   ✓ (∃x)~(Wxj →x = f)
              ✓ ~(Waj →a = f)
                 Waj
                 ~(a = f)
              ✓ Waj →Ca
                 / \
              ~Waj Ca
                X ✓ Ca →a = f
                      / \
                   ~Ca   a = f
                    X   X

7.   ✓ (∃x)(∃y){[Rx & [Ry & ~(x = y)]] & (z)[Rz →(z = x ∨ z = y)]}
                   Rj   /∴   (∃x){Rx & ~(x = j)}
                 ✓ ~(∃x){Rx & ~(x = j)}
                 ✓ (x)~{[Rx & ~(x = j)]}
      ✓ (∃y){[Ra & [Ry & ~(a = y)]] & (z)[Rz →(z = a ∨ z = y)]}
       ✓ [Ra & [Rb & ~(a = b)]] & (z)[Rz →(z = a ∨ z = b)]
              ✓ Ra & [Rb & ~(a = b)]
                 (z)[Rz → (z = a ∨ z = b)]
                       Ra
              ✓ Rb & ~(a = b)
                 Rb
                 ~(a = b)
              ✓ ~(Ra & ~(a = j)
                 / \
              ~Ra   ✓ a = j
                X   ✓ ~(Rb & ~(b = j)
                       / \
                    ~Rb   b = j
                     X   a = b
                          X

9.   ✔(Rf & ~Gf) & (x){[Rx & ~(x = f)]↦ Gx}
    ✘(x)[(Rx & Gx) →Wxa}
                ✘ Wfj   /∴   (x)[Rx →(Wxa ∨ Wxj)]
            ✔~(x)[Rx →(Wxa ∨ Wxj)]
            ✘(∃x)~[Rx →(Wxa ∨ Wxj)]
                ✔ Rf & ~Gf
        ✘(x){[Rx & ~(x = f)]→ Gx}
                        Rf
                        ~Gf
                ✔~[Rb →(Wba ∨ Wbj)]
                        Rb
            ✔~(Wba ∨ Wbj)
                    ~Wba
                    ~Wbj
                ✔(Rb & Gb) →Wba
                        / \
            ✔~(Rb & Gb)   Wba
                / \   X
            ~Rb   ~Gb
            X   ✔[Rb & ~(b = f)]→ Gb
                            / \
                ✔~[Rb & ~(b = f)]   Gb
                        / \   X
                    ~Rb   b = f
                    X   Wbj
                            X

Glossary

A proposition   In categorical logic, an **A** proposition is a universal affirmative proposition.

Absorption (Abs.)   In propositional logic, absorption is a rule of inference in which a conditional statement is given as a premise; you conclude a conditional statement with the same antecedent, and the consequent is a conjunction of the antecedent and consequent of the given proposition. The form of the rule is: $\alpha \rightarrow \beta \; / \therefore \; \alpha \rightarrow (\alpha \; \& \; \beta)$.

Accent   The fallacy of accent rests upon the ways in which you emphasize the words in a statement or by quoting passages out of context.

Accident   An argument commits the fallacy of accident if it applies a general rule in a case in which that rule does not apply.

Addition (Add.)   In propositional logic, addition is a rule of inference which, given any statement as a premise, allows you to conclude that statement disjoined to *any* other statement. The form of the rule is: $\alpha \; / \therefore \; \alpha \lor \beta$.

Ad hoc Hypothesis   An *ad hoc* hypothesis is a hypothesis posed *solely* to explain why another hypothesis or theory fails in a particular case or kind of case.

Affirmative   If you claim that members of the first class named are members of the second class, the proposition is affirmative in quality.

Ambiguous   A word is ambiguous if it has more than one meaning.

Ampersand (&)   In the symbolic language for propositional logic, the ampersand represents conjunction.

Amphiboly   Amphibolies are arguments based on loose sentence structure. In an argument that commits the fallacy of amphiboly, the referent of a word or phrase is left unclear and the meaning of the phrase shifts in the course of the argument.

Analogy   Analogies are claims of similarity. Analogies can be used to illustrate, to explain, and to argue.

Antecedent   The antecedent of a conditional statement is the phrase following 'if'; in symbolic form, it is the statement to the left of the arrow.

Appeal to Force   The fallacy of appeal to force occurs if you appeal to force or the threat of force to convince someone to accept a conclusion.

Arguing in a Circle   You argue in a circle if you propose a series of arguments in which the conclusion of the last argument was accepted as a premise in an earlier argument.

Argument   An argument is a set of propositions in which one or more propositions (the premises) are said to provide reasons or evidence for the truth of another proposition (the conclusion).

Argument Form   The argument form is the structural pattern of an argument.

Argumentum ad Baculum   See **Appeal to Force.**

Argumentum ad Hominem   See **Personal Attack.**

Argumentum ad Populum   See **Mob Appeal.**

Aristotelian Interpretation of Categorical Logic   The Aristotelian interpretation of categorical logic is an interpretation of categorical logic that ascribes existential import to universal propositions.

Aristotle   A Greek philosopher who lived in Athens from 384 to 322 B.C.; the first person known to treat logic as a formal discipline.

Arrow ($\rightarrow$)   In the symbolic language for propositional logic, the arrow represents the relation of material implication. It is also known as the single arrow.

Association (Assoc.)   In propositional logic, association is an equivalence falling under the Rule of Replacement that allows you to reposition parentheses in a statement in which the only connectives are either wedges or ampersands. The two forms of this equivalence are: $[\alpha \lor (\beta \lor \Gamma)] \leftrightarrow [(\alpha \lor \beta) \lor \Gamma]$ and $[\alpha \ \& \ (\beta \ \& \ \Gamma)] \leftrightarrow [(\alpha \ \& \ \beta) \ \& \ \Gamma]$.

Average   See **Mean, Median, Midrange,** and **Mode.**

Bandwagon   A bandwagon argument is a form of the fallacy of mob appeal—basically, "Everyone's doing it, so you should do it too."

Begging the Question   You commit the fallacy of begging the question if the conclusion of your argument is nothing more than a restatement of one of the premises.

Belief   A belief is a proposition accepted as true.

Biased Sample A survey is based on a biased sample if the population surveyed is not representative of the population the survey purports to represent.

Binary Relation A binary relation is a two-place relation.

Boole, George George Boole was the nineteenth-century British logician and philosopher who is credited with resolving the controversy over the existential import of universal propositions in favor of holding that universal propositions *do not* have existential import.

Boolean Interpretation of Categorical Logic The Boolean interpretation of categorical logic is an interpretation of categorical logic that ascribes existential import *only* to particular propositions.

Bound Variable A bound variable is a variable within the scope of a quantifier.

Categorical Syllogism A categorical syllogism is a special kind of syllogism in which both the premises and the conclusion are categorical propositions, and in which there are three terms, each occurring twice, with each term assigned the same meaning throughout the argument.

Ceremonial Function of Language The ceremonial function of language is the use of language in various ceremonies, including greetings.

Class A class is a collection of objects that have at least one characteristic in common, namely, the class-defining characteristic.

Classical Theory of Probability The classical theory of probability was developed by the seventeenth-century mathematicians Blaise Pascal and Pierre de Fermat. The classical theory is *a priori* insofar as it does not depend on empirical data. It assumes that all possibilities are taken into account and that all possibilities are equal. The mathematical basis for probability theory developed by Pascal and Fermat is also used in the relative frequency theory of probability and the subjective theory of probability.

Collective Use of a Word A word is used collectively if it applies to a class itself—as a whole.

Commissive Function of Language The commissive function of language is to use language to make vows and promises.

Commutation (Com.) In propositional logic, commutation is a statement of logical equivalence found under the Rule of Replacement that allows you to switch the places of statements around a common ampersand or wedge. The two versions of the equivalence are: $(\alpha \lor \beta) \leftrightarrow (\beta \lor \alpha)$ and $(\alpha \ \& \ \beta) \leftrightarrow (\beta \ \& \ \alpha)$.

Complementary Class   For any class C, a complementary class is a class containing all the objects not in C. The complement of the class of green things is the class of nongreen things.

Complex Question   You commit the fallacy of complex question if you implicitly ask two questions at once, one explicitly and one implicitly, and an answer to the explicit question allows you to draw a conclusion regarding the implicit question.

Composition   The fallacy of composition occurs if either (1) you attribute characteristics true of a part to a whole or (2) you claim that something that is true of each member of a class of objects is true of the class as a whole.

Compound Statement   A compound statement is any statement that has another statement as a component.

Conclusion   In an argument, the conclusion is the statement whose truth the argument is attempting to establish.

Conclusion Indicators   Conclusion indicators are words such as 'thus,' 'therefore,' and 'so' that are used to indicate that a statement is the conclusion of an argument.

Conditional Proof   In propositional and predicate logic, you construct a conditional proof by assuming a statement as an additional premise, working out the consequences of this assumption, and discharging the assumption by constructing a conditional statement in which the antecedent is the assumption for conditional proof and the consequent is the conclusion reached in the previous line of the proof.

Conditional Statement   A conditional statement is a statement expressing the relation of material implication. A conditional statement is true except when its antecedent is true and its consequent is false.

Confirmation of a Hypothesis   If an experimental procedure based on a hypothesis yields the predicted consequence, the experiment *tends* to confirm the hypothesis, that is, it provides *some* evidence that the hypothesis is true.

Conjunct   A conjunct is a statement in a conjunction.

Conjunction In propositional logic, conjunction is represented by the ampersand (&). A statement of the form p & q is true if and only if both p and q are true.

Conjunction (Conj.) In propositional logic, conjunction is a rule of inference in which two premises are given and the conclusion is a conjunction of the two premises. The form of the rule is: α, β /∴ α & β.

Connotative Definition A connotative definition is a definition in which the definiens states the connotation of the definiendum.

Connotative Meaning; Connotation The connotative meaning of a term consists of all the characteristics or properties that are common to all the members of the class denoted by a term. Also known as the *intension* of a term.

Consequent In a conditional statement, the consequent is the statement following the word 'then'; in symbolic form, it is the statement to the right of the arrow.

Constructive Dilemma (C.D.) In propositional logic, constructive dilemma is a rule of inference in which the first premise is a conjunction of two conditional statements, the second premise is a disjunction of the antecedents of the conditionals in the first premise, and the conclusion is a disjunction of the consequents of the conditionals in the first premise. The form of the rule is: $(\alpha \rightarrow \beta)$ & $(\Gamma \rightarrow \pi)$, $\alpha \vee \Gamma$ /∴ $\beta \vee \pi$.

Contingent Proposition The truth value of a contingent proposition is determined by whether the proposition corresponds to the world. All simple propositions are contingent.

Contradiction, Contradictories In categorical logic, two statements are contradictories if they are formally related to one another in such a way that if one is true the other must be false. In propositional logic, a contradiction or self-contradiction is a statement that is false solely in virtue of its form.

Contrapositive, Contraposition The contrapositive of a given categorical proposition is formed by replacing the subject term with the complement of the predicate term, and replacing the predicate term with the complement of the subject term. **A** and **O** propositions are logically equivalent to their contrapositives; **E** and **I** propositions are *not* logically equivalent to their contrapositives.

Contrariety, Contraries In Aristotelian logic, contrariety is the formal relationship between two universal propositions with the same subject and predicate terms but opposite qualities such that it is possible for both to be false but not for both to be true. Two propositions so related are known as *contraries.*

Conventional Connotation of a Term The conventional connotation of a term consists of the properties of a thing that the members of a certain linguistic community consider common to the things a term denotes.

Converse, Conversion The converse of a given categorical proposition is formed by reversing the position of the subject and the predicate term. Only E and I propositions are logically equivalent to their converses.

Convertand A convertand is a proposition that is to be converted.

Copula The copula is a form of the verb 'to be.'

Criterion, Criteria A criterion is a standard for judging on a certain topic or subject matter.

Crucial Experiment A crucial experiment is an experiment that provides strong evidence that one of two opposing hypotheses is correct by showing that the predictions of one hypothesis correspond to the observational data whereas the predictions of the other do not.

Deductive Argument A sound deductive argument provides conclusive evidence for the truth of its conclusion.

Deductive Counterexample You construct a deductive counterexample to an argument of a given form by constructing an instance of the same form with true premises and a false conclusion. This shows that the argument form is invalid.

Deductive-Nomological Explanation A deductive-nomological explanation tells why a phenomenon is as it is by showing that the truth of a description of the phenomenon follows deductively from a statement of a natural law and an initial state description (statement of antecedent conditions).

Definiendum The definiendum is the word defined in a definition.

Definiens The word or words that define the definiendum are known as the definiens.

Definite Description   A definite description is a phrase of the form "the so and so." A definite description is a complex linguistic expression that picks out exactly one thing.

Definition by Genus and Difference   A definition by genus and difference is a connotative definition in which the definiendum is treated as the name of a class; in which the definiens identifies a more general class of which it is a part (the genus) and the properties that are unique to that species; and in which the definiens *differentiates* that species from other members of the genus.

Definition by Subclass   A definition by subclass is a denotative definition in which you name the subclasses of a class denoted by a term.

De Morgan's Theorems (DeM.)   In propositional logic, a pair of equivalences falling under the Rule of Replacement specifying (1) that the denial of a conjunction of two propositions is equivalent to the disjunction of the denial of each proposition, and (2) that the denial of the disjunction of two propositions is equivalent to the conjunction of the denial of each proposition. The forms of these two equivalences are:
$\sim(\alpha \,\&\, \beta) \leftrightarrow (\sim\alpha \lor \sim\beta)$ and $\sim(\alpha \lor \beta) \leftrightarrow (\sim\alpha \,\&\, \sim\beta)$.

Denotative Definition   A denotative definition defines a word by reference to objects in the term's denotation.

Denotative Meaning; Denotation   The denotative meaning of a term consists of all the things to which a term is correctly applied. Also known as the *extension* of a term.

Dichotomy   A dichotomy is a division of a class into two mutually exclusive and exhaustive subclasses, that is, a division of a class such that every member of the original class is a member of one of the two subclasses and no member of the original class is a member of both subclasses.

Directive Function of Language   The directive function of language is the use of language to request information, plead for action, and issue orders.

Disjunct   A disjunct is a statement in a disjunction.

Disjunction   Disjunction is represented by the wedge, or vee ($\lor$). A statement of the form "$p \lor q$" is true except when both p and q are false.

Disjunctive Syllogism (D.S.)   In propositional logic, disjunctive syllogism is a rule of inference in which the first premise is a disjunction, the second premise is the negation of the first disjunct in the first premise, and the conclusion is the second disjunct in the first premise. The form of the rule is: $\alpha \vee \beta, \sim \alpha \; / \therefore \; \beta$.

Distribution   A term in a categorical proposition is distributed if and only if it refers to all the members of the class denoted by the term.

Distribution (Dist.)   In propositional logic, distribution is an equivalence falling under the Rule of Replacement that specifies the relationship between a statement conjoined to a disjunction and a conjunction of disjunctions, or a statement conjoined to a disjunction and a disjunction of conjunctions. The two forms of distribution are: $[\alpha \; \& \; (\beta \vee \Gamma)] \leftrightarrow [(\alpha \; \& \; \beta) \vee (\alpha \; \& \; \Gamma)]$ and $[\alpha \vee (\beta \; \& \; \Gamma)] \leftrightarrow [(\alpha \vee \beta) \; \& \; (\alpha \vee \Gamma)]$.

Distributive Use of a Word   A word is used distributively if it applies to each and every member of a class taken individually.

Division   The fallacy of division occurs if either (1) you attribute to a part characteristics that are true only of the corresponding whole or (2) you attribute to a member of a class a property that is true of a class of objects as a whole.

Domain of Discourse   A domain of discourse is a set of objects that are *assumed* to exist for the sake of the argument.

Double Arrow   In the symbolic language for propositional logic, the double arrow represents material equivalence.

Double Negation (D.N.)   In propositional logic, double negation is an equivalence falling under the Rule of Replacement indicating that any statement is equivalent to its double negative. The form of the rule is: $\alpha \leftrightarrow \sim\sim\alpha$.

Drawing an Affirmative Conclusion from a Negative Premise (ACNP)   In categorical logic, a syllogism commits the fallacy of drawing an affirmative conclusion from a negative premise if its conclusion is an affirmative proposition and at least one of its premises is a negative proposition.

Dyadic Relation   A dyadic relation is a two-place relation.

E Proposition   In categorical logic, an E proposition is a universal negative proposition.

Emotive Function of Language   The emotive function of language is the use of language to express or evoke emotions.

Empirical Evidence, Empirical Data   Empirical evidence is evidence drawn from experience; empirical data is data based on empirical experience.

Empty Denotation   A term has an empty denotation if there is nothing it denotes.

Enthymeme, Enthymematic Argument   An enthymeme is an argument in which one of the premises or the conclusion is not stated.

Enumerative Definition   An enumerative definition is a denotative definition in which the definiendum is defined by naming objects in the denotation of the term.

Epithet   An epithet is a descriptive word or phrase used to characterize a person, thing, or idea. You can commit the fallacy of begging the question by ascribing an epithet to a person, thing, or idea that assumes what you are trying to establish.

Equivocate   If you shift from one meaning of a word to another within a piece of discourse, you equivocate.

Equivocation   An argument commits the fallacy of equivocation if the meaning of a word shifts in the context of the argument and the persuasive force of the conclusion depends upon that shift.

Evidence   Evidence is that which tends to prove or disprove the truth of a statement.

Exceptive Proposition   An exceptive proposition is a proposition beginning with 'All except' or 'All but.' Exceptive propositions are complex. "All except *S* are *P*" means *both* "All non-*S* are *P*" and "No *S* is *P*."

Exclusive Premises (EP)   In categorical logic, a syllogism commits the fallacy of exclusive premises if both of its premises are negative.

Existential Fallacy (EF)   In categorical logic under the Boolean Interpretation, a syllogism commits the existential fallacy if its conclusion is a particular proposition and both of its premises are universal propositions.

Existential Generalization (E.G.)   In predicate logic, the rule of existential generalization allows you to introduce the existential quantifier *given that a statement is true of some individual.*

Existential Import   Existential import is the property of a proposition that its truth entails the existence of at least one object.

Existential Instantiation (E.I.)   In predicate logic, existential instantiation is a rule that allows you to eliminate the existential quantifier by introducing a *hypothetical* name to represent the "at least one thing" of which the statement is true. The name introduced must be new to the proof.

Existential Quantifier   In predicate logic, the quantifier in a particular proposition. The symbol of the backward-E ($\exists$) is the existential quantifier.

Explanation   An explanation is a discourse that answers the question why something is as it is.

Exportation   In propositional logic, exportation is a logical equivalence falling under the Rule of Replacement asserting that a conditional statement with a conjunction as an antecedent is logically equivalent to a conditional statement in which the first conjunct is the antecedent and the consequent is a conditional statement in which the second conjunct of the equivalent statement is the antecedent and the consequent of the equivalent statement is the consequent. The form of the equivalence is: $[(\alpha \mathrel{\&} \beta) \to \Gamma] \leftrightarrow [\alpha \to (\beta \to \Gamma)]$.

Extension   The extension of a term consists of all the things to which a term is correctly applied. Also known as the *denotation* of a term.

External Consistency   Experimental evidence is externally consistent with accepted scientific theories when the accepted theories help explain the evidence.

Fallacy   A fallacy is an error in reasoning. It is an argument that seems to be sound but is not. Invalid deductive arguments are formally fallacious: the form of the argument does not guarantee that if the premises are true, the conclusion is also true. Informal fallacies rest on the content of the argument.

Fallacy of Four Terms (4T)   In categorical logic, an argument commits the fallacy of four terms if either there are more than three terms in the argument, or a term is assigned different meanings at different points in the argument. If an argument commits the fallacy of four terms, by definition it is *not* a categorical syllogism.

False, Falsehood   A proposition is false if and only if it does not correspond with the world. Falsehood is a characteristic of a statement or proposition.

False Cause An argument commits the fallacy of false cause if it misidentifies the cause of an event and draws a conclusion.

False Dichotomy An argument commits the fallacy of false dichotomy if it presents two alternatives as the only alternatives with respect to an issue when in fact there are other options, and rejects one of the alternatives and concludes that you must accept the other. What the argument claims is a dichotomy is not.

Fermat, Pierre de Pierre de Fermat was the seventeenth-century French mathematician who, with Blaise Pascal, developed the classical theory of probability.

Figure of a Categorical Syllogism The figure of a categorical syllogism specifies the position of the middle in the syllogism in standard form.

Form of an Argument The form of an argument is the structural pattern of an argument. It is like the design of a house insofar as there may be many arguments of the same form.

Formal Fallacy A formal fallacy is an error in reasoning based solely on the form of the argument, not on its content.

Free Variable In predicate logic, a free variable is any variable not bound by a quantifier.

General Conjunction Rule In the probability calculus, the general disjunction rule allows you to calculate the probability of the second event on the assumption that the first event occurred. Where A and B are two events, the formula for the general conjunction rule is: $P(A \text{ and } B) = P(A) \times P(B \text{ given } A)$.

General Disjunction Rule In the probability calculus, the general disjunction rule allows you to calculate the probability of either of two *independent* events whether or not they are mutually exclusive. Where A and B are two events, the formula for the general disjunction rule is: $P(A \text{ or } B) = P(A) + P(B) - P(A \text{ and } B)$.

Guide Columns In a truth table, guide columns specify the truth values of each of the different simple statements in the argument.

Hasty Generalization An argument commits the fallacy of hasty generalization if a general conclusion—a conclusion pertaining to all or most things of a kind—is based on an atypical case or cases.

Hypothesis A hypothesis is an educated guess or hunch regarding a necessary or sufficient condition for a particular phenomenon or kind of phenomenon.

Hypothetical Syllogism   In propositional logic, the rule of hypothetical syllogism states that given two premises that are conditional statements in which the consequent of the first is the antecedent of the second, the conclusion is a conditional statement in which the antecedent is the antecedent of the first premise and the consequent is the consequent of the second premise. The form of the rule is: $\alpha \to \beta$, $\beta \to \Gamma$ /∴ $\alpha \to \Gamma$.

I Proposition   In categorical logic, an I proposition is a particular affirmative proposition.

Ignoratio Elenchi   See **Irrelevant Conclusion.**

Illicit Process of the Major Term (IMa)   In categorical logic, a syllogism commits the fallacy of illicit process of the major term (illicit major) if the major term is distributed in the conclusion but not in the major premise.

Illicit Process of the Minor Term (IMi)   In categorical logic, a syllogism commits the fallacy of illicit process of the minor term (illicit minor) if the minor term is distributed in the conclusion but not in the minor premise.

Immediate Inference   An immediate inference is an inference you can correctly draw regarding the truth value of a proposition given nothing more than the truth value of one other proposition.

Incomplete Truth Table   An incomplete truth table is a truth table in which you construct the guide columns and the column for the conclusion, and, proceeding from the upper right corner to the lower left, you fill in *only* those rows in which the conclusion is false. Further, you assign truth values to the statements in a row *only* until you find a false premise, and you continue assigning truth values on the table *only* until you find a row in which all the premises are true and the conclusion is false.

Inconsistent; Inconsistency   Two propositions are inconsistent with one another if one asserts what the other denies.

Independent Events   In probability theory, two or more events are independent if and only if the occurrence of any one of them has no influence on the occurrence of any of the others.

Indirect Proof   In propositional and predicate logic, an indirect proof is constructed by assuming the *denial* of the proposition you want to prove as an additional premise and showing that this enlarged set of premises yields a pair of contradictory statements. This procedure shows that the proposition you wanted to prove follows from the original premises.

Inductive Arguments Inductive arguments provide some, but not conclusive, evidence for the truth of their conclusions.

Informal Fallacy An argument commits an informal fallacy if it is psychologically persuasive but not logically persuasive, and its logical error rests on the material presented in the argument.

Informative Function of Language The informative function of language is the use of language to convey information.

Intension The intension of a term consists of all the characteristics or properties that are common to all the members of the class denoted by a term. Also known as the *connotation* of a term.

Internal Consistency A theory is internally consistent if the statements in the theory do not entail self-contradictory statements.

Invalid, Invalidity Invalidity is a characteristic of an argument form. An argument form is invalid if and only if the truth of the premises does not guarantee the truth of the conclusion.

Irrelevant Conclusion You commit the fallacy of irrelevant conclusion if your premises seem to lead you to one conclusion and you draw an entirely different conclusion.

Lexical Definition A lexical definition states the convention governing the use of a word.

Logical Equivalence Two statement forms are logically equivalent if they express the same proposition and if they are true under exactly the same conditions.

Major Premise In a categorical syllogism, the major premise is the premise containing the major term.

Major Term In a categorical syllogism, the major term is the predicate term of the conclusion.

Margin of Error In a survey, the margin of error is the percentage by which past experience suggests actual behavior might deviate from the results of the survey within a certain "level of confidence," which is typically 95 percent. So if the results of a survey show that a certain presidential candidate can expect 48 percent of the votes and the survey has a 2 percent margin of error, this indicates that there is a 95 percent chance that the candidate will receive between 46 and 50 percent of the votes.

Material Equivalence   In propositional logic, material equivalence is represented by the double-arrow ($\leftrightarrow$). A statement of material equivalence is true whenever the truth values of p and q are the same; otherwise it is false.

Material Equivalence (Equiv.)   In propositional logic, material equivalence is a statement of logical equivalence falling under the Rule of Replacement that allows you to introduce or replace a statement containing a double arrow. The two forms of the equivalence are: $(\alpha \leftrightarrow \beta) \leftrightarrow [(\alpha \to \beta) \;\&\; (\beta \to \alpha)]$ and $(\alpha \leftrightarrow \beta) \leftrightarrow [(\alpha \;\&\; \beta) \lor (\sim\alpha \;\&\; \sim\beta)]$.

Material Implication   In propositional logic, material implication is represented by the single arrow ($\to$). A statement of the form "$p \to q$" is true except when p is true and q is false.

Material Implication (Impl.)   In propositional logic, material implication is a statement of logical equivalence falling under the Rule of Replacement that allows you to replace a conditional statement with a disjunction consisting of the denial of the antecedent of the conditional and the consequent or to replace such a disjunction with a conditional statement. The two forms of the equivalence are: $(\alpha \to \beta) \leftrightarrow (\sim\alpha \lor \beta)$ and $(\sim\alpha \to \beta) \leftrightarrow (\alpha \lor \beta)$.

Mean   The mean is the arithmetic average. It is calculated by dividing the sum of the individual values by the total number of individuals in the reference class.

Median   The median of a set of numerical data is the middle value when arranged in ascending order: there are as many values above as below. 'Median' is one of the meanings of 'average.'

Mention   A word is mentioned in a statement if a statement refers to the word itself. By convention, you mention a word by placing it in single quotation marks.

Metaphor   A metaphor is an analogy in which an implicit comparison is made between two things. The statement "Language is a picture of the world" is a metaphorical statement.

Middle Term   In a categorical syllogism, the middle term is the term that is in both premises but not in the conclusion.

Midrange The midrange is the point in the arithmetic middle of a range, and it is determined by adding the highest number in the range to the lowest number and dividing by two. 'Midrange' is one of the meanings of 'average.'

Minor Premise In a categorical syllogism, the minor premise is the premise containing the minor term.

Minor Term In a categorical syllogism, the minor term is the subject term of the conclusion.

Mob Appeal You commit the fallacy of mob appeal by appealing to the emotions of the crowd—the desire to be loved, accepted, respected, etc.—rather than to the relevant facts.

Mode In a set of numerical data, the mode is the value that occurs most frequently. 'Mode' is one of the meanings of 'average.'

Modus Ponens (M.P.) In propositional logic, *modus ponens* is a rule of inference in which the first premise is a conditional statement, the second premise is the antecedent of that conditional, and the conclusion is the consequent of the conditional. The form of the argument is: $p \to q, p \mathbin{/\therefore} q$.

Modus Tollens (M.T.) In propositional logic, *modus tollens* is a rule of inference in which the first premise is a conditional statement, the second premise is the denial of the consequent of that conditional, and the conclusion is the denial of the antecedent of that conditional. The form of the argument is: $p \to q, \sim q \mathbin{/\therefore} \sim p$.

Mood of a Syllogism In categorical logic, the mood of a syllogism consists of the kinds of propositions of which the syllogism is composed. In stating the mood of a syllogism, you state the letter representing the major premise first, then the letter representing the minor premise, and finally the letter representing the conclusion.

Mutually Exclusive Events In probability theory, two or more events are mutually exclusive if and only if they are distinct and the occurrence of one of the events precludes the occurrence of any of the others.

Necessary Condition A necessary condition is a condition is whose absence a given phenomenon will not occur. A necessary condition is expressed by the consequent of a conditional.

Necessary and Sufficient Condition A necessary and sufficient condition is a condition in whose absence a given phenomenon will not occur and in whose presence the phenomenon occurs. A necessary and sufficient condition is expressed by a biconditional.

Negation   In propositional logic, negation is represented by the tilde (~). Placing a tilde in front of a statement changes a true statement into a false statement and a false statement into a true statement.

Negation Rule   In the probability calculus, the negation rule tells you that the probability that some event *A* occurs is equal to one minus the probability that *A* does not occur. The form of the rule is: $P(A) = 1 - P(\text{not}-A)$.

Negative   If you deny that members of the first class named are members of the second, the proposition is negative in quality.

Non Causa Pro Causa ("not the cause for the cause")   This is a variety of the false cause fallacy. If you incorrectly take something to be the cause of something else without any reference or allusion to the temporal order of events, you commit the fallacy of *non causa pro causa*.

Normal Probability Distribution   A normal probability distribution is the mark of a random survey. You have a normal probability distribution if the mean, the mode, the median, and the midrange are the same.

O Proposition   In categorical logic, an **O** proposition is a particular negative proposition.

Objective Connotation   The objective connotation of a term consists of all the characteristics common to all the things a term denotes.

Obverse, Obversion   In categorical logic, the obverse of a categorical proposition is obtained by changing the quality of a given categorical proposition from affirmative to negative and replacing the predicate term with its complement. Every categorical proposition is logically equivalent to its obverse.

Obvertend   The obvertend is a proposition to be obverted.

Operational Definition   An operational definition is a connotative definition in which the definiens specifies an experimental procedure or operation that provides a criterion for the application of a term.

Oppositions   In categorical logic, oppositions are immediate inferences among categorical propositions.

Ostensive Definition   An ostensive definition is a denotative definition in which the definiendum is defined by pointing to objects denoted by the word.

Parameter A parameter is a word or phrase that is added to a statement to specify its domain of discourse.

Particular Affirmative Proposition In categorical logic, a particular affirmative proposition asserts that there is at least one member of the subject class and it is also a member of the predicate class. A particular affirmative proposition can be stated in standard form as "Some *S* is *P*."

Particular Negative Proposition In categorical logic, a particular negative proposition asserts that there is at least one member of the subject class and it is *not* a member of the predicate class. A particular negative proposition can be stated in standard form as "Some *S* is not *P*."

Particular Proposition A particular proposition is a proposition that is true of at least one individual.

Pascal, Blaise Blaise Pascal was the seventeenth-century French philosopher and mathematician who, with Pierre de Fermat, developed the classical theory of probability.

Personal Attack You commit the fallacy of *personal attack* if you attempt to *refute* the conclusion of another person's argument by attacking the person who presented the argument rather than the argument itself.

Post Hoc Ergo Propter Hoc ("before that, therefore because of that") *Post hoc ergo propter hoc* is a variety of the false cause fallacy. If you assume that one event is the cause of another *simply because it occurs first,* you commit the fallacy of *post hoc ergo propter hoc.*

Precising Definition A precising definition is offered to set limits to the definiendum and thereby reduce vagueness.

Predicate Term In a categorical proposition, the predicate term is the term in the predicate place; it is the second term that names a class.

Premise In an argument, a premise is a statement used to provide evidence for the truth of another statement, namely, the conclusion.

Premise Indicators Premise indicators are words such as 'since,' 'because,' and 'given that,' which are used to indicate that a statement is a premise of an argument.

Prenex Normal Form In predicate logic, a statement is in prenex normal form if all the quantifiers are placed to the left of the entire propositional function over which they range. If the quantifier is in the antecedent of a conditional, moving the quantifier outside the farthest left parentheses requires changing the quantity of the quantifier: universal to particular or particular to universal.

Principal Connective In symbolic logic, the principal connective is the connective that holds an entire complex statement together. For example, in the statement "$p \rightarrow (q \ \& \ r)$," the arrow is the principal connective. In "$(p \ \& \ q) \lor (r \rightarrow s)$," the wedge is the principal connective.

Principle of Indifference In the probability calculus, the principle of indifference is the assumption that all possible events in the class under consideration are equally probable.

Probability Calculus The probability calculus consists of those mathematical formulae used to calculate the probability of an event. The probability calculus is common to the classical, relative frequency, and subjective theories of probability.

Proposition A proposition is the information expressed by a declarative sentence or statement.

Propositional Function In predicate logic, a propositional function is a predicate with a variable as its subject.

Propositional Logic Propositional logic is a system of logic in which simple propositions are the fundamental elements of a logical schema.

Quality In categorical logic, the quality of a proposition is either affirmative or negative.

Quantifier The quantifier of a categorical statement tells you how many things the statement refers to. In categorical logic, the universal quantifiers are 'All' and 'No,' and the particular quantifier is 'Some.' In predicate logic, the universal quantifier is a variable in parentheses, and the existential quantifier is the backward-E ($\exists$) followed by a variable.

Quantifier Negation In predicate logic, quantifier negation is a rule that allows you to move the tilde across a quantifier. Moving the tilde across a quantifier changes an existential quantifier to a universal quantifier and changes a universal quantifier to an existential quantifier.

Quantity In categorical logic, the quantity of a proposition tells you how many members of the first class named are or are not members of the second.

Quaternary Relation A quaternary relation is a four-place relation.

Random Sample The sample on which a survey is taken is random if every person or object in the population surveyed has an equal chance of being chosen for the survey.

Red Herring You commit the red herring fallacy if you shift away from the issue under consideration to something different and then draw a conclusion.

Reductio ad Absurdum A *reductio ad absurdum* is literally a reduction to absurdity. It is a proof technique in which an assumption is added to a set of premises, and it is shown that adding the assumption yields a pair of contradictory statements. This shows that the original assumption was false. See also **Indirect Proof.**

Reflexive Relation A relation is reflexive if and only if an object can stand in that relation to itself. The relation of "being the same age as" is an example of a reflexive relation.

Refutation of a Hypothesis If an experimental procedure based on a hypothesis fails to yield the predicted consequence, the experiment refutes the hypothesis, that is, it provides conclusive evidence that the hypothesis is false.

Relation A relation is a predicate of two or more places. For example, the predicates "to the left of" and "between" are relational predicates.

Relative Frequency Theory of Probability The relative frequency theory of probability is based on empirical data. This theory of probability is used in calculating such things as insurance rates.

Restricted Conjunction Rule In the probability calculus, the restricted conjunction rule is used to calculate the probability of two *independent* events. For the events A and B, the probability of both A and B is: $P(A \text{ and } B) = P(A) \times P(B)$.

Restricted Disjunction Rule In the probability calculus, the restricted disjunction rule is used to calculate the probability that either of two or more *mutually exclusive* events occurs. For the events A and B, the probability of either A and B is: $P(A \text{ or } B) = P(A) + P(B)$.

Reverse Truth Table In constructing a reverse truth table, *assume* that all the premises are true and the conclusion is false, then consistently assign truth values to the components in an attempt to show that your assumption is correct. If the argument is invalid, this method allows you to construct one line of a truth table that demonstrates the invalidity. If the argument is valid, it is impossible consistently to assign truth values on the assumption that the argument is invalid.

Rule of Replacement   In propositional logic, the rule of replacement is the rule that logically equivalent expressions may replace each other wherever they occur in a proof.

Rules of Inference   The rules of inference are rules that allow valid inferences from statements assumed as premises.

Sample   A sample is a portion of a certain population of objects or people on which a poll or survey is based.

Scope of a Quantifier   The scope of a quantifier is the propositional function whose variables are so grouped that they are bound by the quantifier.

Simile   A simile is an analogy in which the word 'like' makes the comparison between two things explicit.

Simplification (Simp.)   In propositional logic, simplification is the rule of inference in which the premise is a conjunction and the conclusion is the first conjunct. The form of the rule is: α & β /∴ α.

Singular Proposition or Singular Statement   A singular proposition (statement) makes a claim about an individual, exactly one thing.

Slippery Slope Argument   A slippery slope argument has the following structure. There is a slope—a chain of causes. It is slippery. Therefore, if you take even one step on the slope, you will slide all the way to the bottom. But the bottom is a bad place to be. So, you should not take the first step.

Slippery Slope Fallacy   An argument commits the slippery slope fallacy when (and only when) at least one of the causal relations constituting the slope in a slippery slope argument does not hold.

Some   As used in logic, the word 'some' means at least one.

Sorites   A sorites is a chain of enthymematic syllogisms in which the unstated conclusion of one syllogism is a premise for the next syllogism.

Sound Arguments   Sound arguments are valid deductive arguments with premises that are all true.

Square of Opposition A square of opposition is a diagram showing the immediate inferences that can be drawn given the truth or falsehood of a categorical proposition.

Standard-Form Categorical Statement In categorical logic, a statement is a standard-form categorical statement if and only if: (a) it expresses a categorical proposition; (b) its quantifier is either 'All,' 'No,' or 'Some'; (c) it has a subject and a predicate term; (d) its subject and predicate terms are joined by a copula, a form of the verb 'to be'; and (e) the order of the elements in the statement is: quantifier, subject term, copula, predicate term.

Standard-Form Categorical Syllogism A syllogism is a standard-form categorical syllogism if and only if it fulfills each of the following criteria: (a) it is a categorical syllogism; (b) the premises and conclusion are standard-form categorical statements; (c) the syllogism contains three different terms; (d) each of the terms appears twice in the argument; (e) each term is used with the same meaning throughout the argument; (f) the predicate term of the conclusion appears in the first premise; (g) the subject term of the conclusion appears in the second premise.

Statement A statement is a sentence that is true or false in virtue of the proposition it expresses.

Statement Abbreviation In propositional logic, the uppercase letters (A, B, C, . . .) are statement abbreviations and represent statements in ordinary language.

Statement Variables In propositional logic, the lowercase letters beginning with p (p, q, r, . . .) are statement variables. Statement variables can be replaced by statements of any degree of complexity.

Stipulative Definition A stipulative definition is used to assign a meaning to a new word, to assign a new meaning to a word already in use, or to specify the meaning of a word in a particular context.

Straw Person You commit the straw person fallacy if, in replying to an argument, you either distort the original argument by suggesting that the first arguer accepted a premise that was not explicitly stated and argue that the premise is implausible, or distort the conclusion, argue against the conclusion as you have restated it, and hold your criticisms to apply to the original argument.

Subaltern   In Aristotelian logic, a subaltern is a particular proposition with the same subject and predicate terms and the same quality as a given universal proposition.

Subalternation   In Aristotelian logic, subalternation is an immediate inference between a universal categorical proposition and the corresponding particular proposition of the same quality that allows you to infer the truth of the particular given the truth of the universal or the falsehood of the universal given the falsehood of the particular.

Subcontrariety, Subcontraries   In Aristotelian logic, subcontrariety is a formal relationship between two particular propositions with the same subject and predicate terms but opposite qualities such that it is possible for both to be true but it is not possible for both to be false. Two propositions so related are known as *subcontraries.*

Subject Term   In a categorical proposition, the subject term is the term in the subject place; it is the first term that names a class.

Subjective Connotation   The person-to-person differences in the connotations assigned to a term are known as subjective connotations.

Subjective Theory of Probability   The subjective theory of probability is based on individual beliefs. This theory of probability is used in calculating such things as the outcome of sporting events.

Sufficient Condition   A condition is a sufficient condition for some phenomenon if whenever that condition holds, the phenomenon in question occurs. A sufficient condition is expressed by the antecedent of a conditional.

Suppressed Evidence   An argument that commits the fallacy of suppressed evidence is enthymematic. It states a premise that is true but presupposes an additional premise, a false premise, the truth of which must be assumed as grounds for accepting the conclusion.

Syllogism   A syllogism is a deductive argument consisting of two premises and a conclusion.

Symmetrical Relation   A relation R is symmetrical if and only if when it is true that a stands in relation R to b, it is also true that b stands in relation R to a. The relation of "being a sibling" is a symmetrical relation: if John is a sibling of Mary, then Mary is a sibling of John. The relation of "being older than" is not a symmetrical relation (it is an **asymmetrical** relation): if John is older than Mary, then it is false that Mary is older than John.

Synonymous Definition   A synonymous definition is a connotative definition in which the definiens is a single word that has the same connotation as the definiendum.

Tautology   In propositional logic, a tautology is a statement that is true solely in virtue of its form.

Tautology (Taut.)   In propositional logic, a tautology is a logical equivalence falling under the rule of replacement that indicates (1) that any statement is logically equivalent to a disjunction of that statement with itself and (2) that any statement is logically equivalent to a conjunction of that statement with itself. The two forms of the equivalence are: $\alpha \leftrightarrow (\alpha \lor \alpha)$ and $\alpha \leftrightarrow (\alpha \mathrel{\&} \alpha)$.

Term   A term is a word or phrase that can be the subject of a sentence.

Ternary Relation   A ternary relation is a three-place relation.

Tetradic Relation   A tetradic relation is a four-place relation.

Theory   A scientific theory consists of a number of general, well-confirmed hypotheses that will explain why specific phenomena are as they are.

Tilde (~)   In the symbolic language for propositional logic, the tilde represents negation. The tilde is the only one-place connective in our system.

Transitive Relation   A relation R is transitive if and only if given that a is in relation R to b, and b is in relation R to c, it follows that a is in relation R to c.

Transposition   In propositional logic, transposition is an equivalence falling under the rule of replacement that a conditional is logically equivalent to another statement in which the denial of the consequent of the first is the antecedent and the denial of the antecedent of the first is the consequent. The two forms of the equivalence are: $(\alpha \to \beta) \leftrightarrow (\sim\beta \to \sim\alpha)$ and $(\sim\alpha \to \beta) \leftrightarrow (\sim\beta \to \alpha)$.

Triadic Relation   A triadic relation is a three-place relation.

True, Truth   Truth is a characteristic of a statement or proposition. A proposition is true if and only if it corresponds with the world.

Truth-Functionally Compound Statements   A truth-functionally compound statement is a compound statement in which the truth of the entire statement is determined wholly by the truth values of its component statements.

Truth Table   A truth table represents all logically possible truth values of a statement.

Truth Tree   The truth-tree technique is a purely mechanical method of determining whether an argument in propositional logic is valid and demonstrating that an argument in predicate logic is valid. The truth-tree technique operates by the method of *reductio ad absurdum.*

Truth Value   Truth value is a property of a proposition. The truth value of a proposition is its truth or falsehood.

Undistributed Middle   In categorical logic, a syllogism commits the fallacy of undistributed middle if the middle term is undistributed.

Universal Affirmative Proposition   In categorical logic, a universal affirmative proposition claims that all the members of the subject class are included in the predicate class. A universal affirmative proposition can be stated in standard form as "All *S* is *P.*"

Universal Generalization (U.G.)   In predicate logic, the rule of universal generalization allows you to conclude the truth of a universal proposition on the basis of propositions instantiated in terms of variables.

Universal Instantiation (U.I.)   In predicate logic, the rule of universal instantiation allows you to eliminate the universal quantifier by replacing each variable in the scope of the quantifier by a constant or a variable.

Universal Negative Proposition   In categorical logic, a universal negative proposition holds that no members of the subject class are included in the predicate class. A universal negative proposition can be stated in standard form as "No *S* is *P.*"

Universal Quantifier   In predicate logic, the universal quantifier is a variable placed in parentheses.

Universal Statement   A universal statement makes a claim about every member of its subject class.

Use   A word is used if the truth or falsehood of a statement depends upon the meaning of that word.

Vague   A word is vague if its meaning is unclear or imprecise.

Valid, Validity Validity is a characteristic of an argument form. An argument form is valid if and only if the truth of the premises guarantees the truth of the conclusion.

Venn, John John Venn was a nineteenth-century logician who developed a pictorial means of representing categorical propositions understood according to the Boolean interpretation.

Venn Diagram The Venn diagram is a pictorial means of representing categorical propositions understood according to the Boolean interpretation.

Verbal Disputes Verbal disputes are disputes that rest on alternative meanings of terms rather than a genuine disagreement about the facts.

Wedge In the symbolic language for propositional logic, the wedge (or vee) represents disjunction.

Well-Formed Formula (WFF) I. In propositional logic, a formula is a well-formed formula in our language under the following conditions: (1) any simple proposition is a WFF; (2) if the proposition p is a WFF, then so is $\sim p$; (3) if p and q are WFFs, then so are the following: $(p \ \& \ q)$, $(p \lor q)$, $(p \to q)$, $(p \leftrightarrow q)$; (4) nothing is a WFF unless its being so follows from (1)–(3). II. In predicate logic, a formula is a well-formed formula in our language under the following conditions: (1) atomic expressions: a. individual variables: x, y, z; b. individual constants: a, b, c, . . ., w; c. predicate letters: A, B, C, . . . Z; d. Connectives: i. one-place:$\sim$; ii. two-place: $\&$, $\lor$, $\to$, $\leftrightarrow$; e. grouping indicators: $($,$)$, $[$,$]$, $\{$,$\}$; f. quantifiers: (x), $(\exists x)$; (2) well-formed formulae (WFFs): a. atomic WFFs: i. where Φ is a predicate letter and μ is either an individual constant or an individual variable, then $\Phi\mu$ is an atomic WFF; ii. where Φ is a predicate letter and μ and σ are either individual constants or individual variables, then $\Phi\mu\sigma$ and $\Phi\sigma\mu$ are atomic WFFs; iii. since predicates can be predicates of any degree, where Φ is a predicate letter followed by any number of individual constants or individual variables, μ, σ, τ, . . ., $\Phi\mu\sigma\tau$ . . . is an atomic WFF; b. molecular WFFs: where α and β are WFFs, so are: i. $\sim\alpha$; ii. $\alpha \ \& \ \beta$; iii. $\alpha \lor \beta$; iv. $\alpha \to \beta$; v. $\alpha \leftrightarrow \beta$; c. general WFFs: where Φ is a predicate letter and x is an individual variable, the following are WFFs: i. $(x)(\Phi x)$ is a WFF; ii. $(\exists x)(\Phi x)$ is a WFF; d. nothing is a WFF unless it can be constructed by a finite number of applications of rules a–c.

Whole An object is treated as a whole relative to the various parts of which it is composed.

Bibliography

Adler, Irving. *Probability and Statistics for Everyman.* New York: Signet Books, 1963.

Barnett, Lincoln. *The Universe and Dr. Einstein.* Revised edition. New York: Bantam Books, 1957.

Bentham, Edward. *An Introduction to Logick.* 1773. Reprint edition Menston, England: The Scolar Press, 1967.

Boole, George. *The Mathematical Analysis of Logic: Being an Essay Towards a Calculus of Deductive Reasoning.* Oxford: Basil Blackwell, 1965.

Burlingame, Roger. *Scientists Behind the Inventors.* New York: Avon Books, 1960.

Carroll, Lewis. *Symbolic Logic and the Game of Logic.* New York: Dover Publications, 1958.

Chrucky, Andrew. "Teaching Validity with a Stanley Thermos." *APA Newsletters,* 91, no. 2 (Fall 1992): 114–115.

Dray, William H. *Philosophy of History.* Foundations of Philosophy Series. Englewood Cliffs, NJ: Prentice Hall, 1964.

Fischer, David Hackett. *Historians' Fallacies: Toward a Logic of Historical Thought.* New York: Harper Colophon Books, 1970.

Gale, George. *Theory of Science: An Introduction to the History, Logic, and Philosophy of Science.* New York: McGraw-Hill Book Company, 1979.

Gardner, Martin. *Relativity for the Million.* New York: Pocket Books, 1962.

Govier, Trudy. "*Ad Hominem:* Revising the Textbooks." *Teaching Philosophy* 6 (1983): 13–24.

———. "Worries About *Tu Quoque* as a Fallacy." *Informal Logic* 3 (1981): 2–4.

Hanson, Norwood Russell. *Patterns of Discovery.* London: Cambridge University Press, 1958.

Harré, Rom. *Great Scientific Experiments.* Oxford: Oxford University Press, 1981.

Hempel, Carl G. *Philosophy of Natural Science.* Foundations of Philosophy Series. Englewood Cliffs, NJ: Prentice Hall, 1966.

Keller, Evelyn Fox. *A Feeling for the Organism: The Life and Work of Barbara McClintock*. New York: W. H. Freeman and Company, 1983.

———. *Reflections on Gender and Science*. New Haven, CT: Yale University Press, 1985.

Kuhn, Thomas S. *The Structure of Scientific Revolutions*. 2nd edition, enlarged. In *Foundations of the Unity of Science*, International Encyclopedia of Unified Science, vol. 2, edited by Otto Neurath, Rudolph Carnap, and Charles Morris. Chicago: University of Chicago Press, 1970, pp. 53–272.

Mackie, J. L. "Causes and Conditions," *American Philosophical Quarterly* 17 (1965). Reprinted in *Readings in the Philosophy of Science*, 2nd edition, edited by Baruch A. Brody and Richard E. Grady. Englewood Cliffs, NJ: Prentice Hall, 1989, pp. 235–247.

McNeill, William H. *Arnold J. Toynbee: A Life*. New York: Oxford University Press, 1989.

Mill, John Stuart. *A System of Logic, Ratiocinative and Inductive: Being a Connected View of the Principles of Evidence and the Methods of Scientific Investigation*. 8th edition. New York: Harper & Brothers, Publishers, 1895.

Quine, Willard Van Orman. *Word and Object*. Cambridge: M.I.T. Press, 1960.

Quine, W. V., and J. S. Ullian. *The Web of Belief*. New York: Random House, 1970.

Roll, Charles W., and Albert H. Cantril. *Polls: Their Use and Misuse in Politics*. New York: Basic Books, 1972.

Silverberg, Robert. *The Mound Builders*. Athens: Ohio University Press, 1970.

Thorne, Alice. *The Story of Madame Curie*. New York: Scholastic Book Services, 1959.

Von Wright, Georg Henrik. *A Treatise on Induction and Probability*. Patterson, NJ: Littlefield, Adams, & Co., 1960.

Webb, Kenneth, and Harry P. Hatry. *Obtaining Citizen Feedback: The Application of Citizen Surveys to Local Governments*. Washington, DC: The Urban Institute, 1973.

Index